MX 0302809 7

AF443733

ARTIFICIAL INTELLIGENCE RESEARCH AND DEVELOPMENT

Frontiers in Artificial Intelligence
and Applications

Series Editors: J. Breuker, R. López de Mántaras, M. Mohammadian, S. Ohsuga and W. Swartout

Volume 100

Recently published in this series

Vol. 99.   D. Šuc, Machine Reconstruction of Human Control Strategies
Vol. 98.   H. Fujita and P. Johannesson (Eds.), New Trends in Software Methodologies, Tools and Techniques – Proceedings of Lyee_W03: The Second International Workshop on Lyee Methodology
Vol. 97.   H.U. Hoppe et al. (Eds.), Artificial Intelligence in Education – Shaping the Future of Learning through Intelligent Technologies
Vol. 96.   S. Handschuh and S. Staab (Eds.), Annotation for the Semantic Web
Vol. 95.   B. Omelayenko and M. Klein (Eds.), Knowledge Transformation for the Semantic Web
Vol. 94.   H. Jaakkola et al. (Eds.), Information Modelling and Knowledge Bases XIV
Vol. 93.   K. Wang, Intelligent Condition Monitoring and Diagnosis Systems – A Computational Intelligence Approach
Vol. 92.   V. Kashyap and L. Shklar (Eds.), Real World Semantic Web Applications
Vol. 91.   F. Azevedo, Constraint Solving over Multi-valued Logics – Application to Digital Circuits
Vol. 90.   In preparation
Vol. 89.   T. Bench-Capon et al. (Eds.), Legal Knowledge and Information Systems – JURIX 2002: The Fifteenth Annual Conference
Vol. 88.   In preparation
Vol. 87.   A. Abraham et al. (Eds.), Soft Computing Systems – Design, Management and Applications
Vol. 86.   R.S.T. Lee and J.H.K. Liu, Invariant Object Recognition based on Elastic Graph Matching – Theory and Applications
Vol. 85.   J.M. Abe and J.I. da Silva Filho (Eds.), Advances in Logic, Artificial Intelligence and Robotics – LAPTEC 2002
Vol. 84.   H. Fujita and P. Johannesson (Eds.), New Trends in Software Methodologies, Tools and Techniques – Proceedings of Lyee_W02
Vol. 83.   V. Loia (Ed.), Soft Computing Agents – A New Perspective for Dynamic Information Systems
Vol. 82.   E. Damiani et al. (Eds.), Knowledge-Based Intelligent Information Engineering Systems and Allied Technologies – KES 2002
Vol. 81.   J.A. Leite, Evolving Knowledge Bases – Specification and Semantics
Vol. 80.   T. Welzer et al. (Eds.), Knowledge-based Software Engineering – Proceedings of the Fifth Joint Conference on Knowledge-based Software Engineering
Vol. 79.   H. Motoda (Ed.), Active Mining – New Directions of Data Mining
Vol. 78.   T. Vidal and P. Liberatore (Eds.), STAIRS 2002 – STarting Artificial Intelligence Researchers Symposium
Vol. 77.   F. van Harmelen (Ed.), ECAI 2002 – 15th European Conference on Artificial Intelligence
Vol. 76.   P. Sinčák et al. (Eds.), Intelligent Technologies – Theory and Applications
Vol. 75.   I.F. Cruz et al. (Eds.), The Emerging Semantic Web – Selected Papers from the first Semantic Web Working Symposium
Vol. 74.   M. Blay-Fornarino et al. (Eds.), Cooperative Systems Design – A Challenge of the Mobility Age
Vol. 73.   H. Kangassalo et al. (Eds.), Information Modelling and Knowledge Bases XIII

ISSN 0922-6389

Artificial Intelligence Research and Development

Edited by

Isabel Aguiló

*Departament de Matemàtiques i Informàtica,
Universitat de les Illes Balears, Palma, Illes Balears, Spain*

Llorenç Valverde

*Departament de Matemàtiques i Informàtica,
Universitat de les Illes Balears, Palma, Illes Balears, Spain*

and

M. Teresa Escrig

*Departament d'Enginyeria i Ciència dels Computadors,
Universitat Jaume I, Castellón, Spain*

IOS Press

Ohmsha

Amsterdam • Berlin • Oxford • Tokyo • Washington, DC

ISBN 1 58603 378 6 (IOS Press)
ISBN 4 274 90622 1 C3055 (Ohmsha)
Library of Congress Control Number: 2003111592

Publisher
IOS Press
Nieuwe Hemweg 6B
1013 BG Amsterdam
The Netherlands
fax: +31 20 620 3419
e-mail: order@iospress.nl

Distributor in the UK and Ireland
IOS Press/Lavis Marketing
73 Lime Walk
Headington
Oxford OX3 7AD
England
fax: +44 1865 75 0079

Distributor in the USA and Canada
IOS Press, Inc.
5795-G Burke Centre Parkway
Burke, VA 22015
USA
fax: +1 703 323 3668
e-mail: iosbooks@iospress.com

Distributor in Japan
Ohmsha, Ltd.
3-1 Kanda Nishiki-cho
Chiyoda-ku, Tokyo 101-8460
Japan
fax: +81 3 3233 2426

LEGAL NOTICE
The publisher is not responsible for the use which might be made of the following information.

PRINTED IN THE NETHERLANDS

Preface

The CCIA'2003 Catalan Conference on Artificial Intelligence took place at the Universitat de les Illes Balears (UIB) on 22-24 October, 2003, organized by the Catalan Association of Artificial Intelligence (ACIA) and the Mathematics and Computer Science Department of the UIB. The main aim of the 6th Catalan Conference on Artificial Intelligence was to promote collaborations among research groups in the community and the interchange of ideas, allowing researchers to get a quick overview of the local state of the art.

In this regard it is of particular interest to encourage links between researchers of different areas of Artificial Intelligence who have common problems and frequently use similar techniques. The conference included seven sessions of presented papers, two poster sessions and three invited speakers dealing with various aspects of the topics: Professor E. Trillas from the Universidad Politécnica de Madrid and Professors J. Amat and Ton Sales from the Universitat Politècnica de Catalunya. Eighty-two papers were submitted. The program committee selected 50 of them, after considering the reviews provided by at least two referees for each paper. Among these 50 accepted papers, 44 were original papers and therefore they were included in this volume. The number of submitted papers and the number of rejected papers has increased compared to the last conference.

In this volume, final versions of the accepted papers incorporating the reviewers' comments have been included. We have arranged the contents into seven subject areas:

In section 1, Information Fusion and Aggregation, there are four papers on applications of aggregation: two on multicriteria decision making, one on RNA structures and one on fuzzy morphology. The remaining paper is more theoretical and deals with dispersion measurement.

Many papers were received in the second and third subject areas, of which six on Robotics (Section 2) and eight on Computer Vision (Section 3) were included in this volume. The topics of these papers range from control architectures to world modelling and from segmentation and matching to physics based vision.

Section 4, Multi-agent Systems, includes four papers on the different applications of multi-agent systems for controlling network protection, configuration at the knowledge level and defining security measures in a medical system.

Section 5, Machine Learning, includes five papers in such diverse areas as inductive learning, learning algorithms based on kernels, clustering techniques, weighting approach and creative evolution.

In the area of Problem Resolution in AI, many different papers were received. Section 6 includes ten of them: six containing theoretical results and the other four combining theoretical with practical results.

In section 7, Constraint Reasoning and section 8, Planning, six papers were included, five of which contain theoretical results and the sixth combines branch and bound algorithms with branching heuristics.

We would like to express our sincere gratitude to all the authors and the invited speakers for making the conference and this book possible with their contributions and participation. We sincerely thank the members of the organizing and program committee, and the reviewers, for their efforts in helping with the preparation of this event. Finally, we would like to recognize the effort made by the Sponsors of the Conference.

The global assessment of the contributions contained in this volume is positive. They give a representative sample of the current state of the art in the Catalan Artificial Intelligence Community.

October 2003
I. Aguiló
Program Co-Chair
CCIA'2003

Conference Organization

CCIA 2003 was organized by the Departament de Matemàtiques i Informàtica, Universitat de les Illes Balears (UIB) and the Asociació Catalana d'Intel·ligència Artificial

General Chair
Llorenç Valverde Garcia (UIB)

Program Committee

Isabel Aguiló Pons (UIB)

Teresa Escrig Monferrer (UJI)

Referees

Núria Agell (ESADE)

Joseph Aguilar (Tou-UPC)

M. Isabel Alfonso (UA)

Cecilio Angulo (GREC-UPC)

Ester Bernardó (EALS-URL)

Vicent Botti (UPV)

Tomasa Calvo (UAH)

Jaume Casasnovas (UIB)

Nuria Castell (UPC)

Andreu Català (UPC)

M. Teresa Escrig (UJI)

Gabriel Fiol (UIB)

Pilar Fuster (UIB)

Ana García (UPM)

Luis A. García (UJI)

Rafael García (UdG)

Josep M. Garrell (Salle-URL)

Elisabet Golobardes (Salle-URL)

Yolanda González (UIB)

Manolo González (UIB)

Antoni Grau (ESAI-UPC)

M. Angeles López (UJI)

Beatriz López (UdG)

R. López de Mantaras (CSIC)

Lluís Marquez (UPC)

Joan Martí (UdG)

Isabel Aguiló (UIB)

Mario Martín (UPC)

Gaspar Mayor (UIB)

Joaquím Melendez (UdG)

Josep Miró (UIB)

Margarita Miró (UIB)

Antonio Moreno (URV)

Gabriel Oliver (UIB)

Eva Onaindia (UPV)

Xavier Parra (GREC-UPC)

Francisco Perales (UIB)

Filiberto Pla (UJI)

Enric Plaza (CSIC)

Monique Polit (Uper)

Josep Puyol (IIIA-CSIC)

David Riaño (URV)

Horacio Rodriguez (UPC)

Xavier Rovira (ESADE)

Miquel Sánchez (UPC)

Carles Sierra (IIIA-CSIC)

M. Toro (U.Sevilla)

Vicenc Torra (IIIA-CSIC)

Joan Torrens (UIB)

Enric Trillas (UPM)

Magdalena Valls (UdL)

Llorenç Valverde (UIB)

Jordi Vitrià (CVC-UAB)

Organization Committee

Isabel Aguiló

Jaume Casasnovas

Gabriel Fiol

Pilar Fuster

Ricardo Galli

Rut Garí

Javier Martín

Margalida Mas

Margaret Miró

Gabriel Oliver

Jaume Suñer

Joan Torrens

Llorenç Valverde

Manolo González

Sponsoring Institutions

Departament de Matemàtiques i Informàtica, Universitat de les Illes Balears

Associació Catalana d'Intel·ligència Artificial

Caja de Ahorros del Mediterráneo

Conselleria d'Innovació i Indústria del Govern de les Illes Balears

Conselleria d'Educació i Cultura del Govern de les Illes Balears

Contents

Section 6. Problem Resolution in AI

1. Information Fusion and Aggregation

Artificial Intelligence Research and Development
I. Aguiló et al. (Eds.)
IOS Press, 2003

T-quasi-concave dispersion measures

Isabel Aguiló, Javier Martín, Gaspar Mayor and Jaume Suñer
Dept. of Mathematics and Computer Science
University of the Balearic Islands
07071-Palma de Mallorca. Spain
{dmiiap0,javier.martin,gmayor,jaume.sunyer}@uib.es

Abstract. In this paper we generalize the concept of quasi-concavity for dispersion measures by means of the use of t-norms. Thus we study symmetric functions with extremal values defined on the set of n-dimensional probabilistic vectors satisfying a property which we call T-quasi-concavity. Furthermore we relate this property to other well-known ones like Schur-concavity and monotonicity.

Keywords: dispersion measure, t-norm, Schur-concavity, quasi-concavity.

1 Introduction

Many aggregation functions (weighted means, OWA operators) use in their definition lists of weights, that is, numbers $w_1, \ldots, w_n \in [0, 1]$ such that $\sum_{i=1}^{n} w_i = 1$. In [7] a method to obtain lists of weights associated to OWA operators is given. In consists of solving the mathematical programming problem of finding the list of weights with a given degree of optimism ("orness") which has maximum entropy. This is a desirable situation, because it means that, within the restrictions given by the type of operator we want, we will obtain the operator with the weights of the list as uniformly distributed as it is possible. The same problem has been studied in [1] for the case of multidimensional OWA operators. In both cases, the Shannon's entropy ([8] has been used, but there is not any reason for using this dispersion measure. In this way, we can find a study of different dispersion measures in [5].

It is usual to consider different types of concavity for the study of dispersion measures. In this sense, in [6] the concept of uncertainty measure is given by means of Schur-concavity. In [4] it is proved that concavity plus symmetry give Schur-concavity and thus uncertainty measures. Moreover, in [5] it is shown that it is sufficient to consider quasi-concavity (plus symmetry) to obtain Schur-concavity.

Nevertheless the quasi-concavity property is very restrictive, in the sense that it provides few dispersion measures. In this paper, we propose to substitute the condition of monotonicity used to define dispersion measures by different types of concavity and study the relations between the types of dispersion measure we obtain.

Next we present the definitions and known results which we will use throughout all the paper. They can be found mainly in [5], [6] and [2].

For each $n \geq 2$, let us consider the following set L of n-dimensional lists:

$$L = \{x = (x_1, \ldots, x_n) \in [0,1]^n : \sum_{i=1}^{n} x_i = 1\}.$$

Observe that L is a convex part of $[0,1]^n$, specifically it is the convex closure of the lists $\delta_1 = (1,0,\ldots,0), \delta_2 = (0,1,0,\ldots,0), \ldots, \delta_n = (0,\ldots,0,1) : L = <\delta_1,\ldots,\delta_n>.$

Definition 1. *Given two lists $x, y \in L$, we say that $x \leq_d y$ if and only if for all $i = 1, \ldots, n$ is $x_i \leq y_i \leq \frac{1}{n}$ or $x_i \geq y_i \geq \frac{1}{n}$.*

Remark
It is easy to see that $\leq_d$ is a partial order over L with the list $(\frac{1}{n}, \ldots, \frac{1}{n})$ as a maximum element and that, if we call $weight(x) = |\{i : x_i \neq 0\}|$, for each $x \in L$, then x is minimal if and only if $weight(x) < n$ and $x_i > \frac{1}{n}$ for all $x_i \neq 0$.

Given $x \in L$ such that $x_1 \leq \ldots \leq x_n$, let $p_x = \max\{i : x_i \leq \frac{1}{n}\}$. Then $1 \leq p_x \leq n$, and $p_x = n$ if and only if $x = (\frac{1}{n}, \ldots, \frac{1}{n})$.

In this paper we are interested in the study of a class of functions $D : L \longrightarrow \mathbb{R}$. In [6] it is introduced the concept of uncertainty measure as a function of this class satisfying the Shur-concavity, defined as follows:

Definition 2. *We say that a function $D : L \longrightarrow \mathbb{R}$ is Schur-concave if when $x \succ y$, then $D(x) \leq D(y)$, where $x \succ y$ (x dominates y) means that there exists a doubly stochastic matrix $n \times n$, A, such that $y = x A$.*

On the other hand, the quasi-concavity is defined as follows:

Definition 3. *A function $D : L \longrightarrow \mathbb{R}$ is quasi-concave if, for any $x, y \in L$ and $a \in [0,1]$,*

$$D((1-a)x + ay) \geq \min(D(x), D(y)).$$

Remark
Let $D : L \longrightarrow \mathbb{R}$.

1) If D is concave (that is $D((1-a)x + ay) \geq (1-a)D(x) + aD(y)$ for all $a \in [0,1]$), then D is quasi-concave.

2) For each $c \in \mathbb{R}$, let us consider $L_c = \{x \in L : D(x) \geq c\}$ (the c-cut of D). Then:

   a) If $c \leq c'$, then $L_c \supset L_{c'}$,

   b) L_c is a convex set for each $c \in \mathbb{R}$ if and only if D is quasi-concave.

The concept of c-cut gives us an interesting result to verify whether a function $D : L \longrightarrow \mathbb{R}$ is Schur-concave. Given $x = (x_1, \ldots, x_n) \in L$, we will call $Conv(x)$ the convex closure of $(x_{\pi(1)}, \ldots, x_{\pi(n)})$ for all permutations π of $1, \ldots, n$. We need previously two results to make more easy to use the dominance relation and the order $\leq_d$. The proofs of the following proposition can be found in [5].

Proposition 1. *a) If $x \leq_d y$, then $y \in Conv(x)$.*

b) Given $x, y \in L$, we have:

$$x \succ y \Longleftrightarrow y \in Conv(x).$$

Now we can give the proposition which relates the Schur-concavity with the c-cuts.

Proposition 2. *A function $D : L \longrightarrow \mathbb{R}$ is Schur-concave if and only if, for all $x \in L$, $Conv(x) \subset L_{D(x)}$.*

In [5] we give the following definition of a dispersion measure is defined as follows, and then the monotonicity condition with quasi-concavity and Schur-concavity condition are compared.

Definition 4. *A function $D : L \longrightarrow \mathbb{R}$ is a dispersion measure if it satisfies the following conditions:*

1) Simmetry: for any list $x \in L$ and for any permutation π of $1, \ldots, n$,

$$D(x_1, \ldots, x_n) = D(x_{\pi(1)}, \ldots, x_{\pi(n)})$$

2) Extremal values: for all $(x_1, \ldots, x_n) \in L$,

$$D(1, 0, \ldots, 0) \leq D(x_1, \ldots, x_n) \leq D(\tfrac{1}{n}, \ldots, \tfrac{1}{n}).$$

3) Monotonicity: if $x \leq_d y$, then $D(x) \leq D(y)$.

Specifically, in [5] it is proved that a function D satisfying conditions (1) plus quasi-concavity is Schur-concave and this implies that D is a dispersion measure.

2 T-**Quasi-concavity**

Observe that the definition of quasi-concavity (def. 3) means that the image through D of any intermediate point of the segment with extremes x and y must be greater than or equal to the image of $D(x)$ and $D(y)$ through the t-norm MIN. Now we propose to substitute MIN by any other t-norm T and study the relations between T-quasi-concave dispersion measures for different t-norms T. First of all, we give the definition of T-quasi-concave dispersion measure

Definition 5. *A function $D : L \longrightarrow [0, 1]$ is a T-quasi-concave dispersion measure if it satisfies the following conditions:*

1) Simmetry: for any list $x \in L$ and for any permutation π of $1, \ldots, n$,

$$D(x_1, \ldots, x_n) = D(x_{\pi(1)}, \ldots, x_{\pi(n)})$$

2) Extremal values: for all $(x_1, \ldots, x_n) \in L$,

$$0 = D(1, 0, \ldots, 0) \leq D(x_1, \ldots, x_n) \leq D(\tfrac{1}{n}, \ldots, \tfrac{1}{n}) = 1$$

3) D is T-quasi-concave: for any $x, y \in L$ and $a \in [0, 1]$,

$$D((1 - a)x + ay) \geq T(D(x), D(y)).$$

Since for any t-norm T, $T(x, y) \leq \min(x, y)$ $\forall x, y \in [0, 1]$, we immediately obtain

Proposition 3. *If $D : L \longrightarrow [0, 1]$ is quasi-concave, then D is T-quasi-concave.*

As we know (see [5]), any quasi-concave dispersion measure is Schur-concave. Thus, both the Schur-concave dispersion measures and the T-quasi-concave ones contain all the quasi-concave dispersion measures. We want to determine what is the relation between Schur-concave dispersion measures, T-quasi-concave dispersion measures and monotonic dispersion measures.

We must distinguish two situations: when D equals 1 only on the point $(\tfrac{1}{n}, \ldots, \tfrac{1}{n})$ and when there exists a point in L different from $(\tfrac{1}{n}, \ldots, \tfrac{1}{n})$ where D also equals 1.

Definition 6. *Given a dispersion measure $D : L \longrightarrow [0, 1]$, the kernel of D is the set*

$$Ker(D) = \{x \in L : D(x) = 1\}$$

As a first example, we are going to analize what happens with the zero t-norm. Recall that

$$Z(x, y) = \begin{cases} x & \text{if } y = 1 \\ y & \text{if } x = 1 \\ 0 & \text{if } x \neq 1 \text{ and } y \neq 1 \end{cases}$$

Definition 7. *A function $D : L \longrightarrow [0, 1]$ is Z-quasi-concave if, for any $x, y \in L$ and $a \in [0, 1]$,*

$$D((1 - a)x + ay) \geq Z(D(x), D(y)).$$

Observe that this definition is equivalent to

$$D(x) = 1 \implies D((1 - a)x + ay) \geq D(y) \quad \forall y \in L, \ \forall \lambda \in [0, 1]$$

In particular, if we take $x = (\tfrac{1}{n}, \ldots, \tfrac{1}{n})$, we obtain that D must be non decreasing over any segment with final extreme $(\tfrac{1}{n}, \ldots, \tfrac{1}{n})$.

Proposition 4. *If $Ker(D) = \{(\tfrac{1}{n}, \ldots, \tfrac{1}{n})\}$, then any monotonic dispersion measure is Z-quasi-concave.*

Proof. If $x = (\frac{1}{n}, \ldots, \frac{1}{n})$, $\forall \lambda \in [0,1]$ and $\forall y \in L$, $(1-\lambda)x + \lambda y \geq_d y$ since $\forall y_i \leq \frac{1}{n}$, $\frac{1}{n} \geq (1-\lambda)\frac{1}{n} + \lambda y_i \geq y_i$, and for $y_i > \frac{1}{n}$, $\frac{1}{n} < (1-\lambda)\frac{1}{n} + \lambda y_i < y_i$. Then, if D is monotonic, $D(1-\lambda)x + \lambda y \geq D(y)$. $\qquad\square$

Remarks

1) As a consequence of this proposition, if $Ker(D) = \{(\frac{1}{n}, \ldots, \frac{1}{n})\}$, any Schur-concave dispersion measure is Z-quasi-concave.

2) If $|Ker(D)| > 1$, then the monotonicity does not imply the Z-quasi-concavity. Let us see a counter-example in the case $n = 3$. Let us consider the dispersion measure

$$D(x_1, x_2, x_3) = \begin{cases} 1 & \text{if } x_1 = \frac{1}{3} \text{ or } x_2 = \frac{1}{3} \\ & \text{or } x_3 = \frac{1}{3} \\ 0 & \text{in any other case} \end{cases}$$

Observe that D is monotonic because it could only fail in the case that an element of the kernel could be less than or equal to an element out of the kernel. But this is impossible since

$$(\frac{1}{3}, a, 1-a) \leq_d (y_1, y_2, y_3) \longrightarrow y_1 = \frac{1}{3}$$

and $(y_1, y_2, y_3) \in Ker(D)$.

On the other hand, D is not Z-quasi-concave because if we take $x = (\frac{1}{3}, 0, \frac{2}{3})$ and $y = (0, \frac{1}{3}, \frac{2}{3})$, we obtain $D(x) = D(y) = 1$ but, if $\lambda = \frac{1}{2}$, $\frac{1}{2}x + \frac{1}{2}y = (\frac{1}{6}, \frac{1}{6}, \frac{2}{3})$ and $D(\frac{1}{2}x + \frac{1}{2}y) = 0 < D(y)$.

3) The Z-quasi-concavity does not imply the monotonicity as we will see with a counter-example. Let us consider the dispersion measure

$$D(x_1, x_2, x_3) = \begin{cases} 0 & \text{if } x \in \Delta \\ \frac{1}{2} & \text{if } x \notin \Delta \cup \{(\frac{1}{3}, \frac{1}{3}, \frac{1}{3})\} \\ 1 & \text{if } x = (\frac{1}{3}, \frac{1}{3}, \frac{1}{3}) \end{cases}$$

where $\Delta = \{0 \leq x_1 \leq \frac{1}{3}, 0 \leq x_2 \leq x_1\} \cup \{0 \leq x_1 \leq \frac{1}{3}, \frac{2}{3} - x_1 \leq x_2 \leq 1\} \cup \{\frac{1}{3} \leq x_1 \leq \frac{2}{3}, \frac{2}{3} - x_1 \leq x_2 \leq \frac{1}{3}\} \cup \{\frac{2}{3} \leq x_1 \leq 1, 0 \leq x_2 \leq 1 - x_1\} \setminus \{(\frac{1}{3}, \frac{1}{3}, \frac{1}{3})\}$.

D is clearly Z-quasi-concave, but it is not monotonic since $D(0.1, 0.2, 0.7) = \frac{1}{2}$ and $D(0.3, 0.2, 0.5) = 0$ but $(0.1, 0.2, 0.7) \leq_d (0.3, 0.2, 0.5)$.

4) So far, we have related the Z-quasi-concavity with the monotonicity. Now we will deal with the Schur-concavity. We know (see [5]) that the Schur-concavity implies the monotonicity. Thus in the case that $Ker(D)$ consists only of the point $(\frac{1}{n}, \ldots, \frac{1}{n})$, the Schur-concavity implies the Z-quasi-concavity. In the other case, if $|Ker(D)| > 1$, then the Schur-concavity

does not imply the Z-quasi-concavity. Let us consider again an example in the case $n = 3$. Let us take the dispersion measure

$$D(x_1, x_2, x_3) = \begin{cases} 1 & \text{if } x \in \nabla \\ \frac{1}{2} & \text{if } x \in \Delta \\ 0 & \text{in any other case} \end{cases}$$

where $\nabla = \{x_1, x_2, x_3 \leq \frac{1}{2}\}$ and $\Delta = \{x_1, x_2, x_3 \geq \frac{1}{6}\} \setminus \nabla$.

D is Schur-concave but it is not Z-quasi-concave since $D(\frac{1}{12}, \frac{1}{12}, \frac{10}{12}) = \frac{1}{2}, D(\frac{1}{2}, 0, \frac{1}{2}) = 1$ but

$$D(\tfrac{1}{2}(\tfrac{1}{12}, \tfrac{1}{12}, \tfrac{10}{12}) + \tfrac{1}{2}(\tfrac{1}{2}, 0, \tfrac{1}{2})) = D(\tfrac{7}{24}, \tfrac{1}{24}, \tfrac{16}{24}) = 0 < D(\tfrac{1}{12}, \tfrac{1}{12}, \tfrac{10}{12}).$$

3 T-quasi-concave dispersion measures on L_3

Let us consider now $L_3 = \{(x, y, z) \in [0, 1]^3 : x + y + z = 1\}$. Given a t-norm T, we say that a function $D : L_3 \longrightarrow [0, 1]$ is a T-quasi-concave dispersion measure if it satisfies the following conditions:

1) Symmetry: for any $(x_1, x_2, x_3) \in L_3$ and for any permutation π of $\{1, 2, 3\}$,

$$D(x_1, x_2, x_3) = D(x_{\pi(1)}, x_{\pi(2)}, x_{\pi(3)})$$

2) Extremal values: for all $(x_1, x_2, x_3) \in L_3$,

$$D(1, 0, 0) \leq D(x_1, x_2, x_3) \leq D(\tfrac{1}{3}, \tfrac{1}{3}, \tfrac{1}{3}).$$

3) $D(x, y, z) = 1 \iff x = y = z = \frac{1}{3}$

4) For all $A, B \in L_3$ and $\lambda \in [0, 1]$, $D((1 - \lambda)A + \lambda B) \geq T(D(A), D(B))$.

As shown in [5], it is very useful to use the representation given in Figure 1 for the case $n = 3$.

By symmetry, we can only take into account the third part of L_3 formed by lists (x, y, z) such that $x, z \geq y$. A good way to simplify the study of T-quasi-concave dispersion measures in this context is through the following change of variables. Given a point $P = (x, y, z)$ in this region, let a, b be as in Figure 2.

Then the new variables are $p_1 = \sqrt{3}a$, $p_2 = \sqrt{3}b$. For example, if $P = (1/3, 1/3, 1/3)$, we have $p_1 = p_2 = 1$, and if $P = (1/2, 0, 1/2)$, $p_1 = p_2 = 1/2$. With these new variables, we can represent the points P of this region of L_3 as points $(p_1, p_2) \in [0, 1]^2$ such that $p_1 + p_2 \geq 1$.

A few calculations give the relations:

$$p_1 = 1 + y - z, \; p_2 = 1 + y - x$$

and, conversely,

$$\begin{cases} x = \frac{p_1 - 2p_2 + 2}{3} \\ y = \frac{p_1 + p_2 - 1}{3} \\ z = \frac{2 - 2p_1 + p_2}{3} \end{cases}$$

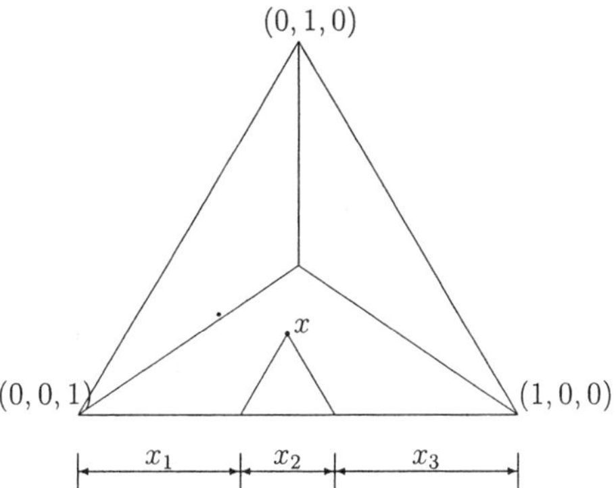

Figure 1: Barycentric coordinates

Let us consider now the family

$$\mathcal{D}_{T,i} = \{D : L_3 \longrightarrow [0,1] \; T - \text{quasi-concave disp. measure} : D(x,x,z) = 3x \forall x \in [0,\tfrac{1}{3}]\}$$

Observe that this condition, with the new variables, indicates that $D(p_1, 1) = p_1$, $\forall p_1 \in [0,1]$. We are now going to see how to construct the minimum T-quasi-concave dispersion measure of this family. We have to impose that D satisfies $D(P) \geq T(D(A), D(B))$ for all $A \in \{x = y\}$ and $B \in \{y = z\}$ such that the segment $\bar{AB}$ passes through the point P. Figure 3 shows this situation in the unit square.

The general equation of a straight line passing through the point (p_1, p_2) is $y - p_2 = m(x - p_1)$. Then

$$\begin{cases} y = 1 & \longrightarrow \quad x_A = \frac{1-p_2}{m} + p_1 \\ x = 1 & \longrightarrow \quad y_B = p_2 + m(1 - p_1) \end{cases}$$

Thus we have to impose that

$$D(p_1, p_2) \geq T(\frac{1 - p_2}{m} + p_1, p_2 + m(1 - p_1))$$

for all permisible m. It is not difficult to show that we obtain the minimum dispersion measure D if we take

$$D(p_1, p_2) = \max_m T(\frac{1 - p_2}{m} + p_1, p_2 + m(1 - p_1))$$

We will call $D_{T,i}$ this dispersion measure. A straightforward calculations show that $D_{T,i}$ is, in fact, T-quasi-concave.

We are going now to generalize this construction. Let $f : [0, \tfrac{1}{3}] \longrightarrow [0,1]$ be a continuous and strictly increasing T-morphism such that $f(0) = 0$ and $f(\tfrac{1}{3}) = 1$. Let us now consider the

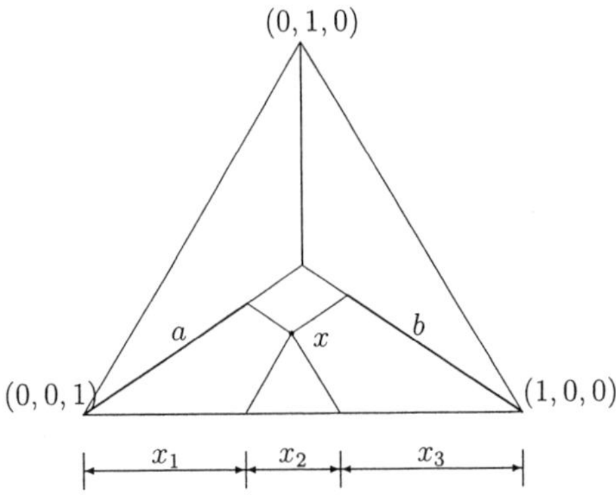

Figure 2: Variables a, b

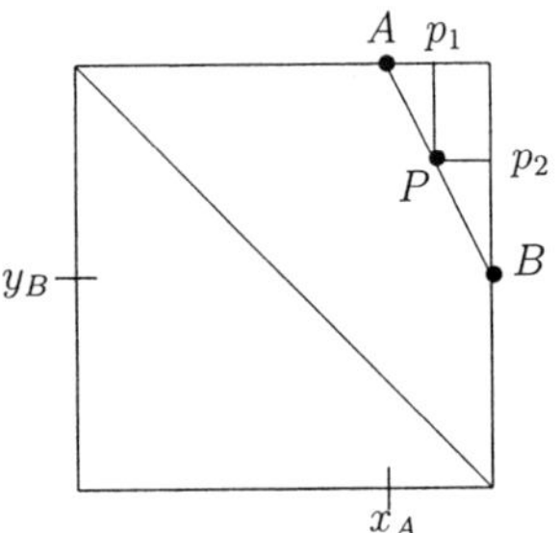

Figure 3: Unit square

family

$$\mathcal{D}_{T,f} = \{D : L_3 \longrightarrow [0,1] \; T - \text{quasi-concave disp. measure} : D(x,x,z) = f(x) \; \forall x \in [0,\tfrac{1}{3}]\}$$

We are going to define the minimum dispersion measure $D_{T,f}$ of this class. Given $(x,y,z) \in L_3$, let $(x',x',z') \in L_3$ be the unique point such that $D_{T,i}(x',x',z') = D_{T,i}(x,y,z) = 3x'$. Then we define $D_{T,f}(x,y,z) = f(x')$. Let us prove that $D_{T,f}$ is the minimum dispersion measure of the class $\mathcal{D}_{T,f}$. First of all, we have to prove that $D_{T,f}$ is a dispersion measure: if $A, B \in L_3$, then any point P of the segment $\overline{AB}$ satisfies that $D_{T,f}(P) \geq T(D_{T,f}(A), D_{T,f}(B))$. We can suppose that $A = (a,a,1-2a)$ and $B = (1-2b,b,b)$, that is, A belongs to the segment of vertices $(0,0,1)$ and $(\tfrac{1}{3},\tfrac{1}{3},\tfrac{1}{3})$ and B to the segment with vertices $(1,0,0)$ and $(\tfrac{1}{3},\tfrac{1}{3},\tfrac{1}{3})$. Let $(p,p,1-2p)$ the unique point of the segment of vertices $(0,0,1)$ and $(\tfrac{1}{3},\tfrac{1}{3},\tfrac{1}{3})$ such that $D_{T,i}(P) = D_{T,i}(p,p,1-p)$. Let $g : [0,1] \longrightarrow [0,1]$ be defined by $g(x) = f(\tfrac{x}{3})$. Then

$$D_{T,i} \text{ is } T\text{-quasi-concave} \implies D_{T,i}(P) \geq T(D_{T,i}(A), D_{T,i}(B)) \implies 3p \geq T(3a, 3b)$$

$$\implies g(3p) \geq g(T(3a, 3b)) = T(g(3a), g(3b)) \implies f(p) \geq T(f(a), f(b))$$

$$\implies D_{T,f}(P) \geq T(D_{T,f}(A), D_{T,f}(B))$$

In order to prove that $D_{T,f}$ is the minimum dispersion measure of the class $\mathcal{D}_{T,f}$, we need to introduce a new dispersion measure. Given $(x, y, z) \in L_3$, let $(x', x', z') \in L_3$ be the unique point such that $D(x, y, z) = D(x', x', z') = f(x')$. Then we define $D_{-1}(x, y, z) = 3x'$. Let us prove that $D_{-1} \in \mathcal{D}_{T,f}$. We have to see that $D_{-1}(P) \geq T(D_{-1}(A), D_{-1}(B))$. But

$$D \text{ is } T\text{-quasi-concave} \implies D(P) \geq T(D(A), D(B)) \implies f(p) \geq T(f(a), f(b))$$

$$\implies g(3p) \geq T(g(3a), g(3b)) = g(T(3a, 3b)) \implies 3p \geq T(3a, 3b)$$

$$\implies D_{-1}(P) \geq T(D_{-1}(A), D_{-1}(B))$$

Let us now prove that $D_{T,f}$ is the minimum dispersion measure, that is, if $D \in \mathcal{D}_{T,f}$, then $D(x, y, z) \geq D_{T,f}(x, y, z) \; \forall (x, y, z) \in L_3$.

Since $D_{-1} \in \mathcal{D}_{T,i}$, we will have $D_{-1}(x, y, z) \geq D_{T,i}(x, y, z)$. Then, if $D_{T,i}(x, y, z) = D_{T,i}(x'', x'', z'') = 3x''$, we will have $3x' \geq 3x''$, and this implies that $f(x') \geq f(x'')$, because f is increasing. Finally, $D(x, y, z) = f(x') \geq D_{T,f}(x, y, z) = f(x'')$.

As a consequence of this construction, we can state the following proposition:

Proposition 5. *Let $D : L_3 \longrightarrow [0, 1]$ symmetric, with extremal values and such that $Ker(D) = \{(\frac{1}{3}, \frac{1}{3}, \frac{1}{3})\}$ and $D(x_1, x_1, 1 - 2x_1) = f(x_1)$ for all $x_1 \in [0, \frac{1}{3}]$. Then if D is T-quasi-concave, $D \geq D_{T,f}$.*

3.1 Product t-norm

Let us apply now this construction to the t-norm $\Pi(x, y) = x \cdot y$. We have:

$$f(m) = \Pi(\tfrac{1-p_2}{m} + p_1, p_2 + m(1 - p_1)) = (\tfrac{1-p_2}{m} + p_1) \cdot (p_2 + m(1 - p_1))$$

$$= \tfrac{(1-p_2)p_2}{m} + p_1 p_2 + (1 - p_2)(1 - p_1) + m p_1(1 - p_1)$$

The maximum is taken in $m = -\sqrt{\frac{(1-p_2)p_2}{(1-p_1)p_1}}$ and thus

$$D_{\Pi,i}(p_1, p_2) = 1 - p_1 - p_2 + 2\left[p_1 p_2 - \sqrt{p_1 p_2(1 - p_1)(1 - p_2)}\right]$$

Remarks

Let us observe

1) $D_{\Pi,i}(p_1, 1) = D_{\Pi,i}(1, p_2) = 1$.

2) $D_{\Pi,i}$ is symmetric with respect to $\{x = z\}$, that is $D_{\Pi,i}(p_1, p_2) = D_{\Pi,i}(p_2, p_1)$.

3) Obviously, $D_{\Pi,i}$ is Π-quasi-concave.

4) If $p_2 = p_1$, $D_{\Pi,i}(p_1, p_1) = 1 - 4p_1(1 - p_1)$.

5) With the barycentric coordinates, $p_1 = 1 + y - z, p_2 = 1 + y - x$ and

$$D_{\Pi,i}(x, y, z) = 2 \left[y^2 + xz - xy - yz - \frac{x}{2} + y \right.$$
$$\left. - \frac{z}{2} + \frac{1}{2} - \sqrt{(1 + y - z)(1 + y - x)(z - y)(x - y)} \right]$$

6) $D_{\Pi,i}$ is not quasi-concave as the c-cuts are not convex sets:

$$D_{\Pi,i}\left(\frac{1}{2\sqrt{3}}, \frac{1}{2\sqrt{3}}, 1 - \frac{1}{\sqrt{3}}\right) = D_{\Pi,i}\left(1 - \frac{1}{\sqrt{3}}, \frac{1}{2\sqrt{3}}, \frac{1}{2\sqrt{3}}\right) = \frac{\sqrt{3}}{2}$$

but the half point of the segment determined by these two extremes has a dispersion of $D_{\Pi,i}\left(\frac{1 - \frac{1}{\sqrt{3}}}{2}, \frac{1}{\sqrt{3}}, \frac{1 - \frac{1}{\sqrt{3}}}{2}\right) = 0.75$ and does not belong to $L_{\frac{\sqrt{3}}{2}}$.

7) $D_{\Pi,i}$ is not Schur-concave because, for example, if we take $x = \left(\frac{1}{4}, \frac{1}{4}, \frac{1}{2}\right) \in L$, $Conv(x) \not\subset L_{D_{\Pi,i}(x)}$: the point $y = \left(\frac{3}{8}, \frac{1}{4}, \frac{3}{8}\right) \in Conv(x)$, but $D(y) = 0.5625 < D(x) = 0.75$.

8) $D_{\Pi,i}$ is not monotonic since $\left(\frac{1}{2\sqrt{3}}, \frac{1}{2\sqrt{3}}, 1 - \frac{1}{\sqrt{3}}\right) \leq_d \left(\frac{1}{3}, \frac{1}{2\sqrt{3}}, \frac{2}{3} - \frac{1}{2\sqrt{3}}\right)$ but $D_{\Pi,i}\left(\frac{1}{2\sqrt{3}}, \frac{1}{2\sqrt{3}}, 1 - \frac{1}{\sqrt{3}}\right) = \frac{\sqrt{3}}{2}$ is greater than $D_{\Pi,i}\left(\frac{1}{3}, \frac{1}{2\sqrt{3}}, \frac{2}{3} - \frac{1}{2\sqrt{3}}\right) = 0.756185$

Thus we have proved that the Π-quasi-concavity does not imply quasi-concavity, nor Schur-concavity nor monotonicity.

3.2   Łukasiewicz t-norm

Let us consider now the t-norm $W(x, y) = \max\{x + y - 1, 0\}$. In this case,

$$f(m) = W\left(\frac{1 - p_2}{m} + p_1, p_2 + m(1 - p_1)\right) = \max\left\{p_1 + p_2 - 1 + \frac{1 - p_2}{m} + m(1 - p_1), 0\right\}$$

The maximum is taken in $m = -\sqrt{\frac{1 - p_2}{1 - p_1}}$ and thus

$$D(p_1, p_2) = p_1 + p_2 - 1 - 2\sqrt{(1 - p_1)(1 - p_2)}$$

Remarks

Let us observe that

1) $D(p_1, 1) = D(1, p_2) = 1$.

2) D is symmetric with respect to $\{x = z\}$, that is $D(p_1, p_2) = D(p_2, p_1)$.

3) Obviously, D is W-quasi-concave.

4) If $p_2 = p_1$, $D(p_1, p_1) = \max\{4p_1 - 3, 0\}$ and $D(p_1, p_1) > 0 \iff p_1 > \frac{3}{4}$.

5) With the barycentric coordinates, $p_1 = 1 + y - z, p_2 = 1 + y - x$ and

$$D(x, y, z) = \max\{1 + 2y - x - z - 2\sqrt{(z-y)(x-y)}, 0\}$$

6) D is not quasi-concave as the c-cuts are not convex sets:

$D(\frac{1}{2\sqrt{3}}, \frac{1}{2\sqrt{3}}, 1 - \frac{1}{\sqrt{3}}) = D(1 - \frac{1}{\sqrt{3}}, \frac{1}{2\sqrt{3}}, \frac{1}{2\sqrt{3}}) = \frac{\sqrt{3}}{2}$ but the half point of the segment with these two extremes has $D(\frac{1 - \frac{1}{\sqrt{3}}}{2}, \frac{1}{\sqrt{3}}, \frac{1 - \frac{1}{\sqrt{3}}}{2}) = 0.732051$ and does not belong to $L_{\frac{\sqrt{3}}{2}}$.

7) D is not Schur-concave because, for some $x \in L$, $Conv(x) \not\subset L_{D(x)}$.

8) D is not monotonic since $(\frac{1}{2\sqrt{3}}, \frac{1}{2\sqrt{3}}, 1 - \frac{1}{\sqrt{3}}) \leq_d (\frac{1}{3}, \frac{1}{2\sqrt{3}}, \frac{2}{3} - \frac{1}{2\sqrt{3}})$ but $D(\frac{1}{2\sqrt{3}}, \frac{1}{2\sqrt{3}}, 1 - \frac{1}{\sqrt{3}}) = \frac{\sqrt{3}}{2} > D(\frac{1}{3}, \frac{1}{2\sqrt{3}}, \frac{2}{3} - \frac{1}{2\sqrt{3}}) = 0.739713$

9) D is not Π-quasi-concave: $\Pi(D(\frac{1}{2\sqrt{3}}, \frac{1}{2\sqrt{3}}, 1 - \frac{1}{\sqrt{3}}), D(1 - \frac{1}{\sqrt{3}}, \frac{1}{2\sqrt{3}}, \frac{1}{2\sqrt{3}})) = \left(\frac{\sqrt{3}}{2}\right)^2 = 0.75 > D(\frac{1 - \frac{1}{\sqrt{3}}}{2}, \frac{1}{\sqrt{3}}, \frac{1 - \frac{1}{\sqrt{3}}}{2}) = 0.732051$

10) Since $\Pi \geq W$, we have that Π-quasi-concavity implies W-quasi-concavity.

Thus we have proved that any Π-quasi-concave dispersion measure is W-quasi-concave, but the W-quasi-concavity does not imply quasi-concavity, nor Schur-concavity nor monotonicity.

4   Conclusions

In this paper we have generalized the concept of quasi-concavity for dispersion measures by means of the use of t-norms, specially the more usual ones, $T = Z, \Pi, W$. We have characterized the Z-quasi-concavity, and for the other t-norms we have found the minimum T-quasi-concave dispersion measures. We have also studied the relations between all of them as well as the quasi-concavity, the Schur-concavity and the monotonicity.

A future study should be to complete the characterization of Π-quasi-concavity and W-quasi-concavity. This study would involve in some way the generalization of Schur-concavity by means of t-norms.

5   Appendix

In this appendix we give examples of dispersion measures indicating in each case the properties of the dispersion measure considered. The list has been done for the case when $Ker(D) = \{(\frac{1}{n}, \ldots, \frac{1}{n})\}$ as it seems to be more usual.

1) Quasi-concave: $$D(x_1, \ldots, x_n) = 1 - (\bigvee x_i - \bigwedge x_i).$$

2) Schur-concave and Π-quasi-concave, not quasi-concave:

$$D(x_1, x_2, x_3) = \begin{cases} 3 \cdot \bigwedge x_i & \text{if } p_x \geq 2 \\ \max\left\{0, 2 - 3 \cdot \bigvee x_i\right\} & \text{if } p_x = 1 \end{cases}$$

3) Monotonic and W-quasi-concave, not Π-quasi-concave nor Schur-concave:

$$D(x_1, \ldots, x_n) = x_{(1)} + \cdots + x_{(p_x)}$$

4) Z-quasi-concave, not monotonic nor W-quasi-concave:

$$D(x_1, x_2, x_3) = \begin{cases} 1 & \text{if } x = (\tfrac{1}{3}, \tfrac{1}{3}, \tfrac{1}{3}) \\ \tfrac{1}{2} & \text{if } x \in \{0 < x_{(1)} = x_{(2)} < \tfrac{1}{3}\} \\ 0 & \text{in any other case} \end{cases}$$

5) Π-quasi-concave, not monotonic:

$$D(x_1, x_2, x_3) = 2\left[x_2^2 + x_1 x_3 - x_1 x_2 - x_2 x_3 - \frac{x_1}{2} + x_2 - \frac{x_3}{2} + \right.$$
$$\left. + \frac{1}{2} - \sqrt{(1 + x_2 - x_3)(1 + x_2 - x_1)(x_3 - x_2)(x_1 - x_2)} \right]$$

6) W-quasi-concave, not Π-quasi-concave nor monotonic:

$$D(x_1, x_2, x_3) = \max\{1 + 2x_2 - x_1 - x_3 - 2\sqrt{(x_3 - x_2)(x_1 - x_2)}, 0\}$$

References

[1] M. Carbonell, M. Mas and G. Mayor, On a class of monotonic extended OWA operators, Proceedings of the FUZZIEEE-97 **3**, Barcelona (1997) 1695-1700.

[2] I. Couso and P. Gil, Characterization of a family of entropy measures, Proc. of the IPMU'98, Paris (1998) 1053-1059.

[3] A. DeLuca and S. Termini, A definition of a non-probabilistic entropy, Information and Control **20-4** (1972) 301-312.

[4] W. Gehrig, On a characterization of the Shannon concentration measure, in Functional Equations: History, Applications and Theory (J. Aczél, editor), D. Reidel Publishing Company (1984) 191-206.

[5] Javier Martín, Gaspar Mayor and Jaume Suñer, On Dispersion Measures, Mathware & Soft Computing **8-3** (2001) 227-237.

[6] D. Morales, L. Pardo and I. Vajda, Uncertainty of Discrete Stochastic Systems: General Theory and Statistical Inference, IEEE Trans. on Systems, Man, and Cybernetics-Part A: Systems and Humans **26-6** (1996) 681-697.

[7] M. O'Hagan, Using maximum entropy-ordered weighted averaging to construct a fuzzy neuron, Proceedings 24th Annual IEEE Asilomar Conf. on Signals, Systems and Computers, Pacific Grove, CA, (1990) 618-623.

[8] C.E. Shannon, A mathematical theory of communication, Bell Syst. Tech. J. **27** (1948), 379-423 and 623-656.

Artificial Intelligence Research and Development
I. Aguiló et al. (Eds.)
IOS Press, 2003

Distances between possibilistic descriptions of RNA structures

Jaume Casasnovas*, Joe Miró*, Francesc Rosselló*
Dep. de Matemàtiques i Informàtica, Universitat de les Illes Balears,
E-07122 Palma de Mallorca, Spain.
{dmijcc0,dmijmj0,dmifrl0}@clust.uib.es

Abstract. We present possibilistic RNA primary structures as representations of the imprecise knowledge of the composition of RNA molecules. These are a special type of Sadegh-Zadeh's fuzzy genomes, and in particular they are points of a Kosko hypercube of adequate dimension. But, against what happens in probabilistic representations, in possibilistic RNA primary structures it is biologically plausible to assume that the possibility of a given nucleotide in a given position is independent of the possibility of the same or other nucleotides in other positions. This motivates the definition of metrics to quantify their similarity by aggregating pseudodistances defined at the level of possibilistic distributions representing imprecisely known nucleotides. We show some applications of these facts.

1 Introduction

As is well known, an RNA molecule can be viewed as a chain of (ribo)nucleotides with a definite orientation. Each of these nucleotides is characterized by the base attached to it, which can be adenine (A), cytosine (C), guanine (G), or uracil (U). Thus, an RNA molecule with N nucleotides can be mathematically described as a word of length N over the alphabet $\{A, C, G, U\}$. This chain of bases is called the *primary structure* of the molecule. Unfortunately, determining experimentally which base is present in each position in an RNA molecule often cannot be done with total reliability, and the available data may allow only a degree of certainty in a given description. Treating this situation probabilistically, we would be able to award a value between 0 and 1 to each possible sequence, but we would not be able to study similarities and differences between sequences.

Sadegh-Zadeh [20, 21] has recently introduced a new way of looking at imprecisely known nucleic acid (DNA or RNA) molecules, reminiscent of probabilistic profiles in computational biology [9], that allows the definition and use of distances, entropies, etc. within this degree of certainty. This author represented a polynucleotide of length N as a vector of length $4N$ with entries in $[0, 1]$. The first four entries in this vector represent the probability that the first symbol is A, C, G, or U (T, in DNA), respectively, the next four numbers represent the same thing for the second symbol, and so forth. For example, our knowledge of

---

*This work has been partially supported by Spanish Government grants of the DGES, BFM2000-1113-C02-01 y BFM2000-1114.

the composition of a *codon* (an RNA sequence of length $N = 3$) could be represented by a 12-dimensional vector

$$(1/3, 2/3, 0, 0, 0, 0, 1, 0, 1/3, 1/6, 1/3, 1/6).$$

In this vector we read, for instance, that the first base in the codon cannot be a G (or rather, that the probability of it being a G is zero) and that the probability of the third symbol being a C is 1/6. This vector could actually have been obtained as the probabilities which the different bases appear with in the three positions of those codons coding for the aminoacid arginine, which are

$$CGA, CGC, CGG, CGU, AGA, AGG.$$

But it can also be obtained by any other method, as for instance as a profile resulting from a multiple sequence alignment, or as the result of a sequencing procedure.

The vectors introduced by Sadegh-Zadeh can be understood as the coordinates of points in the unit hypercube $[0, 1]^{4N}$ of dimension $4N$, but it can also be understood as a fuzzy set defined over a universe of $4N$ elements and values in $[0, 1]$. The connection between points of a hypercube $[0, 1]^{M}$ and fuzzy sets defined on a set of M elements was introduced by Kosko [11], and so these unit hypercubes are also dubbed *Kosko's hypercubes*. The interpretation of imprecisely known RNA or DNA sequences as points of $[0, 1]^{4N}$ allows the introduction of metric concepts such as distances and similarities to compare descriptions of sequences, as well as related notion like for instance midpoints [15]. Besides, the interpretation as fuzzy sets, allows us to apply concepts such as the entropy of a fuzzy set to the description of a polynucleotide. Sadegh-Zadeh described the relationships among these concepts.

In [6] we proposed an alternative way of modelling our imprecise knowledge of an RNA molecule by means of a point in Kosko's hypercube, using possibilistic descriptions instead of probabilistic ones. In this approach, each position in the sequence defining the primary structure of the RNA molecule of length N defines a *possibilistic distribution* over the alphabet $\{A, C, G, U\}$, i.e., a mapping $\pi_i : \{A, C, G, U\} \to [0, 1]$, for each position $i = 1, \ldots, N$, such that at least one of the elements in the alphabet has image 1.

One of the most important features of possibilistic descriptions of RNA molecules is that, depending on how they have been obtained (for instance, through sequencing experiments [2]), it is biologically plausible to assume that the possibility that a given base appears in a given position of the sequence is independent of the possibility that the same or some other base appears in another position. This simplifies the computation of the possibility of events related to the composition of a possibilistic description of an RNA molecule, using the theory and tools introduced in [7, 8]. Notice moreover that this independence assumption is false for probabilistic descriptions, and this falsehood lies at the base of the search algorithms for biologically relevant subsequences using Hidden Markov Models and other higher order probabilistic methods [9].

In this paper we deal with the definition of metric concepts between possibilistic descriptions of RNA molecules of a fixed length N considered as points in $[0, 1]^{4N}$. We propose here that the nature of these descriptions, obtained by attaching in an ordered way possibilistic distributions over $\{A, C, G, U\}$, one for each position in the chain of nucleotides, motivates the use of pseudodistances that quantify the similarity of these "single-position" possibilistic distributions and then to aggregate them to define a distance between the points in the hypercube corresponding to full-length molecules. Of course, the way of performing this is not unique [23], as was already pointed out by Sadegh-Zadeh [20].

The use of distances allows the definition and computation of magnitudes like entropies, differences, etc. [20], but it can also be used in the study of RNA secondary structures in the presence of uncertainty. In the cell and *in vitro*, an RNA molecule folds into a three-dimensional structure which is held together by weak interactions called *hydrogen bonds* between pairs of nucleotides that are far apart in the chain [19, 22]. Most of these bonds form between *Watson-Crick complementary bases*, i.e., between A and U and between C and G, but a far from negligible amount of bonds also form between other pairs of bases [24]. The *secondary structure* of an RNA molecule is a simplified model of this three-dimensional structure, consisting roughly of the set of its hydrogen bonds or *contacts*.

These RNA secondary structures usually are described by means of suitable (to the purposes of the description) contact matrices [5, 13, 19]. In their simplest description, one uses the adjacency matrix of the graph defined by the contacts on the set of nodes corresponding to the nucleotides: $(a_{i,j})_{i,j=1,\ldots,N}$ with $a_{i,j} = 1$ if there is a contact between the i-th and the j-th nucleotides, and $a_{i,j} = 0$ otherwise. We could represent our uncertain knowledge of a secondary structure by replacing the entries in this adjacency matrix by new entries yielding the possibility of a contact between the corresponding nucleotides. If we also introduce a possibility distribution on $\{A, C, G, U\}^2$ that associates to every pair of bases the possibility of a contact between them (for instance, 1 to Watson-Crick complementary pairs and lower values to other pairs [24]), then we shall be able to compute the possibility that an imprecisely known primary structure folds into an imprecisely known secondary structure, both possibilistically described.

It is actually the possibility of making the step from primary to secondary structures that motivates us to consider here only RNA molecules. But it should be clear that everything we shall discuss in this paper concerning RNA primary structures can also be translated *mutatis mutandi* to other contexts, like for instance DNA molecules (as words over $\{A, C, G, T\}$ or simply over $\{\text{Pur}, \text{Pyr}\}$), proteins (as words made of aminoacids or of equivalence classes of them, like for instance the usual 8-letter chemical alphabet or the 3-letter structural alphabet), genes (as words made of codons), etc.: actually, the concept of a fuzzy word that we introduce in Sect. 3 can be applied to all these settings. On the other hand, our discussion of RNA secondary structures can also be generalized to models of protein three-dimensional structures, but this generalization is not straightforward, as most (if not all) of these models are not simply graphs capturing the neighborhood of monomers [22].

2 Preliminaries

2.1 Possibility measures

We recall from [7, 8] several notions and facts related to possibility distributions.

Definition 1. *Let Ω be a finite set, whose subsets are generically called* events. *A function* $\Pi : P(\Omega) \to [0, 1]$ *is a* possibility measure *when it satisfies the following conditions:*

- $\Pi(\emptyset) = 0; \; \Pi(\Omega) = 1;$

- *for every* $B_1, B_2 \subseteq \Omega$, $\Pi(B_1 \cup B_2) = \Pi(B_1) \vee \Pi(B_2)$.

If $\Pi : P(\Omega) \to [0, 1]$ *is a possibility measure, the mapping* $\pi : \Omega \to [0, 1]$ *defined by* $\pi(a) = \Pi(\{a\})$ *for every* $a \in \Omega$ *is a* possibility distribution.

Proposition 2. *If a mapping* $\pi : \Omega \to [0,1]$ *is such that there exists some* $a \in \Omega$ *with* $\pi(a) = 1$, *then the function* $\Pi : P(\Omega) \to [0,1]$ *defined by* $\Pi(B) = \bigvee\{\pi(a)|a \in B\}$ *is a possibility measure, and the corresponding possibility distribution is* π.

Definition 3. *If* Π *is a possibility measure on* Ω *and* A *and* B *are events, the* possibility *of* A conditioned to B *is a solution of the equation*

$$\Pi(A \cap B) = \Pi(B) \wedge x$$

and will be denoted by $\Pi(A|B)$

Conditioned possibilities are not unique. For instance, Dubois and Prade take the greatest solution of this equation.

Definition 4. *An event* A *is* independent *of an event* B *if*

$$\Pi(A \cap B) = \Pi(A) \wedge \Pi(B),$$

in which case we take $\Pi(A|B) = \Pi(A)$.

2.2 RNA secondary structures

From now on, and for every positive integer N, let $[N]$ denote the set $\{1, \ldots, N\}$.

Definition 5 ([5, 19]). *An* RNA secondary structure *of length* N *is an undirected graph without multiple edges or self-loops* $\Gamma = ([N], Q)$, *for some* $N \geq 1$, *whose arcs* $\{j, k\} \in Q$, *called* contacts, *satisfy the following three conditions:*
   i) For every $j \in [N]$, $\{j, j+1\} \notin Q$.
   ii) For every $j \in [N]$, *if* $\{j, k\}, \{j, l\} \in Q$, *then* $k = l$.
   iii) For every $\{i, j\}, \{k, l\} \in Q$, *if* $i < k < j$, *then* $i < l < j$.

We shall denote a contact $\{j, k\}$ by $j \cdot k$ or $k \cdot j$, without distinction.

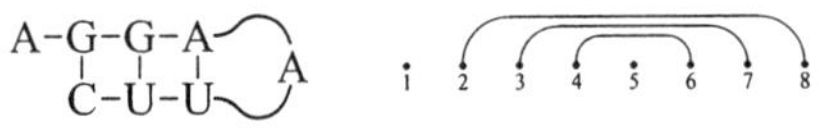

Figure 1: Short RNA strand and a graphical representation of its secondary structure.

As we have mentioned in the introduction, RNA secondary structures are a simplified model of the three-dimensional structures which RNA molecules fold into. Condition (i) in the previous definition translates the impossibility of a hydrogen bond between two consecutive bases; condition (ii), usually called the *unique bonds condition*, translates the fact that if two bases bond, then neither one of them can bond with any other base; and condition (iii) forbids the existence of the so-called *pseudo-knots*. Although "real" RNA three-dimensional structures may violate the unique bonds condition [1, 14] and may contain pseudo-knots [10], the conventional definition of RNA secondary structure includes these restrictions because they allow to use divide-and-conquer strategies in the development of algorithms for predicting RNA secondary structures [25]: pseudo-knots and contacts violating the unique bonds condition are then considered to be part of the *tertiary structure* of the molecule.

We can represent such an RNA secondary structure Γ by means of its adjacency matrix $M(\Gamma) = (a_{i,j})_{i,j=1,\ldots,N}$, where $a_{i,j} = 1$ if $i \cdot j \in Q$, and $a_{i,j} = 0$ otherwise. For instance, the following matrix represents the secondary structure shown in Fig. 1.

$$
\begin{pmatrix}
0 & 0 & 0 & 0 & 0 & 0 & 0 & 0 \\
0 & 0 & 0 & 0 & 0 & 0 & 0 & 1 \\
0 & 0 & 0 & 0 & 0 & 0 & 1 & 0 \\
0 & 0 & 0 & 0 & 0 & 1 & 0 & 0 \\
0 & 0 & 0 & 0 & 0 & 0 & 0 & 0 \\
0 & 0 & .0 & 1 & 0 & 0 & 0 & 0 \\
0 & 0 & 1 & 0 & 0 & 0 & 0 & 0 \\
0 & 1 & 0 & 0 & 0 & 0 & 0 & 0
\end{pmatrix}
$$

3 Possibilistic RNA secondary structures as points in Kosko's hypercube

If we consider the alphabet $\{A, C, G, U\}$, each letter can be represented by a binary 4-tuple with only one element equal to 1. Let us represent A by $(1,0,0,0)$, C by $(0,1,0,0)$, G by $(0,0,1,0)$, U by $(0,0,0,1)$. Then every RNA primary structure of length N can be represented by the concatenation of the N binary 4-tuples corresponding to its nucleotides, with the same order as they appear in the molecule once an orientation has been fixed. This yields a binary vector of length $4N$ such that in every group of entries of indexes $4m + 1, 4m + 2, 4m + 3, 4m + 4$, $m = 0, \ldots, N - 1$, there is exactly one 1, the remaining entries in every such group being 0. For instance,

$$(1, 0, 0, 0, 0, 0, 0, 1, 0, 0, 1, 0)$$

represents the primary structure AUG (the only codon corresponding to the aminoacid methionine).

Since every binary vector of length $4N$ defines a point in the $4N$-dimensional unit hypercube $[0, 1]^{4N}$, we conclude that each RNA primary structure defines a point in this hypercube. But, of course, not every point in $[0, 1]^{4N}$ corresponds to an RNA primary structure: actually, only some of its corners.

This could be done with every *alphabet* Σ, say with m letters: we could represent each letter in it by a different binary m-tuple with one and only one 1, and then we could represent every word of length N over Σ as binary vector of length mN, which would correspond to some corner of Kosko's hypercube $[0, 1]^{mN}$.

We want to model now the imprecise knowledge of the letter in some or each position of a word over Σ by means of fuzzy words. To do this, we define first a *fuzzy letter* in Σ as a fuzzy subset of it, i.e. a mapping $\mu : \Sigma \to [0, 1]$. If Σ has m elements, then, after fixing an ordering of these elements, every fuzzy letter in it can be understood as a point in the unit hypercube $[0, 1]^m$: if $\Sigma = \{L_1, \ldots, L_m\}$, with the order given by the subscripts, then we can identify a fuzzy letter $\mu : \Sigma \to [0, 1]$ with the point

$$(\mu(L_1), \ldots, \mu(L_m)) \in [0, 1]^m.$$

Now, by a *fuzzy word* of length N over the alphabet Σ we understand a sequence $(\mu_1, \ldots, \mu_N)$ of fuzzy letters in Σ. If we concatenate the representations of the fuzzy letters of a fuzzy word as points in $[0, 1]^m$, in the order as they appear in the fuzzy word, we obtain a representation of this fuzzy word as an element of Kosko's hypercube $[0, 1]^{mN}$:

$$(\mu_1(L_1), \ldots, \mu_1(L_m), \mu_2(L_1), \ldots, \mu_N(L_m)).$$

Consider now the alphabet $\Sigma_{RNA} = \{A, C, G, U\}$ representing the bases that can be attached to ribonucleotides; we assume its elements ordered in the usual alphabetic order: set in the sequel $L_1 = A$, $L_2 = C$, $L_3 = G$ and $L_4 = U$. Then, we define a *fuzzy RNA primary structure* as a fuzzy word over this alphabet: fuzzy letters in Σ_{RNA} will be called *fuzzy nucleotides*. Every such a fuzzy RNA primary structure of length N corresponds to a point in $[0, 1]^{4N}$ and, conversely, every point in this unit hypercube represents one, and only one, fuzzy RNA primary structure of length N.

Fuzzy RNA primary structures represent the incomplete knowledge of RNA molecules at the nucleotide level: the i-th fuzzy nucleotide in such a fuzzy RNA primary structure grasps the information we have about which is (or, rather, can be) the base lying in the i-th position of the corresponding RNA molecule.

The incomplete knowledge modelled by means of RNA primary structures can have different sources, and then different meanings. For example, it can be given through a probabilistic profile [9]: given a set of aligned RNA molecules of the same length N without gaps, every fuzzy nucleotide can represent the frequency of each base in the corresponding position of the primary structure; for instance, in the introduction we gave such a profile for the set of all arginine codons. In this kind of applications, it is natural to impose on the fuzzy letters forming the fuzzy RNA primary structures to be actually probability distributions over the alphabet Σ_{RNA}.

But in other applications it can be more convenient to take these fuzzy letters to be possibilistic distributions. This can be the case when the information is the result of a non-conclusive sequencing experiment [2], or when some features of the secondary structure of the molecule are known, which impose restrictions of the primary structures [14], or in general when what we want to stress or evaluate is the possibility of a certain base in a certain position, rather than its probability.

Thus, we define a *possibilistic RNA primary structure* of length N as a sequence $(\pi_1, \ldots, \pi_N)$ of possibility distributions on the alphabet $\{A, C, G, U\}$. We shall represent a possibilistic RNA primary structure $(\pi_1, \ldots, \pi_N)$ by means of the point

$$(\pi_1(L_1), \ldots, \pi_1(L_4), \pi_2(L_1), \ldots, \pi_N(L_4)) \in [0, 1]^{4N};$$

notice that its projection onto every four-dimensional subspace

$$x_1 = \ldots = x_{4m} = 0$$
$$x_{4m+5} = \ldots = x_{4N} = 0,$$

for every $m = 0, \ldots, N - 1$, has at least one coordinate equal to 1, and that this characterizes those points in Kosko's hypercube arising from possibilistic RNA primary structures.

For instance

$$(0, 0.5, 0, 1, 0, 0, 0, 1, 1, 0.1, 0.5, 1)$$

corresponds to

$$\pi_1(A) = 0, \pi_1(C) = 0.5, \pi_1(G) = 0, \pi_1(U) = 1$$
$$\pi_2(A) = 0, \pi_2(C) = 0, \pi_2(G) = 0, \pi_2(U) = 1$$
$$\pi_3(A) = 0.5, \pi_3(C) = 0.1, \pi_3(G) = 0.3, \pi_3(U) = 1.$$

This possibilistic RNA primary structure can be viewed as representing the possibilities which the different bases appear with in the three positions of those codons coding for the leucine aminoacid in a compositionally biased RNA molecule poor in C and G bases. But, again, it could be the result of any other reasoning or experiment.

4   Aggregation of pseudodistances

Several definitions of distance on the unit hypercube can be found in the literature that have a sense when they are applied to compare fuzzy RNA primary structures [3, 17]. Among others, let us mentions the following ones: given

$$x = (x_1, \ldots, x_n), y = (y_1, \ldots, y_n) \in [0, 1]^n,$$

- *Minkowski's distances*: For every $p \in \mathbb{Q}$,

$$d_p(x, y) = (\sum_{i=1}^{n} |x_i - y_i|^p)^{1/p}.$$

In particular, when $p = 1$, we have *Hamming's distance*

$$d_1(x, y) = \sum_{i=1}^{n} |x_i - y_i|.$$

In [17], Nieto *et al* propose the following normalization of the latter:

$$d_N(x, y) = \frac{\sum_{i=1}^{n} |x_i - y_i|}{\sum_{i=1}^{n} (x_i \vee y_i)}.$$

This is equal to the *degree of difference* as defined in [20, Def. 8]. Other normalizations of Hamming's distance had been proposed earlier; see [3, §3.1] and the references quoted therein.

- The *maximum distance*:

$$d_\infty(x, y) = \bigvee_i |x_i - y_i|.$$

These definitions assume an homogeneity in the composition of vectors x and y. But vectors in $[0, 1]^{4N}$ corresponding to possibilistic RNA primary structures are not homogeneous. The first four entries correspond to the information we have about the first nucleotide in the primary structure, the next four entries correspond to the information we have about the second nucleotide in it, and so on. Moreover, and as we mentioned in the introduction, it is acceptable to assume that the first four entries are independent of the next four ones and so on. This motivates that, in order to compare possibilistic RNA primary structures, instead of using distances defined globally, we consider more suitable to aggregate, in the sense of [23], pseudodistances depending only on corresponding fuzzy nucleotides. We can actually go one step beyond and to aggregate pseudodistances defined componentwise.

Given two possibilistic RNA primary structures $\Pi = (\pi_1, \ldots, \pi_N)$ and $\Pi' = (\pi'_1, \ldots, \pi'_N)$, let, for every $i = 1 \ldots, N$ and for every $k = 1, \ldots, 4$,

$$d_{H,i,k}(\Pi, \Pi') = |\pi'_i(L_k) - \pi_i(L_k)|, \qquad d_{N,i,k}(\Pi, \Pi') = \frac{|\pi'_i(L_k) - \pi_i(L_k)|}{\pi'_i(L_k) \vee \pi_i(L_k)},$$

$$d_{C,i,k}(\Pi, \Pi') = \frac{|\pi'_i(L_k) - \pi_i(L_k)|}{\pi'_i(L_k) + \pi_i(L_k)}, \qquad d_{N,i}(\Pi, \Pi') = \frac{\sum_{k=1}^{4} |\pi'_i(L_k) - \pi_i(L_k)|}{\sum_{k=1}^{4} \pi'_i(L_k) \vee \pi_i(L_k)},$$

$$d_{BC,i}(\Pi, \Pi') = \frac{\sum_{k=1}^{4} |\pi'_i(L_k) - \pi_i(L_k)|}{\sum_{k=1}^{4} \pi'_i(L_k) + \sum_{k=1}^{4} \pi_i(L_k)}$$

Proposition 6. *For every i (and for every $k = 1, \ldots, 4$, when necessary), the mappings $d_{H,i,k}$, $d_{N,i,k}$, $d_{P,i,k}$, $d_{N,i}$ and $d_{P,i}$ are pseudodistances on the set of possibilistic RNA primary structures of length N.*

The pseudodistances $d_{N,i,k}$ and $d_{N,i}$ correspond to the one-dimensional and four-dimensional versions of Nieto et al's distance d_N mentioned above; the pseudodistances $d_{C,i,k}$ are the one-dimensional version of the Canberra metric [12], and $d_{BC,i}$ is the Bray-Curtis, or Wiskonsin, distance [4, 18].

Proposition 7 (cf. [23]). *Let $F : [0,1]^{4N} \to [0, +\infty]$ be a non-decreasing mapping such that:*

i) $F(0, \ldots, 0) = 0$

ii) F is subadditive, i. e., if $c_i \leq a_i + b_i$ for every $i = 1, \ldots, 4N$, then

$$F(c_1, \ldots, c_{4N}) \leq F(a_1, \ldots, a_{4n}) + F(b_1, \ldots, b_{4N})$$

Then the function
$$d(\Pi, \Pi') = F(d_{1,1}(\Pi, \Pi'), \ldots, d_{N,4}(\Pi, \Pi'))$$

is a pseudodistance of possibilistic RNA primary structures.
*   If F satisfies moreover that*

iii) $F(c_1, \ldots, c_{4N}) = 0$ *implies* $c_1 = \ldots = c_{4N} = 0$

then d is a distance.

It is easy to check that conditions (i) to (iii) in the previous proposition are satisfied, among others, by the following mappings $[0,1]^{4N} \to [0, +\infty]$:

- $F_h(x_1, \ldots, x_{4N}) = \sum_{i=1}^{4N} x_i.$

- $F_\omega(x_1, \ldots, x_{4N}) = \sum_{i=1}^{4N} \omega_i x_i$ if $\omega_i \neq 0$ for every i.

- $F_p(x_1, \ldots, x_{4N}) = (\sum_{i=1}^{4N} c_i^p)^{1/p}$ for every $p \in \mathbb{N}$.

- $F_\infty(x_1, \ldots, x_{4N}) = \bigvee_{i=1}^{4N} x_i.$

If we apply a function F_a from this list to every 4-tuple $(x_{4m+1}, \ldots, x_{4(m+1)})$, $m = 0, \ldots, N - 1$, and next we apply another function F_b (not necessarily the same) to the resulting N-tuple, we obtain a new function $F_{a,b}$ also satisfying conditions (i) to (iii).

This allows us to define distances between possibilistic RNA primary structures of length N in an asymmetrical way. To begin with, we can aggregate first by means of a certain F_a and for each m, distances $d_{X,m,j}$, $X = H, N, P$, $j = 1, \ldots, 4$, to define distances between fuzzy nucleotides on the same position of the chain. Then we can aggregate, by means of another certain F_b, the N-tuple of pseudodistances between fuzzy nucleotides obtained in this way, or an N-tuple of distances $d_{N,i}$ or $d_{BC,i}$.

In this way we obtain, among others, the following distances between possibilistic RNA primary structures of length N:

- $d_{h,h,H}(\Pi, \Pi') = \sum_{i=1}^{N} \sum_{k=1}^{4} d_{H,i,k}(\Pi, \Pi')$ (the usual Hamming distance)

- $d_{\infty,\infty}(\Pi, \Pi') = \bigvee_{i=1}^{N} \bigvee_{k=1}^{4} d_{i,k}(\Pi, \Pi')$.

- $d_{\infty,h,N}(\Pi, \Pi') = \sum_{i=1}^{N} (\bigvee_{k=1}^{4} d_{N,i,k}(\Pi, \Pi'))$.

- $d_{h,\infty,P}(\Pi, \Pi') = \bigvee_{i=1}^{N} (\sum_{k=1}^{4} d_{P,i,k}(\Pi, \Pi'))$.

- $d_{p,\infty,N}(\Pi, \Pi') = \bigvee_{i=1}^{N} (\sum_{k=1}^{4} (d_{N,i,k}(\Pi, \Pi')^p)^{1/p})$ if $p \in \mathbb{N}$.

But notice that many other distances are obtained in this way, and that several distances, as for instance d_P, cannot be obtained in this way.

For example, in the last section we gave the possibilistic RNA primary structure

$$\Pi_{Le} = (0, 0.5, 0, 1, 0, 0, 0, 1, 1, 0.1, 0.5, 1)$$

representing the leucine codons in an RNA molecule poor in C and G bases. A similar description for the isoleucine codons could be

$$\Pi_{Ile} = (1, 0, 0, 0, 0, 0, 0, 1, 1, 0.5, 0, 0).$$

Then, for instance,

$$d_{\infty,h,H}(\Pi_{Le}, \Pi_{Ile}) = 2, \; d_{h,\infty,H}(\Pi_{Le}, \Pi_{Ile}) = 2.5,$$
$$d_{\infty,h,N}(\Pi_{Le}, \Pi_{Ile}) = d_{\infty,h,P}(\Pi_{Le}, \Pi_{Ile}) = 3,$$
$$d_{h,h,H}(\Pi_{Le}, \Pi_{Ile}) = 6.8, \; d_{h,h,P}(\Pi_{Le}, \Pi_{Ile}) = 6.66$$

5 Some applications

5.1 Possibility of a given sequence

We assume henceforth that, in a possibilistic description of an RNA molecule, the possibility that a given base appears in a given position is always independent of the possibility that the same or some other base appears in another position of the sequence.

Thus, given a possibilistic RNA primary structure $\Pi = (\pi_1, \ldots, \pi_N)$ and a (crisp) RNA primary structure $\underline{L} = L_1 \ldots L_N$ of the same length N, we can compute the possibility value of $\underline{L}$ relative to Π by means of

$$Pos(\underline{L}, \Pi) = \bigwedge_{i=1}^{N} \pi_i(L_i);$$

see [7, 8]. This clearly allows us to talk about "the most possible" RNA molecules relative to a given possibilistic RNA primary structure, which can be moreover obtained in linear time.

5.2 Possibility of a secondary structure

By a *possibilistic RNA secondary structure* we understand a fuzzy graph

$$\Gamma_\pi = ([N], \pi : [N] \times [N] \to [0, 1]),$$

for some $N \geq 1$, satisfying the following conditions:

i) For every $i, j \in [N]$, $\pi(i, i) = 0$ and $\pi(i, j) = \pi(j, i)$ (the graph is undirected and without self-loops).

ii) For every $i \in [N]$, $\bigvee_{j=1}^{N} \pi(i, j)$ is either 0 or 1 (if i can possibly contact with some other node, then $\pi(i, -)$ defines a possibility distribution on $[N]$; this relaxes the unique bonds condition).

iii) For every $j \in [N]$, $\pi(j, j+1) = 0$ (contacts between consecutive vertices are impossible).

iv) For every $i, j, k, l \in [N]$, if $i < k < j < l$, then $\pi(i, j) \wedge \pi(k, l) = 0$ (pseudo-knots are impossible).

We can represent a possibilistic RNA secondary structure by means of its adjacency matrix $(\pi(i, j))_{i,j=1,\dots,N}$: this matrix is symmetrical, it has zeros on the main diagonal as well as immediately above and below it, and each row and column containing some non-zero entry contains some 1.

On the other hand, let $\kappa : \{A, C, G, T\}^2 \to [0, 1]$ be a symmetric possibilistic distribution that captures the possibility of a contact between a pair of bases. For instance, it could assign 1 to pairs of Watson-Crick complementary pairs (A,U), (U,A), (C,G) and (G,C), and lower values to other pairs, established through stereochemical considerations [24].

Then, again under a suitable independence hypothesis, we can compute the possibility value of the folding of a given possibilistic RNA primary structure $\Pi = (\pi_1, \dots, \pi_N)$ into an imprecisely known secondary structure described by a possibilistic RNA secondary structure Γ_π of the same length, by means of

$$Pos(\Gamma_\pi, \underline{L}) = \bigwedge_{\substack{1 \le i,j \le N \\ \pi(i,j) > 0}} \left(\pi(i, j) \wedge \bigvee_{k,l=1}^{4} \left(\pi_i(L_k) \wedge \pi_j(L_l) \wedge \kappa(L_k, L_l) \right) \right).$$

As special cases, we obtain a formula for the possibility value $Pos(\Gamma_\pi, \underline{L})$ of the folding of a given RNA molecule $\underline{L} = L_1 \dots L_N$ into a secondary structure described by a possibilistic RNA secondary structure Γ_π of the same length,

$$Pos(\Gamma_\pi, \underline{L}) = \bigwedge_{\substack{1 \le i,j \le N \\ \pi(i,j) > 0}} \left(\pi(i, j) \wedge \kappa(L_i, L_j) \right),$$

as well as for the possibility value $Pos(\Gamma, \Pi)$ of a given secondary structure $\Gamma = ([N], Q)$ on a given possibilistic RNA primary structure $\Pi = (\pi_1, \dots, \pi_N)$,

$$Pos(\Gamma, \Pi) = \bigwedge_{ij \in Q} \left(\bigvee_{k,l=1}^{4} \left(\pi_i(L_k) \wedge \pi_j(L_l) \wedge \kappa(L_k, L_l) \right) \right).$$

These formulas allow to adapt easily Nussinov's, Zuker's and others' dynamic programming algorithms [25] to compute optimal and suboptimal solutions to the problem of finding those most possible secondary structures on a given possibilistic RNA primary structure.

5.3   *Possibilistic descriptions within a known distance*

Let Π and Π' be two possibilistic RNA primary structures of length N and assume we know the value $D = d_\infty(\Pi, \Pi')$. Then $d_{i,k}(\Pi, \Pi') \le D$ and hence

$$(\pi_i(L_k) - D) \vee 0 \le \pi_i'(L_k) \le (\pi_i(L_k) + D) \wedge 1.$$

for every $i = 1, \ldots, N$ and $k = 1, \ldots, 4$. If D is small, this yields sharp lower and upper bounds for each value $\pi'_i(L_k)$. These bounds can be incorporated into the formulas given in the previous subsections, to bound for instance the possibility value of a given RNA molecule relative to Π' in terms of D and its possibility value relative to Π, or to bound the possibility value of a secondary structure relative to Π in terms again of D and its possibility value relative to Π:

- Given an RNA primary structure $\underline{L}$, we have that

$$|Pos(\underline{L}, \Pi') - Pos(\underline{L}, \Pi)| \leq D.$$

- Given a RNA secondary structure Γ, we have that

$$|Pos(\Gamma, \Pi') - D - Pos(\Gamma, \Pi)| \leq D.$$

6 Conclusions

We have presented possibilistic descriptions of RNA molecules as fuzzy words and of RNA secondary structures as secondary graphs. We have also defined metrics on possibilistic RNA primary structures by aggregating pseudodistances at the level of nucleotides.

We have opted to compare possibilistc RNA primary structures by means of metrics but metrics are probably too restricted for this purpose. It is an interesting open problem to compare fuzzy genomic sequences by aggregating suitable similarity relations.

Acknowledgements: We thank an anonymous referee for his comments which have led to a remarkable improvement of this paper. We would also like to thank F. Sebastiá for several useful comments.

References

[1] R. T. Batey, R. P. Rambo, J. A. Doudna, Tertiary motifs and folding of RNA, Angew. Chem. Int. Ed. **38** (1999), 2326–2343.

[2] D. S. Blackman, *The logic of biochemical sequencing*. CRC Press (1994).

[3] I. Bloch, On fuzzy distances and their use in image processing under imprecision. Pattern Recognition **32** (1999), 1873–1895.

[4] J. R. Bray, J. T. Curtis, An ordination of the upland forest communities of southern Wisconsin, Ecological Monographs **27** (1957), 325–349.

[5] J. Casasnovas, J. Miró, F. Rosselló, On the algebraic representation of RNA secondary structures with G.U pairs. To appear in Journal of Mathematical Biology

[6] J. Casasnovas, J. Miró, F. Rosselló, Probabilistic and possibilistic descriptions of RNA's primary and secondary structures. Proceedings of Iberamia 2002, Workshop "Bioinformatics and A.I.", 3–12.

[7] L. M. de Campos, J. F. Huete, Independence concepts in possibility theory I. Fuzzy Sets and Systems **103** (1999), 127–152.

[8] L. M. de Campos, J. F. Huete, Independence concepts in possibility theory II. Fuzzy Sets and Systems **103** (1999), 487–505.

[9] R. Durbin, S. Eddy, A. Krogh, G. Mitchinson, *Biological sequence analysis*. Cambridge Univ. Press (1998).

[10] C. Haslinger, P. F. Stadler, RNA structures with pseudo-knots: Graph-theoretical, combinatorial, and statistical properties, Bull. Math. Biol. **61** (1999), 437–467.

[11] B. Kosko, *Neural networks and fuzzy systems*, Prentice-Hall (1992).

[12] G. N. Lance, W. T. Williams, A general theory of classificatory sorting strategies I: Hierarchical systems. The computer journal **9** (1967), 373–380.

[13] Y. Magarshak, C. J. Benham, An algebraic representation of RNA secondary structures. J. of Biomolecular Structures & Dynamics **10** (1992), 465–488.

[14] P. B. Moore, Structural motifs in RNA. Annual Review of Biochemistry **68** (1999), 287–300.

[15] J. J. Nieto, A. Torres, Midpoints for fuzzy sets and their application in medicine. Artificial Intelligence in Medicine (2002)

[16] J. J. Nieto, A. Torres, The fuzzy polynucleotide space: Basic Properties. Bioinformatics **19** (2002), 587–592.

[17] J. J. Nieto, A. Torres, M. M. Vázquez-Trasande, A metric space to study differences between polynucleotides. To appear in Applied Mathematics Letters.

[18] C. P. Pappis, N. I. Karacapilidis, A comparative assessment of masures of similarity of fuzzy values. Fuzzy Sets and Systems **56** (1993), 171–174.

[19] C. Reidys, P. F. Stadler, Bio-molecular shapes and algebraic structures. Computers & Chemistry **20** (1996), 85–94.

[20] K. Sadegh-Zadeh, Fuzzy genomes. Artificial Intelligence in Medicine **18** (2000), 1–28.

[21] K. Sadegh-Zadeh, Advances in Fuzzy Theory. Artificial Intelligence in Medicine **15** (1999), 309–23.

[22] P. Schuster, P. F. Stadler, Discrete models of biopolymers. To appear in Handbook of Computational Chemistry (M.J.C. Crabbe, M. Drew and A. Konopka, eds.), Marcel Dekker (in press).

[23] A. Pradera, E. Trillas, E. Castiñeira, On Distances Aggregation. Proceedings of IPMU2000 (Madrid, July 3-7), 693–700

[24] E. Westhof, V. Fritsch, RNA folding: beyond Watson-Crick pairs. Structure with Folding & Design **8** (2000), R55–R65.

[25] M. Zuker, The use of dynamic programming algorithms in RNA secondary structure prediction. In Mathematical methods for DNA sequences (M. Waterman, ed.), CRC Press (1989), 159–184.

Artificial Intelligence Research and Development
I. Aguiló et al. (Eds.)
IOS Press, 2003

Algebraic Properties of Fuzzy Morphological Operators based on Uninorms

M. González[†][*]**, D. Ruiz**[†]**, J. Torrens**[†]
[†] *Dpt. de Ciències Matemàtiques i Informàtica*
Universitat de les Illes Balears. Edifici A. Turmeda
Crta. de Valldemossa, Km. 7.5.
E-07122 Palma de Mallorca. Spain.
dmimgh0@clust.uib.es; daruz@yahoo.com; dmijts0@clust.uib.es

Abstract. In this paper, an approach to fuzzy mathematical morphology based on conjunctive uninorms is studied. It is proved that the most suitable conjunctive uninorms to be used in this framework are two special kinds of both, representable and idempotent uninorms. For these operators, it is proved that the most usual algebraic and morphological properties are preserved, such as, duality, monotonicity, interaction with union and intersection, invariance under translating and scaling, local knowledge property, extensivity, idempotence, and many others.

Keywords: Fuzzy mathematical morphology, erosion, dilation, uninorms, representable and idempotent uninorms, implicators.

1 Introduction

The identification of objects, object feature extraction and anomalies detection in automated industrial processes are closely connected with the recognition of shapes and therefore with the recognition or vision systems. In this context the mathematical morphology is a useful tool for extraction image components that are useful in the representation and description of region shapes, such as boundaries, skeletons, and convex hull. The basic tools of mathematical morphology are the morphological operations. A morphological operation P transforms the structure that we want to analyze A (an image) by means of a small object B, called "structuring element", with we want to probe the structure of A, into a new object $P(A, B)$ (a new image). The basic morphological operations are the dilation and erosion. These operations are based on set theory and were originally developed for binary images (black and white) and afterwards successfully extended to gray-scale images.

Nevertheless, the shapes in an image are not always crisply defined, and uncertainty can arise within each level of image analysis and pattern recognition. It can occur at the low-level in the raw sensor output, and it can be extended all the way through intermediate and higher levels. A recognition or computer vision system must have sufficient flexibility for

---

[*]Corresponding author

processing the uncertainty in any of these levels, so that the system could retain as much of the information content of the data as possible, at each level. As the first essential step of a recognition or vision system is the feature extraction, the method used should have a provision for representing and manipulating the uncertainties. Fuzzy set theory provides a mechanism to represent and manipulate uncertainty and ambiguity. Fuzzy operators and their properties as well as fuzzy inference rules have found considerable applications in image analysis and pattern recognition (see [11],[2] and references therein).

In order to do that, the fuzzy mathematical morphology is an alternative extension of binary morphology to gray-scale morphology using concepts and techniques from fuzzy set theory. Several researchers have introduced alternative morphological operations. Bloch and Maître [1] follow an approach using t-norms and the associated model implicator, with an involutive negator. Fuzzy set inclusion was used by Zadeh, Sinha & Dougherty, Kitainik and Bandler & Kohout in order to define fuzzy morphological operators. The "Minkowsky addition" was initially used by De Baets et al. in [7],[8]. A detailed account can be found in [11], [2] and references therein. In this paper we focus our attention in the general framework for fuzzy mathematical morphology constructed by De Baets in [3] where he uses "conjunctors" and "implicators" in order to define "fuzzy erosion" and "fuzzy dilation", without forcing duality relationships between these operators, and obtaining good properties for the corresponding fuzzy closing and fuzzy opening operators.

Our goal is to study this general framework when we use conjunctive uninorms. A first tentative appears in [9] where De Baets et al. use conjunctive uninorms and its residual implicators to construct the fuzzy morphological operators. Taking into account that duality and idempotency are indispensable for the further development of fuzzy mathematical morphology, it is proved in [9] that left-continuous, conjunctive, representable uninorms are suitable to be used in this framework. But there is another class of conjunctive uninorm being also suitable in this way as we prove here: some idempotent ones. Then, the aim of this paper is the construction of a fuzzy morphology based on conjunctive uninorms, including the representable and the idempotent ones, taking into account the morphological and algebraic properties of the fuzzy morphological operators and going so far than De Baets in [9].

The paper is organized as follows. In the next Section we review the basic definitions and properties of fuzzy logical operators needed in the subsequent sections. In Section 3, we present the general framework initiated by De Baets in [3]. We will discuss, in Section 4, the algebraic and morphological properties satisfied by the fuzzy morphological operators based on left-continuous conjunctive uninorms, following a similar structure than the used in Chapter 1 of [11]. The paper ends with some conclusions and the future work.

2   Fuzzy logical operators

Let us recall the fuzzy logical operators that we will use throughout the paper. More details on these operators can be found for instance in [12].

Definition 1. *A decreasing and involutive unary operator $\mathcal{N}$ on $[0,1]$ with $\mathcal{N}(0) = 1$ and $\mathcal{N}(1) = 0$ is called a strong negation.*

Definition 2. *An increasing binary operator $\mathcal{C}$ on $[0,1]$ is called a conjunctor if it satisfies*

$$\mathcal{C}(0,1) = \mathcal{C}(1,0) = 0 \quad and \quad \mathcal{C}(1,1) = 1.$$

Definition 3. *A binary operator $\mathcal{I}$ on $[0, 1]$ is called an implicator if it is decreasing with the first partial map, increasing with the second one and it satisfies*

$$\mathcal{I}(0, 0) = \mathcal{I}(1, 1) = 1 \quad and \quad \mathcal{I}(1, 0) = 0.$$

One can construct conjunctors and implicators from each other. On one hand, given an implicator $\mathcal{I}$ and a strong negation $\mathcal{N}$ the binary operator defined by

$$\mathcal{C}_{\mathcal{I},\mathcal{N}}(a, b) = \mathcal{N}(\mathcal{I}(a, \mathcal{N}(b)))$$

is a conjunctor. On the other hand, given a conjunctor $\mathcal{C}$ and a strong negation $\mathcal{N}$ the binary operator defined by

$$\mathcal{I}_{\mathcal{C},\mathcal{N}}(a, b) = \mathcal{N}(\mathcal{C}(a, \mathcal{N}(b)))$$

is an implicator. Another way to construct implicators from conjunctors is by residuation. Given a conjunctor $\mathcal{C}$ the binary operator

$$\mathcal{I}_{\mathcal{C}}(a, b) = \sup\{c \in [0, 1] \mid \mathcal{C}(a, c) \le b\}$$

is an implicator called the residual implicator of $\mathcal{C}$.

A special kind of conjunctors is given by the well known t-norms. In fact, fuzzy morphological operators are usually constructed from t-norms and, a special kind of them, the nilpotent ones, has been proved to be the most useful in this framework (see for instance [11]). However, a generalization of t-norms has appeared and has been studied in [10]:

Definition 4. (See [10]) *A uninorm is a two-place function $U : [0, 1] \times [0, 1] \longrightarrow [0, 1]$ which is associative, commutative, increasing in each place and such that there exists some element $e \in [0, 1]$, called the neutral element, such that $U(e, x) = x$ for all $x \in [0, 1]$.*

It is clear that the function U becomes a t-norm when $e = 1$ and a t-conorm when $e = 0$. For any uninorm we have $U(0, 1) \in \{0, 1\}$ and a uninorm U is said conjunctive when $U(1, 0) = 0$ and disjunctive when $U(1, 0) = 1$. Moreover, a uninorm U is said to be idempotent whenever $U(x, x) = x$ for all $x \in [0, 1]$.

This kind of operators results specially interesting because of their behavior: like a t-norm in $[0, e]^2$ and like a t-conorm in $[e, 1]^2$.

There are three known classes of conjunctive uninorms ([4]): uninorms in $\mathcal{U}_{\min}$, representable uninorms and idempotent uninorms. The first two classes have been already used in fuzzy morphology in [9]. Since left-continuity is essential in order to have "good" properties, and there is no left-continuous uninorms in the class $\mathcal{U}_{\min}$, we will only use here representable and idempotent, conjunctive uninorms. Of course, a fuzzy morphology can be done using also uninorms in $\mathcal{U}_{\min}$, but all properties stated and proved in this paper where left-continuity is required can fail, for this kind of logical operators. Let us recall here the definitions and characterizations of representable and idempotent uninorms, but more details of these classes can be found in [10] and [5] respectively.

Definition 5. *Let $e \in (0, 1)$ and let $h : [0, 1] \to [-\infty, +\infty]$ be a strictly increasing, continuous function with $h(0) = -\infty$, $h(e) = 0$ and $h(1) = +\infty$. The binary operator $\mathcal{U}$ defined by*

$$\mathcal{U}(a, b) = h^{-1}(h(a) + h(b))$$

for all $(a, b) \in [0, 1]^2 \setminus \{(0, 1), (1, 0)\}$ and $\mathcal{U}(0, 1) = \mathcal{U}(1, 0) = 0$ is a conjunctive uninorm with neutral element e. This kind of uninorms are usually called representable uninorms.

Theorem 2.1. *A conjunctive uninorm $\mathcal{U}$ with neutral element $e \in (0,1)$ is representable if and only if it is strictly increasing and continuous on $(0,1)^2$ and there is a strong negation $\mathcal{N}$ with $\mathcal{N}(e) = e$, such that for any $(a,b) \in [0,1]^2 \setminus \{(0,1),(1,0)\}$*

$$\mathcal{U}(a,b) = \mathcal{N}(\mathcal{U}(\mathcal{N}(a),\mathcal{N}(b))).$$

Theorem 2.2. *Let $\mathcal{U}$ be a representable uninorm with additive generator h, then its residual implicator $I_{\mathcal{U}}$ is given by*

$$I_{\mathcal{U}}(x,y) = \begin{cases} h^{-1}(h(y) - h(x)) & \text{if } (x,y) \in [0,1]^2 \setminus \{(0,0),(1,1)\} \\ 1 & \text{otherwise} \end{cases}$$

Following with the idea to have the "good" properties derived from left-continuity, we will only use in this paper left-continuous, conjunctive, idempotent uninorms. However, note again that any other kind of conjunctive, idempotent uninorms (see [13]) can also be used in the same way.

Theorem 2.3. *A binary operator $\mathcal{U}$ is a left-continuous idempotent uninorm with neutral element $e \in (0,1)$ if and only if there exists a decreasing function $g : [0,1] \to [0,1]$ with fix point e, satisfying $g^2(x) \geq x$ for all $x \leq g(0)$ and $g(x) = 0$ for all $x > g(0)$ such that, for all $x,y \in [0,1]$, $\mathcal{U}$ is given by*

$$\mathcal{U}(x,y) = \begin{cases} \min(x,y) & \text{if } y \leq g(x) \text{ and } x \leq g(0) \\ \max(x,y) & \text{elsewhere} \end{cases}$$

Note that given any strong negation $\mathcal{N}$ we obtain a left-continuous idempotent uninorm just taking $g = \mathcal{N}$, that we will denote by $\mathcal{U}^{\mathcal{N}}$. On the other hand, the residual implicator of an idempotent uninorm is given by

Theorem 2.4. *Let $\mathcal{U}$ be any idempotent uninorm with $g(0) = 1$. The residual implicator $I_{\mathcal{U}}$ is given by:*

$$I_{\mathcal{U}}(x,y) = \begin{cases} \min(g(x),y) & \text{if } y < x \\ \max(g(x),y) & \text{if } y \geq x \end{cases}$$

Proposition 2.5. *Let $\mathcal{U}$ be a conjunctive uninorm and $I_{\mathcal{U}}$ its residual implicator.*

- *The second partial map of $I_{\mathcal{U}}$ is right-continuous and for all $x,y \in [0,1]$,*

$$y \leq I_{\mathcal{U}}(x,\mathcal{U}(x,y)).$$

- *If $\mathcal{U}$ is left-continuous then so is the first partial map of $I_{\mathcal{U}}$, $I_{\mathcal{U}}$ satisfies the exchange principle:*

$$I_{\mathcal{U}}(x, I_{\mathcal{U}}(y,z)) = I_{\mathcal{U}}(y, I_{\mathcal{U}}(x,z)),$$

and also the following properties:

$$\mathcal{U}(x, I_{\mathcal{U}}(x,y)) \leq y, \quad I_{\mathcal{U}}(\mathcal{U}(x,y),z) = I_{\mathcal{U}}(x, I_{\mathcal{U}}(y,z))$$

for all $x,y,z \in [0,1]$.

3 Fuzzy morphological operators

From the definition of classical erosion and dilation ([11]) it is clear that the intersection and inclusion of sets play a major role. The idea of De Baets ([3]) was to fuzzify the underlying logical operations, i.e. the Boolean conjuntion and the Boolean implication, to obtain a successful fuzzification. An n-dimensional gray-scale image is model as an $\mathbb{R}^n \to [0,1]$ function. It is required that the gray values of the image belong to the real unit interval in order to consider an image as a fuzzy object. Taking two n-dimensional images A and B, a conjunctor C and an implicator $\mathcal{I}$, we have the following definitions:

Definition 6. *The fuzzy dilation $D_C(A, B)$ and fuzzy erosion $E_\mathcal{I}(A, B)$ of A by B are the gray-scale images defined by*

$$D_C(A, B)(y) = \sup_x C(B(x - y), A(x)) \tag{1}$$

$$E_\mathcal{I}(A, B)(y) = \inf_x \mathcal{I}(B(x - y), A(x)). \tag{2}$$

Definition 7. *The fuzzy closing $C_{C,\mathcal{I}}(A, B)$ and fuzzy opening $O_{C,\mathcal{I}}(A, B)$ of A by B are the gray-scale images defined by*

$$C_{C,\mathcal{I}}(A, B)(y) = E_\mathcal{I}(D_C(A, B), -B)(y) \tag{3}$$

$$O_{C,\mathcal{I}}(A, B)(y) = D_C(E_\mathcal{I}(A, B), -B)(y). \tag{4}$$

Note that the reflection $-B$ of a n-dimensional fuzzy set B is defined by $-B(x) = B(-x)$, for all $x \in \mathbb{R}^n$.

Obviously, since a conjunctive uninorm is a conjunctor, we can use conjunctive uninorm and related implicators to define fuzzy morphological operators following the previous definitions. Next, we investigate which conjunctive uninorms need to be chosen in order to preserve the algebraic and morphological properties, such as, duality, monotonicity, interaction with union and intersection, invariance under translating and scaling, extensivity and idempotence, inclusion properties, commutativity and associativity of the fuzzy dilation, combinations of dilation and erosion, local knowledge property and adjunction property.

4 Algebraic properties of morphological operators using idempotent uninorms

In this section we will give sufficient and/or necessary conditions on the conjunctive uninorms in order to guarantee similar properties as in the binary and gray-scale mathematical morphology.

Given a strong negation $\mathcal{N}$, we define by $(co_\mathcal{N} A)(x) = \mathcal{N}(A(x))$ the $\mathcal{N}$-complement $co_\mathcal{N} A$ of a fuzzy set A. Two fuzzy morphological operations P and Q are called $\mathcal{N}$-dual if for any two gray-scale objects A and B it holds that $P(A, B) = co_\mathcal{N} Q(co_\mathcal{N} A, B)$.

All results in this paper are concerning to a left-continuous conjunctive uninorm and its residual implicator $\mathcal{I}_\mathcal{U}$. However, it is known that the fuzzy dilation and fuzzy erosion are $\mathcal{N}$-dual if and only if $\mathcal{I} = \mathcal{I}_{C,\mathcal{N}}$ (or equivalently $C = C_{\mathcal{I},\mathcal{N}}$), moreover, if the fuzzy dilation and fuzzy erosion are $\mathcal{N}$-dual, then also the fuzzy closing and fuzzy opening are $\mathcal{N}$-dual [3]. Hence, to have duality between our fuzzy morphological operators, we need to use conjunctive uninorms satisfying

$$\mathcal{I}_\mathcal{U} = \mathcal{I}_{\mathcal{U},\mathcal{N}}.$$

It is proved in [6] that this always occurs for representable conjunctive uninorms taking as strong negation the operator obtained from the additive generator h of $\mathcal{U}$ by

$$\mathcal{N}(a) = h^{-1}(-h(a)).$$

Moreover, the same property is also satisfied if we choose a strong negation $\mathcal{N}$ and the corresponding conjunctive, left-continuous, idempotent uninorm $\mathcal{U}^{\mathcal{N}}$ (see again [6] or [13] for a proof in a more general setting). Thus, these two kinds of conjunctive uninorms are the most suitable in our framework.

Note that next propositions (from 4.1 to 4.7) are actually particular cases of those stated, for instance in [11]. Thus either, we do not include their proof or we only note that the used class of uninorms satisfies the properties required on the conjunctor.

Proposition 4.1. *Let $\mathcal{U}$ be a conjunctive uninorm and $I_{\mathcal{U}}$ its residual implicator. It holds: the fuzzy dilation $D_{\mathcal{U}}$ is increasing in both arguments, the fuzzy erosion $E_{\mathcal{I}}$ is increasing in the first argument and decreasing in the second one, the fuzzy closing $C_{\mathcal{U},\mathcal{I}_{\mathcal{U}}}$ and the fuzzy opening $O_{\mathcal{U},\mathcal{I}_{\mathcal{U}}}$ are both increasing in the first argument.*

The following two propositions concern interaction properties with Zadeh's union and intersection. For an arbitrary family $(A_i)_{i\in I}$ of fuzzy sets the Zadeh union and intersection are defined by: $\cup_{i\in I}A_i(x) = \sup_{i\in I} A_i(x)$ and $\cap_{i\in I}A_i(x) = \inf_{i\in I} A_i(x)$.

Proposition 4.2. *Let $\mathcal{U}$ be a left-continuous, conjunctive uninorm and $I_{\mathcal{U}}$ its residual implicator. Let A be a gray scale image and let B be a gray-scale structuring element. Further, let $(A_i)_{i\in I}$ be an arbitrary family of gray-scale images and let $(B_i)_{i\in I}$ be an arbitrary family of gray-scale structuring elements. Then it holds*

$$D_{\mathcal{U}}\left(\bigcup_{i\in I} A_i, B\right) = \bigcup_{i\in I} D_{\mathcal{U}}(A_i, B), \qquad D_{\mathcal{U}}\left(A, \bigcup_{i\in I} B_i\right) = \bigcup_{i\in I} D_{\mathcal{U}}(A, B_i),$$

$$E_{I_{\mathcal{U}}}\left(A, \bigcup_{i\in I} B_i\right) = \bigcap_{i\in I} E_{I_{\mathcal{U}}}(A, B_i), \qquad E_{I_{\mathcal{U}}}\left(\bigcap_{i\in I} A_i, B\right) = \bigcap_{i\in I} E_{I_{\mathcal{U}}}(A_i, B).$$

Proof Since $\mathcal{U}$ is left-continuous, the second partial map of $I_{\mathcal{U}}$ is right-continuous and the first one is left-continuous by Proposition 2.5 and thus, the results follow easily from definitions. $\qquad\square$

Proposition 4.3. *Let $\mathcal{U}$ be a conjunctive uninorm and $I_{\mathcal{U}}$ its residual implicator. Let A be a gray scale image and let B be a gray-scale structuring element. Further, let $(A_i)_{i=1}^{k}$ be a finite family of gray-scale images. Then it holds*

$$C_{\mathcal{U},\mathcal{I}_{\mathcal{U}}}\left(\bigcup_{i=1}^{k} A_i, B\right) \supseteq \bigcup_{i=1}^{k} C_{\mathcal{U},\mathcal{I}_{\mathcal{U}}}(A_i, B), \qquad O_{\mathcal{U},\mathcal{I}_{\mathcal{U}}}\left(\bigcup_{i=1}^{k} A_i, B\right) \supseteq \bigcup_{i=1}^{k} O_{\mathcal{U},\mathcal{I}_{\mathcal{U}}}(A_i, B),$$

$$C_{\mathcal{U},\mathcal{I}_{\mathcal{U}}}\left(\bigcap_{i=1}^{k} A_i, B\right) \subseteq \bigcap_{i=1}^{k} C_{\mathcal{U},\mathcal{I}_{\mathcal{U}}}(A_i, B), \qquad O_{\mathcal{U},\mathcal{I}_{\mathcal{U}}}\left(\bigcap_{i=1}^{k} A_i, B\right) \subseteq \bigcap_{i=1}^{k} O_{\mathcal{U},\mathcal{I}_{\mathcal{U}}}(A_i, B).$$

The translation $T_v(A)$ of a fuzzy set A by $v \in I\!\!R^n$ is defined by $T_v(A)(x) = A(x - v)$, the scaling $H_\lambda(A)$ of a fuzzy set A by $\lambda > 0$ is defined by $H_\lambda(A)(x) = A(\frac{1}{\lambda}(x))$. It follows, from [11] (see also [3]) that all four basic fuzzy morphological operators are invariant under translation and scaling.

Proposition 4.4. *Let $\mathcal{U}$ be a conjunctive uninorm and $I_\mathcal{U}$ its residual implicator. Let A be a gray-scale image, let B be a gray-scale structuring element and let $v \in \mathbb{R}^n$. Then it holds:*

$$D_\mathcal{U}(T_v(A), B) = T_v(D_\mathcal{U}(A, B)), \qquad D_\mathcal{U}(A, T_v(B)) = T_{-v}(D_\mathcal{U}(A, B)),$$
$$D_\mathcal{U}(T_v(A), T_v(B)) = D_\mathcal{U}(A, B).$$

The fuzzy erosion $E_{I_\mathcal{U}}(A, B)$ satisfies the same relations. The fuzzy closing $C_{\mathcal{U}, I_\mathcal{U}}$ holds

$$C_{\mathcal{U}, I_\mathcal{U}}(T_v(A), B) = T_v(C_{\mathcal{U}, I_\mathcal{U}}(A, B)), \qquad C_{\mathcal{U}, I_\mathcal{U}}(A, T_v(B)) = C_{\mathcal{U}, I_\mathcal{U}}(A, B),$$
$$C_{\mathcal{U}, I_\mathcal{U}}(T_v(A), T_v(B)) = T_v(C_{\mathcal{U}, I_\mathcal{U}}(A, B)),$$

the fuzzy opening $O_{\mathcal{U}, I_\mathcal{U}}$ satisfies the same relations than the previous ones.

Proposition 4.5. *Let $\mathcal{U}$ be a conjunctive uninorm and $I_\mathcal{U}$ its residual implicator. Let A be a gray-scale image, let B be a gray-scale structuring element and let $\lambda > 0$. Then it holds:*

$$D_\mathcal{U}(H_\lambda(A), H_\lambda(B)) = H_\lambda(D_\mathcal{U}(A, B)), \quad C_{\mathcal{U}, I_\mathcal{U}}(H_\lambda(A), H_\lambda(B)) = H_\lambda(C_{\mathcal{U}, I_\mathcal{U}}(A, B)),$$
$$E_I(H_\lambda(A), H_\lambda(B)) = H_\lambda(E_I(A, B)), \quad O_{\mathcal{U}, I_\mathcal{U}}(H_\lambda(A), H_\lambda(B)) = H_\lambda(O_{\mathcal{U}, I_\mathcal{U}}(A, B)).$$

Just as in the binary and the classical gray-scale cases, this property also holds for $\lambda < 0$. For $\lambda = -1$, we obtain the following special case.

Proposition 4.6. *Let $\mathcal{U}$ be a conjunctive uninorm and $I_\mathcal{U}$ its residual implicator. Let A be a gray-scale image and let B be a gray-scale structuring element, then it holds*

$$-D_\mathcal{U}(A, B) = D_\mathcal{U}(-A, -B), \qquad - E_I(A, B) = E_I(-A, -B),$$
$$-C_{\mathcal{U}, I_\mathcal{U}}(A, B) = C_{\mathcal{U}, I_\mathcal{U}}(-A, -B), \qquad - O_{\mathcal{U}, I_\mathcal{U}}(A, B) = O_{\mathcal{U}, I_\mathcal{U}}(-A, -B).$$

The principle of local knowledge for the fuzzy dilation and fuzzy erosion is expressed in the following proposition, and is adapted from [3]. We put $d_B = \sup B = \{x \in \mathbb{R}^n \mid B(x) > 0\}$.

Proposition 4.7. *Let $\mathcal{U}$ be a conjunctive uninorm and let $I_\mathcal{U}$ be its residual implicator. Let A be a gray-scale image, let B a gray-scale structuring element and let Z be a binary mask. Then it holds:*

$$D_C(A \cap Z) \cap E_{I_\mathcal{U}}(Z, d_B) = D_C(A, B) \cap E_{I_\mathcal{U}}(Z, d_B),$$
$$E_{I_\mathcal{U}}(A \cap Z) \cap E_{I_\mathcal{U}}(Z, d_B) = E_{I_\mathcal{U}}(A, B) \cap E_{I_\mathcal{U}}(Z, d_B).$$

The following results are again similar to those stated in [11], but in this case an adapted proof for uninorms is required and consequently it is included. The extensivity of the fuzzy dilation and the anti-extensivity of the fuzzy erosion is ensured by the next proposition.

Proposition 4.8. *Let $\mathcal{U}$ be a conjunctive uninorm with neutral element $e \in\ ]0, 1[$, let $I_\mathcal{U}$ be its residual implicator and let B a gray-scale structuring element such that $B(0) = e$. Then the following inclusions hold:*

$$E_{I_\mathcal{U}}(A, B) \subseteq A \subseteq D_\mathcal{U}(A, B).$$

Proof As $\mathcal{I}_\mathcal{U}$ is the residual implicator of $\mathcal{U}$, it satisfies $\mathcal{I}_\mathcal{U}(e, x) = x$ for all x. Then

$$E_{\mathcal{I}_\mathcal{U}}(A, B)(y) = \inf_x \mathcal{I}_\mathcal{U}(B(x - y), A(x)) \leq \mathcal{I}_\mathcal{U}(B(0), A(y)) = \mathcal{I}_\mathcal{U}(e, A(y))$$
$$= A(y) = \mathcal{U}(e, A(y)) = \mathcal{U}(B(0), A(y)) \leq \sup_x \mathcal{U}(B(x - y), A(x))$$
$$= D_\mathcal{U}(A, B)(y). \qquad \square$$

Proposition 4.9. *Let $\mathcal{U}$ be a left-continuous conjunctive uninorm and $I_\mathcal{U}$ its residual implicator, let A be a gray-scale image and let B be a gray-scale structuring element, then it holds*

1. *The fuzzy closing $C_{\mathcal{U},\mathcal{I}_\mathcal{U}}$ is extensive: $A \subseteq C_{\mathcal{U},\mathcal{I}_\mathcal{U}}(A, B)$.*

2. *The fuzzy opening $O_{\mathcal{U},\mathcal{I}_\mathcal{U}}$ is anti-extensive: $O_{\mathcal{U},\mathcal{I}_\mathcal{U}}(A, B) \subseteq A$.*

3. *The fuzzy closing and the fuzzy opening are idempotent, i.e.:*

$$C_{\mathcal{U},\mathcal{I}_\mathcal{U}}(C_{\mathcal{U},\mathcal{I}_\mathcal{U}}(A, B), B) = C_{\mathcal{U},\mathcal{I}_\mathcal{U}}(A, B), \quad O_{\mathcal{U},\mathcal{I}_\mathcal{U}}(O_{\mathcal{U},\mathcal{I}_\mathcal{U}}(A, B), B) = O_{\mathcal{U},\mathcal{I}_\mathcal{U}}(A, B).$$

Proof The first property follows from definition and taking into account that by Proposition 2.5 $I_\mathcal{U}$ satisfies, for all $(x, y) \in [0, 1]^2$

$$y \leq \mathcal{I}_\mathcal{U}(x, \mathcal{U}(x, y)).$$

Similarly, 2 can be derived from the fact that by left-continuity $\mathcal{U}$ satisfies

$$\mathcal{U}(x, \mathcal{I}_\mathcal{U}(x, y)) \leq y.$$

In order to prove 3, we have one inclusion immediately using 1:

$$C_{\mathcal{U},\mathcal{I}_\mathcal{U}}(C_{\mathcal{U},\mathcal{I}_\mathcal{U}}(A, B), B) \supseteq C_{\mathcal{U},\mathcal{I}_\mathcal{U}}(A, B).$$

The other inclusion is a consequence of the anti-extensivity of the fuzzy opening, the definitions of the fuzzy operators and the monotonicity of the fuzzy erosion, that is

$$C_{\mathcal{U},\mathcal{I}_\mathcal{U}}(C_{\mathcal{U},\mathcal{I}_\mathcal{U}}(A, B), B) = E_{\mathcal{I}_\mathcal{U}}(D_\mathcal{U}(C_{\mathcal{U},\mathcal{I}_\mathcal{U}}(A, B), B), -B)$$
$$= E_{\mathcal{I}_\mathcal{U}}(D_\mathcal{U}(E_{\mathcal{I}_\mathcal{U}}(D_\mathcal{U}(A, B), -B), B), -B) = E_{\mathcal{I}_\mathcal{U}}(O_{\mathcal{U},\mathcal{I}_\mathcal{U}}(D_\mathcal{U}(A, B), -B), -B)$$
$$\subseteq E_{\mathcal{I}_\mathcal{U}}(D_\mathcal{U}(A, B), -B) = C_{\mathcal{U},\mathcal{I}_\mathcal{U}}(A, B). \qquad \square$$

Proposition 4.10. *Let $\mathcal{U}$ be a conjunctive uninorm, with neutral element $e \in\,]0, 1[$ and let $I_\mathcal{U}$ be its residual implicator. Let A be a gray-scale image and let B be a gray-scale structuring element such that there exists $z \in \mathbb{R}^n$ where $B(z) = e$, then it holds*

$$E_{\mathcal{I}_\mathcal{U}}(A, B) \subseteq D_\mathcal{U}(A, B).$$

Proof Analogous to the proof of Proposition 4.8. $\qquad \square$

Proposition 4.11. *Let $\mathcal{U}$ be a conjunctive uninorm, with neutral element $e \in\,]0, 1[$ and let $I_\mathcal{U}$ be its residual implicator. Let A be a gray-scale image and let B be a gray-scale structuring element such that $B(0) = e$, then it holds*

$$D_\mathcal{U}(A, B) \supseteq C_{\mathcal{U},\mathcal{I}_\mathcal{U}}(A, B), \quad D_\mathcal{U}(A, B) \supseteq O_{\mathcal{U},\mathcal{I}_\mathcal{U}}(A, B), \quad D_\mathcal{U}(A, B) \supseteq O_{\mathcal{U},\mathcal{I}_\mathcal{U}}(A, -B),$$
$$E_{\mathcal{I}_\mathcal{U}}(A, B) \subseteq O_{\mathcal{U},\mathcal{I}_\mathcal{U}}(A, B), \quad E_{\mathcal{I}_\mathcal{U}}(A, B) \subseteq C_{\mathcal{U},\mathcal{I}_\mathcal{U}}(A, B), \quad E_{\mathcal{I}_\mathcal{U}}(A, B) \subseteq C_{\mathcal{U},\mathcal{I}_\mathcal{U}}(A, -B).$$

Proof We only prove the first inclusion since the other follows similarly. For all $y \in \mathbb{R}^n$ we have:

$$C_{\mathcal{U},\mathcal{I}_\mathcal{U}}(A,B)(y) = \inf_x \mathcal{I}_\mathcal{U}(B(y-x), \sup_z \mathcal{U}(B(z-x), A(z)))$$

$$\leq \mathcal{I}_\mathcal{U}(B(0), \sup_z \mathcal{U}(B(z-y), A(z))) = \sup_z \mathcal{U}(B(z-y), A(z)) = D_\mathcal{U}(A,B)(y). \quad \square$$

Proposition 4.12. *Let $\mathcal{U}$ be a conjunctive uninorm, with neutral element $e \in]0,1[$ and let $I_\mathcal{U}$ be its residual implicator. Let A be a gray scale-image and let B be a gray-scale structuring element such that $B(0) = e$, then it holds that*

$$E_{\mathcal{I}_\mathcal{U}}(A,B) \subseteq O_{\mathcal{U},\mathcal{I}_\mathcal{U}}(A,B) \subseteq A \subseteq C_{\mathcal{U},\mathcal{I}_\mathcal{U}}(A,B) \subseteq D_\mathcal{U}(A,B).$$

Proof It is obvious by joining some of the results in the propositions above. $\quad \square$

Proposition 4.13. *Let $\mathcal{U}$ be a left-continuous conjunctive uninorm, and let A, B and C be gray-scale images. Then it holds that*

$$D_\mathcal{U}(A, D_\mathcal{U}(B,C)) = D_\mathcal{U}(D_\mathcal{U}(A,B), -C)$$

and

$$D_\mathcal{U}(A,B) = -D_\mathcal{U}(B,A).$$

Proof Using left-continuity, it follows easily from the associativity and the commutativity of the uninorm $\mathcal{U}$. $\quad \square$

Combinations of dilations and erosions are addressed in the next propositions.

Proposition 4.14. *Let $\mathcal{U}$ be a left-continuous conjunctive uninorm, let $I_\mathcal{U}$ be its residual implicator and let A, B and C be gray-scale images. Then it holds:*

$$D_\mathcal{U}(D_\mathcal{U}(A,B),C) = D_\mathcal{U}(D_\mathcal{U}(A,C),B), \; E_{\mathcal{I}_\mathcal{U}}(E_{\mathcal{I}_\mathcal{U}}(A,B),C) = E_{\mathcal{I}_\mathcal{U}}(E_{\mathcal{I}_\mathcal{U}}(A,C),B).$$

Proof Using Proposition 4.6 and the previous one we obtain the first equality:

$$D_\mathcal{U}(D_\mathcal{U}(A,B),C) = D_\mathcal{U}(A, D_\mathcal{U}(B,-C)) = D_\mathcal{U}(A, -D_\mathcal{U}(-C,B))$$
$$= D_\mathcal{U}(A, D_\mathcal{U}(C,-B)) = D_\mathcal{U}(D_\mathcal{U}(A,C),B).$$

To prove the second part, note that since $\mathcal{U}$ is left-continuous, the residual implicator $I_\mathcal{U}$ satisfies the exchange principle (see Proposition 2.5) and also, its second partial map is right-continuous. Then, applying definitions and using these facts the results follows. $\quad \square$

Proposition 4.15. *Let $\mathcal{U}$ be a left-continuous conjunctive uninorm and let $I_\mathcal{U}$ be its residual implicator. Then it holds:*

$$E_{\mathcal{I}_\mathcal{U}}(A, D_\mathcal{U}(B,-C)) = E_{\mathcal{I}_\mathcal{U}}(E_{\mathcal{I}_\mathcal{U}}(A,B),C).$$

Proof Using Proposition 2.5 and the properties of the implicator $I_\mathcal{U}$ we have:

$$
\begin{aligned}
E_{\mathcal{I}_\mathcal{U}}(A, D_\mathcal{U}(B, -C))(y) &= \inf_x \mathcal{I}_\mathcal{U}(D_\mathcal{U}(B, -C)(x - y), A(x)) \\
&= \inf_x \mathcal{I}_\mathcal{U}(\sup_z \mathcal{U}(C(-z + x - y), B(z)), A(x)) \\
&= \inf_x \inf_z \mathcal{I}_\mathcal{U}(C(-z + x - y), \mathcal{I}_\mathcal{U}(B(z), A(x))) \\
&= \inf_{z'} \inf_x \mathcal{I}_\mathcal{U}(C(z' - y), \mathcal{I}_\mathcal{U}(B(x - z'), A(x))) \\
&= \inf_{z'} \mathcal{I}_\mathcal{U}(C(z' - y), \inf_x \mathcal{I}_\mathcal{U}(B(x - z'), A(x))) \\
&= \inf_{z'} \mathcal{I}_\mathcal{U}(C(z' - y), E_{\mathcal{I}_\mathcal{U}}(A, B)(z')) = E_{\mathcal{I}_\mathcal{U}}(E_{\mathcal{I}_\mathcal{U}}(A, B), C)(y). \qquad \square
\end{aligned}
$$

Although fuzzy dilation and erosion, for a suitable election of the conjunctor and the implicator, are dual, this does not mean that one can freely perform cancellation on fuzzy morphological equalities. In particular, the equality $A = E_\mathcal{I}(B, C)$ does not necessarily imply $D_C(A, -C) = B$. However, the following proposition indicates that a containment relationship is still maintained.

Proposition 4.16. *Let $\mathcal{U}$ be a left-continuous conjunctive uninorm and let $I_\mathcal{U}$ be its residual implicator. Then it holds:*

$$
A \subseteq E_{\mathcal{I}_\mathcal{U}}(B, C) \Leftrightarrow D_\mathcal{U}(A, -C) \subseteq B.
$$

Proof From the definition of $\mathcal{I}_\mathcal{U}$ we have that, for all x, y, $z \in [0, 1]$.

$$
\mathcal{U}(x, z) \le y \Leftrightarrow z \le \mathcal{I}_\mathcal{U}(x, y)
$$

and, from this equivalence, the result follows trivially. $\qquad \square$

5   Conclusions and future work

We have proved that it is possible to use left-continuous conjunctive uninorms in order to construct a fuzzy mathematical morphology satisfying the same properties than in binary and gray-scale classical mathematical morphology. Moreover, we have proved that the properties needed in order to obtain a "good" morphology are satisfied in both cases:

- When we use a representable uninorm $\mathcal{U}$ with additive generator h and the strong negation given by
$$
\mathcal{N}(a) = h^{-1}(-h(a)).
$$

- When we use the left-continuous, idempotent uninorm $\mathcal{U}^\mathcal{N}$ associated to a strong negation $\mathcal{N}$.

In particular using this kind of uninorms we have duality and idempotence of the fuzzy morphological operators, moreover we have anti-extensivity of the fuzzy opening and extensivity of the fuzzy closing. Intuitive requirements on the effects of the transformations such as expanding, contracting and filtering correspond to these algebraic properties. Namely, extensivity express that a transformation expands a set, whereas anti-extensivity formalizes contracting. Moreovedr all these properties jointly with increasingness are the mathematical properties necessary for representing filtering. Then, these results lead us to the possibility of deriving fuzzy morphological filters having the same properties as in the classical morphology. On the other hand, from Proposition 4.8 it follows that $D_{\mathcal{U}}(A, B) \setminus E_{\mathcal{I}_{\mathcal{U}}}(A, B)$ will serve as an edge detector of the image A (as a fuzzy morphological gradient). Also, Proposition 4.4 and Proposition 4.5 shows that the fuzzy morphological operators are invariant under translation and scaling. Invariance under translation implies that the fuzzy morphological operations are independent of the choice of the origin, while invariance under scaling means that these operations are independent of the used scale. Thus, the structuring element only depend on its shape and this can be exploted for directional transformation, which are useful in granulometry.

The next step is to study the effect of the neutral element election in practical cases; that is, the implementation of the fuzzy operators using different uninorms changing its neutral element. The study of closed and open objects, as well as the use, in shape recognition and image analysis, of fuzzy morphological filters based on these fuzzy morphological operators, will be done in future works.

Acknowledgements

The first author has been partially subsidized by CICYT under grant TIC2001-0931 and the third one by the DGI grant BFM2000-1114.

References

[1] Bloch I., Maître H., Fuzzy mathematical morphologies: a comparative study, *Pattern Recognition*, Vol. 28, No. 9 (1995), 1341 - 1387.

[2] Cheng H.D., Jiang X.H., Wang J., Color image segmentation: advances and prospects, *Pattern Recognition*, 34 (2000), 2259 - 2281.

[3] De Baets B., *Fuzzy Morphology: a logical approach*, in : "Uncertainty Analysis in Engineering and Sciences: Fuzzy Logic, Statistics, and Neural Network Approach", Kluwer Academic Publishers, 1997.

[4] De Baets B., Uninorms: the known classes, in *Proc. Third International FLINS Workshop on Fuzzy Logic and Intelligent Technologies for Nuclear Science and Industry* (Antwerp, Belgium), World Scientific, 1998.

[5] De Baets B., Idempotent uninorms, *European J. Oper. Res.*, **118** (3), pp. 631-642, 1999.

[6] De Baets B., Fodor, J., Residual operators of uninorms, *Soft Computing*, Vol. 3 (1999), 89 - 100.

[7] De Baets B., Kerre E., Gupta M., The Fundamentals of Fuzzy Mathematical Morphologies Part I: Basics Concepts, *International Journal of General Systems*, Vol. 23 (1995), 155 - 171.

[8] De Baets B., Kerre E., Gupta M., The Fundamentals of Fuzzy Mathematical Morphologies Part II: Idempotence, Convexity and Decomposition, *International Journal of General Systems*, Vol. 23 (1995), 307 - 322.

[9] De Baets B., Kwasnikowska N., Kerre E., *Fuzzy Morphology based on uninorms*, in : "Seventh IFSA World Congress", 215 - 220, Prague, 1997.

[10] Fodor J.C., Yager R.R., Rybalov A., Structure of Uninorms, *Int. J. of Uncertainty, Fuzziness and Knowledge-based Systems*, **5** N.4, pp. 411-427, 1997.

[11] Kerre E., Nachtegael M. (Eds.), *Fuzzy Techniques in image processing*, Studies in fuzziness and soft computing, vol. 52, Springer-Verlag, 2000.

[12] Klement E.P., Mesiar R., Pap E., *Triangular norms*, Kluwer Academic Publishers, Dordrecht, 2000.

[13] Ruiz D., Torrens J., Residual implications and co-implications from idempotent uninorms, *Accepted in AGOP'2003*.

Artificial Intelligence Research and Development
I. Aguiló et al. (Eds.)
IOS Press, 2003

Choquet integral based models for general approximation

Yasuo Narukawa[1], Vicenç Torra[2]
[1] *Toho Gakuen*
3-1-10 Naka, Kunitachi, Tokyo, 186-0004 Japan
e-mail: narukawa@d4.dion.ne.jp

[2]*Institut d'Investigació en Intel·ligència Artificial - CSIC*
Campus UAB s/n, 08193 Bellaterra (Catalonia, Spain)
e-mail: vtorra@iiia.csic.es,

Abstract. In this paper we study decision making models based on aggregation operators and, more specially, on Choquet integrals. The motivation of our work is to study the modeling capabilities of these operators and to build models that can approximate arbitrary functions. We describe and study two models that are universal approximators.

1 Introduction

Recent work on decision making models has been centered on the so-called multi-step Choquet integrals [5, 8, 11]. This is a model defined as a composition of Choquet integrals (CI) in such a way that the output of some Choquet integrals are used as the input for some other integrals. See Figure 1.

In general, in a multi-step aggregation process, the outcome is obtained through a succession of partial aggregations where low level aggregated values are combined in higher levels until a single result is obtained. In this way, the model is like an acyclic directed graph in which nodes correspond to aggregation operators and edges to information transmission. A multi-step Choquet integral model corresponds to the case when Choquet integrals are the solely used type of aggregation operator.

Choquet integrals [2] are powerful aggregation operators that extend, among others, weighted means. One of Choquet integral main characteristics is that they permit users to express interactions among the criteria being aggregated. This is achieved by means of fuzzy measures and integrals. While weights in a weighted mean weighting vector are defined for individuals or criteria (or information sources), fuzzy measures are defined for sets of sources. In this way, interactions can be expressed with a suitable definition of fuzzy measures.

In a multi-step model, the usual situation is that the architecture (the underlying structure of the model) and the parameters of the aggregation operators are constant and thus are not affected by actual computations. This is, for example, the case of multi-step Choquet integrals. In this model, fuzzy measures are fixed when the model is settled.

In this work we study the modeling capabilities of models based on Choquet integrals. We study the case of multi-step choquet integrals with non-monotonic measures and we propose the so-called multi-knowledge k-step choquet integral. We prove that both models can

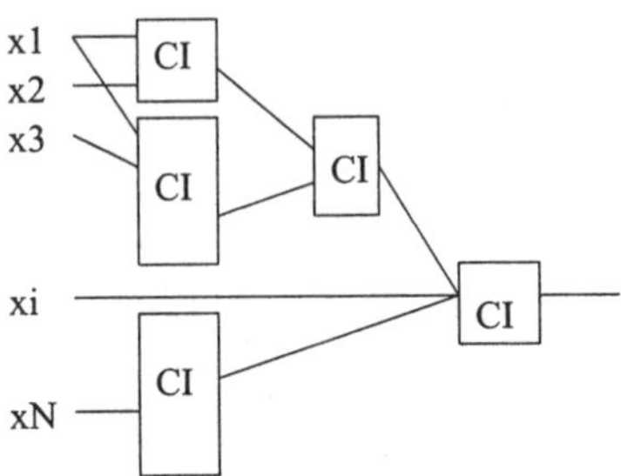

Figure 1: Multi-step Choquet integral

approximate functions at the desired level of detail. Therefore, models do not restrict to approximate monotonic functions.

The structure of the paper is as follows. In Section 2 we review basic concepts and results about fuzzy measures. Then, in Section 3 we prove that multi-step choquet integrals with non-monotonic measures can approximate arbitrary functions. Then, in Section 4 we define a new model that restricting choquet integrals to have monotonic measures can also approximate arbitrary functions. The paper finishes in Section 5 with some conclusions.

2   Preliminaries

In this section we review fuzzy measures, multi-step Choquet integrals for values in $\mathbb{R}^+$ and their generalization to values in $\mathbb{R}$.

Definition 1. *A fuzzy measure μ on a set X is a set function $\mu : \wp(X) \to \mathbb{R}^+$ satisfying the following axioms:*

(i) $\mu(\emptyset) = 0$ (boundary conditions)

(ii) $A \subseteq B$ implies $\mu(A) \leq \mu(B)$ (monotonicity)

It is usual to consider an additional boundary condition for fuzzy measures when considering decision problems. This is, the measure of the whole set is one ($\mu(X) = 1$). Nevertheless, this condition is not considered in this work to avoid restricting the model.

Definition 2. *Let μ be a fuzzy measure on X with $|X| = N$, then the* Choquet integral *of a function $f : X \to \mathbb{R}^+$ with respect to the fuzzy measure μ is defined by:*

$$CI_\mu(f) = \sum_{i=1}^{N} [f(x_{s(i)}) - f(x_{s(i-1)})]\mu(A_{s(i)}) \tag{1}$$

where $f(x_{s(i)})$ indicates that the indices have been permuted so that $0 \leq f(x_{s(1)}) \leq \cdots \leq f(x_{s(N)}) \leq 1$, $A_{s(i)} = \{x_{s(i)}, \ldots, x_{s(N)}\}$ and $f(x_{s(0)}) = 0$.

The Choquet integral is defined on $\mathbb{R}^+$. The following extensions on real numbers $\mathbb{R}$ have been considered in the literature:

Definition 3. *Šipoš integral (or symmetric extension):*

$$\check{S}I_\mu(f) = CI_\mu(f^+) - CI_\mu(f^-)$$

Asymmetric integral:

$$AI_\mu(f) = CI_\mu(f^+) - CI_{\bar{\mu}}(f^-)$$

where $\bar{\mu}$ is the conjugate fuzzy measure defined by $\bar{\mu}(A) := \mu(X) - \mu(A^c)$ and f^+ and f^- are defined as $f^+ := f \vee 0$ and $f^- := -(f \wedge 0)$. In the sequel, we will also use CI to refer to the second integral as this is the usual definition of Choquet integral on real numbers.

The following propositions hold for the Choquet and Šipoš:

Proposition 1. *Given a function f on X and a fuzzy measure μ on $\wp(X)$, the following holds:*

$$\check{S}I_\mu(-f) = -\check{S}I_\mu(f)$$

$$AI_\mu(-f) = -AI_{\bar{\mu}}(f)$$

Next we will define the multi-step Choquet integral.

Definition 4. *[8, 12]* Let $\mathcal{I}$ be a functional $\mathcal{I} : \mathbb{R}^+ \to R_+$. A 1-step Choquet integral is defined by

$$\mathcal{I}(x) = C_\mu(x)$$

for $x \in \mathbb{R}^+$, and a given μ. The functional $\mathcal{I}$ is said to be a k-step Choquet integral if there exist a natural number m_k, $k_j(k_j < k)$ step Choquet integrals $\mathcal{I}_j : \mathbb{R}^+ \to R_+$ for $j = 1, \ldots, m_k$ and a fuzzy measure μ_k on $2^{\{1,\ldots,m_k\}}$ such that $k = \max\{k_j | j = 1, \ldots, m_k\} + 1$ and

$$\mathcal{I}(x) = C_{\mu_k}(\mathcal{I}_j(x)).$$

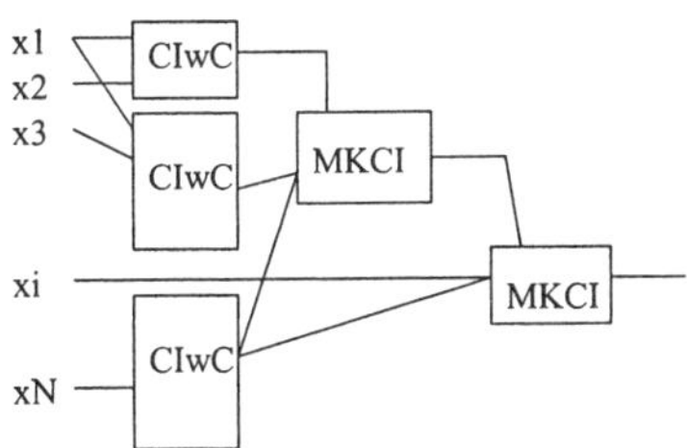

Figure 2: Multi-step Choquet integral with meta-knowledge and constant

Figure 2 shows a multi-step model that uses the previous integrals. However, this model is not appropriate for approximating arbitrary functions when measures are monotone. In the rest of this paper we consider two alternative approaches for tackling this problem.

First we consider the same structure with non-monotonic measures. Then, we introduce an alternative model that only uses monotonic measures. The Meta-Knowledge K-Step Choquet Integral (MKKSCI model). This latter model (see Figure 3) uses as input values not only the values s but also the values $-s$. To do so, the model extends the set X into X^* and the function s into s^*. Then, the set X^* contains two elements $(-1, x_i)$ and $(1, x_i)$ for each x_i in X (these two elements are denoted, respectively, pi and ni in Figure 3). Once the elements are defined, the function s^* assigns $s(x_i)$ and $-s(x_i)$ to each element $(1, x_i)$ and $(-1, x_i)$. Thus, s^* is a function on X^*.

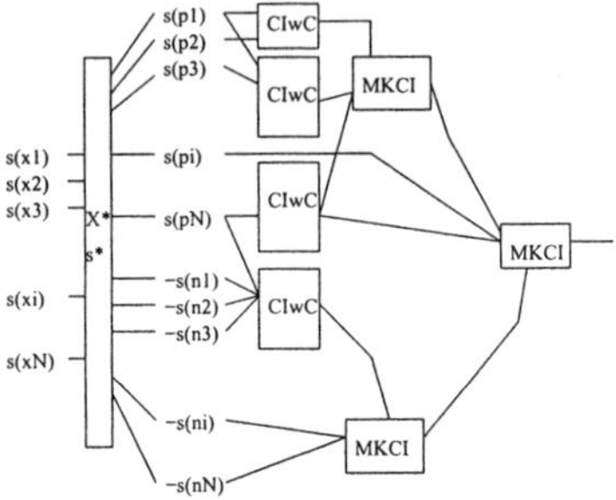

Figure 3: Example of Meta-Knowledge K-Step Choquet Integral (MKKSCI model): pi and ni are elements of X^*

3   On multi-step Choquet integrals

We start defining the Choquet integral with Meta-Knowledge. This is one of the basic elements in the Meta-Knowledge K-Step Choquet Integral (MKKSCI model) defined in Section 4. The rationale of this integral is to allow that the outcome of one step influences the parameters (the fuzzy measure) of the next step. This is similar in spirit to the *meta-knowledge* type of *multi-step inference systems* [4, 14].

Definition 5. *Let X be a set, μ be a fuzzy measure on $\wp(X)$ and let s be a function from X to $\mathbb{R}$, then the* Choquet integral with meta-knowledge *(MKCI)* $\alpha \in \mathbb{R}$ *with respect to μ is defined as the Choquet integral of s with respect to $\alpha \cdot \mu$. This is:* $CI_{\alpha \cdot \mu}(s)$.

The next lemma is obvious from the definition of Choquet integral.

Lemma 1. $CI_{\alpha \cdot \mu}(s) = \alpha CI_{\cdot \mu}(s)$. *for $\alpha \in \mathbb{R}$.*

Definition 6. *We say that a fuzzy measure μ is a $0-1$ fuzzy measure if $\mu(A) = 1$ or $\mu(A) = 0$ for $A \in \wp(X)$. Let $B \in \wp(X)$. We say that a fuzzy measure N_B on X is $0 - 1$ necessity measure if*

$$N_B(A) = \begin{cases} 1 & B \subset A \\ 0 & o.w. \end{cases}.$$

Let $C \subset B$. $0 - 1$ fuzzy measure $\mathcal{N}_C$ of C generated by $0 - 1$ necessity measure is defined by

$$\mathcal{N}_C = \sup_{B \in C} N_B$$

where N_B is a $0 - 1$ necessity measure.

The next lemma is shown in [10] using the topological setting.

Lemma 2. *Let μ be a fuzzy measure on $(X, \wp(X))$. There exist $a_1, a_2, \cdots a_m \geq 0, C_1, C_2, \cdots C_m \subset$* $\wp(X)$ *such that*

$$\mu = \sum_{i=1}^{m} a_i \mathcal{N}_{C_i}.$$

Applying the above lemma, we have the next theorem.

Theorem 1. *The Choquet integral is a two step Choquet integral such that the first step is the MKCI with respect to 0-1 necesity measures and the second step is a Choquet (Lebesgue) integral with respect to a probability P.*

Proof. Let f be a function $f : X \to \mathbb{R}^+$. Applying Lemma 2, there exist $a_1, a_2, \cdots a_m \geq 0$, $C_1, C_2, \cdots C_m \subset \wp(X)$ such that

$$CI_\mu(f) = \sum_{i=1}^{m} CI_{a_i \mathcal{N}_{C_i}}(f).$$

Let $\mu(X) = a$. We have $\sum_{i=1}^{m} a_i = a$. Define a probability P by $P(i) = a_i / a$. Then we have

$$CI_\mu(f) = \sum_{i=1}^{m} CI_{a \mathcal{N}_{C_i}}(f) P(i) = CI_{P(i)}(CI_{a \mathcal{N}_{C_i}}(f)).$$

$\square$

Definition 7. *[9] Let X be a set, μ be a fuzzy measure on $\wp(X)$ and let s be a function on X, then the* Choquet integral with constant *(CIwC) $\beta \in \mathbb{R}$ with respect to μ is defined as the Choquet integral of s with respect to μ plus β. This is: $CI_\mu(s) + \beta$.*

Lemma 3. *Let $Y \subset \mathbb{R}^n$ be a compact set and $g : Y \to \mathbb{R}^+$ be a nonnegative continuous function. Then for arbitrary $\epsilon > 0$, there exists a finite family of affine functions f_i, $(i = 1, 2, \ldots, N)$ and a $0 - 1$ fuzzy measure μ on $\wp(\{1, 2, \ldots, N\})$ such that*

$$|g(x) - CI_{\mu(i)}(f_i(x)))| < \epsilon$$

for all $x \in Y$.

Proof. Since Y is compact, for arbitrary $\epsilon > 0$, there exist a piecewise linear function f such that

$$|g(x) - f(x)| < \epsilon$$

for $x \in Y$. Then applying Ovchinnikov' theorem [13], there exists finite family $\{f_i\}$ of linear (affine) functions such that

$$f(x) = \vee_{j \in J} \wedge_i f_i(x)$$

for $x \in Y$. Then the function f can be represented as a Choquet integral with respect to a $0 - 1$ fuzzy measure [6, 9].

$\square$

To present a general approximation theorem, we define the non-monotonic fuzzy measure [7] with bounded variation.

Definition 8. *Non monotonic fuzzy measure μ with bounded variation is defined by $\mu = \mu_1 - \mu_2$, where μ_1 and μ_2 is (monotone) fuzzy measures.*

Let f be a real-valued function on X and μ is non-monotonic fuzzy measure. The Choquet integral CI_μ with respect to non montonic fuzzy measure μ is defined by

$$C_\mu(f) := C_{\mu_1} - C_{\mu_2}.$$

Since every affine function is represented as Choquet integral with respect to non-monotonic fuzzy measure with constant, we have the next theorem.

Theorem 2. *Let $Y \subset \mathbb{R}^n$ be a compact set and $g : Y \to \mathbb{R}^+$ be a nonnegative continuous function. Then for arbitrary $\epsilon > 0$, there exists fuzzy measures $\mu_{1,k}$, $(k = 1, 2, \ldots, N)$ on $\wp(\{1, 2, \ldots, n\})$ and a $0 - 1$ fuzzy measure μ on $\wp(\{1, 2, \ldots, N\})$ such that*

$$|g(x) - CI_{\mu(i)}(CI_{\mu_{1i}(j)}(x_j))| < \epsilon$$

for all $(x_j)_{j=1,\ldots,n} \in Y$, where $CI_{\mu_{1i}(j)}(x_j)$ is "Choquet integrals with constant".

Example 1. *Suppose that a compact set $Y \subset \mathbb{R}$ and a nonnegative continuous function $g : Y \to \mathbb{R}^+$ is defined as the figure below. Then for $\epsilon > 0$, there exists a finite family of affine functions f_i, $(i = 1, 2, \ldots, 4)$ such that*

$$|g(x) - ((f_1 \vee f_2) \wedge (f_3 \vee f_4))(x)| < \epsilon$$

for all $x \in Y$. Then define a $0 - 1$ fuzzy measure by $\mu(A) := 1$ if $A \supset \{1, 2\}$ or $A \supset \{3, 4\}$ and $\mu(A) := 0$ if otherwise. Then we have

$$((f_1 \vee f_2) \wedge (f_3 \vee f_4))(x) = C_\mu(f_i(x)).$$

On the other hand, each f_i can be represented as Choquet integral with constant.

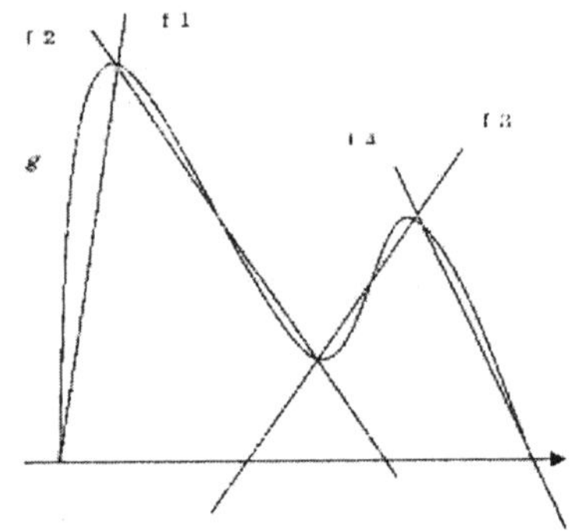

Figure 4:

μ on $\wp(\{1, 2, \ldots, N\})$
such that

$$|g(x) - CI_{\mu(i)}(f_i(x)))| < \epsilon$$

for all $x \in Y$.

Corollary 1. *Let $Y \subset \mathbb{R}^n$ be a compact set and $g : Y \to \mathbb{R}$ be a continuous function. Then for arbitrary $\epsilon > 0$, there exists a finite family of linear functions f_i, $(i = 1, 2, \ldots, N)$ and non-monotonic fuzzy measures μ on $\wp(\{1, 2, \ldots, N\})$ such that*

$$|g(x) - CI_{\mu_{(i)}}(f_i(x)))| < \epsilon$$

for all $x \in Y$.

4 The MKKSCI model

Definition 9. *Let X be a finite set. Then, the $* -$ extension of X is defined by $X^* := \{-1, 1\} \times X$. Let s be a function from X to $\mathbb{R}$. Then, the $* -$ extension of s is defined as follows:*

$$s^*((1, x)) = s(x)$$

$$s^*((-1, x)) = -s(x).$$

We now define the cc-complement, a function on the set X^* that is needed latter on and give some basic results related to this complement.

Definition 10. *Let X^* be a $*-$extension of a finite set X, then the cc-complement, denoted by cc_e, of an element $x^* = (a, x)$ of X^* is defined by (note that $a \in \{-1, 1\}$ and $x \in X$):*

$$cc_e(x^*) = cc_e((a, x)) = (-a, x)$$

and its extension to sets, denoted by, cc_s is defined by:

$$cc_s(A) = \cup_{a \in A} cc_e(a)$$

for all $A \subseteq X^*$.

For the sake of simplicity, we will use cc instead of cc_e and cc_s in both cases when no confusion arises.

Note that $cc((1, x)) = (-1, x)$ and $cc((-1, x)) = (1, x)$.

The next proposition is obvious from the definition.

Proposition 2. *The cc-complement satisfies the following properties:*

$$cc_s(\emptyset) = \emptyset$$

$$cc_e(cc_e((a, x))) = (a, x) \text{ for all } (a, x) \in X^*$$

$$cc_s(cc_s(A)) = A \text{ for all } A \subseteq X^*$$

$$A \subseteq B \subseteq X^* \text{ implies } cc_s(A) \subseteq cc_s(B)$$

Proposition 3. *Let s^* be the $*$-extension of the function $s : X \to \mathbb{R}^+$, then, the following property holds:*

$$s^*(x) = -s^*(cc(x)) \text{ for all } x \in X^*$$

Definition 10 is used below to define the so-called cc-complement of a fuzzy measure.

Definition 11. *Let μ_1 and μ_2 be a fuzzy measure on $(X, \wp(X))$, where X is a finite set. Let X^* be a *-extension of X. Then, the *-extension μ^* on X^* of two fuzzy measures μ_1 and μ_2 is defined as follows:*

$$\mu^*((\{1\} \times A) \cup (\{-1\} \times B) \cup (\{-1, 1\} \times C)) := \mu_1(A \cup C) - \mu_2(B \cup C),$$

where $A, B, C \subset X$ are pairwise disjoint.

It follows from the definition of μ^* that

$$\mu^*(\{1\} \times A) = \mu_1(A), \mu^*(\{-1\} \times A) = -\mu_2(A), \mu^*((\{-1, 1\} \times A) = \mu_1(A) - \mu_2(A)$$

$$\mu^*((\{1\} \times A) \cup (\{-1\} \times B)) = \mu_1(A) - \mu_2(B)$$

for A and $B \in \wp(X)$ and $A \cap B = \emptyset$.

Let $\alpha \geq 0$. It follows from the definition of s^* that $\{s^* > \alpha\} = \{1\} \times \{s(x) > \alpha\} \cup \{-1\} \times \{-s(x) > \alpha\}$. Since $\{s(x) > \alpha\} \cap \{-s(x) > \alpha\} = \emptyset$, we have $\mu^*(\{s^* > \alpha\}) = \mu_1(\{s(x) > \alpha\}) - \mu_2(\{-s(x) > \alpha\})$. Therefore we have the next proposition:

Proposition 4. *Let μ_1, μ_2 be a fuzzy measure on $X, \wp(X)$ and s be a real valued function on X with $s^* \geq 0$. Then we have $CI_{\mu^*}(s^*) = CI_{\mu_1}(s^+) - CI_{\mu_2}(s^-)$. Especially, if $\mu_1 := \mu$ and $\mu_2 := \bar{\mu}$ then we have $CI_{\mu^*}(s^*) = AI_\mu(s)$ and if $\mu_1 := \mu$ and $\mu_2 := \mu$ then we have $CI_{\mu^*}(s^*) = \check{S}I_\mu(s)$.*

The proposition above says that the *-extension is a natural extension of both Symmetric and Asymmetric Choquet integrals, moreover CPT functional [15]. If we consider a real-valued function f on X^* with $f(1, x) = f(-1, x) > 0$ for all $x \in X$, we have $CI_{\mu^*}(f) = \min_{x \in X} f(1, x)$ when μ^* is the *-extension of the fuzzy measures $\mu_1 := \mu$ and $\mu_2 := \bar{\mu}$.

Definition 12. *Let cc denote the cc-complement in X^*, then, the cc-complement of a fuzzy measure μ on X^{cc} is defined by:*

$$\mu^{cc}(A) = \mu(cc(A))$$

Proposition 5. *The cc-complement μ^{cc} of a fuzzy measure μ is a fuzzy measure.*

Proof. To prove this proposition, we need to prove boundary conditions and monotonicity.

1. $\mu^{cc}(\emptyset) = \mu(cc(\emptyset)) = \mu(\emptyset) = 0$

2. If $A \subseteq B$ then $cc(A) \subseteq cc(B)$. Therefore, applying the monotonicity of μ, we have that $\mu(cc(A)) \leq \mu(cc(B))$ and, thus, $\mu^{cc}(A) \leq \mu^{cc}(B)$.

$\square$

Definition 13. *Let X be a finite set and let s be a function from X to $\mathbb{R}$, let X^* the *-extension of X and s^* the $* -$ extension of s. Then, Meta-Knowledge K-Step Choquet Integral (MKKSCI model) of a function s is defined as the k-step integral of s^* on X^* where the integrals are either "Choquet integrals with constant" or "Choquet integrals with meta-knowledge".*

4.1 Properties of the MKKSCI model

Now, we consider some of the properties of this model.

Proposition 6. *The MKKSCI model generalizes the multi-step Choquet integral.*

Now, we prove that the Choquet integral of a function f on X^* can be equivalently expressed in terms of its negation $-f$ and the cc-complement.

Proposition 7. *Let X be a finite set and X^* be its $* -$ extension, let s be a function from X to $\mathbb{R}$ and s^* its $* -$ extension, let μ be a fuzzy measure on X^* and μ^{cc} its cc-complement, then the following holds for all functions s:*

$$CI_\mu(s^*) = CI_{\mu^{cc}}(-s^*)$$

Proof. To prove this proposition, we consider the integrals of $f = s^*$ and $f' = -s^*$. This is:

$$\sum_i [f(x_{s(i)}) - f(x_{s(i-1)})]\mu(A_{s(i)}) =$$

$$= \sum_i [f'(x_{s'(i)}) - f'(x_{s'(i-1)})]\mu^{cc}(A_{s'(i)})$$

It is clear, that proving the equality

$$[f(x_{s(i)}) - f(x_{s(i-1)})]\mu(A_{s(i)}) =$$

$$[f'(x_{s'(i)}) - f'(x_{s'(i-1)})]\mu^{cc}(A_{s'(i)})$$

for all i proves the proposition.

We consider the following steps:

1) $f(x_{s(i)}) = f'(x_{s'(i)})$ because according to Proposition 3, $f((a,x)) = -f((-a,x)) = f'((-a,x))$ for all $x \in X$ and $a \in \{-1, 1\}$. Note that this implies that f and f' have exactly the same elements so, when ordered, the i-th ordered element in f corresponds to the i-th ordered element in f'.

2) Therefore, to prove this proposition, it is enough to prove that $\mu(A_{s(i)}) = \mu^{cc}(A_{s'(i)})$ for all i. This, using μ^{cc} definition, is equivalent to: $\mu(A_{s(i)}) = \mu(cc(A_{s'(i)}))$. Thus, proving $A_{s(i)} = cc(A_{s'(i)})$, the proposition is proven.

3) Now, note that $A_{s(i)} = \{x | f(x) \geq f(x_{s(i)})\}$ and that $A_{s'(i)} = \{x | f'(x) \geq f'(x_{s'(i)})\}$ and that the values $f(x_{s(i)})$ and $f'(x_{s'(i)})$ are equal (this is proven above). Equivalence between $A_{s(i)}$ and $cc(A_{s'(i)})$ follows from:

   For all $(a_i, x_i) \in A_{s(i)}$, we have that $f((a_i, x_i)) \geq f(x_{s(i)})$, and, from Proposition 3, $f((a_i, x_i)) = f'((-a_i, x_i))$. Therefore, $f((a_i, x_i)) = f'((-a_i, x_i)) \geq f(x_{s(i)}) = f'(x_{s'(i)})$. This implies that $(-a_i, x_i)$ is also in $A_{s'(i)}$. So, $cc(a) \in A_{s'(i)}$ for all $a \in A_{s(i)}$.

   For all $(a_i, x_i) \in A_{s'(i)}$, we have that $f'((a_i, x_i)) \geq f'(x_{s'(i)})$ and, again from Proposition 3, $f'((a_i, x_i)) = f((-a_i, x_i))$. Therefore, $f((-a_i, x_i)) \geq f'(x_{s'(i)}) = f(x_{s(i)})$ and, thus $(-a_i, x_i) \in A_{s(i)}$. So, $cc(a) \in A_{s(i)}$ for all $a \in A_{s'(i)}$.

$\square$

In the rest of this section we prove that the MKKSCI model can also be used to approximate an arbitrary function. The approach is similar to the proof in [3] about NetFAN as an universal approximator. Similar results about fuzzy controllers can be found in [1].

Theorem 3. *For any given real continuous function g on a compact domain $Y \subseteq \mathbb{R}^n$ and arbitrary $\epsilon > 0$, there exists a MKKSCI $f \in F$ with F being the set of all $MKKSCI$ such that $sup_{y \in Y}|f(y) - g(y)| < \epsilon$*

The proof of this theorem is based on Stone-Weierstrass theorem:

Theorem 4. *Let $F(Y)$ be a set of real continuous functions on a compact domain Y. If:*

(1) *F is an algebra, i.e. the set F is closed under addition, multiplication, and scalar multiplication, and*

(2) *F vanishes at no point Y, i.e., for each $y \in Y$ there exists $f \in F$ such that $f(y) \neq 0$, and*

(3) *F separates points on Y, i.e. for each $s, t \in Y$, $s \neq t$ there exists $f \in F$ such that $f(s) \neq f(t)$,*

then the uniform closure of F consists of all real continuous functions on Y, i.e. F is dense in $C(Y)$, which is the set of all continuous functions on Y.

To prove this theorem, we need to prove that $F(Y)$ is a set of real continuous functions and that the previous three conditions hold. As MKKSCI is a real continous function, we just need to prove the last conditions. We start proving that the MKKSCI model satisfies the last two conditions. We state them as lemmas.

Lemma 4. *F vanishes at no point Y*

Proof. This is to prove that for each $y \in Y$ there exists $f \in F$ such that $f(y) \neq 0$. It is clear that a Choquet Integral with a non-zero constant satisfies this condition. $\square$

Lemma 5. *F separates points on Y*

Proof. This is to prove that for each $s, t \in Y$, $s \neq t$ there exists $f \in F$ such that $f(s) \neq f(t)$. A Choquet integral with the fuzzy measure μ_{sepY} defined below satisfies this condition.

As s and t are defined on the $* - extension$ X^*, the measure is defined on $\wp(X^*)$. In particular, let $i = arg\min_i\{s(x_i) \neq t(x_i)\}$ then, μ_{sepY} is the 0-1 necessity measure $N_{\{x_i\}}$. $\square$

Now, we turn into the first condition of Theorem 4. It can be decomposed into the following three ones:

(1.1) the set F is closed under addition

(1.2) the set F is closed under multiplication

(1.3) the set F is closed under scalar multiplication

We establish them as three independent lemmas below.

Lemma 6. *The set F is closed under addition.*

Proof. We need to prove that given f_1 and f_2 in F, $f_1 + f_2$ is also in F. Then, given f_1 and f_2 in F, we consider them as the input of a Choquet integral f_c with and additive measure with $\mu(\{f_1\}) = \mu(\{f_2\}) = 1$. Naturally, f_c is in F and is equivalent to $f_1 + f_2$. $\qquad\square$

Lemma 7. *The set F is closed under multiplication.*

Proof. We need to prove that given f_1 and f_2 in F, $f_1 \cdot f_2$ is also in F. To do this, we use a MKCI. Then, given f_1 and f_2 in F, we consider f_1 as the input of a single-input MKCI and f_2 as its meta-knowledge. Naturally, the corresponding fuzzy measure is defined with $\mu(\{f_1\}) = 1$ and, therefore, we are computing the Choquet integral of f_1 with respect to $f_2 \cdot \mu$. So, the result is in F and is equivalent to $f_1 \cdot f_2$. $\qquad\square$

Now, we turn into the proof that F is closed under scalar multiplication. To prove it, we need the following result:

Proposition 8. *Let X be a finite set and X^* its $* -$ extension, let μ be a fuzzy measure on X^* and μ^{cc} be its cc-complement, then all functions s on X satisfy:*

$$-CI_\mu(s^*) = CI_{(\bar{\mu})^{cc}}(s^*)$$

where s^* is the $* -$ extension of s, and CI is the AI when applied to negative values.

Proof. From Proposition 1 (recall that CI corresponds to AI when negative values are used), we have that

$$-CI_\mu(f) = CI_{\bar{\mu}}(-f)$$

and from Proposition 7

$$CI_{\bar{\mu}}(-f) = CI_{(\bar{\mu})^{cc}}(f)$$

Therefore, the proposition is proven. $\qquad\square$

Lemma 8. *The set F is closed under scalar multiplication.*

Proof. We need to prove that given f_1 in F, $f_1 \cdot \alpha$ is also in F. It is enough to prove that given a Choquet integral f_1 with fuzzy measure μ_1 (and constant β_1), it is possible to build a Choquet integral f_c such that its output is $f_1 \cdot \alpha$. We distinguish three cases for α:

If α is positive, use a Choquet integral with $\mu'_{f_1} = \alpha \cdot \mu_{f_1}$ (see Lemma 1), and $\beta = \alpha \cdot \beta_1$.

If α is -1, then, applying Proposition 8, we build an expression for $-f_1$ (if the Choquet integral is with constant β_1, then use a Choquet integral with constant $\beta = \alpha \cdot \beta_1$).

If α is negative but $\alpha \neq 1$, then we combine the two cases above. $\qquad\square$

5 Conclusions

In this paper we have studied the construction of models based on aggregation operators. We have shown that the models are universal approximators and, therefore, they can be used for approximating arbitrary functions.

Acknowledgements

Comments and suggestions by Prof. Toshiaki Murofushi are gratefully acknowledged. Partial support by the European Community under contract "CASC" IST-2000-25069 and by MCyT and FEDER fund under the project "STREAMOBILE" (TIC2001-0633-C03-02) is acknowledged as well.

References

[1] J.J.Buckley, Sugeno type controllers are universal controllers, *Fuzzy Sets and Systems* 53 (1993) 299-303

[2] G. Choquet, "Theory of Capacities", *Ann. Inst. Fourier* 5 (1954) 131-296.

[3] O. Huwendiek, W. Brockmann, Function approximation with decomposed fuzzy systems, *Fuzzy Sets and Systems* 101 (1999) 273-286.

[4] L. Magdalena, Hierarchical fuzzy control of a complex system using meta-knowledge. *Proc. 8th Int. Conf. Information Processing and Management of Uncertainty in Knowledge-Based Systems*, Madrid, Spain, 2000, pp. 630-637.

[5] R. Mesiar, D. Vivona, Two-step integral with respect to fuzzy measure, *Tatra Mt. Math. Publ.* 16 (1999) 359–368.

[6] T. Murofushi, K. Fujimoto, and M. Sugeno, Canonical separated hierarchical decomposition of Choquet integral over a finite set, *International Journal of Uncertainty, Fuzziness and Knowledge-Based Systems*, vol. 6, no.3 (1998) pp.257-272

[7] T. Murofushi, M. Sugeno, M. Machida: Non-monotonic fuzzy measures and the Choquet integral, *Fuzzy Sets and Systems*, 64:1 (1994) 73-86.

[8] T. Murofushi, Y. Narukawa, A characterization of multi-step discrete Choquet integral, *6th Int. Conf. Fuzzy Sets Theory and Its Applications, Abstracts*, 2002, p. 94.

[9] T. Murofushi, Y. Narukawa, A characterization of multi-level discrete Choquet integral over a finite set (in Japanese). *Proc. of 7th Workshop on Evaluation of Heart and Mind*, 2002, pp. 33-36.

[10] Y. Narukawa, *A Study of Fuzzy Measure and Choquet Integral* (in Japanese), Master Thesis, Tokyo Institute of Technology, 1990.

[11] Y. Narukawa, V. Torra, Twofold integral and Multi-step Choquet integral, *Proc. AGOP*, 2003, in press.

[12] Y. Narukawa, T. Murofushi, The n-step Choquet integral on finite spaces, *Proc. 9th Int. Conf. Information Processing and Management of Uncertainty in Knowledge-Based Systems*, 2002, pp. 539–543.

[13] S. Ovchinnikov, Max-min representation of piecewise linear functions, *Contributions to Algebra and Geometry*, 43 (2002) 297–302.

[14] V. Torra, A Review of the Construction of Hierarchical Fuzzy Systems, *Int. J. of Intel. Systems*, 17:5 (2002) 531-543.

[15] A. Tversky and D. Kahneman, Advances in prospect theory: cumulative representation of uncertainty, *Journal of Risk and Uncertainty*, 5, 1992, pp 297-323.

Describing Preferences with a Negation-based Vocabulary

Aïda VALLS[1], Vicenç TORRA[2]

[1] *Dept. Computer Science and Mathematics, Universitat Rovira i Virgili*
Avda.Països Catalans, 26, 43007 Tarragona, Catalonia, Spain
[2] *Artificial Intelligence Research Institute, CSIC*
Campus UAB, s/n, 08193 Bellaterra, Catalonia, Spain
avalls@etse.urv.es; vtorra@iiia.csic.es

Abstract. This paper explains a method for describing a set of ordered alternatives with a qualitative preference vocabulary. This is needed at the last stage of a decision making process, when after aggregating and ranking a set of alternatives, we have to select the most appropriate terms to describe the global preference value of each alternative. We present a method based on the representation of the semantics of the terms by means of negation functions.

1. Introduction

In this paper we will face a decision problem in which we have to rank a set of alternatives that are described by many qualitative preference criteria. We will follow an approach based on the Utility Theory called *ClusDM*. It consists of three stages: Aggregation / Ranking / Explanation [9]. The two initial stages will be briefly introduced, however, in this paper we will concentrate on the Explanation stage, where an appropriate term to describe each alternative must be found.

We have concentrated on the development of decision support methods that deal with qualitative preferences, that is, with criteria using a predefined set of linguistic terms. For example: {excellent, good, poor, bad, terrible}. So, we will consider a scenario in which the user will provide us several qualitative preference criteria describing a set of alternatives. In fact, each preference criterion is giving a possible ranking of the alternatives. Thus, the goal is to find a ranking of the alternatives considering all the criteria. This is a multicriteria optimisation problem that usually does not have a solution that agrees with all the criteria. What we do is to build a ranking that agrees as much as possible with as many criteria as possible.

To operate with qualitative scales, we must know the meaning of each term. Several approaches to the definition of the underlying semantics of a scale can be found in the literature. They can be classified as follows [8]:

- **Explicit semantics**: A mapping exists that translates each linguistic term into a numerical or fuzzy value. Operations on the linguistic values are defined on terms of the corresponding operations in the numerical or fuzzy scale (f.i [2]).
- **Implicit semantics**: Operations are defined assuming an implicit mapping function from the original scale into a numerical one. The typical case is to replace each term by its position in its domain (f.i. [4]).

- **Operations restricted on the ordinal scale**: New operations in a given scale are only defined in terms of operations axiomatically defined in that scale. Allowed operations are maximum, minimum, t-norm, t-conorm and operations defined from them (f.i. [3],[6]).

Working on any of these settings has advantages and disadvantages. In the case of explicit semantics, operations are well defined and sound. However, the experts are required to supply additional information, in particular, they must provide a mapping for each scale. Implicit semantics provide easy to use operations but, instead, semantics is coded - and fixed- in the operators. Counterintuitive results can be obtained if the application does not follow the assumptions considered. Operators restricted on the ordinal scale also lead to sound results. Nevertheless, some of the basic operations are difficult to be defined by non-experienced users, as their meaning is sometimes difficult to grasp.

We propose a different approach based on a semantics expressed with negation functions [12]. The negation-based semantics uses the concept of antonym following [1]. So, the negation of each term is interpreted as its antonym. In this paper we will give a detailed explanation of this approach, which is an alternative to the explicit semantics because it builds an explicit mapping from the set of linguistic terms into the unit interval. This mapping is inferred from a negation on the set of terms. The user is only required to supply a negation function instead of a complete explicit mapping from terms to numbers.

1.1 Negotation based semantics for linguistic terms

In [7] a new class of negation functions over linguistic terms is introduced in order to allow non-equal informativeness without requiring experts to supply detailed information on the semantics of the terms. With this approach an expert can provide additional information about the meaning of the terms in a more natural way. Being $T=\{t_1, t_2, ..., t_n\}$ the vocabulary of one criterion, this negation function is defined from the set of terms T to $\wp(T)$ (i.e., parts of T).

Definition 1. A function *Neg* from T to $\wp(T)$ is a negation function if it satisfies:

C0) *Neg* is not empty and convex
C1) if $t_i < t_j$ then $Neg(t_i) \geq Neg(t_j)$ for all $t_i, t_j \in T$
C2) if $t_i \in Neg(t_j)$ then $t_j \in Neg(t_i)$

For a vocabulary T, the semantics of a term is understood as a subset of the unit interval. Let $I(t_i)$ be the subset attached to term t_i; in this case the set $P = \{I(t_0),...,I(t_n)\}$ corresponds to the semantics of all terms in T. It is assumed that $\cup_{I \in P} I = [0,1]$ and $I(t_i) \cap I(t_j) = \varnothing$. Given a negation function, there are several consistent semantics. In particular, we can have the semantics given in Eq.1, where |X| stands for the cardinality of the set X. Then, using this intervals we can associate a number in [0,1] to each term, $p_i = (m_i + M_i)/2$.

$$I(t_i) = [m_i, M_i] = \left[\frac{\sum_{t < t_i} |Neg(t)|}{\sum_{t \in T} |Neg(t)|}, \frac{\sum_{t \leq t_i} |Neg(t)|}{\sum_{t \in T} |Neg(t)|} \right] \tag{1}$$

1.2 Structure of the paper

Although this paper is devoted to explain the last stage of the decision process, Section 2 makes a brief description of the previous stages. Section 3 defines the distance measure used to select the vocabulary that will be used to explain the result. Section 4 presents the method to attach a term to each set of alternatives. Section 5 gives some details about the inclusion of new terms in the vocabulary. The semantics of this vocabulary is built in Section 6. The following section defines some measures to evaluate the explanation procedure. To conclude, Section 8 makes some comments about the whole process.

2. Overview of the ClusDM method

We have designed a multicriteria decision making method called *ClusDM* (Clustering for Decision Making). *ClusDM* is able to deal with discrete sets of alternatives described with different types of scales (i.e. different numerical scales, different qualitative vocabularies, Boolean data, etc.).

Multicriteria decision aid methods (MCDA) are usually classified into two families: (i) *Aggregation* approaches, based on the Multi-Attribute Utility Theory, and (ii) *Order-focussed* approaches, based on Outranking relations [14]. ClusDM belong to the first family. The multi-attribute utility theory is based on the idea that any decision maker attempts unconsciously to maximise some function that aggregates the utility of each different criterion. The different methods consider different forms for this function. Then the decision making is done in two steps:

- *Aggregation*: a global value for each alternative is computed using an aggregation operator that calculates a global utility value for the alternative considering all the criteria at the same time.
- *Ranking*: the global utility values are used to find the best alternative or to rank them.

ClusDM uses classical Artificial Intelligence clustering algorithms to aggregate the heterogeneous values of the different criteria and obtains a partition of the alternatives in as many clusters as values in the vocabularies [11]. The ranking step is done using the prototypes of these clusters [13]. At the end of this stage, each cluster has a position z in the interval $[0,1]$.

We have added a third stage, called Explanation, that is the one that attaches the most suitable linguistic term to each cluster, according with the ranking positions. These terms define a new preference criterion that summarises the original criteria and expresses the global preference degree of each alternative.

3. Distance between vocabularies

Once we know which is the ranking of the partition of the alternatives according to the criteria, we must determine which is the vocabulary that we want to use to describe the classes of this partition.

We propose the use of one of the vocabularies of the original criteria, because those terms will be familiar to the user. To select the most appropriate vocabulary we have defined a distance between two vocabularies, V_A and V_B as $d_v: V_A, V_B \to \Re$.

First, we define a *centre function* as a function that assigns to each value x_i in $[0,1]$ another value in $[0,1]$ that is the value of the central point of the interval $(m,M]$ to which x_i

belongs to. This centre function is a left continuous step function. Having two vocabularies, V_A and V_B, we denote A and B their corresponding centre functions, such that, for any $x \in [0,1]$, $A : x \to a_x$ and $B : x \to b_x$, where a_x is the central point of the interval of A to which x belongs, and b_x is the central point of the interval of B to which x belongs. So, we can measure the similarity between vocabularies as follows:

$$d_v(V_A, V_B) = d_v(A, B) = \left[\int_0^1 d^2(a_x, b_x) dx \right]^{1/2} \tag{2}$$

where $d^2(a_x, b_x) = (a_x - b_x)^2$. Notice that $d(a_x, b_x) = \sqrt{(a_x - b_x)^2}$ is the Euclidean distance between two points.

Proposition 1. $d_v(V_A, V_B)$ is a distance.

Proof. To prove that $d_v(V_A, V_B)$ is a distance we check the three properties: positivity, symmetry and triangular inequality.

(1) Positivity.

According to the definition of $d_v(V_A, V_B)$, the result cannot be negative, $d_v(V_A, V_B) \geq 0$.

Let's proof that if $d_v(V_A, V_B) = \left[\int_0^1 d^2(a_x, b_x) dx \right]^{1/2} = 0$ then $V_A = V_B$

We will show that when $d_v(V_A, V_B) = 0$, for any $x \in (0,1]$, $d^2(a_x, b_x) = 0$, which means that a_x and b_x are always equal ($V_A = V_B$).

Let us suppose that there exists $x' \in (0,1]$, such that $d^2(a_{x'}, b_{x'}) = (a_{x'} - b_{x'})^2 \neq 0$, as A and B are left-continuous step functions, for any $x' \in (0,1)$, there exists an $x'' \in (0,1)$, $x'' < x'$ such that $(a_x - b_x)^2 = (a_{x'} - b_{x'})^2$ for any $x \in [x'', x']$. So,

$$\int_0^1 d^2(a_x, b_x) dx \geq \int_{x''}^{x'} d^2(a_x, b_x) dx = \int_{x''}^{x'} (a_x - b_x)^2 dx = \int_{x''}^{x'} (a_{x'} - b_{x'})^2 dx = (a_{x'} - b_{x'})^2 (x'' - x')$$

as $(x'' - x') > 0$ and $(a_{x'} - b_{x'})^2 \neq 0$, we have that this expression is positive, $\int_0^1 d^2(a_x, b_x) dx \geq (a_{x'} - b_{x'})^2 (x'' - x') > 0$, which contradicts the original assumption $d_v(V_A, V_B) = \left[\int_0^1 d^2(a_x, b_x) dx \right]^{1/2} = 0$. So, it is not possible to find any $x' \in (0,1]$ such that $d^2(a_{x'}, b_{x'}) = (a_{x'} - b_{x'})^2 \neq 0$. Therefore, $a_{x'} = b_{x'}$ $\forall x' \in [0,1]$, i.e. $V_A = V_B$

(2) Symmetry.

For any V_A, V_B, $d_v(V_A, V_B) = d_v(A, B) = \left[\int_0^1 d^2(a_x, b_x) dx \right]^{1/2} =$

$$= \left[\int_0^1 d^2(b_x, a_x) dx \right]^{1/2} = d_v(B, A) = d_v(V_B, V_A) \text{ since } d^2(a_x, b_x) = (a_x - b_x)^2 \text{ is symmetric.}$$

(3) Triangle inequality. We want to show that : $d_v(V_A, V_B) \le d_v(V_A, V_C) + d_v(V_C, V_B)$.

We know that $d(a_x, b_x) \le d(a_x, c_x) + d(c_x, b_x)$ $\forall x \in [0,1]$, because it is a distance. From this inequality we can have, $d^2(a_x, b_x) \le (d(a_x, c_x) + d(c_x, b_x))^2$ or $d^2(a_x, b_x) \le$ $\le d^2(a_x, c_x) + d^2(c_x, b_x) + 2d(a_x, c_x) \cdot d(c_x, b_x)$. So, if we introduce the bounded integral in each operand, $\int_0^1 d^2(a_x, b_x) dx \le \int_0^1 d^2(a_x, c_x) dx + \int_0^1 d^2(c_x, b_x) + 2\int_0^1 d(a_x, c_x) \cdot d(c_x, b_x) dx$, the inequality is also true.

Since $\int_0^1 d(a_x, c_x) \cdot d(c_x, b_x) dx \le \left(\int_0^1 d^2(a_x, c_x) dx \cdot \int_0^1 d^2(c_x, b_x) dx \right)^{1/2}$, we have that

$$\int_0^1 d^2(a_x, b_x) dx \le \int_0^1 d^2(a_x, c_x) dx + \int_0^1 d^2(c_x, b_x) + 2\left(\int_0^1 d^2(a_x, c_x) dx \cdot \int_0^1 d^2(c_x, b_x) dx \right)^{1/2} \text{ or}$$

$$\int_0^1 d^2(a_x, b_x) dx \le \left[\left(\int_0^1 d^2(a_x, c_x) dx \right)^{1/2} + \left(\int_0^1 d^2(c_x, b_x) \right)^{1/2} \right]^2 \text{ which is exactly the triangle}$$

inequality property: $\left[\int_0^1 d^2(a_x, b_x) \right]^{1/2} \le \left[\int_0^1 d^2(a_x, c_x) \right]^{1/2} + \left[\int_0^1 d^2(c_x, b_x) \right]^{1/2}$

$\square$

Proposition 2. The maximum value of d_v is 0.25.

Proof. The difference between the centres of two overlapping intervals reaches its maximum when these intervals are large and are positioned far from one to each other. The maximum length of the intervals is achieved having the minimum number of terms. That is, having a vocabulary with only 1 term, and the other one with 2 terms (Fig.1).

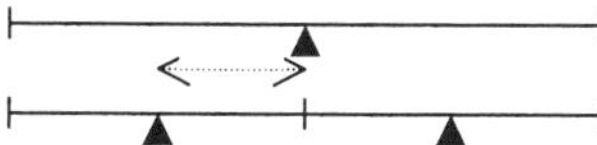

Fig. 1. Maximum distance between overlapping negation-based intervals

In this situation, the maximum difference of the centres is 0.25 for all the points in the domain [0,1]. Therefore, for all x in [0,1], we have $d^2(a_x, b_x) = 0.25^2 = 0.0625$ that can be substituted to d_v to obtain the maximum distance: $d_v(V_A, V_B) = \left[\int_0^1 0.0625 dx \right]^{1/2} = 0.25$ $\square$

4. Selecting the most appropriate term for each cluster

Having found the best preference vocabulary, we have to assign a term of this vocabulary to each cluster, so that this term describes the suitability of the cluster to be a solution of the decision problem. We must note that we can only use each term once, because if more than one cluster receives the same term, they will be indistinguishable. Assuming that each cluster has a position, z, in the interval [0,1], we have designed a methodology following some intuitive assumptions:

- no cluster with a position $z<0.5$ will receive a positive term ($p_i>0.5$)
- no cluster with a position $z>0.5$ will receive a negative term ($p_i<0.5$)
- if a cluster is near the centre, 0.5, it will receive the neutral term ($p_i=0.5$)
- the neutral term will have a negation equal to itself

According to these requirements, the following procedure has been considered:

1. Find the cluster with a position $z=0.5 \pm \xi$, which will be denoted $C_{neutral}$
2. If it exists then assign to it the neutral term, $t_{neutral}$ (if the vocabulary does not have a neutral term, it is required to the user). For further calculations, we consider that $C_{neutral}$ is positioned in $z=0.5$.
3. Divide the clusters into two groups:
   Positive Clusters (positioned between 0.5 and 1) and
   Negative Clusters (positioned between 0 and 0.5)
4. Divide the vocabulary into two groups:
   T_{sup} = Positive Terms (best than $t_{neutral}$, $p_i>0.5$) and
   T_{inf} = Negative Terms (worse than $t_{neutral}$, $p_i<0.5$)
5. If the granularity of any group is smaller than the number of clusters of the corresponding group, apply the algorithms Making_new_terms and Make_names until we have the same number of terms than clusters.
6. Apply the algorithm Explain_result to the 2 groups independently.

After presenting the general procedure for selecting terms, in the rest of the paper will detail the algorithms mentioned above. The Explain_result algorithm receives a set of ordered clusters and the vocabulary given by the expert.

```
Algorithm Explain_result is
    k := number of clusters to be explained
    if k=number of terms then
        Assign these k terms to k clusters
    else
        C_best := the best cluster of the set
            While k>0 do
            Take all those terms in the vocabulary that have at least k-1
            worse terms [t_a..t_b]. Moreover, t_a should not be better than any
            previously assigned term.
            If z(C_best) ∈ [I(t_a)∪...∪I(t_b)] then
                C_best takes the term corresponding to this interval
            else
                if z(C_best)>I(t_a) then
                    C_best takes t_a (the best possible term)
                elsif z(C_best)<I(t_b) then
                    C_best takes t_b (the worst possible term)
                end if
            end if
            k := k - 1
            If k = number of terms after the assigned term then
                Assign these k terms to the k remaining clusters
                k := 0
            else
            Take the cluster that follows C_best in the ranking, and call it
        C_best
                end if
            end while
    end if
end algorithm.
```

This algorithm pretends to give the most appropriate term to each cluster maintaining always the ranking among them. However, we suppose that the decision maker is particularly interested in knowing which are the best alternatives, because he is trying to make a good decision. Thus, we start the process with the selection of the most suitable term for the first cluster in the ranking, provided that we leave enough terms for the rest of clusters.

5. Adding terms to the vocabulary

As it has been pointed out in the previous section, if we have more positive clusters than positive terms or more negative clusters than negative terms, we cannot describe all the clusters. To sort this out, we have designed a method for creating new terms using the ones that we have in the vocabulary. The key idea is to split some terms up and use a qualifier to distinguish the two new parts. So, the problem is reduced to the selection of the terms most adequate to be split.

As we have some information (given by the negation function) about the meaning of the terms in a vocabulary, we can use it to guide the process. A term that has more than one term in its negation indicates that there are slight differences between some of the alternatives assigned to it, in some sense, there is a gradation in the meaning of the term, and each degree corresponds with a term in the negation. Under this interpretation, this term is a candidate to be split up.

```
algorithm Making_new_terms is
  repeat
        {t_left, t_right}:=split the most
                suitable term, t_k
        T := remove t_k from T
        T := add t_left and t_right to T
  until have the desired number of terms
end algorithm.
```

In [12] this process is explained in more detail. In short, we compare each possible ordered set of terms (the initial + one candidate cut) to the ordered partition of alternatives that we are trying to describe. The closest one determines the cut we are going to do. If more cuts are needed, the process is repeated. To compare two vocabularies we use again the distance function (Eq.2), $d_v: V_A, V_B \rightarrow \Re$.

However, it is possible to have some situations where the negation cannot produce the number of new terms required [10]. For example, when the negation function is the classical one, we cannot obtain any new term because all have the same dimension. Then, if the clusters obtained are concentrated on one side of the vocabulary (if they are mainly good or bad), we will have a lack of terms. To sort it out, we propose to identify the term that has a larger number of clusters to explain, $t_i=[m_i, M_i]$, and split it up to obtain $[m_i, c_i]$ and $[c_i, M_i]$. In order to obtain the most accurate cut point, c_i, we will use the position of the clusters in [0,1]. Let us suppose that we have 3 clusters (α, β and γ) positioned like it is shown in Fig.2:

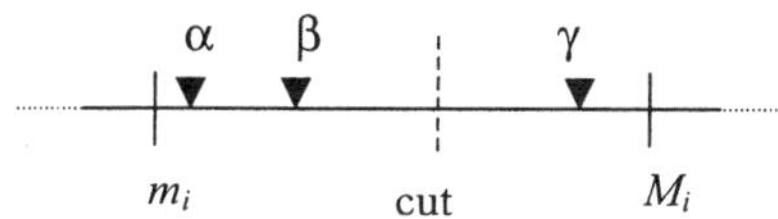

Fig. 2. Selected cut point for the interval $[m_i, M_i]$

The most suitable cut point is the one between the two clusters that are more distant from each other. That is, in Fig.2 we decide to break up the interval just in the middle between β and γ, because the meaning of these two clusters is more different than the meaning of β with respect to α.

In any case, each time we split a term up, two new terms are needed. The method to create new terms for the new intervals in a vocabulary is not trivial, because they should be in accordance with the rest. For this reason, our third algorithm (Make_names) does not invent them, it introduces linguistic hedges (e.g. *very*, *not-so*, ...) in order to distinguish the different grades in the meaning of the term.

To keep the structure of the qualitative vocabularies, we have decided that the neutral term (if exists) it is never split up, since its meaning is that its negation is itself, and an split will end with this property. The rest of the vocabulary is divided in two sets, T_{inf} and T_{sup}, as explained before. Notice that, this algorithm assumes that we will only cut a term once or twice. That is, we will not generate more than 3 terms from a single one. We consider that if more than 3 terms must be obtained, we should ask the decision maker in order to obtain more appropriate terms.

```
algorithm make_names is
 if t∈T_inf then
        if t hasn't been previously split then
            return {very-t,t} being very-t<t
        else /* very-t already exists */
            return  {t, not-so-t} being t < not-so-t
        end if
   else   /* t∈T_sup */
        if t hasn't been previously split then
            return {t,very-t} being t<very-t
        else /*very-t already exists*/
            return  {not-so-t,t}  being not-so-t<t
        end if
   end if
end algorithm.
```

6. Building the negation function of the new criterion

Once we have got the terms that constitute the vocabulary of the new preference criterion, we have to determine their semantics. If the consensus partition were identical to the expert's one, the meaning of the terms would not change, but this will usually not be the case. The meaning of the terms has to be built knowing the alternatives that each term is now describing.

To calculate the new negation function, first we have to attach a numerical interval in $[0,1]$ to each term, $I(t_i)$, using Equation 1. The disjoint intervals are built with the positions of the prototypes of the clusters in the unit interval. Following the fuzzy approach of [15], we consider that the terms have a triangular membership function (except in the extremes), where the prototype of each cluster will have the maximum membership value, which is 1. To build those fuzzy sets, if some of the terms of the vocabulary have not been used to explain the clusters obtained in the previous stages, we include a new imaginary cluster with a prototype positioned in the centre of the interval corresponding to this term. Then, the negation function is built with the real and imaginary prototypes. The additional prototypes are located in the centre in order to try to avoid the changes in the limits of the terms that are not used in the result, since we do not know what should be their meaning in the new criterion.

In order to keep the neutral term centred in 0.5, we begin the process of building the fuzzy sets from the middle. In Fig.3 we have an example with four real clusters represented with triangles and three imaginary prototypes indicated with squares. We can see that to establish the point where the membership function attached to the central term reaches 0 is determined by the second imaginary prototype, because it is the closest one to 0.5.

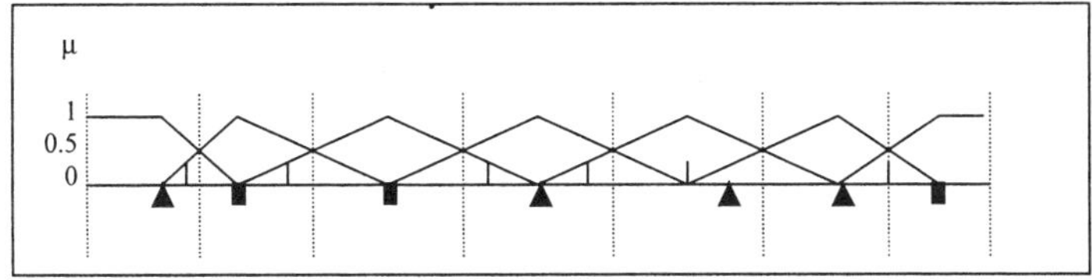

Fig. 3. Fuzzy sets corresponding to an example with 4 clusters (*the squares indicate imaginary prototypes for unused terms, the triangles are the positions of the clusters after the ranking*)

Since the similarity function of the neutral term must be symmetrical, we have that the end of the membership function in the right is established at the same distance to the centre than the prototype in the left. Once the fuzzy set of the neutral term has been fixed, we continue with the rest of the membership functions as explained before. In Fig.3, it can be also observed that, in general, the middle point between two consecutive projections is the one that has membership equal to 0.5. These are the points usually corresponding to the limits of intervals.

Finally, when each term has its corresponding interval in the new criterion, $I(t_i)$, the negation of each one can be built using Equation 3.

$$\text{Neg}(t_i) = \{ \, t_j \mid I(t_j) \cap 1\text{-}I(t_i) \neq \varnothing \} \tag{3}$$

where $1\text{-}I(t_i)$ is the interval between $1\text{-}\max(I(t_i))$ and $1\text{-}\min(I(t_i))$.

7. Evaluation of the quality

MCDA is now paying attention to measuring the trustworthiness of the ranking produced by a decision support tool. In this line, we have defined a global goodness measure for the whole *ClusDM* process.

$$G_{ClusDM} = \omega_1 G_{Agg} + \omega_2 G_{Rank} + \omega_3 G_{Terms} + \omega_4 G_{Neg} \tag{4}$$

where ω_i are the degrees of importance given to each step of the decision making process. For example, increasing ω_1 the user may indicate that obtaining very good and compact clusters is the best option, although it implies a change in the vocabularies and semantics. Weights must hold that $\sum \omega_i = 1$.

With respect to the Explanation stage, in Equation 4 we have two different measures to evaluate the goodness of the new vocabulary and semantics. We should see if this new vocabulary could be misinterpreted. That is, if we are using some words that the decision maker will understand with a different meaning, we can induce him to an error. So, we propose to compare the new criterion with the ones in the initial decision matrix that have some terms in common with it, $C_{common}=\{c_i, c_j, ..., c_k\}$. Obviously, the vocabulary from which we have generated the new one will be in this set.

With Equation 5 we propose to use the distance d_v to measure the differences in the meaning of the terms in each vocabulary. The larger the differences (remember that the distance d_v gives values in [0,0.25]), the more confusing the result may be. Therefore, when the result is 1, we have a perfect correspondence between the terms in all the experts.

$$G_{Terms} = 1 - \frac{\sum_{c_i \in C_{common}} d_v(c_{new}, c_i) \big/ 0.25}{cardinality(C_{common})} \tag{5}$$

Once we have given a linguistic term to each cluster, we evaluate their appropriateness. The position of each cluster before and after the explanation stage can be compared. The ranking stage provides a numerical position in [0,1] for each set of alternatives, z, which is used to select the most appropriate label from the vocabulary. After the explanation process, the position of some clusters may have changed due to the different meaning of the terms. That is, the intervals induced by the negation function may not have the cluster at the centre of the interval.

$$G_{Neg} = 1 - \frac{\sum_{j=1}^{r} |z(j) - (m(j) + M(j))/2|}{r} \tag{6}$$

Equation 6 compares the position of the alternatives before and after the introduction of the negation-based semantics. Being j the prototype of one cluster, $[m(j), M(j)]$ is the interval corresponding to the term assigned to this cluster using the new negation function.

8. Final remarks

We have presented a methodology for describing the degree of preference of a set of alternatives based on a new representation for the semantics of linguistic values. The method requires that the Aggregation and Ranking stages produce an ordered set of clusters. Then, the Explanation stage shows the degree of preference over the clusters.

It must be noted that, during the execution of the process, it will be necessary to relax some definitions. For example, in Equation 3, a small intersection should be ignored. In general, if we have 7 terms in the vocabulary each one covers a 14% of the domain, we recommend to ignore overlappings smaller than 0.02 (1/7 of the length of a term). At the end, the intervals induced by the new negation may be slightly different to the ones we have used to build the function. That is, we have a partition given by fuzzy sets applied to the prototypes of the clusters, which is not exactly the same that the one induced by the negation function assigned to the new preference criterion (obtained using Equation 1). However, we have seen that the differences are small [9].

ClusDM pretends to be a useful recommender tool for decision makers. Our main aim has been to present the results using a linguistic vocabulary easily understandable by the user. The different goodness values can be used by the decision maker to have an idea of the quality of the different stages of the process. In addition, the overall goodness value can be also understood as the weight attached to the new preference criterion obtained.

Apart from that, our method is able to provide some additional information during the execution of the multiple criteria analysis (e.g. a list of conflicting alternatives or the degree of agreement of the original criteria with respect to the new global criterion). The importance of providing additional explanations of the results obtained with the decision model is a problem frequently considered in the Artificial Intelligence community [5].

References

[1] de Soto, A.R., Trillas, E.: On antonym and negate in fuzzy logic, *International Journal on Intelligent Systems*, vol.14:3 (1999) 295-303

[2] Dubois, D., Prade, H.: *Fuzzy sets and sytems:Theory and applications*, Academic Press (1980)

[3] Godo, L., Torra, V.: On aggregation operators for ordinal qualitative information, *IEEE Transactions on Fuzzy Systems*, vol.8:2 (2000) 143-154

[4] Herrera, F., Herrera-Viedma, E.: Aggregation operators for linguistic weighted information, *IEEE Trans.on Systems, Man and Cybernetics*, vol.27 (1997) 646-656

[5] Papamichail, H.N.: Explaining and justifying decision support advice in intuitive terms, *13th European Conf on Artificial Intelligence*, (1998) 102-103

[6] Sugeno, M.: *Theory of fuzzy integrals and its applications*, PhD. Dissertation. Tokyo Institute of Technology, Japan (1974)

[7] Torra, V.: Negation functions based semantics for ordered linguistic labels, *Int. Journal of Intelligent Systems*, vol.11 (1996) 975-988

[8] Torra, V.: Aggregation of linguistic labels when semantics is based on antonyms, International *Journal of Intelligent Systems*, vol.16:4 (2001) 513-524

[9] Valls, A.: *ClusDM: a multiple criteria decision making method for heterogeneous data sets*, Ph.D. Thesis, Universitat Politècnica de Catalunya, Spain (2002) ISBN: 84-688-1348-6

[10] Valls, A., Torra, V.: *Reaching consensus when experts use different linguistic terms*, Proceedings of the European EUSFLAT-ESTYLF Joint Conference (1999) 147-150

[11] Valls, A., Torra, V.: Using classification as an aggregation tool in MCDM, *Fuzzy Sets and Systems*, vol.115-1, Special issue on Soft Decision Analysis (2000) 159-168

[12] Valls, A., Torra, V.: *Explaining the consensus of opinions with the vocabulary of the experts*, International Conference on Information Processing and Management of Uncertainty in Knowledge Based Systems (IPMU), vol.2 (2000) 746-753

[13] Valls, A., Torra, V.: *Fusion of qualitative preferences with different vocabularies*, 5th AI Catalan Conference, Spain (2002). Lecture Notes on Computer Science, Springer-Verlag [7] Ref dels autors

[14] Vinke, P.: *Multicriteria decision aid*, John Wiley & Sons (1992)

[15] Yuan, Y., Shaw, M. J.: Induction of fuzzy decision trees, *Fuzzy Sets and Systems*, vol.69 (1995) 125-139

2. Robotics

Artificial Intelligence Research and Development
I. Aguiló et al. (Eds.)
IOS Press, 2003

Evolutionary Tuning of the Control Architecture of an Underwater Cable Tracker*

Javier ANTICH and Alberto ORTIZ
University of the Balearic Islands
Maths and Computer Science Department
{javi.antich, alberto.ortiz}@uib.es

Abstract. Nowadays, the surveillance and inspection of underwater installations, such as power or telecommunication cables and pipelines, are carried out by trained operators who, from the surface, control a Remotely Operated Vehicle (ROV) with cameras mounted over it. This is a tedious, time-consuming and expensive task, prone to errors mainly because of loss of attention or fatigue of the operator and also due to the typical low quality of seabed images. In this paper, a behavioural control architecture for visually guiding an Autonomous Underwater Vehicle (AUV) to detect and track a cable laid on the seabed is presented. Additionally, the results of an efficient off-line tuning method based on evolutionary theory are discussed. Such results were obtained by using a 3D simulation environment which incorporates the hydrodynamic model of a real underwater vehicle called GARBI.

1 Introduction

The feasibility of an underwater installation can only be guaranteed by means of a suitable inspection programme. This programme must provide the company with information about potential hazardous situations or damages caused by the mobility of the seabed, corrosion, or human activities such as marine traffic or fishing. Nowadays, the surveillance and inspection of these installations are carried out using video cameras attached to ROVs normally controlled by operators from a support ship. Obviously, this is a tedious task because the operator has to concentrate for a long time in front of a console, which makes the task highly prone to errors mainly due to loss of attention and fatigue. Besides, undersea images possess some peculiar characteristics which increase the complexity of the operation: blurring, low contrast, non-uniform illumination and lack of stability due to the motion of the vehicle, just to cite some of them. Therefore, the automation of any part of this process can constitute an important improvement in the maintenance of such installations with regard to errors, time and monetary costs.

The special visual features that artificial objects have allow distinguishing them from the rest of objects present in a natural scenario even in very noisy images. In our case, the rigidity and shape of the underwater cable can be exploited by a computer vision algorithm to discriminate it from the surrounding environment. This fact makes feasible the automatic guidance of an AUV by means of visual feedback to carry out maintenance/inspection tasks.

---

*This study has been partially supported by project CICYT-DPI2001-2311-C03-02 and FEDER funding.

Following this strategy, a novel approach to the problem of detecting and tracking an underwater cable by analysing the image sequence from a video camera attached to an ROV was described in [10], being afterwards improved and optimised in [2, 11].

In this study, a first approximation to the control architecture for locating and tracking the cable autonomously on the basis of the aforementioned vision system is presented. On the other hand, an evolutionary strategy to carry out the tuning of such control system is also described and its implementation discussed.

The proposed control architecture is reactive to produce timely robotic response in a dynamic and unstructured world such as the submarine. Schema theory [3] has been applied in its implementation together with the motor schema methodology adopted by Arkin in [4]. Simplicity, modularity and robustness are the most important characteristics of this behavioural architecture.

As for the evolutionary tuning strategy, a genetic algorithm [8] based on bit representation, one-point crossover, bit-flip mutation changing the step size, and tournament selection has been designed in order to optimize the control system according to a minimum mission duration criterion. It is important to note that the performance of the evolutionary algorithm has been improved by using specific knowledge of the problem.

The whole system has been validated using a 3D object-oriented simulator consisting of an AUV dynamic model, a low-level controller, the control architecture, the vision system, and a virtual OpenGL-based underwater environment through which the vehicle navigates. The AUV model used is based on the real dynamics of a vehicle designed and built by the Computer Vision and Robotics research group of the University of Girona (Spain) named GARBI. Information about the method followed to model and estimate the dynamics of the vehicle can be found in [13].

The rest of the paper is organized as follows: the control architecture is described in section 2, while the tuning strategy is discussed in section 3; section 4 shows experimental results; and, finally, section 5 presents some conclusions and future work.

2　Control Architecture

2.1　General Description

Robot control is the process of taking information about the environment, through the sensors of the robot, processing it as necessary to decide how to act, and then executing those actions by means of the available effectors to achieve the set of goals corresponding to a user-specified mission. Nowadays, there is a small number of fundamentally different classes of robot control methodologies (see [6, 12, 14], among many others), usually embodied in particular control architectures, which can be roughly classified as: deliberative/hierarchical, behavioural/reactive, and hybrid. However, only the two last ones are suitable to deal with complex, non-structured, and changing worlds, like the majority of underwater environments. In order to control the navigation of an underwater cable tracker, the paper proposes a complete behavioural control architecture based on Motor Schemas with 3D potential fields. Simplicity and modularity have been the key factors to choose this approach.

In this context, behaviours are the basic building blocks to carry out robotic actions, representing each of them the reaction to a stimulus. Behavioural responses are all coded as 3D vectors whose orientation denotes the direction to be followed by the vehicle while the magnitude expresses the strength of the response against other behavioral commands. The output vectors generated by the architecture's active behaviours are asynchronously channelled into a cooperative coordination mechanism that combines them in order to obtain the final control system response. More precisely, the characteristic gain value associated to each behaviour is used as a multiplier before the addition. In this way, it is usual that safety and dominant behaviours possess the highest gains. In spite of this simple rule, the tuning of these values is, in general, a difficult task that requires either experimental work and an experienced system designer. As it has been said before, a solution to the "by hand" tuning problem for our particular case is going to be presented in section 3.

2.2　Mission Stages

Throughout a mission, the AUV passes through several stages: diving, sweeping, tracking and homing. In the first one, the AUV, after having been released from the support ship, goes down until reaching a certain distance to the seabed. The second and third stages comprise, respectively, searching for the cable in a predefined exploration area and tracking it afterwards. Finally, the vehicle returns to the starting point after having achieved the limits of the exploration area while tracking the cable.

2.3　Behaviour Description

Taking into account this general way of action for the AUV, the control architecture makes use of a total of six behaviours. Some of them appear in the classical literature about behavioural architectures, but others are specific of this application. They all are described in the following:

- *Stay on region* prevents the AUV from straying from the area to be explored. The behaviour is exclusively activated when the vehicle is close to the limits of the exploration area. In such a case, a vector that moves the vehicle away from those limits is generated, being its magnitude directly related to the corresponding distance: the closer to the limits, the larger the magnitude.

- *Avoid obstacles* allows the vehicle to avoid navigational barriers such as rocks, algae or, even, other possible cooperating vehicles. In this case, a vector in the opposite direction to the obstacles is generated. The magnitude of the vector is again variable, now according to the distance that separates the AUV from the obstacles ahead.

- *Avoid the past* is intended to avoid the known trapping problem characteristic of reactive strategies [5]. For such a purpose, a local map of the most recent AUV's path is used. When it is detected that the vehicle remains in essentially the same area for a long time, this behaviour becomes active generating a vector whose direction favours the exploration of new regions of the environment. In this case, the magnitude of the vector is proportional to the size of the area where the vehicle has been trapped into.

- *Cable detection and tracking* moves the vehicle strategically through the exploration area in search of a sufficient evidence of the presence of the cable. Specifically, after having acquired the working depth through a vertical path from the surface, the AUV executes the sweeping stage performing a zigzag movement on the exploration area until the cable is found. Although other more optimised strategies could have been devised, it is important to notice that it has been assumed a total lack of information about the location of the cable, so that there are no many more alternatives but an exhaustive or near-exhaustive search.

Once the cable has been detected, the tracking stage starts. At this point, the AUV can be oriented in any one of the two possible –and opposite– directions to start tracking the cable. The particular choice is based on a predefined parameter which establishes a certain range of preferred orientations.

Along the tracking, two different tasks are sequentially executed: the first one tries to keep the cable oriented vertically in the captured images, while the second task intends to maintain the cable in the central area of the images. In this way, improvements in both the cable visual detection and the longitude and smoothness of the vehicle's path are expected.

As it can be anticipated in a real application, anomalous situations can arise. In particular, the cable can disappear from the images because the AUV's course has drifted apart from the actual cable location. In such cases, a suitable recovery mechanism is activated, consisting in making the behaviour return to its internal search state, where the vehicle acquires the aforementioned zigzag movement. However, now the area to be explored is reduced using the vehicle's trajectory during the past tracking stage. This trajectory is fitted by a straight line and a new search zone is determined computing the intersection between such line and the limits of the exploration area (see fig. 1). Note that the dimensions of that zone can be readjusted according to the AUV's manoeuvrability.

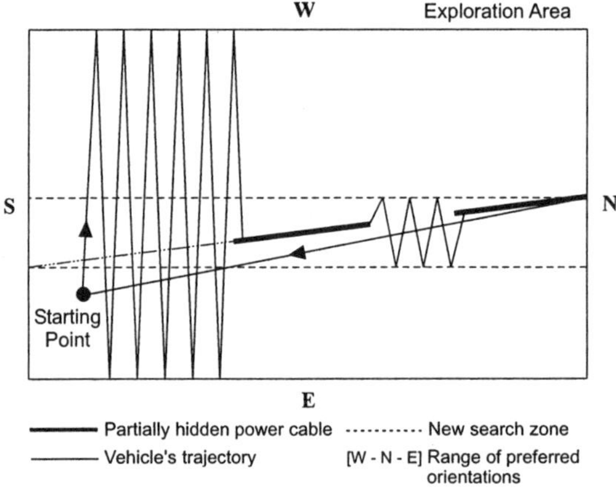

Figure 1: AUV's trajectory for a typical mission (notice how the cable is lost once and tracked again).

- *Keep distance to seabed* tries to keep the distance to the seabed constant in order to keep the apparent width of the cable in the images also constant. In this way, the vision system can assume that the separation between both sides of the cable is nearly constant, and use this information to reduce its probability of failure. Sonars or, in case they cannot bring accurate enough measures, the acoustic positioning system, are expected to supply the required distance to the seabed.

- *Go home*, finally, makes the vehicle go to the starting point of the mission. Two different steps are carried out: first, the AUV approximates to the goal point keeping a certain distance to the seabed; afterwards, it goes up until the sea surface is reached. In both cases, the magnitude of the output vector is proportional to the proximity to the intermediate/final goals considered.

Fig. 2 summarizes the way how the aforementioned components of the control architecture are organized. As it can be seen, a supervisor has been added. From a functional point of view, this component just activates and deactivates behaviours depending on the mission stage where the vehicle is, in order to avoid conflicts among them. It can be considered, therefore, as the first step towards a future hybrid control architecture. For additional information on the subject, the reader is referred to [1].

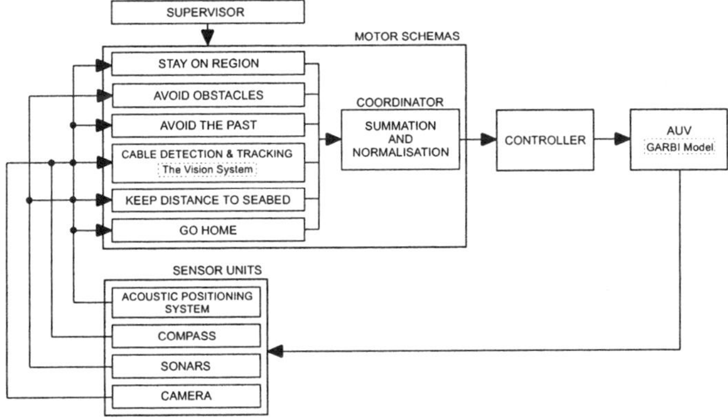

Figure 2: Components of the system.

3 Off-line Tuning Strategy

John Holland showed in his book "Adaptation in Natural and Artificial Systems" in 1975 how the evolutionary process can be applied to solve a wide variety of problems using a highly parallel technique called *genetic algorithm* (GA). They constitute a class of gradient descent methods where a high-quality solution is found by applying, over a series of generations, a set of biologically-inspired operators to points within a specific search space [4]. The goodness or fitness of each individual of the population —set of points in the search space— is computed using an evaluation function that measures how well it solves the target problem. Those individuals which represent a better solution to the problem have more chances to reproduce and be part of the next generation. Over generations, it is expected that the population progressively improves the quality of its set of solutions. In spite of this fact, it is important to note that this evolutionary technique does not guarantee to achieve an optimal global solution but it generally produces very good solutions within reasonable amounts of time for certain problem spaces.

In this paper, a genetic algorithm has been used to find a near-optimal set of behaviour gain values for the previously described control architecture. A mission duration minimization criterion has been applied. Fig. 3 shows a high-level description of the structure of this particular genetic algorithm, where $P(t)$ denotes a population of μ individuals at generation t. Each individual, or chromosome using the classical terminology, represents a potential solution to the problem at hand and is implemented as a fixed-length string over the alphabet $\{0,1\}$. The utilization of binary representation derives from the *schema theory* [7]. The length L of the bit string associated to each chromosome directly depends on the number of variables of the problem. In our case, there will be *a priori* as many variables as behaviours in the control architecture. Given a variable x_i that can take values from a domain $Di = [u_i, v_i] \subseteq \mathbf{R}$ with a precision p —number of places after the decimal point—, the number of bits required to code it is computed according to equation 1. On the other hand, the mapping from a binary j-length substring ss corresponding to the variable x_i into a real number is shown in equation 2.

```
Procedure GA
Begin
     t := 0
     Initialize P(t)
     Repair      P(t)
     Evaluate    P(t)
     While (not terminate) Do
     Begin
          t := t + 1
          Select   P(t) from P(t-1)
          Alter    P(t)
          Repair   P(t)
          Evaluate P(t)
     End
End
```

Figure 3: Structure of the genetic algorithm.

$$min\left(j \in \mathbf{N}^+ \mid \left((v_i - u_i) \cdot 10^p\right) + 1 \leq 2^j \right) \tag{1}$$

$$x_i = u_i + (v_i - u_i) \cdot \frac{\left(ss_{j-1} \ldots ss_0\right)_{10}}{2^j - 1} \tag{2}$$

The genetic algorithm begins generating an initial population of chromosomes by randomization. Immediately afterwards, a reparation step is executed on the resultant population. At this point, the chromosomes are strategically altered, without loss of information, in order to satisfy a set of basic constraints dependent on the problem at hand. Fundamentally, a value interchange among the constrained variables of each chromosome is carried out with that purpose. This initialization phase finishes measuring the fitness of the solutions obtained by means of simulation experiments. More precisely, each chromosome is assessed computing the time d that the AUV needs to carry out a representative mission using the coded behaviour gains. Details of the heuristic evaluation function can be found in equation 3, where d_r is a reference duration whose value is obtained by simulating the mission considered on the basis of a set of manually tuned gains.

$$f(\vec{x}) = \begin{cases} 0 & \text{if the vehicle collides} \\ 0.1 & \text{if } d > 1.25 \cdot d_r \\ 0.1 + \frac{0.9 \times (1.25 \cdot d_r - d)}{0.25 \cdot d_r} & \text{otherwise} \end{cases} \tag{3}$$

Once the genetic algorithm has been initialised, new generations of chromosomes are obtained by iteratively executing four different steps: reproduction, variation, reparation and evaluation. In the first one, a new population is formed by choosing chromosomes according to the tournament selection method. Specifically, it works by taking a random uniform sample of a certain size $q > 1$ from the population, selecting the best of these q chromosomes to survive in the next generation, and repeating the process until the new population is filled. It is important to note that this popular selection method has shown to be both easy to implement and computationally efficient. On the other hand, an accurate control of the selective pressure has been allowed by increasing or decreasing the tournament size q. In the second step, the bit string encoding of the members of the new population is altered using two genetic operators: mutation and a standard one-point crossover (see [7, 8], among many others, to obtain detailed information on the latter operator). The former is performed on a bit-by-bit basis. The probability of mutation p_m gives us information about the expected number of mutated bits per chromosome ($p_m \cdot L$). In our case, following the Mühlenbein's formula, p_m has been fixed to $\frac{1}{L}$. The excellent properties of this value can be found in [9]. As for the mutation step size, it changes depending on the fitness of each chromosome. Given the binary j-length substring corresponding to the variable x_i of a certain chromosome $\vec{x}$, the mutation probability of the bit k ($0 \leq k < j$) of such substring is determined on the basis of equation 4. The next two steps, reparation and evaluation, have been previously explained.

$$
p_m(k) = \begin{cases} \text{if } f(\vec{x}) < 1 & \dfrac{(k+1)-k \cdot f(\vec{x})}{\sum_{l=0}^{j-1}(l+1)-l \cdot f(\vec{x})} \cdot (p_m \cdot j) \\[3ex] \text{if } f(\vec{x}) \geq 1 & \dfrac{(j-k)-(j-k-1) \cdot (2-f(\vec{x}))}{\sum_{l=0}^{j-1}(j-l)-(j-l-1) \cdot (2-f(\vec{x}))} \cdot (p_m \cdot j) \end{cases} \tag{4}
$$

4 Experimental Results

In order to validate the proposed system and the evolutionary tuning strategy, a 3D object-oriented simulator has been implemented using C++ together with the OpenGL graphics library. The simulator, named NEMO$_{CAT}$ (Navigational Environment MOdeller, Control Architecture Tester), incorporates the dynamic model of the underwater vehicle GARBI (see fig. 4), making thus the simulations more realistic.

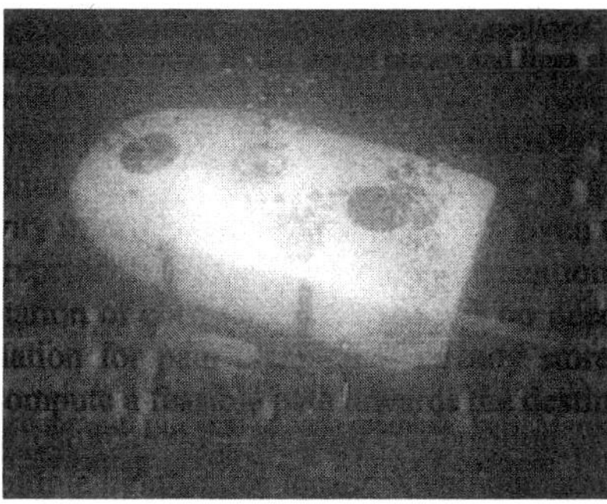

Figure 4: The underwater vehicle GARBI.

Fig. 5 shows a global view of the simulation environment. In such figure, the environment where the vehicle navigates appears in the rightmost window, while the window at the left-lower corner shows the image captured by the camera. On top, some data about the state of the vehicle and about the control architecture are displayed.

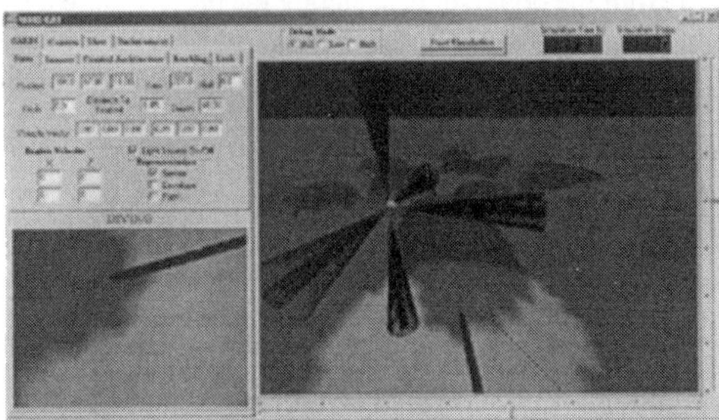

Figure 5: The simulation environment NEMO$_{CAT}$.

Initially, gain values of the architecture's behaviours were experimentally determined on the basis of a heterogeneous set of missions. Table 1 shows the results of this tedious task. Different views of the AUV's trajectory for a representative mission using the behaviour gains specified in the aforementioned table are displayed in fig. 6. As it can be seen, the AUV, after the diving stage, is trapped into a box-shaped canyon. The activation of the "avoid the past" behaviour allows the vehicle to escape from this undesirable situation. Then, the characteristic zigzag movement of the sweeping stage is resumed. When tracking, the cable is lost on one occasion and subsequently tracked again after a restricted search process carried out on a small region of the exploration area. The mission finishes with the return of the vehicle to the starting point.

Table 1: Experimental behaviour gain values

Behaviour	Gain
Stay on Region	2.00
Avoid Obstacles	6.00
Avoid the Past	2.25
Cable Detection and Tracking	1.50
Keep Distance to Seabed	2.75
Go Home	1.25

In order to prove the feasibility and robustness of the proposed off-line tuning strategy, the results for the previous mission are discussed next. First of all, it is important to note that the feasibility of the evolutionary approach for tuning mainly depends on the time required to simulate the mission. In general, a high percentage of this time comes from the image processing task associated to the vision subsystem. For this reason, a big effort has been done in that direction to significantly reduce —more than 95%— the cost of such task from the point

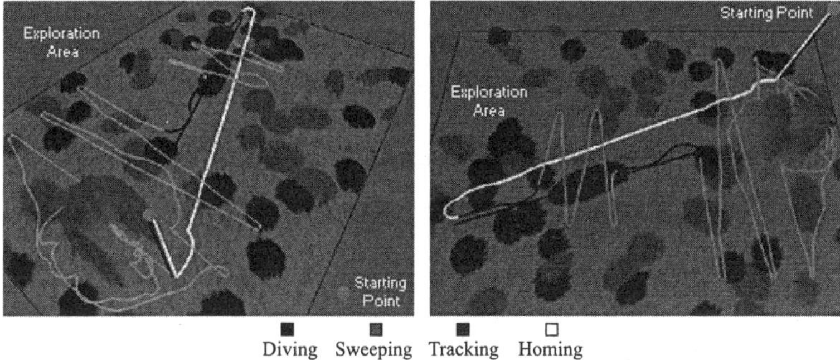

Figure 6: AUV's path using experimental gains.

of view of the execution time. Pre-computed information is used with this purpose. Specifically, a finite set of points is uniformly distributed on the virtual underwater environment and several images are taken in each point varying the camera orientation. All the images captured are next analysed by the vision system and cable detection results are saved. In this way, information about the cable, if any, can be immediately obtained in an approximated way knowing the position and orientation of the AUV inside the underwater environment. Fig. 7 shows the AUV's trajectory for the mission under consideration following the previously explained time-reduction strategy. The experimental behaviour gains were used.

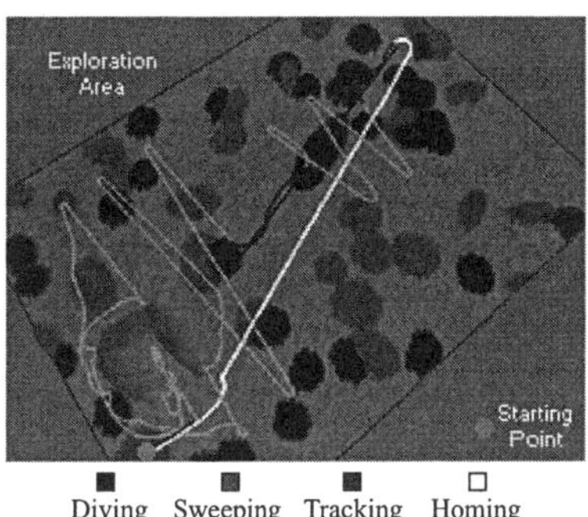

Figure 7: Results in fast mode.

Referring to the tuning, it is also important to note that only the gains of the next three behaviours have been genetically adjusted: "avoid obstacles", "avoid the past" and, finally, "cable detection and tracking". In this way, it is intended to focus the optimization problem on that subset of variables whose tuning is more complex due to their high interdependency. Consequently, the search space is considerably reduced. On the other hand, the gain values are required to satisfy equation 5 at every stage for every chromosome of the population.

$$Gain_{AvoidObstacles} > Gain_{AvoidPast} > Gain_{CableD\&T} \tag{5}$$

As for the parameters of the genetic algorithm, the most important ones are listed in table 2. Note that the domain upper limit of the problem variables has been established taking into account the maximum velocity (rpm) of the vehicle's thrusters.

Table 2: Genetic algorithm parameters

Parameter	Value
Variable domain	$[0, 7.2]$
Variable precision	2
Number of generations	50
Population size	50
Tournament size	3
Probability of mutation	$\frac{1}{L} = \frac{1}{30}$
Probability of crossover	$\frac{1}{3}$

Several results of the evolutionary process are presented in the following. On the one hand, a graphical representation of the average fitness of the population over generations is shown in fig. 8. As it was expected, the quality of the solutions obtained tends to improve as the genetic algorithm progresses. It is important to note that at the end of the process, all the members of the resultant population are, from an average point of view, reasonably better than the initially proposed experimental solution (average fitness higher than 1). On the other hand, table 3 shows the *best-so-far* chromosome for this run, which reduces the duration of the mission about 12%. Finally, a view of the optimised AUV's trajectory is displayed in fig. 9.

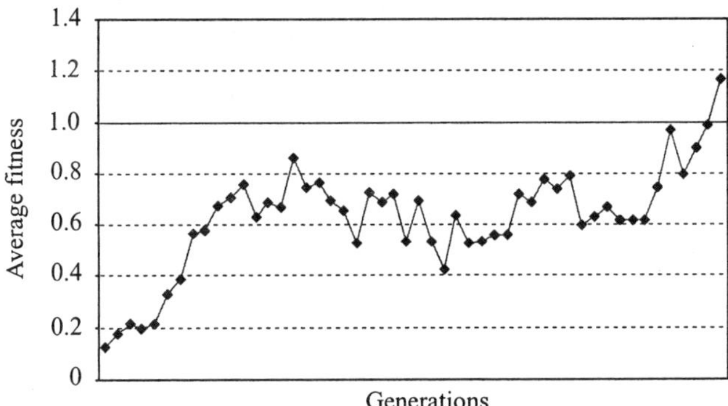

Figure 8: Average fitness over generations.

In order to illustrate the validity of the solution obtained, two more complex alternative missions have been defined. In the first one (see fig. 10(a)), the curvature of the cable becomes more significant. As for the second one (see fig. 10(b)), a special texture, created by manually applying a mosaicking process to an excerpt of an image sequence of a real cable, has been mapped on the seabed of the simulated underwater environment. For each case, the duration of the mission has been respectively reduced more than 4% and 6% with regard to the "by hand" tuning reference.

Table 3: Genetic algorithm output

Behaviour	Gain
Avoid Obstacles	5.58
Avoid the Past	2.97
Cable Detection and Tracking	2.38

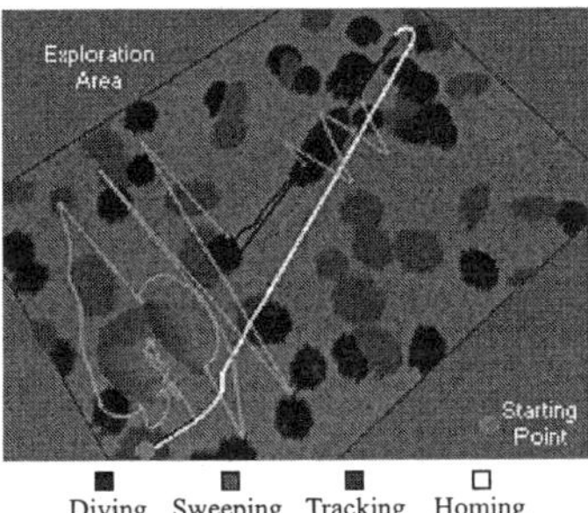

Figure 9: Optimised AUV's path.

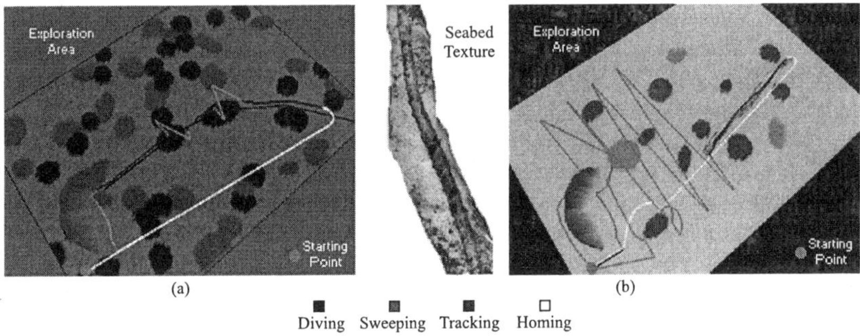

Figure 10: Results for two alternative missions.

5 Conclusions and Future Work

A behaviour-based control architecture for locating and tracking an underwater cable on the basis of a vision subsystem has been presented. The study has been completed by proposing an evolutionary off-line strategy to tune such control system according to a mission duration minimization criterion. Interesting results have been obtained using a 3D OpenGL-based simulator called NEMO$_{CAT}$.

As future work, the control system will be validated with a prototype of AUV, which our research group SRV is working on at the present. On the other hand, new evaluation functions will be tested to optimize the behaviour gains based on other criteria such as the minimization of the AUV's battery consumption. Afterwards, an effort will be done to suitably combine those basic functions.

Acknowledgements

The authors of this study would like to thank the members of the Computer Vision and Robotics research group of the University of Girona (Spain) for providing them with the hydrodynamic model of their underwater vehicle GARBI.

References

[1] J. Antich and A. Ortiz. Behaviour-based control of an underwater cable tracker. Technical Report A-4-2003, DMI (UIB), 2003.

[2] J. Antich and A. Ortiz. Underwater cable tracking by visual feedback. In *Proceedings of the 1st Iberian Conference on Pattern Recognition and Image Analysis*, LNCS 2652, pages 53–61, 2003.

[3] R. Arkin. *Neuroscience in motion: the application of schema theory to mobile robotics*. Plenum Press, New York, 1989.

[4] R. Arkin. *Behavior-based robotics*. MIT Press, Cambridge, Massachusetts Institute of Technology, 1998.

[5] T. Balch and R. Arkin. Avoiding the past: a simple but effective strategy for reactive navigation. In *Proceedings of the Intl. Conference on Robotics and Automation*, pages 678–685, 1993.

[6] È. Coste-Manière and R. Simmons. Architecture, the backbone of robotic systems. In *Proceedings of the Intl. Conference on Robotics and Automation*, pages 67–72, 2000.

[7] J. Holland. *Adaptation in Natural and Artificial Systems*. University of Michigan Press, Ann Arbor, 1975.

[8] Z. Michalewicz. *Genetic Algorithms + Data Structures = Evolution Programs*. Springer-Verlag Berlin Heidelberg, 1996.

[9] H. Mühlenbein. How genetic algorithms really work — Part I: Mutation and hillclimbing. In *Proceedings of the 2nd Conference on Parallel Problem Solving from Nature*, pages 15–25, 1992.

[10] A. Ortiz, G. Oliver, and J. Frau. A vision system for underwater real-time control tasks. In *Proceedings of Oceans*, pages 1425–1430, 1997.

[11] A. Ortiz, M. Simó, and G. Oliver. A vision system for an underwater cable tracker. *Intl. Journal of Machine Vision and Applications*, 13(3):129–140, 2002.

[12] P. Ridao, J. Batlle, J. Amat, and G. N. Roberts. Recent trends in control architectures for autonomous underwater vehicles. *Intl. Journal of Systems Science*, 30(9):1033–1056, 1999.

[13] P. Ridao, J. Batlle, and M. Carreras. Dynamics model of an underwater robotic vehicle. Technical Report IIiA 01-05-RR, UdG, 2001.

[14] K. Valavanis, D. Gracanin, M. Matijasevic, R. Kolluru, and G. Demetriou. Control architectures for autonomous underwater vehicles. *IEEE Control Systems Magazine*, 17:48–64, 1997.

Artificial Intelligence Research and Development
I. Aguiló et al. (Eds.)
IOS Press, 2003

An Intelligent System for Simultaneous World Modelling and Localization

Antoni BURGUERA, Yolanda GONZÁLEZ, Gabriel OLIVER

Mathematics and Computer Science Department
Universitat de les Illes Balears, Ctra. Valldemossa Km. 7,5
07071 Palma de Mallorca, Spain
{a.burguera, y.gonzalez, goliver}@uib.es

Abstract. The navigation ability is the main feature that sets autonomous mobile robots apart. It is widely accepted that navigation is the methodology that permits to guide a robot around its environment using sensor information. Without this ability, the robot has to resort on inefficient strategies such as random motion. The control architecture, which is the framework where the navigation ability is implemented, is strongly influenced by the environment representation and the knowledge of the robot position. This paper presents a straightforward system that permits both incrementally robust map building and vehicle relocation simultaneously while navigating by combining dead reckoning and landmark based navigation methods. The design and implementation of a hybrid three-layer control architecture which fully integrates the system is also exposed, as well as the experimental results obtained testing it on a versatile simulation environment.

1 Introduction

An intelligent mobile robot must be able to perceive its environment, reasoning about its state, and acting according to a prescribed action. Therefore, mobile robots pose a unique challenge to artificial intelligence and robotics researchers.

The navigation ability is the main feature that sets autonomous mobile robots apart. It is widely accepted that navigation is the methodology that permits to guide a robot around its environment using sensor information. Without this ability, the robot has to resort on inefficient strategies such as random motion.

According to Nehmzow [9], there are four competences related to the navigation ability: map-building, self-localization, map interpretation and path planning. Map-building competence refers to the construction of an environment representation. Self-localization refers to the ability of the robot to know its position in the map. Finally, map interpretation refers to the ability of the robot to use the map for navigation tasks such as path planning.

Dead reckoning and landmark based navigation are the most usual methods for a robot to navigate. The main problem of the first one is the accumulation of a drift error because it is based on path integration. Landmark based systems may produce a way-point based navigation if a sparse set of landmarks is used.

Moreover, when the environment is partially or totally unknown it is desirable for the system to solve simultaneously map-building and self-localization tasks [13]. This open problem is known as SLAM: Simultaneous Localization and Mapping [6].

A critical point for SLAM systems is the environment representation. Two main approaches can be distinguished: topological [8, 5] and metric [7, 10]. The first one represents the navigation space as connections between landmarks. In the other one, the environment is represented as a regular map.

The right choice of the control architecture, which is the framework where the navigation ability is implemented, can help the specification, implementation and validation of intelligent mobile robot systems.

Hybrid deliberative-reactive control architecture style emerged in the 1990's and continues being the most widely accepted paradigm of research in this field. Hybrid architectures combine the use of reactive behaviors [1] in the lower layer with high level planning layers.

Some examples of well known intelligent mobile robots are *RHINO*, *Dervish* or *Xavier*, whose control architectures are explained in [2].

This paper presents the three-layer hybrid architecture named ATHRAIA, able to safely guide an autonomous mobile robot although the environment is unknown. ATHRAIA deals with the four navigation competences described above. Both metric and topological environment representations are obtained while navigating. The navigation method proposed uses both dead reckoning and landmark based techniques. The first one permits ATHRAIA to estimate the robot pose at any moment, while the second one makes ATHRAIA able to correct the errors in the robot pose estimation.

The simulation environment SEFIRoT and the real robot CABRIT have been developed in order to test the system. Some experiments have been conducted and the results obtained are also shown.

The document is structured as follows: section 2 overviews the control architecture, section 3 details the navigation process, section 4 describes the environment representation and the pose correction process, section 5 shows the experimental platforms, section 6 states the experimental results and conclusions are explained in section 7.

2 Control Architecture

ATHRAIA (*Advanced Three-layer Hybrid Robot Architecture for Intelligent Autonomy*) is a control architecture that guides mobile robots safely planning the paths to accomplish a mission. While doing that, ATHRAIA maps the environment and corrects the robot position errors. Moreover, ATHRAIA is able to perform the above mentioned tasks without previous information of the environment. As a matter of fact, the robot doesn't know its initial position in the environment.

The fact that both map building and position correction are done simultaneously while navigating, with no *a priori* information, makes ATHRAIA a suitable SLAM-oriented [11, 6, 12] control architecture.

The mission is specified by the user and it is composed by a set of spatial points that must be sequentially reached by the robot. Each mission point has a user defined margin of tolerance so the robot doesn't has to pass exactly on the mission point coordinates. Because of the sequentiality of the mission execution, ATHRAIA only takes into account one mission point at a time, called the *Active Mission Point*.

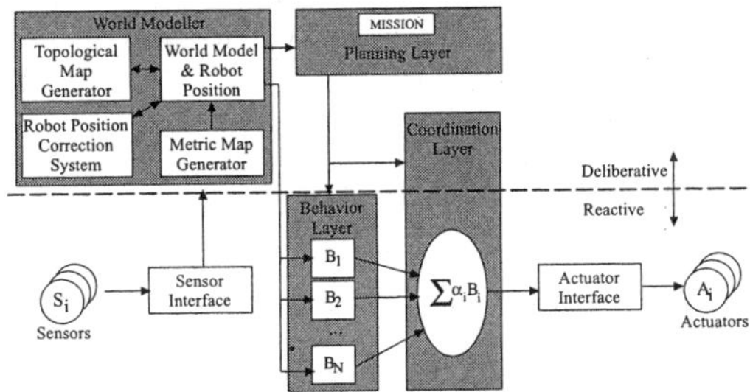

Figure 1: Block diagram of ATHRAIA

ATHRAIA (fig. 1) is composed of a *World Modeller* and the three layers: *Behavior Layer*, *Coordination Layer* and *Planning Layer*. The Behavior Layer and a subset of the Coordination Layer modules are in charge of the reactive tasks. The rest of the Coordination Layer, the Planning Layer and the World Modeller make the deliberative tasks possible.

The World Modeller, which uses a metric and a hybrid metric-topological representation of the environment, is in charge of both world modeling and robot position correction, as will be described in section 4.

The three layers, using the information contained in the World Model, are in charge of the navigation process, and are described in the next section.

3 Navigation

The ability of ATHRAIA to navigate in an intelligent and safe way through complex environments is accomplished by its three layers, which are described next. By accessing robot pose and mapping information in the World Model they are able to perform an accurate navigation.

The Behavior Layer: It is composed of behaviors which use the sensor information processed by the World Modeller and the path generated by the Planning Layer. At the moment three behaviors have been implemented: the *Go To* behavior, the *Avoid Obstacles* behavior and the *Avoid the Past* behavior.

The Coordination Layer: It produces a vehicle movement direction vector by combining the outputs of the behaviors. This direction is communicated to the robot through the Actuator Interface. ATHRAIA uses a collaborative coordination method consisting on a weighted mean of the behavior outputs.

The deliberative part of the Coordination Layer is able to dynamically change the weights assigned to the behaviors by using a Finite State Machine and a set of Monitors.

The Finite State Machine, defined by the user, is composed by a set of states and a set of conditional transitions between states. One and only one of the states can be active at a time.

Each state has associated an N-dimensional vector, being N the number of behaviors present in the Behavior Layer. Each vector component represents the desired weight for each behavior when the state is active. Thus, the only possible change in behaviors weights is due to a change of state in the Finite State Machine.

Each transition has an associated condition. If the condition is satisfied then the active state changes to the one pointed by the transition. Conditions are specified using boolean operations on the *Monitors* outputs.

The Monitors produce a boolean output based on the environment observation through the World Model, the system state and their internal parameters. The internal parameters depend on the type of monitor and can be selected by the user.

At the moment, three types of monitors are defined:

DOM: Distance to Obstacle Monitor. Its output is *true* when there are obstacles inside a user-defined area surrounding the robot. The use of this monitor allows the Finite State Machine to, for instance, disable all behaviors except the Avoid Obstacles one when there are obstacles too close to the robot.

EZM: Explored Zone Monitor. Its output is *true* when the robot has been moving in the same area for a time. Both area dimensions and time are defined by the user. The use of this monitor allows the Finite State Machine, among others, to increment the Avoid the Past behavior weight when the vehicle has been moving into a small region for a large amount of time.

GDM: Goal Distance Monitor. Its output is *true* when the robot is approaching the *Goal Point*, which is the high-level path point communicated by the Planning Layer. This monitor is used in combination with DOM to deal with situations where the goal point is close to an obstacle. The GDM behavior could be in charge of decreasing the Avoid Obstacles behavior weight when approaching a goal point and the DOM of increasing it again if an obstacle is too close.

The structure of ATHRAIA allows both the addition of more monitor types and the use of multiple monitors of the same type with different internal parameters. The Finite State Machine is also user-definable.

The Planning Layer: The Planning Layer is responsible for the path generation between the robot position and the Active Mission Point while monitoring if the current path has became invalid. The generated path is composed by a sequence of spatial points. One and only one of the path points is communicated to the rest of ATHRAIA layers. This point is called the *Active Path Point*. When the robot approaches the Active Path Point, it is changed to be the next point in the path sequence.

The Behavior Layer and the Coordination Layer by themselves are able to guide the robot in a safe way by avoiding obstacles and driving the robot through mission points using the processed sensor information generated by the World Modeller. The Planning Layer has a global view of the known environment and generates plans which are communicated to the other layers, adding intelligence to ATHRAIA.

A detailed description of the ATHRAIA navigation processes can be found in [3].

4   The World Modeller

The World Modeller builds both metric and topological maps of the environment and uses them to correct the estimated vehicle position. All the tasks performed by the World Modeller are executed while the robot navigates and are fully integrated into the control architecture.

The World Modeller is composed by the *Metric Map Generator*, the *Topological Map Generator*, the *Robot Position Correction System* and the *World Model*.

The World Model stores mapping information and robot pose estimation. In the present implementation the World Model is obtained from acoustical range finders, odometry and magneto-inductive compass data. The dead reckoning sensors are used to estimate the vehicle pose. The mapping information is generated incrementally during navigation by the Metric

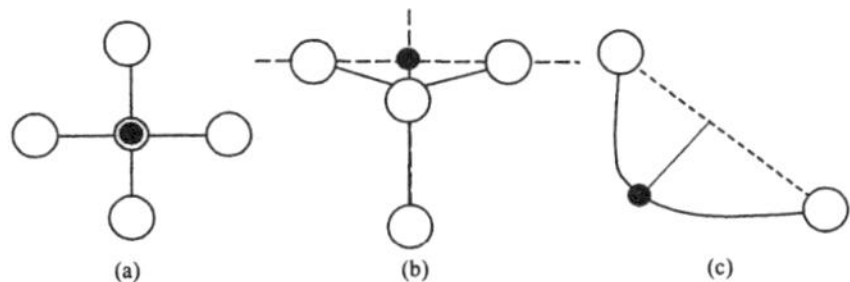

Figure 2: Graphs and Base Points for: a) X-junctions, b) T-junctions and c) L-corners.

Map Generator and the Topological Map Generator.

The Metric Map Generator processes the acoustical range finder information and builds a local vehicle-centered occupancy grid. Data about observed, unobserved and recently visited regions is also stored.

The Topological Map Generator and the Robot Position Correction System are explained below.

Readers are directed to [4] to find a complete description of the world modelling tasks.

4.1　Topological Map Generator

The Topological Map Generator takes information from the occupancy grid in order to build the topological map of the environment.

It is composed by two modules: the *landmark detector* and the *map builder*.

For the context of this paper, we will distinguish between *landmarks* and *nodes*. Although both are defined by the same features, a landmark is a temporary item, being observed by the robot at a certain time, and a node is a permanent item. When the system decides that a landmark can be introduced in the World Model, it becomes a node in the topological map.

4.1.1　Landmark detection

The Landmark Detector is able to identify landmarks using the structure of the area where the robot is, as measured by the echo-sounder array. At the moment, the landmarks used are T-junctions, X-junctions, L-corners and corridors but the system allows the addition of different types such as H-junctions or U-turns in an easy way.

The information associated to a landmark consists of its estimated position, the error in this estimation and its class (X-junction, T-junction, L-turn or corridor). A robot centered area of the occupancy grid, called *Interest Zone* is analyzed by means of computer vision techniques. These techniques generate a graph description of the Interest Zone, making ATHRAIA able to robustly identify and classify the landmarks while navigating with incomplete environment information.

A point is selected by the landmark detector in order to fix the landmark position. This point is called the *Base Point* and its global position has to be stable in further landmark detections. Fig. 2 shows the graphs and the selected Base Points for the X-junctions, T-junctions and L-corners landmarks.

The extraction of additional information from the graph description of the landmark, and the use of other types of landmarks is now under study.

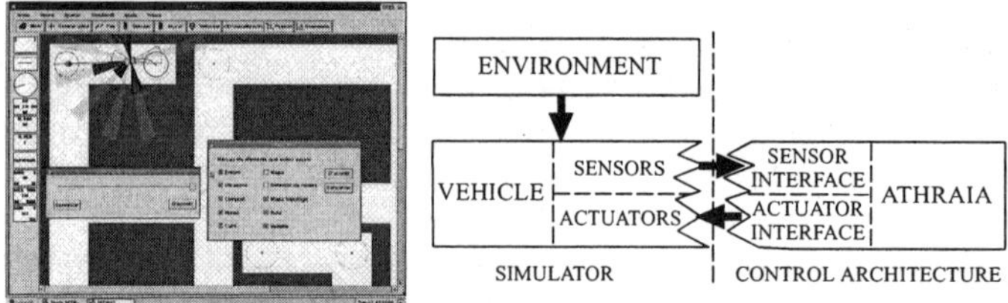

Figure 3: SEFIRoT, the simulation environment.

4.1.2   Topological map building

Topological map building operates by performing exploration of the environment guided by the control architecture criteria and recording place descriptions and place connections.

The Landmark Detector communicates to the Topological Map Builder the landmark currently observed. The Topological Map Builder distinguishes between two kinds of landmarks: *Node Landmarks* (T-junctions, X-junctions and L-corners) and *Transition Landmarks* (corridors).

The Topological Map Builder decides if the landmark has to be introduced in the map and become a node. The process consists on checking for a Transition Landmark after a Node Landmark detection. Only after a Transition Landmark is detected a new Node Landmark can be found. When a Node Landmark is found, it can be introduced in the map as a node or be used for position correction purposes, as described next. Connections in the topological map are inserted between couples of consecutively detected nodes.

4.2   Robot Position Correction

The Robot Position Correction System corrects the error in the vehicle estimated position by associating the currently observed landmark with the nodes present in the topological map. The error correction is made at the same time as the vehicle navigates.

As soon as a Node Landmark is detected, the system starts the data association process in order to determine if can be a new node or not. If not, a position correction is done.

Estimations of the maximum position error of the vehicle and the topological nodes are calculated. When a position correction has to be done, the system corrects the topological node or the vehicle position according to these estimations, as described in [4].

5   Experimental platform

This section describes SEFIRoT, the simulation environment, and CABRIT, the real robot, both used to test ATHRAIA.

5.1   The simulation environment: SEFIRoT

SEFIRoT (*Simulation Environment For Intelligent Robot Testing*) is a graphical interactive simulation environment for mobile robot and control architecture testing (fig. 3). Through this tool the user is able to change the simulation parameters easily, even during the simulation,

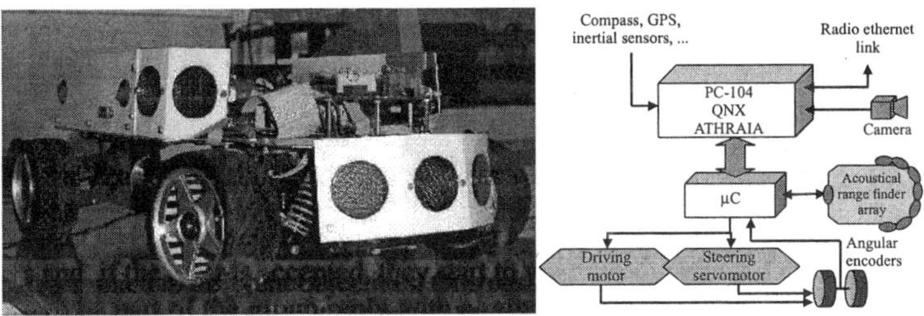

Figure 4: The CABRIT robot.

and to access the simulation results through graphical items at any moment. The information to be displayed can be selected through the GUI, being the user able to concentrate on specific aspects of the simulation.

The simulation can run either in automatic or step-by-step modes, being the simulation speed configurable. Both robot position and orientation can be changed by the user in order to simulate robot pose errors.

SEFIRoT has been developed on the QNX Real Time Operating System using the Photon GUI. It allows both experimentation with real time artificial intelligence concepts present in ATHRAIA and calibration of the system parameters to be used in real experiments with CABRIT.

SEFIRoT is composed of a mobile robot simulator and an implementation of the ATHRAIA control architecture (fig. 3). It has been implemented using object oriented techniques, that makes the adaptation of the ATHRAIA code easy to run on the real robot CABRIT.

By using script files the user can configure the following three groups of parameters:

Vehicle parameters: The kinematics of the vehicle can be specified by defining its speed, acceleration and steering capabilities. The sensors (at the moment, acoustical range finders, odometry and compass) and the vehicle shape, which is important for collision detection purposes, can also be accurately defined, including noise models.

Environment parameters: These parameters allow the system to have an accurate model of the environment. At the moment the free and the occupied space of the world can be easily defined in a global coordinate system. The scale of this system is configurable, so different environments can be modelled. The inclusion of different materials for obstacles and floor conditions (so different sensor and actuator responses can be tested) is now under study.

Control architecture parameters: All the ATHRAIA parameters (behavior weights, finite state machine, path finding criteria, mission, ...) can be configured and tested under SEFIRoT.

The following four groups of outputs are available at any moment during a simulation:

World Model: It includes the metric and the topological maps, and the position corrections. Both real and estimated vehicle position errors are also available.

Simulated sensors: The output of the simulated sensors is available, and can be analyzed in order to improve the sensor models.

ATHRAIA outputs: The behavior, coordination and planning layer outputs (such as behaviors output vectors, coordinator state and generated paths) are also available to the user.

Simulation results: Some other outputs, such as the real path followed by the vehicle or the real time spent for the mission execution, are also provided by SEFIRoT.

The experiments conducted using SEFIRoT are described in section 6.

5.2   The robot: CABRIT

CABRIT (*Car Based Robot for Intelligent Transport*) is a car-like mobile robot (fig. 4), developed in the *Systems, Robotics and Vision group* of the University of the Balearic Islands. It is equipped with eight acoustical range finders, a magneto-inductive compass, two optical encoders placed at the steering wheels, a microcontroller based board and a Pentium based PC-104 board. For the time being, only the above mentioned sensors are used. It is under development the improvement of the system capabilities with a communication link and more sensors like GPS, cameras or inertial sensors (fig. 4).

The PC-104 board runs the the ATHRAIA code under QNX.

Except for the compass, the hardware interface between the sensor and actuator groups and the PC-104 board is accomplished by the microcontroller based board. This board is able to manage the acoustical range finders, the optical encoders and the electric motors of the vehicle according to the orders received from the PC-104 through the parallel port.

The compass used is a serial device that communicates directly to the PC-104 using an RS-232 link.

The modularity of the control architecture and the fact that both the simulator and the robot run the same operating system allow the use of SEFIRoT code slightly adapted for CABRIT.

The most important changes that have been done involve the sensor and the actuator interfaces. They have been successfully tested, and now the rest of the control architecture is being evaluated on the CABRIT robot.

In the CABRIT implementation the interfaces have to send and receive information through the PC-104 communication ports.

6   Experimental results

Experimental results obtained by executing missions on SEFIRoT are presented in this section. The execution of the sensor and actuator interfaces programmed on the real robot CABRIT is also discussed.

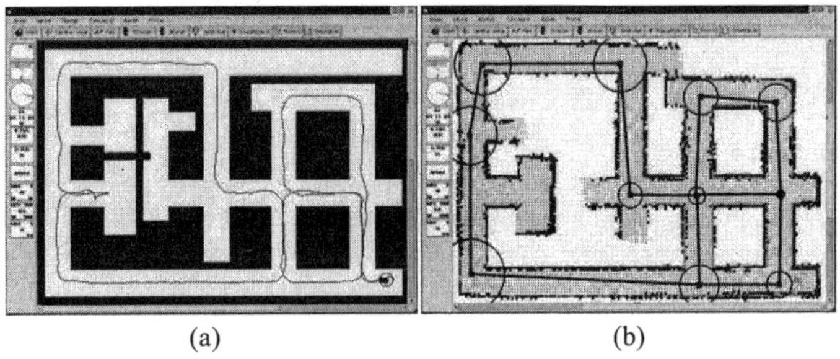

(a)   (b)

Figure 5: a) A simulated environment and the trajectory followed by the robot. b) The occupancy grid and topological map generated by ATHRAIA.

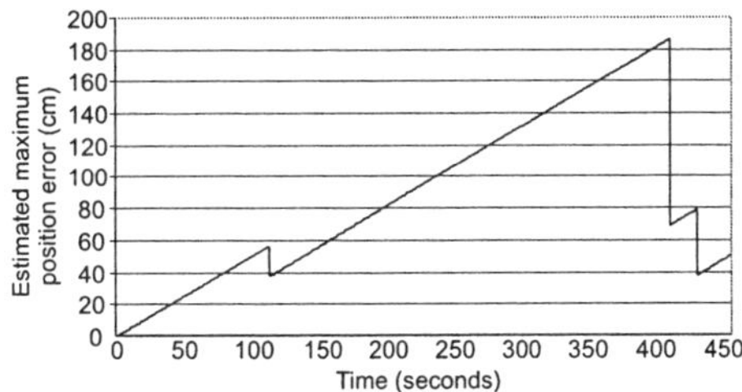

Figure 6: Maximum estimated position error during mission execution.

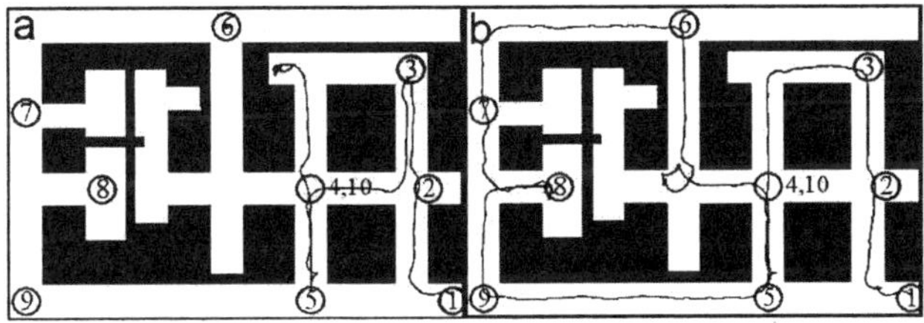

Figure 7: Mission solving: the robot has to reach the mission points in the order they are numbered. (a) Only reactive modules (b) Reactive and deliberative modules

Fig. 5-a shows one of the simulated environments used in the presented experiments. Main corridors in this environment are 2 meters wide. The simulated robot successfully reached the set of areas specified in the mission. It has followed the path shown as the thin black line in fig. 5-a moving autonomously with a maximum speed of 0.4 m/s. Although all the described landmarks have been used to build the topological map, only X-junctions have been used for error correction because of the strength of their Base Point.

The robot built the occupancy grid and the topological map shown in fig. 5-b with no *a priori* knowledge about the environment or its location in it. Circles surrounding the topological nodes represent their position error estimation, and the dotted regions represent the observed cells of the occupancy grid.

Fig. 6 shows the estimated maximum position error of the robot during the simulation. In this experiment, the error corrections allow to reduce this error to less than 40 cm when a landmark is redetected. Between 114 seconds and 413 seconds the robot is traveling by the region on the left of the environment where no redetection could be done. Thus, the maximum error increases linearly.

Experiments conducted in other simulated environments demonstrate the robustness of the system. The results obtained show that in the first exploration of these environments near the 90% of the existing landmarks are detected. This rate increases to the 100% if two explorations are conducted.

Some other experiments have been done in order to demonstrate the ability of ATHRAIA to solve complex missions. These experiments show that, while the system is able to safely navigate with only the reactive modules (fig. 7-a), the deliberative modules add the intelligence necessary to successfully navigate in complex environments (fig. 7-b).

Finally, experiments conducted on CABRIT demonstrate that the sensor and actuator interfaces, which replace the SEFIRoT ones, work properly in the real robot implementation.

Real data from sensors is successfully obtained and now the full ATHRAIA code running on the real robot CABRIT is being tested.

7 Conclusions

In this paper a flexible and robust control architecture able to guide a robot intelligently through complex environments while mapping them and correcting the vehicle position has been presented. Our work is focused both in a control architecture able to provide the robot with an intelligent behavior and a landmark based navigation system able to bound the drift error produced by the dead reckoning techniques and to build complex representations of the environment.

The system has been tested on two experimental platforms: a versatile simulation environment under QNX and a real robot. The simulation environment has been used in order to test ATHRAIA real time artificial intelligence concepts and to calibrate the system parameters to be used in the robot.

The experimental results demonstrate the ability of ATHRAIA to successfully generate topological and metric maps. Reliable and intelligent guidance and relocation performance have also been tested and shown.

References

[1] R. C. Arkin. *Behavior-Based Robotics*. The MIT Press, 1998.

[2] R. P. Bonasso, D. Kortenkamp, and R. Murphy. *Artificial intelligence and mobile robots: case studies of successful robot systems*. The MIT Press, 1998.

[3] A. Burguera, Y. González, and G. Oliver. ATHRAIA: A hybrid control architecture for a world modeller robot. *Europeran Conference on Mobile Robots, Radziejowice (Poland)*, 2003.

[4] A. Burguera, Y. González, and G. Oliver. A robust system for localization and mapping while navigating. *Eleventh International Conference in Advanced Robotics, Coimbra (Portugal)*, 2003.

[5] H. Choset and K. Nagatani. Topological simultaneous localization and mapping (SLAM): Towards exact localization without explicit localization. *IEEE Transactions on Robotics and Automation*, 17:125–137, April 2001.

[6] G. Dissanayake, O. Newman, S. Clark, H. Durrant-Whyte, and M. Csorba. A solution to the simultaneous localization and map building (SLAM) problem. *IEEE Transactions on Robotics and Automation*, 17(3):229–241, June 2001.

[7] A. Elfes. Sonar-based real-world mapping and navigation. *IEEE Journal of Robotics and Automation*, 3(3):249–265, 1987.

[8] B.J. Kuipers. The spatial semantic hierarchy. *Artificial Intelligence*, 119:191–233, 2000.

[9] U. Nehmzow. Map building through self-organization for robot navigation. *Lecture Notes in Artificial Intelligence 1812*, pages 1–22, 2000.

[10] A.C. Schultz and W. Adams. Continuous localization using evidence grids. *IEEE International Conference on Robotics and Automation*, pages 2833–2839, 1998.

[11] R. Smith, P. Cheeseman, and M. Self. A stochastic map for uncertain spatial relationships. *4th International Symposium on Robotic Research, MIT Press*, 1987.

[12] J. Tardós, J. Neira, P. M. Newman, and J. J. Leonard. Robust mapping and localization in indoor environments using sonar data. *International Journal of Robotics Research*, 21(4):311–330, April 2002.

[13] S. Thrun, D. Fox, W. Burgard, and F. Dellaert. Robust monte carlo localization for mobile robots. *Artificial Intelligence*, 128(1-2):99–141, 2000.

Artificial Intelligence Research and Development
I. Aguiló et al. (Eds.)
IOS Press, 2003

Evolving a Multiagent System for Landmark-based Robot Navigation

Dídac BUSQUETS, Ramon LÓPEZ DE MÀNTARAS, Carles SIERRA
Artificial Intelligence Research Institute (IIIA)
Spanish Council for Scientific Research (CSIC)
Campus UAB, 08193 Bellaterra, Spain

Abstract In this paper, we build upon a multiagent architecture for unknown environments landmark based navigation. In this architecture, each of the agents in the navigation system has a bidding function that is controlled by a set of parameters. We show here the good results obtained by an evolutionary approach that tunes the parameter set values for two navigation tasks.

Keywords: Multiagent systems, Robotics, Evolultive computation

1   Introduction

In landmark-based navigation, the robot must be able to start in an unknown location and navigate to a desired target using visually-acquired landmarks. The specific scenario that we are studying assumes that there is a target landmark that the robot is able to recognize visually. The target is visible from the robot's initial location, but it may subsequently be occluded by intervening objects. The challenge for the robot is to acquire enough information about the environment (locations of landmarks and obstacles) so that it can move along a path from the starting location to the target position. The robot should do this quickly but safely.

Each of the agents in the navigation system has a bidding function that is controlled by a set of parameters. These parameters need to be tuned to achieve the best performance of the Navigation system and of the overall system. Adjusting these parameters manually can be very difficult, particularly because of the tradeoffs confronting the top-level agents. An alternative to manual tuning is to employ an evolutionary approach to tune them. This paper describes this approach.

Section 2 is devoted to relevant related work. The multiagent architecture of the navigation system is described in Section 3. Section 4 describes each one of the agents and their bidding parametric functions. Section 5 describes the evolutionary approach to tune these functions. Finally, the experimental results are discussed in Section 6.

2   Related work

Since Brooks proposed the subsumption architecture [4], many other coordination mechanisms for robotic systems have been proposed (Maes [11], Arkin [2]). Regarding multiagent architectures, Liscano et al [8], Isik [9], and Stentz [16], among others, use hierarchical centralized architectures with arbitration to decide which activity takes control of the robot. Our approach, based on a bidding mechanism, is completely decentralized, which means that the broadcast of information is not hierarchical. This approach is easier to program and is more flexible and extensible than centralized approaches. A similar model was proposed by Rosenblatt [14] in CMU's DAMN project, in which voting was used to coordinate a set of modules to control the robot. Moreover, a running project at CMU also uses a market-oriented approach to model the cooperation of a team of robots [5].

The map building approach we use is based on the work by Prescott [13], who proposed a network model that stores the spatial relationships among landmarks for robot navigation. By matching a perceived landmark with the network, the robot can find its way to a target, provided it is represented in the network. While Prescott's approach is quantitative, ours uses a fuzzy extension of his model to work with fuzzy qualitative information about distances and directions. Levitt and Lawton [10] also proposed a qualitative approach to the navigation problem, but assume unrealistically accurate distance and direction information between the robot and the landmarks. Another qualitative method for robot navigation was proposed by Escrig and Toledo [7], using constraint logic. However, they assume the robot has some a priori knowledge of the spatial relationship of the landmarks, whereas we build these relationships whilst exploring the environment.

There is a vast literature on evolutionary approaches to parameter optimization. For this reason we will not single out any particular work. Nonetheless, an application of genetic algorithms to a similar problem on path planning was done in [15] where the low-level parameters tuned correspond to an insect-inspired pheromone based model defining a potential field over the space, whereas our approach is based on a group of deliberative agents. Also in [1] an evolutionary approach to the generation of an optimal colony of robots is presented.

3   The multiagent architecture

The architecture is composed of three systems (see Figure 1). Each system competes for two available resources: motion and vision. The Pilot is responsible for all motions of the robot. It selects these motions to carry out commands from the Navigation system and (independently) to avoid obstacles. The Vision system is responsible for identifying and tracking landmarks (including the goal). Finally, the Navigation system is responsible for choosing higher-level robot motions to move the robot to a specified goal. This requires requesting the Vision system to identify and track landmarks, to build a map of the environment, and requesting the Pilot to move the robot toward the goal position or toward some intermediate target position.

From this brief description, two observations can be made. First, these three systems must cooperate to achieve the overall task of reaching the goal landmark position. For instance, the Pilot needs the Vision system to identify obstacles, and it needs the Navigation system to select

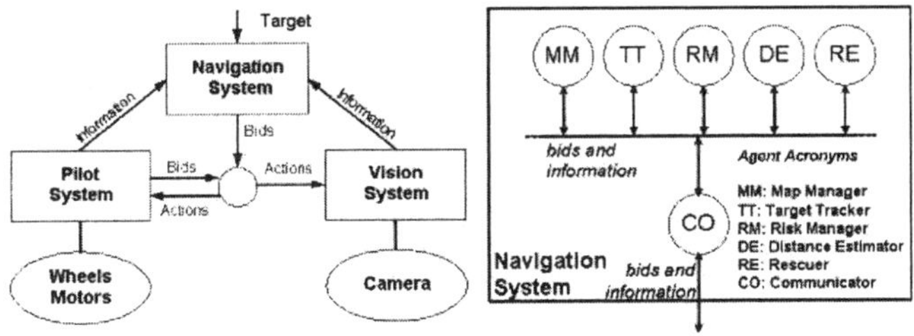

Figure 1: *Left:* Robot architecture. *Right:* Multiagent navigation system

a path to the goal. Second, the systems are also competing —there are some tradeoffs between them. For example, both the Pilot and the Navigation system compete for the Vision system. The Pilot needs vision for obstacle avoidance, while the Navigation system needs vision for landmark detection and tracking.

To manage this cooperation and competition, we use a bidding mechanism. Each system generates bids for the services offered by the Pilot and Vision systems. The service actually executed by each system depends on the winning bid at each point in time.

The Navigation system itself is also implemented as a MAS (see Figure 1). This system is composed of six agents with the following responsibilities: keep the target located with maximum precision and reach it (*Target Tracker*), keep the risk of losing the target low (*Risk Manager*), recover from blocked situations (*Rescuer*), keep the error in the distance to landmarks low (*Distance Estimator*), and keep the information on the map consistent and up-to-date (*Map Manager*). There is an additional agent, *Communicator*, which manages the communication between the Navigation system with the other systems. As with the overall system, the Navigation system employs a bidding mechanism to coordinate these agents. Each agent bids for the action it wants the robot to perform. These bids are sent to the *Communicator* agent, which determines the winning action. The selected action is then sent as the Navigation system's bid for the services of the Vision and Pilot systems. Each action can involve a combination of requests to the Vision and the Pilot systems. The resulting bids coming from the agents depend on bidding functions associated to each agent. These functions depend on the values of different sets of parameters. These values affect the overall performance of the navigation system. Since a manual adjustment is extremely difficult we propose to employ a genetic algorithm to find optimal sets of values. Next section describes the bidding functions in detail and the rest of the paper is devoted to describe this evolutionary approach and the results of our experiments.

For map representation and wayfinding, we have extended Prescott's beta-coefficients system [13]. Prescott's model stores the relationships among the landmarks in the environment to build a map. The location of a landmark is encoded based on the relative locations (headings and distances) of three other landmarks. This relationship is unique and invariant to viewpoint. Once this relationship has been stored, the location of each landmark can be computed from the locations of the three landmarks encoding it, no matter where the robot is located as long as the robot can compute the heading and distance to each of the three landmarks.

As the robot explores the environment, it stores the relationships among the landmarks it sees. This creates a network of relationships among the landmarks in the environment. If this network is sufficiently-richly connected, it provides a computational map of the environment. Given the headings and distances to a subset of currently-visible landmarks, the network allows to compute the locations of all landmarks, even if they are currently not visible.

Prescott's model assumes that the robot is able to measure the exact location of the landmarks. But this is not the case in our robot: the vision system gives only imprecise information about the location of the landmarks, and we cannot rely on the odometry of the robot, as it is also imprecise. To deal with this imprecision, our extended model represents all the network coordinates as fuzzy numbers and carries out all map computations using fuzzy arithmetic [3]. The focus of this paper is on the evolutionary approach to tune the agents' bidding behaviour. For this reason, from now on, we will skip the details of the map representation and management.

4   The Agents

The navigation system is decomposed into five different agents that are responsible for different tasks, which when coordinated by the *communicator* provide the desired effect of leading the robot to a desired target. As mentioned before, each agent has certain parameters which affect its bidding behaviour. The agents and their parameters are described next.

4.1   Map Manager (**Parameters** : none)

This agent is responsible for maintaining the information of the explored environment as a map. Since the map manager does not bid, there are no parameters to tune and therefore it is not on the focus of this paper. The details of the map management algorithmics are also not given here due to space limitations.

4.2   Target Tracker (**Parameters**: $\alpha, \beta, \kappa_1, \kappa_2$)

The goal of this agent is to keep the target located at any time. The imprecision U_a associated with the location of the target is computed as a function on the size of the angle arc, ϵ_α calculated from the robot's current position to where the target is thought to be located, and the agent acts to keep the imprecision as low as possible. The bids for moving towards the target start at the value κ_1 and decrease polinomically to 0, depending on the parameter α. The rationale of this is that when the imprecision about the target location is low, this agent is confident about the target position and therefore bids high to move towards the target. As the imprecision increases, this confidence decreases and so does the bid. Bids for looking at the target increase from 0 to a maximum of κ_2 and then decrease again to 0. The rationale behind this is that when the imprecision is low there is no urgency in looking to the target as its location is known with high precision. This urgency starts to increase as the imprecision increases. When the imprecision reaches a level in which the agent has no confidence on the target location it starts decreasing the bid so as to give the opportunity to better informed agents to win the bid. The equations involved are :

$$U_a = (\epsilon_\alpha / 2\pi)^\beta$$
$$bid(move(\epsilon_\alpha)) = \kappa_1 (1 - U_a^{1/\alpha})$$
$$bid(look(\epsilon_\alpha)) = \kappa_2 \sin(\pi U_a)$$

where β controls the shape of the imprecision function.

4.3 Distance Estimator (*Parameters* : κ, ϕ, δ)

The goal of this agent is to keep the distance error to the target landmark as low as possible. This agent plays a very important role at the beginning of the navigation. When analysing the first viewframe to obtain the initial landmarks, the error in distance is maximal, there is no reference view to obtain an initial estimation of the distance to the target. This agent generates high bids to move orthogonally with respect to the line connecting the robot and the target in order to get another view on it and establish an initial estimation of the distances to the target. Similarly, when a target switch is produced (by the intervention of the Rescuer) this agent may become relevant again if the distance value to the new selected target is very imprecise. Again, the same process will have as consequence a decrease in the new target distance error.

We model distance imprecision as the size of the support of the fuzzy number modeling distance. We note ϵ_t the imprecision error to the current target. Thus, the imprecision in distance to the target can be modeled as $U_d = 1 - 1/e^{\kappa \epsilon_t}$ where κ is a parameter that changes the shape of U_d; high values of κ gives faster increasing shapes. At the beginning of a run the *distance* is the fuzzy number $[0, \infty]$, $\epsilon_t = +\infty$ and hence $U_d = 1$.

This agent is relevant when the imprecision is very high. Its action is to bid to move the robot in an orthogonal direction using as bid the value of U_d, that is:

$$bid \left(move \left(\epsilon_\alpha + \frac{\pi}{2} \right) \right) = U_d$$

This agent is also responsible for deciding (up to a certainty degree ϕ) whether the robot is *at target*. It considers that the robot has reached the target if the upper bound of the α-cut of level ϕ of the fuzzy number modeling the distance to the target is less than δ times the body size of the robot.

4.4 Risk Manager (*Parameters* : $\gamma_A, \gamma_B, \gamma_r$)

The goal of this agent is to keep the risk of losing the target as low as possible. To do so, it tries to keep a reasonable amount of landmarks, as non collinear as possible, in the surroundings of the robot. The less landmarks around, the more risky is the current situation and the higher the probability of losing the target. Also, the more collinear the landmarks the higher the error in the location of the target and thus the higher the imprecision on its location.

We model the risk as a function that combines: 1) the number of landmarks ahead (elements in set A), 2) the number of landmarks around (elements in set B), and 3) their "quality"(q_A and q_B). These qualities are computed by the *Map Manager*. A minimum risk of 0 is assessed when there are at least four visible landmarks in the direction of the movement and minimally collinear. A maximum risk of 1 is assessed when there are no landmarks ahead nor around:

$$R = 1 - \min\left(1, q_A\left(\frac{|A|}{4}\right)^{\gamma_A} + q_B\left(\frac{|B|}{4}\right)^{\gamma_B}\right)$$

The values γ_A and γ_B determine the relative importance of the position of landmarks (ahead or around).

Given that the robot cannot decrease the collinearity of the landmarks, the only way to decrease the risk level is by increasing the number of landmarks. We privilege the fact of having landmarks ahead by bidding

$$bid\left(look\left(random\left(\left[-\frac{\pi}{4},+\frac{\pi}{4}\right]\right)\right)\right) = \gamma_r \cdot R$$

for the action of looking at a random direction in front of the robot and tyring to identify the landmarks in that area, and

$$bid\left(look\left(random\left(\left[+\frac{\pi}{4},+\frac{7\pi}{4}\right]\right)\right)\right) = \gamma_r \cdot R^2$$

(which is obviously smaller than $\gamma_r \cdot R$) for the action of looking at a random direction around the robot and trying to identify landmarks, where γ_r is a parameter to control the maximum value of the bidding function.

4.5 Rescuer (**Parameters** : $\overline{I}_a, \overline{R}$)

The goal of the Rescuer agent is to rescue the robot from problematic situations. These situations may happen due to three reasons. First, the pilot can lead the robot to a position with an obstacle ahead. Second, the imprecision of the location of the target (see Section 4.2) is over the threshold $\overline{I}_a$. Finally, the robot can be at a very risky place, that is a place where the risk to get lost (see Section 4.4) is over a threshold $\overline{R}$. If any of these situations happen, the rescuer agent asks the Map Manager for a diverting target and communicates it to the other agents. The algorithm uses a stack where the different diverting targets are stacked, to avoid repeating them.

5 Evolving the Multiagent system

As we have already mentioned, trying to manually find the best values for the parameters of the bidding functions is an extremelly difficult task. In this section we follow an evolutionary approach to do this optimization.

5.1 Representation

We seek to optimize the navigation system with respect to its 10 parameters: Target tracker (α, β, κ_1, κ_2), Distance Estimator (κ), Risk manager (γ_A, γ_B, γ_r), and Rescuer ($\overline{U}_a$, $\overline{R}$). ϕ and δ are fixed to 0.7 and 2 respectively since they do not affect the efficiency of the system. We use a real valued chromosome, each chromosome being a vector in 10 dimensions. The initial population is generated randomly.

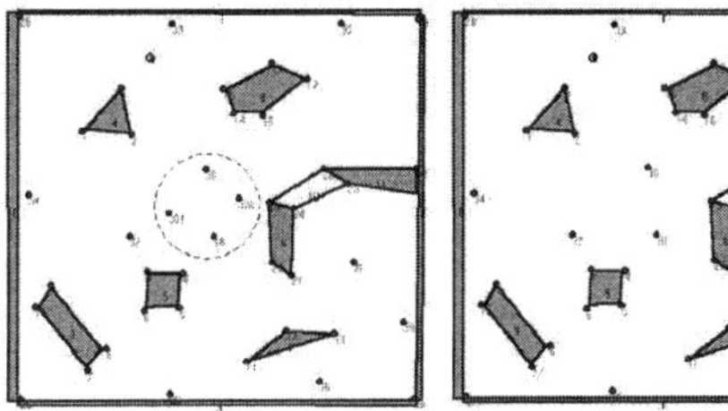

Figure 2: Cluster C1 (left) and C2 (right). White polygons are non occluding obstacles.

5.2 Navigation Tasks

For a given environment we consider two different navigation tasks. Each one of them with a different level of complexity. The best parameter set may change depending on the complexity of the task. We conjecture that the parameters found depend mainly on the complexity of the navigation task and not so much on the structure of the overall environment. This complexity is dependent, though not equal, to the cartographic complexity of the world in which the agent moves, and is based on the following factors: (1) number of visible landmarks at any time, (2) density of obstacles in the region of navigation, and (3) visibility of the target at any time.

Using this notion of navigational complexity, the total space of all navigation tasks can be split into two representative classes: going towards the target free of obstacles, and reaching targets located behind obstacles. In our experiments we use clusters C_1 and C_2 (encircled targets in Figure 2) as representatives of the two task complexity classes. The best parameter set is determined for both these classes. The aim of the experiments is to endow the navigation system of the robot with the capability to switch between these two parameter sets according to the actual task complexity it is facing.

5.3 Evaluation

Each individual in the population specifies a particular parameter set for the system, and is evaluated by running a simulation with the specified parameters in a given environment. Consider that the agent navigates from an initial position p_0 to the target cluster C containing the n target positions $(t_1, t_2, ..., t_n)$ and that it takes d_i steps to reach the target t_i from p_0 with a success value s_i. A threshold is defined for the number of steps that are taken to reach the target, above which the agent is said to have failed in its attempt to navigate to the target i.e. its success value is 0, otherwise it is 1.

This formalization gives the clues to define the fitness function, f, that permits the selection of the best parameter sets. It is clear that the average cost, $\bar{c}$, of reaching a target from the initial position p_0 is defined as the summation of the steps required to reach each target divided by the number of targets. Similarly, we can naturally define the average success, $\bar{s}$. The best behaviour for a navigation system is the one that has a high success rate with a low average cost and with a low standard deviation σ_c for this average cost:

$$\overset{\longleftarrow \text{TT} \longrightarrow}{} \quad \overset{\text{DE}}{} \quad \overset{\longleftarrow \text{RM} \longrightarrow}{} \quad \overset{\longleftarrow \text{RE} \longrightarrow}{}$$

$$\boxed{\alpha} \;\; \boxed{\beta} \;\; \boxed{\kappa_1} \;\; \boxed{\kappa_2} \;\; \boxed{\kappa} \;\; \boxed{\gamma_A} \;\; \boxed{\gamma_B} \;\; \boxed{\gamma_r} \;\; \boxed{\bar{I}_a} \;\; \boxed{\bar{R}}$$

Figure 3: Chromosome with the set of parameters

$$\bar{c} = \frac{\sum_{i=1}^{n} d_i}{n} \qquad \bar{s} = \frac{\sum_{i=1}^{n} s_i}{n} \qquad f = \frac{\bar{s}}{\bar{c} + \sigma_c}$$

5.4   Evolution

We follow an elitist approach. That is, from a population of individuals, the fittest individual is passed to the next generation. The remaining individuals form the pool from which the new generation offsprings are created. We randmonly select two individuals from the mating pool whose fitness is over a randomly determined value. Then we apply crossover and mutation on them to generate new individuals.

5.5   Crossover

A simple two point crossover is used with the two parents exchanging their genetic material between two randomly generated breakpoints in the gene string. Chromosomes are broken only at agent boundaries (see Figure 3). The idea is that one of the parents may have good genes for a particular agent while the other parent may have good genes for another agent. This way the crossover could result in an offspring having a higher fitness value than both its parents.

5.6   Mutation

The mutation operator for the genetic algorithm has been adopted from the Breeder Genetic Algorithm [12]. Given any set of parameters as a chromosome, we can view it as a point x within a 10 dimensional space. Using our mutation operator, we seek to search for optimality within a "small" hypercube centered at x. How small this hypercube is, depends on the ranges in each parametric dimension within which we allow the chromosome to mutate. The parametric dimensions are not homogeneous, hence mutation ranges differ for each dimension, being directly proportional to the variance allowed in that parameter. Another feature of this mutation operator is that while it searches within the hypercube centered at x, it tests more often in the very close neighbourhood of x, the idea being that, while we want to conduct a global search for optimum using our recombination, mutation is used for a more restricted local search. Having understood the broad features which the mutation operator should demonstrate, we formally define the mutation as follows:

Given a chromosome x, each parameter x_i is mutated with probability 0.1. The number of parameters being 10 implies that at least one parameter will be probably mutated. Further, given the mutation range for the parameter x_i as $range_i$, the parameter x_i is mutated to the value x_i^* given by $x_i^* = x_i \pm range_i \cdot \rho$. As previously discussed, ρ should be such that it lies between 0

Cluster	α	β	κ_1	κ_2	κ	γ_A	γ_B	γ_R	$\overline{U_a}$	$\overline{R}$
Cluster1	1.731	2.03	0.314	0.493	0.355	0.240	0.521	0.054	0.386	0.215
Cluster2	1.231	2.12	1.0	0.564	0.178	1.377	4.39	0.707	0.871	0.906

Table 1: Optimal parameter values for each of the clusters for one execution of the GA over 100 generations

and 1 (to generate the hypercube centered at x) and also it should probabilistically take on small values so as to test more often in the close neighbourhood of x. This is realized by computing ρ from the distribution $\rho = \sum \alpha_j 2^{-j}$, where each α_j is probabilistically either 0 or 1.

5.7 Diversity

The convergence of the genetic algorithm is estimated through its population diversity. Initially, the population has a high diversity since all the individuals are randomly selected. As the algorithm converges, the individuals in the population converge towards the best solution, thus decreasing the diversity. In our case, the individuals are points in a heterogeneous dimension space, with α, β, γ_A and $\gamma_B \in \Re^+$ while the other parameters ranging between 0 and 1. Hence we use the Mahalanobis distance measure to determine the diversity of a population [6].

The Mahalanobis distance takes into account the heterogeneity in dimensions and correspondingly scales each dimension while estimating the distance between two points. Given a set of data points $\{z_i\}$ with each data point z_i being an n-tuple $\langle z_{ij} | 1 \leq j \leq n \rangle$, the Mahalanobis distance d_m between two points z_k and z_l is given as $d_m(z_k, z_l) = (z_k - z_l)^T \Sigma^{-1} (z_k - z_l)$. Here Σ is the $n \times n$ variance-covariance matrix for the given data points. To compare the diversity of populations across generations, the covariance matrix is computed taking into account all the chromosomes over all generations. The diversity of a population is then calculated as the average Mahalanobis distance of each chromosome from the mean chromosome.

6 Results

The genetic algorithm was run on the two task complexity classes represented by the target clusters C_1 and C_2 in our simulator. The population size was of 20 individuals, and we ran the genetic algorithm for 100 generations. The initial position was the same for both with the crossover and the mutation rates being 0.8 and 0.1 respectively. In the algorithm, four of the parameters — α, β, γ_A and γ_B lie on the positive real axis and hence we have to choose an upper limit on the real line. This upper limit is important since a low upper limit value implies that we implicitly restrict our real valued parameters to that limit, while a high upper limit value may increase the number of generations for which the genetic algorithm may have to be run since the initial random generation will be very disperse. α and β are exponents of numbers less than 1 and hence their large values will not be useful. Keeping these factors in consideration, the upper limit value has been fixed to 5 in our simulations.

The genetic algorithm converges to an optimal solution for each cluster as can be seen in Figures 4-6 (these graphics are for Cluster C_1; similar results were obtained for Cluster C_2). The optimal values for some of the parameters differ significantly for the two clusters as shown

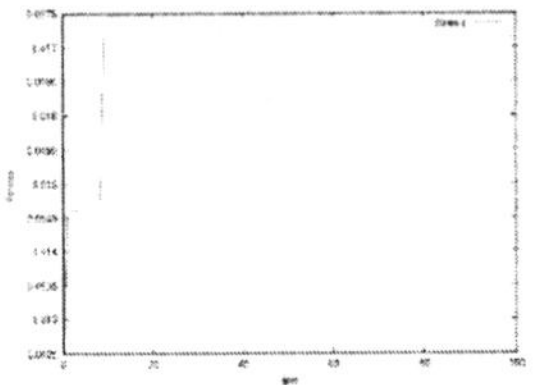

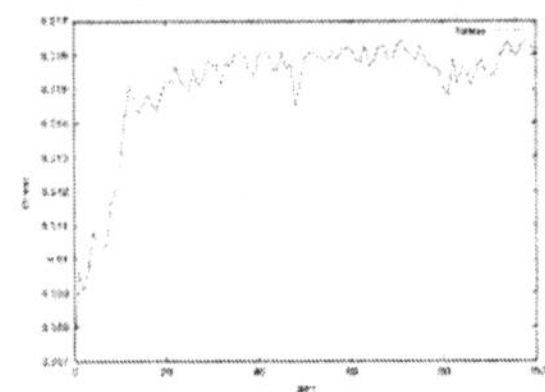

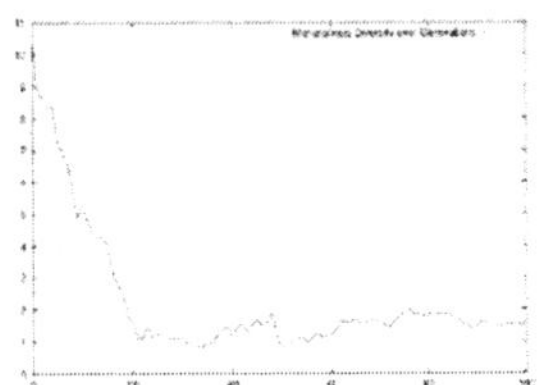

Figure 4: Fitness of the fittest individual along generations (cluster C_1)

Figure 5: Average fitness of the population along generations (cluster C_1)

Figure 6: Mahalanobis diversity (cluster C_1)

	Going to C_1			Going to C_2		
	$\bar{s}$	$\bar{c}$	f	$\bar{s}$	$\bar{c}$	f
C_1 set	1	50.5	0.017	0.5	127.5	0.003
C_2 set	0.5	42.5	0.011	1	122	0.007
HT set	0.5	69	0.005	0	–	0

Table 2: Results obtained by the different parameter sets

in Table 1. The parameters associated to the bidding function of the *Risk Manager* agent differ the most between the two clusters. This is so because the Risk Manager is very sensible to the complexity of the task. The more obstacles, the higher the risk of losing sight of landmarks.

In order to check the results obtained for each of the clusters, we have tested the two parameter sets found by the genetic algorithm on the two different navigation tasks (going to cluster C_1 and going to cluster C_2). We have also tested our original parameter set, which we set by hand, on the same two navigation tasks. The results obtained by each set on each of the tasks are shown in Table 2. For each task, the mean average success value ($\bar{s}$), average cost ($\bar{c}$) and the fitness value (f) is computed. As expected, the parameter set found for cluster C_1 performs perfectly when going to cluster C_1 and it only reaches the targets of cluster C_2 50% of the times. On the other hand, the parameter set found for cluster C_2 reaches the targets of cluster C_2 all the times, while it only reaches the targets of cluster C_1 50% of the times. Finally, the hand-tuned parameter set reaches 50% of the times the targets of cluster C_1, and never reaches the targets of cluster C_2. Therefore, the evolutionary approach has improved the global navigation behaviour.

In Figures 7 and 8 we can see some paths followed by the robot using each of the parameter set on each of the tasks. Succesful paths are only shown for those parameter set with a success value of 1. Otherwise, an example of a failing path (marked with a cross at its end) is shown.

We are currently testing the parameter sets on a real robot, and we will analyse the generality, in terms of different environments and starting point, of the parameters obtained by the GA.

7 Acknowledgements

This work has been partially supported by the Spanish MCYT project ARGOS (DPI2000-1352-C02-02). Dídac Busquets enjoys a CIRIT doctoral scholarship 2000FI-00191.

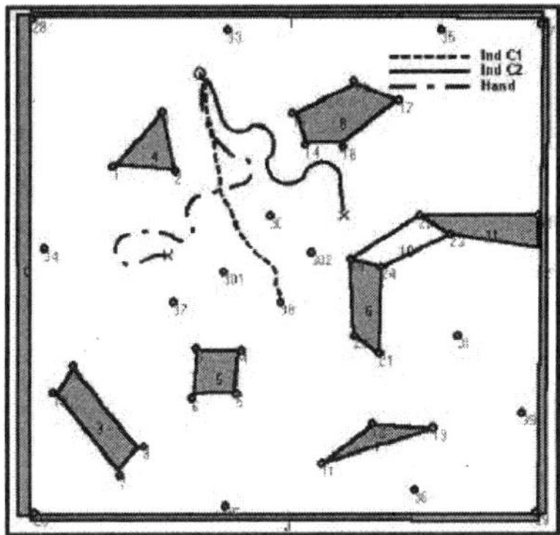

Figure 7: Going to C_1

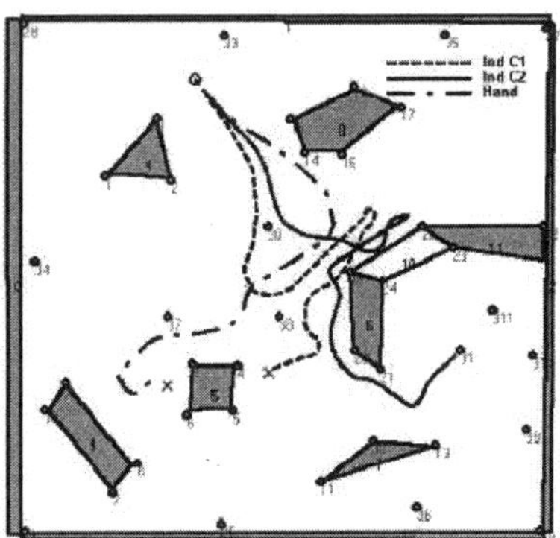

Figure 8: Going to C_2

References

[1] Arvin Agah and George A. Bekey. A genetic algorithm-based controller for decentralized multi-agent robotic systems. In *IEEE International Conference on Evolutionary Computation*. IEEE, 1996.

[2] R.C. Arkin. Motor schema-based mobile robot navigation. *International Journal of Robotics research*, 8(4):92–112, 1989.

[3] G. Bojadziev and M. Bojadziev. *Fuzzy sets, fuzzy logic, applications*, volume 5 of *Advances in Fuzzy Systems*. World Scientific, 1995.

[4] R. Brooks. A robust layered control system for a mobile robot. *IEEE Journal of Robotics and Automation*, RA-2(1):14–23, 1986.

[5] M.B. Dias and A. Stentz. A market approach to multirobot coordination. Technical report, Robotics Institute, CMU, 2001.

[6] R. O. Duda, P. E. Hart, and D. G. Stork. *Pattern Classification*. John Wiley & Sons, Inc., 2001.

[7] M. Teresa Escrig and F. Toledo. Autonomous robot navigation using human spatial concepts. *International Journal of Intelligent Systems*, 15:165–196, 2000.

[8] R. Liscano et al. Using a blackboard to integrate multiple activities and achieve strategic reasoning for mobile-robot navigation. *IEEE Expert*, 10(2):24–36, 1995.

[9] C. Isik and A.M. Meystel. Pilot level of a hierarchical controller for an unmanned mobile robot. *IEEE J. Robotics and Automation*, 4(3):241–255, 1988.

[10] T.S. Levitt and D.T. Lawton. Qualitative navigation for mobile robots. *Artificial Intelligence Journal*, 44:305–360, 1990.

[11] P. Maes. The dynamics of action selection. In *Proc. of IJCAI'89*, pages 991–997, 1989.

[12] H. Muhlenbein and D. Schlierkamp-Voosen. The science of breeding and its application to the breeder genetic algorithm (bga). *Evolutionary Computation*, 1(1):335–360, 1993.

[13] T.J. Prescott. Spatial representation for navigation in animats. *Adaptive Behavior*, 4(2):85–125, 1996.

[14] J. Rosenblatt. Damn: A distributed architecture for mobile navigation. In *Proceedings of the 1995 AAAI Spring Symposium on Lessons Learned from Implemented Software Architectures for Physical Agents*. AAAI Press, March 1995.

[15] John Sauter, Robert Matthews, H. van Dyke Parunak, and Sven Brueckner. Evolving adaptive pheromone path planning mechanisms. In *Proc. of AAMAS'02*, pages 434–440, Bologna, July 2002. ACM Press.

[16] A. Stentz. The codger system for mobile robot navigation. In C.E. Thorpe, editor, *Vision and Navigation, the Carnegie Mellon Navlab*, pages 187–201, Boston, 1990. Kluwer Academic Pub.

Artificial Intelligence Research and Development
I. Aguiló et al. (Eds.)
IOS Press, 2003

Qualitative Spatial Reasoning for Robot Path Planning

M. Teresa ESCRIG MONFERRER[†]**, Pablo FELIP MONFERRER**[‡]

Universitat Jaume I

[†]*Engineering and Computer Science*
Department
e-mail: escrigm@icc.uji.es

[‡]*Programming Languages & Computer*
Systems Department
e-mail: felipp@lsi.uji.es

Campus Riu Sec E-12071 Castellón (Spain)
phone: +34 964 728303- fax: +34 964 728486

Abstract. Uncertain information provided by robot sensors has been successfully managed with quantitative probabilistic approaches, although at a high computational cost, since neither discerning of irrelevant data nor any kind of reasoning is performed.

Recent techniques of robot navigation integrate and hybrid information management (quantitative and qualitative). Despite preliminary results, they only use qualitative spatial representation and no qualitative reasoning at all.

This document focuses on discussing the applicability of Qualitative Spatial Reasoning in the field of autonomous robotics and introduces a novel strategy and an algorithm to perform such reasoning for robot path planning.

Keywords: Qualitative Reasoning, Spatial Reasoning, Robot Path Planning.

Introduction

Traditional quantitative methods for robot navigation demand precise and reliable metrics to account for the robot path. For instance, techniques such as the configuration space [1], the generalized cones [2], the segmented model [3], the grid-based model [4] or the convex cell model [5] perform well in low uncertainty, thoroughly known environments, where the whole workspace can be perceived from any place.

Quantitative probabilistic approaches have been developed in recent years to cope with partial and inaccurate information in real world robot navigation [6], [7] and [8]. Systems founded on these approaches typically demand a huge amount of computational resources. We could say that they are based on "force" algorithms, since they do not usually discard information that may not be relevant for a given situation to reduce computational load. Although impressive results have been attained, a dead end seems to be not much further away along this line of research.

The use of common sense, human-like reasoning on selected data extracted from all the imprecise and incomplete information that the robot can take in from the environment is another path where researchers are blazing new trails in robot navigation.

In fact, many qualitative models for dealing, in a clever way, with uncertain and imprecise spatial knowledge have been developed so far [9], [10], [11], [12], [13], [14],

[15], [16], [17], [18], [19], [20]. Most of these qualitative robot navigation models have only been applied to simulated robots, which move along virtual environments, almost always assuming a completely unrealistic high resolution and error-free sensorial input.

Recent works in real robot navigation in unknown environments merge qualitative and quantitative techniques to deal with incomplete and imprecise knowledge [21], [22], [23], [24], [25]. They demonstrate preliminary results that are not up to the level of performance of their probabilistic, quantitative counterparts. Besides that, they use only qualitative or hybrid spatial representation (qualitative spatial information augmented with metric data) with little or no trace of spatial reasoning.

At the same time, several qualitative models have been developed to represent and reason with spatial and temporal concepts such as orientation in 2-D [26], [27], [28], [29], [30], [31], orientation in 3-D [32], named distances [33], [34], [35], [36], compared distances [37], cardinal directions [38], velocity [39], topology [40] and topology extended with time [41]. The concept of qualitative motion has been modelled in [17], [42] and [15] as a sequence of changes in position, taking into account conceptual neighbourhood.

Researchers supporting these models hold a strong intuition that the use of qualitative reasoning techniques will enhance the "abilities" of robot path planning and navigation algorithms. They will provide the robot with superior reasoning, and therefore with more intelligent behaviour. However, the step to use this kind of qualitative spatial thinking has not been taken yet, maybe because an important question has not been answered, that is: When is it necessary to use qualitative reasoning process in robot path planning and navigation? The present paper tries to give an answer to this issue.

1. Qualitative Representation versus Qualitative Reasoning

The concept of reasoning seems obvious when considered from the point of view of a human being. Reasoning is an intellectual faculty by which conclusions are drawn from premises.

Qualitative Spatial Reasoning (QSR from now on) is, perhaps, the most common way of modelling commonsense reasoning in the spatial domain. A qualitative representation can be defined as that representation which makes only as many distinctions as necessary to identify objects, events, situations, etc. in a given context. Qualitative models are suitable for further reasoning with partial information in a robust manner, in such cases when complete information is either unavailable or too complex to be efficiently managed.

Nevertheless, a suitable representation is not enough to make robots capable of reasoning, so these two concepts should not be mistaken: when a QSR system analyses interrelated facts that encode spatial information, it infers new ones that were not available in the beginning.

1.1. Qualitative Reasoning: an Intuitive Approach

Let us focus on the following statements that represent spatial knowledge:

a) My house lies south east of the stadium, far away from it and close to a supermarket.
b) There is a cinema between the supermarket and my house.

After composing the information expressed in (a) and (b), (c) and (d), amongst other facts, can immediately be inferred (see figure 1):

a) The supermarket lies south east of the stadium and, possibly far away from it.
b) The cinema is near the supermarket.

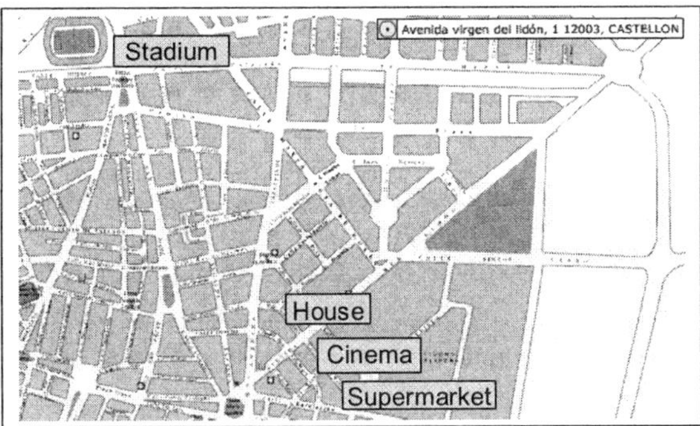

Figure 1. A possible disposition of places after QSR on statements (a) and (b).

These facts have been obtained by qualitatively reasoning about the initial statements. For humans it is just commonsense thinking, for an artificial system the process is accomplished by means of inference techniques. Deduced facts become part of the already known spatial information and thus can be used for further reasoning.

1.2. Formalization of Qualitative Reasoning

QSR involves reasoning with qualitative spatial information. This means that the way spatial data is encoded as well as the mechanisms to make reasoning possible have to be defined in a formal manner.

An algebra is needed to explicitly account for the qualitative representation of each spatial aspect. This algebra comprises (1) the meaning of the relations or constraints amongst objects, (2) the number of spatial objects involved in the relation and (3) the operations involving these relationships which can be defined.

An example of a model of qualitative spatial information representation is Freksa and Zimmerman's fine qualitative orientation model [30], which we will use to represent spatial knowledge later on this article. In this model, the orientation of an object c with respect to (*wrt*) the reference system defined by two points, a and b (*c wrt ab*), is represented in a qualitative manner. Space is therefore divided in fifteen regions (figure 2) by the imaginary line between a and b and the two perpendicular lines at both points. Two qualitative spatial regions, A and B, are conceptual neighbours if, and only if, in a continuous translation from a position of the qualitative region A to a position in qualitative region B, there does not exist a position belonging to another qualitative region C.

Given *c wrt ab*, five more relations can be obtained by permutation of a, b and c, as shown in table 1:

Table 1. Freksa and Zimmerman's qualitative orientation model relations.

c wrt ab	Original relation
c wrt ba	Inverse operation
a wrt bc	Homing
a wrt cb	Homing-inverse
b wrt ac	Shortcut
b wrt ca	Shortcut-inverse

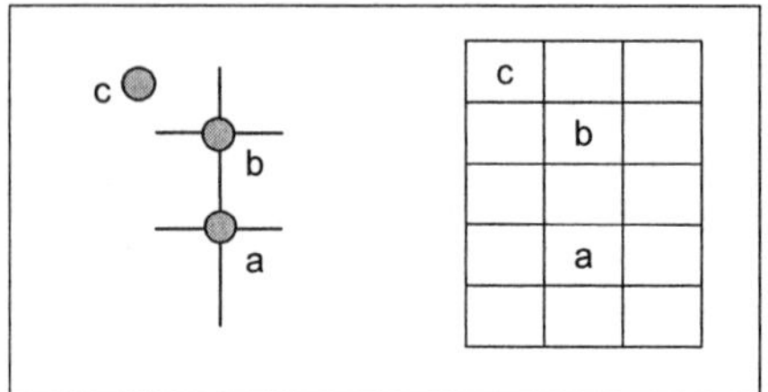

Figure 2. Reference system (left) and iconic representation (right).

Reasoning is defined in a two-step process. First, by means of the Basic Step of Inference Process (BSIP), given two relationships that relate three objects A, B, and C (one object is shared among the two relationships, for instance B), the third relationship, between objects A and C will be found (figure 3).

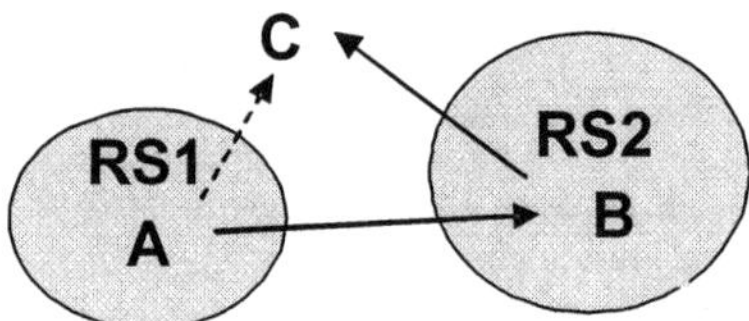

Figure 3. Basic Step of Inference process.

For example, in Freksa and Zimmerman's fine qualitative orientation model, given *c wrt ab* and *d wrt bc*, the BSIP involves obtaining *d wrt ab* (figure 4).

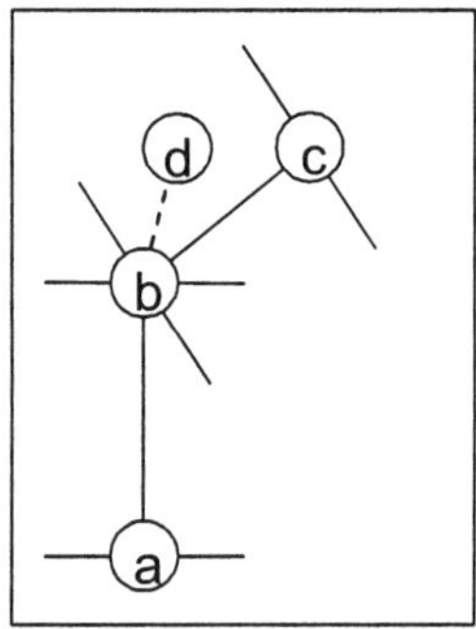

Figure 4. BSIP in Freksa and Zimmerman's fine qualitative orientation model.

The second step is the Full Inference Process (FIP): When several relationships among spatial landmarks are provided, the FIP will repeat the BSIP as many times as possible.

2. Robot Path Planning Using Cognitive Maps

Cognitive maps represent spatial information in the form of some sort of sketch (figure 5) or graph (figure 6) that contains qualitative information and partial or no metric data about the robot world. A typical cognitive map is a graph where each node represents a distinctive place and arcs amongst nodes are indicative of connectivity between places.

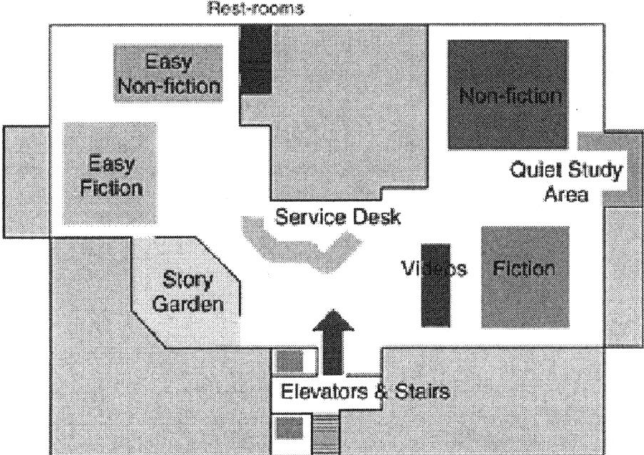

Figure 5. Schematic map of a library. Different places are shown, although sizes and distances may be heavily distorted.

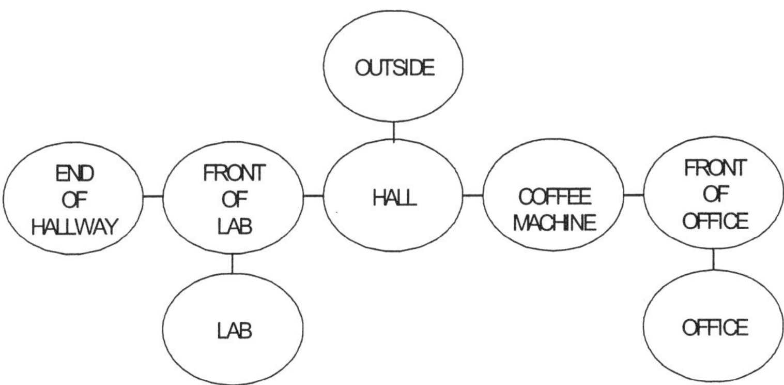

Figure 6. Typical topological map. Nodes depict places and lines show connectivity.

When a cognitive map is fed into a robot, be it manually provided or just acquired by exploration and perception, path planning is just a matter of going from place to place according to the connectivity information stored in the map. Even though qualitative spatial information is used to represent the world (the aforementioned connectivity, coarse distance, qualitative orientation of corridors, etc.), there is no need for spatial reasoning at this stage. All the information for path planning is already stored in the map; the route planner simply uses it to compute a feasible path towards the destination place.

3. Robot Path Planning Using Qualitative Reasoning

Qualitative reasoning seems to be of some help when the robot has to deal not only with accurate information about its surroundings, but also with partial or imprecise data. In these cases, some sort of spatial reasoning process could be performed:

❏ *At high scale*: for instance, when trying to plan the route from the main hall of a building to a certain office (global path-planning).

❏ *At small scale*: when planning and performing local navigation *inside* a certain localization or place to circumvent obstacles or simply wander inside a small scale space such as a room to reach particular positions or traverse doors (local path planning).

Since a global path-planning task with a final goal can be easily split down in several subtasks attained by local navigation feats and the lack of complete information is very likely in real word dynamic scenarios, this paper will focus on this latter type of reasoning.

3.1. An Example of QSR for Path Planning

To illustrate QSR in path planning, let us define a scenario consisting of a room with just one door, an obstacle in the middle of the room and a robot that tries to advance in a collision-prone direction to reach the door on the opposite wall. This robot should go around the obstacle and target the door once the object has been left behind.

When the robot (represented by point r) approaches the object, it extracts reference points a and b from it by means of its perceptual system (figures 7 and 8).

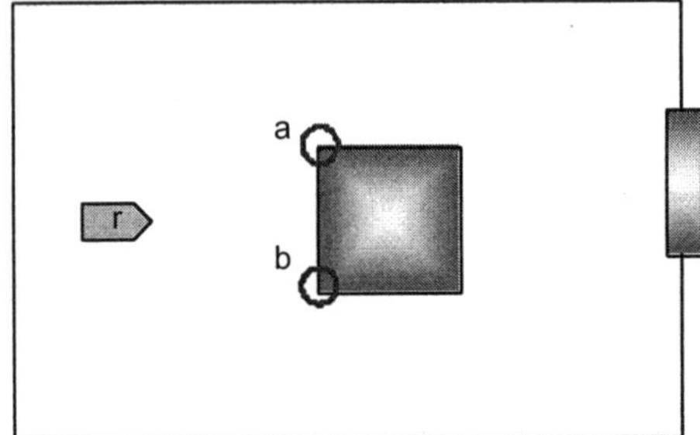
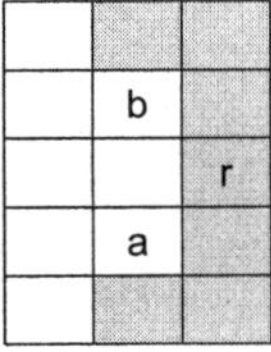

Figure 7. The robot (r) approaches the obstacle.   **Figure 8**. Iconic representation for r *wrt ab*

By exploiting conceptual neighbourhood, the robot knows that he has to turn the corner around either b or a, traversing darker regions in figure 8. Let's assume it tries b (figure 9).

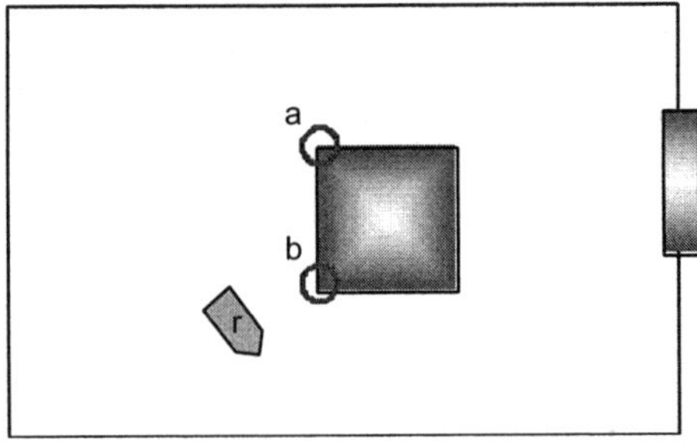

Figure 9. Turning round the corner.

Now, two new points enter the robot's sensorial horizon, first c and then d (figure 10). At this point the robot is qualitatively located with respect to both reference systems (figures 11 and 12). Its new goal will be passing between c and d, as the end of the obstacle is also detected, but where is d? Points b and c have already been tracked for a while, but d has just appeared. To improve reliability, spatial reasoning can be used to locate *d wrt bc*.

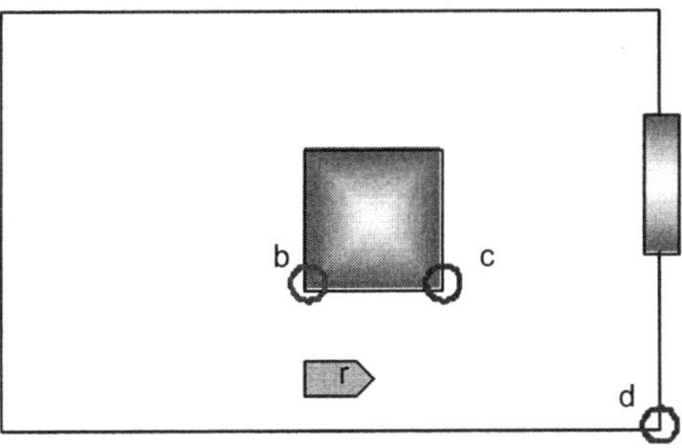

Figure 10. Leaving obstacle aside.

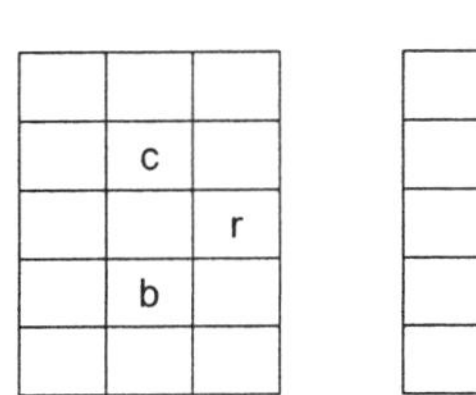

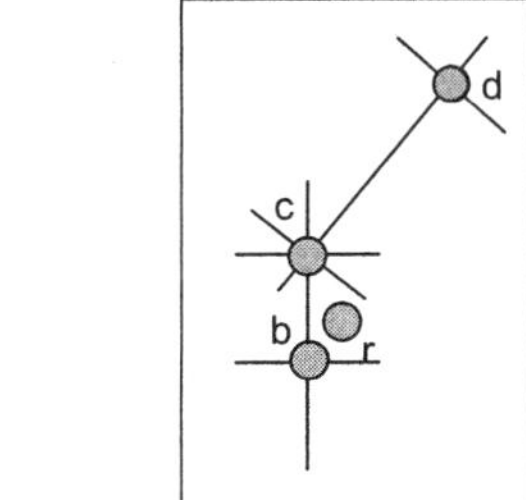

Figure 11. *r wrt bc* (left) and *r wrt cd* (right)　　**Figure 12.** Representation of *r wrt bc* and *r wrt cd.*

To obtain *d wrt bc*, *r wrt cd* has to be transformed by means of shortcut into *d wrt cr*:

$$r \text{ } wrt \text{ } cd \Rightarrow (\text{shortcut}) \Rightarrow d \text{ } wrt \text{ } cr$$

Now composition can be used to perform the BSIP [20] using Freksa & Zimmerman's fine qualitative orientation model composition table, as shown in figure 13.

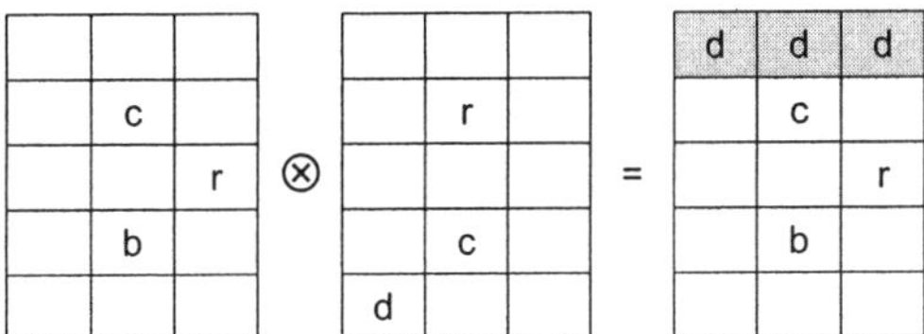

Figure 13. Composition of *r wrt bc* and d *wrt cr.*

In this case, since d might be in any of the darker coloured regions in figure 13 (there is not enough information to locate d wrt bc), disjunction appears. The new goal for the robot at this moment is to traverse the ambiguous regions where d could be until new perceptual information confirms that the line c-d has been traversed (figure 14).

Figure 14. Traversing c-d.

An analogue reasoning process could be performed now with recently discovered point e, which is a part of the door (figures 15 and 16):

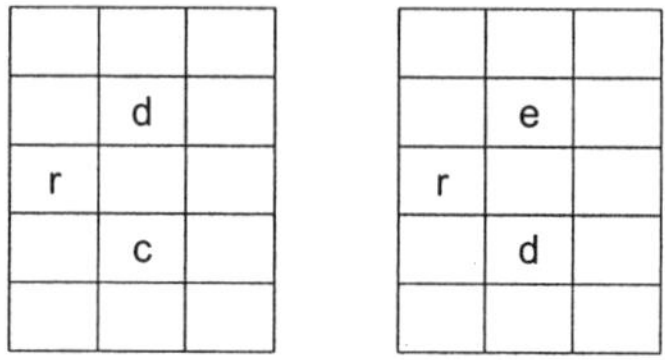

Figure 15. r *wrt cd* (left) and r *wrt de* (right).

r wrt de ⇨ (shortcut) ⇨ *e wrt dr*

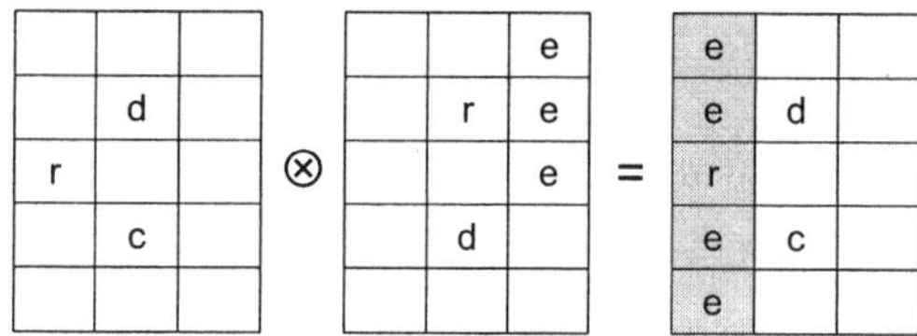

Figure 16. Composition of r *wrt cd* and e *wrt dr*.

Now, the robot detects point f and heads for the door, passing between e and f (figure 17).

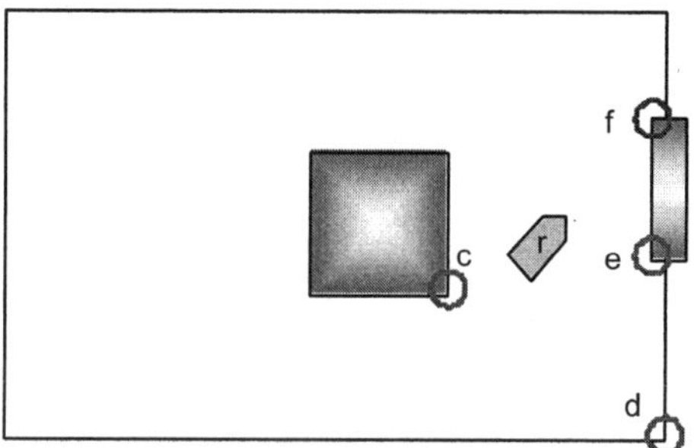

Figure 17. Moving towards e-f.

3.2. An Algorithm for Local Path Planning Based on QSR

According to the example shown, the strategy to perform path planning consists of:

- ❑ The acquisition of perceptual information and the extraction of significant points.
- ❑ The construction of reference systems using new and old points.
- ❑ The integration of reference systems so that a goal for the path planner can be established.
- ❑ The search of a route in the integrated reference system from the actual position of the robot towards the goal region or regions, if disjunction appears (in this latter case perceptual information is crucial to identify the right place). This search is performed exploiting conceptual neighbourhood on the iconic representations of the composed reference systems earlier shown (figures 13, 16).

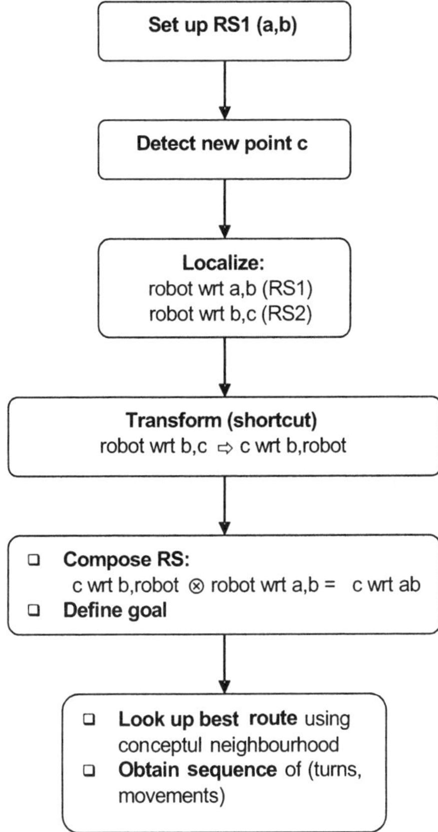

Figure 18. Algorithm for local path planning.

The route is explained in terms of qualitative turns at 90° to convey bearing, and forward movements that represent travel from one conceptual region to the next neighbouring one in the heading of the robot (figure 19).

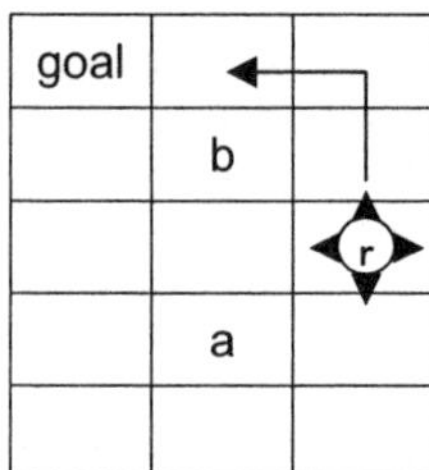

Figure 19. Orientation of the robot (r) in the composed reference system.

4. Conclusions and future work

We believe that this paper justifies the use of Qualitative Spatial Reasoning, and not only qualitative spatial representation, for robot path planning. A novel approach to navigate in local environments using QSR has been explained, and a preliminary algorithm to demonstrate it has also been presented. QSR can significantly improve robustness of mobile robots when wandering along partially unknown dynamic environments, such as those encountered in the real world.

There is much work left to be done on this subject. The selection of points with which reasoning is performed is not trivial at all. Points are now selected as they are perceived, which seems quite a logical approach. Nonetheless, the formalization of strategies for (optimal) point selection, as well as the demonstration of the validity of a particular choice, is a task to deal with. In the same sense, the way reference systems are constructed so that they are used for the definition of a particular goal for the robot deserves further consideration.

The depth of reasoning is something that has not been mentioned, either. QSR has only been performed using the BSIP, so far. How and when a full inference process should be performed is left to be analysed in the near future.

The integration of the local path planning approach shown here with a lower-level sensorimotor system and a higher-level path planner that constructs global routes is another delicate matter that needs to be analysed.

Tests will soon start to be carried out in virtual environments and real-world robots in our lab to check for the validity of the method shown in this paper.

Acknowledgments

We would like to acknowledge the help and cooperation of all the members of the Intelligent Control System group of Jaume I University of Castellón, and their regular participation in meetings, which their contributions make so intellectually stimulating.

References

[1] Lozano-Pérez, T., "Automatic Planning of Manipulator Transfer Movements", IEEE Transactions on Systems Mans and Cybernetics, SMC-11(10):681-698, October 1981.
[2] Brooks, R. A., "Solving the find-path problem by good representation of free space", in Proc. AAAI-82.
[3] Crowley, J. L., "Navigation for an intelligence mobile robot". IEEE Journal of Robotics and Automation, RA-1(1):31-41, 1985.

[4] Moravec, H. P. and Elfes, A., "High resolution maps from wide angle sonar", in IEEE International Conference on Robotics and Automation, pag. 116-121, 1985.
[5] Giralt, G., Sobek, R., and Chatila, R., "A multi-level planning and navigation system for a mobile robot". In IJCAI-79, pag. 335-337, 1979.
[6] Thrun, S. et al., "Map learning and high-speed navigation in RHINO", in Artificial Intelligence and Mobile Robots, D. Kortenkamp, A.P. Bonasso, R. Murphy (eds.), The MIT Press, 1998.
[7] Nourbakhsh, I., "Dervish: An office.navigating robot, in Artificial Intelligence and Mobile Robots, D. Kortenkamp, A.P. Bonasso, R. Murphy (eds.), The MIT Press, 1998.
[8] Koening, S., Simmons, R.G., "Xavier: A robot navigation architecture based on partially observable markov decision process models", in Artificial Intelligence and Mobile Robots, D. Kortenkamp, A.P. Bonasso, R. Murphy (eds.), The MIT Press, 1998.
[9] Kuipers, B., "Modeling spatial knowledge", Cognitive Science, 2:129-153, 1978.
[10] Davis, E., "Representing and Acquiring Geographic Knowledge". Morgan Kaufmann Publishers, Inc., Los Altos, California, 1991.
[11] Kuipers, B., Byun, Y., "A Robust, Qualitative Method for Robot Spatial Reasoning", Proceedings of the seventh National Conference on Artificial Intelligence, pag. 774-779, 1988.
[12] Kuipers, B.J. & Levitt, T.S., "Navigation and Mapping in Large-Scale Space", AI Magazine, 1988.
[13] Sutherland, K. T. and Thompson, W. B., "Inexact Navigation". In Proceedings of the IEEE Robotics and Automation, pag. 1-7, 1993.
[14] Zheng, J. Y. and Tsuji, S., "Panoramic Representation for Route Recognition by a mobile robot". International Journal of Computer Vision, 9(1):55-76, October, 1992.
[15] Schlieder, C, "Representing Visible Locations for Qualitative Navigation". In Proceedings of the III IMACS International Workshop on Qualittive Reasoning and Decision Technologies —QUARDET'93—, pag. 523-532, 1993. CIMNE, Barcelona.
[16] Jungert, E., "Extended sysmbolic projections as a knowledge structure for spatial reasoning". In kittler, J., editor, 4th International Conference on Pattern Recognition, Volume 301 of Lecture Notes in Computer Science, pag. 343-351, Springer, Berlin, 1988.
[17] Holmes, P.D. & Jungert, R.A., "Symbolic and Geometric Connectivity Graph Methods for Route Planning in Digitized Maps", in IEEE Transactions on Pattern Analysis and Machine Intelligence, vol. 14, No. 5, May 1992.
[18] Dai, D. and Lawton, D. T., "Range-free qualitative navigation". In Proceedings of the IEEE Robotics and Automation, pag783-790, 1993.
[19] Park, Il-Pyung, "Qualitative Environmental Navigation: Theory and Practice". PhD thesis in the Graduate School of Arts and Sciences, Columbia University, 1994.
[20] Escrig, M.T., Toledo, F., "Qualitative Spatial Reasoning: theory and practice. Application to Robot Navigation". IOS Press, Frontiers in Artificial Intelligence and Applications, ISBN 90 5199 4125. 1998.
[21] Zanichelli, F., "Topological maps and robust localization for autonomous navigation", IJCAI workshop on Adaptive spatial representations of dynamic environments, 1999.
[22] Musto, A. et al., "From motion observation to qualitative representation", in C. Freksa, C. Habel, C. Hendel (eds.), Spatial Cognition II. LNCS-Series, Springer Berlin, Heidelberg, New York, 2000.
[23] Musto, A. et al., "Qualitative and Quantitative representations of Locomotion and their application in robot navigation", in Proceedings of the IJCAI-99, Morgan Kaufman Publishers, 1999.
[24] Tomatis, N, Nourbakhsh, I, Arras, K., Siegwart, R, "A Hybrid Approach for Robust and Precise Mobile Robot Navigation with Compact Environment Modeling". In

Proceedings of the 2001 IEEE International Conference on Robotics & Automation Seoul, Korea • May 21-26, 2001

[25] Remolina, E., Kuipers, B., "Towards a general theory of topological maps". Submitted to Artificial Intelligence Journal, 2002.

[26] Guesgen, H.W., "Spatial reasoning based on Allen's temporal logic", Technical Report TR-89-049, International Computer Science Institute, Berkeley, 1989.

[27] Jungert, E., "The Observer's Point of View: An Extension of Symbolic Projections", in International Conference GIS -From Space to Territory: Theories and Methods of Spatio-Temporal Reasoning in Geographic Space. Volume 639 of Lectures Notes in Computer Science. Ed. Springer-Verlag, 1992.

[28] Mukerjee, A., Joe, G., "A Qualitative Model for Space". In 8th-AAAI, pag. 721-727, 1990.

[29] Freksa, C., "Using Orientation Information for Qualitative Reasoning", in A. U. Frank, I. Campari, and U. Formentini (editors). Theories and Methods of Spatio-Temporal Reasoning in Geographic Space. Proceedings of the International Conference on GIS-From Space to Territory, Pisa, volume 639 of Lecture Notes in Computer Science, pag. 162-178, 1992. Springer, Berlin.

[30] Freksa, C., Zimmermann, K., "On the Utilization of Spatial Structures for Cognitively Plausible and Efficient Reasoning", Proceedings of the IEEE International Conference on Systems, Man and Cybernetics, pag. 18-21, 1992.

[31] Hernández, D. "Qualitative Representation of Spatial Knowledge". In volume 804 in Lecture Notes in AI. Ed. Springer-Verlag, 1994.

[32] Pacheco, J., Escrig, M.T., Toledo, F., "A model for representing and reasoning with 3-D Qualitative Orientation", in Proceedings of the 9th Conference of Spanish Association of Artificial Intelligence, October 2001.

[33] Zimmermann, K., "Enhancing Qualitative Spatial Reasoning Combining Orientation and Distance", in Frank, A. U. and Campari, I. (eds.). Spatial Information Theory. A Theoretical Basis for GIS. European Conference, COSIT'93, pag. 69-76, Marciana Marina, Italy, Volume 716 of Lecture Notes in Computer Science. Springer, Berlin.

[34] Jong, J. H., "Qualitative Reasoning About Distances and Directions in Geographic Space". Ph.D. thesis. Department of Surveying Engineering. University of Maine, 1994.

[35] Clementini, E., Di Felice, P., Hernández, D., "Qualitative Representation of Positional Information", TR FKI-208-95, Technische Universität München, 1995.

[36] Escrig, M.T., Toledo, F., "Autonomous Robot Navigation using human spatial concepts". International Journal of Intelligent Systems, Vol.15, No.3, March 2000, pp.165-196, 2000. ISBN 0884-8173.

[37] Escrig, M.T., Toledo, F., "Reasoning with compared distances at different levels of granularity", in Proceedings of the 9th Conference of Spanish Association of Artificial Intelligence, October 2001.

[38] Frank, A. "Qualitative Spatial Reasoning about Distance and Directions in Geographic Space". In Journal of Visual Languages and Computing 3, pag. 343-373, 1992.

[39] M.T. Escrig, and F. Toledo, "Qualitative Velocity". Lecture Notes in Artificial Intelligence, vol.2504, Springer-Verlag, pp.29--39, 2002.

[40] Isli, A., Museros, L., Barkosky, T. and Reinhard, M., "A Topological Calculus for Cartographic Entities. Conceptualizang". Lecture Notes in Artificial Intelligence 1849. Springer-Verlag, pp. 225--238, ISBN: 3-540-67584-1, Germany, 2000.

[41] Museros, L. and Escrig, M.T., "Modeling Motion Qualitatively: Integrating Space and Time". Lecture Notes in Artificial Intligence, vol. 2504, Springer-Verlag, pp. 64--74, 2002.

[42] Zimmerman, K., Freksa, C., "Qualitative Spatial Reasoning Using Orientation, Distance and Path Knowledge", in Proceedings of the 13th. International Joint Conference on Artificial Intelligence. Workshop on Spatial and Temporal Reasoning, 1993.

Artificial Intelligence Research and Development
I. Aguiló et al. (Eds.)
IOS Press, 2003

Multi-Robot Task Allocation Strategies Using Auction-Like Mechanisms

José Guerrero, Gabriel Oliver
Dept. de Matemàtiques i Informàtica, Universitat de les Illes Balears (UIB),
Cra. de Valldemossa, km 7.5, 07122, Palma de Mallorca (SPAIN)
{jose.guerrero,goliver}@uib.es

Abstract. Task allocation is a complex and open problem for multi-robot systems. In this paper, we present three strategies for dynamically allocating tasks in a colony of mobile robots. The system is partially inspired on auction and thresholds-based methods and tries to determine the optimum number of robots that are needed to solve specific tasks, or sub-goals, in order to minimize the execution time of a mission. The method has been extensively tested for a modification of the well-known foraging task. Initial situations with different combinations of workload and work capacity have been used to test the proposed solution on robot teams with different homogeneities. Experimental results are presented to show the benefits of the proposed methods.

1 Introduction

Multi-robot systems can provide several advantages over single-robot systems: robustness, flexibility and efficiency among others. To benefit from these potential aspects the robots must cooperate to carry out a common mission. It is well known that several problems have to be solved to archive this aim. Some tasks can be carried out by a single robot but if two or more robots can cooperate, the task can be archive faster. In this situation, the following question has to be answered: How many robots and which of them do we need to optimize the execution time of this task?. As it has been demonstrated in different studies, if the number of robots is increased with wrong criteria, the execution time can increase, among other causes, due to the interference effect. Interference is the result of competition for the shared resources, especially the physical space and the robots themselves. In [10] it is shown how the interference can affect the execution time of the foraging tasks and how increasing the number of robots also causes the time to finish the mission to increase. Besides, if a certain task captures the attention of an excessive number of robots, other tasks can be forsaken. Therefore, our challenge is to design a distributed system to coordinate a heterogeneous robot team working in an unknown and dynamic environment. We mainly focus on the task allocation, that is, selecting the best robot or robots to perform a specific task.

In this paper, we propose and evaluate a first version of a decentralized method of task allocation for groups of heterogeneous robots executing foraging-like tasks. Our method is partially inspired in both the auction-based works [7], [6] and the threshold models of the swarm intelligence approach [4]. Thus, strategy presented here are hybrid solutions between those approaches. Special attention will be focused on deciding the optimal number of robots to execute a specific task. This problem is closely connected with the diversity level of the team of robots, as will be shown later. To measure the heterogeneity of the robot collectivity we use, among others, the social entropy proposed by T. Balch [3]. We will also study the relation between this metric and some of our architecture parameters. Also, three different variations or strategies of our method are presented: "no monitoring and no preemption", "monitoring and no preemption" and "monitoring and preemption". The differences among these three strategies lie in the capacity of monitoring the task progress and in the group preemption ability. The preemption ability is the capacity for change the task assigned to a robot.

In the system presented here, when a robot detects a non-assigned task tries to organize a working group. This group consists of all the robots that will cooperate to execute the specific task. One of the robots of this group will be the leader. The leader will decide how many robots and which of them will be needed to execute the task. To select these robots the leader starts an auction process, similar to [7]. The auction mechanism does not allow deciding how many robots will form the group. Thus, to take this decision, the leader together with the auction mechanism has to calculate the ratio between the work to do and the work capacity of the robots in the group. One of the objectives of the leader is to create a group as reduced as possible with the maximum work capacity. It is important to mention that the number of robots of the group can vary during the task execution. As it will be shown, during the mission, the leader can accept more robots as members of the group while other robots can abandon it too. In non preemption executions a robot can only abandon its task to became leader and create its own group. On the other hand, the preemption approach implements an inter-group or inter-leader negotiation mechanism. During this negotiation the leader can transfer one or more of its robots to another group. The experiments shown here are inspired on the so-called foraging or transportation tasks. In the present case, each robot has a limited load capacity (work capacity). If a robot can't load the full object, it loads a portion of the weight, goes to the delivery point and comes back for more.

The rest of this paper is organized as follows: section 2 presents some relevant work in the field of multi-robot task allocation; section 3 describes our methods and their implementation; section 4 shows the experiments carried out to validate the different approaches; section 5 explains some conclusions and future work is stated.

2 Related work

The computer engineering community has done a lot of research to solve the task allocation problem. In recent years, some studies on multi-robot systems have used some similar ideas to solve the problem of how robot teams can distribute their individual work capacity to efficiently achieve a common task. This section shortly relates some of those researches that have inspired us. These approaches are the marked-based systems, inspired in the economy markets, and the threshold-based systems, inspired in the swarm intelligence paradigm.

The marked-based approaches are based in a negotiation between the robots to cooperate [7], [6]. The robots act as self-interest agents and try to maximize their own benefits and reduce the costs. When a robot executes a task it can obtain a benefit but it also has to pay an execution cost. The cost may be, for example, the distance between the robot and the target point, and the profit could be the reduction in the global work to be executed by the robots. If each robot, as self-interest agent, reduces its own cost and maximizes its benefit, the profit for the whole system will be maximized. The robots can subcontract part of the task execution to other robots. The subcontracted robots can carry out the task with a lower cost or higher benefit. Finally, the profit is distributed among all the robots which cooperated during the execution. Thus, the overall system profit is increased thanks to the robot cooperation.

Dias and Stenz [6] have proposed cooperation mechanisms based on the marked-based metaphor. In the same line, Gerkey and Mataric are working on auction-based mechanisms [7]. In these systems the robots bid for the tasks. The robot with the highest bid wins the auction process and gets the task. The bids are adjusted to the robots' interest (capacity) to carry out the goal. Thus, when a robot finds a task, it can start an auction process and subcontract its execution to other robots.

Other works can be found in the literature inspired in some biology metaphors. One of the best known are the so-called swarm intelligence paradigm systems, which are inspired in the collective behaviour of insect colonies like ants and wasps. To implement these systems some authors make use of the response thresholds systems [4], [9]. In these systems, each robot has a stimuli associated with each task to execute. The stimuli value depends on some intrinsic parameters of the robots and the tasks. When the level of the stimuli exceeds a threshold, the robot starts its execution. A pure threshold-based system dosen't requires communication mechanisms between robots and therefore, there are no negotiation protocols. Recently, some authors include a very simple communication mechanism to improve the system performance [1] . In this system the robots can exchange the information about the task location, but any negotiation protocol is implemented.

The pure threshold-based systems don't require any kind of communication mechanisms. Therefore, they are not limited by the bandwidth communication restrictions and they are very scalable. Nonetheless, a disadvantage of these systems is the absence of knowledge about the other robots. Thus, a robot can decide by itself to execute a task when other option could be better. Moreover, using a pure threshold-based system the execution of plans shared by several robots would be very difficult. The marked-based systems do not have this limitation but they require communication mechanisms. These communication requirements limit the system scalability. It has to be pointed out that both for threshold-methods and marked-based methods, a function has to be designed to quantify the cost and the profit values of a task. This function is task dependent, thus, when the robot team executes a different task, a new functions has to be used. In [4] a comparison between biology-based and marked-based task allocation algorithms is presented. The experiments shown in that paper are performed with industrial manipulators and they conclude that the performance of both, biology-based and marked-based systems is very similar.

Our approach is partially inspired in the auction mechanisms and, consequently, the best robot for a specific task can be chosen. However, while previous works cannot determine the optimal number of robots to execute a task, our method allows deciding this number as a function of both the amount of work required to complete the task and the work capacity of the robots involved in the auction process. Moreover, during the leader to leader negotiation the robots bid using a threshold-based like equation. Thus, this paper try to shows the initial works to create an hybrid system which will combine the advantages of both, threshold and market-based systems.

3 Working group leading, formation and updating

The coordination mechanisms description, including the groups' formation, the leading, the membership policy, the task assignment and the preemption strategies is described in the following paragraphs.

3.1 Single robot to leader negotiation

This section describes the negotiation that is carried out between each single robot and one group's leader. This negotiation level corresponds to a non preemption strategy, and therefore it doesn't allow the exchange of robots (work capacity) between groups.

In an initial stage, each robot is looking for a task. When a robot finds a new task by itself, it will try to lead it. As there can be only be one leader per task, the candidate will first check if this task is assigned to any other robot or not. If there are two or more robots requesting the leadership of the same task, it will be assigned to the 'best' robot. To determine their suitability, we evaluate each candidate using a measure that depends on the specific task to do. During our experiments this measure is the robots' load capacity.

When a robot is promoted to leader of a task, it evaluates the work needed to carry it out. Then, it will create, if necessary, the work group; that is, the set of robots that will cooperate to execute this specific task. In that case, the leader must decide which is the optimum group size. In this paper, we propose the leader to decide, as it will be exposed in the auction mechanism, using the following equation:

$$TH_g = \frac{taskWorkLoad}{\sum_{1 \leq i \leq N} workCapacity_i} < TH \tag{1}$$

Where $taskWorkLoad$ is the amount of work required to finish the assigned task that is calculated by the leader. N is the number of robots of the group and $workCapacity_i$ is the individual work capacity of the ith robot. Finally, TH is the group threshold; this value is a parameter that will be used to compare the efficiency of the group formation policy. Using equation (1) the leader fixes the maximum ratio between work to do and available work capacity and, therefore, it fixes the maximum number of robots that will be part of the group. This concept is similar to the response threshold of the swarm intelligence algorithms, where the stimulus for each robot is a combination of its load capacity and the taskWorkLoad. In the present case, the decision process is also centralized on the leader.

The leader monitors the task execution, thus, in any time the leader knows the current value of the taskWorkLoad parameter of the equation (1). Obviously, the value must decrease as the execution progress. The practical problem is how can the leader monitor this progress?, and is it necessary to monitor the progress?. Section 4 shows the impact of the monitor process over the execution time.

To select the robots that will be part of its group the leader uses an auction process. Unlike other auction-based methods, we use the inequality (1) to select the robots. This process is as follows:

- *Auction beginning*: the leader sends a massage to inform that it has found a new task and needs to form a working group.

- *Bids*: each robot without any assigned task (robots that are not part of any group) sends to the leader its work capacity.

- *Auction finishing*: after a fixed time has passed, the leader closes the auction and doesn't accept more bids.

- *Selecting the robots*: the leader selects the robots with the highest work capacity provided the inequality (1) is verified.

- *Agreement and refuse negotiation*: The leader sends an agreement massage to the selected robots and, if the offer is accepted, they start to work for the group. The robots that do not accept to be part of the group reply with a refuse message and the leader subtracts their work capacity from the group capacity. A robot can refuse an offer if it joined another group or it became a leader task during the auction process.

If after this process the equation (1) is not fulfilled, the leader starts a new auction round. This new auction round will include a leader to leader negotiation as will be explained in section 3.2. When the task is finished, the working group is dissolved immediately.

Using only this kind of negotiation, the size of the group can vary during the execution of the task by means of two mechanisms. Group size can be reduced by a robot segregation process. If a non-leader robot, which is part of a group, finds a new task, it will try to leave its present group and become a leader of the new task. When this situation occurs, the segregated robot communicates this circumstance to its old leader which will recalculate equation (1) for the new situation of its group and, eventually, can initiate a new auction process. On the other hand, the size of the group can increase thanks to a robot aggregation process. This process takes place when after a certain time has passed a robot does not have any task to execute. Then, it sends a message asking for a task. If a leader receives one of these messages, it accepts the robot in its group if the group size is less than a fixed number. Using this mechanism, the inactive robots are avoided. A new mechanism to modify the group size will be included thanks to the leader to leader negotiation.

3.2 Leader to leader negotiation: Preemption

The leader to leader negotiation allows the exchange of robots between groups. If after the single robot to leader negotiation the equation (1) is not fulfilled, the group's leader tries to contract the robots which are working in another task. To select these robots, each leader bids for the task using both its robots load capacity, as in the previous negotiation, and its working group energy. Using the operating systems vocabulary, during the experiments this kind of algorithm will be called strategies with preemption.

The working group energy is a measure to indicate the group's tendency to send its robots to another group. A group with a high energy value is a potential sender of robots to other tasks and, on the other hand, a low energy value indicates that this group is a receptor of new robots. The energy is calculated using the following equation:

$$E_g = \frac{GroupSize}{TH_g} \tag{2}$$

Where $GroupSize$ is the number of group robots and TH_g is obtained from equation (1). A high value of TH_g indicates that the group has a low value of work capacity compared with the task to carry out. In this case the group needs more robots and, therefore, the energy is low. Moreover, the leader has to try to create a group with the minimum number of robots to reduce the interference effect between robots. Thus, a group with a lot of robots needs to reduce this number, and this means a higher energy value.

The energy concept is similar to the stimulus intensity value used by some threshold based algorithms [4]. Using stimulus the robots have to belong to a specific cast or group with its particular characteristics. Nevertheless, using the energy concept, each robot has its own load capacity and it is not necessary a preliminary division in groups. Finally, the main difference between the threshold and energy strategies lies in the fact that the energy value will be used as the bid value in an action process, and therefore, the decisions will be taken knowing its impact over the others groups. In a pure threshold based system this decision is reactive and it is taken in independence from the others groups.

To select robots from other groups the leader uses another auction process. This process is as follow:

- *Auction beginning*: if the equation (1) is not fulfilled after the previous auction process, the leader sends a 'leader to leader' negotiation request.

- *Bids*: each leader sends the value of its energy and the information about the robots of the group; this is, the identification of each robot and its load capacity. A robot only can abandon a group after a fixed time passed since its incorporation. During the experiments this time is equal to 85 units. As in the previous auction process, if a robot without any assigned task received this message, it sends its load capacity.

- *Close Auction*: after a fixed period of time the leader closes the action and doesn't accept more bids.

- *Selecting robots without assigned task*: first of all the leader selects the robots without any assigned task and with the higher load capacity.

- *Selecting robots associated to a previous group*: if the equation (1) is not fulfilled, the leader selects the robots sent by the others leaders. The goal of this selection is create a more stable system. By the way, a system where the groups have low energy will be more stable than a system made up of groups with high energy. A more appropriate definition of system stability is now under study.

The leader, before starting the auction process, pre-selects the robots that will participate in the auction process. A robot from another group is pre-selected if reassigning it to the new group produces a reduction of the maximum value of the global energy; that is, if the following condition is verified:

$$MAX(E_{g1}, E_{g2}) > MAX(E'_{g1}, E'_{g2}) \qquad (3)$$

Where $MAX(v1, v2)$ returns the maximum value of v1 and v2. E_{g1} is the energy of the acceptant group and E_{g2} is the energy of the requesting group before the transaction. E'_{g1} and E'_{g2} are the predicted energies after the transaction. Therefore, the left side of the equation (3) is the current state of the system and the right side represents the situation after the robot selection. Finally, O is the perceptual overhead produced by the group change. This factor avoids the robot selection when the benefit obtained by the group is very low. During the experiments the overhead is equal to 50% and, therefore, the O value is equal to 1,5. The selected robots bid during the auction process not only using its work capacity, like in the single robot to leader negotiation, but using the following value:

$$B = workCapacity * E'_{g2} \qquad (4)$$

Where $WorkCapacity$ is the individual work capacity of the robot and E'_{g2} is the energy of the robot's group if this robot is selected. The robot with a higher bid is selected. The action process finished when the equation (1) is fulfilled or when no more robots validate the equation (3). This auction process allows selecting the best robot between all the pre-selected candidates. If after this process the equation (1) is not fulfilled another auction process is started.

4 Experiments and validation

This section explains the experiments carried out to validate our approach. It is also shown how the value of the group threshold and the social entropy of the group affect the execution time. We have also evaluated the impact of the task work load monitoring and the effects of the leader to leader negotiation over the team. All the experiments have been done using the RoboCoT environment. The mission to be carried out by the robots is a modification of the classical foraging task.

4.1 Measure of the homogeneity of the collective

It has to be emphasized that each robot can have a different work capacity. Thus, we have focused part of our study on the measure of the performance of the collective while its homogeneity is changed. To characterize the homogeneity of the collective of robots we use two entropy measures. On the one hand, the simple entropy measure based on the Shannon's information entropy:

$$H = \sum_{1 \leq i \leq M} p_i \log_2(\frac{1}{p_i}) \qquad (5)$$

where M is the number of classes of robots and p_i is the proportion of robots in the ith class. On the other hand, social entropy as formulated by Balch [3] extends simple entropy to take into account the quantitative differences between groups. In our experiments, these differences are the work capacity of each robot; therefore, two robots belong to the same group if they have the same work capacity.

4.2 Platform and task description

We use as test bed a multi-robot simulator called RoboCoT (Robot Colonies Tool). RoboCoT is a software tool developed and used by the authors at the University of the Balearic Islands that allows testing the performance of individual or colonies of mobile robots in a very flexible, fast and non-expensive way. This simulator implements robots that work according to a control architecture based on behaviours, as they were introduced by Ronald C. Arkin [2]. It has been widely proved that efficient robot navigation capabilities can be obtained at

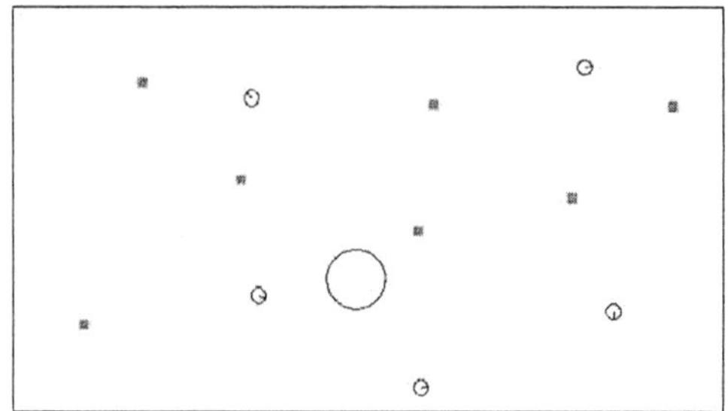

Figure 1: Example of initial situation of the experiments.

Table 1: Robots' load capacities used during the experiments. R1..R5 represent the robots' load capacities. The H represents the simple entropy of the configuration and SH the social entropy.

Configuration	R1	R2	R3	R4	R5	H	HS
1 (Homogeneous)	3	3	3	3	3	0	0
2	1	1	1	1	11	0,72	7,22
3	1	1	3	5	5	1,52	4,49
4	1	2	3	4	5	2,32	2,32

a reasonable low computational cost with such architectures. A detailed discussion about the RoboCoT architecture can be found in [8].

The task to be carried out by the robots is described as follows: some randomly placed robots must locate objects, randomly placed too, and carry them to a common delivery point. Figure 1 shows a typical initial situation, where the squares represent the objects to collect, the delivery point is the big circle in the middle of the image and the robots are the little circles. Each object to gather has a weight and each robot has a load capacity. The robot load capacity is the amount of weight that it can carry. If a robot cannot carry the entire object at once, it takes a part of it, goes to the delivery point and comes back to the object for more bits. Therefore, unlike a classical foraging task, the objects can be transported by the robots in little transportable bits. It is obvious that in this kind of experiments, a robot can always complete any specific task, carrying bit by bit all the objects to the delivery point. However, if several robots cooperate, the task can be done faster. During the experiments, the taskWorkLoad value is the object weight and the workCapacity of a robot is its load capacity.

In all the experiments presented here, we have used seven objects to load and five robots. The objects' weights are: 1, 3, 5, 5, 8, 10 and 15 units. All the robots have the same sensorial, behavioral and communication capabilities, and they only differ in their load capacity. To study the impact of the robots' homogeneity over the execution time we have used four different configurations or combinations for the load capabilities of the robots. Table 4.2 shows these configurations, the load capacities of the robots, and the value of simple (H) and social (SH) entropy of the robot community. For each configuration, we have used as values for the group threshold (TH): 0, 1, 2, 3. In addition, we have executed the experiments without communication between robots. In the case TH=0, equation (1) has not been used, and therefore the number of robots per group is not limited. We have repeated each experiment 56 times using 14 different environments. The environments are different because of the initial placement

Table 2: Mean of the execution time for the experiments using a no monitoring and no preemption strategy. The "No Comm." row represents the experiments executed without communication. C1..C5 represent the robots configurations

-	C1	C2	C3	C4
No Comm.	996,6	1384,3	1002,3	1079,8
TH=0	934,4	1060,6	948,3	947,5
TH=1	919,2	1047,3	964,1	886,5
TH=2	878,7	1043,4	852,7	970,3
TH=3	892,4	1081,5	886,2	893

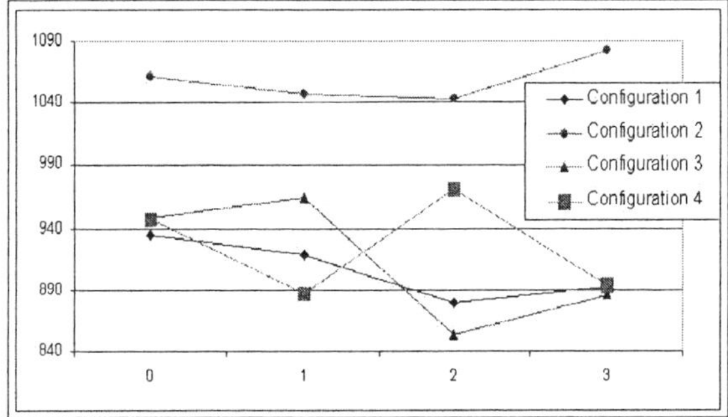

Figure 2: Execution time as a function of robot configuration for a no monitoring and no preemption strategy.

of the robots and the objects. To evaluate the impact of both, work load monitoring and leader to leader negotiation (preemption), three different strategies have been tested: no monitoring and no preemption, monitoring and no preemption and monitoring and preemption.

4.3 No monitoring and no preemption strategy

Using a no monitoring and no preemption strategy the group's leader can not monitor the progress of the task. It only can detect when the task is finished. Therefore, the value of the task work load of equation (1) is fixed during all the execution. Also, the leader to leader negotiation, presented in section 3.2 is not implemented. As it can be seen, this is the simplest strategy presented in this paper.

Table 4.3 and figure 2 show the mean of the execution time of the experiments. As it can be seen in this table, in most cases equation (1) involves the reduction of the execution time compared to the system with null threshold (TH=0). The configuration with the highest social entropy (SH) presents the lowest benefits due to the use of threshold. In this configuration the highest benefit reaches the 1,6% (TH=2), but when TH=3 the time is increased a 2%. On the another hand, the configuration 3 presents the highest benefit (10,1%) when TH=2 and the configuration 4 presents the highest increase (2,4%) when TH=2. As it can be seen, the use of communication produces a considerable reduction of the execution time in all the cases, and this time increases as the social entropy (SH) grows. The figure 2 also shows that the worst case is always the configuration with the highest social entropy value (configuration 2).

Table 3: Mean of the execution time for the experiments using a monitoring and no preemption strategy. C1..C5 represent the robots configurations

-	C1	C2	C3	C4
TH=0	934,4	1060,6	948,3	947,5
TH=1	869,9	1019,4	930,3	863,7
TH=2	905,8	996,8	880,8	950,5
TH=3	904,1	1044,3	922,8	910,1

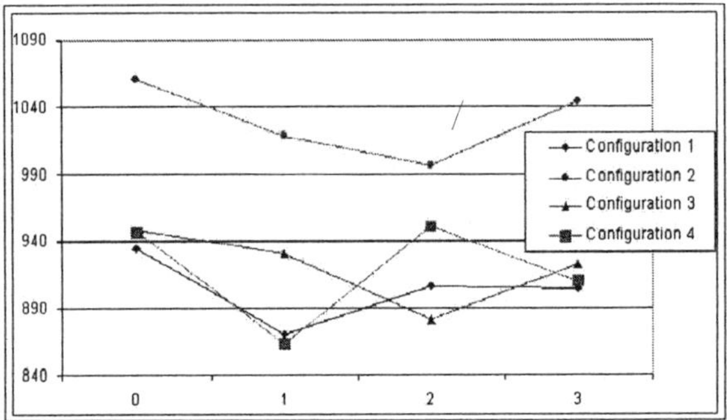

Figure 3: Execution time as a function of robot configuration for a monitoring and no preemption strategy.

4.4 Monitoring and no preemption strategy

Figure 3 and table 4.4 show the mean of the execution time of our monitoring and no preemption strategy experiments. If these results are compared with the no monitoring and no preemption strategy results, it can be seen that for all configurations the worst execution time is reduced. This effect is more evident in the configuration 2. Nonetheless, the better execution time is increased in some cases. For example, for the configuration 3 the better case is 880,8 but during the no monitoring experiments this time was 852,7. Therefore, the monitoring task produces a "smoothing" effect over the execution time, but, in general, it seems that a little reduction of the execution time is produced.

4.5 Monitoring and preemption strategy

Monitoring and preemption strategy implements both the leader monitoring capacity and the leader to leader negotiation process. Thus, this is the most sophisticate strategy that we present here. Figure 4 and table 4.5 show the execution time for the experiments and, as it can be seen, the results are similar to those of the previous strategy. The main difference appears during the configuration with the highest simple entropy (configuration 4) where, in general, the execution time is reduced. Also, a reduction of the execution time is produced when the threshold is equal to 2. We expect that the leader to leader negotiation is especially useful if a priority is associated to each task. Thus, if a robot finds a high priority task, it can negotiate the temporary cession of some robots that are executing lower priority tasks using the leader to leader negotiation mechanism.

Table 4: Mean of the execution time for the experiments using a monitoring and preemption strategy. C1..C5 represent the robots configurations

-	C1	C2	C3	C4
TH=0	944,4	1099,8	957,9	955,6
TH=1	930,1	1026,6	969,4	874,8
TH=2	917,6	996,5	891,1	885,8
TH=3	890,9	1066,9	910,2	881,9

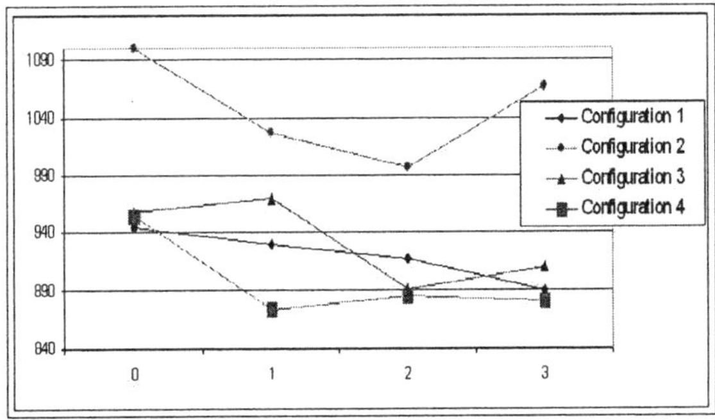

Figure 4: Execution time as a function of robot configuration for a monitoring and preemption strategy.

5 Conclusion and future work

This paper presents a simple and efficient way to solve the task allocation problem and, more specially, to decide how many robots are needed to execute a specific task. Our algorithms adapt the classical auction using some threshold-based systems concepts to find the optimal number of robots. In addition, our method allows both changing the robots assigned to a task as new objectives are found and interchanging robots between working groups. Thus, we have provided a faster and flexible way to regulate the optimal number robots as a function of the kind of the task and the available robots. Three versions of our mechanism have been proposed and tested using several environments. All the cases have been tested using a modification of the classical foraging task to allow a higher cooperation degree between robots. The execution results of this task prove that our mechanism reduces the mission's execution time.

This paper presents a work in progress that has some challenging aspects to add and to improve. For the time being we are focused on a deep analysis of the data available, obtained from a huge set of experiments that should take us to a precise understanding of the relations between heterogeneity and group thresholding as well as robot segregation, aggregation and preemption processes or auction algorithms. We are working on developing a better definition of system stability. As it can bee seen in section 4, the execution time of the mission is not modified by the leader to leader negotiation. The next kind of mission to implement by our system will include tasks with priorities. We expect that in this kind of environment the preemption strategy will be very useful. Thus, if a leader finds a high priority task, it could ask for help to other groups with lower priority tasks and some of their robots could temporarily be transferred to the demanding leader. Another aspect we are working on is the replacement of the leader mechanisms. These strategies should be activated when the leader robot faults and should improve the robustness of the system. Finally, another aspect of the systems that should be improved is the use of a non fixed threshold. Dynamic thresholding techniques in the line of those exposed in [5] will be tested.

Acknowledgments

This work has been partially supported by project CICYT-DPI2001-2311-C03-02 and FEDER fundings.

References

[1] W. Agassounon, A. Martinoli, "Efficiency and Robustness of Threshold-Based Distributed Allocation Algorithms in Multi-Agent Systems", First Int. Joint Conf. on Autonomous Agents and Multi-Agents Systems, (2002), 1090–1097.

[2] R.C. Arkin, *"Behaviour-Based Robotics"*, The MIT Press, (1998).

[3] T. Balch, "Social Entropy: A New Metric for Learning Multi-Robot Teams", *10th international Florida Artificial Intelligence Research Society Conference*, CA:AAAI Press, (1997).

[4] E. Bonabeau, A. Sobkowski, G. Theraulaz and J. L. Deneubourg, "Adaptive Task Allocation Inspired by a Model of Division of Labor in Social Insects", *Bio Computation and Emergent Computing*, edited by D. Lundh, B. Olsson, Narayanan, Singapore: World Scientific, (1997), 36-45.

[5] M. Campos, E. Bonabeau, G. Théraulaz and J. L. Deneubourg, "Dynamic Scheduling and Division of Labor in Social Insects", *Adaptive Behavior*, Vol. 8-2, (2001), 83–92.

[6] M.B. Dias and A. Stentz, "A Free Market Architecture for Distributed Control of a Multirobot System", *6th International Conference on Intelligent Autonomous Systems*, Venice (Italy), (2000), 115–122.

[7] B. P. Gerkey and M. J. Matarić, "Sold!: Auction methods for multi-robot coordination", *IEEE Transactions on Robotics and Automation, Special Issue on Multi-robot Systems*, Vol. 18, No. 5, (2002), 758–768.

[8] J. Guerrero, G. Oliver and A. Ortiz, "On Simulating Behaviour-based Robot Colonies in the Clasroom", *First EURON Workshop on Robotics Education and Training*, Weingarden (Germany), (2001), 91–98 .

[9] M. J. Krieger, J. G. Billeter and L. Keller, "Ant-like task allocation and recruitment in cooperative robots", *Nature 406*, (2000), 992–995, .

[10] Kristina Lerman, Aram Galstyan, "Mathematical Model of Foraging in a Group of Robots: Effect of Interference", *Autonomous Robots 13 (2)*, (2002), 127–141.

Artificial Intelligence Research and Development
I. Aguiló et al. (Eds.)
IOS Press, 2003

Model of a Place-Sensor System for Self-Localization of an Autonomous Mobile Robot

Gracián TRIVIÑO [†], Antonio RUIZ [†], Sergio GUADARRAMA Cotado [†] Rut GARÍ [††]
† Dept. Tecnología Fotónica. Universidad Politécnica de Madrid
†† Dept. Matemàtiques i Informàtica. Universitat de les Illes Balears

Abstract. A model of the system formed by the ultrasonic sensors of a mobile robot that measures the distances to walls in the place where the robot is located is presented. The model is based on the utilization of a set of fuzzy rules that are useful to represent the knowledge that the robot has to manage during self-localization process. To make viable the building of this model, the number of needed variables to define the system behavior has been strongly reduced, so that the combinatory explosion of rules number which is characteristic of this kind of models is controlled. An algorithm used for learning the fuzzy rules weights is presented and results of the model experimentation with a real robot are shown as well.

1 Introduction

One of the most important capacities that an autonomous mobile robot (AMR) should have is the self-localizing in its physical environment. In general, the robot should be capable to get an environment map by itself and then use it to estimate its own position with respect to the objects represented in it [3].

The classical tools of measuring used by an AMR in order to get by itself in the interior of a closed place are: odometric sensors to measure its relative position with respect to a point given as a reference, and ultrasonic sensors to measure the distance to walls and other objects around it.

These measurement instruments have a reduced cost and are quite easy to use. But, unfortunately, the results they give contain important lacks of precision.

On the one hand it must be taken into account the precision problems inherent in robot mechanisms:

Odometric sensors have a limited resolution. This fact causes that the imprecision of data which represents the relative position grows up while distance and number of maneuvers increase. Furthermore, there is a possibility that wheels skid depending on ground surface characteristics [2].

Measure of ultrasounds time of flight has imprecision inherent in to the measure instrument. Apart of the committed error in the time measure due to electronic limitations, the signal emitted forms an opened solid angle which does not permit to know exactly in which point of the arc formed by the front of waves the object that has returned the echo is located [9].

On the other hand, one must keep in mind the imprecision related to the physical characteristics of objects that form the place. Obtained measures are limited to the time of flight of the first received echo and, therefore, only correspond to the distance of the first obstacle detected. The intensity of the received echo depends on the incidence angle of the signal on the obstacle surface. An incidence angle too opened over a polished plain surface may cause either the obstacle can not be detected or a false echo appears due to echo reflection in another object encountered during the echo return trajectory. In a real closed place, different kinds of materials with different characteristics to absorb or reflect the signal have to be considered [8].

As a consequence these considerations, we can say the system relating the AMR position with the distances obtained using ultrasonic sensors in a closed place is, in general, not continuous and not linear. In the last decade some approximations of the AMR self-localization problem have been published, but definitive solutions have not been found [2] [5] [6].

In this work we propose to analyze some ways of representing the information that an AMR obtain of the place-sensor integrated system, emphasizing that obstacles and sensors characteristics must be both considered as a whole. The aim is modeling the system formed by a specific closed place when it is measured using sensors with specific characteristics.

The desired result can be expressed as a function that, using as input the distances to objects surrounding the robot, approximately provides the position o positions in which the robot may be located:

Approximated position = F (set of distances).

This work continues the line of previous works of the authors about this topic [11] [10].

Figure 1. The robot Sancho2

2 System definition

2.1   Use of a real robot

Although the investigation of new methods for AMR self-localization is frequently carried out using simulators, it is generally accepted that the use of these simulators should be limited to the preliminary phase of this type of developments.

In this work, a robot named Sancho2 has been used (see Figure 1), which has been designed and built by authors. This robot incorporates odometric sensors in the motorized wheels and twelve ultrasonic sensors distributed in angles of 30° around it (see Figure 2).

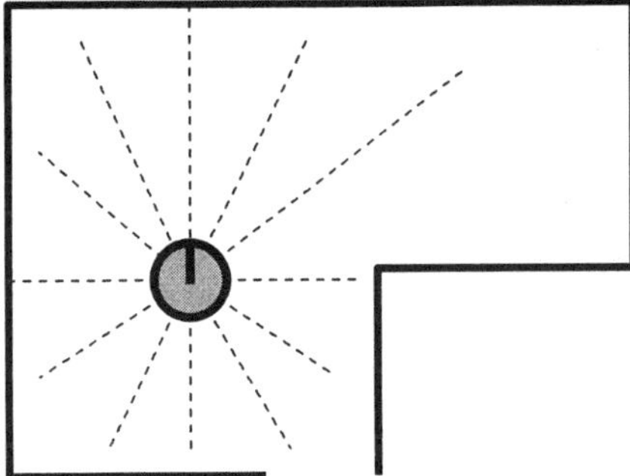

Figure 2. Twelve ultrasonic sensors

The odometric sensors have a resolution of 4 cm and the ultrasonic sensors have a beam opening angle of 30°. The behavior of this robot can be programmed using the portable computer included in its structure. A set of software tools, including the necessary functions to control the AMR movement and to use the available sensors, have been incorporated.

2.2   Utilization of a real closed place

By means of these resources, the robot has been programmed to carry out a series of measures in a place where the area is limited by the furniture of a room in the University.

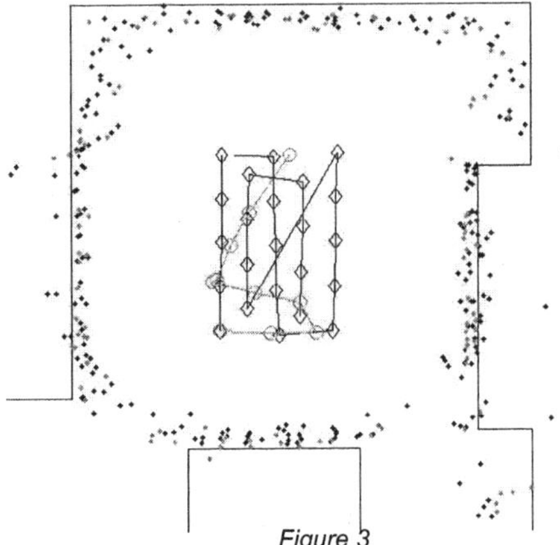

Figure 3

This closed place has approximated dimensions of 200 x 250 cm. The walls of this place are formed by different materials including several polished surfaces that can provoke outliers because ultrasonic signal bounces.

2.3   The set of measures

The robot has been programmed to follow a route measuring the distances in the twelve directions around (d1, d2... d12) and taking down its position and orientation (x, y, θ). In this way, a data set, that we have called *trace*, is formed containing n vectors of the form:

$$(x, y, \theta, d1, d2, .. d12) \, .$$

In order to delimit the problem complexity, some periodical corrections of data associated with the estimated positions by odometry have been performed to guarantee that annotated positions in the *trace* were free of significant errors.

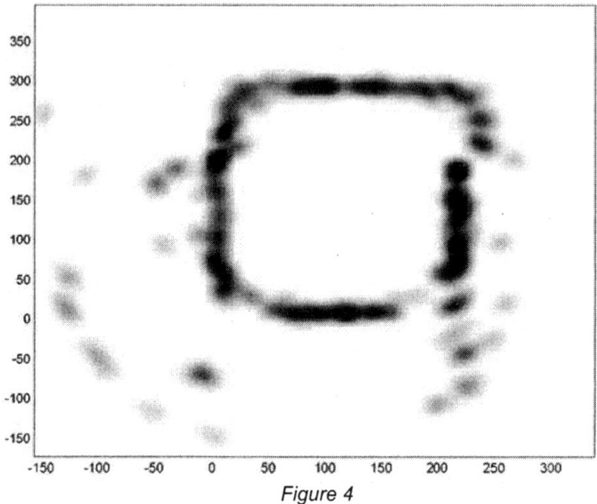

Figure 4

During the robot activity we have to distinguish two modes: Exploration mode, in which the robot has to learn the map of the place; and Navigation mode, during which the robot will use the learnt map to self-localize. In order to get a set of data useful for our experiments, in Exploration mode, a *trace* has been obtained by following a route of points uniformly distributed forming a grid in the chosen area for experimentation. For the Navigation phase, the *trace* has been obtained by performing a random trajectory into a domain delimited by the explored area. In Figure 3, data obtained from maneuvers and measurements carried out have been represented. Over a schematic map of the place, the robot and obstacles positions detected by ultrasounds are represented (the points are actually the centers of the 30° arcs corresponding to ultrasonic signals). The *trace* corresponding with Exploration phase is represented with rhombus, while Navigation phase *trace* is represented with circles.

Information of received echoes from obstacles delimiting the place can be used to obtain an approximated representation of the place geometry. A widely extended technique is to use the so called *occupancy grid map* [4]. Using the available set of measures, a grid is constructed in such a way that every cell contains a number between 0 and 1, which represents the available certainty about whether this cell is occupied by an obstacle. We have used this representation in order to verify that the available data were enough to represent the closed place geometry. Figure 4 shows an *occupancy grid map* of the place used during the experimentation, where the possibility that cells are occupied by an obstacle is represented by different grey color intensities. In this figure, the limits of place can be recognized and also it can be observed as some outliers appear because of presence of bounces.

2.4   Possibility map

The model of system we are building can be seen like a relation between two vectors. Input variables are the twelve distances *(d1, d2 ... d12)* that the robot measures in every visited point, while output variables are grouped in the triplet (x, y, θ) that represents the robot position and orientation. The relation between these variables could be given by a correspondence expressed as:

$$(x, y, \theta) = F\ (d1, d2, ...d12)\ .$$

One important characteristic of this system is that, in general, this relation is not univoque. For a certain distances vector used as input variable, due to the data uncertainty and possible symmetries in the place geometry, several robot positions could be considered as valid output vectors.

To represent all possible solutions and be able to include the grade of certainty with which these positions are known, in this work we will make use of the idea of *possibility map*. In parallel with the occupancy grid concept, this kind of map uses a grid, covering the place dimensions, indicating in every cell the possibility to be the robot current position.

3 Model of the place-sensor system

Before introducing our proposal, let's go to briefly analyze other two possible previous approximations to the problem solution.

3.1   Direct interpolation

An intuitive first approximation consists of using directly the *trace*, which has been obtained during the Exploration phase, as the only representation of the available information about the system.

Suppose the robot is in an unknown position (x_t, y_t) and obtains a vector of twelve distances $V_t = (d1, d2... d12)$. The first basic idea consists of to estimate the robot position by interpolating the coordinates of the k nearest neighbor vectors that are available in the *trace*.

This approach implies to consider the system is linear in the trial point neighborhood and that the set of samples is dense enough to cover the neighborhood of every trial point. Due to the studied system is neither continuous nor linear this approximation to the model requires a huge amount of data in order to have enough points density covering the whole place area.

3.2   Map Matching

The second approximation to the problem is based on using an *occupancy grid map* as it has been described above. In contrast to the previous solution, this type of representation permits synthesize the accumulated information from a samples set in such a way that the data structure size is kept constant while the precision of the representation achieved increases with the number of samples. To use this type of map during the robot self-localization process the so called "map-matching" technique is used.

The twelve distances obtained in an unknown position permit to obtain a partial map (an occupancy grid) of the obstacles surrounding the robot. In order to find the possible robot position, a scan is performed superimposing as a mask this partial map over all the possible positions in the complete map of the place, and then to evaluate the coincidence grade to get the possibility map [2] [6].

Although this solution improves the former proposal performances, the scanning of a enough number of points and the operations of maps comparison have an important computational load which limit its application for controlling the AMR navigation in real time conditions.

4 Model based in fuzzy rules

The proposal presented in this job consists of using a set of fuzzy rules in order to build a compact and robust enough representation of the available information about the integrated place-sensor system. The idea of approximating an unknown function by a set of fuzzy rules has been extensively studied [7] [1]. The main problem of this approach is the combinatory explosion that is produced in the number of rules which are needed to define the system behavior.

Therefore the main difficulty for designing this type of model is the selection of the set of variables and the definition of the best way of using them. Indeed, since a systematic process for designing the most suitable variables set does not exist, this work is considered to be more an art than a science [12].

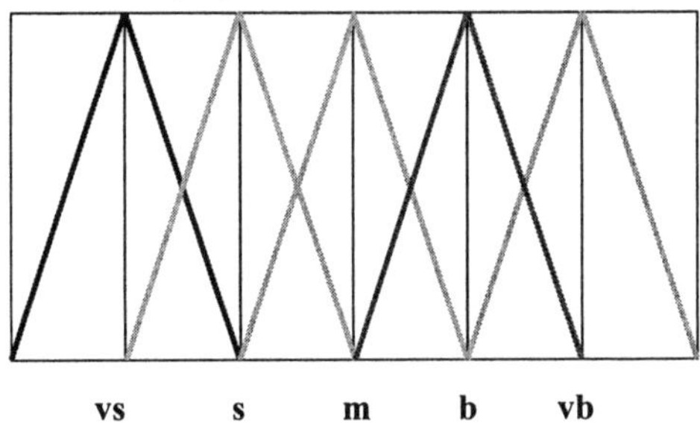

Figure 5. Linguistic labels

4.1   Definition of the linguistics labels

As an initial step we are going to use the five linguistic labels showed in figure 5 to obtain the fuzzy values of every variable involved in the model definition: coordinates, angle and distances. These labels are:

vs (very small), s (small), m (medium), b (big), vb (very big) .

Using these linguistic labels, it is possible to write down the following general set of rules to estimate the robot position:

IF (d1 IS vs) AND... (d12 IS vs) THEN (x IS vs) AND (y IS vs) AND (θ IS vs)

IF (d1 IS s) AND... (d12 IS vs) THEN (x IS vs) AND (y IS vs) AND (θ IS vs)
IF (d1 IS m) AND... (d12 IS vs) THEN (x IS vs) AND (y IS vs) AND (θ IS vs)
...

The number of fifteen variables combined with five linguistics labels provides a set with a total of 5^{15} possible rules.

Using this rules set it will be necessary evaluate the answer for a known input vector. Unfortunately, as it has been anticipated, in general, for every input vector a total of 2^{15} rules are fired due to the defined labels are overlapped in grade 1. So, one can see that the solution to the problem following this way requires the use of a huge amount of processing resources.

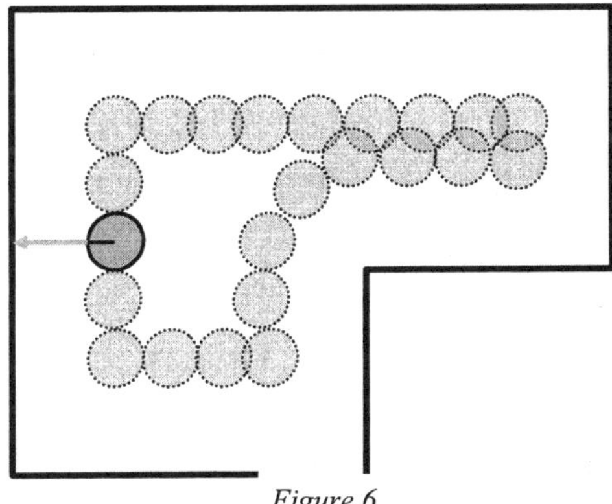

Figure 6

4.2 *Reduction of variables number*

The aim now is to find the way of controlling the combinatory explosion of the rules number. The strategy is to analyze and use for this propose the specific characteristics of the system which is being considered.

Since the number of five linguistics labels for variable suggested at the beginning is likely not to admit any kind of reduction, the easiest option to reduce the computational charge is the reduction of the variables number.

In order to do it, we have considered eliminating the *orientation* variable of the output vector. The idea consist of reducing the data about robot position to coordinates (x, y) in a self-localization process first phase. The *orientation* would be obtained using additional data generated from a posterior exploration maneuver.

Next step, in order to reduce the number of antecedent variables, is to identify a set of variables which must be independent of robot orientation. To start, we have chosen the next option:

The shortest distance of the 12 available ones

This distance can be interpreted as the radio of the maximum circle free of obstacles rounding the robot, as well [11]. Figure 6 shows how the possible robot positions are limited once the value of this variable is known.

For completing the set of used variables as antecedents, we add the two next variables:

The longest distance of the 12 available ones

and

The angle that the two directions corresponding to these distances form

In Figure 7, measures corresponding with different robot positions using a simple square place are indicated. Intuitively, it seems that this set of variables will quite help to determine the robot position in the place area.

A last correction has still to be made. As we have said before, an inconvenient is that during the measurement of distances by ultrasounds, it is relatively frequent that some false measurements appear due to that some signal bounce has been produced. In order to solve this problem, we have corrected the initial idea substituting the value of the longest and shortest distances for the averaged values of three consecutives measures, so introducing a low pass filter in the finally used variable value.

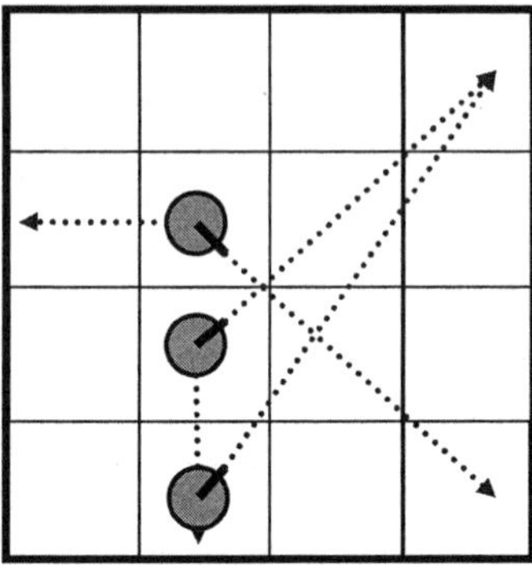

Figure 7

Therefore, the distances vector, corresponded to the input variables, is reduced to the tri-dimensional vector:

$$(d_{max}, d_{min}, ang)$$

And the coordinates vector to a bi-dimensional one:

$$(x, y) .$$

Let D_{max}, D_{min} and ANG the sets of membership functions associated to rules antecedents,

$$D_{max} = \left\{ \mu_{vs}^{max}, \mu_{s}^{max}, \mu_{m}^{max}, \mu_{b}^{max}, \mu_{vb}^{max} \right\},$$
$$D_{min} = \left\{ \mu_{vs}^{min}, \mu_{s}^{min}, \mu_{m}^{min}, \mu_{b}^{min}, \mu_{vb}^{min} \right\},$$
$$ANG = \left\{ \mu_{0}^{ang}, \mu_{60}^{ang}, \mu_{120}^{ang}, \mu_{180}^{ang}, \mu_{240}^{ang}, \mu_{300}^{ang} \right\}$$

Where the set of triangular labels for the distances represented in Figure 5 are kept on using and six labels more also triangular with base of 60° are used for the angle.

Let X and Y the sets of membership functions corresponding to consequents:

$$X = \left\{ \mu_{vs}^{X}, \mu_{s}^{X}, \mu_{m}^{X}, \mu_{b}^{X}, \mu_{vb}^{X} \right\},$$
$$Y = \left\{ \mu_{vs}^{Y}, \mu_{s}^{Y}, \mu_{m}^{Y}, \mu_{b}^{Y}, \mu_{vb}^{Y} \right\}.$$

For every variable, the label domain is chosen in such a way that exactly covers the available training values.

So, the new rules set with which we will work are:

IF (d_{max} IS D_{max}) AND (d_{min} IS D_{min}) AND (ang IS ANG) THEN (x IS X) AND (y IS Y)

We have now a total number of 5*5*6*5*5 = 3750 rules, hardly more reduced number than the one obtained by the initial variables set.

The next step is to use a learning process which permits to assign the suitable weight to rules in order to resultant rules set, with weights non zero, is the desired model of the system.

4.3   Rules weight calculus

The technique used in this work to implement the rules is the Mandani implication with the minimum t-norm and maximun t-conorm [12]. According to this procedure, for a training values vector

$$v_t = (d_{max}, d_{min}, ang, x, y)$$

And for every rule

IF (d_{max} IS D_{max}) AND (d_{min} IS D_{min}) AND (ang IS ANG) THEN (x IS X) AND (y IS Y)

The accomplishment grade of antecedents is

$$W_{antec,t} = \min\left(\mu^{max}(d_{max}), \mu^{min}(d_{min}), \mu^{ang}(ang)\right)$$

While the accomplishment grade of consequents is

$$W_{consec,t} = \min\left(\mu^{X}(x), \mu^{Y}(y)\right).$$

The rule fired factor for this vector is

$$\delta_{i,t} = \min\left(W_{antec}, W_{consec}\right),$$

And the rule weight is obtained by the union of contributions of all fired training values:

$$\delta_i = \max\left(\delta_{i,t}\right).$$

5 Experimentation results

From the initial 3760 rules, using the *trace* obtained during the Exploration phase as the set of training data and following the described procedure, a set of 280 rules with weight non zero has been obtained. This set of rules is the desired model of the specific integrated place-sensor system that we have used for experiment.

For every position (x_t, y_t), a possibility matrix has been obtained according to the expresion:

$$POS(x, y) = \sum\left(\min\left(W_{antec}, W_{consec}\right)\right) * \delta_i .$$

That is, every grid point (x,y) has been assigned to the sum of contributions of every fired rules in that point.

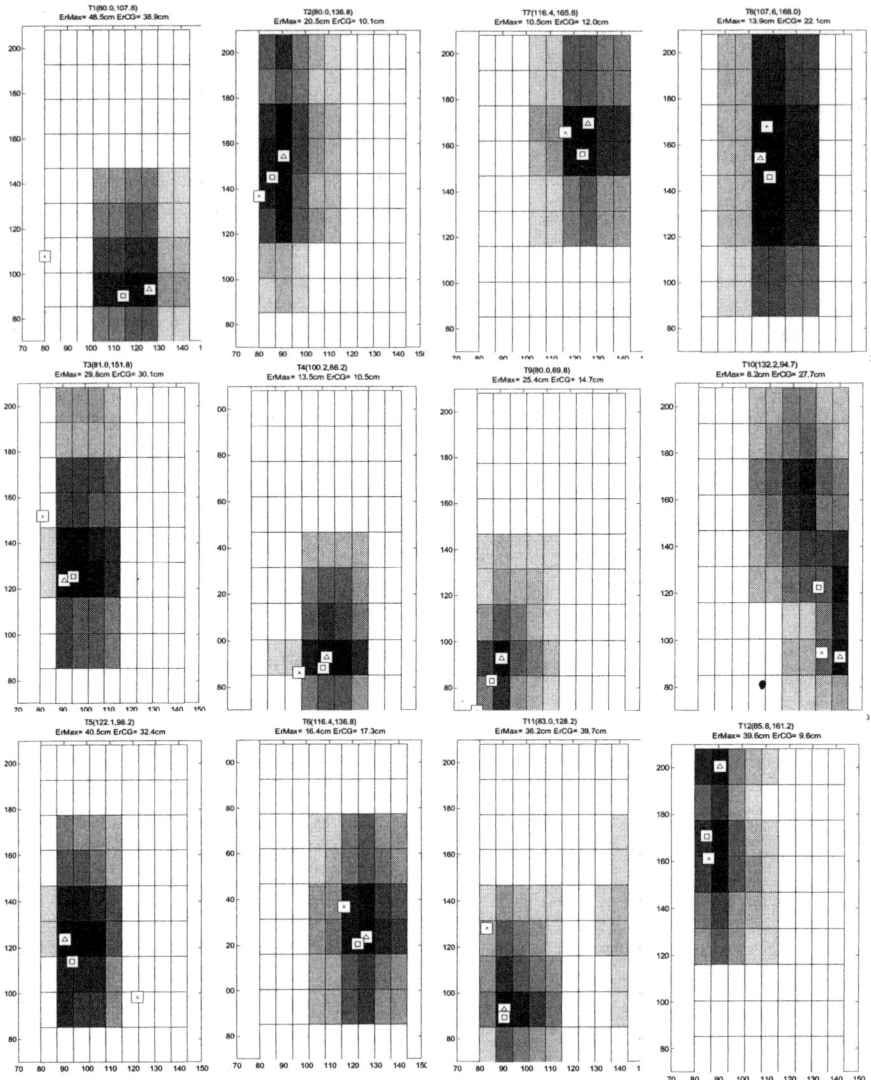

Figure 8. Maps of possibility obtained in different robot positions

The sequence of figures in Figure 8 shows the *Possibility maps* obtained as a result of the model application when distances corresponding to a set of 12 positions in the Navigating *trace* has been introduced to it. In every figure, the robot is represented by cross, the triangle symbolizes the maximum of possibility value and the square the gravity center of maximums.

6 Conclusion

A proposal to create a place-sensor system model based on the use of a fuzzy rules set has been presented. Some experimental results with a real robot has been obtained, which show the viability of the proposed proposal. It has been proved that fuzzy logic is a useful tool to represent the uncertainty inherent in a system like this. In this case, fuzzy logic has been used successfully to fusion information obtained from different samples, to calculate the weights of a set of rules in the Exploration mode and to calculate *Possibility* values when estimating the robot position in the Navigating mode.

In next works, we will propose ourselves to explore the evolution of the possibility map following the AMR movement. Furthermore, we also propose ourselves to study new learning methods exploiting the relations between this type of rules set and neuronal nets.

Acknowledgements

This work has been supported by the "Plan Nacional de I+D" of spanish MCYT as part of the project TIC 2000-1420.

References

[1] Berthold M. & Hand D.J., *Intelligent data analysis.* Springer-Verlag, 1999.

[2] Borenstein J. & Everett H.R. & Feng L., *Navigating Mobile Robots.* A. K. Peters, 1996.

[3] Dudek G. & Jenkin M., *Computational Principles of Mobile Robotics*, Cambridge University Press, 2000.

[4] Elfes A., Sonar based real world mapping and navigation, *IEEE Journal of robotics and automation,* Vol. RA-3, N° 3, June 1987.

[5] Fox D. & Burgard W. & Dellaert F. & Thrun S., "Montecarlo Localization: Efficient Position estimation for Mobile Robots", *Proc. of the Sixteenth National Conference on Artificial Intelligence (AAAI-99)*, pp 343-9, Orlando, Florida, 1999.

[6] Gutmann J. & Schlegel C., *AMOS: Comparison of Scan Matching Approaches for Self-Localization in Indoor Environments*, 1st Euromicro Workshop on Advanced Mobile Robots (EUROBOT'96), pp 61-67, Kaiserslautern, GERMANY, October 9-11,1996.

[7] Kosko B., *Fuzzy engineering*, Prentice Hall, 1997.

[8] Leonard J.J. & Durrant-Whyte H.F, *Directed Sonar Sensing for Mobile Robot Navigation,* Kluwer Academia Publishers, 1992.

[9] Nehmzov U., *Mobile Robotics. A Practical Introduction.* Springer-Verlag, 2000.

[10] Ruiz A. & Triviño G. & Crespo J.C., Zonas de Confirmación de Ruta en autolocalización de robots móviles autónomos (in spanish), Actas de la IX Conferencia de la Asociación Española para la Inteligencia Artificial CAEPIA-TTIA 2001, Vol I, pp 695-704, Noviembre 2001.

[11] Triviño G. & Ruiz A., A Mobile Robot World Model Using Fuzzy Labels, *Proceedings of the Eighth International Conference on Information Processing and Management of Uncertainty in Knowledge-based Systems IPMU*, Vol. 3, pp. 1634-1639, Julio 2000.

[12] Yager R.R. & Filev D.P., *Essentials of fuzzy modeling and control*, Willey and Sons, 1994.

3. Computer Vision

Artificial Intelligence Research and Development
I. Aguiló et al. (Eds.)
IOS Press, 2003

Elastic Matching and Retrieval of IVUS Images Using Contextual Information

Jaume Amores[†], Petia Radeva[†]
[†]*Computer Vision Center, Dept. Informàtica, UAB, Bellaterra, Spain*
jaume@cvc.uab.es

Abstract. We present a registration and retrieval algorithm of medical images. We use rich descriptors based on both local and global (contextual) information, and at the same time we use a cooperative-iterative strategy in order to get a good set of correspondences as well as a good final transformation. We focus on a novel type of images for registration: IntraVascular UltraSound (IVUS) images, a promising technique of analyzing the coronary vessels. Registration is performed as a first step towards retrieval, and we present quantitative results on an IVUS database of images.

There is a wide range of applications of medical image registration and we refer to books such as [9] for a list. We apply registration to IntraVascular UltraSound images (IVUS), a powerful imaging modality for analysis and diagnosis of coronary vessels. The image is obtained inserting a catheter along the coronary vessel, with a transducer on its tip. The transducer emits ultrasonic pulses as it rotates and the tissues around the vessel reject part of them, allowing the generation of an image tangential to the vessel that displays the different types of tissues and other biological structures lying around the vessel.

We refer to [3] for a comprehensive study of IVUS. The structure and composition of atherosclerotic plaques play important roles in coronary artery disease study and in the outcomes of coronary interventions, hence a system that accurately retrieves these cases is interesting.

In figure 1 we can see an IVUS image with the catheter in its center represented by a circle with high intensity and a point (the tip) in its center. Around the catheter there is the blood in the lumen of the vessel. In this picture there are two kinds of biological structures: the adventitia tissue, represented by a big region of high intensity and fine texture; and two calcium plaques, represented by thin regions of intensity equal or greater than the adventitia and with shadow windows (dark regions) beyond it. The shadow beyond calcium plaque is critical for recognizing it. It is produced by the high echogenic impedance of calcium which makes the ultrasound wave to be rejected almost entirely and hence without achieving the part beyond it.

Registration of IVUS images has the same range of applications as in the rest of modalities, but in concrete we use it as a first step towards performing retrieval. The IVUS technique produces images with quite particularities and noise, which makes it an interesting case to study. Creating a retrieval system of IVUS images is a good way to analyze IVUS images automatically. Although there are a huge number of works in the area of Registration and Retrieval of Medical Images ([4], [9]), we do not know previous approaches neither to the problem of matching IVUS images between them nor to the problem of retrieving IVUS images from a database of IVUS images.

Given a pair of images I_1 and I_2, registration consists on finding the structures analog in both

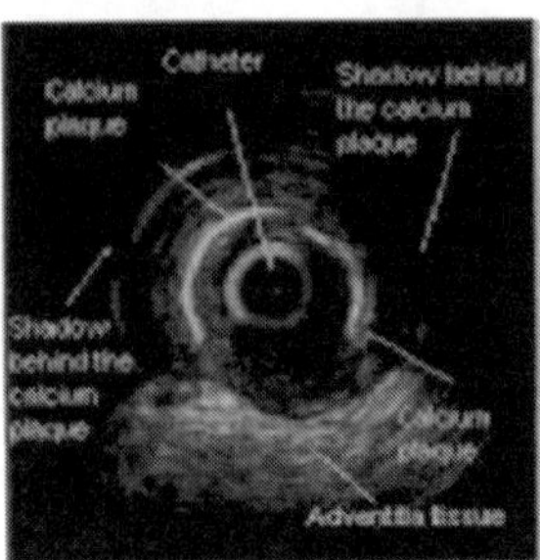

Figure 1: IVUS image with different structures

images and computing a transformation of the coordinates of I_1 that aligns its structures to the analogs ones of image I_2. For doing so we take point mapping as general structure of our algorithm, see [7] for a definition of this approach and [1] for a detailed explanation of the steps. In general registration algorithms can be classified by the type of transformation they perform: simple rigid transformations consisting of rotation and translation, or more complex elastic transformations such as the ones achieved by variational approaches, which do not enforce any form on the transformation while still preserving the topology of the object.

Many works on medical image registration are focused on rigid parts where the tissues are constrained by a skeleton behind them, for example in brain MRIs, or radiographies. In these cases simple rigid transforms are suitable. Medical images of non-rigid bodies such as coronary vessels present features quite different as they do not have any characteristic spatial configuration forced by the squeleton. Given the high variability inter and intra subject of those medical images, we perform elastic matching following a variational approach for computing the transformation.

Opposite to many works on medical images such as brain MRIs, which take a grid of characteristic points over all the image, we only extract a small set of characteristic points from the boundaries of the salient regions we want to match together. This approach makes the algorithm faster and avoids the necessity of employing a multi-resolution scheme. Given the type of images we deal with, we must choose quite a rich set of descriptors which not only take into account the local statistics near the characteristic point (local descriptors) but also the context of the point (global or contextual descriptors) that give information of how other structures are located around the point and where the point is located at its own structure. Graphs are the most traditional tool for taking into account the context of some object. However, they are very dependent on an accurate segmentation, and this makes them little robust. We instead make use of the so-called correlograms (see [5]) in order to take account of the context of points, extending the shape-context descriptor of Belongie et al [5] to cope with gray level images. Correlograms in 2-D allow us to match the couple of images coarsely coping with the spatial distribution of structures, but have the draw-back of including some information about the 2-D shape of the contours not interesting in our case. Thus we extend the contextual information using shape invariant 1-D correlograms after a coarse alignment [2]. The use of these two types of context descriptors as well as local descriptors make our feature space quite rich.

Yet, the set of correspondences obtained with this set of descriptors is not enough to compute directly the final transformation based on them. As indicated by Brown [7], whenever there is little independent information to compute the correspondences directly, it is good to use a cooperative-iterative algorithm, which consists on using the transformation to give information about a new set of correspondences, which at the same time will produce a new transformation and so on, iterating the algorithm. We use a feedback scheme similar to the one used by Rangarajan et al. in [8], but extended to deal with gray level images and without an annealing framework, as the combination of contextual and local descriptors give us enough information to seek for an accurate transformation in a more straightforward manner. Finally we perform registration as a first step towards making retrieval, comparing the homologous regions matched and the degree of matching for computing the distance between a pair of images.

The article is organized as follows: section 2 describes the registration method, section 3 describes the retrieval method, section 4 shows the results obtained and the paper finishes with conclusions and future work.

1 Registration method

Coronary vessels present all their structures of interest around the interface between lumen and adventitia, what we call the wall of the vessel. Thus, in our case the set of characteristic points to be extracted from each image will be placed along this boundary. We first extract the catheter of the image, apply an anisotropic diffusion [11] of the resulting IVUS image and let a snake grow from its interior to the wall of the vessel. Finally, we sample the boundary points and this will be our set of characteristic points. The next step will be to extract the feature vectors associated to each characteristic point.

1.1 Feature space

We compute local feature vectors associated to each characteristic point and then based on them compute 2-D correlograms and 1-D correlograms [1, 2]. Local feature vectors aim at characterizing the biological structure where the point lies, whereas correlograms will put the points into context. Summarizing, associated to each characteristic point x_i we are going to use three different feature vectors: our local feature vector l_i, a 2-D correlogram v_i, and an 1-D correlogram w_i. We will now describe each of them in turn.

In IVUS images, regions such as calcium plaque are characterized by the gray level they have inside them and the gray level they cause outside them because of their echogenic impedance. Thus a good descriptor of the structure the point is at, is the gray level profile along the line perpendicular to the wall from the point towards the outside part of the vessel. We measure a set of statistics over this profile and its first derivative which conform our local feature vector [1].

Correlograms consist of partitioning the image in cells distributed radially around its origin, which is the current point we are describing. In fig. 2-a we can see a correlogram, a partition of the image in sectors or cells, each one accounting for some part of the image at a specified range of angles and radius, taking as origin a characteristic point x_i. The radial length of the cells grows with logarithmical rate from the origin towards outside, giving more importance to the near context of the point.

In every cell of the correlogram, we compute a statistic such as the mean over the local

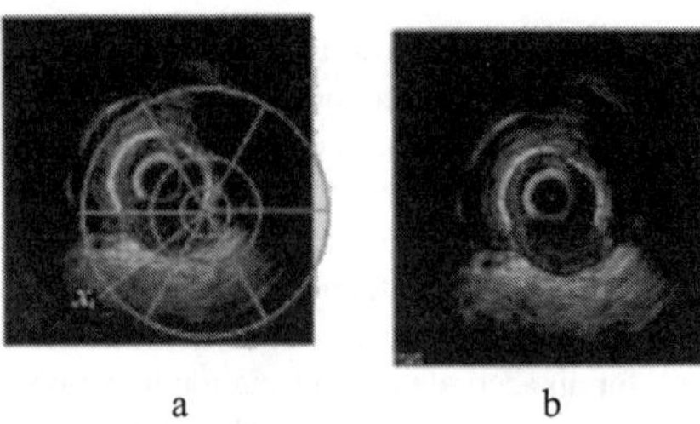

a　　　　　　　　　　b

Figure 2: 2-d Correlogram with 6 intervals of angles and 3 intervals of radius (a), and 1-d Correlogram (b)

feature vectors of the points that lie inside the cell. Let v_i be the 2-D correlogram associated to x_i. Let $\{x_{u_1}, x_{u_2}, \ldots, x_{u_t}\}$ be the characteristic points which lie in the u cell of v_i. We take the local feature vectors associated to these characteristic points: $\{l_{u_1}, l_{u_2}, \ldots, l_{u_t}\}$ and compute a mean over each of their characteristics. Let every local feature vector l_k have d characteristics: $l_k = (l_{k1}, l_{k2}, \ldots, l_{kd})\ \forall k$. Let $c_{uj} = mean(\{l_{u_1 j}, l_{u_2 j}, \ldots, l_{u_t j}\})$, the mean over the j characteristic of the local feature vectors $\{l_{u_1}, l_{u_2}, \ldots, l_{u_t}\}$. If we have r cells for every correlogram, we can express the 2-D correlogram associated to the characteristic point x_i as $v_i = (c_{11}, c_{12}, \ldots, c_{1d}, c_{21}, c_{22}, \ldots, c_{2d}, \ldots, c_{r1}, c_{r2}, \ldots, c_{rd})$.

The 1-D correlogram is a division in cells but now of the contour curve where we have our characteristic points (see fig. 2-b). Let w_i be the 1-D correlogram for the characteristic point x_i. We can express the contour curve as a function $\varphi : [0, 1) \rightarrow \mathbb{R}^2$ depending on an internal parameter $s \in [0, 1)$: $\varphi(s) = (x, y)$. We take as intern parameter s an approximation to the arc-length of the curve, and such that $\varphi(0) = x_i$. Then we take as cells of the 1-D correlogram a set of intervals $I_u \subset [0, 1)\forall u, \bigcup I_u = [0, 1), I_u \bigcap I_v = \emptyset \leftrightarrow u \neq v$. This correlogram is not based on the local feature vectors directly but on a classification result of the characteristic points using these local feature vectors. For all the points that fall inside one cell of a correlogram w_i, we count how many of these points belong to the same type of structure and this is the value associated to this cell.

The 1-D correlogram does not take into account the particular shape peculiarities of two structures to be aligned. Once we have put the structures close by using the 2-D correlogram, which take account of the 2-D distribution of structures, we finish an accurate matching of points from two analog structures by using the 1-D correlogram. This descriptor accounts mainly for the position of the point along the boundary of the structure it belongs to, saying intuitively if this point is at one extremum (and in which extremum it is) or if it is near the center of the structure. Thus extremum points from both structures are matched together, central points together, and so on.

1.2　Iterative scheme and final registration algorithm

The registration algorithm follows the point mapping paradigm [7]: extract a set of characteristic points or landmarks from both images, based on a set of descriptors associated to them, compute the distance in the feature space between every pair of landmarks and based on this distance obtain a set of correspondences from landmarks in the first image (the *query image*) to landmarks in the second image (the *complementary image*) that globally minimizes the distance. The latter is an assignment optimization algorithm, and can be resolved by the hungarian's method. Based on this set of correspondences we produce a transformation of the query image onto the complementary image. We make use of Thin Plate Splines (TPS) [6], which allows different degrees of approximation [5], making the transformation more coarse and global at initial steps and refining it locally in later steps.

We apply first a coarse alignment using as feature vectors only the 2-D correlograms, which accounts globally for the 2-D distribution of structures and put analog structures close enough. After this coarse alignment, we perform a more accurate alignment allowing more local and fine deformations. The second more accurate alignment is performed based on a combination of 1-d correlograms and local feature vectors, and restricting the mapped points not to lie far away from mapped positions given by the coarse alignment. 1-d correlograms are not so noisy as 2-d correlograms, but are only appropriate after a global alignment achieved by the use of the 2-d correlograms. Let I_1 be the query image and I_2 be the complementary. For any pair $x_i \in I_1, y_j \in I_2$, the distance between them is computed as $d_{class} + d(w_i, w_j)$, where the distance $d(w_i, w_j)$ is the χ^2 distance (see [5]) between the 1-D correlograms of both points, and d_{class} is infinite if both points do not belong to the same type of structure (class), and 0 if they do. By adding d_{class} we are restricting the correspondences to match always points belonging to the same structure.

Both transformations, the global and coarse first transformation and the more accurate second transformation are obtained by a cooperative and iterative algorithm [7] for obtaining a reliable set of correspondences based on correspondences that are not free of irregularities, and at the same time allowing an accurate final alignment. The idea of cooperation between neighbor points is based on the fact that if one point x_i is matched with y_i, a neighbor point x_{i+1} of x_i should not be matched with a point y_j too far away from y_i. Let a couple of points $x_i \in I_1$ and $y_j \in I_2$, and let its distance in the feature space be d_{ij}. We have such a distance for every possible couple of points. After obtaining an initial set of correspondences based on these distances, we make a transformation by TPS. Let $f(x_i)$ be the mapping of x_i by the TPS. We recompute the distance between every couple of points $(x_i \in I_1, y_j \in I_2)$ as $d_{ij} + \alpha \| f(x_i) - y_j \|$. With these new distances we compute a new set of correspondences that produce a new transformation and this is iterated several steps. The TPS do not allow two neighbor points x_{i+1} of x_i to be mapped far away from each other. Thus, by adding to the set of distances the term $\alpha \| f(x_i) - y_j \|$ for the point x_i and $\alpha \| f(x_{i+1}) - y_j \|$ for the point x_{i+1}, we are biasing both points towards the same region of I_2. The parameter α indicates how much we rely on the last transformation. If the last transformation is very accurate, we take as α a high value, restricting the corresponding points $y_j \in I_2$ to be near the mapped points $f(x_i)$. Thus, as the process makes the transformations better, we must increase this parameter through the successive iterations, beginning with a small value. Also the regularization degree of the TPS becomes smaller as the set of correspondences is better, as a high regularization is only needed to approximate coarsely noisy correspondences. Thus we decrease the regularization through the successive iterations.

Both types of correlograms depend on the spatial distribution of the characteristic points. As the spatial distribution of the points become modified by the successive mappings, we must recompute these correlograms through successive iterations of the algorithm.

2   Retrieval method

The registration step gives us a transformation T function which maps every point x of I_1 to the domain $\Omega \subset \mathbb{R}^2$ of I_2. From this transformation we must obtain a correspondence function $\phi : \{1, 2, \ldots, n\} \rightarrow \{1, 2, \ldots, m\}$, where $\{1, 2, \ldots, n\}$ are the indexes of the characteristic points $\{x_1, x_2, \ldots, x_n\}$ of I_1; and $\{1, 2, \ldots, m\}$ are the indexes of the characteristic points $\{y_1, y_2, \ldots, y_m\}$ of I_2. $\phi(i)$ must assign one index i to only one index j, but not necessarily all the indexes $i \in \{1, 2, \ldots, n\}$ must be assigned because we allow outliers not to be matched to any point (see [1] for an explanation about how we deal with outliers). This function is computed by assigning to x_i the point from $\{y_1, y_2, \ldots, y_m\}$ that lies more close to its mapped position $T(x_i)$. This is achieved through the hungarian's algorithm, the assignment method used before in the registration, but now taking as distance measures simply the euclidean distance between mapped points in $\mathbb{R}^2$ and destination points $\{y_1, y_2, \ldots, y_m\}$.

Given the correspondence function ϕ computed, we compute the similarity between images I_1 and I_2 based on the feature vectors of the characteristic points matched. This similarity computation is the key to performing the retrieval. To be more precise let $\{x_1, x_2, \ldots, x_n\}$ be the set of characteristic points from I_1 and $\{y_1, y_2, \ldots, y_m\}$ be the set of characteristic points from I_2. Let f_{1i} be some feature vector (such as the local feature vector) associated to the i-th characteristic point of the image I_1, x_i. Let f_{2j} be the same kind of feature vector associated to the j-th characteristic point of the image I_2, y_j. The contribution of this type f of feature vector to the distance between both images is $D_f = \sum_{i \in M_1} \left\| f_{1i} - f_{2\phi(i)} \right\|$, where $M_1 \subset \{1, 2, \ldots, n\}$ is the subset of the indexes $\{1, 2, \ldots, n\}$ associated to the characteristic points from I_1 that have any matching in ϕ, i.e. indexes of points which are not considered outliers.

As explained before we have three types of feature vectors: local feature vectors, l, 2-d correlograms v and 1-d correlograms w. Local feature vectors account for the class of the region where the point lies, 2-d correlograms account for a distribution in the plane of the different regions around the current point, and 1-d correlograms account for shape invariant distributions of the regions along the boundary of the vessel, which allow mainly to take into account characteristics such as the length of the calcium plaque regions where the points are located, as well as the position of the point along the region: in one extremum, in the middle or in the center.

We let each of these types of feature vectors to have its constribution distance to the total distance computed between the pair of images I_1 and I_2. We add also into this distance the geometric distance between the mapped points of I_1 and their corresponding ones of I_2, in order to know if the two images have been allowed to match closely. This distance can be expressed as $D_{geom} = \sum_{i=1}^{n} \left\| T(x_i) - y_{\phi(i)} \right\|$. Finally we add a contribution from the energy of the deformation. High energy means a great degree of deformation for matching both images, indicating that the matching is not very natural. In summary, we have as distance between I_1 and I_2 a weighted sum of individual contributions: $D = \alpha_l D_l + \alpha_v D_v + \alpha_w D_w + \alpha_{geom} D_{geom} + \alpha_E D_E$, where D_l is the distance due to the local feature vector and α_l its weight, D_v is the distance due to the 2-d correlogram, $alpha_v$ its weight, D_w is the distance due to the 1-d correlogram , $alpha_w$ its weight; and the other two distances and their α parameters take into account respectively the geometric distance and the energy of the deformation, and their weights. This set of weights is adjusted so that the retrieval result is optimal.

3　Results

We show first the necessity of using contextual as well as local information, and the necessity of using as contextual information not only the 2-D correlograms but also 1-D correlograms. Then we provide quantitative results on retrieval of IVUS images using our approach.

In fig. 3 we can see a first couple of IVUS images with two calcium plaques, one on the left and the other one on the right. The IVUS image of 3-(a) corresponds to the query image, and the IVUS image of 3-(b) to its complementary image. In fig. 3-(c) we show the anisotropic diffusion of the query image and superposed in red the boundary of the vessel from which we extract the characteristic points. In fig. 3-(d) we show the anisotropic diffusion of the complementary image and superposed in red the boundary of the vessel from which we extract the characteristic points. In fig. 7 we see the final set of correspondences.

In fig. 4 we compare the result of the first coarse transformation using contextual information (2-D correlograms) and using only local information (our local feature vectors). We show transformation results on the anisotropic diffusion of the images because it is visually more clear. In 4-(a) we show the anisotropic diffusion of the query transformed by the coarse mapping. In 4-(b) we show the complementary image with the edges of the transformed query image superposed in red. We can see how both calcium plaques are mapped close, as well as the adventitia tissue. In 4-(c) and 4-(d) we show the same coarse transformation using only local feature vectors. We can see that one of the calcium plaques has not been mapped closed to any of the calcium plaques of the complementary image.

In fig. 5 we see how the set of correspondences using only a 2-D correlogram is more noisy than using a combination of 1-D correlogram and local feature vectors.

In fig. 6 we compare the result of the transformation obtained in the second step using 1-D correlograms and including the classification information by the distance d_{class} (see previous section), with a transformation obtained by the same algorithm but using 2-D correlograms and including also the classification information. As can be seen the transformation using 2-D correlograms is more inaccurate and produce an irregular warping with the noise seen in the images. The irregular warping is due to be using a low regularization degree of the TPS based on a too noisy set of correspondences for such a small degree of regularization. Finally we see results for another couple in fig. 8.

Now we give a series of quantitative results of our registration and retrieval system. Our database of IVUS images, collected for testing our system, comprise 168 images classified in two classes: images of diseased coronary vessels having calcium plaque and images of healthy vessels without any calcium plaque. Images with calcium plaque are further characterized by using a set of global descriptors whose values are assigned manually by physicians to each of the images, so that a complete dissimilarity measure between each pair of images can be computed based on a human's expert criteria. The characteristics used to discriminate among vessels with calcium are the length of the calcium plaque, the degree of embracement of the plaque around the vessel, the number of plaques and the thickness of the plaques. With this set of characteristics every image of a diseased vessel has a vector of characteristics assigned to it. We then compute the distance between every pair of images of diseased vessels as the euclidean of the vectors assigned to each of them. Although we are mainly interested in an accurate retrieval of images of diseased vessels, due to the clinical importance of determining the extent of the plaque, its disposition and thickness; we also want our system to differentiate among diseased and healthy images. Thus half the set of images are from diseased vessels and the other half from healthy ones. We put the manual distance between any

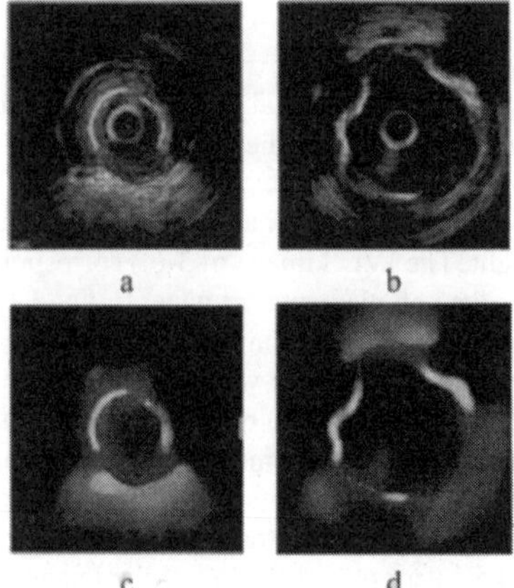

Figure 3: Query and its complementary IVUS (a)-(b). Their anisotropic diffusion results (c)-(d)

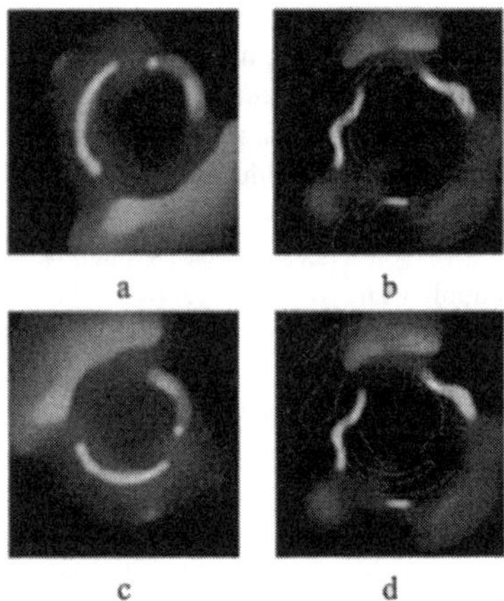

Figure 4: Coarse alignment (first step of the algorithm) using first contextual information (a)-(b), and then only local information (c)-(d)

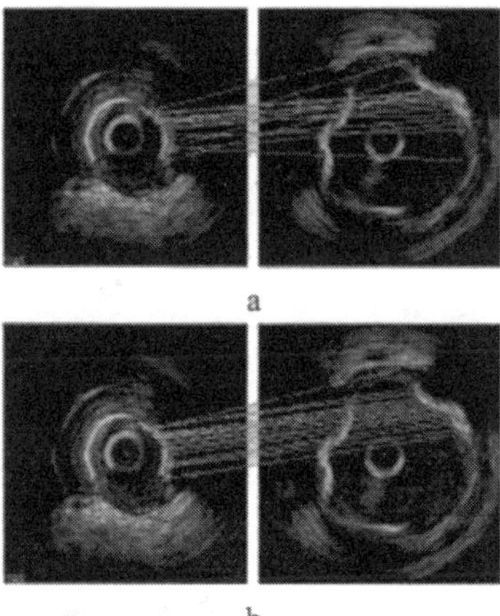

Figure 5: Correspondences with only 2-D correlograms (a) and correspondences with 1-D correlograms and local feature vectors (b)

image from a diseased vessel and any image from a healthy image to a much higher value than any possible distance between two images of the same category. As we are not interested in discriminating between different IVUS images from healthy vessels we put the distance between every pair from the set of healthy vessel images to zero.

For assessing the rate of success of the retrieval system we use the physician-based dissimilarity measure explained above and see how close the automatic dissimilarity measure is to the assigned one. We present to the system a query image and use our retrieval similarity measure to assign a distance from every image from the database to the query. Then the images are sorted in increasing order of similarity, and the first most similar K images are presented to the user in order of similarity. We want to know what is the value of K for which an image very similar to the query is included. Let I_i be the query and I_j the complementary. We regard I_j as being very similar to the query if the physician-based dissimilarity measure $g(i,j)$ between both images is below a threshold. In our case this threshold is 1, as we have observed that below this threshold the similarity between the images is quite high. In average the value of K obtained through this procedure is 3. For $K = 2$ the percentage of times that one such image is included is 71%. In fig. 9 we can see three examples of retrieval. On the right hand we have the query image and on the left hand the three images most similar to the query. The weights obtained for the different distance components are: $\alpha_l = 0.15, \alpha_v = 0.6, \alpha_w = 0.05, \alpha_E = 0.14, \alpha_{geom} = 0$.

The frequency of times in which the first image selected is from the same category (diseased or healthy) than the query is 87.5%.

4   Conclusions and Future Work

We apply registration to a novel type of medical images, IntraVascular UltraSound (IVUS) images, images of highly elastic bodies and quite difficult to analyze. These types of images need of a rich feature space, using not only local information around the point but also

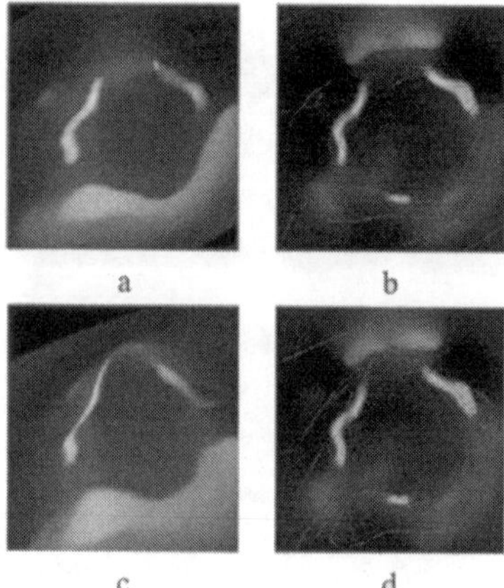

Figure 6: Second transformation using first in 1-D correlograms (a)-(b), and then 2-D correlograms (c)-(d)

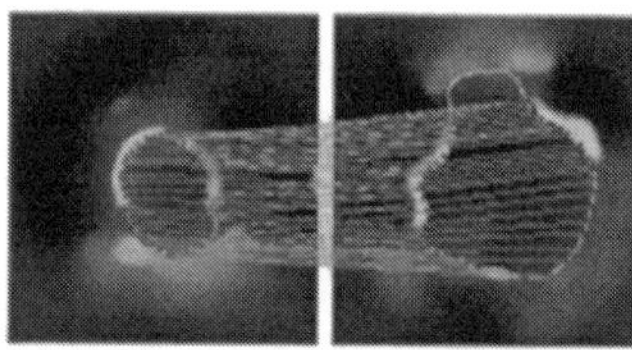

Figure 7: Final set of correspondences of the first pair of images

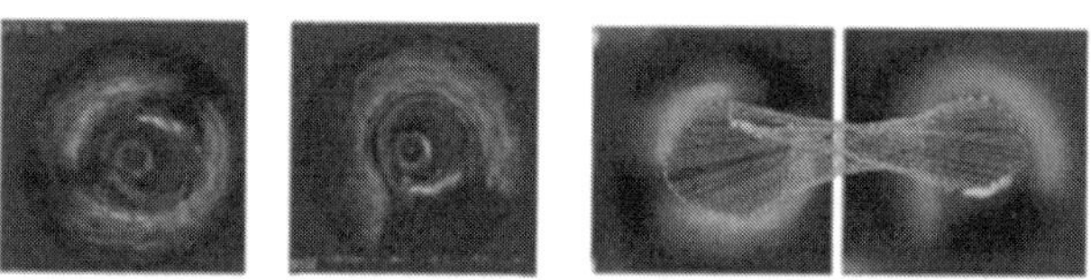

Figure 8: Query (a), complementary (b), and final set of correspondences on their anisotropic diffusions (c)

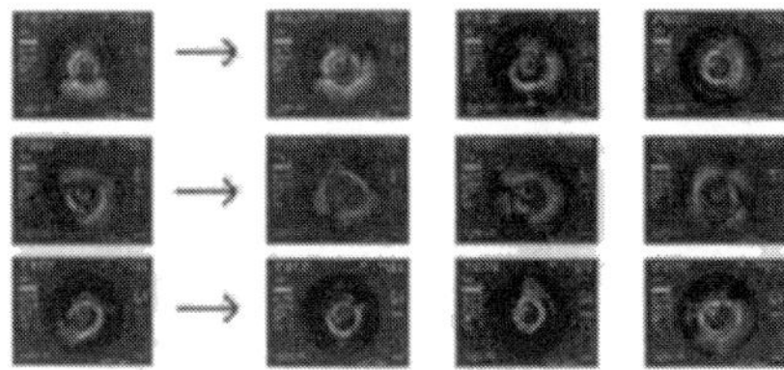

Figure 9: Retrieval example

providing context or global information relative to this point. Instead of using graphs as a traditional technique, we extend the work of Belongie et al. [5] using a modification of their correlograms in order to cope with gray level images, and adding a second contextual information, shape invariant 1-d correlograms. We use these rich set of descriptors along with a cooperative-iterative scheme similar to the one used by Rangarajan et al. [8], but designed to cope with gray level images, and without the deterministic annealing framework they use, as the combination of contextual and local information give us enough information to seek for an accurate transformation in a more straightforward manner. The combination of rich descriptors, a variational approach such as TPS and the use of an iterative-cooperative scheme give our algorithm robustness as well as accuracy, the result not depending on accurate classifications of all the points.

As future work we must first of all include textural information in the computation of the local information, as we believe it fundamental in order to increase the richness of the descriptors and include more tissues. We want to work on a retrieval system where first the set of possible images to match the query be filtered using rough descriptors. Then the registration would be done between a small set of images and the query, using a simple measure as the one explained above.

We are also investigating other variational approaches, apart from TPS, as TPS has the drawback that does not make difference between an irregular set of correspondences and a set of correspondences which lead to a high deformation of the object. We refer to [1] for a detailed explanation.

Acknowledgments

This work is supported by Ministerio de Ciencia y Tecnologia of Spain, grant TIC2000-1635-C04-04

References

[1] J.Amores, P. Radeva. *Elastic Matching Retrieval in Medical Images using contextual information.* CVC. Tech Report September 22nd 2002.

[2] J.Amores, P. Radeva. *Non-Rigid Registration of Vessel Structures in IVUS Images.* IbPRIA 2003. Accepted

[3] Boston Scientific Europe. *Beyond Aniography. Intravascular Ultrasound: State of the Art.* August 22nd 1998. XX Congress of the ESC. Vol 1.

[4] J.B. Antoine-Mantz and M.A. Viergever. *A survey of medical image registration.* Medical Image Analysis (1998) Vol. 2, num. 1, pp 1-37.

[5] S.Belongie, J. Malik, and J.Puzicha. *Shape Matching and object recognition using shape contexts.* Technical Report UCB//CSD-00-1128, UC Berkeley, 2001.

[6] F. L. Bookstein. *Principal warps: Thin-plate splines and the decomposition of deformations.* IEEE TPAMI, 11(6):567585, June 1989.

[7] L. Brown. *A Survey of Image Registration Techniques.* ACM Computing Surveys, 24(4): 325-376, 1992.

[8] H. Chui and A. Rangarajan. *A new algorithm for non-rigid point matching.* Proc. CVPR, 2000, Vol. 2, pp. 40-51.

[9] Hajnal, Hill and Hawkes. *Medical Image Registration*, The Biomedical Engineering Series, 2001.

[10] A. Pentland and S. Sclaroff. *Closed-form solutions for physically based shape modelling and recognition.* IEEE. TPAMI 13(7):715-729.

[11] J.Weickert. *Anisotropic Diffusion in Image Processing.* PhD. Thesis, Kaiserslautern University, 1996.

Artificial Intelligence Research and Development
I. Aguiló et al. (Eds.)
IOS Press, 2003

Robust segmentation of scenes with colour mark

Pilar Arques, Mar Pujol, Ramón Rizo

Departamento de Ciencia de la Computación e Inteligencia Artificial. University of Alicante

{arques,mar,rizo}@dccia.ua.es

Abstract

Image segmentation is the first step for pattern recognition. Our work is based in Markov Random Fields and its associated energy function to find an optimal image segmentation applying the simulated annealing algorithm. Thus, using this segmentation as a starting point, in a future work we propose to recognize all the objects in the image. The images to recognize contain traffic signals, to help in mobile robot guiding.

Key words: Segmentation, Markov Random Fields, Simulated Annealing, Energy Function.

1 Introduction

The shape of an object can be described either in terms of its boundaries or in terms of the region that it occupies. Shape representation based on boundary information requires image edge detection and following. Region-based shape representation requires image segmentation in several homogeneous regions.

Image regions are expected to have homogeneous characteristics of intensity, texture, ... which are different in each region. These characteristics form the feature vectors that are used to discriminate one region from each other.

The image segmentation is a process which divides a scene in a set of disjoint subsets; we want to use these segmentation a step in object recognition, and these recognition will be used for mobile robot guiding, thus our work is focused in indoor and outdoor images with a traffic signal.

To use the image segmentation as a first step for object recognition we need that this segmentation divides the image in well-defined and perfectly distinguishable regions.

Object recognition is a wide concept and is applied to several fields of investigation. We are focused in objects which are useful in a mobile robot guiding, objects like traffic signals.In a future work we will try to recognize these signals.

The robustness of the model based on Markov Random Fields if verified applying it to segmentation of outdoor and indoor scenes taken during the navigation of an autonomous vehicle.

Section 2 introduces the color model, section 3 deals with the segmentation algorithm: Scaling, Pre-segmentation MPMT, Post-processing MPMT, Markov Random Fields, section 4 shows the results obtained, for indoor and outdoor images and finally, section 5 explains the conclusions and the future work.

2   The Colour Model

The red, green and blue (RGB) [3], [7] colour model is an additive model; the intensities of the primaries colours are added to produce the other colours. We could present this model with the unitary cubre which define the Red, Green and Blue axis. The origin of the axes is the black colour and the vertex in coordinates $(1,1,1)$ is the white colour. The cube vertex are the primary colours and rest vertex are the complementary colour for each primary colour.

Each colour point in the cube boundaries could be represented as a set of three coordinates (R,G,B) where these coordinates have values from 0 to 1. Thus, colour C_λ is represented in RGB components as:

$$C_\lambda = R\mathbf{R} + G\mathbf{G} + B\mathbf{B} \tag{1}$$

The main diagonal of the cube, with equal amounts of each primary colour, represents the gray levels: black is $(0,0,0)$ and white is $(1,1,1)$.

In our algorithm we calculate de distance between region, the measure of the distance between region is made based on the intensity of the pixels in the image. So two pixels are from a same region if their intensities are similar, and two pixels are from different regions if their intensities are disparate.

We choose the RGB colour model because its geometric representation is a cube and we can measure the colour difference between two pixels using the Euclidean distance.

$$D(x_{(r,g,b)}, y_{(r,g,b)}) = \\ \sqrt{(y_r - x_r)^2 + (y_g - x_g)^2 + (y_b - x_b)^2} \tag{2}$$

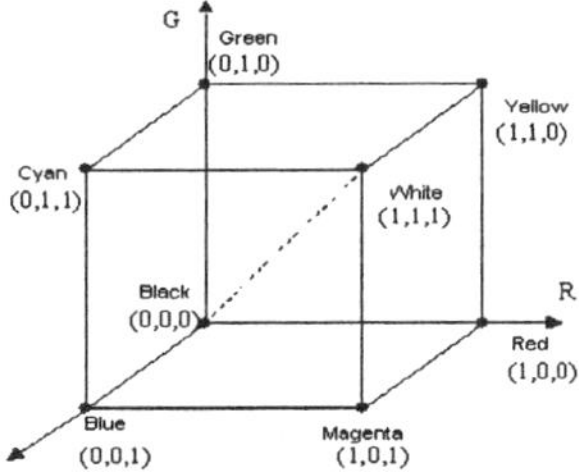

Figure 1: RGB colour model

Thus, we consider two pixels are part of the same region when the distance between them are less than a threshold.

There are a great influence of brightness in RGB colour model to calculate the closeness or the distance between two colours. There is no problem in our images because we want to join intensities with the same brightness or darkness, since as a traffic signal is situated in a visible zone and with bright colours to avoid the influence of luminosity or the absence of luminosity.

3   Segmentation Algorithm

The segmentation algorithm which we based on applies the next processes:

- Image scaling.

- Pre-segmentation MPMT.

- Post-processing MPMT.

- Markov Random Fields.

    - Construction of the adjacency graph.

    - Application of the energy function to joint or disjoint regions. (Simulated Annealing Algorithm).

3.1   Image scaling

Due to the temporal cost of working with real images, we deal with scaled images. The scale consists in the elimination of columns and rows, depending on a scale factor. Thus we reduce both the original size and the detail level of the image.

We are dealing with a kind of images for which is not necessary to have a complete knowledge of the objects at a high detail, we really need to perfectly define the objects using our segmentation, and we gain this goal even scaling the images and loosing some non-significant information of the object.

3.2 Pre-segmentation MPMT

The MPMT algorithm [8] labels an image using a single scan process, providing an oversegmentation of the image. This algorithm divides the image into subareas (2x2) (called windows) assigning one of the 12 partition modes to each window. The joint or disjoint of two pixels to form a single region depends on the distance in intensity of these pixels. If the distance is less than a given threshold these pixels form a region.

<table>
<tr><td>

select a window 2x2
assign the partition mode to this window
if all the pixels are labeled
*   assign a new label if it is an inconsistent case*
if there are pixels without a label
*   assign the correct label for each case*
if the whole image is covered
*   stop*
otherwise
*   select a new window 2x2*

</td></tr>
</table>

Table 1: Pre-segmentation MPMT Algorithm

The threshold selection [1] depends on how detailed you want the segmentation. As we commented in the previous section, we want to increase the sharpness of the objects in the image instead of the details of the objects, so we use a threshold as big as possible to join similar intensities. We establish the threshold in a experimental form; we suppose that two intensities are similar if its distance is less than 12% of the maximum distance.

3.3 Postprocessing MPMT

The presegmentation process make a single scan of the image and at the same time make the regions divisions, so in few cases generate isolated points in the image; these isolated points blurring the image. The number of regions increase a lot with the regions of one pixels, so that the adjacency graph is distorted.

Thus, we make a postprocessing algorithm (See Table 2). This algorithm increase the speed of the segmentation algorithm.

```
if Area(Rᵢ)==1 then
    for all Neighbour(Rᵢ)
        calculate Distance(Rᵢ,Rⱼ)
        choose Minimum Distance
    if Minimum Distance < Threshold then
        Label(Rᵢ)=Label(Rⱼ)
        calculate
        (Mᵣ(Rⱼ), M_g(Rⱼ), M_b(Rⱼ))
        Area(Rⱼ)++
    otherwise
        Label(Rᵢ)=Label(Rⱼ)
        Area(Rⱼ)++
```

Table 2: Post-processing MPMT

With this algorithm the object features are clearly obtained.

3.4 Markov Random Fields

In the pre-segmentation process, the algorithm make a single scan of the image, so we obtain a oversegmentation. The process is very fast but it is not efficient enough to make a recognition.

We need to perform a new process to clearly define all the boundaries of the objects. We use the Markov Random Fields concept [5] [6] to obtain an optimal segmentation.

Theorem (Hammersley-Clifford).

If F is a Markov Random Field on a lattice S with respect to the neighborhood system G, the probability distribution of the configuration generated by it always have a definite form, which is a Gibbs distribution:

$$P(f) = \frac{1}{Z}exp - \frac{1}{T}U(f) \tag{3}$$

where:

- f Labels of the regions in the image.

- $U(f)$ is an energy function.

- Z is a normalizing constant.

- T temperature.

The goal is to find an optimal label assignment, of maximum probability, thus we minimize the energy function.

$U(f)$ is obtained adding the clique functions $V_c(f)$,

$$U(f) = \sum_c V_c(f) \tag{4}$$

where C ranges over the cliques associated with the given neighborhood system.

Given a neighborhood system on a lattice, we define a clique C as either a single site, or a set of sites of the lattice, such that all the sites that belong to C are neighbours of each other.

The first step is constructing an adjacency graph between regions, the second step is deciding if two regions should or should not be join using an energy function.

3.4.1   Adjacency Graph

The adjacency graph shows the relation between all the regions formed after the presegmentation process. It means that the adjacency graph shows the neigbours system defined in this image during the presegmentation process.

This graph changes dynamically as regions join to make a new region.

3.4.2   Energy Function

The energy function is our criterion function used to make a decision about whether two regions should or should not be joined.

To correctly define the energy function we will focus on colour similarity to join or disjoin regions. As we are working with RGB colour model, the difference between two intensities is calculated using the Euclidean distance.

The definition of the energy function is:

$$U(CE/R, F) = \sum_c V_c(CE/R, F) \tag{5}$$

where: CE the current label configuration, R the region process, a measure of the region's homogeneity and F the boundary process, a measure of the discontinuity in the limits of adjacents regions.

The initial energy function is computed by adding the tonality differences of the neighbouring regions

Where $F = \{F_{red}, F_{green}, F_{blue}\}$ is the set of region processes

where $F_i =$ is the average of intensity of the region i.

We can define the spectral characteristics of the region R_i as:

$F_i = \{F_{red}, F_{green}, F_{blue}\}$

For an optimal segmentation, we must take into consideration the next constraints:

- Homogeneous spectral characteristics provide a segmentation in single regions.

- In the common boundary between two regions there must be strong discontinuities of intensity values.

so we define a clique function of region c as:

$$\sum_{R_i \in C} \sum_{\substack{R_j \in C \\ R_j \neq R_i}} |F_i - F_j| \tag{6}$$

We use this equation to calculate the initial energy function in the adjacency graph.

We add the boundary process to this measure, as result we obtain the influence of to joint two regions, either as an individual process of these two region as the collect process in all the adjacency graph.

The next energy function is the result of joining two regions:

$$\sum_{R_i \in C} \sum_{\substack{R_j \in C \\ R_j \neq R_i}} |F_i - F_j| + NAdy_{i,j}|F_i - F_j| \tag{7}$$

where $NAdy_{i,j}$ is the maximum number of adjacencies between regions R_i and R_j

Thus, two regions should be joined if the global energy function decreases, and if the global energy function increases, these two regions shouldn't be joined.

Simulated Annealing is the algorithm used to calculate the minimum energy function, [2], Table 3 explains this algorithm.

> *Assign initial temperature T and assign F_s*
> en F $\forall s$
> *for each F_s in F*
> *   change its label to anyone of its neighbours*
> *   calculate the energy*
> *   if the energy decrease*
> *   join this two regions*
> *   re-calculate the adjacency graph*
> *   if the energy becomes stabilized*
> *   exit*
> *otherwise*
> *   lower the temperature*
> *   go back to step 2*

Table 3: Simulated Annealing Algorithm

4   Results

We use outdoor and indoor images for the experimentation. In every image there is a traffic signal because our future work will deal with recognizing the signals to help in mobile robot guiding.

For each view we shown a sequence of three images, the first one is the original image, the second one corresponds to the segmentation obtained after the process (we only show the boundaries between regions), and the third one shows the segmentation image using the colour corresponding to each region. (The colour of the region using our energy function).

The algorithm implementation is made using Java, so the results could not be considered done in real time. Now we are transform the implementation to C++ to improve our time results.

4.1   Outdoor Images

In outdoor images we can see the luminosity influence, unifying regions due to its brightness or its darkness. All these images are taken without flash in a sunny day and in a bright environment.

We can appreciate in every image that the objects in the segmentation image are well-defined, and the colours of the segmentation image are also correct.

We must mention the loosing of information of small objects.It is abso-

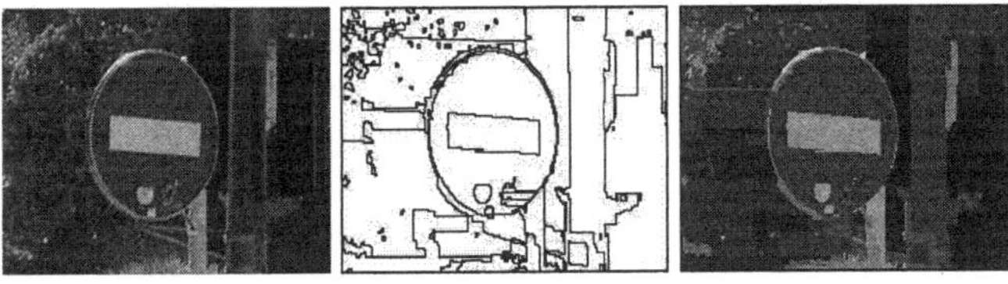

Figure 2: Image 1

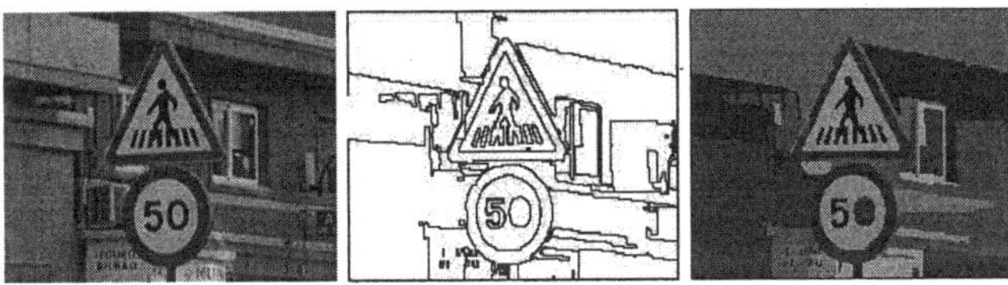

Figure 3: Image 2

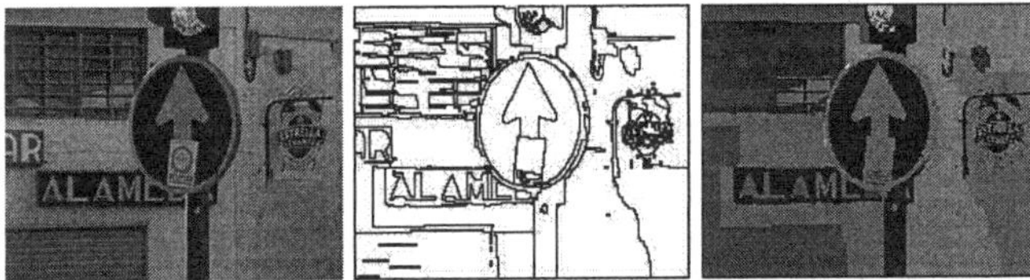

Figure 4: Image 3

lutely voluntary, because our interest is focused on the signal in the image, an that signal is perfectly defined using our algorithm, as we can see in all the figures. If we need either more information or more details of the objects, we must fit the threshold to join or disjoin regions, because the detail level is in inverse relation with the unifying threshold: the smaller the threshold the higher the details.

4.2   Indoor images

In indoor images we must bear in mind the great influence of shadows, so all the images are taken with artificial light and in absence of natural light.

In this images we can appreciate how two region form a new larger region depending on its luminosity.

To compare the indoor experiments we take images with flash and without flash. As results show, image segmentation with flash is better and clearer than image segmentation without flash.

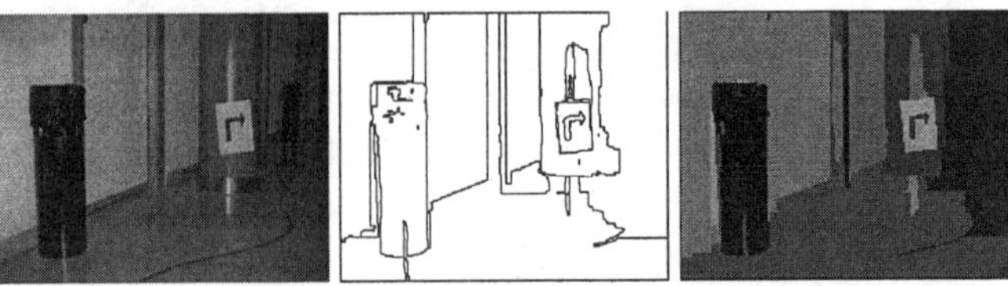

Figure 5: Indoor image (with flash)

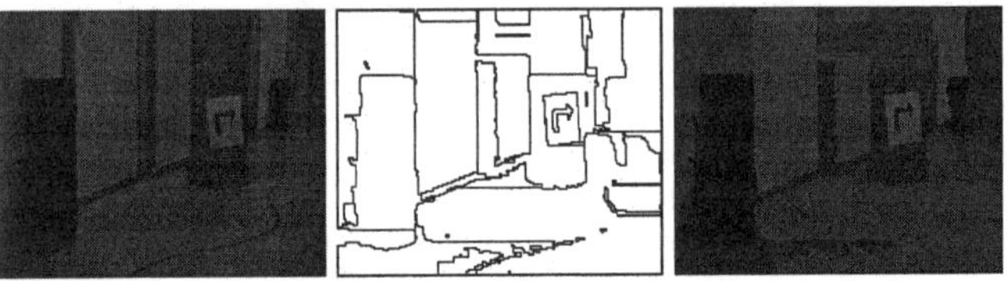

Figure 6: Indoor image (without flash)

5   Conclusions and future work

Luminosity is an important factor to join or disjoin regions. We work with traffic signal images, either outdoor or indoor; in these images the traffic signal is highlighted in the scene, because is the object to recognize in a future work.

We can see the clarity of the signal in the image, either outdoor or indoor.

We have achieved our goal, as we have an optimal segmentation, with a correct definition of the signal trace.

Using this segmentation in the future we want:

- To create an image data base of traffic signals.

- To study the best classificator for this kind of images.

- To take the colour information of the original image to accelerate the object search and its recognition.

- To use the inicial image histogram, to automatically calculate the threshold, depending on the image luminosity and intensity.

- To make a comparative study applying the energy function to different colour models.

Acknowledgements

This work has been supported by the spanish "Comisión Interministerial de Ciencia y Tecnología" (CICYT), project number TIC2001-0245-C02-02.

References

[1] Arques, P et al, Procedure of annealing for image segmentation:energy function with robust features. *Proceedings of the VIII Symposium Nacional de Reconocimiento de Formas y Análisis de Imágenes*, 1 (1999), 19 - 26.

[2] Azencott, R., *Simulated Annealing. Parallelization Tecniques*, John Wiley & Sons, 1999.

[3] Foley, Van Dam, Feiner y Huges, *Computer Graphics: Principles and Practice*, Addison Wesley, 1990.

[4] Hearn y Baker, *Gráficas por computadora*, Prentice Hall, 1995.

[5] Li, S.Z., *Markov Random Field Modelling in Computer Vision*, Springer-Verlag, 1995.

[6] Modestino, J.W. and Zahng, J., A Markov Random Field Model-based approach to image interpretation. *IEEE Transactions on Pattern Analysis and Machine Intelligence*, 14, (1994), 969 - 976.

[7] Pitas, *Digital Image Processing Algorithms and Applications*, John Wesley & sons, 2000.

[8] Suk, M.S. and Chung, S.M., A new image segmentation technique based on Partition Mode Test, *Pattern Recognition*, 16 (1983), 469 - 480.

Artificial Intelligence Research and Development
I. Aguiló et al. (Eds.)
IOS Press, 2003

Disparity estimation in stereoscopic vision by *simulated annealing*

Patricia COMPAÑ, Rosana SATORRE, Ramón RIZO

Group i3a: Industrial Computing and Artificial Intelligence
Departament of Computer Science and Artificial Intelligence
University of Alicante
{patricia, rosana, rizo}@dccia.ua.es

Abstract. This paper presents a correspondence algorithm for stereo vision based on an integrated model that includes several units corresponding to different stages: features extraction, minimization of an energy function using simulated annealing, multiresolution and interpolation. Firstly the original images are scaled down to considerably reduce their size. From the reduced images a disparity map is obtained, which is used as the basis to develop the complete process. For this reason an energy function is built and minimized using a multiresolution scheme. The energy function integrates features such as grey level, non parametric transforms, edges, smoothness and uniqueness. The obtained disparity for every resolution is interpolated to work with the following resolution. Our model produces a dense disparity map. The algorithm has been tested with different kinds of real images to show its flexibility.

Introduction

Our brains obtain two similar images of a scene, as if they had been taken from two nearby points on the same horizontal level, this is due to the position and the control of our eyes. Two objects at a different distance from the observer have different relative positions in their retinal images. The brain is able to measure this difference (retinal disparity) and to use it to estimate the depth [9]. The retinal disparity depends on the distance to the fixing instant. To be able to use the binocular capacity to detect depth, an organism must have a binocular visual field, that is, an overlap region of visibility between both eyes. Every animal has a different binocular visual field size. In general, predators have their eyes at the front and so they have large binocular visual fields. On the other hand, their prey typically have their eyes at the side of their heads so they have small binocular visual fields, if any. Stereoscopic vision is a set of techniques that try to recover three-dimensional information from two or more views of a scene. In this process some different stages can be distinguished:

- Calibration of intrinsic and extrinsic parameters involved in the stereoscopic geometry.
- Rectification of the epipolar geometry to simplify the search done when solving the problem of correspondence.
- Correspondence of tokens of the images to obtain a disparity map. Our three-dimensional perception of the world is due to how our brain interprets the difference between the retinal position of correspondent items: the disparity. This problem is considered the main difficulty in stereo vision (Figure 1).

- Reconstruction of the three-dimensional scene, that is, obtaining the depth from the disparity.

1. The correspondence problem

This problem can be seen as a search problem: given an element in the left image, a corresponding element in the right image must be searched.

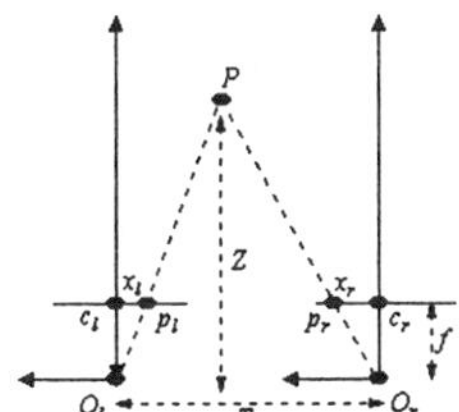

Fig. 1. p_l and p_r correspond to 3D point P

From a human point of view, the process of stereoscopic vision is so natural that we cannot appreciate its complexity unless we try to automate it. Uniqueness, smoothness and epipolar geometry are some of the physical constraints that are usually established to make the correspondence search easier.

1. Epipolar geometry: for a given point in the left image, all possible matching points in the right image lie on a line. Therefore, the dimension of the space of search is reduced from two to one dimension. The epipolar constraint is, of course, symmetrical, that is, for a point in the right image, all possible matching points in the left image also lie on a line.
2. Uniqueness: when we are working only with opaque objects, a point in the left image should have only one matching point in the right image, at the most. This is not true in general for transparent objects.
3. Smoothness: this constraint is based on the fact that the world is mainly made of smooth surfaces.

The correspondence algorithms are usually classified into two main groups: those based on correlation and others based on features.

In correlation based methods, the elements to match are fixed-size windows in the image. The similitude criterion is a measure of the correlation between windows in both images. The corresponding element is given by the windows that maximize the similitude criterion within a search region.

The feature based algorithms firstly extract some predefined features and then, they try to match them.

The correspondences based on regions are included in the family of feature based methods. In general, the higher the semantic level of the primitive, the more robust the obtained correspondences are, although some important drawbacks can appear: extracting the primitives can be more difficult and the disparity map is more disperse. In [8] an interesting review of the region based correspondence problem is shown.

A widely used technique is dynamic programming [5], [6] and [2]. These kinds of algorithms are characterized by a global cost function that is minimized.

For a long time several researchers have considered the possibility of including multiresolution models for the detection of correspondence in a stereo pair in order to obtain an estimation of depth in a three-dimensional scene. In [12] an integrated scheme including multiresolution is used. In this example a new approach is formulated and developed. It integrates several units implied in stereo vision: feature extraction, matching and interpolation. An energy function is built for every unit and every resolution and it is minimized in an integrated manner so that it produces a dense disparity map.

In [7] the authors worked simultaneously with several scales of the image and obtained an error function defined for every scale. They used and compared two methods (GRAPHSEARCH algorithm [11] and gradient fall) to find the correct correspondence between two images.

Other researches have found that better results are obtained using more than two images. Ayache [1] describes a trinocular stereo system in which the initial correspondences between features for cameras 1 and 2 are tested in a verification step that examines a specific point in the third image.

In section 2 an energy function is described to formulate the correspondence problem. The algorithm that is used to minimize the energy function and to obtain the disparity map is explained in section 3. Section 4 presents the applied multiresolution scheme. Finally, in section 5 some experiments are shown.

2. Energy function

The energy function minimized by the simulated annealing algorithm is made up of five terms, each one weighted by a control parameter (γ_n). Eq. (1) defines this function.

$$U(p) = \sum_{n=1}^{5} \gamma_n U_n(p) \qquad \qquad (1)$$

Notation is shown in Table 1.

Table 1. Notation of the energy function

II	Left image
ID	Right image
(p_x, p_y)	Coordinates of pixel p
N(p)	Neighbourhood environment of p
vL(p), vR(p)	Vertical edges of the images, it has a value of 1 if there is an edge between the pixels (p_x, p_y) and (p_x, p_y-1), and 0 else.
hL(p), hR(p)	Horizontal edges of the images, it has a value of 1 if there is an edge between the pixels (p_x, p_y) and (p_x-1, p_y), and 0 else
disp	Disparity map
$\delta(a,b)$	Function that returns 1 if a=b and 0 else
τ	Absolute value of the difference of the grey level between two points
$\Xi(p, N(p))$	Census transform of p
H(v1, v2)	Hamming distance between two vectors of bits

The term U_1 is the correspondence cost at intensity level at the selected pixel. Instead of comparing a pixel in the left image with a pixel in the right image, a neighbourhood environment around the pixel p is considered.

$$U_1(p) = \sum_{N(p)} \tau(p,q)\,|\,(p \in II) \wedge (q \in ID) \wedge \tag{2}$$
$$(p_x = q_x) \wedge (q_y = p_y + disp(p))$$

In previous works [4] the squared difference between intensity values has been used instead of the absolute value of the difference, but we have verified that the absolute value works better when there are outliers.

The term U_2 is the correspondence cost of the Census transform [14]. It is a non parametric measure of the local special structure. The value of this transform depends on the comparison of the intensity value of a pixel with the intensity values of the pixels in the neighbourhood. The value of the transform for a pixel in the left image must be very similar to that of the corresponding pixel in the right image.

$$U_2(p) = \sum_{N(p)} H(\Xi(p,N(p)),\Xi(q,N(q)))\,| \tag{3}$$
$$(p \in II) \wedge (q \in ID) \wedge (p_x = q_x) \wedge (q_y = p_y + disp(p))$$

The term U_3 is the correspondence cost at edge level. Information about horizontal and vertical edges is used. It can be assumed that if there is an edge in the left image, there should also be an edge in the right image, corresponding to the first one but with a displacement of the amount of pixels determined by the disparity.

$$U_3(p) = \sum_{N(p)} (1 - \delta(vL(p),vR(q))) + (1 - \delta(hL(p),hR(q))) \tag{4}$$
$$|\,(p \in II) \wedge (q \in ID) \wedge (p_x = q_x) \wedge (q_y = p_y + disp(p))$$

The term U_4 refers to the smoothness constraint: it is assumed that the disparity varies in a smooth manner between edges. This term does not assume the smoothness when a vertical edge is found in the image. We can expect to have different disparity values in two positions when there is an edge between them.

$$U_4(p) = (disp(p) - disp(q))^2 * (1 - vL(p)) + \tag{5}$$
$$(disp(p) - disp(r))^2 * (1 - vL(r))\,|$$
$$(p_x = q_x) \wedge (q_y = p_y - 1) \wedge (p_x = r_x) \wedge (r_y = p_y + 1)$$

The last term includes the uniqueness constraint. If we are working only with opaque objects, every point in the left image should have a unique corresponding point in the right image. This is not true for transparent objects. It means that if the disparity in columns j^{th} and q^{th} is obtained for any row i then, as the uniqueness constrain states, j+disp(i,j) ≠ q+disp(i,q).

$$U_5(p) = \sum_{q=ini}^{fin} \delta(p_y + disp(p), q_y + disp(q))\,|\,(p_x = q_x) \tag{6}$$

3. Simulated Annealing

A stochastic relaxation method called simulated annealing (SA) is used to obtain a global or quasi-global solution depending on a cooling factor. The algorithm tries to minimize an energy function that includes a measure of the similitude error between corresponding points. There are many versions of SA algorithm: Metropolis algorithm, Creutz algorithm, Boltzman machine, Gibbs Sampler, etc. In this study, we have used the **Metropolis algorithm** [10]. Every pixel is visited and its disparity value is modified by another value belonging to a maximum range of disparity.

Considering the previously defined energy function, the algorithm is applied iteratively. The proposed algorithm is shown in Table 2.

Table 2. SA algorithm

Pas 1	Assign initial temperature T
Pas 2	For each pixel p in the disparity map 1. Change its disparity value for another in the given range 2. Calculate $\triangle U$ 3. If $\triangle U < 0$, accept the new value; else, accept if $e^{-\triangle U/T} > \xi$, where ξ is a random value in [0,1].
Pas 3	Cool the system by $0 < k < 1$ so that $T_{k+1} = kT_k$ and go to step 2 during a fixed amount of iterations

4. Multiresolution

The multiresolution scheme is usually represented as a pyramidal structure (Figure 2) where the peak of the pyramid represents the maximum level of scale and the base is the image in its original scale.

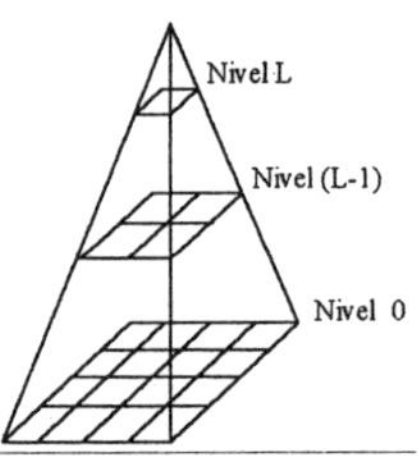

Fig. 2. Pyramidal structure

The multiresolution methods are based on the analogy that can be establish between the operations done in a rough grid of a region and the more global calculations done in a finer grid of the same region [13]. Two ways of transforming a grid into another of a different resolution level can be considered:

- By **sampling**: From the unscaled image some pixels are selected. This procedure is shown in Figure 3.
- By **block averages**: Some blocks are formed from the unscaled image and their average is calculated. Then the scaled image is built with these values.

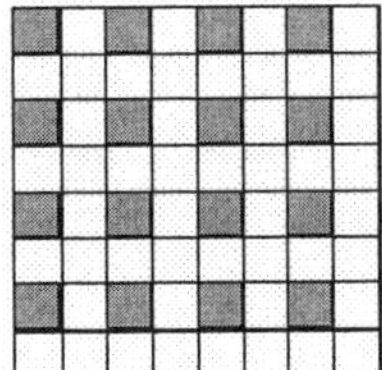

Fig. 3. Resolution transformation by sampling

In our studies we have used the sampling method.

The proposed method to estimate the disparity can be described as follows:

- At the roughest level of resolution (pyramid peak) the optimal solution can be obtained quickly because of the small amount of elements that are in the allowed disparity space.
- At intermediate levels of resolutions, the previous level solution is used to interpolate an initial estimation. The method is then applied to calculate the optimal solution.
- The same process in continued until level 0 of complete resolution (pyramid base) is achieved.

A median filter is applied at every disparity estimation resulting from each scale level. The median filter make the intensity of the pixels smoother in relation to their neighbourhood, eliminating the isolated outliers.

4.1 Interpolation

Multiresolution models require an interpolation technique that allows the results of the method at one level to be used at the next level. Some interpolation techniques have been defined: linear interpolation, Bessel interpolation, Hermite interpolation, and so on. We have used linear interpolation.

5. Experiments and results

Some experiments conducted with real images are shown. The images belong to several types, both interior and exterior. The main goal of selecting such different kinds of images is to prove the flexibility of our method.

The images have been taken with a Digiclops interface IEEE 1394 camera with a resolution of 240×320 pixels. In the different experiments, the images have been scaled by a factor of 2^4 to apply the multiresolution scheme. Moreover, a range of maximum disparity has been fixed in every stereo pair.

The first example is shown in Figure 4. The parameters that have been used are: $\gamma_1=1$, $\gamma_2=150$, $\gamma_3=150$, $\gamma_4=100$ i $\gamma_5=150$. During the scale process we have worked with images at a resolution of 120×160 (scale 2^1), 60×80 (scale 2^2), 30×40 (scale 2^3) and 15×20 (scale 2^4). The allowed disparity range is 25. Figure 5 (a) shows the disparity map using the model without multiresolution. The results obtained using multiresolution with 5 levels is presented in Figure 5 (b). In this figure and in the others, the brighter the intensity is, the nearer the object is. The darkest areas represent the most distant objects.

(a) Left image   (b) Right image

Fig. 4. Pair of stereo images

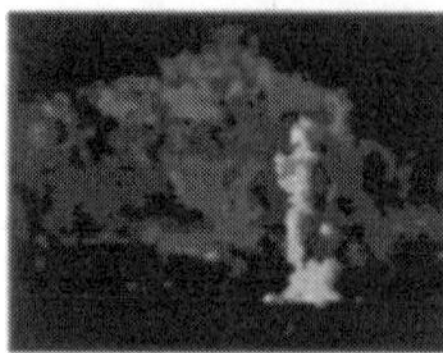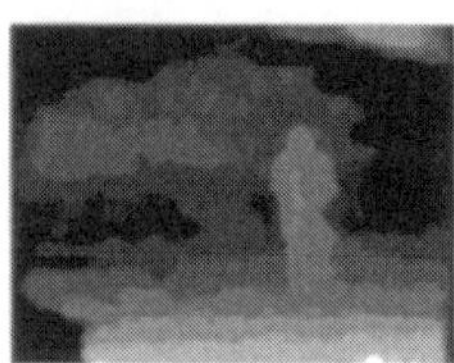

(a) Without multiresolution   (b) With multiresolution

Fig. 5. Disparity maps for the stereo map in Figure 4

The second experiment presents a stereo map taken in an interior scene (Figure 6). Figure 7 shows the intermediate disparity maps resulting from applying the algorithm at several resolutions. The parameters are the same as in the previous experiment. The final result is shown in Figure 6 (d). The allowed range of disparity is 40.

(a) Left image   (b) Right image

Fig. 6. Pair of stereo images for experiment 2

The execution time for both stereo pairs is 23 seconds. This time refers to an Athlon XP 1700 processor.

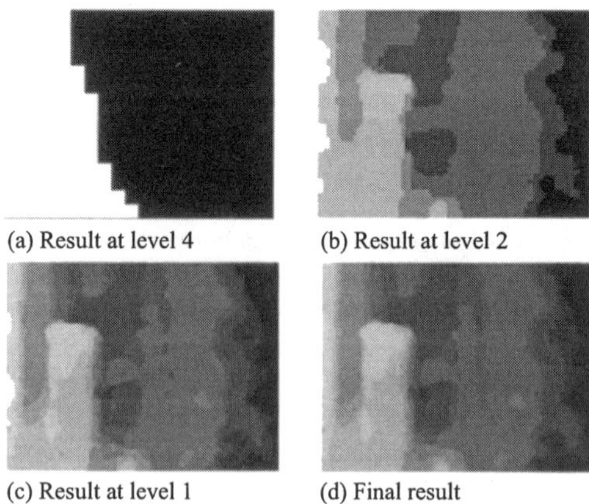

(a) Result at level 4   (b) Result at level 2

(c) Result at level 1   (d) Final result

Fig. 7. Intermediate disparity maps for stereo pair 2

In some previous studies, we have worked with energy functions applied to the complete image, but we have verified that using an energy function defined for pixels decreases the computational cost of the method.

We have included intensity features, edges, non parametric transforms, smoothness constrains and uniqueness restrictions to construct a robust energy function. The fact that humans are able to determine the disparity in a better way when there are edges can constitute evidence that a mechanism based on edges must be included in a stereo algorithm.

We believe that colour features would also allow a better discrimination of pixels, and so we are working to adapt this model to colour images.

6. References

[1]   N. Ayache. Artificial Vision for Mobile robots: Stereo Vision and Multisensory Perception. The MIT Press, 1990.

[2]   P. Belhumeur and D. Mumford. "A bayesian treatment of the stereo correspondence problem using half-occluded regions". Proc. International Conference on Computer Vision and Pattern Recognition IEEE, 1992

[3]   C. Chang and S. Chatterjee. "Multiresolution stereo – A bayesian approach". International Conference on Pattern Recognition, pp. 908-912, 1990.

[4]   P. Compañ, R. Satorre, C. Villagrá and R. Rizo "Visión estereoscópica en un modelo multirresolución". Actas de la IX Conferencia de la Asociación Española para la Inteligencia Artificial, pp. 1291-1300, 2001

[5]   I. J. Cox, S. L. Hingorani and S. B. Rao. "A maximum likelihood stereo algorithm. Computer Vision and Image Understanding. Vol 63:3, pp. 542-567. 1996.

[6]   D. Geiger, B. Ladendorf and A. Yuille. "Occlusions and binocular stereo". International Journal of Computer Vision, 14, pp 211-226, 1995

[7]   M. Lew, K. Wong and T. Huang. "Multi-scale stero matching". Int. Conference on Pattern Recognitiion, pp. 600-623, 1992.

[8]   M. A. López. "Visión estereoscópica basada en regiones: estado del arte y perspectivas de futuro". Actas de IX Conferencia de la Asociación Española para la Inteligencia Artificial, 2001.

[9]   D. Marr and T. Poggio. "A theory for human stereo vision". Proceeding Roy. Soc Lond. B. pp. 301-328. 1979.

[10]   N. Metropolis. "Equation of state calculations by fast computing machines". Journal Chem., 21, pp. 1087-1091,1953.

[11]   N. Nilsson. Principios de Inteligencia Artificial. Díaz de Santos, 1987.

[12]   K. Sunil and U. Desai. "New algorithms for 3D surface description form binocular stereo using integration". Journal of the Franklin Institute, 1994.

[13]   D. Terzopoulos. "Image analysis using multigrid relaxation methods". IEEE Transactions on Pattern Analysis and Machine Intelligence, 1986

[14]   R. Zabih and J. Woodfill. "Nom-parametric transforms for computer visual correspondence". Proccedings of the Third European Conference on Computer Vision, pp 151-158, 1994.

Artificial Intelligence Research and Development
I. Aguiló et al. (Eds.)
IOS Press, 2003

A Human Action Comparison Framework for Motion Understanding

Jordi Gonzàlez, Javier Varona, F.Xavier Roca and J.J. Villanueva
Computer Vision Center & Dept. d'Informàtica,
Edifici O, Universitat Autònoma de Barcelona (UAB), 08193 Bellaterra, Spain
{poal, xaviv, xavir, villanueva}@cvc.uab.es

Abstract. In this paper, we consider *Motion Understanding* as the generation of textual descriptions from image data, in which human behavior analysis is involved. Specifically, existing human action recognition methods provide narrations by using verbs. However, the temporal and spatial evolution of recognized actions should be addressed in order to enhance action descriptions by using adverbs. Thus, we propose to achieve a more accurate annotation by providing a human action comparison framework to better reflect the underlying differences between several performances.

1 Introduction

Motion Understanding is commonly defined as the generation of textual descriptions from image data. Therefore, there is an abstraction process from raw video signals to high-level, qualitative descriptions. Such descriptions require to associate natural language components, such as verbs, adverbs, nouns and adjectives, to observation of temporal variations.

Specifically, we are interested in those image sequences in which humans are involved. Within this context, we define a human action as a process of human performing that has a significance to our system. Thus, an action is considered as a sequence of human movements, which can be described in terms of attitudes or motion characteristics [3]. Typical actions are running, jumping or bending.

Currently, most effort has been spent in developing suitable algorithms for human action recognition (a recent review can be found in [15]). As a result, human behavior narrations are generated by using motion verbs. However, no additional characteristics about a specific human action performance are derived afterwards. That means, the *temporal* and *spatial* evolution of such recognized actions are not exploited to enhance action descriptions by using adverbs or adjectives, for example. Therefore, our aim is to describe *how* an action is being performed, once we know *which* action is being performed.

In this paper, we first justify the *key-frame* concept within the human action representation domain. Subsequently, we review our proposal to human action modeling, which exploits such a key-frame concept. Thus, spatial variability of human actions is demonstrated to be handled. Based upon this representation, we subsequently enhance such human action model to achieve temporal invariance. As a result, we present a human action comparison framework in order to further derive the underlying differences between several performances. Lastly, conclusions are provided.

2 Background

We define an action as a sequence of time-ordered body posture configurations. If one considers the complete set of body postures for a given action sequence, several postures are found to be repeated. A posterior analysis determines that there exists a more reduced group of human postures that do not appear as frequently as the redundant ones, which are found to *identify* an action. They give enough information to state, by only considering these reduced group of human postures, which action is being performed. But also, these characteristic human postures can be used to *discriminate* between different actions.

Such capabilities argue for representing an action by selecting few frames from the entire sequence. It can be found in the literature an increasing number of papers which attempt to perform human action tracking and recognition by only considering few poses. In [1], human motion tracking is applied during a gymnastic exercise which is known in advance. Tracking is performed by using a set of key-frames for each exercise, which are computed beforehand. Also in [2], few body poses are considered to achieve human action recognition. However, no criteria is used to select the key-frames, which are found randomly. In [8], key-frames are called *exemplars*, which are selected from a sequence of frames using the k-means algorithm based on an error distortion measure. Exemplars are used to recognize humans from walking action sequences. In [13], human action tracking and recognition is performed by considering a set of stored key-frames. However, it is not clear how many key-frames are required for a given tennis stroke, due to the fact that they are provided beforehand.

3 Human Action Modeling

In this section, we briefly revise our proposal to human action modeling. In order to use a suitable action representation, several criteria have been applied: to require few parameters to describe each human posture; to include any posture which is plausible to appear in a performance of given action; to exclude those postures which have not been presented during the learning step; to be independent of the duration of any action performance to be learnt; and to preserve the order in which the variation of the human posture has been observed during an action performance.

3.1 Parametric Eigenspaces

Consider an action as a sequence of human postures. Each human posture model is based on a stick figure, which is composed of ten rigid parts (torso, head, two for each leg and two for each arm) and six joints, similar to that presented in [5]. A sequence of n frames corresponding to a performance of a given action is considered to be composed of a set of body posture configurations $\mathbf{S}_j = \{\mathbf{x}_1, \mathbf{x}_2, ..., \mathbf{x}_n\}$, where

$$\mathbf{x}_i = (\mathbf{u}_i, \Theta_i)^T. \tag{1}$$

Θ_i corresponds to the ten angle values which define the limb configuration of the stick figure, and $\mathbf{u}_i$ corresponds to the hip center coordinates.

An action $\mathbf{A}$ is learnt using r different real world sequences $\mathbf{A} = \{\mathbf{S}_1, \mathbf{S}_2, ..., \mathbf{S}_r\}$. In order to provide a proper learning set which is generic enough, the same action is performed several times by different actors of different sizes. For our experiments, 25 performances for each action were recorded. As a result, nearly 2000 frames are included for each action. Note

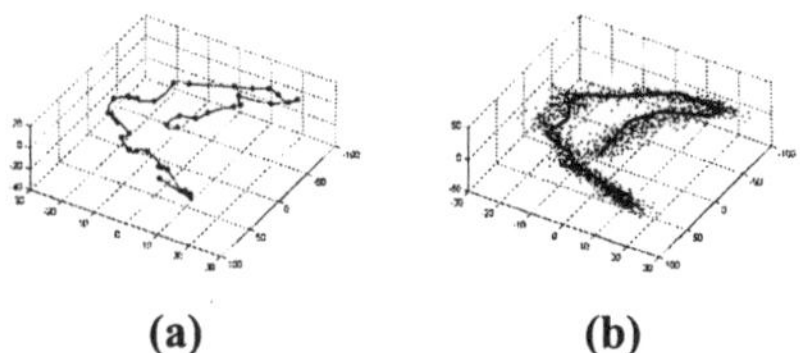

(a)   (b)

Figure 1: Parametric eigenspace for the bending action. Only the three most prominent dimensions are displayed. **(a)** Manifold obtained by interpolation between the projections (black dots) of the postures of a single performance. **(b)** Manifold (thick line) obtained by interpolation between the means of pose distributions [4].

that each performance sequence is not compulsory to contain the same number of frames. Afterwards, the components of x_i of a given frame are found by manual annotation. Thus, errors in the training set are avoided.

Such a learning data set is used to compute the action class Ω_A called *aSpace* and defined as:

$$\Omega_A = (\mathbf{E}, \Lambda, \bar{\mathbf{x}}), \tag{2}$$

where $\mathbf{E} = (e_1, ..., e_m)$ corresponds to the eigenvectors of the reduced space, Λ to the m largest eigenvalues and $\bar{x}$ to the mean body posture configuration for that action. A more detailed description about *aSpaces* can be found in [6].

Using such an action model, each body human posture configuration x_i of a performance $\mathbf{S}_j$ of our learning set $\mathbf{A}$ is projected to the eigenspace Ω_A. As projections y_i of consecutive human postures are strongly correlated, we consider such projections as the control values for a interpolating curve $\mathbf{g}_j(p)$, which is computed using a standard cubic-spline interpolation algorithm [11] (see Fig. 1.**(a)**). This process is repeated for each performance of the learning set, thus obtaining r manifolds:

$$\mathbf{g}_j(p), \qquad p \in [0, 1], \qquad j = 1, ..., r, \tag{3}$$

where p refers to the variation of the pose over time, which is normalized for each performance. Afterwards, for each performance $\mathbf{S}_j$, points lying in the manifold $\mathbf{g}_j(p)$ are indexed by their parameter p. Therefore, it is possible to compute the mean manifold for the action Ω_A:

$$\bar{\mathbf{g}}(p) = \frac{1}{r} \sum_{j=1}^{r} \mathbf{g}_j(p), \qquad p \in [0, 1], \tag{4}$$

where $\bar{\mathbf{g}}(p)$ is obtained by interpolating between these means using a standard cubic-spline interpolation algorithm. Fig. 1.**(b)** shows the point clouds in the *aSpace* corresponding to the bending action and its interpolated parametric curve $\bar{\mathbf{g}}(p)$.

This action representation is not influenced by the duration of a performance (expressed in seconds or number of frames). Unfortunately, this resulting parametric manifold is highly rough. The problem arises from the fact that any subject performs an action in the way he or she is used to. Furthermore, it is highly unlikely that the same actor performs different times the same action in a completely similar manner. So we need to determine how a *prototypical action* representation can be derived by considering individual and highly variable performances as the learning set. Consequently, only few human posture configurations will be considered to represent a given action, which will constitute the *key-frame* set for that action.

Figure 2: Key-frames found for a bending action.

3.2   Automatic Key-Frame Selection

As expounded before, when an action sequence is analyzed, quite few characteristic body postures can be found. From a probability point of view, characteristic postures are the least likely body postures exhibited during the action performances. So we need to represent the action in terms of a probability distribution in order to compute the likelihood that a sample $\mathbf{x}_j$ is an instance of the action class Ω_A, that is, $P(\mathbf{x}_j|\Omega_A)$. Low values actually correspond to less repetitive samples, that is, very characteristic postures for that action. Thus, by selecting those samples that are less likely, we assure that they provide most entropy of such an action class.

Note that the *aSpace* can also be used to compute the action class conditional density $P(\mathbf{x}_j|\Omega_A)$, assumed to be Gaussian [4]. Consequently, we compute the likelihood values for the sequence of pose-ordered points $\mathbf{x}_j$ in the $\bar{\mathbf{g}}(p)$ manifold. Due to high-dimensionality of the data, we apply an efficient and robust manner to compute such a likelihood, proposed in [9]. As a result, an estimation of the Mahalanobis distance, which considers only the largest eigenvalue eigenvectors of the eigenspace, is applied for each point of the manifold $\bar{\mathbf{g}}(p)$ (see [14] for details). Thus, we obtain a distance function that estimates the likelihood value for each posture. Note that this distance measurement is also related to important changes of direction of the manifold.

Applying a pose ordering to each distance, peaks of this function correspond to locally maximal distances or, in other words, to the least likely samples. So each peak of the distance function corresponds to a key-frame $\mathbf{k}_i$, and the number of key-frames k is determined by the number of peaks. Thus, we obtain the set $\mathbf{K}_A = \{\mathbf{k}_1, \mathbf{k}_2, ..., \mathbf{k}_k\}$ of time-ordered key-frames for the action A. Examples of key-frames obtained from the manifold computed in bending *aSpace* are shown in Fig. 2.

3.3   Parametric Action Representation

Once the key-frames have been selected, a new manifold is obtained by interpolating between the key-frame set using a standard cubic-spline interpolation algorithm. This interpolated parametric curve is referred as the *parametric action representation* or *p–action*, and is defined as a function of the pose p:

$$\mathbf{f}^A(p), \qquad p \in [0, 1], \tag{5}$$

which can be written explicitly as (assuming that three eigenvectors are enough for representing the *aSpace*):

$$\mathbf{f}^A(p) = (u(p), v(p), w(p)), \tag{6}$$

which represents three equations, one for each eigenvector (i.e. dimension of the *aSpace*):

$$u(p) = a_u p^3 + b_u p^2 + c_u p + d_u. \tag{7}$$

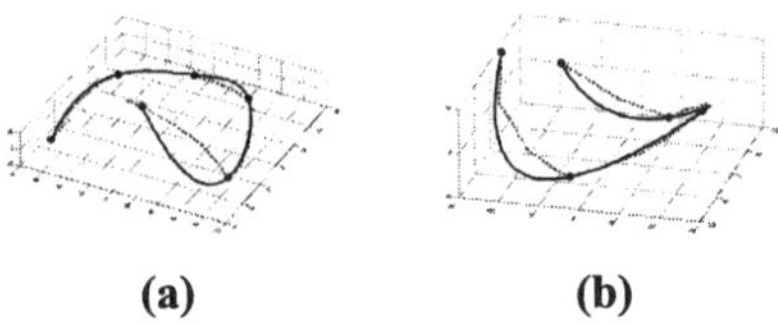

(a)   (b)

Figure 3: *P-actions* obtained by interpolation (solid curve) of the key-frames (black dots) found in $\bar{\mathbf{g}}(p)$ (dot curve) for bending **(a)** and running **(b)** actions.

As shown in Fig. 3, $\mathbf{f}^A(p)$ represents a manifold which *smooths* the manifold $\bar{\mathbf{g}}(p)$: by using interpolation, we attain a reduction of the roughness derived from the learning set. Mathematically, smoothness is determined by how many derivatives of the curve equation are continuous: by using cubic splines, second-order continuity between segments is attained.

The break points of the spline correspond to the projections of the key-frames found before. Consequently, the curve is made up of several segments, which correspond to transitions between key-frames: each segment represents how the body posture evolves from one key-frame to its next in temporal order.

4   Towards Human Action Comparison

Note that, by considering the *p-action* representation depicted above, only the first step for human action comparison has been made. The problem arises from the fact that any subject performs an action in the way he or she is used to. Furthermore, it is highly unlikely that the same actor performs different times the same action in a completely similar manner. As a result, both spatial and temporal variability of human actions should be handled.

Spatial invariance has already been achieved by considering the key-frame set. Instead of modeling the complete set of feasible postures which an actor could adopt while performing an action, our human action model is based upon the most characteristic posture configurations repeated during several performances, because any new subject can include posture configurations not presented in the learning set.

On the other hand, in order to cope with temporal variability, the speed at which the parameter p is increased has to be under control too. However, this is not straightforward, due to the difference between a change in p and the corresponding change in distance along the curve. Thus, an algorithm for stepping along the curve in equal increments is required, but also for speeding up and slowing down. In the next section, we enhance the *p–action* representation by incorporating existing animation strategies which allow to control the speed at which synthetic animated sequences are generated. Thus, we will attain a synchronization algorithm to derive differences between several performances.

4.1   *Arc length parameterization of* p–actions

Within the computer animation domain, speed invariance is commonly achieved by considering the distance along the curve of interpolation or, in our case, by establishing a reparameterization of the *p–action* by arc length [7]. Thus, the animator can specify the relative velocities that the variation of the body posture should have along the *p–action*. For example, stepping along the curve at equally spaced intervals of arc length will result in a synthetic action at a constant speed.

Therefore, consider the manifold computed in the previous chapter, $\mathbf{f}^A(p)$. We will require of a reparameterization in terms of the arc length s. Usually, this step is difficult or impossible for many types of curves, so several approximate techniques have been developed (see [10] for details). For our purposes, to establish the relationship between parametric values and arc length is enough. We do not need an arc length parameterization where a unit change in the parameter value results in a unit change in the curve length [12]. By describing how the length varies with the parametric variable, we could determine afterwards from that curve an arc length parameterization.

The easiest way for establishing the correspondence between p and s is to sample the curve at a multitude of parametric values $\mathbf{p}$. The arc length is then estimated by computing the length of the curve between adjacent points, as shown next.

The length s of a curve from a point p_1 to p_2 is found by evaluating the arc length integral:

$$s = \int_{p_1}^{p_2} \left| \frac{d\mathbf{f}^A}{dp} \right| dp. \tag{8}$$

Consequently, the total length s_{end} of the curve is derived as:

$$s_{end} = \int_0^1 \left| \frac{d\mathbf{f}^A}{dp} \right| dp. \tag{9}$$

Assuming that the *aSpace* is well-represented by the three largest eigenvalue eigenvectors, the derivative of the curve is defined as three equations, from Eq. (6):

$$\frac{d\mathbf{f}^A}{dp} = \left(\frac{du(p)}{dp}, \frac{dv(p)}{dp}, \frac{dw(p)}{dp} \right), \tag{10}$$

and

$$\left| \frac{d\mathbf{f}^A}{dp} \right| = \sqrt{ \left(\frac{du(p)}{dp} \right)^2 + \left(\frac{dv(p)}{dp} \right)^2 + \left(\frac{dw(p)}{dp} \right)^2 }. \tag{11}$$

Note that each equation of Eq. (6) is defined as in Eq. (7). Consequently, the derivative of each dimension is found as:

$$\frac{du(p)}{dp} = 3\, a_u p^2 + 2\, b_u p + c_u. \tag{12}$$

Consider $\mathbf{p} = \{p_1, p_2, ..., p_n\}, p_i \in [0,1]$ the parametric values to be sampled being selected in increasing order. For each p_i, its corresponding arc length $s_i \in [0, s_{end}]$ is calculated using Eqs. (8), (11) and (12), in order to compute $\mathbf{s} = \{s_1, s_2, ..., s_n\}$. This calculation can be achieve recursively [10, 12]:

$$\begin{aligned} s_1 &= 0, \\ s_i &= s_{i-1} + \left| \frac{d\mathbf{f}^A(p_i)}{dp} \right| (p_i - p_{i-1}), \qquad i = 2, ..., n. \end{aligned} \tag{13}$$

As this is done, a table is built up of arc lengths indexed by parametric values. Note that the arc length is strictly monotonically increasing function of $\mathbf{p}$, and when $p_n = 1$, then $s_n = s_{end}$. Arc length values are normalized so that $s_{end} = 1$.

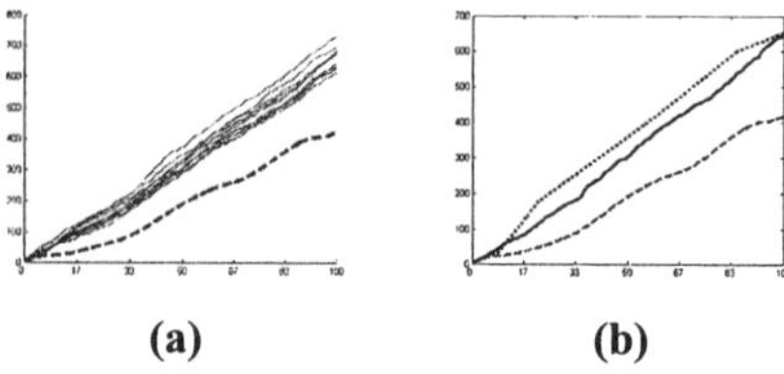

(a)   **(b)**

Figure 4: Manifolds parameterized by arc length (parametric value p vs. arc length s). Left figure **(a)** represents several performances parameterized by arc length (solid lines). The dashed curve represents the *p–action*, with a reduced total length due to the interpolation process between key-frames. Right figure **(b)** represents the manifold $\mathbf{f}^A(p)$ (dashed line), a new performance (solid line) and the synchronization of the new performance against $\mathbf{f}^A(p)$ (dotted line). See text for details.

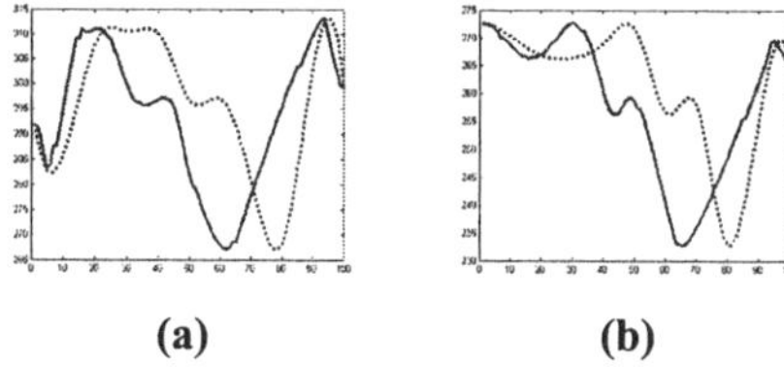

(a)   **(b)**

Figure 5: Comparison of both parameterizations (parametric value p and arc length s). Left figure **(a)** represents the variation of the angle of the left lower arm when the *p–action* is sampled using p (dotted line) and s (solid line) as parametric value. Right figure **(b)** corresponds to the angle of the left lower leg.

This table is then searched for obtaining the arc length given a parametric value. If the parametric value is not present at the table, an interpolation step is made between the arc lengths corresponding to entries on either side of the given parametric value. The reverse situation (given an arc length, how to obtain its corresponding parametric value) is handled in a similar manner.

Fig. 4.**(a)** represents several performances parameterized by arc length. Variation of the total arc length of such performances is due to the different postures exhibited. The dashed curve represents the *p–action*, with a reduced total length due to the interpolation process between key-frames (the *p–action* manifold is smoother than any performance manifold).

Once the *p–action* has been parameterized by arc length, it is possible to control the speed at which the curve is traversed. Fig. 4.**(b)** shows a new performance sampled at different speeds (solid and dotted lines).

However, speed control is under the time space, which is different to the curve space. So it is required to relate arc length with time, that is, to produce a distance-time function $s(t)$. Thus, at a given time t_i, the desired distance traveled along the space curve is obtained using $s(t_i)$. Then, using the arc length table computed before, the parametric value p is found.

For example, sampling at equally spaced values of arc length will evolve to constant-velocity motion. In such a case, Fig. 5 shows the angle values of the left lower arm and left lower leg during the bending *p–action*, as a result of choosing equally spaced samples using p and s parameterizations. By considering the arc length parameterization, the temporal evolution of the posture is achieved to occur at any user-specified speed.

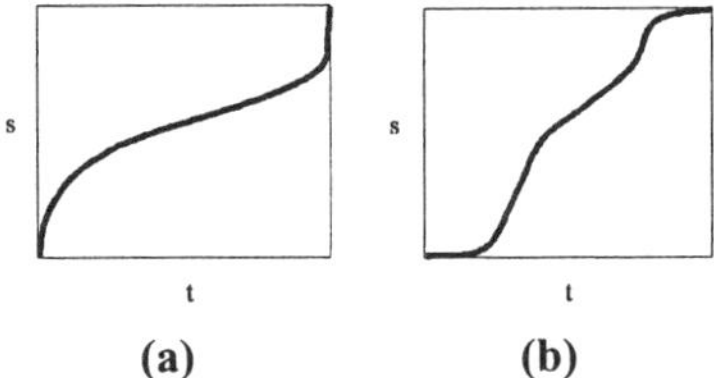

Figure 6: Distance-time functions. Left figure **(a)** represents a performance which starts and ends abruptly. Right figure **(b)** shows a performance which smoothly starts and stops.

Usually, the distance-time function is built analytically or by using a curve-editing tool. However, several assumptions are required to be contemplated [10]. For example, the distance-time function should be monotonic in t and continuous. But also, the common assumption is that the entire arc length of the curve should be traversed during the given total time. This means that:

$$s(0) = 0,$$
$$s(t_{end}) = s_{end}, \tag{14}$$

where $s_{end} = 1$ due to the normalization step described above, and $t_{end} = 1$. Obeying these normalization steps involves that distance-time curves can be reused with other *p–action* curves. Examples of distance-time functions are shown in Fig. 6.

Once we can determine the non-uniform speed at which any performance is played, we next proceed to modify the speed at which a new performance is sampled in order to synchronize it to our action model.

4.2 Comparison of performances

There are several applications which are interested in the analysis of a performance. Training of physically disabled persons and athletic performance analysis, for example, require of a comparison measure between different performances of the same action in order to improve the efficiency of an action performance. In other words, we will be able to determine "how well" a performance has been executed with respect to a reference model (in this paper, the *p-action*).

Using the arc length parameterization and the key-frames, a correspondence algorithm will be presented to establish a comparison measure between the *p-action* and any new performance of the same action. Thus, we can compare how the angles of the limbs evolve during any performance with respect to our model. The idea arises from the principle that any performance of a given action should present the key-frames of such an action. Thus, the key-frames will be considered as the reference postures in order to *adjust* the new performance to our action model. Therefore, the goal is to select a set of partition points of the new performance manifold, so that the key-frames are equally spaced in both manifolds.

Let be

$$\mathbf{g}(p), \qquad p \in [0, 1], \tag{15}$$

the manifold of the new performance in the *aSpace* parameterized by p (the posture configuration over time), as defined in Eq. (6).

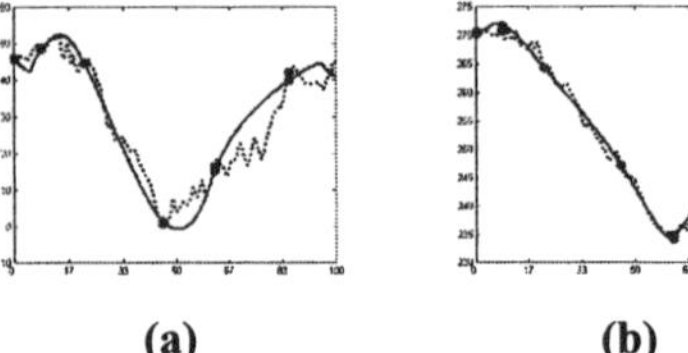

(a)   **(b)**

Figure 7: Synchronization of a new performance with the *p–action* $\mathbf{f}^A(p)$. The variation of the angles for the right arm **(a)** and for the right upper leg **(b)** during a new performance (dotted line) and during the *p–action* (solid line) is shown. By adjusting the key-frames (dots), the correspondence for both manifolds is established.

In order to compare two parametric curves, the correspondence process begins with the identification of the key-frames in the performance manifold. So, for each key-frame of the action, $\mathbf{K}_A = \{\mathbf{k}_1, \mathbf{k}_2, ..., \mathbf{k}_k\}$, we select the closest projection by using the Euclidean distance,

$$p_{\mathbf{k}_i} = \arg\min_p \| \mathbf{g}(p) - \mathbf{k}_i \|, \qquad p \in [0,1], i = 1, ..., k. \tag{16}$$

Thus, we obtain the set of projections $\mathbf{p}_\mathbf{k}^g = \{p_{\mathbf{k}_1}, p_{\mathbf{k}_2}, ..., p_{\mathbf{k}_k}\}$ which corresponds to the most characteristic postures (in temporal order) found in the new performance. Let be

$$\mathbf{s}_\mathbf{k}^g = \left\{ s_{\mathbf{k}_1}^g, s_{\mathbf{k}_2}^g, ..., s_{\mathbf{k}_k}^g \right\} \tag{17}$$

the arc lengths corresponding to the key-frames found in the new performance.

The second step is centered on determining each arc length in the *p–action* which corresponds to the key-frames, thus obtaining,

$$\mathbf{s}_\mathbf{k}^f = \left\{ s_{\mathbf{k}_1}^f, s_{\mathbf{k}_2}^f, ..., s_{\mathbf{k}_k}^f \right\}. \tag{18}$$

Now, let generate a sequence of consecutive arc lengths in the new performance so that $\mathbf{s}_\mathbf{k}^g$ be equally spaced as $\mathbf{s}_\mathbf{k}^f$. That is, let s_r be the sequence of r consecutive equally spaced arc lengths taken between $s_{\mathbf{k}_i}^f$ and $s_{\mathbf{k}_{i+1}}^f$. Similarly, by considering r consecutive equally spaced arc lengths between $s_{\mathbf{k}_i}^g$ and $s_{\mathbf{k}_{i+1}}^g$, we are actually sampling the new performance manifold so that the key-frames of both manifolds are time-coincident.

Fig. 4.**(b)** showed the manifold $\mathbf{f}^A(p)$ (dashed line), a new performance (solid line) and the synchronization of the new performance against $\mathbf{f}^A(p)$ (dotted line). Actually, we are modifying the speed at which a performance is sampled so that its key-frames coincide in time with the key-frames of the *p–action*.

In Fig. 7, the synchronization of a new performance with the *p–action* is displayed. The variation of the angles for the right arm (fig. 7.**(a)**) and for the right upper leg (fig. 7.**(b)**) during a new performance (dotted line) and during the *p–action* (solid line) is shown. The key-frames (dots) establish the correspondences for both manifolds. Thus, a comparison measure between new performances and our action model is attained.

As a result of such a synchronization process, differences between a performance and the prototypical action can be derived by analyzing the resulting angle variation curves. Such differences can be associated with natural language terms related to speed, naturalness, or suddenness, for example.

5 Conclusions

In this paper, we have developed a human action representation which allows to compare performances in order to further derive textual descriptions. Once human action recognition has been achieved, a more detailed analysis of an input performance will help to determine how the performance has been played with respect to our action model. As a result of such a comparison, the next step is centered on generating an accurate description of the performance by describing the quickness, naiveness, and brusqueness, for example.

6 Acknowledgements

This work has been supported by project TIC2000-0382 of spanish CICYT.

References

[1] K. Akita. Image sequence analysis of real world human motion. *Pattern Recognition*, 17(1):73–83, 1984.

[2] J. Ben-Aire, Z. Wang, P. Pandit, and S. Rajaram. Human activity recognition using multidimensional indexing. *IEEE Trans. Pattern Analysis and Machine Intelligence*, 24(8):1091–1104, 2002.

[3] A.F. Bobick and J. Davis. The representation and recognition of movement using temporal templates. *IEEE Trans. Pattern Analysis and Machine Intelligence*, 23(3):257–267, march 2001.

[4] H. Borotschnig, L. Paletta, M. Prantl, and A. Pinz. Appearance-based active object recognition. *Image and Vision Computing*, 18:715–727, 2000.

[5] J. Cheng and M.F. Moura. Capture and represention of human walking in live video sequences. *IEEE Transactions on Multimedia*, 1(2):144–156, 1999.

[6] J. Gonzàlez, X. Varona, F.X. Roca, and J.J. Villanueva. *aSpaces*: Action spaces for recognition and synthesis of human actions. In *Proc. Second International Workshop on Articulated Motion and Deformable Objects (AMDO 2002)*, pages 189–200, Palma de Mallorca, Spain, 2002.

[7] B. Guenter and R. Parent. Computing the arc length of parametric curves. *IEEE Computer Graphics and Applications*, 10(3):72–78, May 1990.

[8] A. Kale, N. Cuntoor, and R. Chellappa. A framework for activity-specific human recognition. In *Proceedings of the International Conference on Acoustics, Speech and Signal Processing*, volume 4, pages 3660–3663, Orlando, FL, May 2002.

[9] B. Moghaddam and A. Pentland. Probabilistic visual learning for object representation. *IEEE Trans. Pattern Analysis and Machine Intelligence*, 19(7):696–710, 1997.

[10] R. Parent. *Computer Animation. Algorithms and Techniques*. Morgan Kaufmann Publishers, San Francisco, CA, 2002.

[11] W. Press, B.P. Flannery, S.A. Teukolsky, and W.T. Vetterling. *Numerical Recipes in C*. Cambridge University Press, Cambridge, 1988.

[12] C.L. Sabharwal. An intelligent approach to discrete sampling of parametric curves. In *Proceedings of the 1993 ACM/SIGAPP symposium on Applied computing*, pages 397–401. ACM Press, 1993.

[13] J. Sullivan and S. Carlsson. Recognizing and tracking human action. In *Proceedings of the seventh European Conference Computer Vision (ECCV'02)*, pages 629–644, Copenhagen, Denmark, 2002.

[14] X. Varona, J. Gonzàlez, F.X. Roca, and J.J. Villanueva. Automatic selection of *keyframes* for activity recognition. In *Proc. First International Workshop on Articulated Motion and Deformable Objects (AMDO 2000)*, pages 173–181, Palma de Mallorca, Spain, 2000.

[15] L. Wang, W. Hu, and T. Tan. Recent developments in human motion analysis. *Pattern Recognition*, 36(3):585–601, 2003.

Artificial Intelligence Research and Development
I. Aguiló et al. (Eds.)
IOS Press, 2003

On the Feature Extraction for Gender Recognition Using the Nearest Neighbor Approach

David Masip[†], Jordi Vitrià[†]
Centre de Visió per Computador (CVC), Dept. Informàtica.
Universitat Autònoma de Barcelona
Bellaterra, Spain, 08193
{davidm, jordi}@cvc.uab.es

Abstract We propose an analysis of different face processing techniques for gender recognition problems. Prior research works show that support vector machines achieve the best classification results. We will show that a nearest neighbor classification approach can reach a similar performance or improve the SVM results, given an adequate selection of features of the input data. This selection is performed using a dimensionality reduction technique based on a modification of nonparametric discriminant analysis, designed to improve the nearest neighbor classification. The choice of nearest neighbor is specially justified by the use of a large database. We also analyse a nonlinear algorithm, locally linear embedding, and its supervised version. Given that this technique is focused in preserving the local configuration of the neighborhood of each point, it should be a priori a good dimensionality reduction technique to extract good features for nearest neighbor classification. A complete comparative study with the most important face processing techniques is also performed.

Keywords: Feature extraction, Dimensionality reduction, Gender Recognition, Nonparametric Discriminant Analysis, Nearest Neighbor Rule.

1 Introduction

The last years, computational resources are becoming smaller as well as more powerful. This evolution will allow the progressive introduction of technology in our every day life and new applications dealing with cameras will emerge. Some of the most important are related to face classification techniques. Typical examples are face recognition applied to security systems, face verification in authentication schemes, face and gesture analysis in user friendly interfaces, and gender and ethnicity recognition for applications of reactive publicity. In this paper we will deal with a gender recognition problem. We will show different schemes to solve it, and the results can be taken into account as a benchmark of techniques when we need to solve more general face classification tasks.

We propose a nearest neighbor approach for gender recognition. This election can be justified by the use of large face databases, and by taking advantage of proper feature extraction techniques. We will evaluate different feature extraction techniques applied to NN classification of gender in human faces, showing that nearest neighbor approach can compete with the best techniques for this task, such as PCA (see [1]) and Support Vector Machines (see [2]). To extract the optimal features for nearest neighbor classification we will evaluate linear and nonlinear techniques, and we will also show that the adequate modification of a discriminant analysis algorithm can provide the best features for NN classification. The main goal of this modification is minimize the intra-class variations, while the extra-class variance is maximized.

Data dimensionality reduction techniques have often been used in pattern recognition, and have been applied to different objectives. One possible application is to use these techniques for data compression reducing the amount of data of each sample by projecting the sample in a reduced space. Another application is the improvement of the classification algorithms by selecting the features that best separate the different classes, or simply reducing the noise present in natural images. Sometimes the reduction of dimensionality helps the training of the classifier too, by reducing the number of parameters to estimate.

Perhaps the most popular technique applied to face classification is Principal Component Analysis and eigenfaces [3, 4]. The goal in PCA is to find a linear projection to a low dimensional subspace, trying to preserve the maximum amount of variance of the input data. Other criteria can be applied to find the optimal projection, such as statistical independence (Independent Component Analysis [5]) and nonnegativity (Nonnegative Matrix Factorization[6]). If we take into account the labels of the training samples in the dimensionality reduction process, we can find the most discriminative features in a reduced space, where the distance between class samples is maximized. The classic discriminative technique is Fisher Linear Discriminant [7]. But FLD has two important drawbacks: the resulting dimensionality is upper bounded by the number of classes, and this complicates its application to the gender recognition problem (where there are only two classes). FLD also assumes Gaussian densities distributions in sample data, which degrades the performance in the case of more general distributions. In the next section we will introduce the Nonparametric Discriminant Analysis [8], and our modification of the original algorithm to overcome this drawbacks.

Another approach to dimensionality reduction is the use of nonlinear techniques. One of them is Locally Linear Embedding (LLE [9]), which will be analysed in section 3. The goal of LLE is to find the low dimensional space that best preserves the local configuration of each point with respect to its nearest neighbors, so we expect that the use of this technique will we useful for a nearest neighbor classification. We also evaluate a simple supervised version of the algorithm [10] which improves considerably the results.

In section 4 we will show some preprocessing and postprocessing steps to improve the NN classification, reducing the noise present in the data samples and using a combination of classifiers. In Section 5 we will show the face database and the gender recognition experiments performed. The final conclusions are shown in the last section.

2 Discriminant Analysis

As we use NN as classification rule, a proper feature extraction algorithm is needed, and Discriminant Analysis can be very useful for this task. In this section we will introduce classic Fisher Discriminant Analysis, to show later how its nonparametric extension can solve the main drawbacks of FLD: gaussian distribution assumption and reduced dimensionality of the generated subspaces. We will also show our modification of classic NDA [8], which is expected to improve the NN classification.

Table 1: General algorithm for solving the discriminability optimization problem stated in equation (2).

---

1. Given X the matrix containing data samples placed as N D-dimensional columns, S^I the within class scatter matrix, and M maximum dimension of discriminant space,

2. Compute eigenvectors and eigenvalues for S^I. Make Φ the matrix with the eigenvectors placed as columns and Λ the diagonal matrix with only the nonzero eigenvalues in the diagonal. M^I is the number of non-zero eigenvalues.

3. Whiten the data with respect to S^I, to obtain M^I dimensional whitened data,

$$Z = \Lambda^{-1/2}\Phi^T X.$$

4. Compute S^E on the whitened data.

5. Compute eigenvectors and eigenvalues for S^E and make Ψ the matrix with the eigenvectors placed as columns and sorted by decreasing eigenvalue value.

6. Preserve only the first $M^E = \min\{M^I, M, \mathrm{rank}(S^E)\}$ columns, $\Psi_M = \{\psi_1, \ldots, \psi_{M^E}\}$ (those corresponding to the M^E largest eigenvalues).

7. The resulting optimal transformation is $\hat{W} = \Psi_M^T \Lambda^{-1/2}\Phi^T$ and the projected data, $Y = \hat{W}X = \Psi_M^T Z$

2.1 Fisher Discriminant Analysis

The goal of discriminant analysis is to find the features that best separate the different classes. One of the most used criterions $\mathcal{J}$ to reach it is to maximize:

$$\mathcal{J} = tr(S^E S^I) \tag{1}$$

where the matrices S^E and S^I, generally represent the scatter of sample vectors between different classes and within a class respectively. It has been shown (see [11, 12]) that the $M \times D$ linear transform that satisfies:

$$\hat{W} = \arg \max_{W^T S^I W = I} tr(W^T S^E W) \tag{2}$$

optimizes the separability measure $\mathcal{J}$. This problem has an analytical solution based on the eigenvectors of the scatter matrices. The algorithm presented in table 1 obtains this solution [12]. The most widely spread approach for defining the within and between class scatter

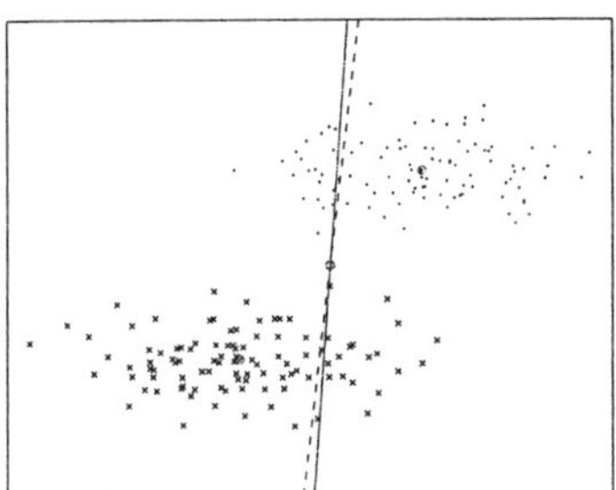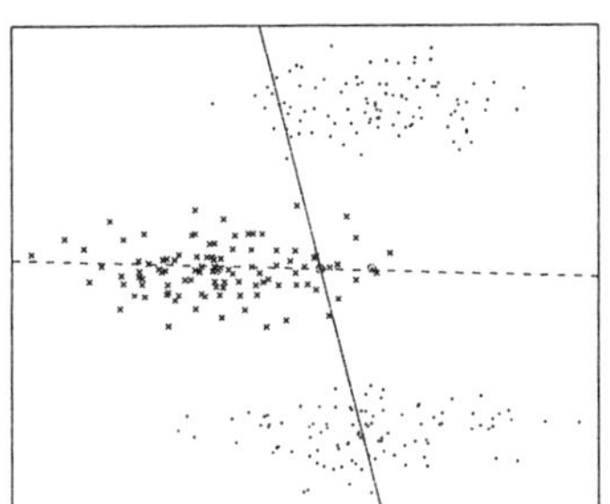

Figure 1: First directions of NDA (solid line) and FLD (dashed line) projections, for two artificial datasets. Observe the results in the right-hand figure, where the FLD assumptions are not met.

matrices is the one that makes use of only up to second order statistics of the data. This was done in a classic paper by Fisher [7] and the technique is referred to as Fisher Discriminant Analysis (FLD). In FLD the within class scatter matrix is usually computed as a weighted sum of the class-conditional sample covariance matrices. If equiprobable priors are assumed for classes C_k, $k = 1, \ldots, K$ then

$$S^I = \frac{1}{K} \sum_{k=1}^{K} \Sigma_k \tag{3}$$

where Σ_k is the class-conditional covariance matrix, estimated from the sample set. The between class-scatter matrix is defined as,

$$S^E = \frac{1}{K} \sum_{k=1}^{K} (\mu_k - \mu_0)(\mu_k - \mu_0)^T \tag{4}$$

where μ_k is the class-conditional sample mean and μ_0 is the unconditional (global) sample mean.

Notice the rank of S^E is $K - 1$, so the number of extracted features is, at most, one less than the number of classes. Also notice the parametric nature of the scatter matrix. The solution provided by FLD is blind beyond second-order statistics. So we cannot expect our method to accurately indicate which features should be extracted to preserve any complex classification structure.

2.2 Nonparametric Discriminant Analysis

In [8] Fukunaga and Mantock present a nonparametric method for discriminant analysis in an attempt to overcome the limitations present in FLD. In nonparametric discriminant analysis the between-class scatter S^E is of nonparametric nature. This scatter matrix is generally full rank, thus loosening the bound on extracted feature dimensionality. Also, the nonparametric structure of this matrix inherently leads to extracted features that preserve relevant structures for classification. We briefly expose this technique, extensively detailed in [12].

In NDA, the between-class scatter matrix is obtained from vectors locally pointing to another class. This is done as follows. The extra-class nearest neighbor for a sample $x \in C_k$ is defined as $x^E = \{x' \in \overline{C_k} / \|x' - x\| \leq \|z - x\|, \forall z \in \overline{C_k}\}$. In the same fashion we can define the set of intra-class nearest neighbors as $x^I = \{x' \in L_c / \|x' - x\| \leq \|z - x\|, \forall z \in C_k\}$.

From these neighbors, the extra-class differences are defined as $\Delta^E = x - x^E$ and the intra-class differences as $\Delta^I = x - x^I$. Notice that Δ^E points locally to the nearest class (or classes) that does not contain the sample. The nonparametric between-class scatter matrix is defined as (assuming uniform priors),

$$S^E = \frac{1}{N} \sum_{n=1}^{N} (\Delta_n^E)(\Delta_n^E)^T \tag{5}$$

where Δ_n^E is the extra-class difference for sample x_n.

A parametric form is chosen for the within-class scatter matrix S^I, defined as in (3). Figure (1) illustrates the differences between NDA and FLD in two artificial datasets, one with Gaussian classes where results are similar, and one where FLD assumptions are not met.

For the second case, the bimodality of one of the classes displaces the class mean introducing errors in the estimate of the parametric version of S^E. The nonparametric version is not affected by this situation.

We now make use of the introduced notation to examine the relationship between NN and NDA. This results in a modification of the within class covariance matrix which we also introduce.

Given a training sample x, the accuracy of the 1-NN rule can be directly computed by examining the ratio $\|\Delta^E\|/\|\Delta^I\|$. If this ratio is more than one, x will be correctly classified. Given the $M \times D$ linear transform W, the projected distances are defined as $\Delta_W^{E,I} = W\Delta^{E,I}$. Notice that this definition does not exactly agree with the extra and intra-class distances in projection space since, except for the orthonormal transformation case, we have no warranty on distance preservation. Equivalence of both definitions is asymptotically true. By the above remarks it is expected, that optimization of the following objective function should improve or, at least not downgrade NN performance,

$$\hat{W} = \arg \max_{E\{\|\Delta_W^I\|^2\}=1} E\{\|\Delta_W^E\|^2\} \tag{6}$$

This optimization problem can be interpreted as: find the linear transform that maximizes the distance between classes, preserving the expected distance among the members of a single class. Considering that,

$$E\{\|\Delta_W\|^2\} = E\{(W\Delta)^T(W\Delta)\} = \mathrm{tr}(W^T\Delta\Delta^T W) \tag{7}$$

where Δ can be Δ^I or Δ^E. Replacing (7) in (6) we have that this last equation is a particular case of eq. (2). Additionaly, the formulas for the within and between class scatter matrices are directly extracted from this equation. In this case, the between-class scatter matrix agrees with (5), but the within-class scatter matrix is now defined in a nonparametric fashion,

$$S_w = \frac{1}{N}\sum_{n=1}^{N} \Delta_n^I \Delta_n^{I^T} \tag{8}$$

Given that we have an optimization problem of the form given in (2) the algorithm presented in table (1) can also be applied to the optimization of our proposed objective function (6).

3 Locally Linear Embedding (LLE)

As has been shown NDA and PCA are linear transformations of the input data applied to dimensionality reduction. The goal of LLE [9] is to find a mapping from a high dimensional space to a low dimensional one too, but performed in a nonlinear way. Sometimes the high dimensional data lies in a nonlinear manifold which can be represented using less dimensions than the dimensionality of the original points. To reach this objective, LLE takes into account the restriction that neighborhood points in the high dimensional space must remain in the same neighborhood in the low dimensional space, and placed in a similar relative spatial situation (it doesn't change the local structure of the nearest neighbors of each point).
Given N D-dimensional training images as input vectors x_n to the LLE technique, a 3 step algorithm detailed in table 2 is performed to find the low dimensional space.

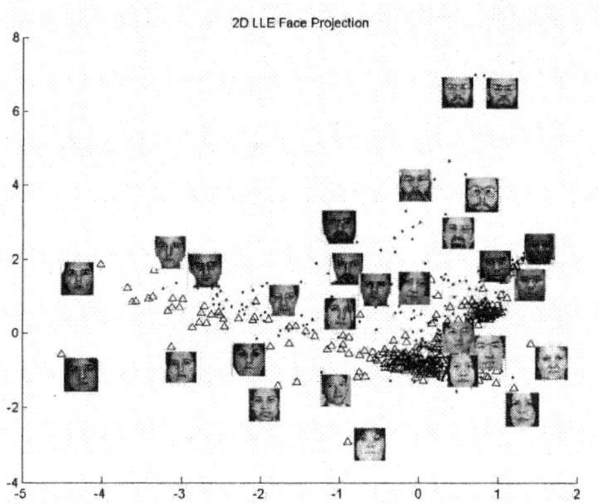

Figure 2: 2-dimensional reduction of faces using LLE. Original faces are plotted near each reduced point. Triangles stand for female subjects and dots for male subjects. As can be observed some characteristics as global illumination, beard presence (on the up-right corner), or ethnicity are captured by LLE embedding.

3.1　Supervised LLE

As we are dealing with classification algorithms, an interesting approach is to consider the class membership of the train vectors to achieve class separation [10]. The main difference between LLE and SLLE is the first step of the algorithm, the search of the nearest neighbors. While LLE looks for the K nearest neighbors of each point from the whole data set, SLLE only searches the K nearest neighbors from the set of points belonging to the same class of each point. So the weights computed in the second step encode the best way of reconstructing each point from its nearest neighbors of the same class of the point. The rest of the algorithm is identical to the exposed LLE.

3.2　Projections of the test vectors

As has been shown, the LLE algorithm is a globally nonlinear technique. This property has some advantages when finding the underlaying manifolds, but there's an important drawback when a new point u is entered as a new input to the system. An approximation of the mapping is necessary in order to avoid rerunning the algorithm each time (solving the expensive eigenvector problem). Parametric (probabilistic) and non-parametric models have been used to solve this problem (see [13, 9]).

Another approach [14] is to the find the k nearest neighbors of the new point u using the points of the training set x_n. Then compute the reconstructing weights W_{nk} using this neighbors. And finally compute the coordinates of the point u in the reduced space as:

$$y = \sum_{j=1}^{k} W_j \cdot y_{N(j)} \tag{12}$$

Table 2: LLE Algorithm

---

1. First we compute the K nearest neighbors of each point.

2. Capture the local geometry of the input data, using a set of W coefficients per each point, corresponding to the weights W_{nk} that best reconstruct the vector x_n from its K nearest neighbors x_{n_k}, minimizing the error reconstruction equation:

$$\varepsilon(W) = \sum_{n=1}^{N} |x_n - \sum_{k=1}^{K} W_{nk} x_{n_k}|^2 \tag{9}$$

To find the vectors that minimize this equation, a least-squares problem must be solved. For more details see [13].

3. In the last step the coordinates of each point in the low dimensional space $d' \ll D$ are computed as the vectors y_n that best minimize the equation:

$$\theta(y) = \sum |y_i - \sum W_{nk} y_{n_k}|^2 \tag{10}$$

The weights found during the previous stage are constant, and we want to find the low dimensional outputs y_n that best reconstruct each vector using the information of these weights, which capture the local geometric properties of each point in the original space.A new sparse matrix M is created and defined as:

$$M_{ij} = \delta_{ij} - W_{ij} - W_{ji} + \sum_{k=1}^{K} W_{ki} W_{kj} \tag{11}$$

It can be proved that the output vectors y_n are the $d'+1$ eigenvectors of the matrix M associated to the lowest eigenvalues (see [13, 9] for more details).

---

where $y_{N(j)}$ are the points in the low dimensional space corresponding to the used nearest neighbors of the point u in the high dimensional space.

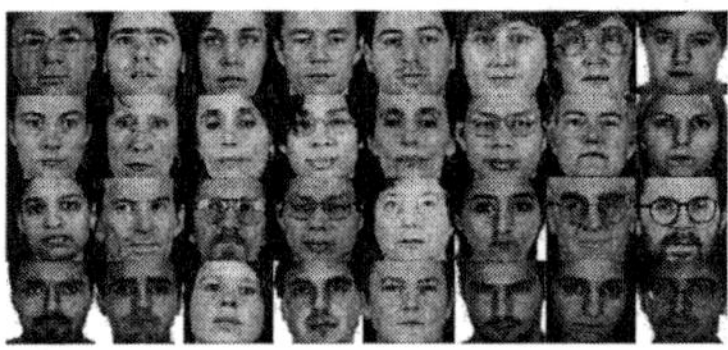

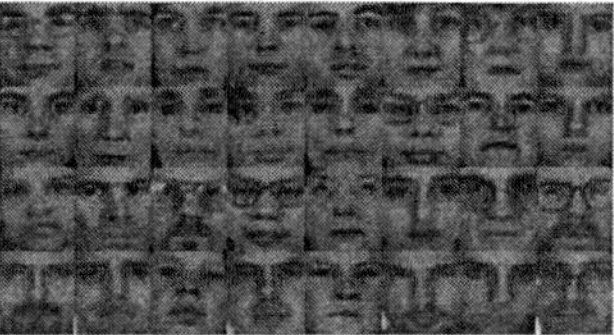

(a) Original Images   (b) Processed images

Figure 3: Examples of face images used in the experiment before and after applying the mean-variance normalization.

4 Improving the Performance

In order to improve the performance of LLE and NDA algorithms, we have analysed the use of a preprocessing step in both algorithms. The NDA algorithm tries to maximize the mean distances to the nearest neighbors of the extra class vectors, while minimizes the distances between vectors of the same class. This criterion is very useful to discriminate and classify samples, but it can be seriously affected by the noise present in the most part of the natural images. To solve this problem we have added an initial PCA dimensionality reduction step, which filters the noise preserving the most part of the data variance. Using the first 300 principal components with the face data set, the 98% of the variance is preserved, and we have seen that any choice from 200 to 400 principal components yield similar results after NDA reduction and NN classification. We realized experimentally that this stage improves considerably the results of NDA, so we have merged the NDA projection matrix with the PCA basis to construct the final projection.

Another approach to improve the results is the use of a combination of classifiers as a postprocessing step. Two different techniques can be useful for this task, boosting [15] and bagging [16]. The goal of boosting is to combine a set of weak classifiers in order to get a classifier with better performance. On the other hand bagging tries to improve the performance by bootstrapping the data samples in different sets, and combining the results of the classification using each set, with some rule such as majority voting or simply averaging the results. The goal of bagging is to avoid or reduce the influence of misleading examples, because they can be isolated in a few sets, having low influence in the final voting results. In our classification scheme it's difficult to use boosting, because the hypothesis of a weak classifier assumed in boosting is not fulfilled. Bagging, on the other hand, can be very useful in the NDA scheme (as we will show in the results). We have broken the training set into subsets, and we have learned the NDA algorithm in each one using low dimensionality (≈ 10). Then we have used the NN rule to classify each projected sample, and we have combined the results using majority voting. The final result shows that bagging increases a little bit the performance of our scheme. The use of bagging has also another important advantage, the lower computational cost due to perform the dimensionality reduction using reduced subsets, and to lower dimensionality spaces.

5 Gender recognition experiment

We are facing a gender recognition problem, so we have tested our modification of the NDA algorithm and the LLE nonlinear projection for this purpose. We have also compared the results with other spread classification algorithms.

5.1 Image database

In this experiment, we have used a face database composed of samples of two different internet available faces databases, the AR Face database [17] and XM2VTS database [18]. As a preprocessing step, all images have been aligned, manually selecting the center pixel of each eye, and translating and resizing the face image with respect to eye distance. Once face images have both eyes in the same position, they have been cropped to a 40-by-32 thumbnail. Then a global mean-variance normalization has been performed. The final data set consist of 3461 1280-dimensional vectors. As can be seen in fig. (3) we have tried to avoid the presence of hair information in the final face database, what makes the problem more difficult to solve [2].

The error rates shown in the results were estimated with five-fold cross validation. The 3461 data samples were broken in 5 sets, 4 of them used for training, and the other one used for testing (we repeated it for the 5 sets and averaged the results). We have built the sets in a pseudo random way, following three basic restrictions:

1. The same number of male and female should appear in each set.

2. Faces from the same person can not be present in more than one set, in order to avoid person recognition instead of gender recognition.

3. The number of faces of each database should be very similar for each group.

As can be seen in table (3), our modification of NDA algorithm improves the results of classic dimensionality reduction techniques, PCA and FLD. We can see how FLD performs worse than nearest neighbor classification in the original space. This happens due to the limitations of FLD when non-gaussian data is used, and due to the fact of dealing with a two class problem, the resulting 1-dimensional projected space is not enough to separate both classes. NDA algorithm overcomes these drawbacks. We also show the results obtained using the standard NDA without mean-variance normalization (NDA-WN) in the data set. We have tested all the algorithms using this non normalized set and the accuracies decreased significantly, except for the NDA technique.

We have also added a bagging step to improve the NDA results. The training set has been broken in 49 subsets and we have trained a NDA reduction to a 16 dimensional space in each set. The final label assignation is obtained by majority voting. This technique has achieved the best results in our experiments, even slightly better than SVM. Another important advantage of the NDA algorithm, is that it's able to reach the best performance even in very reduced spaces. As we can see in fig. (4), in a 20-dimensional space it reaches accuracies close to 90%, with low computational cost.

On the other hand we can see how LLE is a bad algorithm to use in gender classification [1] unless we use the supervised version of the technique. Initially we thought that the preservation of the local configuration of each point would improve the results of a nearest neighbor classifier, but the results are far from the other analysed techniques. As can be seen in fig. (2) LLE projection captures data related to global illumination, ethnicity, gesture, beard, but it doesn't allow good gender discrimination with a nearest neighbor approach. We can also see in the results how the supervised version of LLE achieves performances close to the other analysed techniques, specially in low dimensional subspaces.

Table 3: Gender recognition accuracies

Algorithm	Accuracy
NN	86.28
PCA	86.57
SVM	90.95
FLD	81.30
LLE	76.27
NDA	90.56
Bagged NDA	91.76
NDA-WN	88.81
SLLE	87.12

6 Conclusions

In this paper we have compared different nearest neighbor classification approaches for gender recognition and classification problems in general. We emphasize the importance of ex-

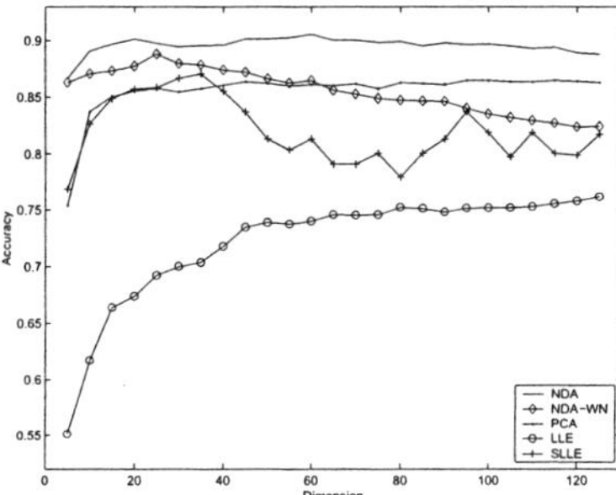

Figure 4: Recognition rate as a function of final dimension

tracting good features of the high dimensional data, focused on improve the NN classification . In particular we have analysed a modification of non parametric discriminant analysis algorithm, which obtains the best accuracies in our experiments. The results obtained show that the use of NDA allows the best classification rates even in low dimensional subspaces and using non preprocessed data , which makes the algorithm computationally efficient.
Another important consideration is the use of bagging to improve the results, and even make the algorithm computationally more efficient due the fact of working with reduced subsets of the training data. This efficiency could allow the use of the algorithm in real time environments.
We also show the performance of the LLE algorithm for the same purpose. Initially, we thought that LLE could be the ideal representation for a nearest neighbor approach due to its interesting property of conserving the local geometry of close points. The results have shown that this technique achieves poor accuracies unless we use its supervised version.

Acknowledgment

This work is supported by grant TIC2000-0399-C02-01, and Ministerio de Ciencia y Tecnologia, Spain.

References

[1] A. B. Graf and F. A. Wichmann, "Gender classification of human faces," vol. 2525, pp. 491–501., nov 2002.

[2] M. B. and Yang, "Learning gender with support faces," *IEEE Trans. Pattern Anal. Machine Intell.*, vol. 24, no. 5, pp. 707–711, jan 2002.

[3] M. Turk and A. Pentland, "Eigenfaces for recognition," *Journal of Cognitive Neuroscience*, vol. 3, no. 1, pp. 71–86, 1991.

[4] M. Kirby and L. Sirovich, "Application of the karhunen-loeve procedure for the characterization of human faces," *IEEE Trans. Pattern Anal. Machine Intell.*, vol. 12, no. 1, pp. 103–108, Jan 1990.

[5] A. Hyvarinen, J. Karhunen, and E. Oja, *Independent Component Analysis.*   John Wiley and Sons, 2001.

[6] D. D. Lee and H. S. Seung, "Learning the parts of objects with nonnegative matrix factorization," *Nature*, vol. 401, pp. 788–791, July 1999.

[7] R. Fisher, "The use of multiple measurements in taxonomic problems," *Ann. Eugenics*, vol. 7, pp. 179–188, 1936.

[8] K. Fukunaga and J. Mantock, "Nonparametric discriminant analysis," *IEEE Trans. Pattern Anal. Machine Intell.*, vol. 5, no. 6, pp. 671–678, nov 1983.

[9] R. S. T. and S. L. K., "Nonlinear dimensionality reduction by locally linear embedding," *Science*, vol. 290, pp. 2323–2326, 2000.

[10] K. O. Okun O and P. M, "Supervised locally linear embedding algorithm," in *Proc. of the 10th Finnish Artificial Intelligence Conference*, Oulu, Finland, Dec 2001.

[11] P. Devijver and J. Kittler, *Pattern Recognition: A Statistical Approach.* London, UK: Prentice Hall, 1982.

[12] K. Fukunaga, *Introduction to Statistical Pattern Recognition*, 2nd ed. Boston, MA: Academic Press, 1990.

[13] S. L. K. and R. S. T., "Think globally, fit locally: Unsupervised learning of nonlinear manifolds," University of Pennsylvania, Tech. Rep. CIS-02-18, 2002.

[14] D. de Ridder and R. P. Duin, "Locally linear embedding for classification," Delft University of Technology, Tech. Rep., 2002.

[15] R. E. Schapire, "A brief introduction to boosting," in *IJCAI*, 1999, pp. 1401–1406.

[16] M. Skurichina and R. P.W.Duin, "Bagging, boosting and the random subspace method for linear classifiers," *Pattern Analysis and Applications*, vol. 5, pp. 121–135, 2002.

[17] A. Martinez and R. Benavente, "The ar face database," Computer Vision Center, Tech. Rep. 24, june 1998.

[18] J. Matas, M. Hamouz, K. Jonsson, J. Kittler, Y. Li, C. Kotropoulos, A. Tefas, I. Pitas, T. Tan, H. Yan, F. Smeraldi, J. Bigun, N.Capdevielle, W. Gerstner, S. Ben-Yacoub, Y. Abdeljaoued, and E. Mayoraz., "Comparison of face verifiacation results on the xm2vts database," in *ICPR*, Jul 1999.

Artificial Intelligence Research and Development
I. Aguiló et al. (Eds.)
IOS Press, 2003

Quasi-Simultaneous Motion Segmentation and Estimation Using an Iterative Region Growing Algorithm

Raul Montoliu and Filiberto Pla
Dept. Lenguajes y Sistemas Informaticos
Universitat Jaume I. 12071 Castellon

Abstract. This paper presents a new framework for the motion segmentation and estimation task on sequences of two grey images without a priori information of the number of moving regions present in the sequence. The proposed algorithm uses temporal information, by using an accurate Generalized Least-Squares Motion Estimation process and spatial information by using an iterative region growing algorithm. The initial regions of pixels are obtained from a given grey-level segmentation process. The performance of the algorithm is tested on synthetic and real images with multiple objects undergoing different types of motion.

1 Introduction

Segmentation of moving objects in a video sequence is basic task for several applications of computer vision, e.g. a video monitoring system, intelligent-highway system, tracking, airport safety, surveillance tasks and so on. In this paper, Motion Segmentation, also called spatial-temporal segmentation, refers to labelling pixels which are associated with different coherently moving objects or regions in a sequence of two images. Motion Estimation refers to assigning a motion vector to each region (or pixel) in an image.

Perfoming Motion Estimation and Motion Segmentation simultaneously falls in a *Hen-and-egg* problem. It is due to the fact that data classification and parameter estimation strongly depend on each other. It is known that, on the one hand, if the data is well-classified, i.e, we know which pixel support which model, then it is easy to obtain accurate estimated for the parameters. On the other hand, if we know accurate estimates of the parameters, then it is straightforward to classify the pixels into the models.

The Motion Segmentation and Estimation problem has been formulated in many different ways ([5], [11], [6], [3]). We choose to approach this problem as a multi-structural parametric fitting problem. In this context, the segmentation problem is similar to robust statistical regression. The main difference is that robust statistical regression usually involves statistics for data having one target distribution and corrupted with random outliers. Motion segmentation problems usually have more than one population with distinct distributions and not necessarily with a population having absolute majority.

The problem of fitting an a priori known model to a set of noisy data (with random outliers) was studied in the statistical community for a number of decades. One important contribution was the Least Median of Squares (LMedS) robust estimator but it has the break down point of 50%. This means that LMedS technique needs the population recovered to have at least a majority of 50% (plus 1). Other robust estimators have been developed in order to overcome this problem, which is frequently encountered in different computer vision tasks. They are Adaptive Least k-th Order residual (ALKS) [7] and Minimum Unbiased Scale Estimator (MUSE) [8]. These techniques minimize the k-th order statistic of the square residuals where the optimum value for the k is determined from the data. The problem of both techniques is the estimation of the correct value of k suffers high computation effort.

To overcome the computational complexity Bab-Hadiashar and Suter presented a method named Selective Statistical Estimator (SSE) [1] which is a variation of the Least K-th order statistic data regression where the user proposes the value k as the lower limit of the size populations one is interested in. All the Motion Segmentation LKS-based algorithms start selecting an initial model using random sampling, and classifying all the pixels into this model using a scale measure. With the remaining pixels the process is repeated until all the pixel have been classified. The main problem of these algorithms is that there are frequently pixels that can be more suitable to belong to a model but they have been classified in an earlier model.

Danuser and Stricker [4] presented a similar framework for parametric model fitting. Their algorithm has a fitting step that is one component of the algorithm which also collect model inliers, detects data outliers and determines the a priori unknown total number of meaningful models in the data. They apply a quasi simultaneous application of a general Least Squares fitting while classifying observations in the different parametric data models. They applied their algorithm to multiple lines and planes fitting tasks. The most important advantages with respect to LKS-based algorithms are the use of an exchange step, that permits change of observation among models, and the use of a inliers/outliers classification process, which increases the accuracy of the segmentation.

In [9] a quasi-simultaneous motion segmentation and estimation method based on a parametric model fitting algorithm was presented. The method accurately estimates the affine motion parameters using a generalized least squares fitting process. It also classifies the pixels into the motion models present in two consecutive frames. This algorithm uses each pixel of the image as observation. It suffers from problems of isolated points because it does not use neighbourhood information and need good initial models to obtain the final motion segmentation. Nevertheless, it indicates that the quasi-simultaneous application of the inliers/outliers classification algorithm and the accurate motion estimator can be useful to be applied in Motion Segmentation tasks.

This paper presents a Motion Segmentation and Estimation algorithm that, instead of using the pixel as observation, it uses regions of pixels. The use of regions made the segmentation more spatial consistent. In addition, the algorithm uses neighbourhood constraints to collect new inliers to the model, only regions that are neighbour of the model are considered to be inliers. This algorithm also erases the need of a previous good segmentation of the models, and allow extracting the model without a priori information of the number of moving regions present in the sequence.

The rest of the paper is organized as follows: Section 2 explains the complete Motion Segmentation and Estimation algorithm. Section 3 presents a set of experiments in order to verify the results obtained with our approach. Finally, some conclusions drawn from this work are described.

2 Algorithm Outline

In this paper we use the term **Model** as a structure with two elements, the first is a parametric motion vector and the second is a list of regions of the image that support the parametric motion vector. We refer as **Region** to a set of pixels with grey-level coherence.

The input of the algorithm are two images of a sequence, the first one I_1 captured at time t and the second one I_2 captured at time $t + 1$. The output of the algorithm are a motion-based segmentated image I_s and a list of motion parameters corresponding at each model in I_s. For the sake of clarity, we describe the proposed algorithm in 6 steps:

1. **Preliminaries**: In this step, I_2 is segmented using a given grey level segmentation algorithm. The regions obtained are used as input of the algorithm. An adjacency graph of the previous segmentation is created. In addition, the spatial derivates of the images I_1 and I_2 are estimated.

   The purpose of the grey-level segmentation process is to classify the pixels into regions. Our Motion Segmentation algorithm requires that each segmented region should not have pixels belonging to more than one final motion models. Any grey level segmentation algorithm that fulfill the previous constraint can be used. A sieve-based grey level segmentation algorithm [2] has been used, since it produces a hierarchical representation of the image with different segmentations that differ in the region size. A segmentation with small regions must be used to fulfill the constraint.

2. **Get Initial Model**: The aim of this process is find the best possible start point to the global Motion Segmentation and Estimation algorithm. A good initial model is made up of a set of regions that have a high likelihood to belong to the same model. The process starts selecting a region randomly. A model with this region and its neighbours is formed. The motion is estimated for this model using the process in subsection 2.2. A goodness measure GM is calculated for this model. The previous step is repeated q times. The model with the best goodness measure is selected as the initial model.

   The goodness measure is calculated using the following expression: $GM = ((1 - l_{avg}) * 2 + (l_{best} - l_{worst}))$ where l_{avg} is the average of the likelihood $L_{M_n}(R)$ for each region R using the motion model M_n (see subsection 2.1), l_{best} is the highest likelihood of the regions and l_{worst} is the lowest likelihood of the regions. Therefore, the best initial model is the one which has the less GM.

3. **Improve the model**: An iterative classification process (see subsection 2.1) is started in order to find the inliers and to reject outliers between the k regions that make up the initial model. With the set of resulting regions, we start another classification process with the neighbours of the last inserted regions not yet processed. This classification step continues until there are not more new neighbour regions to be processed.

4. **Exchange of regions**: If a valid model M_n has been extracted, then a region exchange procedure is started. The goal of this procedure is to reclassify regions that have been captured by an early model M_m where $m < n$. A region is moved if it lies closer to the new extracted model and there is a neighbour relationship between the region and the new model. If all the regions of the model M_m lie closer to the new Model M_n then the model M_m is deleted. When for each region of model M_m we can not decide if it lies closer to

the model M_m or to the model M_n, then the models are merged, that is, it is considered both models have similar motion parameters.

5. **Repeat**: Go to step 2 and repeat the same process with another initial model if any. If there is any problem estimating the motion of some model, e.g. not enough texture information, not enough number of observations, etc., the regions of this model are moved to a set called *regions with problems* (RWP).

6. **End**: When all possible models have been extracted, the models that only have one region are tested in order to try to merge them with their neighbour models. In addition, for each region in the RWP set is tested in order to move it into some of the models in its neighbourhood.

2.1   Inliers/Outliers Classification

The aim of this process is to classify the regions of a model (according to its motion parameters) in two sets, inliers: regions that support the motion parameters and outliers: regions that do not support them. The loop of this classification process consists of:

1. Estimate the motion parameters using all the pixels belonging to the regions of the model (see subsection 2.2).

2. Look for outliers into the regions of the model, if there are outliers, improve the motion parameters using only the remaing regions. A region R is considered outlier (with respect to model M_n) if the likelihood of region R belonging to a model M_n is lower than a threshold.

3. Test each outlier if it can be now considered inlier according to the new estimated parameters. If there are new inliers, the parameters are improved again. A region R is considered inlier (with respect to model M_n) if the likelihood of the region R belonging to a model M_n is higher than a threshold.

4. Go to step 2 and repeat until there are not changes in the set of regions of the model.

In order to estimate a likelihood of a region R belonging to a model M_n, the next expressions are used:

$$L_{M_n}(R) = \left(\sum_{p_i \in R} L_{M_n}(p_i)\right)/N_R$$

$$L_{M_n}(p_i) = e^{-0.5 * \frac{F_{M_n}^2(p_i)}{\sigma_2}}$$

(1)

where N_R is the number of pixels of the region R. For each pixel p_i belonging to the region R the likelihood $L_{M_n}(p_i)$ of the pixel belonging to a model M_n is calculated. This likelihood ([3]) has been modelled as a gaussian like function where $F_{M_n}(p_i)$ is the residual for the pixel p_i of the objective function using the motion parametric vector of the model M_n. A region is considered as inlier when this measure is higher than a threshold and it is considered as outlier when its measure is lower than a threshold.

2.2 *Motion Estimation*

The Generalized Least Squares (GLS) algorithm is used in order to obtain the motion parameters of a model. The GLS algorithm [4] is based on minimizing an objective function O over a set S of r observation vectors, $S = \{L_1, \ldots, L_r\}$.

$$O = \sum_{L_i \in S} (F_i(\chi, L_i))^2 \tag{2}$$

where $\chi = (\chi^1, \ldots, \chi^p)$ is a vector of p parameters and L_i is a vector of n observation $L_i = (L_i^1, \ldots, L_i^n)$, $i = 1 \ldots r$.

The equation (2) is non-linear, but it can be linearized using the Taylor expansion and neglecting higher order terms. This implies that an iterative solution has to be found. At each iteration, the algorithm estimates $\Delta\chi$, that improves the parameters as follows: $\chi_{t+1} = \chi_t + \Delta\chi$. The increment $\Delta\chi$ is calculated (see [4]) using the following expressions:

$$\Delta\chi = \left(A^T(BB^T)^{-1}A\right)^{-1} A^T(BB^T)^{-1}W$$

$$B = \begin{pmatrix} B_1 & 0 & 0 & 0 \\ 0 & B_2 & 0 & 0 \\ \cdots & \cdots & \cdots & \cdots \\ 0 & 0 & 0 & B_r \end{pmatrix}_{(r \times (r \times n))}$$

$$A = \begin{pmatrix} A_1 \\ A_2 \\ \cdots \\ A_r \end{pmatrix}_{(r \times p)} \qquad W = \begin{pmatrix} w_1 \\ w_2 \\ \cdots \\ w_r \end{pmatrix}_{(r \times 1)} \tag{3}$$

$$B_i = \left(\frac{\partial F_i(\chi_t, L_i)}{\partial L_i^1}, \ldots, \frac{\partial F_i(\chi_t, L_i)}{\partial L_i^n} \right)_{(1 \times n)}$$

$$A_i = \left(\frac{\partial F_i(\chi_t, L_i)}{\partial \chi^1}, \ldots, \frac{\partial F_i(\chi_t, L_i)}{\partial \chi^p} \right)_{(1 \times p)}$$

$$w_i = -F_i(\chi_t, L_i)$$

In motion estimation problems ([10]) the objective function is based on the assumption that the grey level of all the pixels of a region remains constant between two consecutive images. The objective function is expressed as follows:

$$O = \sum_{L_i \in S} (F_i(\chi, L_i))^2 = \sum_{L_i \in S} (I_1(x_i', y_i') - I_2(x_i, y_i))^2 \tag{4}$$

where $I_1(x_i', y_i')$ is the grey level of the first image in the sequence at the transformed point x_i', y_i', and $I_2(x_i, y_i)$ are the grey level of the second image in the sequence at point x_i, y_i. Here, for each point i ($i = 1 \ldots r$, being r the number of pixels) the vector of observations $L_i = (x_i, y_i, I_2(x_i, y_i))$ has three elements ($n = 3$): column, row and grey level of second image at these coordinates.

The motion parameters vector, χ, depends on the motion model being used. The affine motion model is used in this work, which is able to cope with translations, scaling, rotation

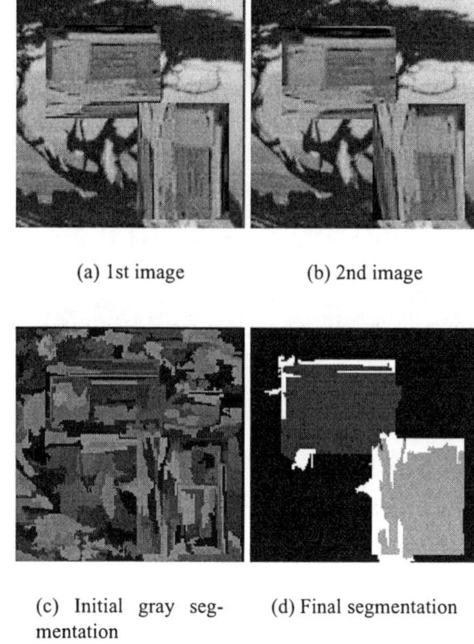

(a) 1st image   (b) 2nd image

(c) Initial gray seg-   (d) Final segmentation
mentation

Figure 1: Both images of the synthetic sequence and results

and shear of images and is defined with a vector of $\chi = (a_1, b_1, c_1, a_2, b_2, c_2)$, $(p = 6)$. The affine motion model relates the transformed coordinates x_i', y_i' to each point x_i, y_i as follows:

$$x_i' = a_1 x_i + b_1 y_i + c_1$$
$$y_i' = a_2 x_i + b_2 y_i + c_2 \tag{5}$$

Therefore, in our motion estimation problem, B_i, A_i and w_i are expressed as follows:

$$B_i = \left(a_1 I_x^1 + a_2 I_y^1 - I_x^2, b_1 I_x^1 + b_2 I_y^1 - I_y^2, -1.0 \right)_{(1 \times 3)}$$
$$A_i = \left(x_i I_x^1, y_i I_x^1, I_x^1, x_i I_y^1, y_i I_y^1, I_y^1 \right)_{(1 \times 6)} \tag{6}$$
$$w_i = - \left(I_1(x_i', y_i') - I_2(x_i, y_i) \right)$$

where I_x^1, I_y^1, are the gradient of first image at the pixel (x_i', y_i') in x and y direction, and I_x^2, I_y^2, are the gradient of second image at the pixel (x_i, y_i) in x and y direction.

3   Experimental Results

In order to show the performance of the approach presented, two types of experiments have been done. In the first experiment, synthetic sequences have been used, where the results

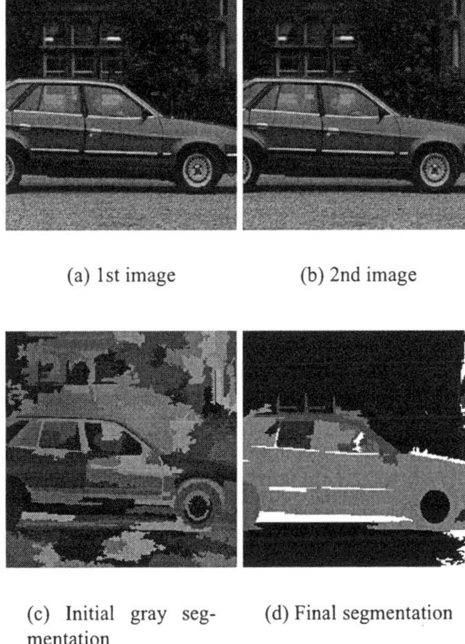

(a) 1st image   (b) 2nd image

(c) Initial gray seg-   (d) Final segmentation
mentation

Figure 2: Both images of the real sequence and results

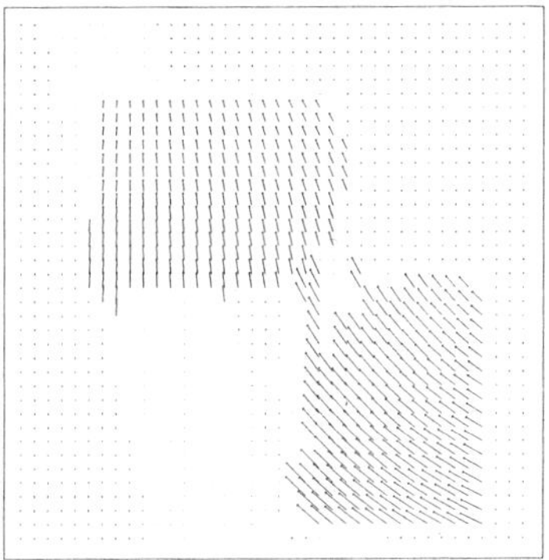

Figure 3: Optic Flow computed from results of the synthetic sequence

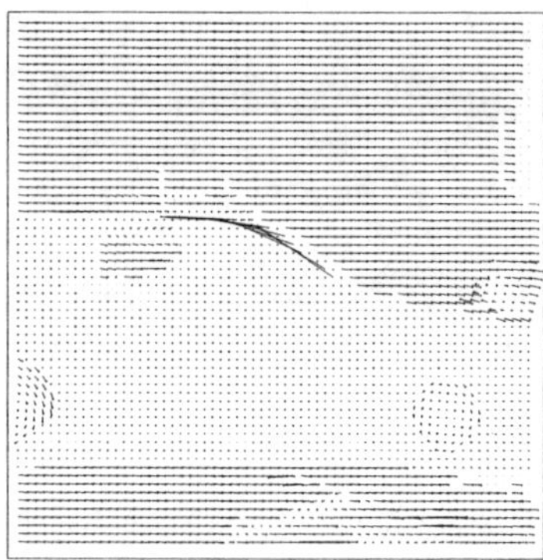

Figure 4: Optic Flow computed from results of the real sequence

of the motion segmentation and the motion parameters of each model are known. In this synthetic sequence three different motion models can be found. The first is the background, which does not perform motion, i.e. it is static. The second motion model performs a change of scale and the third corresponds to a rotational motion.

In the second experiment real scenes are used, where the final motion segmentation and the motion parameters of each model are unknown. The main motions of the real scene are the background produced by the camera motion, the motion of the car and the motion of the wheels.

Figure 1 shows both images of the synthetic sequence, the initial gray segmentation used and the final segmentation obtained, where each final motion model is labelled with a different RGB color. Figure 2 shows both images of the real sequence, the initial gray segmentation used and the final segmentation obtained. White pixels in subfigures 1d and 2d are the ones that have not been classified in any model. These regions correspond mainly to regions belonging to occluded areas due to the motion and to regions that do not fulfill the requirement of belonging only to a model, i.e. some pixels belong to a model and some other belong to a different model.

Figures 3 and 4 show the optic flow for both sequences. They have been computed using the motion parameters of each model in all the pixel belonging to them. They are presented in order to illustrate the motion models estimated.

In order to test the accuracy of the model, two measures have been calculated. P_{WS} is the percentage of pixels that have been well-classified with respect to an ideal segmented image. P_{WME} is the percentage of pixels where the motion have been well estimated. For this purpose, the second image of the sequence is compared with a new image generated from the first image of the sequence using the motion parameters of each motion model found. So, P_{WME} is the percentage of pixels where the difference of grey level in both images is less than a threshold, i.e. the percentage of static pixels.

For the synthetic sequence $P_{WS} = 91.5\%$ and $P_{WME} = 99.7\%$. The three motion models have been accurately segmentated and their corresponding motion parameters are also accurately estimated. The main difficulties in the synthetic sequence are the regions that have pixels belonging to more than one model and the regions in occluded areas due to the motion. They have been correctly classified as member of the outliers set.

For the real sequence $P_{WME} = 88.1\%$. The main motions of this sequence have been segmentated, they are the background and the motion of the car. The main difficulties with the real scene are the motion of the wheels, since although our method has detected a rotational motion, it has less magnitude than real. Nevertheless, interesting results have been obtained in the windows, detecting the motion of the background and the motion of the driver. The outliers are also mainly detected in regions that have pixels belonging to more than one final model and in the regions in occluded areas.

4 Conclusions

In this paper, a motion segmentation and estimation algorithm has been presented, which can extract different moving regions of the scene quasi-simultaneously and without a priori information of the number of moving objects. The main properties of our approach are:

- A GLS Motion Estimation algorithm is used, which produces accurate estimation of the motion parameters.

- The classification process which collects inliers, rejects outliers and exchanges regions among models allows to improve motion segmentation.

- It uses regions of pixels instead of pixels as observations and neighbour information, that improves the spatial consistency.

Future work must be study improvements in our algorithm in order to deal with regions from the given grey-level segmentation having pixels belonging to more than one motion models.

Acknowledgments

This work has been partially supported by project CTIDIB/2002/333 from the *Conselleria de Educació Cultura i Ciència*, Generalitat Valenciana

References

[1] Alireza Bad-Hadiashar and David Suter. Robust motion segmentation using rank ordering estimators. In *Third Asian Coference on Computer Vision ACCV98, Honk Kong*, 1998.

[2] J. Andrew Bangham, Javier Ruiz Hidalgo, Richard Harvey, and Gavin Cawley. The segmentation of images via scale-space trees. In J.N.Carter and N.S.Nixon, editors, *Proceedings of British Machine Vision Conference*, volume 1, pages 33–43, Southampton, UK, September 1998.

[3] M. Bober and J. V. Kittler. Estimation of complex multimodal motion: An approach based on robust statistics and hough transform. *IVC*, 12(10):661–668, December 1994.

[4] G. Danuser and M. Stricker. Parametric model-fitting: From inlier characterization to outlier detection. *PAMI*, 20(3):263–280, March 1998.

[5] M. Irani, B. Rousso, and S. Peleg. Computing occluding and transparent motion. *IJVC*, 12(1):5–16, February 1994.

[6] Jong Bae Kim and Hang Joon Kim. Effient region-based motion segmentation for a video monitoring system. *Pattern Recognition Letters*, 24:113–128, 2003.

[7] Kil-Moo Lee, Peter Meer, and Rae-Hong Park. Robust adaptive segmentation of range images. *IEEE Transactions on Pattern Analysis and Machine Intelligence*, 20(2):200–205, 1998.

[8] James V. Miller and Charles V. Stewart. Muse: Robust surface fitting using unbiased scale estimates. In *Computer Vision and Pattern Recognition 1996*, pages 300–306, 1996.

[9] R. Montoliu and F. Pla. Multiple parametric motion model estimation and segmentation. In *ICIP01, 2001 International Conference on Image Processing*, volume II, pages 933–936, October 2001.

[10] R. Montoliu, V.J. Traver, and F. Pla. Log-polar mapping in generalized least-squares motion estimation. In *Proccedings of 2002 IASTED International Conference on Visualization, Imaging, and Image Processing (VIIP'2002)*, pages 656–661, September 2002.

[11] F. Odone, A. Fusiello, and E. Trucco. Robust motion segmentation for content-based video coding. In *RIAO 2000 6th Conference on Content-Based Multimedia Information Access*, pages 594–601, 2000.

Estimation of Scene Lighting Parameters and Camera Dark Current[*]

Alberto ORTIZ and Gabriel OLIVER
Mathematics and Computer Science Department
University of the Balearic Islands (UIB)
Cra. de Valldemossa, km 7'5
07071 Palma de Mallorca (Spain)
{alberto.ortiz,goliver}@uib.es

Abstract Assuming a model composed of parallel directional lighting and ambient illumination, this paper presents a method using a spherical calibration object to estimate the orientation of directional lighting together with the strengths of both light sources, and even their colour if a colour camera is employed. Furthermore, a model of the operation of current CCD cameras has been considered in order to account for the camera noise that corrupts digital pixel values. Experimental results related to the robustness of the method are included at the end of the paper.

1 Introduction

Vision algorithms relying on the physics of image formation often need to gather some data about the particular imaging infrastructure. Aspects such as the spectral composition of lighting illuminating the scene or the geometry of the lighting configuration are of highest importance for *shape from shading, shape from photometric stereo* or *physics-based image segmentation* algorithms [4]. Assuming a model composed of directional lighting and ambient illumination, this paper presents a method using a spherical calibration object to estimate the direction related to directional lighting together with the strengths of both light sources, and even their colour if a colour camera is employed. As most physics-based vision algorithms do, directional lighting is assumed to be parallel, or, in other words, the light source is assumed distant. Furthermore, the method proposed has been developed not only taking into account the interaction of light with the calibration object, but also considering the operation of current CCD cameras in order to account for the camera noise that corrupts digital pixel values. To this end, the model presented in [1], after some adaptations, has been incorporated to the estimation method.

Previous work on the subject mainly lies on the fields of shape from shading [9] and shape from photometric stereo [4]. On those research areas, a number of algorithms for estimating the direction associated to a parallel light source prior to shape reconstruction from monochrome images have been devised. Research on colour vision [2] has also provided some methods for, mainly, estimating the spectral composition of light sources. Recently, a method for calibrating multiple light source locations without assuming parallel lighting has

---

[*]This study has been partially supported by project CICYT-DPI2001-2311-C03-02 and FEDER fundings.

been published [6]. The method presented in this paper can work with both monochrome and colour cameras, considers ambient lighting, estimates either lighting strength and direction, and has been devised in connection with a camera noise model.

The rest of the paper is organized as follows: section 2 describes the model of image formation, including a CCD camera noise model adapted from the one published in [1]; section 3 describes the method for estimating scene lighting parameters, while section 4 shows how to measure the *dark current* of a CCD, a parameter essential for estimating the strength of ambient illumination; section 5 presents an example of estimation together with some robustness measures about the method; and, finally, conclusions appear in section 6.

2 Image formation

2.1 Interaction of light with matter

In general, when light interacts with matter, two reflection components must be taken into account [7]: the interface or specular reflection, and the body or diffuse reflection. Besides, it is generally accepted that final reflection is an additive composition of the body and interface components, as it is expressed in equation 1:

$$L_p(\lambda) = \overbrace{m_b(p)\,[E_{dp}(\lambda)\rho_{bp}(\lambda)]}^{L_{bp}(\lambda)} + \overbrace{m_i(p)\,[E_{dp}(\lambda)\rho_{ip}(\lambda)]}^{L_{ip}(\lambda)}, \tag{1}$$

where $L_p(\lambda)$ is the light reflected by the surface at a given scene point p and for a certain wavelength λ, and L_{bp} and L_{ip} are, respectively, the body and interface components of the radiance. With a reasonable degree of accuracy [7], each component $L_{jp}(j \in \{b, i\})$ can be modeled as the product of two terms: $C_j(\lambda) = E_{dp}(\lambda)\rho_{jp}(\lambda)$, expressing the fraction of the incoming (directional) light $E_{dp}(\lambda)$ which is conveyed by that reflection component due to the material reflectance $0 \le \rho_{jp}(\lambda) \le 1$; and $m_j(p)$, which is a geometrical factor depending on the surface geometry at point p.

This model can be improved by incorporating an ambient lighting term $L_{ap}(\lambda) = E_a(\lambda)\rho_{bp}(\lambda)$, representing light coming from all directions in equal amounts which increases scene radiance independently of local surface geometry:

$$L_p(\lambda) = \overbrace{E_a(\lambda)\rho_{bp}(\lambda)}^{L_{ap}(\lambda)} + \overbrace{m_b(p)\,[E_{dp}(\lambda)\rho_{bp}(\lambda)]}^{L_{bp}(\lambda)} + \overbrace{m_i(p)\,[E_{dp}(\lambda)\rho_{ip}(\lambda)]}^{L_{ip}(\lambda)}. \tag{2}$$

This model is a better approximation of daylight, that contains directional light from a point source (E_{dp} term), the sun, and ambient light from the sky (E_a term), and of light in a room, which comes from (directional) light fixtures (E_{dp} term) and from inter-reflections on walls and other objects (E_a term).

Because of its properties, the geometrical term of the body reflection is usually modeled by the Lambert's cosine law: $m_b(p) = \cos\theta_p$, where θ_p is the angle between the direction towards the light source at p, $s(p)$, and the surface normal at p, $n(p)$, and thus, if $\|s(p)\| = 1$ and $\|n(p)\| = 1$, $m_b(p) = s(p)^T \cdot n(p)$. In contrast, many models exist for the geometrical term of the interface reflection. As a discussion about it is out of the scope of this paper, the reader is referred to [9].

2.2   CCD basics

An analogy which is quite useful to understand the operation of a CCD compares it with a mechanism to measure the spatial distribution of rainfall over a field. The mechanism consists of an array of buckets which are placed over a grid of conveyor belts laid on the field, in such a way that, after a storm, the buckets are transferred to a metering station where the amount of water in each bucket is measured. In this way, each measurement represents the amount of rainfall at a particular location on the field.

In a CCD, light sensitive elements etched on a thin wafer of silicon play the role of buckets producing, in this case, a measure of the spatial distribution of incident light. The measurement process relies on the photoelectric effect by which the energy associated with photons striking the CCD reacts with the silicon exciting electrons from the valence band to the conduction band and producing electron-hole pairs. The photon-generated electrons (photoelectrons) are then collected in one of many discrete collection sites. To obtain colour images, either the incoming light is split in several colours and projected onto as many CCDs as colour bands, or colour filters are placed on top of collection sites, specializing thus the collection site for a certain colour band.

For every wavelength, the number of photoelectrons collected at each site is linearly dependent on the number of photons per unit time and per unit area striking the silicon. Although, generally speaking, one can say every photon generates one electron-hole pair, there are deviations which degrade the efficiency of the charge generation process such that incomplete conversions of photons into electrons occur. This degradation is characterized by a figure of merit called *quantum efficiency* defined as the number of electrons created per incident photon at a given wavelength.

An electronic representation of the spatial distribution of the light incident on the CCD is finally obtained by integrating photoelectrons in the individual collection sites over a fixed time interval. The resultant image is next read out site by site in a sequential way through a process known as charge coupling, by means of a number of charge transfer techniques which preserve the separation of individual charge packets. The fraction of charge which can be effectively transferred between adjacent collection sites is called the *charge transfer efficiency* of the device. As the charge packets leave the array, they enter a charge-to-voltage output amplifier which produces a signal proportional to the amount of charge, from which a final output signal conforming to any of the internationally accepted standards is finally generated.

2.3   Radiometric model of a CCD camera

Ideally, the number of electrons collected at a given cell for colour band c, I^c, can be expressed as:

$$I^c = T \int_\Lambda \left(\int_y \int_x E(x, y, \lambda) s(x, y) q(\lambda) \, dx \, dy \right) \tau^c(\lambda) d\lambda, \tag{3}$$

where (x, y) are continuous coordinates on the sensor plane, λ represents wavelength and Λ stands for the visible spectrum, T is the integration time, $E(x, y, \lambda)$ is the irradiance incident at the collection site, $s(x, y)$ is the spatial response of the collection site, $q(\lambda)$ is the ratio of electrons collected per incident light energy (i.e. it is a sort of quantum efficiency), and $\tau^c(\lambda)$ is the filter transmittance for the c colour channel.

From a theoretical point of view, the relation between the radiance $L_p(\lambda)$ at the scene points p optically reachable from the collection site under consideration and the corresponding irradiance $E(x, y, \lambda)$ involves the interaction with the propagation medium together with the effects of the camera optics on the arriving light through its *point-spread function* and the *lens collection* capability. Assuming a non-attenuating propagation medium and ignoring the blurring and low-pass filtering effects of the point-spread function of the optics in a properly focused camera, the relation between irradiance at the collection site E and scene radiance L was shown to be [3]:

$$E = \frac{\pi}{4}\left(\frac{d}{f}\right)^2 \cos^4 \phi\, L, \tag{4}$$

where d is the effective diameter of the lens according to the optics aperture, f is the focal distance and ϕ is the angle between the ray from the scene point to the center of projection and the optical axis. The quantity $\frac{f}{d}$ is the so-called *F-number*, by which aperture is configured in current cameras. In particular, notice that the higher the F-number, the more attenuated the irradiance E with respect to scene radiance L.

As one might expect, there are several sources of noise in CCD imaging systems which prevent from measuring ideal pixels values [1]:

- Processing errors during CCD fabrication cause small variations in quantum efficiency and charge collection volume from collection site to collection site, so that, even if a CCD is uniformly illuminated, theses variations lead to a site-to-site nonuniformity in collected charge. This spatial irregularity is often referred to as *fixed pattern noise*. Avoiding a certain dependence on wavelength, the number of electrons collected at a site is given by KI^c, where K is a constant associated with the collection site that accounts for the variation in the product of $q(\lambda)$ and $s(x, y)$. In this sense, K can be characterized as having mean 1 and spatial variance σ_K^2.

- Thermal energy in silicon generates free electrons known as *dark current*, which can be stored at collection sites and thus become indistinguishable from photoelectrons. The expected number of dark electrons generated is proportional to the integration time T and is highly temperature dependent. It is well known that for many devices the amount of dark current generated fluctuates slightly from site to site, so that dark current noise is modeled as a random variable $E_{DC} + N_{DC}$ where E_{DC} represents the dark current expected throughout the CCD array and N_{DC} represents a zero mean noise with spatial variance σ_{DC}^2.

- *Shot noise*, also known as photon noise, is a result of the quantum nature of light and characterizes the uncertainty in the number of electrons stored at a collection site. The total number of electrons at the site is known to follow a Poisson distribution so that the total number of electrons integrated at a collection site can be expressed as:

$$(KI^c + E_{DC}) + N_{DC} + N_S^c, \tag{5}$$

where N_S^c would be the zero mean Poisson shot noise with variance $KI^c + E_{DC}$.

- After integration time, the CCD transfers the charge to the output amplifier for readout. Although the charge transfer efficiency of real CCDs is less than 1, they have been quantified above 0.99999. It is reasonable, thus, to assume that all of the charge collected at each site is transferred to the output amplifier.

- The output charge-to-voltage amplifier transforms sequentially the charge collected at each site into a measurable voltage. Due to the operation of the amplifier, a further zero mean noise factor independent of the number of collected electrons N_R is included in the outputting signal. As this signal is later transformed into a video signal suitable to be used by the subsequent processing stages, a combined gain A^c, including the amplifier and the camera circuitry, appears as a multiplicative factor in the final expression for the signal leaving the camera:

$$V^c = (KI^c + E_{DC} + N_{DC} + N_S^c + N_R)\,A^c\,. \tag{6}$$

- Since the analog video signal must be converted to digital form to be used by a computer, a final noise source N_Q appears in the form of the quantization error. Given the quantization step $q = \max\{V\}/2^b$, N_Q can be shown to be a zero mean random variable with a uniform probability distribution over the range $[-\frac{1}{2}q, \frac{1}{2}q]$ and variance $q^2/12$. In this way, the final digital value D^c is given by:

$$D^c = (KI^c + E_{DC} + N_{DC} + N_S^c + N_R)\,A^c + N_Q\,. \tag{7}$$

- Real cameras can be affected by other non-desired effects such as: clipping, when the dynamic range of the camera is overflowed due to an excessive light level; blooming, by which stored charge at a potential well overflows and mixes with charge at other potential wells; spectral sensitivity in the near IR band; and linejitter, corresponding to the uncertainty when separating, by means of a frame grabber, synchronization information from image data of a composite video signal. Since all those effects can be avoided by adequate procedures [5], they are not included in the model.

Now, the digitized signal corresponding to pixel (u, v) can be stated as a random variable $D^c(u, v) = \mu^c(u, v) + N^c(u, v)$:

$$D^c(u, v) = \overbrace{(K(u, v)I^c(u, v) + E_{DC})\,A^c}^{\mu^c(u,v)} + \underbrace{\overbrace{N_S^c(u, v)A^c}^{} + \underbrace{(N_{DC} + N_R)\,A^c + N_Q}_{N_f^c}}_{N_e^c(u,v)}^{N^c(u,v)} \tag{8}$$

where N_e^c depends on the number of collected electrons while N_f^c does not.

3 Estimation of lighting parameters

3.1 Estimation from single band images

Assuming a non-attenuating propagation medium, the number of electrons stored at a collection site (u, v) results from the conversion, through equation 3, of all the light reflected at the set of scene points optically reachable from this image cell, Ω. Equations 2 and 3 can now be combined to yield equation 9, in which the contribution of every reflection component to the pixel value is explicitly stated. If lighting, reflectance and surface geometry does not change much throughout Ω, $I_a^c(u, v)$, the ambient reflection term, $I_b^c(u, v)$, the body reflection term, and $I_i^c(u, v)$, the interface reflection term, all for colour channel c, can be put in the form of equations 10, 11 and 12, respectively. In those equations, $(E_a\rho_b(u, v))^c$,

$(E_d(u,v)\rho_b(u,v))^c$ and $(E_d(u,v)\rho_i(u,v))^c$ represent the joint contribution of lighting and reflectance to the colour of the reflection component. On the other hand, the integration time T (equation 3) and factor $(\pi/4)(d/f)^2$ (equation 4) are assumed to be embedded in $(E_a\rho_b(u,v))^c$, $(E_d(u,v)\rho_b(u,v))^c$ and $(E_d(u,v)\rho_i(u,v))^c$, so that variations in exposure time and lens aperture will yield different values for those quantities.

$$I^c(u,v) = I_a^c(u,v) + I_b^c(u,v) + I_i^c(u,v) \tag{9}$$

$$I_a^c(u,v) = (E_a\rho_b(u,v))^c \tag{10}$$

$$I_b^c(u,v) = m_b(u,v)(E_d(u,v)\rho_b(u,v))^c \tag{11}$$

$$I_i^c(u,v) = m_i(u,v)(E_d(u,v)\rho_i(u,v))^c \tag{12}$$

In case of a matte object of uniform reflectance and a uniform directional light source $(E_d(u,v) = E_d)$, equation 13 provides an expression for D^c which reveals a linear relationship under such circumstances between D^c and m_b for all the object pixels.

$$D^c(u,v) = K(u,v)(E_a\rho_b)^c A^c + E_{DC}A^c + m_b(u,v)K(u,v)(E_d\rho_b)^c A^c + N^c(u,v) \tag{13}$$

The relevance of equation 13 is that, if m_b can be determined for enough object pixels, so that some pairs (m_b, D^c) can be obtained, those (noisy) pairs can be fitted by a straight line $D^c = \alpha + m_b\beta$ which allows estimating $\alpha = (E_a\rho_b)^c A^c + E_{DC}A^c$ and $\beta = (E_d\rho_b)^c A^c$. The noise in the pairs (m_b, D^c), which comes from N^c and the spatial variation in K, can be significantly removed if the D^c values for those pixels corresponding to the same m_b are averaged and this average $\bar{D}^c$ is used in the fitting. If the matte object under consideration is white $(\rho_b(\lambda) = 1)$, once the straight line parameters α and β are known, β is an estimation of the strength of the directional lighting of the scene $E_d^c A^c$, while $\alpha - E_{DC}A^c = E_a^c A^c$ is an estimate of the strength of the ambient illumination, both for colour channel c. Notice, however, that both values include the effect of the lens aperture and the exposure time, since both affect all the light gathered by the camera.

The knowledge about $m_b(u,v) = \cos\theta(u,v) = s(u,v)^T \cdot n(u,v)$ required by the previous procedure implies, in turn, knowledge about $n(u,v)$ and $s(u,v)$ for the same set of pixels. Both problems are revised in turn in the following paragraphs.

On the one hand, $n(u,v)$ can be determined if the object shape is known beforehand, which implies the use of a calibration object. Apart from other strategies, some regular objects allow determining the parameters of their particular shape from their projection in the image. This is the case of a sphere under orthographic projection. In effect, since the projection of the sphere is a circle, the projected radius r and center (u_0, v_0) can be obtained by pointing out three points over the circle contour. From this information, the surface normal vector at every image pixel $n(u,v)$ is given by equation 14:

$$n(u,v) = \left(\frac{u - u_0}{r}, \frac{v - v_0}{r}, \sqrt{1 - \left(\frac{u - u_0}{r}\right)^2 - \left(\frac{v - v_0}{r}\right)^2}\right). \tag{14}$$

On the other hand, if the light coming from the directional light source is assumed distant, $s(u,v)^T \approx s^T = (s_x, s_y, s_z)^T$ throughout the scene. In this way:

$$\cos\theta = \frac{u - u_0}{r}s_x + \frac{v - v_0}{r}s_y + \sqrt{1 - \left(\frac{u - u_0}{r}\right)^2 - \left(\frac{v - v_0}{r}\right)^2}\,s_z. \tag{15}$$

s can now be determined from the intensity pattern of the sphere in the image. In effect, assuming for the moment $N_c(u, v) = 0$ and $K(u, v) = 1$, the level-curve of level L of the image (i.e. $D^c = L$), without considering the background, is given by:

$$L = \mathcal{A} + \left(\frac{u - u_0}{r} s_x + \frac{v - v_0}{r} s_y + + \sqrt{1 - \left(\frac{u - u_0}{r} \right)^2 - \left(\frac{v - v_0}{r} \right)^2} \, s_z \right) \mathcal{B}, \quad (16)$$

where $\mathcal{A} = (E_a \rho_b)^c A^c + E_{DC} A^c$ and $\mathcal{B} = (E_d \rho_b)^c A^c$.

Equation 17 can now be obtained reordering equation 16:

$$\left(\frac{u - u_0}{r} \right)^2 (s_x^2 + s_z^2) + \left(\frac{v - v_0}{r} \right)^2 (s_y^2 + s_z^2) + 2 \left(\frac{u - u_0}{r} \right) \left(\frac{v - v_0}{r} \right) s_x s_y -$$

$$2\mathcal{C} \left(\frac{u - u_0}{r} \right) s_x - 2\mathcal{C} \left(\frac{v - v_0}{r} \right) s_y + \mathcal{C}^2 - s_z^2 = 0, \quad (17)$$

where $\mathcal{C} = \frac{L - \mathcal{A}}{\mathcal{B}}$. This equation defines a rotated conic over the image plane which results to be an ellipse since both eigenvalues of the associated quadratic form are positive. It can be shown that the direction of the minor axis of this ellipse has a slope $\frac{s_y}{s_x}$. Since $\frac{s_y}{s_x} = \frac{-s_y}{-s_x}$, an ambiguity regarding the signs of s_x and s_y results, which can be resolved taking into account that the sphere is a convex surface so that the signs of s_x and s_y coincide with the signs of the components of the vector $(u_e - u_0, v_e - v_0)$, where (u_e, v_e) is the center of the ellipse and also the brightest pixel in the sphere image. In this way, the tilt $\tau = \tan^{-1} \frac{s_y}{s_x}$ of the illumination can be determined completely. Besides, s_z is given by the square root of the quotient between the smallest and the largest eigenvalues of the quadratic form associated to the ellipse. Since $s_z = \cos \sigma$, where σ is the slant of the illumination, now $s^T = (\sin \sigma \cos \tau, \sin \sigma \sin \tau, \cos \sigma)^T$.

Therefore, s can be computed fitting the image points (u, v) corresponding to any level-curve of the sphere image by an ellipse and determining its minor and major axes. Nevertheless, due to N^c and the spatial variation in K, it is better to rather consider the set of image points belonging to the union of level-curves ranging from level L to level $L + \Delta$. Furthermore, the estimation of s is also improved by clustering the set of estimations $\{s^L\}$ obtained from several different level-set curves and taking the mean of the majority cluster.

Once s is known and $n(u, v)$ has been computed for every pixel within the circle enclosed by the circumference defined by r and (u_0, v_0) using equation 14, m_b can be estimated, as well as the lighting parameters $E_a^c A^c$ and $E_d^c A^c$ as described above. Since r and (u_0, v_0) are determined by manually pointing out three points over the contour of the sphere projection, different values for $E_a^c A^c$ and $E_d^c A^c$ can be obtained for the same calibration image depending on the skillfulness of the user. However, the correct parameters are the ones leading to a set of points $(m_b, \bar{D}^c)$ fitting a line with the least fitting error. Therefore, in order to improve the estimations and also to reinforce their repeatability, the user is asked to point out two circumferences so that one is completely included into the other and the right contour is most likely to be among both. All the circumferences among them are then evaluated and the one leading to the best fitting is kept.

3.2 Estimation from colour images

When several colour channels are available, applying the procedure described in section 3.1 gives rise to three estimations of vector s and an estimation of $E_a^c A^c$ and $E_d^c A^c$ for every colour channel. Since, theoretically, all the vectors s should coincide, in this case it is proposed to estimate an only s applying the majority-based clustering procedure mentioned in section 3.1 to the union of the sets $\{s^L\}^c$ available from every colour channel.

Analogously, since the parameters r and (u_0, v_0) should also be the same for all colour channels, the optimization procedure described in section 3.1 is applied to one of the colour channels, and the resultant values for r and (u_0, v_0) are then used for the other colour channels.

4   Estimation of dark current

This section describes a method for estimating the expected value of the dark current of a CCD camera, E_{DC}. In this way, apart from other uses, an estimation of $E_a^c A^c$ can be obtained after executing the straight line fitting procedure described in section 3.1 from $\alpha - E_{DC} A^c = E_a^c A^c$.

Turning again to equation 13, let us assume that several images of the calibration sphere with the same camera and lighting parameters are taken and averaged. In this way, noise N_c vanishes in the average image $\bar{D}^c$ and equation 19 results for $\frac{\bar{D}^c}{A^c}$:

$$\bar{D}^c(u, v) \;=\; K(u, v)(E_a\rho_b)^c A^c + E_{DC} A^c + m_b(u, v)K(u, v)(E_d\rho_b)^c A^c, \qquad (18)$$

$$\frac{\bar{D}^c(u, v)}{A^c} \;=\; K(u, v)\left(m_b(u, v) + \frac{(E_a\rho_b)^c}{(E_d\rho_b)^c}\right)(E_d\rho_b)^c + E_{DC}. \qquad (19)$$

Now, suppose the calibration object is imaged under different lens apertures (i.e. different values of the F-number). In this way, as it was previously mentioned, a different value for $(E_d\rho_b)^c A^c$ and $(E_a\rho_b)^c A^c$ will result for every configuration and, consequently, a different value for $\bar{D}^c$ for every (u, v). The resultant $(E_d\rho_b)^c A^c$ and $(E_a\rho_b)^c A^c$ values keep however constant the quotient $\frac{(E_a\rho_b)^c}{(E_d\rho_b)^c}$ among configurations, since the factor $(\pi/4)(d/f)^2$ in equation 4 changes both quantities equally. Therefore, for the same pixel (u, v), the pairs $\left(\frac{\bar{D}^c(u,v)}{A^c}, (E_d\rho_b)^c\right)$ define a straight line $\frac{\bar{D}^c(u,v)}{A^c} = \delta + \gamma(E_d\rho_b)^c$ with $\delta = E_{DC}$ and $\gamma = K(u, v)\left(m_b(u, v) + \frac{(E_a\rho_b)^c}{(E_d\rho_b)^c}\right)$. Of course, for this method to be applicable, a value for A^c should have been obtained previously to the line fitting, for instance with the method described in [1], section IV.

As well as for the estimation of s from colour images, different estimations of E_{DC} may be obtained for every colour channel. Although this can be acceptable for a 3-CCD colour camera, for 1-CCD colour cameras they should all take the same value. In order to reinforce this fact, a multiple straight line fitting procedure through a common origin is suggested.

5   Experimental results

In order to test the robustness of the estimation procedures described above, several experiments with synthetic and real calibration images were carried out. The real images were captured using a JAI CV-M70 progressive scan colour CCD camera with linear response, a Quartz Colour Pulsar mod. 3130 650 W spotlight and a COMET Matrox frame grabber. In the experimental results below, when giving the orientation of directional lighting, a viewer-oriented coordinate system is assumed. That is to say, the camera lies at the origin, the Z axis coincides with the optical axis and the positive Z semi-axis points from the camera towards the scene.

5.1   Example of dark current estimation

Dark current was measured using 20 different lens apertures. For every case, 10 calibration images were captured and averaged, as suggested in section 4 to remove N_c. The lighting parameters were then estimated for the average images. Gain A^c was also estimated using the procedure presented in section IV of [1]. As a result, the gains for the red, green and blue channels resulted to be $(5.65, 4.91, 6.18) \times 10^{-3}$, respectively. Using all those values, a 3-line common origin fitting according to equation 19 was executed using least squares for a total of 900 evenly distributed image points over the sphere. From them, the mean value of E_{DC} was estimated to be 1733.85 ± 0.07[1] while $\sigma_{DC} = 191.25$. In this way, $E_{DC}A^c$ for the red, green and blue channels resulted to be $(9.79, 8.51, 10.72) \pm (0.00, 0.00, 0.00)$, with a spatial standard deviation of $(1.08, 0.94, 1.18)$.

5.2   Example of lighting estimation

In this section, the whole method of estimation will be illustrated step by step over the image shown in figure 1(top,right). However, before starting the example, it must be said that the calibration setup (see figure 1(top,left)) consists of a matte white sphere lying over a black background to avoid shadows.

During the first step, image level sets above the intensity of the background ($L \geq 25$) and separated $\Delta = 5$ intensity levels are analyzed to determine the light direction, finding the unit directions presented in figure 1(bottom,left). From this set, directions are grouped into clusters and the average of the majority one gives rise to the estimation $(0.05, 0.18, -0.98) \pm (0.00, 0.00, 0.00)$, which represents a cluster of 69 directions out of the 81 level sets considered between the three colour channels.

Next, two circles are given so that the real projection of the sphere is ensured to lie between them (see the white lines in figure 1(top,right)). According to the parameters of both circles, a total of 1563 circles are analyzed and the one leading to the best fitting for the red channel, the one with the highest intensity value over the image, is kept: $r = 111, u_0 = 117, v_0 = 115$. The resultant set of pairs (m_b, D^c) are given in figure 1(bottom,right). For those parameters, the linear correlation coefficient attains a value of 0.999798, while the mean fitting error is 1.121092; both values are involved in the optimization. The process is next applied to the green and blue channels using the same values for $[r; (u_0, v_0)]$. As a result, the directional lighting strength is estimated as $(179.53, 173.25, 154.03) \pm (0.07, 0.08, 0.11)$ while the ambient lighting strength results to be $(66.46, 71.03, 68.20) \pm (0.07, 0.07, 0.07)$ after subtracting dark current.

5.3   Robustness measures

Three experiments to prove the robustness of the lighting estimation procedure are presented in the following. The first one consisted in facing the method against synthetic images with varying levels of zero mean Gaussian additive noise and different light direction tilts (every $45°$, starting from $0°$), but the same strengths for ambient and directional lighting. In figure 2, the plot in the upper row corresponds to the angle in degrees between true and estimated s, the left plots in the middle and lower rows represent the same but for ambient lighting and

---

[1] In all the experimental results, the Standard Deviation Of Mean is given as measure of uncertainty [8].

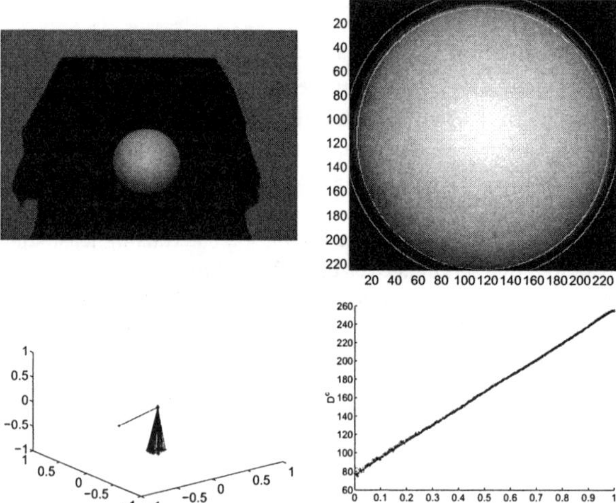

Figure 1: Example of estimation: (top,left) calibration setup; (top,right) calibration image used in the example; (bottom,left) light source directions found; (bottom,right) straight line corresponding to (m_b, D^c) for the red channel.

directional lighting, respectively; finally, the right plots in the middle and lower rows correspond, respectively, to the quotient between the estimated and the real norms of ambient and directional lighting strengths as a percentage ($\|(\widehat{E}_j^R, \widehat{E}_j^G, \widehat{E}_j^B)\| / \|(E_j^R, E_j^G, E_j^B)\| \times 100$, $j \in \{a, d\}$). As it can be seen, some estimation inaccuracies arise in the noiseless case because of quantization errors. On the other hand, observe that estimations for s are quite accurate even for a noise level of $\sigma = 15$. As for E_a and E_d, their estimations are clearly more affected by noise than the estimations for s, so much so that $\sigma = 15$ seems to be the limit of acceptability.

In the second experiment, the 20 average images used to estimate dark current were analyzed to test the robustness of the estimates of s against changes in E_a and E_d. In figure 3, a histogram of the differences between the estimations of s for every pair of images of the set is shown. As it can be appreciated, the difference angle is, on average, around 4.5 degrees.

Finally, in the third experiment, a real calibration image was rotated four times 90 degrees, in order to check the robustness of the estimates of E_a and E_d against changes in s. Results appear in table 1, showing there is no appreciable difference in the estimates for E_a and E_d when, keeping the same lighting strengths, light direction is changed.

6   Conclusions

A method for estimating scene lighting parameters has been presented. The method provides an orientation for the directional lighting and measures of the strength of ambient and directional illumination, up to the factor including the F-number $(\pi/4)(d/f)^2$ and the exposure time T. Besides, camera dark current is also measured to complete the characterization of the illumination. Results about its robustness have shown it very stable as for lighting orientation against changes in lighting strength, and vice versa. Results for synthetic noisy images have also been provided.

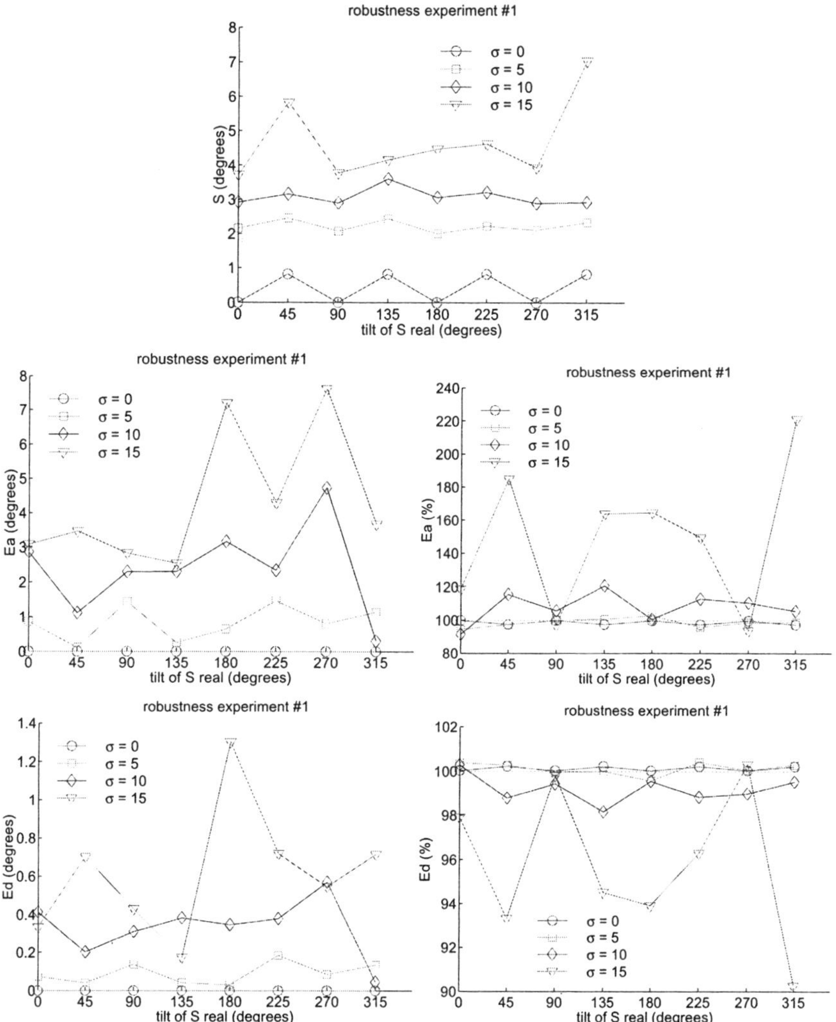

Figure 2: Results for robustness experiment 1: (1st row) angle between true and estimated s; (2nd row) angle between true and estimated E_a (left) and quotient between the norms of estimated and true E_a as a percentage (right); (3rd row) the same as 2nd row but for E_d. (In all the plots, σ is the standard deviation, in intensity levels, of the zero mean Gaussian noise added to images.)

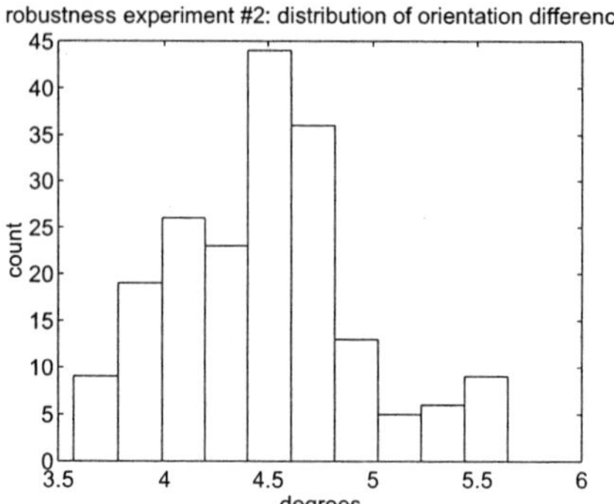

Figure 3: Results for robustness experiment 2.

s	$E_a^c A^c + E_{DC} A^c$	$E_d^c A^c$
(-0.17,0.54,-0.82)	(37.2,38.2,37.0)	(193.9,187.2,172.1)
(-0.54,-0.17, -0.82)	(37.2,38.2,37.0)	(193.9,187.2,172.1)
(0.17,-0.54,-0.82)	(37.2,38.2,37.0)	(193.9,187.2,172.1)
(0.54,0.17,-0.82)	(37.2,38.2,37.0)	(193.9,187.2,172.1)

Table 1: Results for robustness experiment 3. (In the table, c stands for $\{R, G, B\}$.)

References

[1] G. E. Healey and R. Kondepudy. Radiometric CCD camera calibration and noise estimation. *IEEE PAMI*, 16(3):267–276, 1994.

[2] G. E. Healey, S. A. Shafer, and L. B. Wolff. *Physics-based vision: principles and practice*, volume on Color. Jones and Bartlett Publishers, 1992.

[3] B. Horn and R. Sjoberg. Calculating the reflectance map. *Applied Optics*, 18(11):1770–1779, 1979.

[4] R. Klette, K. Schlüns, and A. Koschan. *Computer Vision: Three-Dimensional Data from Images*. Springer-Verlag, 1998.

[5] C. Novak, S. Shafer, and R. Willson. Obtaining accurate color images for machine vision research. In *Proceedings SPIE Perceiving, Measuring and Using Color*, volume 1250, pages 54–68, 1990.

[6] M. Powell, S. Sarkar, and D. Goldgof. A simple strategy for caligrating the geometry of light sources. *IEEE PAMI*, 23(9):1022–1027, 2001.

[7] S. A. Shafer. Using color to separate reflection components. *COLOR Research and Application*, 10(4):210–218, 1985.

[8] J. R. Taylor. *An Introduction to Error Analysis*. University Science Books, 2nd edition, 1997.

[9] R. Zhang, P.-S. Tsai, J. E. Cryer, and M. Shah. Analysis of shape from shading techniques. Technical report, Computer Science Department. University lof Central Florida, 1994.

Artificial Intelligence Research and Development
I. Aguiló et al. (Eds.)
IOS Press, 2003

Cardiac Segmentation with Discriminant Active Contours

Fernando Vilariño, Petia Radeva
Centre de Visió per Computador
Universitat Autònoma de Barcelona. Spain
{fernando,petia}@cvc.uab.es

Abstract Dynamic tracking of heart moving is one relevant target in medical imaging and can be helpful for analyzing heart dynamics in the study of several cardiac diseases. For this aim, a previous segmentation problem of such structures is stated, based on certain relevant features (like edges or intensity levels, textures, etc.) Classical active models have been used, but they fail when overlapping structures or not well-defined contours are present. Automatic feature learning systems may be a powerful tool. Discriminant active contours present optimal results in this kind of problem. They are a kind of deformable models that converge to an optimal object segmentation that dynamically adapts to the object contour. The feature space is designed from a filter bank in order to guarantee the search and learning of the set of relevant features for optimal classification on each part of the object. Tracking of target evolution is obtained through the whole set of images, using information from the actual and previous stages. Feedback systems are implemented to guarantee the minimum well-separable classification set in each segmentation step. Our implementation has been proved with several series of Magnetic Resonance with improved results in segmentation in comparison to previous methods.

Introduction

The problem of heart movement tracking is one important target in order to obtain satisfying dynamic models or volumetric 3D representations. There are particularities inherent to heart imaging in most acquisition formats -magnetic resonance (MR), computerized tomography (CT), intra-vascular ultra-sound (IVUS), etc.- that segmentation has to deal with [10, 18, 19]. Classical active contours [11] are shown to deal with this problem, obtaining good results under some favorable conditions. Active contours evolve from an initial well posed model, attracted by image features -typically edges- [9]. However, when several overlapping biomedical structures are present, image contours have not a good definition, target structure features are not properly contours or volume reconstruction has to be made from several slices (as in MR or CT) [12, 13, 14]. This paper addresses the problem using discriminant active contours [7]. They are a kind of deformable models that converge to an optimal object segmentation that dynamically adapts to the object contour. Feature space is designed from a filter bank -of Gaussian derivatives or log-Gabor filters- in order to obtain the response to a large number of features, and not only contour information. Its coordinates into the feature space characterize each part of the active contour. A dimensionality reduction is implemented by a principal component analysis (PCA) and a Fisher linear discriminant analysis (FLDA). The learning stage poses the optimal projection of the feature space for next steps in segmentation, in which each patch of the active contour will be attracted selectively only by the previously learned features. In addition to this, feedback systems based on trajectories of projected dimensions are implemented to guarantee the minimum well-separable classification set in each segmentation step

1   Our Model of Heart Tracking and 3D Volume Segmentation

Heart tracking is achieved using discriminant active contours. An active contour -or snake [11]- is an elastic curve that evolves from an initial form, being attracted by some features of interest in image (generally, edge points, lines, etc.) [10]. Contour attraction fails when our biomedical structure is close to other structures that could lead the active contour to them. In heart images, the presence of internal structures leads active models to wrong segmentations. In the optimal case, the active contour should learn which are the right targets and find them in an iterative scheme when trying to reach to the tracking or segmentation of a 3D heart volume. To overcome this, several techniques has been developed [19, 20, 21]. Our segmentation model leads each patch of the snake to different features, according to directionality and scale criteria. This set of features is learned in previous steps (see Fig. 1). 3D volume segmentation is obtained by searching the set of features that best separate the patch class. For each segmentation step (slice or tracking frame), active contour patch will be attracted to this feature set, followed by a new learning process. This model lets view each patch of the contour independently, because different patches are attracted by different things -horizontal lines, thinner or thicker contours will not attract patches that define vertical lines-. In addition to this, our model lets the active contour evolve and change its shape as relevant features change for the optimal definition of the segmented biomedical structure contour

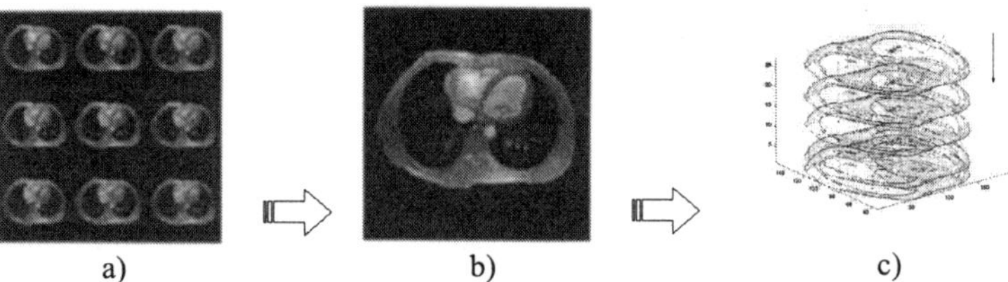

a)   b)   c)

Figure 1: a) Set of cardiac images for tracking. b) Initial stage: one contour is designed by control points that define different patches. c) Patches' features are learned and searched in the next frame. The process is repeated for the whole set.

2   Feature Space Generation

Correct selection of the feature space is a key component of our classification stage. We have tested two different ways of implementation: 1) Using natural basis functions of derivatives of Gaussian $\frac{1}{2\pi\sigma_g}exp\{-\frac{(x^2+y^2)}{2\sigma_g^2}\}$, where σ_g is the standard deviation in x and y directions, and 2) using log-Gabor filters, that are designed in the transformed frequency space by the equation in polar coordinates $G(r_0, \theta_0) = exp\{-\frac{(log(\frac{r}{r_0}))^2}{2(log(\frac{\sigma_r}{r_0}))^2}\}exp\{-\frac{(\theta-\theta_0)^2}{2\sigma_\theta^2}\}$, where θ_0 is the orientation angle of the filter, r_0 is the central radial frequency and σ_θ and σ_r are the angular and radial sigma of the Gaussian. In both cases, associated features have information related to directionality and scale [6].

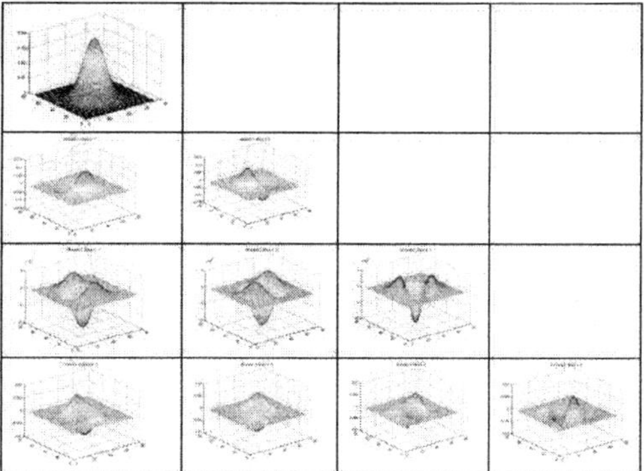

Figure 2: Gaussian bank of filters. Each line represents zero, first, second and third order derivatives, rotated. This set forms a basis for the feature space.

For the derivatives of Gaussian, a minimum set of filters is needed. First, second and third derivatives are used, and response to edge, valley and crest points is obtained. From previous works [6] it is shown that certain number of rotated versions of derivatives of Gaussian work as basis functions, and it is possible to obtain an arbitrary rotation as a linear interpolation of this basis. So, for the first derivative it is enough with 0 and 90 degrees rotated functions, for second derivatives, 0, 60 and 120 degrees rotations are needed, and 0, 45, 90 and 135 degrees for third derivatives [8]. Also, we introduce scale information, and work with 4 different values of scale parameter sigma: 1, 2, 4 and 8. The result is 9*4 = 36 dimensional feature space. Grey level could be also added including the scaled Gaussian filtering, and then a 40-dimension feature space is achieved. Fig.2 shows a graphical representation of the filters set for one scale.

Gabor filters are modulation products of Gaussian and sinusoidal signals [17]. They are Gaussian distributions placed selectively over certain frequency in the space-frequency domain, and they act as band-pass filters responding selectively to one certain orientation. In the case of Gabor and log-Gabor filters, the implementation is built over the Fourier transformed space. Log-Gabor filters are refined versions where normal distribution is calculated over logarithmic space. It is known [4,5] that they are a good mathematical representation of the receptive profiles of visual cortical cells. They cover a larger region of high frequency spectrum, as its transfer function has extended tails at the high frequency end. In both cases, filter bank is built up with rotated versions at different scales. We have to choose a sufficient number of orientations and scales that let us guarantee to cover the higher spectrum without increasing too much the feature space dimensionality. We have chosen 12 rotations, so we will have a filter responding each 15 degrees. Scale information is added by modifying the scale parameter of the Gaussian. Just like in the derivatives of Gaussian case, our implementation includes 4 different scales. In this case, a 12*4=48 dimensions feature space is generated. See Fig. 3 fora graphical representation of these filters.

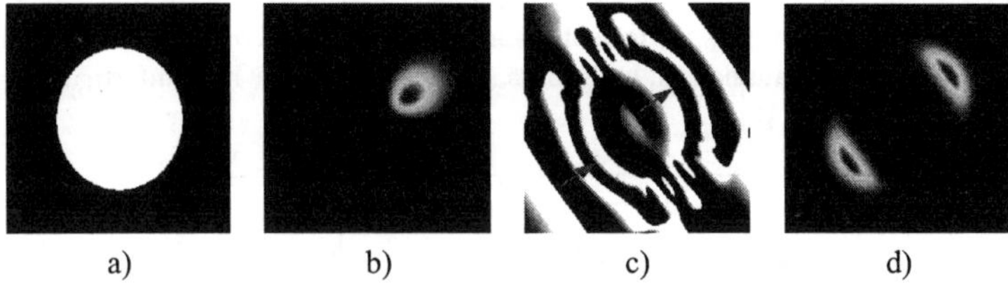

a)   b)   c)   d)

Figure 3: a) A binary image. b) log-Gabor filter in frequency doamain. c) Filter response in phase. d) Filter response in magnitude

3   Feature learning and segmentation

We apply filtering to the whole set of images, obtaining an N*M*D dimensional cube, where N and M represent the image size and D the dimensions number of the feature space. In this cube, each i-plane in z direction is the result of filtering the original image with the i-filter of the filter bank. For the initialization step, an initial active contour is defined over heart contour from a control point set. From this control point set a B-spline is drawn [9], and each control point has a B-spline patch of influence associated. The active contour will be selectively attracted by features of interest that will be different for each patch.

3.1   Features of interest for each patch

Each patch will be attracted by different features. In order to select which are the most relevant ones for each case, we get the feature vectors of every point of each patch, and build up P classification problems where P is the number of patches. For one classification problem, every feature vector from the patch points is set to belong to the patch class, and the rest of contour points is set to belong to its complementary class. We search the best separability between each patch points features and the rest of the contour. The filter bank response has over 40 dimensions, and classification problem becomes difficult to deal with. A dimensionality reduction is implemented by principal component analysis, and a posterior Fisher linear discriminant analysis. PCA is used to obtain the most relevant features set, while FLDA is used in order to achieve the projection in a reduced feature space that performs the best class separability [15] -this problem is stated as the resolution of eigenvalues problem [1, 2]-. In this dimensionality reduction step, we search for the projection matrix that maximizes the distance between the mean of the projection of patch class points and complementary class points. Finally, we obtain a reduced 1D transformed space whose projection vector best separates the features of each contour patch from the rest. Several metrics are tested in order to obtain the best separability. Mahalanobis distance appears to be the best chose, since it takes into account statistical information from the covariance matrix.

3.2   Active contour discriminant feature attraction

In the next segmentation step -a new slice, or tracking frame- we apply the projection vectors found before, and calculate the difference between these projections and the mean of each patch class. This generates P distance maps -one for patch- that will be used as energy images for the active contour. Each patch will be attracted to low energy points on its energy image, that represents points that are closer to its previously learned features. The active contour is guided to its new position around the heart surrounding structure, responding selectively for each patch and ignoring noisy edges and shadows from different anatomical structures. Mahalanobis distance is implemented for the metric [15, 16].

3.3   Optimized discriminant: reducing the number of patch classes

One of the main problems that could arise is the similarity of different patches that actually define the same feature set. This is found when we have two or more patches that define line in some certain orientation. Similar feature defining patches are not needed to be aside, and this adds difficulties. For this case, complementary class of one of these patches will include a number of samples that actually should belong to the patch class. This yields a lower performance on classification and, higher possibility of attraction to points that do not present the searched features. To reduce the number of initial patch classes, a pre-classification step is added. We look for the best separability between all P patches, using the same PCA-FLDA scheme used before. We calculate the mean of projections for each patch and associate the same class to patches whose projected mean difference is less than certain acceptance level. Now, the classification step will not include contiguous patch points into the complementary class. The whole process is repeated for all slices in the volume, and the active contour re-adapts its shape to the new learned features in each segmentation step. Under these conditions, patches are treated like belonging to the same class, i.e., they define the same features, and their points are not included into the complementary class for the discrimination analysis. Just like in the classification step, Mahalanobis distance is used. Higher performance in classification is obtained, and distance maps are less noisy in this way.

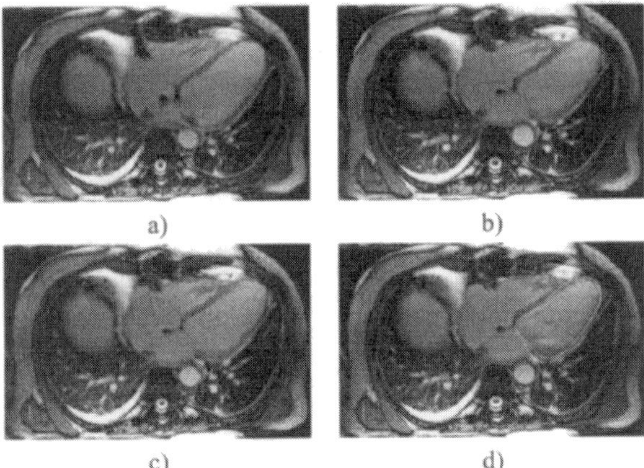

Figure 4: a), b) and c) represent three different frames from one cardiac cycle. d) Discriminant active contours convergence ignoring the noisy structures influence.

4 Experimental Results

We have tested our implementation with different targets for ventricular segmentation and tracking of internal and external walls. We have used MR. Fig 4 shows internal tracking sequence for three frames. For the choice of the bank of filters, we have tested both log-Gabor and Gaussian, finding similar results (in this example, Gaussian filters have been used). The segmentation stage starts in frame 1 with an initial contour that learns the features of interest for any patch. Classification process is done for this first frame, and the projection matrices obtained for each patch reduced 1D space are saved. Now, these projection matrices are used to generate one confidence map in frame 2 for each patch, in which low values are associated to points that are expected to belong to the patch class. The active contour evolves now having into account only relevant features that are locally different, arriving to a final contour segmentation. This contour will be the initial stage for frame 3. Internal structures, textured contours and heart noisy internal zone due to blood flux do not present now a problem for the active contour convergence, so far, its features have been discriminated, they are not relevant and have not effect into the active contour evolution -see Fig. 4-.

5 Conclusions

Efficient ways of segmentation are needed in order to obtain good 3D models of biomedical structures. Active contours are useful for this task, but they are not robust under the specific frame of medical images, where overlapping structures and morphological changes are present at the target structures. Discriminant active contour scheme searches and learns the features that best fit for each patch of the active contour. Feature space is obtained from a filter bank. We have tested derivatives of Gaussians, Gabor and log-Gabor filters, and studied their performance. Dimensionality reduction is achieved through PCA and FLDA. Class-distance maps are implemented testing several metrics and finally using Mahalanobis. Our patch-selective contour convergence to the points of minimum at distance maps yields to improved results in segmentation of biomedical targets with different characterizing features -contours and texture. The patch number optimization improves classification performance. Refined methods for patch number optimization drive to a better classification model.

References

[1] Pentland, A.P. Face recognition using eigenfaces Turk, M.A.Computer Vision and Pattern Recognition, 1991. Proceedings CVPR '91., IEEE Computer Society Conference on , 1991 Page(s): 586 -591

[2] P.N. Belhumeur, J.P. Jespanha, and D.J. Kriegman: Eigen- faces vs. fisherfaces: Recognition using class specific linear projection. PAMI, 19(7):711-720, July 1997.(1982) 315–333

[3] R. Rodriguez-Snchez, J.a. Garcia, J. Fdez-Valdivia, Xose R. Fdez-Vidal: The RGFF Representational Model: A System for the Automatically Learned Partitioning of 'Visual Patterns'.Digital Images October 1999 (Vol. 21, No. 10) pp. 1044-1073R

[4] D.J. Field: Relations between the Statistics of Natural Images and the Response Properties of Cortical Cells, J. Optical Soc. A,. A, vol.4, no. 12, pp.2379-2394. 1987

[5] S. Marcelja, Methematical description of responses of simple cortical cells, J. Opt. Soc. Am, A70, 1297-1300. 1980

[6] Rao, R.P.N. and D.H. Ballard, "Natural basis functions and topographic memory for face recognition," Proc., 14th Int'l. Joint Conf. on Artificial Intelligence, Montreal, August 1995.

[7] Pardo X. and Radeva P., "Discriminant snakes for 3D reconstruction in medical images," in Proceedings of 15th International Conference on Pattern Recognition, 2000, vol. 4, pp. 336–339.

[8] WilliamT. Freeman and Edward H. Adelson. The design and use of steerable filters. IEEE Transactions on Pattern Analysis and Machine Intelligence, 13(9):891–906, September 1991.

[9] A. Blake and Isard. Active Contours. Springer-Verlag, 1998.

[10] T. Cootes, D. Cooper, C. Taylor, and J. Graham. Active shape models - their training and application. Computer Vision and Image Understanding, 61(1):38–59, Jan. 1995.

[11] M. Kass, A. Witkin and D. Terzopoulos, "Snakes: Active Contour Models," First International Conference on Computer Vision, 1987, pp. 259-268

[12] J.M. Pardo, F.Vilariño et al. Applications of deformable models in orthopaedic surgery planning, Journal of Computing and Information Technology. Vol. 6, No. 2, June 1998, pags 191-202.

[13] R. Dosil, J.M.Pardo, A. Mosquera, F. Vilariño. "Modelado 3D Aplicado a Segmentación", X Congreso Nacional de Informática Gráfica. Catellón (Spain), July 2000.

[14] Xu, C. and Prince, J., "Snakes, shapes, and gradient vector flow." IEEE Transactions ofImage Processing, Vol. 7, No. 3, pp. 359-369, March 1998.

[15] R.O. Duda and P.E. Hart. Patter Recognition and Scene Analysis. Wiley New York, 1972

[16] Christopher M. Bishop, Neural Networks for Pattern Recognition, Clarendon Press . Oxford, 1995

[17] R. Mehrotra, K.R Namduri, N. Ranganathan. Gabor Filter-Based Edge Detection. Pattern Recognition. Vol. 25, nno. 12, pp. 1479-1494. 1992

[18] T. McInerney and D. Terzopoulos, "Deformable models in medical image analysis: A survey," Medical Image Analysis 1(2), pp. 91–108, 1996

[19] Wilke et al, Myocardial perfusion reserve: assessment with multisection, quantitative, first-pass MR imaging, Radiology, vol. 204, no. 2, pp. 373-384, 1997.

[20] N. Al-Saadi et al., Noninvasive detection of myocar-dial ischemia from perfusion reserve based on cardio-vascular magnetic resonance, Circulation, vol. 101,pp. 1379-1383, 2000.

[21] L. Spreeuwers and M. Breeuwer, Automatic detection of myocardial boundaries in MR cardio perfusion images, In Proceedings of MICCAI 2001, pages 1228-1231, Utrecht, Netherlands, Oct. 2001.

4. Multi-agent Systems

Describing and Configuring Multi-Agent Systems at the Knowledge Level

Mario Gomez and Enric Plaza
Artificial Intelligence Research Institute IIIA - CSIC
Campus UAB 08193, Bellaterra, Spain
mario/enric@iiia.csic.es

Abstract. Cooperative Problem Solving is usually focused on the coordination and cooperation mechanisms of Multi-Agent Systems, leaving out the user and the problem requirements. This paper introduces the knowledge description level of ORCAS (Open, Reusable and Configurable multi-Agent Systems), a framework to develop MAS applications configurable on demand, according to problem requirements and user preferences. ORCAS introduces the idea of configuring a MAS application at two layers, the knowledge and the operational layers. During the knowledge layer a configuration of MAS components is found, including agent capabilities and domain knowledge; and after that the knowledge configuration is operationalized by a customized team of problem solving agents. This framework is based on applying a knowledge modelling approach to describe Multi-Agent Systems, specifically, it proposes to describe agent capabilities as Problem-Solving Methods.

1 Introduction and motivation

Cooperative Problem Solving(CPS) is usually focused on the coordination and cooperation mechanisms of Multi-Agent Systems (MAS), leaving the user apart. Usually CPS frameworks starts with an agent willing to solve a task and realizing the potential for cooperation [44]. The process until the task to be solved is decided is usually skipped, assuming that it is already hold by the initiator of a cooperative process. Furthermore, task allocation among cooperating agents is typically based on a *preplan* that decomposes a task into subtasks[35], without specifying the algorithms to build the initial plan, neither the criteria to be taken into account. Our approach here is to focus upon these aspects of CPS: How can this initial plan be constructed? Which criteria should guide it? This paper revisits the idea of configuring an application "a la carte" from the point of view of agent provided problem-solving components. It means that a MAS-based application is configured on demand, for each request to solve a problem. For this purpose, we introduce a *Knowledge Modelling Framework* (KMF) to describe Multi-Agent Systems which is based on the ideas brought about by knowledge-based frameworks, specifically it is inspired by the Problem-Solving Methods paradigm[36][3][27], [34] [14].

In addition to give support in the analysis and design stages of MAS development, a formal knowledge-level description of agent capabilities can be used on runtime to reason about agent capabilities dynamically. This feature became specially relevant in the case of open MAS, in which agents can join and exit the system dynamically. Openness involves heterogeneity, therefore open systems have to deal with interoperability issue: how to locate other agents and how to communicate with them successfully. The usual approach to overcome the interoperability problems arising from open environments is that of introducing a mediation layer between requesters and providers of services and the use of shared languages and protocols. It is very useful to have a mediation service in which providers can advertise its capabilities, and the requesters of capabilities may look for appropriate providers for its needs. Usually, this mediation layer is embedded in middle agents[7]. These agents are specialized in reasoning about and coordinating the activities of other agents, engaging them in cooperative problem-solving processes. Typically, the function of a middle agent is to match service-requests with services available in the system. To enable matchmaking, both providers and requesters should share a common language to describe services, which is called an Agent Capability Description Language (ACDL). Our framework extends the notion of an ACDL to include another kind of components in addition to agent capabilities, named *domain models* and *generic tasks*. Such a framework will facilitate the automatic, dynamic configuration of MAS on demand. In addition to provide such a language, this paper explores some directions on using an ACDL. We introduce a model of MAS configuration as a two-layered process: the *knowledge configuration layer* and the *operational layer*. At the *knowledge layer* a configuration of MAS components is found in terms of its descriptions. We call this process *task configuration*. At the *operational layer*, a team of agents is formed and instructed to solve a problem in a cooperative manner, according to the configuration of components. This process is called *team formation*.

2 Knowledge level description of Multi-Agent Systems

Our framework is based on the Problem-Solving Methods(PSM) paradigm, in particular, we follow the software architecture proposed by the UPML framework[12], adapted and extended to deal with *configurable* MAS applications. PSMs describe the reasoning parts of a KBS in a domain independent manner, abstracting the description from the implementation [29].

Figure 1 shows the components we use to describe a system and table 2 summarizes the main features characterizing each component. This architecture provide an effective organization for constructing libraries with large "horizontal cover"[1], thus maximizing reusability and avoiding the brittleness of traditional, monolithic libraries[29]. From a knowledge level view, a task is characterized in terms of a type of problem to be solved (i.e. diagnosis, interpretation, design, planning). This characterization is based on properties of the input, the output, and the nature of the operations that map the input to the output. *Capabilities* are domain independent descriptions of problem-solving methods (i. e search), linked to executable components (i.e. agents). There are two types of capabilities, *task-decomposers*, which decomposes a task into subtasks, and *problem-solving capabilities*, that solve one task without further decomposing it. *Domain models* specify the domain knowledge required by capabilities to solve a task.

The description of any component contains a name, a textual description and some pragmatic attributes (cost, performance measures, classification indexes, reputation, creator, and so on). The description of a problem-solving component (tasks and capabilities) contains a signature specification for the input and the output, and a competence specification de-

---

[1]Horizontal cover refers to the range of problem solving behaviors supported by a library. Actually several libraries of problem-solving components has been described using this approach, like search, classification, diagnosis, parametric design, document analysis, aggregation or CBR

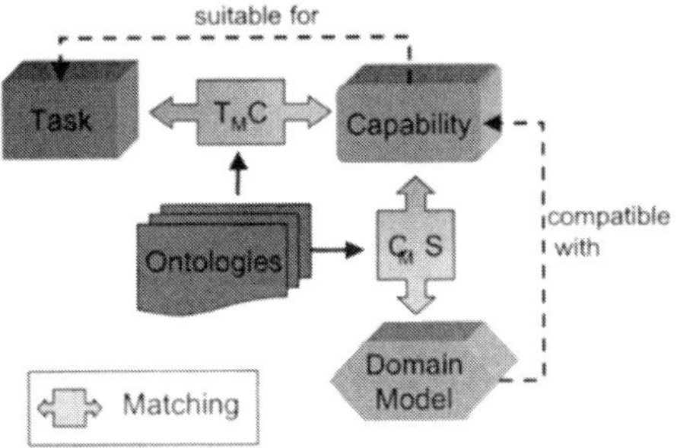

Figure 1: The ORCAS componential architecture

scribing preconditions for the component to be of use, and postconditions or effects of executing it. Signatures relates to data types(input, output) and knowledge structures (knowledge roles). They define the structure of the data and the knowledge required by capabilities to solve problems. Formally, we can describe a problem-solving component P as the tuple $P = \langle in, out, pre, post \rangle$ where $in, out, pre, post \in \mathbb{O}$, i.e. formulae in the object language. We will note an element of the tuple as subscript, e.g. P_{in} is the input signature of P and P_{post} are the postconditions of P.

We deal with four kinds of problem-solving components, namely *task*, and *capability*, which have two further subtypes: *problem-solving capability* and *task-decomposer*: A task (table 2) is a component described with the basic attributes defined by a problem-solving component, thus a task $T \in \mathcal{T}$ is a tuple $T = \langle in, out, pre, post \rangle$. A capability $S \in \mathcal{S}$ does not introduce new items in the tuple of a *problem-solving component*, while a *task decomposer* $D \in \mathcal{D}$ has a new item, *st*, specifying the subtasks into which it decomposes the problem: $D = \langle in, out, pre, post, st \rangle$ where $st \subset \mathcal{T}$. A *problem-solving capability* $S \in \mathcal{S}$ is a component with two new attributes: *knowledge roles* (kr) and *assumptions*(asm). The assumptions declare properties on the domain knowledge that are required by the PSC to be usable; while knowledge roles are inputs to be acquired from some domain knowledge. Thus $S = \langle in, out, pre, post, asm, kr \rangle$ where $asm, kr \in \mathbb{O}$. A domain model $M \in \mathcal{M}$ is a tuple $M = \langle sig, prop, mk \rangle$, is , i.e. it is composed of a signature, a collection of properties, and meta-knowledge (a collection of properties of the domain model assumed to be true).

3 Connecting components

In our framework, a system is composed of some tasks, capabilities and domain models. Nevertheless, an enumeration of classes of components is not enough to describe a system. There is needed some structuring principle: a system is more than a collection of parts, there should exist some organizing principles that regulates the interactions between the parts. The use of a formal language to describe the components and the ontology-based architecture together will support some engineering activities, like component adaptation, interoperation and verification, while improving reuse, scalability and openness.

It has already been introduced the idea that a task is a generalization of a kind of problems, while a capability is just a particular method to solve a class of problems. We say that a

$$
\begin{array}{lll}
Problem-Solving\ Component & P & \langle name, descr, prag \rangle \\
Task & P < T & \langle in, out, pre, post \rangle \\
Capability & P < C & \langle in, out, pre, post \rangle \\
Task-Decomposer & P < C < D & \langle in, out, pre, post, st \rangle \\
Problem-Solving\ Capability & P < C < S & \langle in, out, pre, post, asm, kr \rangle \\
Domain\ Model & M & \langle sig, prop, mk \rangle
\end{array}
$$

Table 1: Types of knowledge components an their main features, where '$<$' means subtype, $st \subset T$, and $in, out, pre, post, asm, kr \in \mathbb{O}$.

capability is suitable for a task if it is able to solve the class of problems defined by that task. Suitability is verified using matching techniques and building mappings between the component's ontologies. The particular "matching" algorithm will depend on the representation formalism chosen as the Object Language, and on the inference mechanism. For example, we use feature-terms and *subsumption*, but is also possible to used First Order Logic and automated theorem proving. Nevertheless, it should be remarked that any "matching" between two components described with independent ontologies may require a *mapping* between both ontologies.

Matching is also required between problem-solving capabilities and domain models. A capability has to declare the concepts of the domain knowledge it needs. We will say that a domain model is compatible with a capability if there is a matching between the knowledge role signature of a capability and the signatures of the domain model. As explained for task-capability matching, a connection between a capability and a domain model expressed with independent ontologies may require a *mapping* in order to interoperate. Furthermore, capabilities can specify *assumptions* over the domain knowledge that should be satisfied. For example, a *query-elaboration* capability may require a *thesaurus* which satisfies that the synonym relation is symmetric.

Figure 1 shows the componential architecture, including the relations (dotted lines) between the components, and the corresponding matchings (arrow-boxes). Matching of components is explained in §5.1

3.1 The role of Ontologies

In this framework we agree with [23] about the potential role of explicit ontologies to support reuse. Definition of what ontologies are is still a debated issue[23]. Nevertheless, in the AI community this term has achieve a considerably attention, and in particular, it is declared as a key issue in maximizing reuse[10][13]. From that view, the main goal of an ontology is to make knowledge explicit and sharable. Furthermore, ontologies are used to enable semantic matching between components[22][31].

Ontology mappings are declarative specification of *matching relations*, which consist of explicit specifications of the transformations required to match elements of one ontology to elements in the other ontology. An example of a mapping is a renaming, but mapping can include any kind of syntactic or semantic transformation: numerical, lexical, regular expres-

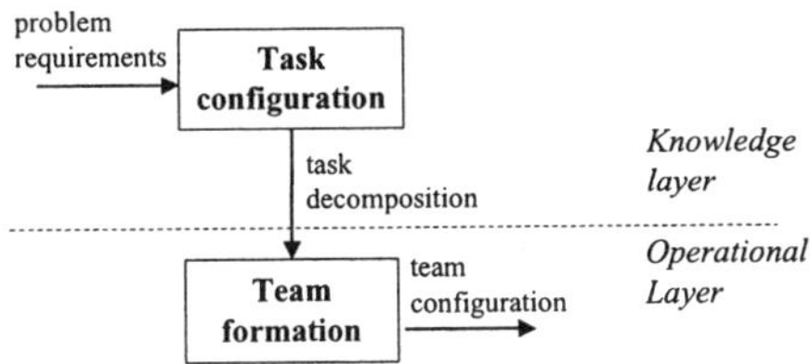

Figure 2: The two layers MAS configuration model.

sions and others. In our framework the components (tasks, capabilities and domain models) can be described with its own, independent ontologies[15]. Therefore, ontology mappings are required to match problem requirements to task (during the problem specification), capabilities to tasks (task-capability matching), and domain models to capabilities(capability-domain matching).

4 Configuration of Multi-Agent Systems

The main idea of ORCAS is to use a specification of each problem at hand to select and execute the most suitable components available. The final result of configuring a MAS application in the context of Cooperative Problem Solving (CPS) will be a team of agents committed to solve a problem together. In ORCAS, MAS applications are configured "on-the-fly", according to the requirements of the problem and the preferences of the requester. As we have introduced previously, ORCAS teams are customized in two steps, task-configuration and team formation. (see figure 2).

(1) Configuration at the *knowledge layer* refers to the process of finding a configuration of components (tasks, capabilities and domain models) according to the specification of the problem to be solved. We call this process *task configuration*, and the result of the process is call a *task-decomposition*: a hierarchical tree where nodes are triplets consisting of a task, a capability suitable for that task, and the domain models describing the knowledge required by the capability.

(2) Configuration at the *operational layer* refers to the process of operationalizing a configuration , which means making ready to be executed; in other words, the operational configuration layer have the function of connecting the components to ensure they can interoperate to solve a problem together. Operationalization of components is very close to the implementation level. In our case, we are particularly interested in multi-agent systems. From our point of view, an operationalization should be understood as a process of enabling the coordination and cooperation of a group of agents to solve a problem according to stated requirements. In particular, we approach this activity as a team-formation process.

Figure 3 shows an example of a task-configuration of the WIM application. This is a configuration for the *Information-Search*(IS) task. IS is decomposed by the *Meta-search* PSM into four subtasks, and each of them has an associated PSM. Notice that some of the tasks have been associated to PSMs requiring some domain knowledge (represented by a domain model), for example, the PSM *Query-expansion-with-thesaurus* requires a *Thesaurus*, like MeSH.

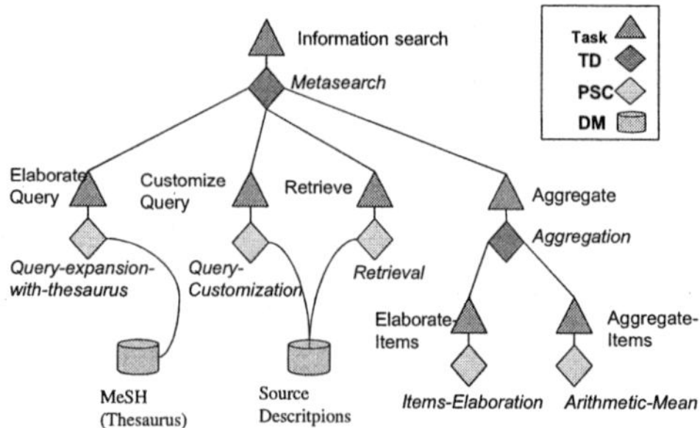

Figure 3: Task-decomposition example

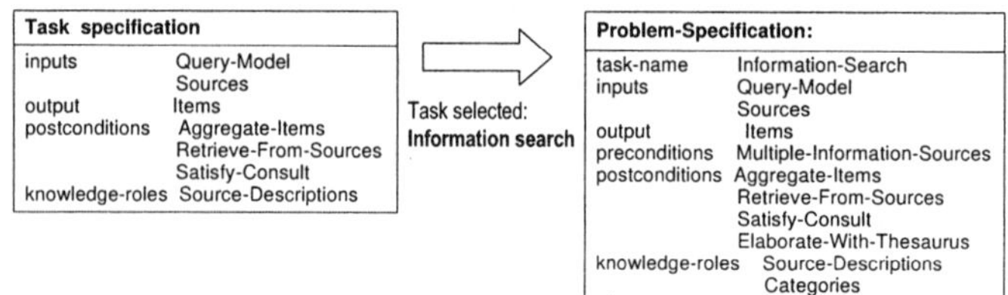

Figure 4: Problem specification

5 Task Configuration

Task configuration has the goal of finding a configuration of agent capabilities and domain models that satisfy the requirements of the problem at hand. First, a task is retrieved characterizing the kind of problem at hand. Problem requirements are specified as signatures (inputs, outputs and domain models) and formulae (preconditions and postconditions) over terms of the task ontology. Problem specification should be made using the same ontologies than tasks and PSMs (or there should exist an ontology mapping between non matching concepts), thus allowing to "match" the problem specification to the agent capabilities.

The input for task configuration is a specification of *problem requirements* composed of a) inputs and outputs, b) the *pre-conditions* that are established to hold, c) the *postconditions* that have to hold when the task was achieved, and d) the *knowledge sources* (domain models) that are available for achieving the task. Figure A4 shows an example of the specification of a problem, using *feature terms* as the object language. The user selects a task from the library of available tasks, afterwards he modifies the requirements to fit better its own needs. In the example the user has selected the task *Information-Search* and has tighten it up by adding one precondition -to search among multiple sources- and one postcondition -to elaborate the query using a thesaurus-. In addition, he has added a domain model called Thesaurus to the knowledge roles. In our implementation, the user is assisted in this activity by a Personal Agent that helps him to specify the problem through a graphical interface.

The output of task configuration is a *task-decomposition-schema* where a) each task has at least an associated capability that can achieve it, b) each problem-solving capability has associated the knowledge it needs, and c) the whole configuration complies to the input requirements.

The task configuration process has been modelled and implemented as a search in the space of partial configurations, where each state represents a partial configuration of capabilities. The main information to be represented in a state is the set of task-capability bindings used in a partial configuration, but it also holds information about the requirements (inputs, pre- and post-conditions, domain models and assumptions), those ones already satisfied and the ones to be yet satisfied. Task configuration uses the problem requirements to generate an initial state. From the initial state, new states are generated until one of the new states is considered a final state, that is defined as a state in which all tasks has been bound to a capability and all the requirements have been satisfied. The new states are generated by binding capabilities to tasks, where binding is achieved by using "component matching", as described below.

We are currently using two configuration techniques: *Search and Subsumes* and *Constructive Adaptation*. The first mode follows a depth-first search method, while the *Constructive-Adaptation* adds CBR retrieval techniques to guide the search process[33].

5.1 Task-PSM matching

Matching of tasks and PSMs is defined in the usual way that matching of components. Task-PSM matching has two parts, signature matching and specification matching. Given ($T \in \mathcal{T}, P \in \mathcal{P}$), where $\mathcal{T}$ is the set of available tasks and $\mathcal{P}$ is the set of available PSMs. We define $\mathcal{P}$ matches $\mathcal{T}$ as:

$$T \preceq_M P = T \preceq_{SIG} P \wedge T \preceq_{SPEC} P$$

Signature matching $\preceq_{SIG}$ requires that their input and output signatures match, and in our context this means that the PSM P has input and output signatures that are equal or that refine those of the task T, i.e. $T \preceq_{SIG} P = T_{in} \preceq P_{in} \wedge T_{out} \preceq P_{out}$. Moreover, specification matching $\preceq_{SPEC}$ requires that a PSM P has weaker preconditions than a task T and stronger postconditions than T, thus: $T \preceq_{SPEC} P = P_{pre} \preceq T_{pre} \wedge T_{post} \preceq P_{post} \wedge P_{asm} \preceq T_{asm}$.

5.2 Capability-Domain Model matching

Although domain models are not problem-solving components (that are domain-independent by design), the concept of matching is very similar. A problem-solving capability $S \in \mathcal{S}$ can use a domain model $M \in \mathcal{M}$ when their signatures match (signature of M may refine signature of R) and when all formulae in S_{asm} are satisfied by $M_{prop} \cup M_{mk}$. More formally we will say that a model satisfies a problem-solving capability when $M \preceq_{SAT} S \Longleftrightarrow (S \preceq_{SIG} M) \wedge (M_{prop} \cup M_{mk} \Longrightarrow S_{asm})$.

6 Problem-Solving Methods as an Agent Service Description Language

According to [5], a language for describing services (agent capabilities fall in this category) should facilitate the automatic location, composition, invocation and monitoring of services. To achieve these goals, it is needed to describe the following aspects of a service: a *service profile* that brings the information needed by service-seeking agents to determine whether the service meets its needs; a *service model* on how does the service works -process and data flow-, which should facilitate service composition and monitoring; and the *grounding*, to specify

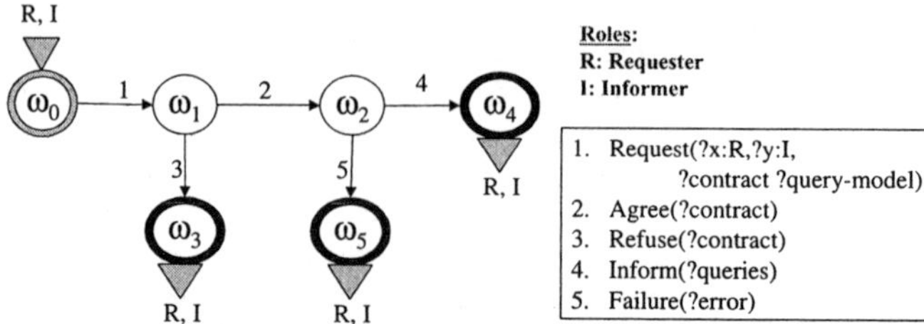

Figure 5: Interaction protocol described with a ISLANDER scene

how to access or invoke a service. The ORCAS framework include these aspects, together with the requirements of "large coverage" and maximization of reuse, that is achieved by decoupling tasks, PSMs and domain models from each other.

In ORCAS, the service profile is specified by the interface(input, output, knowledge roles) and the competence (pre and postconditions); the operational description of a task decomposer is used to specify the service model; and the communication slot of both task decomposers and problem-solving capabilities to define the grounding. Inputs, outputs and knowledge roles are specified by *signatures* in the *object language*; and *preconditions* and *postconditions* are specified as *formulae* in the object language. In our search for an object language providing a tradeoff between expressivity and efficiency we are experimenting with *feature terms*[32], record-like data structures embodying collections of *features* that are a generalization of first order terms[1].

The service grounding is specified at the communication slot of a capability; it specifies the format of the data to be interchanged (for example XML), and the interaction protocol. In ORCAS, interaction protocols are specified using the ISLANDER [8] formalism for describing open agent societies, and in particular, we use ISLANDER scenes to the interaction protocol of a service. A scene describe a pattern of interaction among agent roles as a Finite State Machine, where states represents the state of the communication and transitions are triggered by illocutionary acts or time-outs. Figure 5 shows an example of a ISLANDER scene modelling a typical Request-Inform protocol. There are two roles in these protocols, the requester and the informer, that will be mapped to concrete team-roles during the execution of a capability.

The purpose of the operational description is to specify the data and the control flow between the subtasks of a task decomposition. Some languages has been proposed for this purpose, like KARL[11] and Modal Change Logic[16]. Nevertheless, since we are applying PSM to describe MAS, it seems more appropriate to use agent concepts to describe interaction among subtasks, as the different subtasks may be solved by different agents during the problem-solving process. Such a language must capture dependency relations, temporal relations and parallelism in order to facilitate the operationalization of a configuration during the team formation and the planning stages of CPS. In ORCAS, the operational description of task decomposition is described as a network of tasks: one task for each subtask in the task-decomposition, and transitions between subtasks specifying the control-flow, data-flow and intermediate processing between subtasks. During the execution of a task-decomposition, each of the tasks is substituted by an interaction protocol, the one corresponding to the capability selected for each task. The result then is a network of interconnected scenes describing

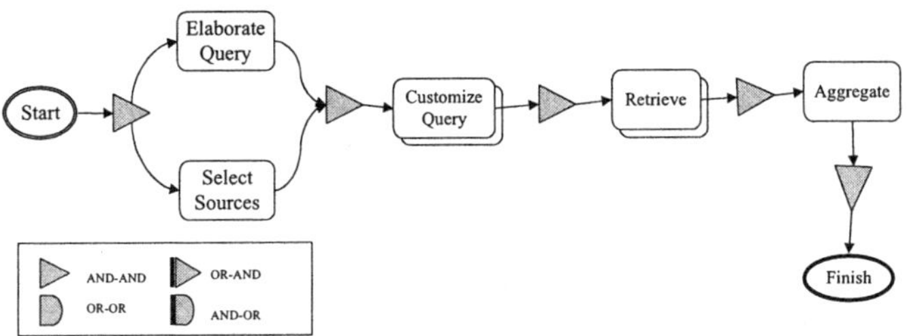

Figure 6: Task-network for a task-decomposer

the necessary communication among agent roles and the intermediate data processing among subtasks. Figure 6 shows such a task.

7   Discussion and conclusions

Therefore, with the introduction of the knowledge level[30] in the development of KBS, the knowledge acquisition phase is no longer seen as a transfer of knowledge, but as a model construction process[4][38]. Knowledge Modelling Frameworks propose methodologies, architectures and languages for analyzing, describing and developing knowledge systems [36][3][27], [34][14]. The goal of a KMF is to provide a conceptual model of a system which describes the required knowledge and inferences at an implementation independent way. This model is intended to support the engineer in the knowledge acquisition phase[6] and to facilitate reuse[10]. The question of reuse has received a lot of attention last years from the knowledge modelling community[2][28][17]. Specifically, the knowledge modelling community has recently focused on ontology-based reuse [26][37]

Surprisingly, knowledge modelling frameworks have been rarely applied in the field of MAS to deal with the reuse and interoperation problems; two exceptions are found in [25][18], which have adapted the CommonKADs methodology [34] for MAS development. Our approach is closer to a more recent framework to configure systems from libraries of reusable problem-solving components called **UPML** [14]. Our main motivation has been to explore the possibilities of knowledge modelling to support the "plug-and-play" and the automatic configuration of applications over distributed libraries of agent provided capabilities in open environments.

Some of our proposals are similar to the research on interoperability among heterogeneous agents. Our way of describing agent capabilities is similar to the LARKS ACDL[40], used in the RETSINA infrastructure[39], but there are some differences: ORCAS states a more clear separation of capabilities(PSMs), tasks and domains. Moreover, while RETSINA lies on planning/schedulling to coordinate problem-solving agents, the ORCAS framework relies on a case-based task-configuration process to support the on-fly configuration of agent teams.

Despite of a lot of research in the field of Cooperative Problem Solving, most of the work done falls into one or more or the stages of the cooperative process as presented in [43], with four stages: recognition, team formation, planning and execution. The problem solving process starts with an agent willing to solve a task and realizing the potential for cooperation.

The process until the task to be solved is decided is usually skipped, assuming that it is already given[44]. Task allocation among cooperating agents is typically based on a preplan that decomposes a task into subtasks[35], without specifying the algorithms to build such plan, neither the criteria to be taken into account. Our approach here is to focus upon these aspects of CPS. How to build this initial preplan, that we call a task-configuration, and how to use such a plan to drive the team formation process. The ORCAS framework provides the representation schemas and the algorithms for obtaining such initial plans according to stated problem requirements. While most approaches are based on planning, we prefer to describe the interactions occurring during cooperative problem solving with a communication oriented-language: ISLANDER, a formal language for describing open agent organizations that supports the automatic verification of the specification[24] and speeds-up development through automated generation of agent-skeletons[41][42].

Another issue is relative to the use of CBR techniques to improve the task-configuration process. In particular, we use CBR retrieval techniques (Constructive-Adaptation[33] to select components according to the similarity of past configurations to the problem at hand.

The framework has been implemented as an electronic institution[9][8] where institutional agents are responsible of mediating between providers and requesters of problem-solving capabilities. The ORCAS e-Institution[21][2] provides the protocols for registering services, configuring tasks and customizing teams of agents to solve those tasks. It is a shell for developing and deploying configurable multi-agent systems in open environments. An application of this infrastructure has been successfully applied to build a configurable meta-search application[19] in a medical domain[20].

References

[1] Josep L. Arcos. *The Noos representation language.* Monografies del iiia, Universitat Politècnica de Catalunya, 1997.

[2] R. Benjamins, D. Fensel, and B. Chandrasekaran. PSMs do IT, 1996. Summary of track on Sharable and Reusable Problem-Solving Methods. KAW'96.

[3] B. Chandrasekaran. Generic tasks in knowledge-based reasoning: High-level building blocks for expert system design. *IEEE Expert*, 1:23–30, 1986.

[4] W. Clancey. The knowlede level reinterpreted. *Machine Learning*, 4:285–291, 1989. cited by studer, benjamins and fensel.

[5] The DAML Services Coalition. DAML-S: Semantic markup for web services, 2001.

[6] W.V. de Velde. *Second generation expert systems*, chapter Issues in Knowledge Level Modelling, pages 211–231. Springer Verlag, 1993.

[7] K. Decker, K. Sycara, and M. Williamson. Middle-agents for the internet. In *Proceedings the 15th International Joint Conference on AI*, 1997.

[8] Marc Esteva, Julian Padget, and Carles Sierra. *Intelligent Agents VIII: Lecture Notes in Artificial Intelligence*, volume 2333 of *Lecture Notes in Artificial Intelligence*, chapter Formalizing a language for institutions and norms, pages 348–366. Springer-Verlag, 2002.

[9] Marc Esteva, Juan A. Rodriguez, Carles Sierra, Pere Garcia, and Josep L. Arcos. On the formal specifications of electronic institutions. In *Agent-mediated Electronic commerce. The European AgentLink Perspective*, volume 1991 of *Lecture Notes in Artificial Intelligence*, pages 126–147, 2001.

---

[2]The ORCAS implemented infrastructure achieved a third price in the Agentcities Technology Competition

[10] D. Fensel. An ontology-based broker: Making problem-solving method reuse work. In *Proceedings Workshop on Problem-solving Methods for Knowledge-based Systems at IJCAI'97*, 1997.

[11] D. Fensel, J. Angele, and R. Studer. The knowledge acquisition and representation language karl. *IEEE Transcactions on Knowledge and Data Engineering*, 10(4):527–550, 1998.

[12] D. Fensel, V. Benjamins, S. Decker, M. Gaspari, R. Groenboom, W. Grosso, M. Musen, E. Motta, E. Plaza, G. Schreiber, S. Studer, and B.J. Wielinga. The component model of UPML in a nutshell. In *Proceedings First Working IFIP Conference on Software Architecture*, 1999.

[13] D. Fensel and V.R. Benjamins. Key issues for automated problem-solving methods reuse. In *Proceedings 13th European Conference on Artificial Intelligence*, 1998.

[14] D. Fensel, V.R. Benjamins, E. Motta, and B.J. Wielinga. UPML: A framework for knowledge system reuse. In *International Joint Conference on AI*, pages 16–23, 1999.

[15] D. Fensel, S. Decker, E. Motta, and Z. Zdrahal. Using ontologies for defining task, problem-solving methods and their mappings. In *Proceedings European Knowledge Acquisition Workshop*, Lecture Notes in Artificial Intelligence, 1997.

[16] D. Fensel, R. Groenboom, and G.R. de Lavalette. Modal change logic (mcl): Specifying the reasoning of knowledge-based systems. *Data and Knowledge Engineering*, 26(3):243–269, 1998.

[17] D. Fensel and E. Motta. Structured development of problem solving methods. *Knowledge and Data Engineering*, 13(6):913–932, 2001.

[18] Norbert Glaser. *Contribution to Knowledge Modelling in a Multi-Agent Framework*. PhD thesis, L'Université Henri Poincaré, Nancy I, France, 1996.

[19] Mario Gomez and Chema Abasolo. Improving meta-search by using query-weighting and numerical aggregation operators. In *Proceedings 9th International Conference on Information Processing and Management of Uncertainty in Knowledge-Based Systems*, 2002.

[20] Mario Gomez, Chema Abasolo, and Enric Plaza. Problem-solving methods and cooperative information agents. *International Journal on Cooperative Information Systems*, 11(3-4):329–354, 2002.

[21] Mario Gomez, Chema Abasolo, and Enric Plaza. ORCAS: Open, reusable and configurable multi-agent systems, 2003. Third price in the Agentcities Technology Competition ATC03.

[22] Nicola Guarino. Semantic matching: Formal ontological distinctions for information organization, extraction, and integration. In M.T. Pazienza, editor, *Summer School on Information Extraction*, pages 139–170. Springer Verlag, 1997.

[23] Nicola Guarino. Understanding, building, and using ontologies: A commentary to using explicit ontologies in kbs development, by van heijst, schreiber, and wielinga. *International Journal of Human and Computer Studies*, (46):293–310, 1997.

[24] Marc-Philipe Huguet, Marc Esteva, Simon Parsons, Carles Sierra, and Michael Wooldridge. Model checking electronic institutions. In *Proceedings of the ECAI Workshop on Model Checking Artificial Intelligence*, 2002.

[25] Carlos Argel Iglesias, Mercedes Garijo, Jose Centeno-Gonzalez, and Juan R. Velasco. Analysis and design of multiagent systems using MAS-common KADS. In *Agent Theories, Architectures, and Languages*, pages 313–327, 1997.

[26] William Grosso John H. Gennari and Mark Musen. A method-description language: an initial ontology with examples. In *Proceedings 11th Workshop on Knowledge Acquisition, Modelling and Management*, 1998.

[27] J. McDermott. Toward a taxonomy of problem-solving methods. In S. Marcus, editor, *Automating Knowledge Acquisition for Expert Systems*, pages 225–256. Kluwer Academic, 1988.

[28] E. Motta. *Reusable Components for Knowledge Modelling*, volume 53 of *Frontiers in Artificial Intelligence and Applications*. IOS Press, 1999.

[29] E. Motta, D. Fensel, M. Gaspari, and A. Benjamins. Specifications of knowledge components for reuse. In *Proceedings of SEKE '99, 1999.*, 1999.

[30] Alan Newell. The knowledge level. *Artificial Intelligence*, 28(2):87–127, 1982.

[31] Massimo Paolucci, T. Kawmura, Terry Payne, and Katia Sycara. Semantic matching of web services capabilities. In *Proceedings of the 1st International Semantic Web Conference*, 2002.

[32] Enric Plaza. Cases as terms: A feature term approach to the structured representation of cases. In *ICCBR*, pages 265–276, 1995.

[33] Enric Plaza and Josep L. Arcos. Constructive adaptation. In S. Craw and A. Preece, editors, *Advances in Case-Based Reasoning. Proceedings 6th ECCBR*, volume 2416 of *Lecture Notes in Artificial Intelligence*, pages 306–320, 2002.

[34] A. Schreiber, Bob J. Wielinga, J. Ackermans, Walter Van De Velde, and R. De Hoog. CommonKADS: A comprehensive methodology for kbs development. *IEEE Expert*, 9(6):28–37, 1994.

[35] Onn Shehory and Sarit Kraus. Methods for task allocation via agent coalition formation. *Artificial Intelligence*, 101(1-2):165–200, 1998.

[36] Luc Steels. Components of expertise. *AI Magazine*, 11(2):28–49, 1990.

[37] R. Studer, H. Eriksson, J. Gennari, S. Tu, D. Fensel, and M. Musen. Ontologies and the configuration of problem-solving methods. In *Proceedings of the 10th Knowledge Acquisition for Knowledge-Based Systems Workshop*, 1996.

[38] Rudi Studer, V. Richard Benjamins, and Dieter Fensel. Knowledge engineering: Principles and methods. *Data Knowledge Engineering*, 25(1-2):161–197, 1998.

[39] Katia P. Sycara, Massimo Paolucci, Martin Van Velsen, and Joseph A. Giampapa. The RETSINA MAS infrastructure. Technical report, Robotics Institute, Carnegie Mellon University, 2001.

[40] Katia P. Sycara, Seth Widoff, Matthias Klusch, and Jianguo Lu. Larks: Dynamic matchmaking among heterogeneous software agents in cyberspace. *Autonomous Agents and Multi-Agent Systems*, 5:173–203, 2002.

[41] Wamberto W. Vasconcelos, Jordi Sabater, Carles Sierra, and Joaquim Querol. Skeleton-based agent development for electronic institutions. In *Proceedings UKMAS*, 2001.

[42] Carles Sierra Wamberto Vasconcelos and Marc Esteva. An approach to rapid prototyping of large multi-agent systems. In *Proceedings of 17th IEEE International Conference on Automated Software Engineering*, pages pages 13–22, 2002.

[43] Michael Wooldridge and Nicholas R. Jennings. Towards a theory of cooperative problem solving. In *Proceedings Modelling Autonomous Agents in a Multi-Agent World*, pages 15–26, 1994.

[44] Michael Wooldridge and Nicholas R. Jennings. The cooperative problem-solving process. *Journal of Logic and Computation*, 9(4):563–592, 1999.

Acknowledgements

The authors would like to thank the Spanish Scientific Research Council for their support. This work has been developed under the the IBROW project (IST-1999-190005).

Artificial-Intelligence Research and Development
I. Aguiló et al. (Eds.)
IOS Press, 2003

Task allocation in rescue operations using combinatorial auctions

Beatriz LÓPEZ, Silvia SUÁREZ, Josep L. DE LA ROSA
Universitat de Girona
Av. Lluís Santaló s/n
17071 Girona, Spain
{blopez, sasuarez, peplluis}@eia.udg.es
http://eia.udg.es/arl/

Abstract. The simulation scenario of RoboCup Rescue is a dynamic and changeable environment, where rescue agents have to mitigate a disaster. Rescue agents tend to carry out the activities nearest to them. This leads to increasing entropy in the organization of rescue activities, with various rescue agents getting involved in the same task. Such a situation is obviously undesirable. This paper provides an approach for distributing rescue agents in a more rational way, by using combinatorial auction techniques to perform task allocation. The RoboCup Rescue platform has been used as the framework for the problem.

Introduction

A disaster environment is a dynamic environment with unpredictable situations. The kinds of rescue activities that take place depend on the kind of disaster that has occurred and can range from rescuing victims, to extinguishing forest fires, re-establishing urban services, cleaning beaches, etc. Rescue resources should be assigned in such a way as to accomplish the various tasks required for optimal recovery from the disaster. Technology should be able to make a contribution in this socially significant situation and to this end, several initiatives have been developed in order to promote research in such complex scenarios. Two examples are Pacifica [3] and RoboCup Rescue [5], both of which provide standard problems in which technologies can be examined and integrated. Such artificial scenarios are restricted to specific domains making the problem easier to tackle. In this study, we worked with RoboCup Rescue.

One of the RoboCup Rescue scenarios is the simulation league where several heterogeneous rescue agents interact with one common purpose: to mitigate the damage caused by an earthquake in a populated city. In such conditions, fire brigades, police forces, and ambulance teams have to be coordinated to rescue victims, extinguish fires and unblock roads. The key issue in this environment is to assign rescue agents to perform these tasks according to the agents' capabilities with the ultimate goal of maximizing the number of rescued victims.

Task allocation is difficult because of the different sources of environmental dynamics. First of all, agents are submitted to continuous danger, so rescue agents can also be injured or even killed. Second, the effects of the disaster are continuous: fires spread if they are not extinguished; burning or weakened buildings may collapse and block roads, etc. And third, the rescue task itself is not known beforehand: civilians in need of rescue are discovered through exploration by the rescue agents.

Most approaches follow a task allocation method based on criteria of distance: each agent performs the task located nearest to them. This leads to increasing entropy in the organization of rescue activities, with various rescue agents getting involved in the same task. This situation is obviously undesirable. In addition to locality, other criteria should be taken into account for task allocation, such as, for example, the presence of other agents acting in the vicinity. There are several techniques for dealing with multiple criteria decision making [4], but, bearing in mind the dynamism of the problem at hand, we think that combinatorial auctions are a good choice for tackling the problem [1,7,9]. In this paper we present such an approach.

This paper is organized as follows: Firstly, the rescue scenario is introduced in section 1. Then, in section 2, we present the concepts of *combinatorial auctions* and the *winner determination algorithm*. In section 3, we describe the application of the algorithm to the RoboCup Rescue domain and in section 4, we illustrate the entire process with an example. Finally, we provide some conclusions and discussions.

1. Rescue scenario

The rescue scenario provided by RoboCup-Rescue [2] is a disaster environment caused by an earthquake (see Figure 1). In this scenario, there are collapsed buildings, fires, and blocked highways, people in a state of panic looking for safe ground, and rescue agents helping victims. Fire brigade agents, police forces and ambulance teams comprise the rescue agents, in addition to central agents made up of the fire, police and ambulance stations. In the current version of the RoboCup Rescue Simulation League, there are initially 72 civilian agents, 5 ambulance team agents, 10 brigade agents, 10 police force agents, 1 ambulance station agent, 1 fire station agent and 1 police station agent in the disaster area. All the agents have the same objective - to minimize the damage and rescue victims within the earthquake scenario.

Fig. 1. Rescue scenario.
Central buildings, rescue agents, houses, civilians, blocked roads
(grey) and fires (from yellow to dark-red). The fire brigade agents are
represented in the simulator viewer by a fire truck, the police agents
are represented by a police car, the ambulance team agents are
represented by an ambulance, and the civilians are represented by
images of people.

1.1 Types of agents

In the simulation environment, there are two main types of agents: rescue agents and
victims (civilians). When the earthquake happens, some civilians can move to nearby
refuges to find safety. However, most of them either die or are buried and injured. The
survival possibilities of the latter depend on the activity of the rescue agents.

The rescue agents are classified into moving and fixed agents (see Figure 2). The moving
rescue agents are the fire brigades, police force and ambulance teams. The fixed agents are
the central agents, i.e. those who cannot move, such as the fire, police and ambulance
stations.

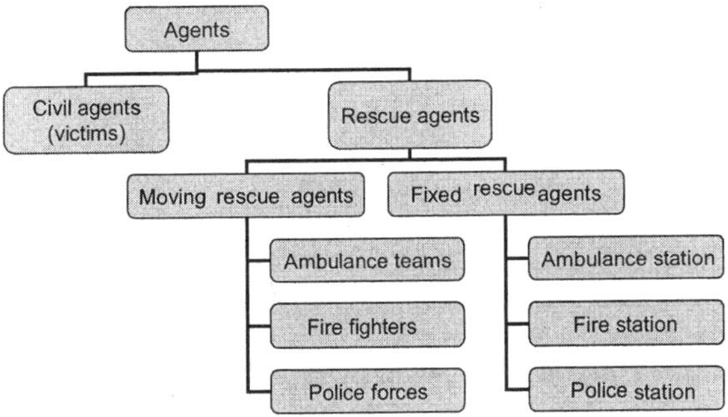

Fig. 2. Types of agents in the RoboCup-Rescue scenario.

1.2 Agents properties

All agents have certain general properties, namely *id, hp, damage, position* and *buriedness*. *Id* is the identification code of the agent. *Hp* measures the remaining life of the agents. *Damage* shows whether or not the agent has been injured. *Position* indicates the location where the agent is in the rescue scenario. Finally, *buriedness* indicates whether the agent can move or is buried under a pile of objects. Other specific properties depend on the type of agent. For example, fire brigade agents have properties such as *water quantity*, which shows how much water is in the tank, and *stretched length* which shows how far their hose can be unreeled [6].

1.3 Agents capabilities

Every type of agent has certain perception, action and communication capabilities, as shown in Table 1. First, *perception capabilities* relate to the limited range of perception that agents have in real situations. Moving agents can see visual information within a radius of 10 meters. Visual information is in terms of collapsed buildings, victim location and so on. Fixed agents cannot perceive visual information.

Secondly, the activities each agent can carry out are constrained by *action capabilities*. Ambulance teams are able to rescue civilians (*load, rescue, unload*). Fire fighters can extinguish fires (*extinguish*) and police forces can clear roads (*clear*) so that other agents can move.

Type	Capabilities
Civilians	Sense, Hear, Move, Say
Ambulance team	Sense, Hear, Move, Say, Tell, Rescue, Load, Unload
Fire brigade	Sense, Hear, Move, Say, Tell, Extinguish
Police force	Sense, Hear, Move, Say, Tell, Clear
Central agents	Hear, Say, Tell

Table 1. Agents' capabilities

Finally, *communication capabilities* constrain the communication among the different types of agents. Agents can exchange messages by voice (*say* and *listen*) and communication services (*tell* and *hear*). In the former, other agents located within a 10-meter radius can perceive the message. In the latter case, the message is perceived by the same type of agents located in a 30-meter radius. Central agents can communicate with other central agents using communication devices (*tell* and *hear*).

An agent is capable of saying or listening to, a maximum of 4 messages in each simulation cycle, within which a decision to perform some action should be taken. This is a tough constraint imposed by the Robocup Rescue simulator which should be taken into account when implementing an appropriate communication strategy (See for example [12].

2. Combinatorial auctions

In an auction, the seller wants to sell certain items and get the highest possible payments for them, while each bidder wants to acquire the items at the lowest possible price. In a sequential auction, the items are auctioned one at a time [1]. In a combinatorial auction, there is one seller (or several sellers acting in concert) and multiple bidders which may place bids on combinations of items [7]. The final objective is to obtain the maximum benefit for the seller by determining the appropriate set of winning bids (i.e., the winners).

There are several approaches for dealing with combinatorial auctions from which we have selected a particular search algorithm for its simplicity and complexity properties (see [9] for a complete analysis of these).

2.1 Winner determination problem

In an auction, it is the auctioneer who determines the winners. A non-combinatorial auction is solved by picking the highest bidder for each item separately, but in a combinatorial auction, deciding who the winner is much harder.

Let's say M is the set of items to be auctioned. Then, an agent i, can place a bid, $b_i(S) > 0$, for any combination $S \subseteq M$.

Let's say $\bar{b}(S)$ is the highest bid price for a combination. If several agents submit the same combination of items, the bid with the highest price is the only one kept, and the others can be discarded as irrelevant (they are less beneficial for the seller). Then, the highest bid price for a combination is:

$$\bar{b}(S) = \max_{i \in bidders} b_i(S) \quad (1)$$

Let W be a partition on the set M so that each item is included in, at most, one of the subsets. Then, $S \in W$. And let A be the set of all possible partitions, that is, $W \in A$.

The goal of the winner determination method is then to find a solution that maximizes the auctioneer's revenue given that each winning bidder pays the prices of her winning bids:

$$\max_{W \in A} \sum_{S \in W} \bar{b}(S) \quad (2)$$

2.2 The search algorithm

According to [9], the optimal winner determination problem can be solved by using a search algorithm. The search space is defined as follows: nodes keep information on bids and paths provide combinations of bids.

The list of bids is denoted by $\{B_1, ..., B_n\}$. Each bid B_j is a tuple $<S_j, \bar{b}_j>$ composed by the set S_j of items in the bid and the price $\bar{b}_j$ of the bid.

Each path is a sequence of disjoints bids, so that no items are shared. That is, for any path $pk = \{B_{k1}, B_{k2}, ... B_{km}\}$, it holds that $S_{k1} \cap S_{k2} \cap ... \cap S_{km} = \varnothing$. A solution is a path in which

$$S_{k1} \cup S_{k2} \cup ... \cup S_{km} \leq M.$$

In order to generate a solution, nodes are generated in lexicographic order of the set of items of the bids. For example, given the following bids:

$B_1 =\ <(319,\ 1230),10>$
$B_2 =\ <(2500,3829),21>$

bid B1 will be selected first, since the first item on the bid combination of B1 is 319, and the first item of B2 is 2500, i.e., $319 < 2500$.

The cost g_k of the path p_k is defined as:

$$g_k = \sum_j \bar{b}_{kj} \quad (3)$$

Obviously, the paths that interest the auctioneer are the ones that lead to a maximum g value.

The heuristics of the search algorithm is defined as $h = g + f$, where g is the cost of the path up to the current node, according to (3), and f is the cost of the bid to be selected, that is, $\bar{b}_i$

3. Application to rescue operations

In this approach each central agent (fire station, ambulance centre and office police) are the auctioneers and each rescue team (fire brigade, ambulance team and police force) are the bidders. The bid items are the tasks and the final objective is to obtain the maximum benefit for the whole system.

At the beginning there are no rescue operations to be performed, since the agents are just exploring the situation in their surrounding area. In order to start the combinatorial auction, the stations need to gather information from the rescue agents in terms of victims, fires and blocked roads.

3.1 Gathering tasks

Ambulance centres decide upon victim operations, fire stations upon fire extinguishing operations and police forces upon road unblocking operations. When an ambulance team discovers a fire, it cannot send this information to the fire station directly (see the description on communication capabilities in the previous section), so a communication strategy is required.

Our communication strategy emphasizes the role of the moving agents in gathering information about tasks for their stations and the role of the fixed agents in passing on this information to the corresponding station. Figures 3 and 4 depict the information flow.

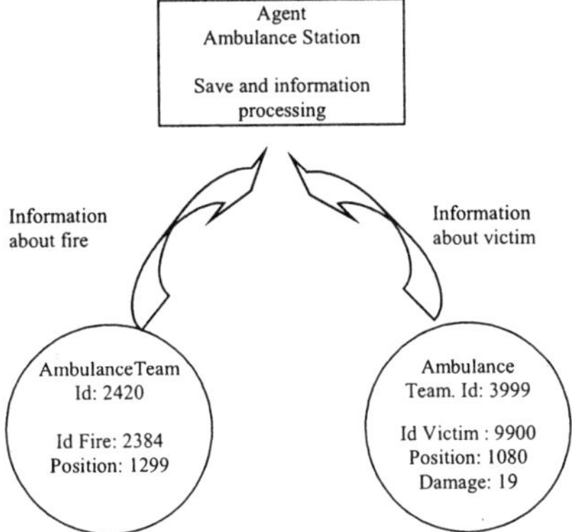

Fig. 3. Information sent to the ambulance station

3.2 Task allocation

When agent stations have information on new tasks, they start the combinatorial auction process. Rescue agents send the central agents their bids corresponding to combinations of tasks to be performed in sequential order. The rescue agents select each activity, taking into account the distance of their location and the place where these are required. Only the activities available in the agents' perception area are taken into account in the bids. In this approach, the rescue agents initially send combinations of the nearest places where it is necessary to perform any task.

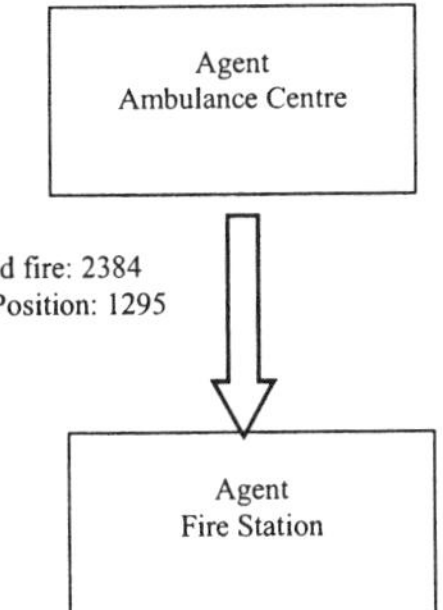

Fig. 4. Information passed from the ambulance to the fire station.

The cost of performing these activities is also included in the bid. It is computed following equation 4, below:

$$\text{Cost estimate} = \sum_i f(Dis, CPT) \quad (4)$$

$$f(Dis, CPT) = Dis * CPT$$

where:
- i = Number of tasks to be performed sequentially.
- Dis = Distance from the agent location to the place where the task will be performed.

- *CPT*= Cost of Performing the Task.

For instance, the CPT of the police agent is the cost required for clearing the road that is provided by the Robocup Rescue simulator (property *repairCost* of the blocked road); the CPT of fire brigades is the degree of fieriness (spelt fieryness in the simulator) that specifies how much a building is burning. If the estimated cost of equation 4 is greater that current agent property (hp, damage) and capabilities (i.e., water quantity), the bid cost is set to ∞.

The $f(Dis, CPT) = Dis*CPT$ function was defined because both the distance and the cost of performing the task are crucial factors in deciding the overall cost.

All bids received by the central station are processed using the *winner determination algorithm* explained in section 3.2. Tasks are selected by ensuring that sets conform to the maximum number of tasks and the minimum cost. Using the algorithm presented in the previous section, the minimum cost is found, rather than the maximum price.

That is, the winner determination consists of finding the solution that minimizes the following:

$$\min_{W \in A} \sum_{S \in W} \bar{b}(S) \quad (4)$$

where

$$\bar{b}(S) = \min_{i \in bidders} b_i(S) \quad (5)$$

4. Example

Let's assume that the fire station has knowledge of four fires in progress in the disaster scenario, identified by 319, 1230, 2500 and 3829; and that there are three fire fighting teams bidding for them (see Figure 5). The set of items to be auctioned is therefore, M={319, 1230, 2500, 3829}. These are the tasks to be performed by fire brigades.

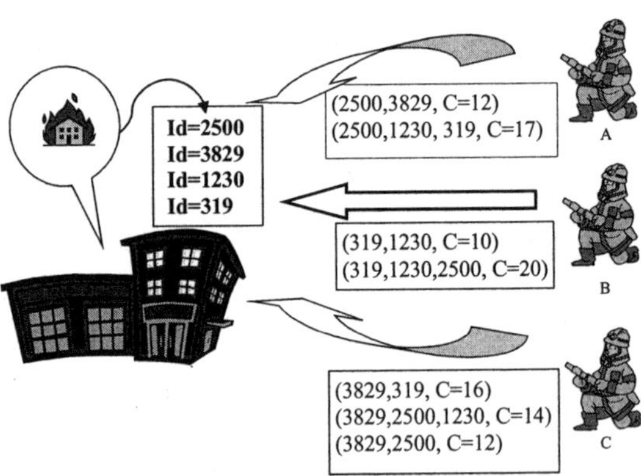

Fig. 5. Fire fighter agents send bids to the fire station

After announcing the tasks, the bids gathered by the fire station are the following:

From agent A:
$B_1 = <S_1, b_A(S_1))>$
$S_1 = \{2500, 3829\}$ $b_A(S_1) = 10$
$B_2 = <S_2, b_A(S_2))>$
$S_2 = \{2500, 1230, 319\}$ $b_A(S_2) = 17$

From agent B:
$B_3 = <S_3, b_B(S_3))>$
$S_3 = \{319, 1230\}$ $b_B(S_3) = 10$
$B_4 = <S_4, b_B(S_4))>$
$S_4 = \{2500\}$ $b_B(S_4) = 20$

From agent C:
$B_5 = <S_5, b_C(S_5))>$
$S_5 = \{3829, 319\}$ $\{b_C(S_5) = 16$
$B_6 = <S_6, b_C(S_6))>$
$S_6 = \{3829, 2500, 1230\}$ $b_C(S_6) = 14$
$B_7 = <S_7, b_C(S_7))>$
$S_7 = \{3829, 2500\}$ $b_C(S_7) = 12$

First of all, we proceed to re-order the different items on each combinatorial auction S, getting the new set of bids shown in the following table.

Bid	S	b
B_1	{2500,3829}	10
B_2	{319,1230,2500}	17
B_3	{319,1230}	10
B_4	{2500}	20
B_5	{319,3829}	16
B_6	{1230,2500,3829}	14
B_7	{2500,3829}	12

We can see that two combinations of items are identical, S_1 and S_7, so the more expensive one S_7 is removed in line with equation (5). The set of bids that make up the winner determination problem is now as follows:

Bid	S	$\bar{b}$
B_1	{2500,3829}	10
B_2	{319,1230,2500}	17
B_3	{319,1230}	10
B_4	{2500}	20
B_5	{319, 3829}	16
B_6	{1230,2500,3829}	14

This is the set of bids that is submitted to the winner determination algorithm, being $W = \{S_1, S_2, S_3, S_4, S_5, S_6\}$.

The search space corresponding to the current data is as follows (Figure 6):

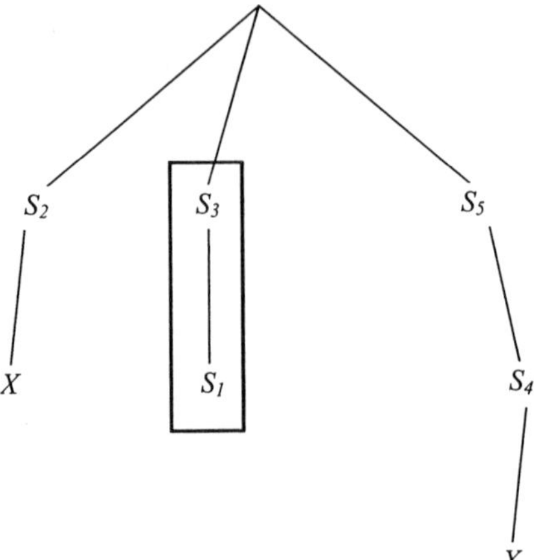

Fig. 6. Search space example

Note that the solution is the path $S_3 \cup S_1$. When applying a heuristic search, S3 is selected as the first node to be expanded since it is the bid with the lowest price. The search tree finally generated is shown below (Figure 7), obtaining the solution $S_3 \cup S_1$:

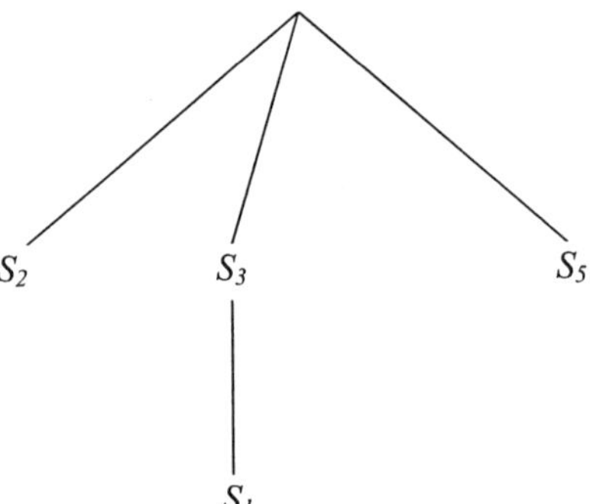

Fig. 7. Search tree example

5. Conclusions and discussion

In this paper we have presented a task allocation strategy for the RoboCup Rescue scenario based on combinatorial auctions. Task allocation helps us to maximize the benefits obtained from the actions performed by each rescue agent. If each agent maximizes their benefits, it is possible to obtain a better global performance from the rescue teams as a whole. We expect that experimental work will corroborate our proposal. In this sense, we are planning to compare the combinatorial auction techniques presented in this paper against multicriteria decision techniques that we have already developed for the same scenario in [12].

There are some previous works, such as [10] and [11] on applying combinatorial auctions to task allocation. In [10], agents are competing for roles. This is quite a different approach to ours. RoboCup Rescue provides agents with fixed rolesthat cannot be changed. So we concentrate on agent distribution. In [11], combinatorial auctions are used as a strategy for exploring the world of RoboCup Rescue. The approach can be complementary to ours in the task gathering phase.

In future work, we are thinking of modifying the search algorithm for winner determination in order to take into account the sequence of the items in the bids. Precedence constraint on tasks is relevant in rescue operations. Recent works, such as [8] can provide useful insights in this area. Other crucial issues, such as pre-emption also need to be solved, in order to deal with environmental dynamics.

Acknowledgments

This work has been supported by the Spanish MCYT project DPI2000-0658.

References

[1] J.A. Rodriguez-Aguilar, F.J. Martin, P. Noriega, P. García, C. Sierra. *Competitive Scenarios for Heterogeneous Trading Agents*. International Conference on Autonomous Agents, 1998, pp. 293-300.

[2] RoboCup-Rescue Official Web Page. http://www.r.cs.kobe-u.ac.jp/robocup-rescue/

[3] Pacifica scenario at the University of Edinburgh. http://www.aiai.ed.ac.uk/~oplan/pacifica/index.html.

[4] A. Valls. *ClusDM: A Multiple Criteria Decision Making Method for Heterogeneous Data Sets*. PhDThesis, UPC, LSI, 2002.

[5] S. Tadakoro, H. Kitano, T. Takahashi, I. Noda, H. Matsubara, A. Shinjoh, T. Koto, I. Takeuchi, H. Takahashi, F. Matsuno, M. Hatayama, J. Nobe, S. Shimada. *"The RoboCup-Rescue Project: A Robotic Approach to the Disaster Mitigation Problem"*. Proc. 2000 IEEE Int. Conf. on Robotics and Automation, April 2000 (ICRA2000).

[6] RoboCup-Rescue Simulator Manual-Versión 0 rev. 4

[7]   S.   de   Vries,   R.   Vohra.   *Combinatorial   Auctions: A   Survey.* http://citeseer.nj.nec.com/cache/papers/cs/19845/http:zSzzSzwww-m9.ma.tum.dezSz~devrieszSzcomb_auction_supplementzSzcomauction.pdf/devries01combinatorial.pdf

[8] A. Babanov, J. Collins, M. Gini. *Scheduling Tasks with Precedence Constraints to Solicit Desirable Bid Combinations*. Accepted, AAMAS'03.

[9] Sandholm Tuomas *Algorithm for optimal winner determination in combinatorial auctions*. Artificial Intelligence 135 (2002), 1-54.

[10] Hunsberger Luke, Grosz Barbara. *A combinatorial auction for collaborative planning*. Proc. of the Fourth International Conference on Multi-Agent Systems (ICMAS-2000), 2000.

[11] Nair Ranjit, Takayuki Ito, Milind Tambe, Stacy Marsella. *Task allocation in the RoboCup Rescue Simulation Domain: A short note*. Proc. International Symposium on RoboCup 2001.

[12] Silvia Suárez, Beatriz Lopez, Josep Lluis De La Rosa. *Co-operation strategies for strengthening civil agents' lives in the RoboCup-Rescue simulator scenario*. Accepted First International Workshop on Synthetic Simulation and Robotics to Mitigate Earthquake Disaster. Padova, Italy. July, 2003.

Artificial Intelligence Research and Development
I. Aguiló et al. (Eds.)
IOS Press, 2003

Security Measures in a Medical Multi-Agent System

Antonio MORENO, David SÁNCHEZ, David ISERN

Research Group on AI, Multi-Agent Systems Group (GruSMA)
Computer Science and Mathematics Department
School of Electrical and Computer Engineering (ETSE)
University Rovira i Virgili (URV)

Abstract. This paper describes the main features of an agent-based application that provides medical services to users. The system contains agents that give information about the medical centres, departments and doctors of a city. These units coordinate their execution in order to offer to the user diverse functionalities such as searching for a medical centre, accessing the medical record or booking a visit to be examined by a doctor. Special attention has been paid to the implementation of security mechanisms that guarantee confidentiality in the access and transmission of data.

Introduction

Distributed systems executing in open environments have been extensively used in the last years, mainly because they allow easy access to users, they have a reduced development cost and they can be deployed on the Internet. These systems allow the possibility of accessing multiple services from Internet, from the basic search for information to the execution of commercial or financial transactions. As these systems may deal with confidential data or perform critical actions, it is necessary to apply mechanisms that guarantee privacy and protection in front of possible attacks from malicious users.

The most typical and studied application field in this area is electronic commerce, that has gained great acceptance due to the market possibilities that it offers to industries. However, the access to any kind of service that deals with critical personal data has to be protected with appropriate security measures. In particular, dealing with an individual's health record through Internet is a very sensitive issue. Recently, an American law [17] defined the rules that software companies have to follow in this field, and the penalties that will be applied to those that do not follow these rules. There also exists a Catalan law [6] that defines the access rights of any patient to his/her medical information.

Within this field, we have developed an agent-based distributed application that provides medical services to users through a remote terminal connected to Internet (e.g. a portable PC, a PDA or a mobile phone) [7]. This system tries to ease the access to medical information (data about medical centres, health records) and to offer the possibility of making some transactions remotely (e.g. book a visit to be examined by a doctor). Security issues are clearly very important in this application, and they have been extensively considered. In [8] there is a more exhaustive review of different problems associated to the use of agents in the medical area, including the management of medical records and the definition of common ontologies. The use of agent technology in the development of this application introduces an innovation in the treatment of security issues. In fact, nowadays there does not exist any universally accepted standard in this area.

This paper provides an accurate study of security problems in a multi-agent system (MAS, [10], [19]) deployed in an open environment (Internet), based on the functionalities provided by the development tool that has been used (JADE [16]). First we explain the features of the implemented system, justifying the choice of agent technology. Then we explain the security model provided by JADE, describing its functionalities but also its important shortcomings. Finally, we explain the security model implemented in our system, detailing the functions provided by JADE as well as the ones that have had to be implemented from scratch to obtain an ad-hoc solution.

1. Description of the Application

The main objectives in the development of the application were the following:

- To design a solution that models accurately the health care organisation, decomposing it in basic units in a three level hierarchy [11] (medical centres, departments and doctors).
- To design an ontology for the medical domain that facilitates information exchange.
- To make the developed components reusable and interoperable with other systems, by using standard protocols and agent communication languages.
- To use security mechanisms that ensure the confidentiality of medical data.

An *intelligent agent* may be defined as a computational process that can perform tasks autonomously. It inhabits a complex and dynamic environment with which it may interact to accomplish a given set of goals [20]. A set of agents that communicate among themselves to solve problems by using cooperation, coordination and negotiation techniques compose a *multi-agent system* (MAS).

Multi-agent systems offer an implementation alternative that certainly fits our needs, because they have the following interesting properties:

- *Modularity*: the different services or functionalities may be distributed among diverse agents, depending on their complexity.
- *Efficiency*: agents may coordinate their activities to perform complex tasks, so that several parts of the same process may be solved concurrently by different agents.
- *Reliability*: any distributed process is more reliable than its centralised counterpart, because there does not exist a single point of failure that may cause the crash of the whole system.
- *Flexibility*: agents may be dynamically created or eliminated according to the needs of the application. Negotiation and knowledge exchange allow the optimisation of shared resources.
- *Existence of a standard*: the FIPA (*Foundation for Intelligent Physical Agents*) [4] is a non-profit foundation based on Geneve (Switzerland). Its main mission is to establish the rules that have to govern the design and implementation of a MAS in order to achieve interoperability among systems. Since 1997 it has been releasing especifications that have been slowly gaining acceptance and have turned into de facto standards in the agents community. Due to this fact, any of our agents is compatible with any other agent that follows the same specifications.

- *Existence of development tools*: JADE (*Java Agent Development Enviroment*) [16] is a programming tool that contains a set of JAVA libraries that facilitate the development of FIPA-compliant MASs. Apart from providing low level agent management functionalities and graphical interfaces that ease development and debugging, it also provides an execution environment for agents. Recently, a JADE plug-in that provides certain security mechanisms, called JADE-S, has been released.

We designed and implemented a MAS with the architecture shown in figure 1. This system contains six different types of agents:

- *Personal Agent* (PA): it provides a graphical interface to the user that facilitates the access to the services offered by the system. It is the only agent that can execute outside the main container of the platform and make remote requests through Internet. Figures 2, 3 and 4 show diverse windows of the interface, used to search for information of medical centres, book a medical visit or look at the medical record.
- *Personal Broker* (PB): it provides a gateway among the PA and the other agents of the system. It controls the access to the system and it also checks the identities of the users (see section 3).
- *Medical Centre Agent* (MCA): it models the organisation of a medical centre.
- *Department Agent* (DEP): it models each department (unit dedicated to a medical specialty) within each medical centre.
- *Doctor Agent* (DA): it simulates the behaviour of each of the doctors belonging to the departments of the medical centres.
- *Database Wrapper* (DW): it controls the access to the database that holds the personal and medical information of each patient.

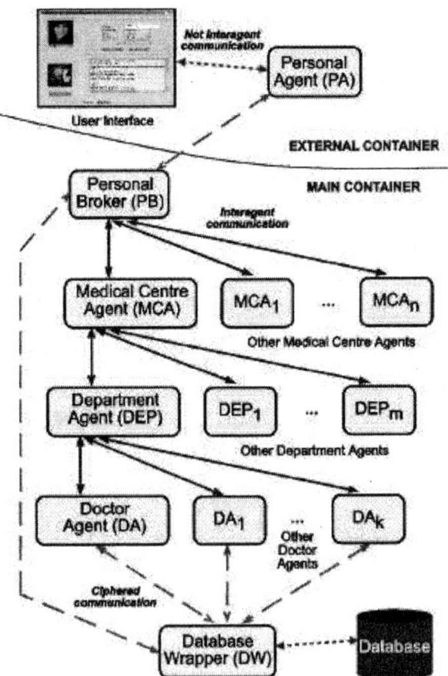

Figure 1. Architecture of the multi-agent system

The basic functionalities provided by the application are the following:

- The user may request information about the available medical centres in a city or region, or about the personnel of a specific medical centre (see figure 2).

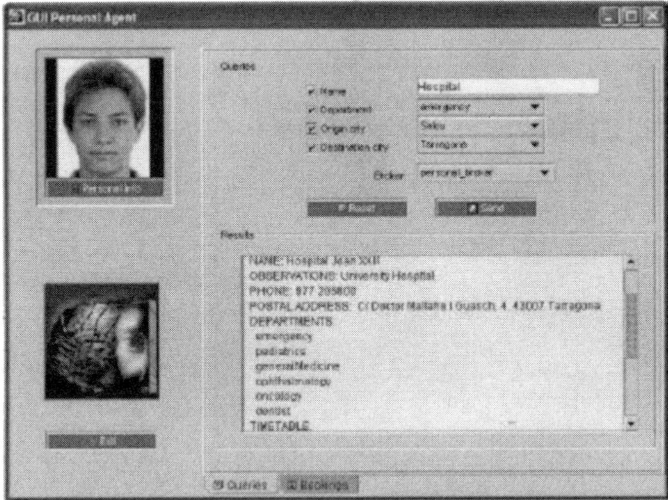

Figure 2. Window to request information

- The user can book a visit to be examined by a particular type of doctor in a specific medical centre (see fig. 3).

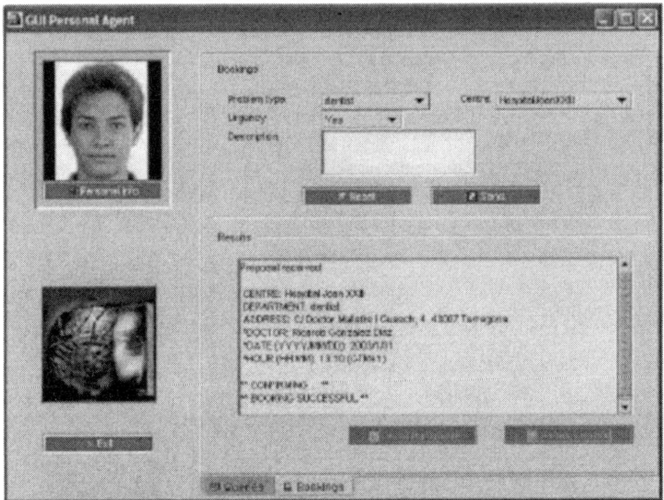

Figure 3. Window to book a visit to a doctor

- The user has a personal and confidential information area that keeps his/her personal data and health record.

- As mandated by the Catalan Law on Information Access Rights [6], the patient may access the data of his/her medical record (see figure 4).

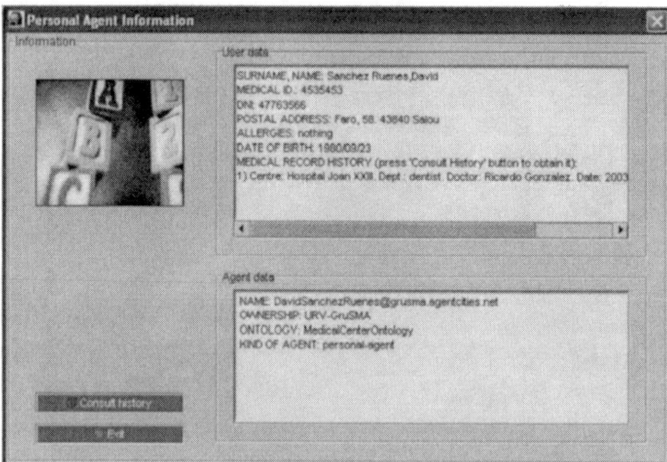

Figure 4. Personal and medical data of the user.

- In the date and time of the scheduled visit, the doctor agent simulates it, storing the results of the examination in the patient's medical record.

2. JADE Security Model (JADE-S)

In order to understand the role of security in the transmission of private and critical information (e.g. health records) through an open environment (e.g. Internet), it is necessary to define the concepts that determine the diverse security levels [3]:

- *Confidentiality:* is the property that ensures that only those that are properly authorised may access the information.
- *Integrity:* is the property that ensures that information cannot be altered. This modification could be an insertion, deletion or replacement of data.
- *Authentication:* is the property that refers to identification. It is the link between the information and its sender.
- *Non-repudiation:* is the property that prevents some of the parts to negate a previous commitment or action.

In the case of a MAS these properties are especially important, due to the autonomy and mobility of agents. A MAS without security support could not be used in an open environment such as Internet if it deals with critical data, because communications could be spied or the identities of the agents could be easily faked.

JADE-S [2] is a plug-in of JADE that allows to add some security characteristics in the development of MAS, so that they can start to be used in real environments. It is based on the Java security model [15] and it provides the advantages of the following technologies:

- JAAS (*Java Authentication and Authorization Service*) [12]: it allows to establish access permissions to perform certain operations on a set of predetermined classes, libraries or objects.

- JCE (*Java Cryptography Extension*) [15]: it implements a set of cryptographic functions that allow the developer to deal with the creation and management of keys and to use encryption algorithms.
- JSSE (*Java Secure Socket Extension*) [14]: it allows to exchange critical information through a network using a secure data transmission (SSL).

2.1 Basic Concepts

A JADE platform may be located in different hosts and have different containers. In order to introduce security in such an open and distributed environment, JADE-S structures the agent platform as a multi-user environment in which all components (agents, containers, etc.) belong to authenticated (through a login and a password) users, who are authorised by the administrator of the system to perform certain privileged critical actions. The general scheme of this environment is shown in figure 5:

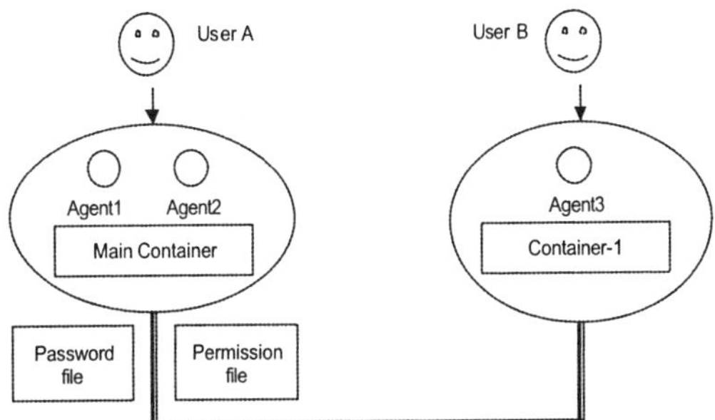

Figure 5. Aspect of a secure agent platform

Thus, in each platform there is a permissions file that contains the set of actions that each user is authorised to perform ([13]).

Internally, an agent proves its identity by showing an Identity Certificate signed by the Certification Authority (provided in a transparent way to the agent when it registers in the system and provides the login and the password of its owner). Using these digitally signed certificates the platform may allow or deny certain actions to each agent.

2.2 Authentication

As explained above, each component of the platform belongs to an authenticated user. The user that boots the platform also owns the AMS[1] and DF[2] agents and the main container.

When a user wants to join the platform (through one of his/her agents), it has to provide his/her login and password. These data are checked with the passwords file contained in the platform, which is stored in a ciphered way, like Unix passwords. The passwords file is unique and is loaded with the main container.

Each agent owned by this user will have an Identity Certificate that contains its name, its owner and the signature of the Certification Authority.

2.3 Permissions and Access Restrictions

In a JADE-S platform the permissions to access resources are given to the different entities by following the mechanism defined by the new system provided by Java (JAAS [12]) for user-based authentication. Thus, it is possible to assign permissions to parts of the code and

---

[1] *Agent Management System*: it stores the addresses of the agents and offers a White Pages service.
[2] *Directory Facilitator*: it is aware of all the services offered by the agents of the system, and it provides a Yellow Pages service.

to its executers, restricting the access to certain methods, classes or libraries depending on who wants to use them. An entity can only perform an action (send a message, move to another container) if the Java security manager allows it. The set of permissions associated to each identity is stored in the access rights file of the platform (which is also unique and is loaded when the platform is booted).

Java provides a set of permissions (apart from those that may be defined by the user) on the basic elements of the language: *AWTPermission, FilePermission, Socket Permission,* etc. Moreover, JADE-S provides other permissions related to the behaviour of the agents: *AgentPermission, ContainerPermission,* etc. Each permission has a list of related actions that may be allowed or denied.

2.4 Certification Authority and Certificates

The Certification Authority is the entity that signs the certificates of all the elements of the platform. To do that, it owns a couple of public/private keys so that, for each certificate, it creates an associated signature by ciphering it with its private key (which is secret). Then, when the identity of an entity has to be checked, the signature may be unencrypted with the public key of the Authority (which is publicly known) and we can check that the identity that the entity wanted to prove matches the one provided by the Authority. The secure platform JADE-S provides a Certification Authority within the main container. Each signed certificate is only valid within the platform in which it has been signed.

2.5 Secure Communication

In order to provide a secure communication between agents located in different hosts or containers, JADE-S uses the SSL protocol *(Secure Socket Layer)* [9] that provides privacy and integrity for all the connections established in the platform. This is a way of being protected against network sniffers.

3. Implementation

In this section we describe in detail all the security mechanisms that have been implemented in the application, including those provided by JADE-S as well as those that have been manually added.

3.1 Access Control

Before using any security mechanism provided by JADE-S on an agent platform, first it is necessary to define a set of default Java permissions that allow to execute the basic code of JADE (including network access, graphical interface, etc.). Recall that the only allowed actions are those explicitly included in the permissions file. These permissions have to appear in the *"basic.policy"* file, which is read by default when the platform is booted.

Having done that, we have built, on top of the security services provided by JADE-S, an access control model that is based on two levels of permissions:

- *Root*: this user has access to all the actions that may be performed on the platform (indicated explicitly one by one in the permissions file).
- *Guest*: the permissions of this user are quite limited. Its agents can only perform the basic actions to request services from the system (send and receive messages).

The content of the passwords file containing these two users has the same format that the UNIX passwords file. This file can be created directly with the UNIX user management capabilities or through the options provided by JADE. The set of permissions of each user is stored in the access policy file associated to the platform. Thus, we associate one of these users to each of the types of agents:

- Internal agents: agents that are executed within the main container of the platform (*Broker, Medical Centres, Departments, Doctors* and *Database Wrapper*). They belong to the *root* user; thus, they do not have any constraint on the actions they can perform. We have taken this decision to facilitate the interaction among them (they can send and receive messages from any agent, or register in the DF or the AMS). As they are internal to the platform (they execute in the main container) and they have been programmed by us, they will not perform any malicious action (kill other agents, deregister other agents, fake the identity of another agent, etc.).
- External agents: the Personal agents, that execute in an external container in another host, belong to this category. They have been associated to the *guest* user, so that they can neither access the main container (to join the other agents) nor access the DF (to modify the information of other agents). They can only communicate with the internal agents through the *Broker*; therefore, they cannot pretend to have the identity of other agents or kill other agents. All these constraints are necessary because we do not have any control over these agents, and they may have been programmed to perform dangerous actions.

3.2 Secure Communication

Apart from the security mechanism implemented through the permission file, we have also taken advantage of the possibility offered by JADE-S of ciphering all the communications using SSL [9].

Even though it is only necessary to encrypt those messages between the main container and the external container (between the *Personal Agent* and the *Broker*) that contain confidential information (medical records), the activation of SSL may only be made globally: we can only cipher all messages or none of them.

Thus, by activating the appropriate option in the JADE initial configuration files in the client (*Personal*) and in the server (platform), *all the communications between the agents of the system will be ciphered* and, therefore, we can safely send the encryption keys or the medical records. This mechanism works if we have previously obtained an identity certificate for the server side (the one that boots the platform), so that SSL may implement authentication. Having this certificate, we can use the *keytool* application (included in the Java distribution) to create a couple of files called *keystore* and *truststore* that have to be included in the execution directory. Certificates are provided freely (for evaluation) by some certificate companies (e.g. Verisign [18]).

It must be remembered that SSL is a protocol that works at the data transport level and, therefore, is transparent to the application. Thus, even though in the development phase we do not have to take it into account, it does not allow us to access the security mechanisms that it incorporates (e.g. the possibility of authentication using certificates).

3.3 JADE-S Shortcomings

Despite its functionalities, it must be stressed that JADE-S is still in an early phase of development and it presents some constraints such as the following:

- SSL can only be globally applied to all messages (not individually or selectively).
- The access permissions are quite generic and limited, and do not allow to define specific actions (e.g. to allow an agent to make queries to the DF but not register in the DF).

- It is not possible to access the information about the identity of the agent from the program.
- We can only define the permissions especified by JADE-S. It is not possible to add new permissions related to the user-defined agents (e.g. about the possibility of requesting a service).

Due to these shortcomings, we have had to add some software security mechanisms to create a reliable and flexible security model.

3.4 Centralised Access Model

One of the main problems of JADE-S is that the permissions that can be defined on the DF (agent that provides information about all the other agents that are executing on the platform) are reduced to the possibility of allowing the reception/sending of messages. However, several actions may be performed on the DF: an agent may register/deregister, or search for other agents that satisfy a given constraint (e.g. that offer a specific service or belong to a certain class). Taking into account that the registration/deregistration operations are critical and that there does not exist any control on the identity of the agent that requests the action, we have had to forbid the access to external agents (*Personal Agents*) to the DF to prevent them for making these actions maliciously (pretending to be other agents). The problem of this approach is that we will no longer be able to search for agents directly, because the communication with the DF is not allowed.

The solution has been to implement a new behaviour in the *Personal Broker* that simulates the functionality of the search process as if it was made directly by the DF. In this way the *Personal Agent* has the possibility of searching for agents without having to talk directly to the DF (the *Broker* provides the gateway).

Another shortcoming of the JADE-S security model is that it does not allow a user to define his/her own permissions for each type of agent (e.g. to control the access to the service of booking visits with doctors). Thus, if we allow the *Personal Agent* to access the *Medical Centres* and the *Database Agent* directly to make a booking or to request information, we can only indicate if the PA can send/receive messages from these agents, but not specify the services that may or may not be requested. Furthermore, in this decentralised model it is more difficult to guarantee security, as it should have to be implemented at different levels. Therefore, we have decided that *Broker* provides a gateway between the *Personal* and the rest of the system, forbidding the communication with any other agent. In this way we can prevent the *Personal* agent from faking the identity of a *Department* when it communicates with a *Medical Centre*, and agents do not have to control the identity of all the senders of the messages they receive.

This centralised model allows us to incorporate all the program security mechanisms described below in a single agent. In this way the rest of the system is not involved in this control and we get a transparent use of the system by external agents, as they only have to communicate with the *Broker* and not with particular agents representing medical centres, departments or doctors. The price to be paid is that the *Broker* has to implement indirectly all the services that are offered to the user, and its implementation gets more complex.

3.5 Software Authentication

JADE-S deals internally with the identities of the users, but this information is not accessible from the program and, as we need to know this information (e.g. to provide the medical records of the users), we had to implement an authentication mechanism.

Classical authentication is based on public key algorithms (in our case RSA), so that each user owns a public key and a private one (which is only known by the agent itself and by the certification authority that generated it). In our case, the keys (managed by the *Database Agent*) are associated to the user from the personal data that it provides when it enters the system. These keys allow the agent to sign the messages that it sends, so that its identity may be checked.

When the user joins the system, the *Database Agent* generates its keys and sends them through the *Broker*. This agent stores the public key of each registered user and sends both keys to the *Personal Agent*. It is not necessary to control in the program the identity of the agent that sends the message (*Database* or *Broker*) with identity certificates, because it is controlled at a lower level (using SSL and JADE-S users management). When the user wants to send a critical message in which it has to prove its identity (e.g. when it wants to access the medical record or request a visit to a doctor), it encrypts the message with its (secret) private key. When *Broker* receives this message, it can check the identity of the sender by using the public key associated to this agent. If the unencrypted content is valid, the identity is deemed correct and the request is processed. If the key does not match the one of the agent or the content of the message has been modified, the result of the unencryption will be wrong and will provoke an exception during the interpretation process, which will cause a denial of the request (see figure 6).

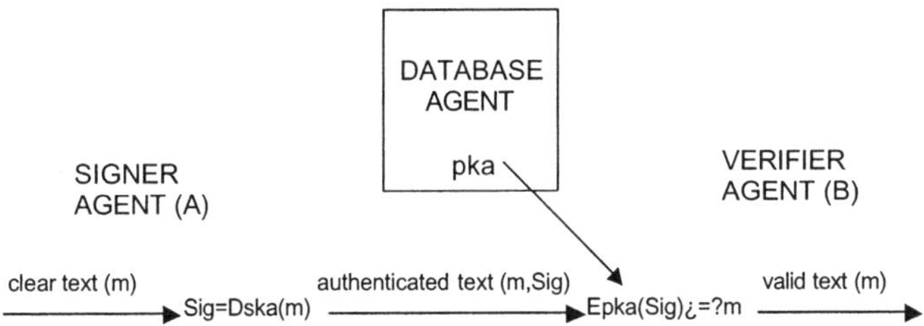

Figure 6. Signing a message with a public key

This mechanism is also used by *Doctors*, to check that only they are allowed to modify the medical records of the patients when they perform a medical examination. In this case, though, keys are not stored, because their data are read statically from a configuration file and are not stored in the database. Thus, keys are valid during the life cycle of the *Doctor* agent (they work as "session keys").

4. Summary and Conclusion

The main features of our security model are the following:

- All the messages exchanged among the agents are encrypted at the transport level, and the server is authenticated with SSL.
- We have established diverse security levels by using different user identities, and associating an owner (identified with a login and a password) to each agent.
- We have defined a set of permissions for each security level through descriptor files.
- It is a centralised access model through the *Broker* agent, that implements a software security control.
- Personal agents cannot communicate directly with any other agent (even with the DF).
- User authentication through the signature of critical messages using a public key mechanism.

We want to argue in this paper that MAS are a good alternative to fully implement complex programs in distributed environments such as Internet. In fact, a complete prototype of the application is permanently running on a server provided by AgentCities in a worldwide agent-based network of services. The project web page [6] contains all the access instructions to be followed to request securely and remotely the services offered by the system.

Even though there is still a lot of work to be done in the security field in MAS, this paper tries to show that it is feasible to apply concepts of information security in these systems. Thus, if FIPA continues developing standards in this field [5] and development tools incorporate these suggestions, it will become possible to develop secure applications in critical domains such as banking or on-line electronic commerce.

Acknowledgments

This system has been developed with the support of *AgentCities.NET* through the deployment grant *"Deployment of agent-based health care services"* ([1]). The authors also acknowledge the support of the Spanish thematic network *"Creación de un entorno innovador para la comunicación de agentes inteligentes"* (MCyT, TIC2001-5108-E).

References

[1] GruSMA web page for AgentCities project: http://grusma.etse.urv.es/~agentcities.

[2] Bellifemine, F. et. al. *JADE Security Administrator Guide*, CSELT S.p.A. and University of Parma, September 2002 (v 2.61), http://sharon.cselt.it/projects/jade/

[3] Domingo, J., Herrera, J., *Criptografia per als serveis telemàtics i el comerç electrònic*, EdiUOC, 1999.

[4] Foundation for Intelligent Physical Agents, web page: http://www.fipa.org

[5] Foundation for Intelligent Physical Agents (2002) *FIPA MAS Security white paper*, FIPA

[6] Generalitat de Catalunya. *Llei sobre els drets d'informació concernent la salut i l'autonomia del pacient, i la documentació clínica*. Law 21/2000, 29th December 2000, Departament de Salut i Seguretat Social, Generalitat de Catalunya. Quaderns de legislació, 31. ISBN 84-393-5459-2.

[7] Moreno, A., Isern, D., Sánchez, D., *Provision of agent-based health care services*, AI-Communications, in press, 2003.

[8] Nealon, J. Moreno, A. *Agent-based health care systems.* In *Applications of Software Agents Technology in the Health Care Domain*, J.Nealon and A.Moreno Eds., Whitestein series in software agent technology, 2003 (in press).

[9] Netscape Communication Corporation, *Introduction to SSL*, available at the web page http://developer.netscape.com/docs/manuals/security/sslin/contents.htm

[10] Poggi, A., Rimassa, G., Tomaiuolo, M., *Multi-User and Security Support for Multi-Agent Systems*, DII – Universitat de Parma, Proceedings of WOA 2001, Modena, Sep 2001.

[11] Servei Català Salut: http://www.gentcat.es/scs

[12] Sun Microsystems, *Authentication and Authorization Service (JAAS)*. Web page: http://java.sun.com/products/jass/index-14.html

[13] Sun Microsystems, *Java Default Policy Implementation and Policy File Syntax*, http://java.sun.com/j2se/1.4/docs/guide/security/PolicyFiles.html

[14] Sun Microsystems, *Java Secure Socket Extension (JSSE) Reference Guide*. Web page: http://java.sun.com/j2se/1.4/docs/guide7security/jsse/SEERefGuide.html

[15] Sun Microsystems, *Java Security*. Web page: http://java.sun.com/security

[16] TILab, Jade, http://sharon.cslet.it/project/jade

[17] US Department of Health and Human Services, *Standards for Privacy and Individually Identifiable Health Information*, Federal Register, volume 65. December 28th, 2000.

[18] Verisign, plana web: http://www.veris ign.com/

[19] Wong, H., Sycara, K., *Adding security and trust to multi-agent systems*, In Proceedings of Autonomous Agents'99, Workshop on deception, fraud and trust in agent societies, pp. 149-161. Seattle, Washington, May 1999.

[20] Wooldridge, M., *An introduction to multiagent systems*, John Wiley Ed., 2002. ISBN 0-471-49691-X.

Artificial Intelligence Research and Development
I. Aguiló et al. (Eds.)
IOS Press, 2003

Multiagent System for Controlling GMPLS Network Protection[*]

Anna URRA, Eusebi CALLE, J. L. MARZO
Institut d'Informàtica i Aplicacions (IIiA)
Universitat de Girona
Avinguda Lluís Santaló s/n, 17071 Girona

Abstract. In this article, we describe the architecture of a system of agents for dynamic management of the probabilities of failures associated with certain links in a GMPLS network environment. The system described here monitors the parameters of failure probability in a network and protects those segments that have the highest failure probabilities. The results show that cooperation between the agents and the GMPLS control plane guarantees a high degree of protection and good resource management.

Introduction

At present, networks require guaranteed quality of Service (QoS) for certain types of traffic. In GMPLS (Generalized Multiprotocol Label Switching) networks, mechanisms have been defined for network management based on routing with protection and network resource management to guarantee the QoS for traffic[1].

There are also some proposals in which agents are used for managing network resources [2,3].

QoS routing algorithms search for the optimum route according to the QoS and the network resources. The protection mechanisms try to minimize the risk of disconnection caused by a link failure. There are various proposals that define algorithms for protection by means of alternative routes, such as, local backup, global backup and reverse backup. These mechanisms come into play the moment the link failure is produced.

There are also proposals of new routing algorithms which take into account the failure probability of the links upon establishing a new route, (origin-destination) the LSP, *Label Switched Path* [4]. A link failure probability (LFP) is assigned to a subset of network links. In this way, the failure probability for the path LSP_FP can be determined. This information is used by the routing algorithm in order to choose the LSP.

The objective is to minimize the number of LSPs that pass through links susceptible to failure.

The initial LFP is worked out according to a series of aspects, such as, for example, the technology (type of cable) or the network provider's own assignation of failure probability (in line with their reliability requirements).

Nevertheless, there are other aspects that may affect the LFP, such as, the type of traffic, failure statistics, etc. which can help to bring about a more efficient and realistic use of failure probabilities.

---

[*]   This work was partially supported by Universitat de Girona (UdG-DinGruRec2003-GRCT40)

In previous work, we developed systems for bandwidth management using distributed agents [5] and multiple control of faults using agents, [6]. In this article, we are concentrating on the application of agents for controlling GMPLS network protection. The multiagent system controls the network protection by monitoring and updating the failure probability and setting up alternative routes using statistics on failure, on the type of traffic and on the technology used in the network.

In this article, we first analyze those aspects thought to determine the LFP value. Then we describe the architecture of the multiagent system designed to adapt the LFP and establish the alternative paths where necessary. Next, we present the comparative results of applying two routing algorithms (the well-known WSP and a variation of it) with no agents applied, and one routing algorithm in which, incorporated in the network, is the multiagent system. Finally, we present our conclusions.

1 Definition of Failure Probability

Initially, the failure probability of a link can be determined directly (for example, when the probability is assigned by the network provider according to their initial needs and reliability requirements. Having said that, this probability does not remain the same as time goes on. In order to calculate a more realistic value of the failure probability, we take into account all of the following three variables which are discussed in detail below:

- Topological changes.
- Failure statistics.
- Type of traffic.

1.1   Topological Changes

A topological change implies the insertion of new links into the network (with or without the addition of new routers) or the modification of the physical medium of the existing link. Generally speaking, topological changes in a network take place over long periods of time. This means that there is little change in failure probability resulting from modifications at the physical level.

Establishing the probability associated with a topological change is carried out directly (Fig. 1).

A link has more or less possibilities of failing depending on the type of physical medium. So, when it comes to establishing or modifying a link, a certain failure probability can be assigned to the link depending on its physical characteristics.

Figure 1 shows the development of the failure probability of a link. Initially, we assign the probability *p1* when inserting the new link into the network at the instant, *t1*. At the instant, *t2*, the physical link is substituted by a link that uses a more secure physical medium. Thus, by improving the physical medium, the failure probability diminishes, and gets a new value, *p2*.

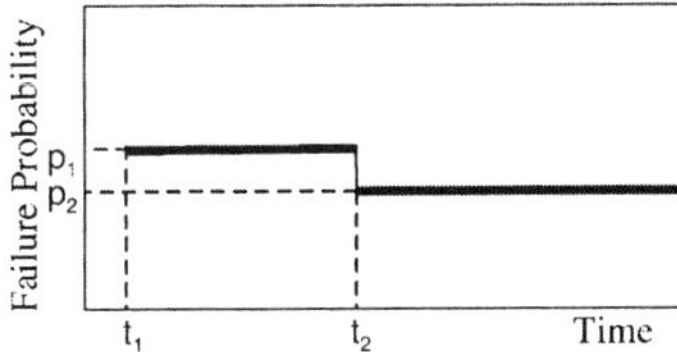

Fig.1 Development of link failure probability caused by topological changes.

1.2   Failure Statistics

The amount of traffic that flows through a link can be monitored and a pattern of its behavior obtained. Using this information, we can find out if there are significant variations occurring in link behavior. At a certain instant, if the statistics increase (for example, in the case of consecutive failures in a short space of time), the possibility of link failure is higher; therefore, this increase must be taken into account in the probability associated with the link. Once the cause of the failure is resolved, the probability returns to the stable value similar to the previous value (see Figure 2).

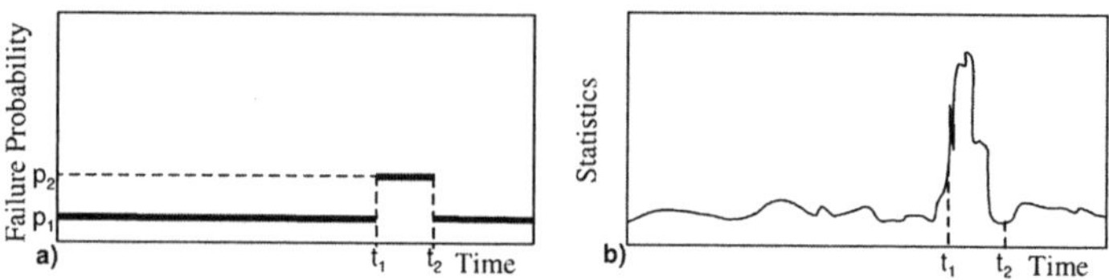

Fig 2 a) Development of failure probabilities according to failure statistics.
b) Development of statistics.

1.3   The Type of Traffic

Depending on the type of traffic that flows through it, a link may need more or less protection. The flow of information that passes through a link is highly variable over time. Various LSPs, with diverse traffic, may pass through it. In this way, the number of LSPs that need protection may begin to increase in one particular link. Hence, if there are two types of traffic, T0 and T1, (T1 with protection requirements, T0, without them), the failure probability is adapted to the number of LSPs with T1 in order to provide them with more protection.

As Figure 3 shows, the changes in probability, bearing in mind the priority traffic, are highly variable. Each time an LSP with T1 containing the link to be protected is established or freed, there is an increase or decrease in the failure probability in this link. The frequency in which LSPs with T1 are established or freed is high with respect to the variations in failure probability generated by the failure statistics (months) or by topological changes in the network (years).

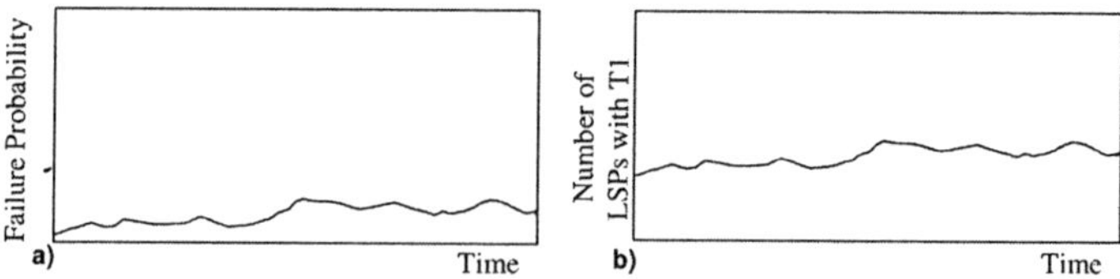

Fig. 3.- a) Development of probabilities according to priority traffic load on the link.
b) Development of priority traffic load on the link.

1.4   Final Link Failure Probability

The variables that determine the failure probability of a link have been described individually. The final probability is a combination of these three variables. Thus, as Figure 4 shows, when a new link is introduced to the network at the instant, *t1*, a probability is assigned to it. From then on, the probability will fluctuate until it becomes more or less stable because of the variations in the priority traffic passing through the link. The probability value will be significantly altered when there is a considerable variation in the statistics, when the link is physically modified or when priority traffic through the link is increased.

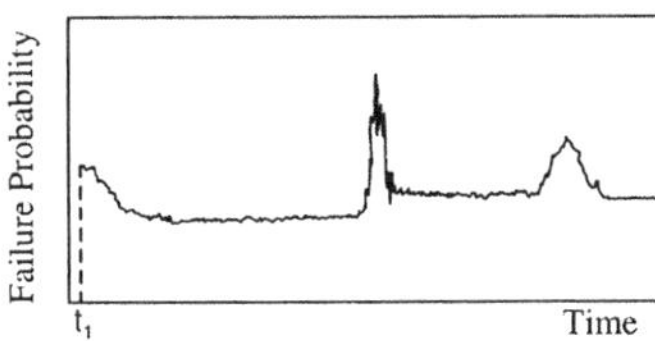

Fig. 4.- Development of link failure probability.

2 Managing Failure Probability

In this section, we define the multiagent system with which these LFPs will be managed. First we describe the operations associated with the system that keeps the LFP updated. Then we will define the classification of agents according to the operations assigned to them and their interaction. Finally, we describe the integration of the agents into the GMPLS network.

2.1   Operations Associated with the System

As we have seen in Section 1, there is a certain amount of information we need to store in order to monitor the link and keep its LFP updated. Maintaining the local information on a link means monitoring the following variables:
- Maintenance of the failure statistics.
- Type of topology.
- Traffic development.

In a GMPLS network, the links may be bi-directional; for this reason, monitoring the LFP variables has to be carried out in the two end nodes of the link. This means we need to establish a final probability from the probabilities indicated by the end nodes.

With this information, decisions can be taken in order to protect the links with a particular LFP. These decisions are:
- Update the LFP of the link when its value varies significantly (modification of the *TE Database*, see section 2.3). This means the routing algorithms will have the most up-to-date information about the network at the moment the LSPs are established, which in turn means that there will be more or less LSPs containing this link, depending on its failure probability.

- Ask the routing entities to establish alternative routes (local backup). This decision is taken when high failure probabilities (greater than x) are detected. This action allows the system to protect the LSPs with priority traffic (T1) passing through the link. Figure 5 shows the points at which the alternative route is established.

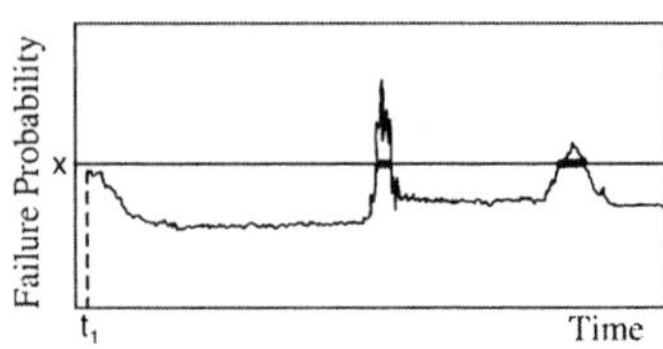

Fig. 5.- Points at which alternative routes are established.

2.2   Agent Classification

The multiagent system, in order to be able to control the points mentioned in section 2.1, is made up of the following agents: probability management agents (PMAs) and protection control agents (PCAs).

The PMAs are positioned in the routers and there is one of them for each link to be protected. A PMA manages the variables (failure statistics, topology, traffic type) and updates the local value of the LFP of the router in which this link is found. Since the links are bi-directional, each one has two PMAs to manage it (one for each end of the link). In this way, the agents that manage the same link have to communicate with each other to reach an agreement on the value of the failure probability.

The PCAs, basically, are responsible for requesting the establishment of alternative routes and updating the values of the network LFPs. There is a PCA for each router where there are links to be protected. This router receives, from the PMAs found in it, the updated information on the LFP. Furthermore, the PCAs are responsible for configuring the PMAs that are in the same router.

2.3   Agent Distribution in the GMPLS Network

The PMAs and PCAs are distributed at application level, as shown in Figure 6. The agent, PCA5, controls a subset of links of the router where it is found through the PMAs.

The information that the PCA needs and updates is found in the GMPLS control plane [7] where the information used by the routing and signaling protocols is found. There are different databases, accessible and updatable by the routing protocols. According to [1], these databases are:
- Topology Database: contains the links, the routers and their connections.
- TE database (Traffic Engineering database or TED): contains the properties of the network resources. Incorporated into this database is the new field in which the LFP is indicated.
- Existing Path Database: contains the information on the active routes and LSPs. This database also includes the LSP_FP.

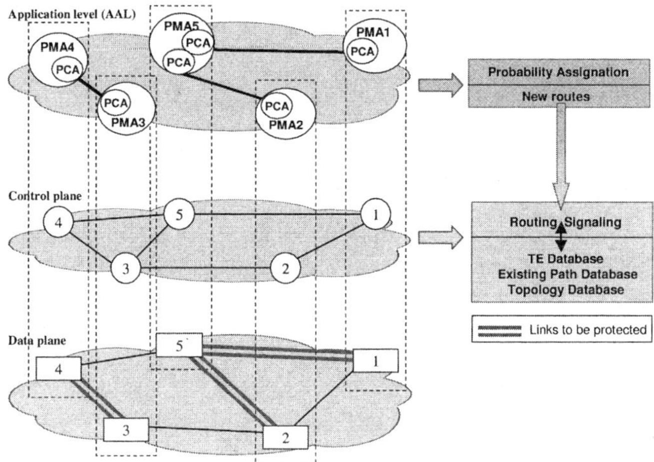

Fig. 6.- Distribution of the agents at application leveling in a GMPLS network.

The PCA updates the information when it detects a significant variation in the link failure probability. The updating of the TE database of the control plane, as in the case of the topology database, is carried out by means of routing protocols such as OSPF or ISIS [1].

To activate the alternative route, the PCAs communicate with the control plane by means of a request for a new LSP to the routing and signaling protocol. Once the alternative route is activated, it will remain active until the failure probability diminishes significantly with respect to the value that activated it. This new route consumes the bandwidth equivalent to the sum of the bandwidth of the LSPs with T1 that pass through the link to be protected. If there is not enough bandwidth in this link, then only a subset of the LSPs with T1 will be protected. While this alternative route is active, the new LSPs with T1 increase the bandwidth of this route wherever possible. The freeing of an LSP with T1 leads to the decrease of the bandwidth reserved in the route, provided that all the LSPs of this type have been protected. Otherwise, the bandwidth is reassigned to the possible LSPs that have not been protected.

3 Results

In this section, we will analyze the results of applying the agents in the assignation of probabilities using algorithms based on WSP [8]. We will analyze two routing algorithms with no agents (WSP and FP), and one of these algorithms with the agents (FPA).

- WSP (Widest Shortest Path): a routing algorithm that determines the LSPs independently of the link failure probabilities.
- FP (Failure Probability): a modification of the WSP where the routing algorithm determines the LSPs, adding the failure probabilities of the links in a GMPLS network. The probabilities are static, that is to say, their value is not effective nor realistic, since the aspects that can make it vary are not taken into account.
- FP with Agents (FPA): the FP algorithm is applied, but, in this case, on the same GMPLS network, we introduce the multiagent system to update the values for the failure probabilities.

The topology used in each of the experiments (Figure 7) and which has been used in many proposals, such as a previous work of ours [8], is as follows:

- 15 nodes and 28 links. The capacity of the links is 1,200 and 4,800 units. Each link is bi-directional. There are four pairs of ingress-egress routers (1-13, 5-9, 4-2, 5-15).
- The bandwidth assigned to the LSPs is uniformly distributed among 10, 20 and 30 units.
- The LSPs arrive according to an exponential distribution of 1 ms. The lifetime of an LSP follows a distribution of 30,000 ms.
- The agents are distributed in routers 1, 3, 9, 10, 11 and 14. These agents control the links that require protection. An initial LSP, shown in Figure 7, has been assigned to these links.
- The agents activate the route when the probability is equal to or greater than 0.007.

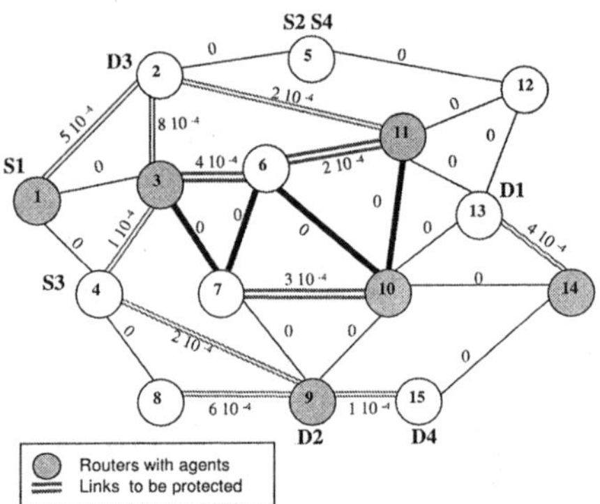

Fig. 7.- Network topology and agent distributions.

Two types of traffic have been defined:

- T0: not priority. Alternative routes are never applied and when the LSP is determined, failure probabilities are not taken into account.
- T1: priority. Alternative routes are applied when appropriate and when the LSP is determined, the failure probabilities will be taken into account (in those algorithms that require them).

In Figure 8 a – b, we analyze the distribution of the number of LSPs with T1 according to their failure probability (LSP_FP). Graph 8a shows the application of a WSP. The distribution of probabilities shows that we obtain a high number of LSPs with high failure probabilities (0.007). This case is especially critical if we distinguish between probabilities calculated by means of agents (3,000 LSPs) or non-updated (static) failure probabilities, where we have 1,000 LSPs with high failure probabilities.

In the FP case, (Figure 8b) we see that the number of LSPs with high failure probabilities decreases with respect to WSP, although there is still a difference between those calculated with real probabilities (i.e., calculated with agents) and those that are not updated.

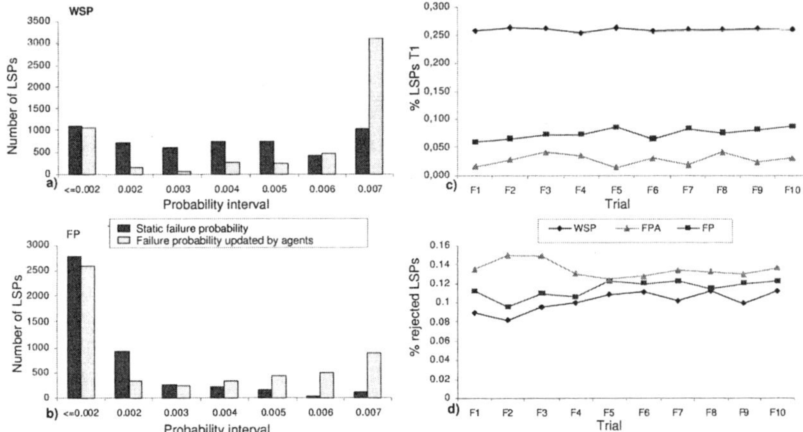

Fig. 8. a)Distribution of the number of LSPs according to failure probabilities when applying WSP.
b) Distribution of the number of LSPs according to failure probabilities when applying FP.
c) Percentage LSPs with failure probabilities greater than 0.007 for priority traffic
d) Percentage of LSPs rejected.

If we apply the FPA (i.e., the FP algorithm on the same network plus the multiagent system) we can see that the number of LSPs with priority traffic and high failure probability decreases considerably with respect to the first two alternatives (see Figure 8c). Hence, we are reducing the probability that an LSP with T1 will fail.

To provide more protection for priority traffic passing through a particular link, the agents establish alternative routes when the link failure probability is high. Having said that, the functionality of the agents in determining the alternative routes means that more bandwidth is consumed, and that there is an increase in the number of LSPs rejected compared to the other algorithms (Figure 8d).

This increase in bandwidth consumption depends on the number of LSPs with T1 that need to be protected and the available bandwidth on the route defined for the alternative route. Likewise, as can be seen in Figure 9, the more LSPs to be protected, the more of them are rejected.

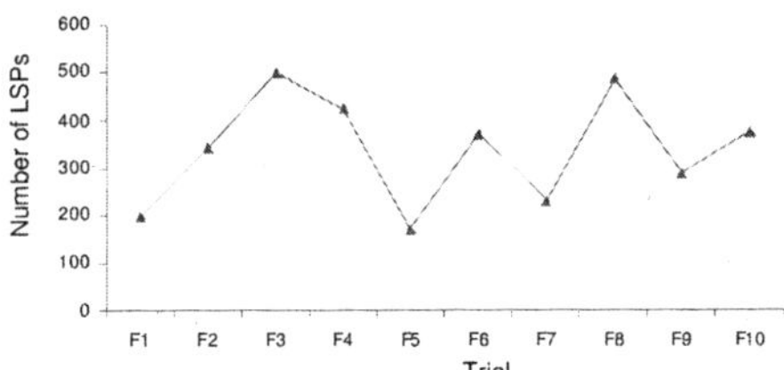

Fig. 9.- Number of LSPs protected with alternative routes.

4 Conclusions

In this article, we have described a multiagent system which monitors link failure probabilities and takes decisions on establishing alternative routes in certain situations.

By incorporating agents that take into account a series of parameters (topology, failure statistics and traffic type), the values obtained for failure probability are more precise, thereby adjusting the degree of real protection given to our network and minimizing the resources given over to protection (i.e., alternative routes), as we have seen in the results of our experiments.

What this system does is to carry out differentiated traffic management, depending on whether or not the traffic has high priority. More protection is offered to high priority traffic. Probability management allows the degree of network protection to be controlled by the service provider, by giving access to updated information on failure probabilities from the agents, such as, for example, the number of LSPs with a high failure probability.

This probability management means that the TE database has more precise information on the current state of the network. As our results have shown, this leads to an improvement in the routing algorithms with QoS – decreasing the number of LSPs that pass through links with particular failure probabilities, or minimizing the failure probability of the LSPs.

References

[1] Sudheer Dharanikota and Raj Jain, *Protection and Restoration in DWDM Networks: Recent Developments and Issues,* Invited paper, SPIE conference 2003

[2] N. Minar, K. H. Kramer, and P. Maes, *Cooperating Mobile Agents for Dynamic Network Routing,* Springer-Verlag, 1999, ch. 12, ISBN: 3-540-65578-6. [Online]. Available: http://www.media.mit.edu/ nelson/research/routes-bookchapter/

[3] R. Onishi, S. Yamaguchi, H. Morino, H. Aida, and T. Saito, *A multi-agent system for dynamic network routing,* IEICE Transactions on Communications, vol. E84-B, n. 10, pp. 2721-2728, Oct 2001.

[4] Florence Touvet, David Harle, *Shared Backup Protection based on Aggregated Information in WDM Networks,* in Proceedings of ICC 2003

[5] Pere Vilà, José L. Marzo, Eusebi Calle, *Dynamic Bandwidth Management as part of an Integrated Network Management System based on Distributed Agents,* IEEE Global Communications Conference (GLOBECOM 2002), Taipei (Taiwan), November 17-21, 2002

[6] E. Calle, T. Jové, P. Vilà, J.L. Marzo, *A Dynamic Multilevel MPLS Protection Domain,* 3rd International Workshop on Design of Reliable Communication Networks, DRCN, Budapest (Hungary), 2001

[7] E. Mannie et al, *Generalized Multi-Protocol Label Switching (GMPLS) Architecture,* Internet Draft. Work in progress. February 2003

[8] J. L. Marzo, E. Calle, C. Scoglio, T. Anjali, *Adding QoS Protection in Order to Enhance MPLS QoS Routing,.* To appear in ICC 2003.

5. Machine Learning

Artificial Intelligence Research and Development
I. Aguiló et al. (Eds.)
IOS Press, 2003

Support Vector Machines over a Discrete Structure: a Kernel for Qualitative Orders of Magnitude Spaces

Núria AGELL[†], Xari ROVIRA[†], Mónica SÁNCHEZ[‡] , Francesc PRATS[‡]
[†]*ESADE, Universitat Ramon Llull. Av. Pedralbes, 62. 08034 Barcelona. Spain*
[‡]*MA2, Universitat Politècnica de Catalunya. Pau Gargallo, 5. 08028 Barcelona. Spain*
{agell, rovira}@esade.edu; {monica.sanchez,francesc.prats}@upc.es

Abstract. This paper is within the domain of the study of learning algorithms based on kernels, precisely of the Support Vector Machines. A kernel is constructed over the discrete structure of absolute orders of magnitude spaces. This kernel is based on an explicit function, defined from the space of k-tuples of qualitative labels to a feature space, which captures the remoteness between the components of the patterns by using certain weights exponentially. A simple example that allows interpreting the kernel in terms of proximity of the patterns is presented.
Keywords: Learning Algorithms, Support Vector Machines, Orders of Magnitude Reasoning.

1. Introduction

The construction of machines able to learn from data is one of the main goals of Artificial Intelligence. Lately different learning machines based on kernels, such as Support Vector Machines (SVM), have been developed and studied in depth because of their numerous applications and their efficiency in the learning process.

One of the more important steps in the construction of Support Vector Machines is the development of kernels adapted to the different structures of the data in real world problems [2], [4], [6].

Within the frame of Artificial Intelligence, a key factor in situations in which one has to obtain some conclusions from imprecise data, is to be able to utilise variables described via orders of magnitude. One of the goals of Qualitative Reasoning is just to tackle problems in such a way that the principle of relevance is preserved [8]; that is to say, each variable involved in a real problem is valued with the required level of precision.

In classification processes the situation in which the numerical values of some of the data are unknown, and only their qualitative descriptions are available - given by their absolute or relative orders of magnitude - is not unusual. In other situations, the numerical values, even though they might be available, are not relevant for solving the proposed problem. This paper starts from *absolute orders of magnitude models* [9], [10], which work with a finite set of symbols or qualitative labels obtained via a partition of the real line, where any element of the partition is a basic label. These models provide a mathematical structure which unifies sign algebra and interval algebra trough a continuum of qualitative structures build from the rougher to the finest partition of the real line. This mathematical structure, the Qualitative Algebras or Q-Algebras, have been studied in depth [1], [10].

In recent studies, some kernels have been constructed over certain discrete structures, such as for example for linguistic text classification [6] and [7]; nevertheless, there is no kernel available to work with data described in a space of orders of magnitude.

This work presents a kernel over a qualitative space of absolute orders of magnitude, based on an explicit function defined over labels. This kernel will be used for classification in learning algorithms based on kernels, in particular in Support Vector Machines, as a part of the development of the MERITO (Analysis and Development of Innovative Soft-Computing Techniques with Expert Knowledge Integration. An Application to Financial Credit Risk Measurement) project, in which different tools for the measurement of the financial credit risk are analysed.

Often, the classification function cannot be expressed as a simple linear combination of the attributes or input variables. Support Vector Machines are learning systems, which use linear functions in a feature space of higher dimension as classification functions by using several kernels [5], [11] and [12].

The mapping between the initial space and the feature space can be defined explicitly in advance, in order to construct an inner product that will give raise to the kernel. However, it is also possible, on the contrary, to construct a kernel directly, which allows for the implicit definition of the function from the data space into the feature space, in which linear learning machines operate. In this work the kernel is constructed following the first option mentioned above.

In Section 2 the absolute orders of magnitude model with granularity n, OM(n), constructed via a symmetric partition of the real line, is presented. Section 3 gives the basic concepts of Support Vector Machines and highlights the importance of kernels for these kinds of learning algorithms. In Section 4 an explicit function from the quantity space into the feature space is defined; in Section 5, this function allows the construction of a kernel to be able to work in spaces OM(n). The paper ends with several conclusions and outlines some proposals for future research.

2 The Absolute Orders of Magnitude Model

In this section the absolute orders of magnitude model is described [1]. The model, which is used, is a generalisation of the model introduced in [10]. The number of labels chosen for describing a determined real problem depends on their characteristics.

The absolute orders of magnitude model of granularity n, OM(n), is defined from a symmetric partition of the real line in $2n+1$ classes:

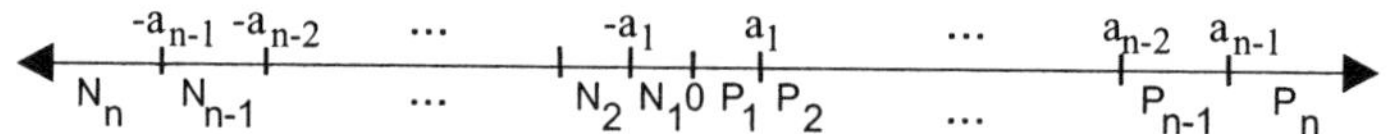

Fig.1. Partition of the real line

where $N_i=[-a_i,-a_{i-1}[$, $0=\{0\}$ and $P_i=]a_{i-1},a_i]$.

Each class is named *basic description or basic element,* and is represented by a label of the set S_1:

$$S_1=\{N_n, N_{n-1}, ..., N_1, 0, P_1, ..., P_{n-1}, P_n\}.$$

Finally, once the partition that defines S_1 is fixed, *the quantity space S is the set of labels in the form [X,Y] for all $X,Y \in S_1$, with X<Y (i.e., x<y for all $x \in X$ and $y \in Y$):*

$$[X,Y] = \begin{cases} X, & \text{if } Y = 0; \\ Y, & \text{if } X = 0; \\ \text{the smallest interval with respect the inclusion containing X and Y,} & \text{if } X \neq 0 \text{ and } Y \neq 0. \end{cases}$$

In S it is defined an order relation $\leq_P$, *to be more precise than*: given $X,Y \in S$, X is more precise than Y ($X \leq_P Y$) if $X \subseteq Y$. In Figure 2 this order relation is represented graphically:

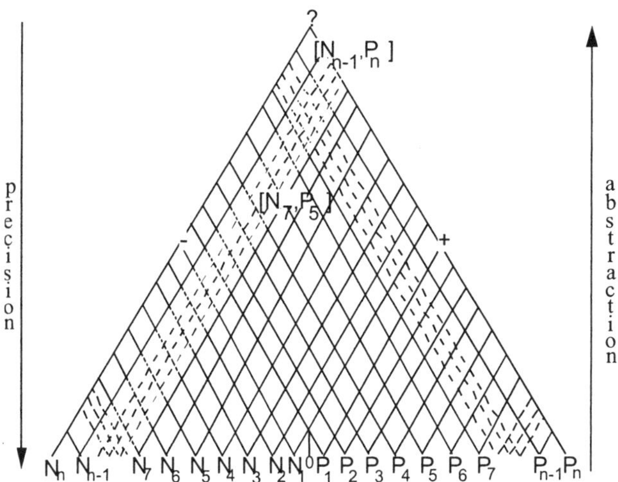

Fig. 2. The order relation $\leq_P$

For all $X \in S-\{0\}$, the *basis of X* is the set $B_X = \{B \in S_1 - \{0\}: B \leq_p X\}$; and for all $X \in S$, the *extended basis of X* is the set $B_X^* = \{B \in S_1 : B \leq_p X\}$.

The *qualitative equality* relation is defined as follows: given $X,Y \in S$, they are q-equals, $X \approx Y$, if there exists $Z \approx S$ such that $Z \leq_P X$ and $Z \leq_P Y$. This means that they have a common basic element, i.e., $B_X^* \cap B_Y^* \neq \varnothing$. The pair $(S, \approx)$ is called a *qualitative space of orders of magnitude*; and, taking into account that it has 2n+1 basic elements, it is said that $(S, \approx)$ has granularity n.

Finally, in order to work with qualitative and quantitative data simultaneously, it is useful to consider the qualitative expression of a set A, denoted by [A] and that it is defined by the most little element of S with respect to the inclusion that contains A.

3. Kernels in Support Vector Machines

In this work a methodology is proposed, which will allow SVM to be used when the input data are described by their orders of magnitude.

Before building an appropriate kernel for this kind of discrete spaces, let us remind ourselves of the basic concepts of Support Vector Machines and kernel functions, introduced by Vapnik et al in [3] and described with more detail in [11].

The SVM are used in learning problems, where the input data are not linearly separable. From a non-linear application the input data are imbedded into a space named feature space, potentially of higher dimension, in which the separability of the data can be obtained in a linear manner. In Figure 3 a scheme of this process can be observed.

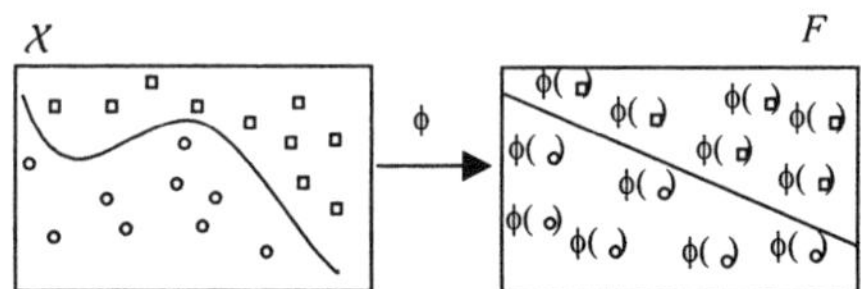

Fig.3. An application from the input space to the feature space

That is to say, noting the input space by X and the feature space by F, a machine of non-linear classification is built in two steps.

First, a non-linear application $\phi: X \to F$ transforms the input data to the feature space, and afterwards an algorithm of linear separation is used in this new space.

An important characteristic of the learning process of a SVM is the fact that only a few elements of the training set are meaningful for the classification. These elements, named *support vectors (SV)*, are ones closest to the separator hyperplane. In Figure 4 the support vectors are doubly marked.

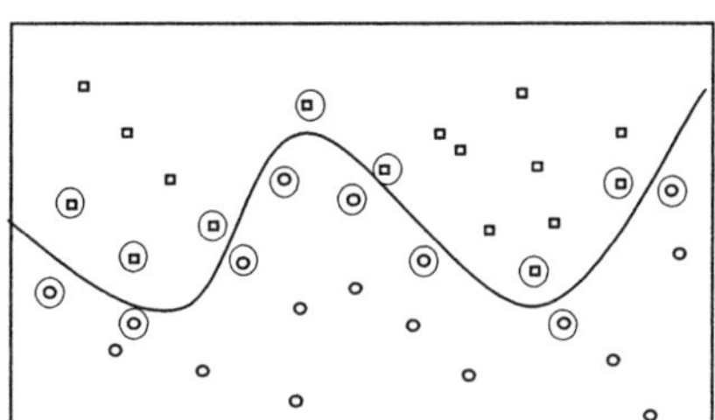

Fig.4. Binary classification of non linearly separable patterns by means of SVM

Let T be the set of input-output training data pairs:

$$T = \{ \ (\mathbf{x}_i, y_i), \ \mathbf{x}_i \in \mathcal{X}, y_i = \{-1,+1 \ \} \ \},$$

where labels +1 and -1 represent the two different classes of objects in $\mathcal{X}$.

Let's assume that the training set is separable by a hyperplane; then the linear decision function can be written as:

$$f(\mathbf{x}) = \mathrm{sign}\left(\sum_{\mathbf{x}_i \in SV} \alpha_i y_i (\mathbf{x}_i \cdot \mathbf{x}) + b \right)$$

where α_i and b are the hyperplane coefficients and $\mathbf{x}_i$ are the elements in T closest to the hyperplane, which have been chosen as support vectors in the learning process. But the choice of a linear function seems to be very restrictive. In the general case of non-linear separability, decision function turns to be a non-linear function which appears by substituting the inner product in $\mathcal{X}$ by an inner product in the feature space F, given by the function K such that:

$$K(\mathbf{x}_i, \mathbf{x}_j) = \phi(\mathbf{x}_i) \cdot \phi(\mathbf{x}_j).$$

Such a function K is called a *kernel*. The name kernel is derived from Integral Operation Theory, and a characterization of this kind of functions is given by Mercer's theorem [11].

This leads to the non-linear decision function:

$$f(\mathbf{x}) = \mathrm{sign}\left(\sum_{\mathbf{x}_i \in SV} \alpha_i y_i K(\mathbf{x}_i, \mathbf{x}) + b \right)$$

A very important advantage of this methodology is that it is not necessary to have an input space with an inner product, i.e. it works for non-Euclidean spaces. Special kernels of that type have been used with many different kinds of data in the input space: to categorize text documents, for protein classification, to classify images, etc., mapping data into a feature space F, which is a Euclidean space. Different applications can be found in [6] and [7].

4 An Explicit Feature Mapping ϕ from a Space $[OM(n)]^k$

Following the method used in [6] to obtain a kernel over a discrete space, and in particular to define a kernel over the space S^k, in this section we define explicitly a feature function ϕ from the quantity space S^k to a feature space F. Further on, the kernel will be obtained from this function ϕ and the inner Euclidian product in F, that is to say, from the following composition:

$$S^k \times S^k \xrightarrow{\phi \times \phi} F \times F \xrightarrow{<,>} R \ .$$

This process begins with the definition of the functions' *basic expansions*, introduced in [1] in the particular case of the expansion of zero. This kind of functions maps each element in S to its extension which is qualitatively equal to a basic element given.

Given $U \in S_1$ we call *U-expansion* the map $\psi_U : S \longrightarrow S$, such that:

$$\psi_U(X) = \mathrm{Min}\{Y \in S : X \leq_P Y \ i \ \ U \leq_P Y\} = [X \cup U].$$

From now on X_U will mean the image of X by Ψ_U. It's easy to see that this map is well defined in the sense that the minimum that is used in the definition exists and it is unique for all $X \in S$. The map satisfies:

a) $X = X_U$, if, and only if, $X \approx U$ (i.e. $U \subset X$)

b) $X \approx X_U$ and $U \approx X_U$

It is necessary to note that X_U does not depend on the values of the landmarks used to determine the real line partition.

Related to this map, and inspired in the definition of qualitative norm introduced in [1], it is defined in S, for a fixed $U \in S_1$, the map *"remoteness with respect to U"*, $a_U : S \longrightarrow N$, such that:

$$a_U(X) = \mathrm{Card}\!\left(B_{X_U}\right) - \mathrm{Card}\!\left(B_X\right).$$

For all $U \in S_1$, the map a_U satisfies:

a) $a_U(X) = 0$, if, and only if, $X \approx U$

b) $a_U(X) = \underset{B \in B_X}{\mathrm{Min}}\, a_U(B)$

For any $X \in S$, the "further" the basics in B_X are with respect to the basic U in the ordered set S_1, the greater is the value of $a_U(X)$.

Finally, and as a prior step for the definition of ϕ, the map ϕ_U associated to any basic element $U \in S_1$ over the space S^k is defined by:

$$\phi_U(\mathbf{X}) = \phi_U(X_1,\dots,X_k) = \left(\lambda^{a_U(X_1)},\dots,\lambda^{a_U(X_k)}\right),$$

for some $\lambda \in\ ]0,1[$. The decay factor λ between 0 and 1 is used in each component to weight the remoteness between two elements in S.

The map ϕ_U transforms each element in S^k into an element in $[0,1]^k$, which reflects the remoteness of **X**'s components with respect to the basic element U. In this way, the components in **X** that are qualitatively equal to U take the value 1 in the corresponding component in $\phi_U(\mathbf{X})$, and less than 1 if they are not. In general, values near 1 in the components of $\phi_U(\mathbf{X})$ mean that respective components of **X** are "close" to U.

Now the explicit feature mapping can already be defined, $\phi : S^k \longrightarrow F$, which will allow moving data from the quantity space S^k to the feature space F.

For all $\mathbf{X} \in S^k$, the vector $\phi(\mathbf{X})$ is:

$$\phi(\mathbf{X}) = \left(\phi_U(\mathbf{X})\right)_{U \in S_1} = \left(\phi_{N_n}(\mathbf{X}),\dots,\phi_0(\mathbf{X}),\dots,\phi_{P_n}(\mathbf{X})\right)$$

where the feature space F of vectors $\phi(\mathbf{X})$ is a subset of $[0,1]^{k(2n+1)}$.

5 Construction of a Kernel in an Orders of Magnitude Space

Once the explicit function ϕ has been defined on the space S^k, the kernel is defined via the Euclidean product existing in the space F; for all **X,Y** belonging to S^k, it is considered:

$$K(\mathbf{X},\mathbf{Y}) = \langle \phi(\mathbf{X}),\phi(\mathbf{Y}) \rangle$$

The explicit kernel expression is as follows: given two k-tuples of qualitative labels, $\mathbf{X} = (X_1,...,X_k)$ and $\mathbf{Y} = (Y_1,...,Y_k)$:

$$K(\mathbf{X},\mathbf{Y}) = \sum_{U \in S_l} \langle \phi_U(\mathbf{X}),\phi_U(\mathbf{Y}) \rangle =$$

$$\sum_{U \in S_l} \left\langle \left(\lambda^{a_U(X_1)},...,\lambda^{a_U(X_k)} \right) \left(\lambda^{a_U(Y_1)},...,\lambda^{a_U(Y_k)} \right) \right\rangle =$$

$$\sum_{U \in S_l} \sum_{i=1}^{k} \lambda^{a_U(X_i)} \lambda^{a_U(Y_i)} = \sum_{U \in S_l} \sum_{i=1}^{k} \lambda^{a_U(X_i)+a_U(Y_i)}$$

From its own definition the function K defined over $S^k \times S^k$ is a kernel and it is not necessary to verify that Mercer conditions are fulfilled [12].

Next, an example with an effective calculus with the kernel considered is given. This example will allow interpreting the results obtained in terms of "remoteness".

Example. Consider an OM(2) space with basic labels $\{N_2, N_1, 0, P_1, P_2\}$ and three patterns $\mathbf{X}$, $\mathbf{Y}$, $\mathbf{Z}$, given by terns of S^3.

Let be, $\mathbf{X}=(P_1,[N_2, N_1],[N_1, P_2])$, $\mathbf{Y}=([P_1, P_2], N_1,0)$ and $\mathbf{Z}=(N_2, P_1,[N_2, N_1])$, then:

$\phi_{N_2}(\mathbf{X})=(\lambda^2,\lambda^0,\lambda^1)$, $\phi_{N_1}(\mathbf{X})=(\lambda^1,\lambda^0,\lambda^0)$, $\phi_0(\mathbf{X})=(\lambda^1,\lambda^1,\lambda^0)$, $\phi_{P_1}(\mathbf{X})=(\lambda^0,\lambda^1,\lambda^0)$, $\phi_{P_2}(\mathbf{X})=(\lambda^1,\lambda^2,\lambda^0)$.

$\phi_{N_2}(\mathbf{Y})=(\lambda^2,\lambda^1,\lambda^3)$, $\phi_{N_1}(\mathbf{Y})=(\lambda^1,\lambda^0,\lambda^2)$, $\phi_0(\mathbf{Y})=(\lambda^1,\lambda^1,\lambda^0)$, $\phi_{P_1}(\mathbf{Y})=(\lambda^0,\lambda^1,\lambda^2)$, $\phi_{P_2}(\mathbf{Y})=(\lambda^0,\lambda^2,\lambda^3)$.

$\phi_{N_2}(\mathbf{Z})=(\lambda^0,\lambda^2,\lambda^0)$, $\phi_{N_1}(\mathbf{Z})=(\lambda^1,\lambda^1,\lambda^0)$, $\phi_0(\mathbf{Z})=(\lambda^2,\lambda^1,\lambda^1)$, $\phi_{P_1}(\mathbf{Z})=(\lambda^2,\lambda^0,\lambda^1)$, $\phi_{P_2}(\mathbf{Z})=(\lambda^3,\lambda^1,\lambda^2)$.

Therefore, it is:

$K(\mathbf{X},\mathbf{Y}) = \langle \phi(\mathbf{X}),\phi(\mathbf{Y}) \rangle = (\lambda^4+\lambda^1+\lambda^4) + (\lambda^2+\lambda^0+\lambda^2) + (\lambda^2+\lambda^2+\lambda^0) + (\lambda^0+\lambda^2+\lambda^2) + (\lambda^1+\lambda^4+\lambda^3) = 3\lambda^4+\lambda^3+6\lambda^2+2\lambda+3,$

$K(\mathbf{Y},\mathbf{Z})= \langle \phi(\mathbf{Y}),\phi(\mathbf{Z}) \rangle = (\lambda^2+\lambda^3+\lambda^3) + (\lambda^2+\lambda^1+\lambda^2) + (\lambda^3+\lambda^2+\lambda^1) + (\lambda^2+\lambda^1+\lambda^3) + (\lambda^3+\lambda^3+\lambda^5) = \lambda^5+6\lambda^3+5\lambda^2+3\lambda$

As can be seen the kernel has been constructed from a function ϕ, which has been defined by means of a set of weights exponentially used. Those exponents capture the concept of "remoteness" of each pattern component with respect to each one of the basic labels. Therefore, the more qualitatively near components two patterns are, the more similar they will be considered to be, because their Euclidian product will be higher.

In the given example, X and Y are two patterns very similar (qualitatively equal component by component); on the contrary, the components of Y and Z are more distant. In Figure 5, the values taken by K(X,Y) and K(Y,Z) can be seen.

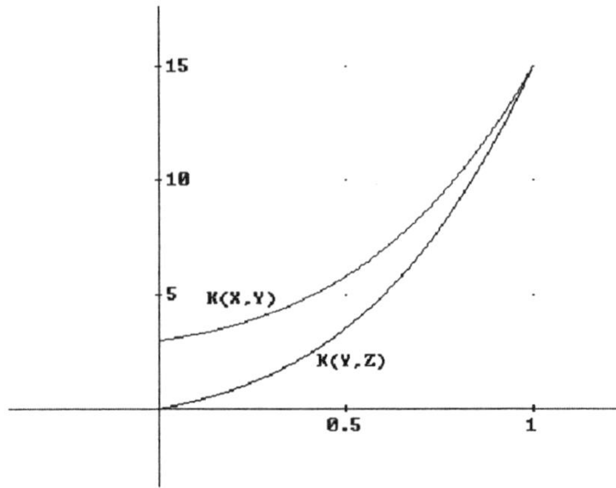

Fig.5. Comparison of the values given by the kernel with respect to parameter λ.

If the functions that represent the values given by the kernel are observed in both cases, it can be seen that, for any value between 0 and 1 given to λ, it is always obtained a greater value in the case of the more similar patterns.

6   Conclusions and Future Research

The present work belongs to a wider project, which aims at motivating, defining and analysing the viability of the use of learning machines in structures defined in orders of magnitude spaces.

The focus of this paper is the construction of a kernel to be used in problems for which the input variables are described in terms of qualitative values of orders of magnitude. For this reason the kernel has been built from a set of weights considered exponentially by an evaluation of its qualitative information. This set of weights captures the known information about de "remoteness" between qualitative values.

Although this paper has focused on a classification problem by using Support Vector Machines, the methodological aspects considered and given can be used in any learning system based on kernels.

As a future work, the implementation of the given method to be applied in problems of classification and multi-classification might be considered.

In particular, and within the MERITO project, supported by the Spanish Ministry of Science and Technology, the methodology given in this paper is going to be used. The project addresses the prediction and measurement of financial credit risk. The results obtained by using input variables defined over orders of magnitude spaces will be compared with the ones obtained by using numerical values.

Considering an OM(n), several concepts can be analysed to measure the degree of "remoteness" or "closeness" between labels, it seems to be reasonable to look for other suitable kernels in these kinds of sets. With regard to open problems and future work, the following comments can be made:

- To define new concepts to measure the degree of "remoteness" or "closeness" between qualitative labels.
- To choose different parameters of decay λ in the Euclidean product expression depending on the length of the intervals defining the basic labels.
- To define new kernels combining numeric and qualitative data.

Acknowledgements

This work was partially supported by the MCyT (Spanish Ministry of Science and Technology) MERITO project (TIC2002-04371-C02).
Cecilio Angulo's valuable remarks and suggestions are gratefully acknowledged.

References

[1] Agell, N. *Estructures matemàtiques per al model qualitatiu d'ordres de magnitud absoluts*. Ph. D. Thesis Universitat Politècnica de Catalunya, 1998.

[2] Angulo, C. *Aprendizaje con màquina núcleo en entornos de multiclasificación*. Ph. D. Thesis Universitat Politècnica de Catalunya, 2001.

[3] Boser, B.E., Guyon, I.M.and Vapnik, V.N. *A training algorithm for optimal margin classifiers*. In D. Haussler, editor, Proceedings of the 5th Annual ACM Workshop on Computational Learning Theory, pp. 144-152. ACM Press, 1992

[4] Burges, C. A tutorial on support vector machines for pattern recognition, Data Mining and Knowledge Discovery, 2 (1998), 1-47.

[5] Cortes, C; Vapnik,V. Support vector networks, *Machine Learning*, 20 (1995), 273–297.

[6] Cristianini, N.; Shawe-Taylor, J. *An Introduction to Support Vector Machines and other Kernel-based learning methods*. Cambridge University Press. 2000.

[7] Lodhi, H; Saunders, C; Sahwe-Taylor, J;Cristianini, N.; Watkins, C. Text Classification Using String Kernels. *Journal of MachineLearning Research,* (2): 419-444, 2002.

[8] Forbus, K. D. Commonsense physics. A: *Annals Revue of Computer Science*. 1988, pàg. 197-232.

[9] Piera, N. *Current Trends in Qualitative Reasoning and Applications*. Monograph CIMNE, núm. 33. International Center for Numerical Methods in Engineering, 1995.

[10]   Travé-Massuyès, L.; Dague, P.; Guerrin, F. *Le Raisonnement Qualitatif pour les Sciences de l'Ingénieur*. Hermès, 1997.

[11] Vapnik, V. *Statistical Learning Theory*. Wiley,1998

[12] Vapnik, V. *The nature of statistical learning theory*, Springer Verlag New York, 1995.

Artificial Intelligence Research and Development
I. Aguiló et al. (Eds.)
IOS Press, 2003

Creative Evolution of Flying Objects

Federico Divina[1] , David Edwards[2] , Sophie Kain[3]
[1] *Department of Computer Science, Vrije Universiteit of Amsterdam*
divina@cs.vu.nl
[2] *Intelligent Systems Lab, School of Mathematical and Computer Science*
Heriot-Watt University
ceedce@macs.hw.ac.uk
[3] *THALES Research and Technology*
Sophie.Kain@uk.thalesgroup.com

Abstract.
Evolutionary computation has been used for optimisation problems since the 1960s,
however it is only recently that these techniques have been used creatively to evolve
novel solutions in design or artistic problems. So called creative evolution has, to date,
shown impressive results in many areas. This paper describes how, by using these techniques, a flying object can be designed. Our aim in this paper is to show that evolution
is capable of exploring the space of possible solutions to a problem providing a range
of solutions that are not limited by "conventional wisdom" and "design fixation". In
this way entirely new methods and principles for solving a problem can be found and
exploited. The results of the experiments indicate that GAs can provide such solutions,
which in the context of this paper means novel forms of flying objects.

1 Introduction

The concept of evolutionary algorithms was first discussed by Turing in 1948 when he proposed "genetical or evolutionary search" and further developed by Bremermann who executed computer experiments using evolution for optimisation in 1962 [7].Three different techniques in this field evolved in the 1960s: in the USA Fogel invented evolutionary programming and Holland introduced genetic algorithms [9, 10, 12], whilst in Germany Rechenberg
and Schwefel introduced evolution strategies [15, 16].

In the early 1990s these three different implementations were merged together under the
heading "evolutionary computation" [1, 2, 3, 5, 11] Around this time Koza added a fourth
technique entitled genetic programming [14].

Until recently evolutionary computation has mainly been used for optimisation in large
solution spaces. In 1999 Bentley introduced the concept of using evolutionary techniques
as an explorer rather than an optimiser [4]. This new area known as "creative evolutionary
systems" can be described as systems which use a computer system to aid creativity to find an
interesting solution to a given problem [6]. In 1999 the use of creative evolutionary techniques
for design was first described by Bentley [4]. The fact that creative evolution originated in the
field of design is unsurprising as design problems tend to be extremely complex with multiple
constraints and a frequent requirement for change. Since 1995 Frazer and his team have been

developing evolutionary architecture systems [13].The results of this work have found many novel and inspiring new architectural structures.

Creative evolution systems have also been used to evolve art, music, coffee tables, buildings, electronic circuits and many more applications [6].For example Dawkins used evolution to evolve art based on pure aesthetics [8].This work inspired Sims to evolve images and animations [17].

In this paper we wanted to explore the creative abilities of evolution. Creativity in this instance means that with the minimum of inductive bias supplied by human input a genetic algorithm can produce a variety of unforeseen solutions, that innovatively address the problem.

This paper discusses how to apply creative evolutionary techniques (in the form of genetic algorithms) to the design of "flying objects" by folding sheets of paper [6]. No initial design, in terms of folds, will be given and no heuristics for good folds will be used. Initial populations will be entirely random. The only evolutionary pressure will be an objective fitness measure made within the experimental environment. No human judgment is used in this fitness measure, and the only bias is that imposed by the experimental environment and the limitations of the folding rules.

The experiments will show how genetic algorithms can be used in a creative manner by successfully producing a variety of developments that improve the flying performance of a folded sheet. This work uses a simple, practical and interesting example to illustrate a little used alternative application of genetic algorithms. This kind of demonstration may encourage the broader use of evolutionary algorithms in this direction.

Previous similar work was carried out by Bentley in his book "Creative Evolution Systems" where he describes how to optimise the amount of time a piece of paper stays in the air when dropped [6]. In that work only the flying time was optimised. In this paper we want to optimise also the distance covered by the objects. Moreover the phenotype used in this paper is different. In [6] the evolved objects consisted of 2-dimensions objects, while in this paper the evolved objects are 3-dimensional.

This paper is organised as follows: a brief description of the genetic algorithms and operators used; design issues such as representation, the fitness function, the experimental set-up; results; the conclusions and future work.

2 Genetic Algorithm

Genetic algorithms (GAs) [11, 12] are stochastic population based search algorithms deriving inspiration from natural evolution and the survival of the fittest principle. A population of individuals evolve through genetic operators, where individuals with higher fitness have more chance of survival. Running GAs on a computer requires a few basic elements:

- a smart representation of the individuals

- a fitness function that evaluates the suitability of each solution

- genetic operators (crossover and mutation)

- a selection function (e.g. roulette wheel, tournament selection...).

We have employed a simple GA for evolving flying objects, whose features are described in the following sections.

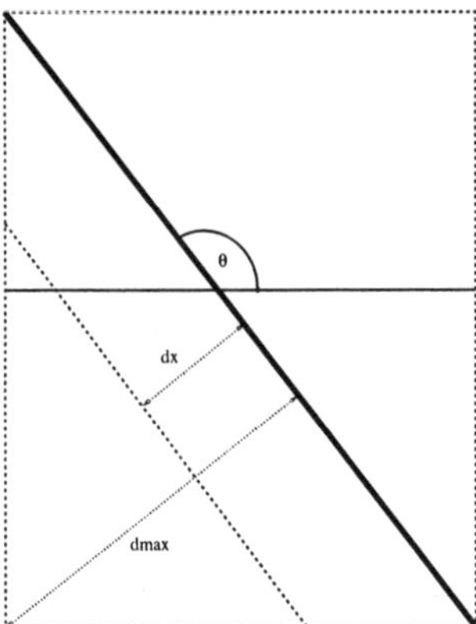

Figure 1: Diagram to show the genotypic line representation

2.1　Representation

On each sheet of paper six labeled lines of different thicknesses were drawn in order to indicate where to fold the paper, in which order and the angle of the fold.

Originally it was considered that the most intuitive way to describe the lines was by representing the line by the two end coordinates x_1, y_1 and x_2, y_2. The folding angle would then be represented by a number between 0 and 4 (where 0=0 degrees, 1=90 degrees, 2=180 degrees, 3= 270 degrees, 4=360 degrees). The folding angle is defined as the angle formed between the printed side of the paper either side of the fold measured at 90 degrees to that fold. Each line would then be given a number to represent the folding order. This representation would require 6 parameters in the phenotype and 34 bits for each line in the genotype (coordinates require 7 bits each, the angle requires 2 bits and the folding order require 4 bits).

An alternative simpler representation and so less computationally expensive is to describe the position of a line (line 1) as shown in figure 1.

In figure 1 θ is the angle of rotation of the line around the center point of the paper from the horizontal. d_x is the displacement of the actual line from the rotated line, and d_{max} is the maximum possible distance from the edge of the paper. For simplicity each line must reach across the entire sheet of paper.

d_x is then calculated as a percentage of d_{max} i.e. $d_{per} = \frac{d_x}{d_{max}} \cdot 100$. The phenotype of each line is then represented by these three parameters θ, d_{per}, $angle$, where $angle$ is the folding angle.

It was realised that a further way of reducing our genotypic bit size was by removing the 180 degree angle which is effectively "no" fold. The "no" fold option was originally considered to be an effective way of varying the number of folds in the phenotype, however the 3rd folding rule (do not fold if the fold would cross a 90 degree angle) discussed below provides this flexibility. The "no" fold option was therefore removed in order to reduce the genotypic bit size from 3 to 2. The folding angles are show in table 1.

Six lines were considered sufficient to create diversity and complexity for the problem. The overall phenotype design can therefore be represented as

Table 1: Chosen representation for the folding angle

Phenotypic Representation	Genotypic Representation	Angle
0	00	0
1	01	90
2	10	270
3	11	360

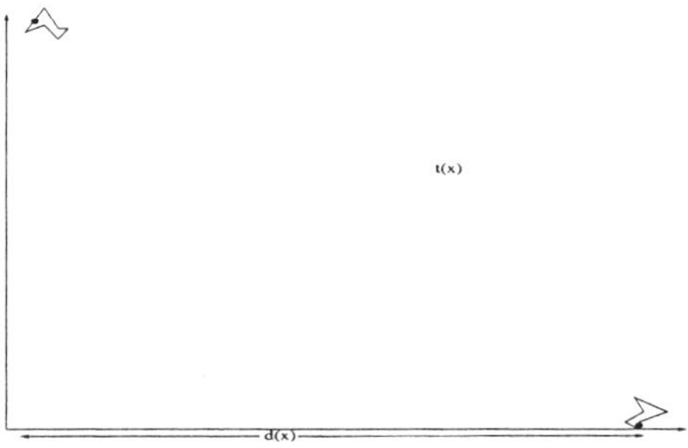

Figure 2: Diagram to show the experimental set-up.

$$(\theta_1, d_{per_1}, angle_1, \ldots \theta_6, d_{per_6}, angle_6).$$

In this representation the order of the folds is included implicitly by the order in which the lines are represented in the genotype.

The genotype was encoded in binary where θ requires 7 bits, d_{per} requires 7 bits and $angle$ requires 2 bits. The complete genotype can therefore be represented by 96 bits.

2.2 Fitness Function

The fitness function used is given in equation 1.

$$f(x) = w_t \cdot t(x) + w_d \cdot d(x) \tag{1}$$

where $f(x)$ is the overall fitness function of x, $t(x)$ is the flying time for test x, $d(x)$ is the distance of test x and w_t and w_d are the weights of the time and distance function respectively. Equation 1 shows that the higher the value of $f(x)$ the fitter the object is. Other possible parameters (e.g. height) that could be included in the fitness evaluation were believed to be considerably less relevant to the flight of an object.

The measurements of $t(x)$ and $d(x)$ are shown in figure 2 and explained in details in section 3.

It was originally considered that the time, $t(x)$, was more important than the distance $d(x)$ because it was thought that this better fits the idea of "flying objects". The weights w_t and w_d were chosen to be 0.8 and 0.2 respectively for the first run. For the second and third runs w_t and w_d were chosen to be 0.2 and 0.8 respectively. The values of the weights were varied and tested for a few trials of the flying objects. The optimal weights were chosen to favour either distance or time without decreasing the importance of the other measure.

2.3   Selection

In order to create offspring, at every generation, n individuals are selected for reproduction. A tournament selection of size four is used for this purpose. Four individuals are selected from the population, and the best one, according to the fitness, is allowed to reproduce. After selection genetic operators are applied to the selected individuals.

2.4   Genetic Operators

A 2-point crossover is adopted for exchanging information between two selected individuals. Two points are randomly selected inside the parents, and two new individuals are created by using the substrings, created by the two randomly chosen points, of the two parents. The 2-point crossover was used because the folding order is encoded as the order that the lines appear in the genotype, consequently, to permit any pair of genes from a single parent to remain in the child a 2-point scheme is needed in preference to the simpler 1-point alternative.

In a further revision of the reproduction, mutation can be applied with a certain probability. Firstly only a classical mutation operator was used. When applied to an individual this operator randomly selects a bit inside the individual and changes its value. In a second time another mutation operator was introduced. This second mutation operator can change the folding order by exchanging the position of two lines in the phenotype.

The crossover operator is applied with a probability equal to 0.8. The new individual is mutated with a probability equal to 0.1. If an individual is mutated, then one of the two mutation operators is applied with equal probability.

However these probabilities are modified in the case when two identical individual are selected for reproduction. In this case one individual is copied into the new population and the other one is mutated before being inserted in the emerging population.

A scheme of the GA employed in this paper is given in the figure 3.

3   Experimental Set-up

Initially two test runs were set up to optimise the weighted fitness function, the size of the initial population and the number of generations. The third run was a complete run.

For the first run the initial population was made up of ten randomly generated individuals and was allowed to evolve for ten generations. The weights w_t and w_d were set to 0.8 and 0.2 respectively, in order to give more importance to the time an object managed to stay in the air.

In a second run the population size was kept to ten, but only five generations were performed. In this run more weight was given to the distance that an individual covered, so the weight w_d was set to 0.8 and the weight w_t to 0.2.

The third and main run had a population size of twenty and the GA was run for twenty generations. The weights w_t and w_d were set to 0.2 and 0.8 respectively.

In order to evaluate an individual, the population was sent to a postscript printer with folding instructions attached. The paper size was set to be standard A4 paper (80g, mm2). Then every individual was thrown three times, and the fitness function was computed for each trial. The mean of the three obtained fitness values was taken as fitness of the individual. Each time the flying object was thrown straight, over-arm at shoulder height with feet square

```
Randomly initialize the population P
repeat
    evaluate P: for each x in P
                compute fitness(x)
    select n individuals from P
            and form n/2 pairs
    for each pair < x,y > do
      if (x = y)
          copy x to the new population P₁
          mutate y
          copy y to P₁
      else
          apply with probability p_c
                crossover to < x,y >
                producing offspring x′,y′
          apply with p_m mutation to x′
          apply with p_m mutation to y′
          copy x′ and y′ to P₁
      let P = P₁
until max number of generation is reached
```

Figure 3: A scheme of the GA employed. p_c and p_m are respectively the crossover probability and the mutation probability. n is set to 20 in the current GA.

on a straight line drawn on the floor. The direction of the throw was chosen by the operator. There was some debate as to whether this operator choice would introduce inconsistencies in the data, however it was concluded that the genetic algorithms would optimise these inconsistencies. The environment for the experiment must have a large area, no obstacles and no wind. The distance $d(x)$ and time $t(x)$ were measured as shown in figure 2. Distance $d(x)$ was measured from the throwing position to the object position and $t(x)$ was measured with a start-stop function on the computer.

For consistency folding rules were agreed. These were:

1. Fold in numerical order;

2. Fold only the visible parts of the folds;

3. Do not fold if the fold would cross a 90 degree angle. (This rule was chosen firstly because it was practically difficult to fold a line that crossed a 90 degree angle, and secondly because in this way a fold can be eliminated);

4. If the line is split into two parts the longer part is folded first and the subsequent parts of the line are folded if rules 1-3 are obeyed.

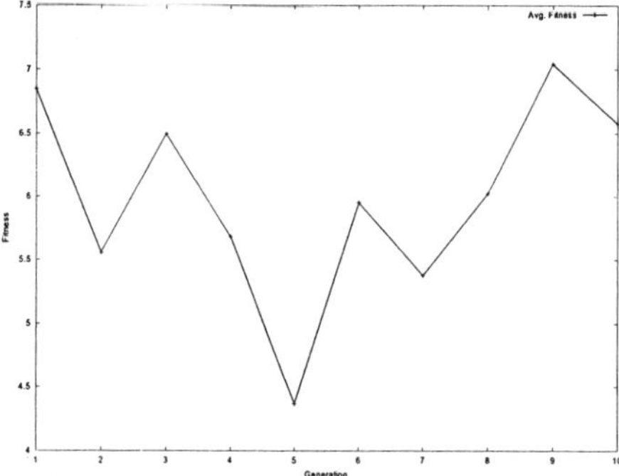

Figure 4: Average fitness of the population evolved in the first run for ten generations.

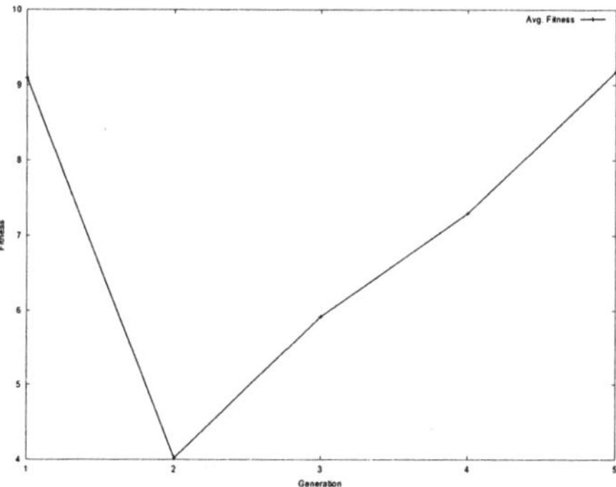

Figure 5: Average fitness of the population evolved in the second run for five generations.

4 Results

Figure 4 shows the mean fitness for the first experimental run with a population size of ten and after ten generations.

These results show that the overall average fitness does not improve over the generations, as expected. This was considered to be because we weighted our fitness function too heavily on time and rather than distance. This weighted the search towards objects which flutter to the ground over a long time and do not effectively fly forward.

The experiment did indicate, however, that diverse solutions were found and that interesting designs began to combine to produce objects with improved performance.

A second run was carried out with a new fitness function were $w_t = 0.2$ and $w_d = 0.8$, in this way the emphasis was put onto the distance rather than the time. The results of the mean fitness for a population size of ten and for five generations is shown in figure 5.

This weighting of the fitness function shows a monotonically increasing average fitness function over the last four generations, suggesting that further generations might continue to produce flying objects of improved fitness.

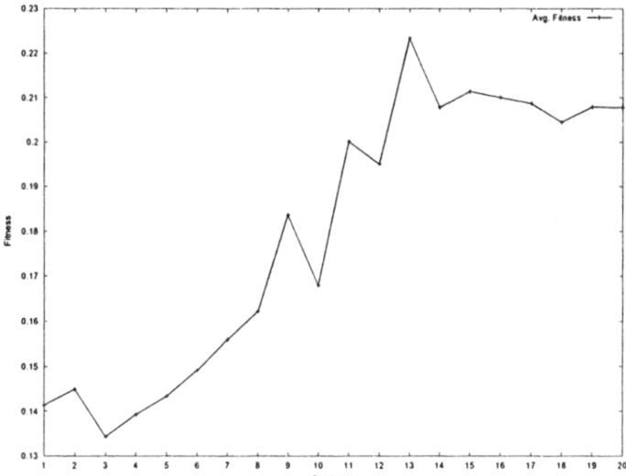

Figure 6: Average fitness of the population evolved in the third run for twenty generations.

This weighting in the second run resulted in flying objects which had a different shape to the first run. This second run preferred severe angles rather than 90 degree angles, leading to more balanced objects which were better able to maintain a straight flight.

The results of the average fitness for the third run with a population size of twenty, twenty generations and with $w_t = 0.2$ and $w_d = 0.8$, are summarised in figure 6.

In the first two runs, the best individuals did not always survive in the subsequent population. With the small population sizes used, the good features present in these individuals were hard to recover. In order to overcome this problem, elitism was adopted in the third run. It was considered that an elitist search keeping the fittest parents in the population could help to drive the search towards a good solution.

Figure 6 clearly shows a steep increase in the average fitness in the first thirteen generations, while from the fourteen generation on the fitness of the population stabilized. Figure 7 shows the best individual obtained in the third run and a picture of the object. The relatively simple shape of this object allows it to spin during its fall towards the ground. In this way the time the object remains in the air is considerably extended.

The graphs showed in figures 4, 5 and 6 are relative to one run of the GA with a single random seed. This choice is due to the high cost of evaluating individuals. Remember that all the individuals of the population has to be tried three times and time and distance have to be taken manually.

In all the runs the environment in which the experiments were performed affected the shape of the evolved objects, e.g a long and narrow room would bias the search toward objects that can fly straight, rather than objects that can spin in the air, since these would bump into the walls.

5 Conclusion & Future Work

The experimental set-up in this paper was limited by the equipment available. A further extension of this work would be to mechanically throw the flying object so that the force behind it can be calculated and any bias removed from the calculation. Similarly an automated system to measure time could be introduced to remove human error. With an automated system

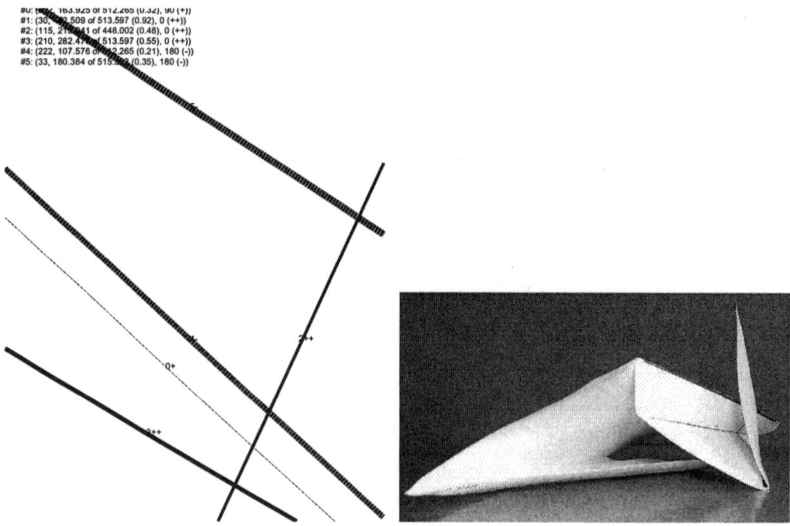

Figure 7: Best individual found in the third run.

it may even be plausible to encode the throwing instructions into the genotype and optimise the force and angle of throw.

When facing real world designs time limitations are a common feature: in this work the most time consuming activity was the construction of the flying objects to assess their fitness. We consider that in future work a similarity measure could be used to indirectly estimate the fitness of some individuals, in order to reduce the number of actual trials. An extended least square fit approach could be used given in equation 2

$$LSF = \sqrt{\sum_{0}^{n} \sum_{1}^{m} \frac{1}{(N_m)^2}(x_{nm} - a_{nm})^2} \tag{2}$$

where x is the phenotype which already has a known fitness function, a is the phenotype of the new individual, N_m are the normalisation coefficients, n is the vector length of the phenotype and m is the number of parameters that describe each line. Using this method for all solutions, those with a fitness below a set threshold (or adaptive with generation) can be considered to be "unfit" and the fitness equal to the estimation given by equation 2 rather than carrying out a trial. This would therefore reduce the overall time to carry out each generation. Other similarity measures could be tested to bench-mark these techniques.

The experiments showed that GAs can be successfully applied to create new, innovative solutions to a problem, without giving any specific knowledge about the problem to be solved. This proves how GAs, but in general EAs, can be helpful for investigating a number of potential solutions, and for providing a variety of interesting designs for a designer to further exploit.

6 Acknowledgments

We would like to thank Domenico Bellomo, Dipartimento di Elettrotecnica ed Elettronica, Politecnico di Bari and Robert Vanyi Department of Theoretical Computer Science, Friedrich-Alexander University for their help in the early stages of this work. Thanks go to the EvoNet, Napier University, Colinton Road 219, Edinburgh, EH14 1DJ, UK where this work was initiated. Thanks also go to Peter Bentley, Department of Computer Science, University College London, London, WC1E 6BT for assistance with the project.

References

[1] T. BÄCK, *Evolutionary Algorithms in Theory and Practice*, Oxford University Press, 1996.

[2] T. BÄCK, D. B. FOGEL, AND Z. MICHALEWICZ, *Evolutionary Computation 1: Basic Algorithms and Operators*, Institute of Physics Publishing, 2000.

[3] ——, *Evolutionary Computation 2: Advance Algorithms and Operators*, Institute of Physics Publishing, 2000.

[4] P. J. BENTLEY, *Evolutionary Design by Computers*, Morgan Kaufmann Publishers Inc., 1999.

[5] P. J. BENTLEY, *Exploring component-based representations - the secret of creativity by evolution?*, in Proc. of the Fourth International Conference on Adaptive Computing in Design and Manufacture (ACDM 2000), 26-28 April 2000.

[6] P. J. BENTLEY AND D. W. CORNE, *Creative evolutionary systems*, Morgan Kaufmann Publishers Inc., 2001.

[7] H. BREMMERMANN, *Optimization through Evolution and Recombination*, M.C. Yovits, G.T. Jacobi and G.D. Goldstein, 1962.

[8] R. DAWKINS, *The Blind Watchmaker*, W.W. Norton & Company, 1986.

[9] D. FOGEL, *Evolutionary computation: Toward a new philosophy of machine intelligence, ieee press*, New, York (1995).

[10] L. J. FOGEL, A. J. OWENS, AND M. WALSH, *Artificial Intelligence through Simulated Evolution*, Wiley, 1996.

[11] D. E. GOLDBERG, *Genetic Algorithms in Search Optimization and Machine Learning*, Addison-Wesley, 1989.

[12] J. H. HOLLAND, *Adaptation in natural and artificial systems*, MIT Press, 1992.

[13] F. J.H., *An Evolutionary Architecture*, Architectural Association, 1995.

[14] J. R. KOZA, *Genetic Programming*, MIT Press, 1992.

[15] I. RECHENBERG, *Evolutionsstrategie*, Friedrich Frommann, 1973.

[16] H. SCHWEFEL, *Evolution and Optimum Seeking*, Wiley, New York, 1995.

[17] K. SIMS, *Artificial evolution for computer graphics*, in Computer Graphics, vol. 25(4), July 1991, pp. 319–328.

Artificial Intelligence Research and Development
I. Aguiló et al. (Eds.)
IOS Press, 2003

Inductive Learning from Incompletely Specified Examples

Gabriel FIOL-ROIG
Computer Science Department,
University of the Balearic Islands,
0712 Palma de Mallorca, SPAIN
e-mail: biel.fiol@uib.es

Abstract. Inductive learning from examples constitutes a pioneering research field of the machine learning area. Most contributions in the field are devoted to situations in which the values of the attributes describing the input examples are assumed to be known. In this respect, a diversity of methods is found; from methods based on well defined values, to techniques considering only approximate descriptions of the real values of attributes, such as probabilistic, fuzzy, rough, … descriptions. In contrast to this kind of methods, research to do with inductive learning techniques from "unknown" or "partially unknown" knowledge about the values of the attributes –also named incompletely specified attributes– have surprisingly received poor attention. Proposing a knowledge representation for incompletely specified attributes is one of the goals of the present work.

The small generality of many inductive learning methods, in the sense that their design is essentially determined by the particular characteristics of the considered knowledge representation, constitutes an important limitation of the applicability of these methods, since the inductive procedure becomes disabled when other different measures to describe the values of the attributes are considered. Overcoming this lack of generality independently of the knowledge description adopted constitutes another motivation of this work, whose central point is made up of two essential notions: the concepts of *attribute basis* [7], [8] and *incomplete knowledge* respectively.

This work presents, on the one hand, a wide bibliographical review on the topic of inductive learning from incompletely specified examples; on the other, a new knowledge representation proposal for incompletely specified attributes allowing an unified algorithm to   generate attribute bases, independently of the considered knowledge description measures, is described.

Introduction

Object Attribute Tables (abreviated OATs), also named Decision Tables or Information Systems by some authors, constitute the input data of inductive learning systems from examples. Each example in an OAT is described by a x-tuple of values corresponding to a set of x attributes, one value for each attribute. However, the existence of unknown or perhaps only partially unknown values for some attributes is a common situation in real world applications, even though the real values of these attributes exist. For example, the value has not been observed clearly by the expert or perhaps was not registered by the sensor. An OAT containing any kind of manifestation of such knowledge for any attribute is called an *incomplete OAT* (also an *incompletely specified OAT*).

The problem of representinng and processing incomplete knowledge in inductive systems is particularly interesting, since neither the reality of things is always completely accessible nor the human capacity of expression and observation is infallible. In section 1, a wide but synthesized review of some interesting works to do with the topic is presented.

1. Bibliographical Review

In [1] a significant contribution describing a variant of the ID3 method [17] is presented. The work includes some additional aspects (in relation to the ID3):

1.- It allows to consider attributes with unknown values through a probabilistic technique.
2.- It offers a binary coding technique for numerical attributes.
3.- It presents a forward pruning technique to treat noisy data.

In relation to the first aspect, a bayesian formalism to handle attributes with unknown values is used, in such a way each original example with an unknown value for a given attribute A is replaced by a collection of examples, associating a value, v, of attribute A, to each example of the collection, weighted by the probalilistic function $p(v/c)$, c being the class or concept associated to the original example. The values of the remaining attributes of the examples of the collection will correspond to those of the original example. That is, the original OAT is extended by replacing unknown values of attributes of the original examples by known ones, weighted by the mentioned probabilistic function.

Two main obstacles have to be faced when applying techniques similar to the one just mentioned:

i.- The uncontrolled growth of the original OAT when considering aspect 1 may cause serious efficiency problems to the inductive process.
ii.- Probabilistic approaches are only suitable when the original OAT constitutes a representative model of the universe.

In [18] a comparative review of several approaches to inductive learning of concepts from examples with unknown attribute values is presented, focussing the discussion on the consideration of the decision tree structure as the induced model. Three problems to do with the inductive process are identified:

a.- Define a test function allowing to select the most adequate attribute of the OAT to be placed at the corresponding place of the decision tree at each step of the inductive process. Such a function must be able to consider attributes with unknown values.

To define such a function some methods adopt solutions such as ignoring those examples of the OAT with unknown attribute values [2], other are based on replacing the unknown values by known ones, for example, the most frequent value [4], etc…

b.- To classify the examples with unknown values once the test function has been defined, in such a way each example is associated with one class. Some strategies ignore such examples [17], whereas other replace unknown values by known ones, most of them based on probabilistic measures [1].

c.- The use of unknown attribute values in decision trees. Only a few notions in the matter have still been properly formalized. In [16] an approach based on exploring all possible branches of the decision tree in hand when an attribute with unknown values is considered, is exposed.

Several works ([3], [5], [10], [11], [14], [20]) on rule generation from incomplete systems in the context of the Rough Sets Theory [13], [14], have been developed. Thus, in [14] a measure of the degree defining how the absence of attribute values affect the generation of consistent rules, is defined.

The method presented in [10] offers a solution to the problem of inductive learning from examples with unknown attribute values based on two essential stages:

Stage 1. Each example containing unknown attribute values is replaced by a set of examples, by substituting each unknown attribute value for all possible values of the corresponding attribute. So, all attribute values of the resultant examples are known. The author of the work supposes that all possible values of an attribute, A, constitute the attribute domain and are known beforehand; moreover, some attribute values of the domain may not appear in the OAT (named Decision Table in the author context).

Stage 2. Once stage 1 has been applied, then create a new OAT, called resultant extended OAT, from those examples of the original OAT without unknown attribute values and the resultant examples of applying stage 1 to the original OAT. The resultant extended OAT is a completely specified OAT, without unknown attribute values. However, inconsistency situations may appear in this new OAT, since possible duplicity of attribute values when replacing unknown values by domain values in stage 1 may cause contradictions. Such problem is faced through the Rough Sets Theory [13], by inducing two sets of rules: "certain" rules, which are categorical and are obtained from the lower approximation of the concepts to be described, and "possible" rules, generated from the upper approximation of the concepts.

Some personal observations to do with each of the just mentioned two stages are esposed next.

In relation to stage 1, the a priori knowledge about the domain of each attribute is required, independently of the knowledge present in the OAT, which may be an impossible requeriment in some problems, particularly in those cases with large attribute domains. On the other hand, processing the resultant extended OAT may cause serious problems, such as:

- An excessive size of the resultant OAT, with the consequent efficiency problems.
- An overabundace of examples in the resultant OAT whose real existence of some of them is perhaps impossible, with the consequent overabundance of information in the induced rules.

The topic of extending an OAT has received special attention in the field of the evaluation of the quality of knowledge bases, whose original ideas are described in [6].

With respect to stage 2, it is our personal opinion that before proceeding to extend the original OAT, a previous stage considering the possibility of inducing only "certain" rules should be included. If such a stage was performed, then the process of extending the original OAT would possibly not be necessary in some cases. The problem of inducing general descripcions of concepts from inconsistent OATs is proposed in [7], showing several alternative solutions to that considered in [10].

Grzymala-Busse and other authors propose, also in the context of the Rough Sets Theory, to model, through fuzzy sets measures, the uncertainty caused by the presence of unknown attribute values [5].

A method based on transforming an incomplete information system into a complete one is presented in [20], where each element of the incomplete system is replaced by the set of possible completely specified elements.

A method to generate all rules from incomplete information systems is exposed in [11]. In this respect, the concept of "completion" of a system δ is defined. A completion of δ is another system δ' such that:

- Known attributes values in δ are also contained in δ',
- Unknown attribute values in δ have been replaced by known domain values in δ'.

The rule generation process of a system δ is based on that of each completion δ', which assumes that attribute domains are known beforehand. The concept of "generalized rule" in an incomplete system is subsequently defined as a rule which is generalized in each completion of the system, showing that the generation of all optimal generalized rules do not require to process every completion, but they can be generated from the original incomplete system. A method based on a boolean reasoning to carry out the just mentioned task is shown.

The concept of definability of a subset of elements in an incomplete information system is exposed in [3]. The purpose of this work is double: on the one hand a propositional language for a binary information system is presented; on the other, two approaches of the concept of definability of a subset X are described in terms of the Rough Sets Theory: the propositional definability of X, which considers only known attribute values of the system, and the strong definability of X, described for both, known and unknown attribute values.

A preprocessing stage of the input examples in order to model uncertainty in terms of the Fuzzy Sets Theory is proposed in [15]. Uncertainty considered in this work arises as a consequence of a discretization process of continuous attributes into intervals –or linguistic elements– representing qualitative values, in such a way each numerical value of an attribute is associated with one interval through a given uncertainty degree, which express the possibility that the numerical value corresponds actually to the associated linguistic element.

As a concluding synthesis, two outstanding aspects must be emphasized when incomplete OATs are present:

1. The language used to express incomplete knowledge about the attribute values.

2. The way which incomplete knowledge is processed by the inductive process.

In relation to the first aspect, it would be desirable to point towards generic languages, allowing a general representation of unknown or partially unknown attribute values independently of the knowledge description measures used. The language proposed in this work is close to the language exposed in [12], being more general than that adopted by the above discussed bibliographical references; moreover, it covers a wide range of real applications.

With regard to the second aspect, the proposed language allows to unify the concepts of incomplete OAT and completely specified OAT under a same treatment, without the need to distinguish when a given attribute value is completely specified or (partially) unknown. In addition, the computational cost to carry out the inductive activity does not suffer any rise when unknown attribute values are present.

2. Theoretical Concepts

The problem studied here can be formally described as follows:

Let $D = \{d_1, d_2, \ldots, d_m\}$ be a set of elements or examples extensionally defined and $R = \{r_1, r_2, \ldots, r_n\}$ a set of attributes also extensionally defined, such that for each $d_j \in D$, $j = 1 \ldots m$, the value of each attribute in R is known. Given w extensionally defined subsets of D, $C_1, C_2, \ldots, C_w$, $C_i \subseteq D$, $i = 1 \ldots w$, $C_i = \{d_a, d_b, \ldots, d_c\}$, find, for each subset C_i, $i = 1 \ldots w$, an optimal intensional description P_i expressed in terms of a subset of attributes R_x, $R_x \subseteq R$; that is, $C_i = \{d_j \in D / P\}$. The term "optimal" does not accept an only definition, of course. In fact, the optimality criterion to consider will depend on the particular problem in hand. However, there may be more than one way to describe subsets C_i under the same optimality criterion considered, and so, more than one subset of attributes of R in terms of which to express the corresponding properties P_i.

Knowledge representation of the above problem is formalized under the name of Object Attribute Table (abreviated OAT), as follow:

Definition 1 (Completely Specified Object Attribute Table). A completely specified OAT, or simply OAT, is a 7-tuple, OAT = <D, R, V, F, C, G, f>, where:

$D = \{d_1, d_2, \ldots, d_m\}$ is a set of elements or concrete portions of knowledge about some concepts.

$R = \{r_1, r_2, \ldots, r_n\}$ is a set of qualities or attributes in terms of which the elements of D are described.

$V = \{V_1, V_2, \ldots, V_n\}$ is a family of sets, one for each attribute $r_i \in R$, V_i being the set of values of attribute r_i appearing in the OAT, also called the domain of r_i.

$F = \{f_1, f_2, \ldots, f_n\}$ is a set of functions defining extensionally the values of attributes $r_i \in R$ for each element $d_j \in D$, that is, $f_i: D \times \{r_i\} \rightarrow V_i$, $i = 1 \ldots n$.

C is a set of w subsets of D, $C = \{C_1, C_2, \ldots, C_w\}$, $1 \leq w \leq m$, $C_i \subseteq D$, $i = 1 \ldots w$, representing each one of which a concept to be intensionally described throug a subset of attributes of R.

f is a function assigning the corresponding concepts to each element $d_i \in D$, that is, $f: D \rightarrow \Pi(C)$, $\Pi(C)$ denoting the set of parts of C.

Finally, $G = \{g_1, g_2, \ldots, g_n\}$ is a set of functions defining, for each attribute value of the attribute domains, the subsets of concepts associated with the value, that is, $g_i: V_i \rightarrow \Pi(\Pi(C))$, so that if $t_p \in V_i$, $g_i(t_p) = \cup_{j=1 \ldots m} f(d_j)$, $\forall d_j$ such that $f_i(d_j, r_i) = t_p$.

Graphically, an OAT can be represented such as figure 1 illustrates, where $t_i^k \in V_k$, $1 \leq k \leq n$, $1 \leq i \leq m$, is the value of attribute r_k associated with element d_i through function f_k; $\{C_i, C_j\} \in \Pi(C)$, is the element of the set of parts of C associated with element $d_i \in D$ through function f, that is, $f(d_i) = \{C_i, C_j\}$. Notice that each row of the OAT contains the complete description of an example or element of D, which can be represented by a n+2 tuple $(d_i, t_i^1, t_i^2, \ldots, t_i^n, \{C_i, C_j\})$. Let $R_x = \{r_a, r_b, \ldots, r_c\}$, $R_x \subseteq R$, a subset of attributes of R; the portion of a row of an OAT made up of attribute values of R_x is called an attribute value tuple of R_x. Thus, considering the n+2 tuple $(d_i, t_i^1, t_i^2, \ldots, t_i^n, \{C_i, C_j\})$, the attribute value tuple of R_x is $(t_i^a, t_i^b, \ldots, t_i^c)$.

D \ R	r_1	r_2		r_k		r_n	$\Pi(C)$
d_1	t_1^1	t_1^2	.	.	.	t_1^n	$\{C_a, C_b, C_c\}$
d_2	t_2^1	t_2^2	.	.	.	t_2^n	$\{C_p\}$
.	.	.				.	.
d_i	t_i^1	t_i^2	.	t_i^k	.	t_i^n	$\{C_i, C_j\}$
d_j	t_j^1	t_j^2	.	.	.	t_j^n	$\{C_i, C_s\}$
.	.	.				.	.
d_m	t_m^1	t_m^2	.	.	.	t_m^n	$\{C_q\}$

Figure 1. Graphical illustration of an OAT

Definition 1 describes OATs whose attribute values are known for any element $d_i \in D$. However, it is not a rule in real world applications. So, a common situation to be faced arises when some attribute values are not completely known for certain elements of D. In such a case the corresponding OAT is said to be an incompletely specified OAT. The concept of incompletely specified OAT is widely treated in section 3.

Selection of a subset of attributes to describe the concepts. Selecting an adequate subset R_x, $R_x \subseteq R$, of attributes to define intensionally the subsets or concepts of C, is one of the main stages of the inductive process. A subset R_x of attributes is said to be able to describe the concepts of C if it allows a consistent description of such concepts, that is, a description without any kind of confussion (contradiction). Such a subset R_x is called an *attribute basis*. However, when an optimality criterion must be satisfied by an intencional description expressed in terms of a subset R_x of attributes, then more restrictive qualities must be demanded from R_x. In this case we say that R_x must be "adequate", in the sense that R_x is able to describe the concepts of C and there exist an intensional description of these concepts satisfying the stablished optimality criterion. In this case, R_x is called an *optimal attribute basis*. A great part of the computational effort of the inductive process is devoted to generating some optimal attribute basis.

Additional literature about the concepts mentioned in this section is found in [7], [8], [9]. From now on the discussion will be focused on incomplete OATs.

3. Incomplete Knowledge

The characteristics determining the incompleteness degree of knowledge about the attribute values of an OAT are given by the accuracy to represent the values of attributes, but not by the description measures adopted to evaluate the real attribute values. For example, the evaluation results can be described through an integer value, a probabilistic value, a simbolic value, a fuzzy value, etc... Thus, the most accurate way to represent a given attribute value is by describing the concrete results of evaluating the real attribute through the considered measures. So, one may say that the value of attribute r_i associated to element d_j is the single value t_j^i, which is for example a continuous value representing the weight of element d_i. On the other hand, the most vague manner to talk about the value of an attribute r_i in an specific situation will consist in not discerning any possible result of the evaluation of r_i, that is, no value of r_i is known. Intermediate ways to represent an incomplete attribute value will consider several possibilities for the value; for example one may not be very sure if the colour of the shirt of Peter is blue, green, or perhaps yellow. Such situations are said to consider only partially unknown attribute values. Although partially unknown attribute values are not precise, they may be useful in several situations, particularly in those cases with a relevant entropy associated with the attributes [19].

Next, the concept of incomplete knowledge about the attribute values of an OAT is formalized. With the aim of avoiding an excessive extension of this work, only discrete attributes will be considered.

Consider a given OAT, and let $r_j \in R$ be an attribute with a discrete domain V_j, $V_j \in V$.

Definition 2 (c_values). Let Vr_j be the value of attribute r_j in a given specific situation. Vr_j can be defined as a subset of the attribute domain V_j, that is, $Vr_j \subseteq V_j$. Value Vr_j is interpreted in logical terms as the disjunction of its values. That is, if $Vr_j = \{v_{ji}, v_{jk}, ..., v_{jp}\}$, $v_{jt} \in V_j$, $t = i...p$, then attribute r_j adopts one of the values included in Vr_j, which can also be written as $Vr_j = v_{ji}$ OR v_{jk} OR ... OR v_{jp}, being OR the logical OR connective. Notice that since attributes can only adopt a single value in a given specific situation, then the OR connective can be replaced by the OREX connective (exclusive OR). Such a value Vr_j is called a *c_value*.

Definition 2 constitutes the starting point in formalizing the concept of incomplete knowledge in relation to the attribute values of an OAT. Notice that nothing has been said about the characteristics of the domain values of attributes, v_{ji}, $v_{ji} \in V_j$; thus, they can be considered as arbitrary values, and so can also be considered the corresponding c values.

From now on, attribute values associated with elements will be interpreted as c_values.

Definition 3 (completely and incompletely specified c_values). Let $V_j = \{v_{j1}, v_{j2}, \ldots, v_{jz}\}$ be the domain or r_j. Consider Vr_j as the c_value of attribute r_j in a given situation. Vr_j is said to be an incompletely specified c_value of r_j if, and only if, $\#Vr_j > 1$, $\#Vr_j$ being the cardinal of Vr_j; otherwise, it is a completely specified c_value. Incompletely specified c_values are also called vague c_values.

Definition 3 formalizes definitively the concept of vagueness of knowledge in relation to the value of an attribute in a given specific situation.

Definition 4 (c_values weight). Let Vr_j be the c_value of r_j in a specific situation. The weight $w(Vr_j)$ of Vr_j is defined as the number of domain values of r_j contained in Vr_j, that is, $w(Vr_j) = \#Vr_j$.

Notice that the vagueness of a c_value Vr_j depends directly on his weight.

Definition 5 (A new representation of the c_values). Let $Vr_j = \{v_{ji}, v_{jk}, \ldots, v_{jp}\}$ be a vague c_value, then Vr_j will also be represented through the simbol $*^j_{i,k,\ldots,p}$.

Definition 6 (c_domains of single attributes). Let r_j be a given attribute of an OAT. The c_domain of r_j, represented by V'_j, is the set of all different c_values of r_j appearing in the OAT.

Note that if V_j is the domain of attribute r_j, then there exist $2^{\#V_j} - (\#V_j + 1)$ possible situations of vagueness for this attribute.

Figure 2 illustrates graphically an OAT with several vagueness situations in describing some attribute values.

R					
D	r_1	r_2	$\cdots$	r_n	$\Pi(C)$
d_1	$\{t^1_1\}$	$\{t^2_1\}$	$\cdots$	$\{t^n_1\}$	$\{C_a, C_b, C_c\}$
d_2	$\{t^1_2\}$	$*^2_{1,3}$	$\cdots$	$\{t^n_2\}$	$\{C_p\}$
$\cdot$	$\cdot$	$\cdot$		$\cdot$	$\cdot$
d_i	$*^1_{2,4,6}$	$\{t^2_i\}$	$\cdots$	$\{t^n_i\}$	$\{C_i, C_j\}$
$\cdot$					
d_j	$\{t^1_j\}$	$\{t^2_j\}$	$\cdots$	$*^n_{i,j}$	$\{C_i, C_s\}$
$\cdot$	$\cdot$	$\cdot$		$\cdot$	$\cdot$
d_m	$\{t^1_m\}$	$\{t^2_m\}$	$\cdots$	$\{t^n_m\}$	$\{C_q\}$

Figure 2. OAT with vague attribute values

Let us observe that $*^1_{2,4,6}$ is a vague value of attribute r_1 associated with element d_i, $*^2_{1,3}$ is the (vague) value of element d_2 for attribute r_2, ... Also observe that completely specified attribute c_values appear in brackets.

To facilitate the formalization of incompletely specified OATs, we will proceed to generalize definition 6 by considering now subsets of attributes over which to define the concept of c_domain, such as definition 7 describes.

Definition 7 (c_domains of subsets of attributes). Let $R_{i,j,\ldots,k} = \{r_i, r_j, \ldots, r_k\}$, $i \neq j \neq \ldots \neq k$, be a subset of attributes of R. The c_domain of $R_{i,j,\ldots,k}$, represented by $V'_{i,j,\ldots,k}$, is the set of all different tuples made up of c_values of $r_i, r_j, \ldots$ and r_k which appear in the OAT. That is, if Vr_i is a c_value of r_i, Vr_j a c_value of $r_j, \ldots$ and Vr_k a c_value of r_k, then a tuple $(Vr_i, Vr_j, \ldots, Vr_k)$ appearing in the OAT represents a c_value of the c_domain of $R_{i,j,\ldots,k}$. Then all these different c_values of $R_{i,j,...,k}$ that appear in the OAT constitute its c_domain. A c_value of a subset $R_{i,j,...,k}$ of attributes will be denoted by $Vr_{i,j,...,k}$.

4. Attribute Bases

The concept of attribute basis is also valid in the case of incompletely specified OATs, having identical meaning than that defined for complete OATs. However, their formalizations differ in some aspects. Particularly, functions $f_i \in F$ and $g_j \in G$, $i, j = 1...n$, and set V of definition 1 must now be defined over attribute c_domains and not on attribute domains. Definition 8 formalizes the concept of incompletely specified OAT in this way.

Definition 8 (incompletely specified OATs). An incompletely specified OAT, abbreviated IS_OAT, is defined as follows:

IS_OAT = <D, R, V', V'$_x$, F', C, G', f>, where D, R, C and f are as in definition 1.

$V' = \{V'_1, V'_2,..., V'_n\}$ represents the set of discrete c_domains of single attributes r_1, $r_2,..., r_n$ respectively, $r_i \in R$, i = 1...n.

$V'_x = \{V'_1, V'_2,..., V'_n, V'_{1,2}, V'_{1,3},..., V'_{i,j,k},..., V'_{1,2,...,n}\}$ represents the set of c_domains of all subsets of attributes of R; note that V'_x contain 2^n-1 c_domains.

$F' = \{f_1, f_2,..., f_n, f_{1,2}, f_{1,3},..., f_{i,j,k},..., f_{1,2,...,n}\}$ is a set of functions defining, for each element of D, the corresponding c_values in relation to any subset of attributes of R, that is, $f_{i,j,...,k}: D \rightarrow V'_{i,j,...,k}$.

$G' = \{g'_1, g'_2,..., g'_n, g'_{1,2}, g'_{1,3},..., g'_{i,j,k},..., g'_{1,2,...,n}\}$ is a set of 2^n-1 functions defining, for each c_value af any c_domain of a subset of attributes, those concepts of C associated with the considered c_value, that is, $g'_{i,j,...,k}: V'_{i,j,...,k} \rightarrow \Pi(\Pi(C))$, so that if $t_p \in V_{i,j,...,k}$, $g_{i,j,...,k}(t_p) = \cup_{j=1...m} f(d_j)$, $\forall d_j$ such that $f_{i,j,...,k}(d_j) = t_p$.

Definition 9 (couples of partially shared c_values). Let $V^a r_i$, $V^b r_i \in V'_i$ two c_values of a same attribute r_i. If $V^a r_i \cap V^b r_i \neq \varnothing$, the $V^a r_i$ and $V^b r_i$ are called a couple of partially shared c_values.

Definition 10 (single contradictory c_values). Let $r_i \in R$ be an attribute of the OAT with c_domain V'_i, and $V^s r_i \in V'_i$ a c_value of domain V'_i. $V^s r_i$ is said to be a contradictory c_value if, and only if, $\#g'_i(V^s r_i) > 1$.

Definition 11 (couples of contradictory c_values). Let $r_i \in R$ be an attribute and V'_i its c_domain. Consider two different c_values, $V^s r_i$ and $V^t r_i$ of domain V'_i, that is, $V^s r_i \in V'_i$, $V^t r_i \in V'_i$. $V^s r_i$ and $V^t r_i$ are said to be a couple of contradyctory c_values if, and only if,

$[(V^s r_i \cap V^t r_i \neq \varnothing)$ AND $((V^s r_i$ is a contradictory c_value) OR $(V^t r_i$ is a contradictory c_value) OR $(V^s r_i$ and $V^t r_i$ are not single contradictory c_values, but $g'_i(V^s r_i) \neq g'_i(V^t r_i)))]$.

Observe that two c_values constitute a couple of contradictory c_values if they do not allow any consistent description of the concepts of C, that is, any description free of contradictions. At the same time, a single c_value describinng two different concepts is a contradictory c_value.

Next, definitions 10 and 11 are generalized for arbitrary subsets of attributes.

Definition 12 (single contradictory tuples). Let $R_{i,j,...,k} = \{r_i, r_j,..., r_k\}$, $R_{i,j,...,k} \subseteq R$, be an arbitrary subset of attributes and $Vr_{i,j,...,j}$ a c_value of $R_{i,j,...,k}$. $Vr_{i,j,...,j}$ is said to be a single contradictory tuple if, and only if, $\#g'_{i,j,...,k}(Vr_{i,j,...,k}) > 1$.

An important property to do with single contradictory tuples manifest that every attribute c_value of any contradictory tuple is a single contradictory c_value.

Definition 13 (couples of contradictory tuples). Let $V^a r_{i,j,\ldots k} = (V^a r_i, V^a r_j, \ldots, V^a r_k)$ and $V^b r_{i,j,\ldots k} = (V^b r_i, V^b r_j, \ldots, V^b r_k)$ two c_values of $R_{i,j,\ldots,k}$. $V^a r_{i,j,\ldots k}$ and $V^b r_{i,j,\ldots k}$ are said to be a couple of contradictory tuples if, and only if,

$[((V^a r_i, V^b r_i), (V^a r_j, V^b r_j),\ldots, (V^a r_k, V^b r_k))$ are couples of partially shared c_values AND $((V^a r_{i,j,\ldots k}$ is a single contradictory tuple) OR $(V^b r_{i,j,\ldots k}$ is a single contradictory tuple) OR $(V^a r_{i,j,\ldots k}$ and $V^b r_{i,j,\ldots k}$ are not single contradictory tuples, but $g'_{i,j,\ldots,k}(V^a r_{i,j,\ldots k}) \neq g'_{i,j,\ldots,k}(V^b r_{i,j,\ldots k})))].$

An important property to do with definition 13 manifest that if $V^a r_{i,j,\ldots k}$ and $V^b r_{i,j,\ldots k}$ constitute a couple of contradictory tuples, then all pairs $(V^a r_i, V^b r_i), (V^a r_j, V^b r_j),\ldots, (V^a r_k, V^b r_k)$ are couples of contradictory c_values.

Definition 14 describes the essential concept of attribute basis in incompletely specified OATs.

Definition 14 (attribute basis). Let us consider a given IS_OAT. Let $R_{i,j,\ldots,k} = \{r_i, r_j,\ldots, r_k\}$, $R_{i,j,\ldots,k} \subseteq R$, be an arbitrary subset of attributes of IS_OAT. $R_{i,j,\ldots,k}$ is said to constitute an attribute basis of IS_OAT if, and only if, neither single contradictory tuples nor couples of contradictory tuples of domain $V'_{i,j,\ldots,k}$ are found in IS_OAT.

5. Conclusions

The basic general questions to do with inductive learning from incompletely specified examples have been exposed, resting on the following two aspects:

 i. On defining a language to represent incompleteness of knowledge.
 ii. On the particular characteristics of the inductive task to process knowledge expressions represented through the defined language.

A wide bibliographical review allowed to bring to light several meaningful needs, among which the lack of generality of most knowledge representation should be emphasized. Each particular work considers, in general, one specific knowledge representation, which depend exclusively on the specific characteristics of the considered problem. Thus, some works make use of probabilistic knowledge on the attribute values, others are about fuzzy descriptions of knowledge, etc.... Such knowledge representations determine the characteristics of the corresponding inductive tasks, to such an extent that inductive processes have been conceived to work for particular representations only.

A generic language to represent incomplete knowledge about the attribute values has been exposed in section 3, in such a way complete and incompletely specified OATs can be treated in an unified way, that is, there is no need to distinguish between completely and incompletely specified attribute values.

However, the presence of incomplete knowledge in an OAT required to redefine the concept of attribute basis, such as it is exposed in section 4, but without affecting the generality level of the original inductive process for optimal bases generation, conceived for complete OATs [7], [8], [9].

Acknowledgements

This work has been partially supported by the University of the Balearic Islands, through the UIB 2003/11 project.

References

[1] Bratko, I., Kononenko, I., Learning Diagnostic Rules fron Incomplete and Noisy Data, Artificial Intelligence and Statistics (1987), pp. 142-153, Phelps (Eds).

[2] Breiman, L., Friedman, J. H., Olshen, R. A., Stone, C. J., Classification and Regression Trees, Belmont, Wadsworth, 1984.

[3] Buszkowski, W., Approximation Spaces and Definability for Incomplete Information Systems, Lecture Notes in Artificial Intelligence, 1424 (1998), pp. 115-122, Springer Verlag.

[4] Clark, P., Niblett, T., The CN2 induction algorithm, Machine Learning, 3 (1989), pp. 261-283.

[5] Chmielewski, M. R., Grzylama-Busse, J. W., Peterson, N. W., Than, S., The Rule Induction System LERS – A Version for Personal Computers, Foundations of Computing and Decision Sciences, Vol. 18, No. 2-3 (1993), pp. 181-212.

[6] Fiol, G., Aguiló, I., On Qualitative Knowledge in a Rule Based Knowledge Base, Proceedings of the IJCAI'93 Workshop on Validation, Verification and Test of Knowledge Based Systems (1993), pp. 27-36.

[7] Fiol, G., Contribution to the Inductive Acquisition of Knowledge, Ph.D. Thesis, Computer Science Department, University of the Balearic Islands, Palma de Mallorca, Spain, 1991.

[8] Fiol, G., Miró-Julià, J., Miró-Nicolau, J., A New Perspective in the Inductive Acquisition of Knowledge from Examples, Lecture Notes in Computer Science, 682 (1992), pp. 219-228, Springer Verlag.

[9] Fiol, G., UIB-IK: A Computer System for Decision Trees Induction, Lecture Notes in Artificial Intelligence, 1609 (1999), pp. 601-611, Springer Verlag.

[10] Grzymala-Busse, J. W., On the Unknown Attribute Values in Induction, Lecture Notes in Artificial Intelligence, 542 (1991), pp. 368-377, Springer Verlag.

[11] Kryszkiewicz, M., Generalized Rules in Incomplete Information Systems, Lecture Notes in Artificial Intelligence, 1325 (1997), pp. 421-430, Springer Verlag.

[12] Lipski, W., On Databases with Incomplete Information, Journal of the Association for Computer Machinery, Vol 28, No. 1 (1981), pp. 41-70.

[13] Pawlak, Z., Rough Sets, International Journal on Computer and Information Sciences, 11 (1982), pp. 341-356.

[14] Pawlak, Z., Rough Sets, Theoretical Aspects of Reasoning About Data, Kluwer Academic Publishers, 1991.

[15] Quafafou, M., Learning Flexible Concepts from Uncertain Data, Lecture Notes in Artificial Intelligence, 1325 (1997), pp. 507-518, Springer Verlag.

[16] Quinlan, J. R., Decision Trees as Probabilistic Classifiers, Proceedings of the 4th International Workshop on Machine Learning (1987), pp. 31-37.

[17] Quinlan, J. R., Induction of Decision Trees, Machine Learning, 1 (1986), pp. 81-106.

[18] Quinlan, J. R., Unknown Attribute Values in Induction, Proceedings of the 6th International Workshop on Machine Learning (1989), pp. 164-168.

[19] Shannon, C. E., A Mathematical Theory of Communication, Bell System Tech. J., 27 (1948), pp. 379-423, 623-656.

[20] Slowinski, R., Stefanowski, J., Rough-Sets Reasoning about Uncertain Data, Fundamenta Informaticae, Vol 27, No. 2-3 (1996), pp. 229-244.

Artificial Intelligence Research and Development
I. Aguiló et al. (Eds.)
IOS Press, 2003

Feature Weighting in IBL: Local vs Global

Héctor Núñez[1], Miquel Sànchez-Marrè[1], Ulises Cortés[1]

[1]*Knowledge Engineering & Machine Learning group, Technical University of Catalonia.*
Campus Nord-Edifici C5, Jordi Girona 1-3,
08034 Barcelona, Catalonia, EU
{hnunez, miquel, ia}@lsi.upc.es

Abstract

This paper tests the power of some global feature weighting techniques against some local feature weighting techniques for predictive tasks within IBL field. The paper analyses several feature weighting approaches, and proposes new feature weighting methods. Three new correlation-based global weighting algorithms and an entropy-based local weighting approach are proposed and tested against other techniques. Predictive tasks have been used to test the performance of the approaches. The testing has been done using several similarity measures, one environmental database and twelve data sets from the UCI Machine Learning Database Repository. Experimental results show that local methods outperform global methods. Specifically, the entropy-based local technique seems to be a good option for feature weighting in IBL.

1 Introduction

A major problem in predictive tasks within instance-based algorithms is to find out which are the relevant features to be taken into account. When experts are available in a particular domain, theses tasks could be easier. But, in general, when there is no expertise available, some automatic methods should be used. Many methods have been proposed and used in the literature for feature relevance specification. One of this kind of techniques is *feature weighting* [Aha, 1998]. Feature weighting consists in the assignment of an importance degree to each one of the available features describing a domain or process. Normally weights are scaled in the range 0..1 or equivalent. Thus, features with lower weights are the less important ones, while high weights mean very important features.

But there is an added problem to evaluate how well the different feature weighting techniques work. They must be evaluated in terms of the performance of a task. In this paper, the predictive task accuracy is used. Even making this decision, there is another key point. Which predictive method should be used? In this study, Instance-Based Learning (IBL), and similarity measures will be used because they are a good technique to make predictions based on previous experience. And experiences are commonly used in many real systems to make accurate predictions, rather than more general knowledge domain theories.

In IBL, similarity is used to decide which instance is closest to a new current case. Thus, this similarity criterion for predictive tasks will be used to evaluate the different weighting techniques in the experimental part.

This paper aims at analysing and studying the performance of several commonly used feature weighting techniques, and proposes new global and local weighting techniques.

The techniques are evaluated in terms of predictive accuracy on unseen cases, measured by a ten-fold cross-validation process.

1.1 Related Work

In recent years, many researchers are focusing on feature weighting. Feature weighting is a very important issue in learning systems. It is intended to give more relevance to those features detected as important, and at the same time, it is intended to give lower importance to irrelevant features. Most general methods for feature weighting use a global scheme. It means to associate a weight to all the space of the feature. If a continuous attribute is present, a discretization pre-process is suggested to allow making weight calculation according to its interval values and his correlation with the value class. The importance of one feature will be determined by the distribution of the class values for that feature. Some work has been done such as the mutual information technique proposed in [*Wettschereck et al.*, 1997], the work reported by Mohri and Tanaka [1994] of his QM2 method and Creecy *et al.* [1992], Relief-F by [Kononenko 1994] and other work in [Kohavi *et al.*, 1997]. On the other hand, local weighting methods assign specific weights to specific values of the attribute. Some works have been done such as the value difference metric of Stanfill and Waltz [1986], the class distribution weighting method of Howe and Cardie [1997], and the per-category feature importance criterion of Creecy *et al.* [1992].

The paper is organized in the following way. Some background and some techniques in global weighting approaches are described in section 2, as well as the new correlation-based global techniques. Section 3 outlines both some background and known methods on local-based weighting techniques, and main features about the new entropy-based local weighting algorithm. Section 4 presents the experimental setup and the results comparing the performance of all feature weighting techniques using several similarity measures tested over thirteen databases. Finally, in section 5 conclusions and future research directions are outlined.

2 Global Weighting Techniques

Global weighting algorithms compute a single weight vector for all cases. A weight is associated to each attribute and this weight is fixed for all the attribute space. There are some research works. Creecy *et al.* in [1992] introduced *cross-category feature importance* (CCF) method. They are trying to assign higher weights to features that occurred in fewer classes. However, this algorithm is not sensitive to the distribution of feature values across classes. Conditional probabilities have been used to assign feature weights. Mohri and Tanaka [1994] reported good performance of his QM2 method that use a set of transformed features based on the originals. The methods selected for the comparison with the new correlation-based methods proposed are the Mutual Information (MI) method, the Class Distribution Weighting (CDW-G). For this reason, these methods are described in detail below.

2.1 Mutual Information

A feature weighting algorithm should assign low weights to features that provide little information for classification and higher weights to features that provide more reliable information. Following this idea, the *mutual information* between the values of a feature and the class of the training examples can be used to assign feature weights. The mutual information is computed as follows [Wettschereck *et al.*, 1997]:

$$w(f) = \sum_{v \in V} \sum_{c_j \in J} p(c_j, x_f = v) * \log\left(\frac{p(c_j, x_f = v)}{p(c_j) * p(x_f = v)} \right)$$

where $p(c_j)$ is the frequency of class c_j among the training set X and $p(x_f=v)$ is the frequency of value v for f among instances in X.

2.2 New Correlation-Based Global Weighting Techniques

The three correlation-based global weighting algorithms developed are based on the idea of assigning higher weights to features showing higher correlation between the value distribution and the class distribution in the sample training set. To achieve this goal the correlation matrix, depicted in table 1, should be used. In our approach, the continuous attributes have to be discretized. Afterwards, a specific weight is assigned, both to discretized continuous attributes or discrete attributes. Next, the new correlation-based global weighting algorithms are described.

Class Distribution Approach (CD)

To implement this global weighting algorithm we have used a new approach based on estimated probabilities and correlation. The calculated values are in the range [0,1] in ascending order of relevance. In our approach, a correlation matrix is filled for each attribute, represented the correlation between attribute's values and class value as show in Table 1.

	C_1	C_2	...	C_n	Value Total
V_1	q_{11}	q_{12}	...	q_{1n}	q_{1+}
V_2	q_{21}	q_{22}	...	q_{2n}	q_{2+}
$\vdots$	$\vdots$	$\vdots$	...	$\vdots$	$\vdots$
V_m	q_{m1}	q_{m2}	...	q_{mn}	q_{m+}
Class Total	q_{+1}	q_{+2}	...	q_{+n}	q_{++}

Table 1. Correlation-Relevance Matrix or Contingency Table for an attribute.

Where:
  V_i is the i value of the attribute, when the attribute is continuous, V_i represents one interval.
  C_j is the class value j
  q_{ij} is the number of instances that have value i (or are in range i for a continuous attribute) and belong to class j.
  q_{+j} is the number of instances of class j.
  q_{i+} is the number of instances that have value i (or are in range i for a continuous attribute).
  q_{++} is the number of instance in the training set.

The information present in the correlation matrix (table 1) has been used for detecting the maximum value at each column (q_{+j}). This value divided by the number of the instances belonging to class j, represent the best prediction of the class j in all the feature space. The main idea is to put together this information for all the class values, in such way that the global weight of the attribute will be higher in the same proportion that the prediction was higher. The computation of prediction is as follows:

$$H_f = \frac{1}{n}\sum_{j=1}^{n}\frac{q_{max,\,j}}{q_{+j}}$$

where,

n is the number of classes

q_{+j} is the total of instances belonging to class j

$q_{max,j}$ is the maximum value of the column j

The number of different values of the feature biases this value, so that, when there are a few values, the lower limit of the prediction will be higher, such as 0.5 for two different values. In fact, the lowest limit will be *1/m*, where m is the number of different feature values. With this in mind, H_f is scaled to obtain the global weight in the range 0..1 for attribute f:

$$W(f)=\frac{H_f-\frac{1}{m}}{1-\frac{1}{m}}$$

Value Distribution Approach (VD)

In the first approach, a weakness is present. It is only taking the best prediction for one class into account according to the values distribution for one attribute in a single class value (a column in the correlation matrix). It is necessary to keep in mind the fact that the same feature value may be distributed among many different classes (a row in the correlation matrix). A second approach is show below, taking into account the distribution of values among classes with the same feature value. So, the value of H_f is given by:

$$H_f=\frac{1}{m}\sum_{i=1}^{m}\frac{q_{i,max}}{q_{i+}}$$

now, the minimum possible value will be: *1/n*, so after the scaling process, the weight is:

$$w(f)=\frac{H_f-\frac{1}{n}}{1-\frac{1}{n}}$$

Class-Value Distribution Approach (CVD)

Two main issues must be taken into account to set appropriates weights: the distribution of the values of the attribute across the classes, and the values associated to a class.

The first one shows how a single attribute's value can determine a class. In the correlation matrix, this can be seen by observing a single row. By observing a column, is it possible to determine the different attribute's values that predict a class. In both cases, it will be ideal to find only one value different to zero in each row and in the column where that value is. This indicates that one attribute's value can predict a single class, and at the same time, one class is determined only by a single attribute's value. The perfect attribute can be seen like a near-diagonal matrix. To take into account both class and values distribution a third approach has been designed:

$$H_f=\frac{1}{n}\sum_{j=1}^{n}\left(\frac{q_{max,j}}{q_{+j}}*\frac{q_{max,j}}{q_{max,+}}\right)$$

With this addition, the minimum possible value obtained is lower that the obtained in the first approach. So, it is necessary to take it into account in the scaling process. Now the lowest limit will be *1/(m*n)*, where m is the number of different feature values and n is the number of classes. The weight of the attribute is finally obtained as:

$$w(f) = \frac{H_f - \frac{1}{m*n}}{1 - \frac{1}{m*n}}$$

In all three approaches, small addends are necessary to prevent possible zero division in very special conditions, when an entire row or an entire column of the correlation matrix is zero.

3 Local Weighting Techniques

Local weighting methods assign specific weights to specific values of the attribute. Is it possible that one attribute could be very useful predicting a class according to one of its values, but when it takes another value, this attribute is not relevant. The value difference metric of Stanfill and Waltz [1986], assigns a different weight to each value of the feature. Howe and Cardie [1997] propose a class distribution weighting method, which computes a different weight vector for each class in the set of training cases using statistical properties of that subset of data. Creecy *et al.* [1992] use per-category feature importance to assign high weights to features that are highly correlated with the class. The methods Value Difference Metric (VDM), and the Class Distribution Weighting (CDW-L) have been selected for a comparison with the new Entropy-Based Local weighting method proposed. For this reason, they are described in detail below.

3.1 Value Difference Metric (VDM)

Stanfill and Waltz proposed the VDM [1986]. In VDM the distance between cases x and y is defined as follows:

$$\text{distance}(x,y) = \sum_{f=1}^{F} w(f, x_f) * \delta(f, x_f, y_f)$$

where:

$$w(f, x_f) = \sqrt{\sum_{j=1}^{n} \left(\frac{C_f(x_f, j)}{C_f(x_f)} \right)^2}$$

$$\delta(f, x_f, y_f) = \sum_{j=1}^{n} \left(\frac{C_f(x_f, j)}{C_f(x_f)} - \frac{C_f(y_f, j)}{C_f(y_f)} \right)^2$$

where F are the number of attributes, x_f and y_f are possible values of an attribute, $C_f(x_f)$ is the number of times that value x_f occurred at an attribute f, and $C_f(x_f, j)$ is the frequency that x_f was classified into the class j at an attribute f.

3.2 Class Distribution Weighting

Howe and Cardie proposed the CDW in [Howe and Cardie 1997]. CDW starts from the premise that the features that are important to match on are those that tend to have different values associated with different classes. For each class C_j there exists a separate vector $\langle W_{f_1 C_j}, ..., W_{f_m C_j} \rangle$ of weights for each feature. The weights are assigned for a particular class on a given feature. The weights are calculated as follows:

$$R_{f_i C_j} = \sum_{h=1}^{r_i} \left| a_h(f_i, C_j) - a_h(f_i, T - C_j) \right|$$

where: $a_h(f_i, C_j)$ is the fraction of instances across the training set where f_i takes on the value v_h and belong to class C_j, $a_h(f_i, T - C_j)$ is the number of instances across the training set where f_i takes on the value v_h and do not belong to class C_j, This yields a raw weight vector $\langle R_{f_1C_j},...,R_{f_mC_j} \rangle$ for each class C_j. The final weights $\langle W_{f_1C_j},...W_{f_mC_j} \rangle$ are simply the raw weights normalized to sum 1. These local weights are used to obtain the global weights (CDW-G) for each feature. The global weights are the average of local weights across all classes to get a single global weight vector. This variant can be expected to perform well in domains where the relevant features are the same for all classes.

3.3 Entropy-Based Local Weigthing (EBL)

Frequently, a single feature may seem irrelevant if you take it in a global way, but perhaps, a range of this feature is a very good selector for a specific class. Our proposal is to assign a high weight to this range, and a low weight to the others. In the tests that have been carried out, entropy values have been used to assign weights to all the ranges. In the following paragraph we present our approach to calculate *local* weights for all values (ranges) and for all attributes. The calculated values are in the range [0,1] in ascending order of relevance. From the correlation matrix, we can obtain the entropy from each value (range):

$$H_{fi} = -\frac{q_{i+}}{q_{++}} \sum_{j=1}^{n} \frac{q_{ij}}{q_{i+}} \log\left(\frac{q_{ij}}{q_{i+}}\right)$$

This entropy H_{fi} belonging to value (range) i from attribute f will be the basis to calculate the weight for the value i following this simple idea. If the value (or range) has a maximum possible entropy ("totally random"), then the weight must be 0. On the other hand, if the value (or range) has a minimum possible entropy ("perfectly classified") then the weight must be 1. The minimum possible entropy is 0 when all the instances with this value (range) belong to the same class. The maximum possible entropy occurs when the instances with this value (range) are equally distributed in all classes and can be calculated as follows:

$$H_{f\max} = -\left(\frac{q_{i+}}{q_{++}}\right) \sum_{j=1}^{n} \left(\frac{\frac{q_{i+}}{n}}{q_{i+}}\right) \log\left(\frac{\frac{q_{i+}}{n}}{q_{i+}}\right)$$

This equation is equivalent to:

$$H_{f\max} = -\frac{q_{i+}}{q_{++}} \log\left(\frac{1}{n}\right)$$

From here, we can interpolate the weight for attribute f value (range) i between 0 and $H_{f\max}$ into the range from 0 to 1:

$$w(f,i) = 1 - \frac{H_{fi}}{H_{f\max}}$$

4 Experimental Setup and Evaluation

A nearest neighbour classifier was implemented, using each one of the nine similarity measures selected from the literature: HVDM, IVDM [Wilson and Martinez 1997], Euclidean, Manhattan, SF [Short and Fukunaga 1981], MRM [Blanzieri and Ricci 1999], Canberra, Clark [Lance and Williams 1966] and *L'Eixample* [Sànchez-Marrè *et al.* 1998], and three discretization methods: CAIM [Kurgan and Cios 2001], Equal Width Intervals, Chimerge [Kerber 1992]. Each measure was tested with no weights, according to the measure distance type. Next tests were carried out to evaluate the generalisation accuracy using both global and local weights, trying to show in an empirical way that the generalisation accuracy can be improved with weights, and specifically with local weights. To test the weighting techniques, Clark, Canberra, SF and MRM similarity measures were left out because they do not work with weights.

Database	Short Name	# Inst	Cont	Disc	NOD	# Class	% Miss
Air Pollution	AP	365	5	0	0	4	0
Auto	AU	205	15	0	8	7	0.004
Bridge	BR	108	3	0	8	3	0.06
Cleveland	CL	303	5	2	6	2	0
Flag	FL	194	3	7	18	8	0
Glass	GL	214	9	0	0	7	0
Hepatitis	HE	155	6	0	13	2	5.7
Horse Colic	HC	351	34	0	0	2	0
Iris	IR	150	4	0	0	3	0
Liver Disord.	LD	345	6	0	0	2	0
Votes	VO	435	0	0	16	2	7.3
Wine	WI	178	13	0	0	3	0
Zoo	ZO	90	0	0	16	7	0

Table 2. Major properties of databases

All tests were performed in one real environmental database plus twelve randomly selected databases from the UCI database repository [Blake and Merz 1998].

Detailed description of the databases is shown in table 2 where number of instances in each database (#Inst.), the number of continuous attributes (Cont), ordered discrete attributes (Disc), not ordered discrete attributes (NOD), number of classes (#Class) and missing values percentage (%Mis.).

To verify the accuracy of the retrieval in a CBR system, a test by means of a 10-fold cross-validation process was implemented. The average accuracy over all 10 trials is reported for each data test, for each similarity measure, and for each weighting scheme. The highest accuracy achieved in each data set is shown in boldface in table 3. The column Aver. shows the average accuracy across all databases for each similarity measure (SM) and weighting algorithm (WA), the column StDev. shows the standard deviation over all averages for each row. For each similarity measure the highest accuracy is in Italics.

5   Conclusions and Future Work

Main conclusions after the analysis of the performance among all weighting schemes and all similarity measures are that, in general, global weighting approach outperforms the unweighted schemes, and that local weighting schemes outperforms both unweighted and global weighting schemes. It can be argued from the table examination, and specifically, from the average accuracy of the local weighting schemes. They always are higher than the other schemes in most of databases and in both measures. These results confirm the importance of weighting schemes in predictive tasks in instance-based algorithms and other domains, as well as in case-based similarity assessment.

To get an insight of the level of significance of this value we have done statistical tests of significance using two-tailed paired t-test and Wilcoxon test to verify whether the differences between *L'Eixample*-EBL combination and the other 48 combinations are really significant. At a 95% level of confidence (on both tests), *L'Eixample*-EBL combination is really significant better than 43 others and only its not significant different from the combinations HVDM-MI, Manhattan-MI, Manhattan-EBL, *L'Eixample*-MI and *L'Eixample*-VDM. If you take a look you can see that the more similar combinations are based in the MI method or EBL method. Taking into account that both MI method and EBL method are based in entropy and information gain measures we can conclude that these kind of methods seem to be very promising in feature weighting methods. This fact is outlined in figures 1a and 1b where the average accuracy over all similarity measures for each database is shown.

A new entropy-based local weighting algorithm (EBL) has been proposed. This local weighting approach seems to be better, in general, than the other weighting schemes with independence of the similarity measure or the discretization method or the database used (see figure 2). Specially, it is very good working with *L'Eixample* measure. For space reasons only the table with CAIM discretization is reported in the paper.

Analysing the results from the different databases, one can state the following conclusions. All databases improve their predictive tasks with weighting schemes, and local weighting techniques are generally even better than global techniques.

SM	WA	Databases													Aver.	StDev
		AP	AU	BR	CL	FL	GL	HE	HC	IR	LD	VO	WI	ZO		
Clark	NA	91.85	68.95	82.00	76.24	48.96	64.47	83.00	73.04	95.33	61.19	93.79	95.97	96.00	79.24	15.30
Canberra	NA	90.91	74.84	81.62	78.54	53.63	68.19	80.66	73.89	93.99	59.37	93.79	97.14	96.00	80.20	14.09
SF	NA	99.72	79.45	84.16	78.24	57.00	78.03	85.16	74.25	**96.00**	62.23	89.44	99.50	94.09	82.87	13.34
MRM	NA	99.72	74.98	84.50	**82.36**	57.47	70.10	**89.16**	66.73	95.33	59.64	92.07	99.50	91.18	*81.75*	14.62
HVDM	NW	90.93	77.77	87.91	77.39	61.00	73.51	76.33	79.80	92.66	63.11	96.95	97.64	97.00	82.46	12.47
	CDWG	94.78	77.77	87.91	79.03	63.63	73.47	76.33	77.01	95.33	66.03	96.42	96.60	98.00	83.25	12.18
	CD	95.64	80.41	89.54	78.03	62.05	73.47	75.66	78.36	95.33	67.50	96.95	97.73	98.00	*83.74*	12.45
	VD	94.24	77.23	88.54	78.69	61.64	73.95	77.00	79.34	94.66	66.34	96.95	97.05	98.00	83.36	12.33
	MI	**100**	79.69	92.54	78.66	63.05	76.25	80.00	76.07	95.33	42.80	**98.89**	98.82	97.00	83.01	16.78
	CVD	98.35	77.77	88.54	78.36	61.59	73.99	75.00	79.97	95.33	64.94	97.47	96.19	96.00	83.35	12.77
HVDM	CDWL	73.35	69.41	88.66	77.86	62.65	32.91	77.47	77.04	93.33	58.02	98.02	97.64	96.00	77.10	18.74
	VDM	93.15	78.52	90.54	78.06	61.98	74.47	75.66	79.53	93.99	63.99	95.89	97.64	97.00	83.11	12.39
	EBL	94.54	78.02	89.54	76.72	61.48	75.85	73.16	79.17	**96.00**	67.76	96.84	99.41	97.00	83.50	12.65
IVDM	NW	81.91	78.23	87.08	72.69	58.39	70.62	80.16	**81.18**	91.99	64.40	97.47	84.37	97.00	80.42	11.78
	CDWG	83.57	78.23	90.08	73.30	60.95	70.14	80.16	76.73	92.66	63.29	96.42	88.85	98.00	80.95	12.02
	CD	84.66	75.36	85.79	73.03	56.74	68.71	83.00	79.23	91.99	66.41	96.42	88.76	97.00	80.55	12.12
	VD	82.74	77.32	87.41	74.72	57.27	68.24	83.16	77.71	91.99	65.27	97.47	87.09	98.00	80.65	12.26
	MI	92.63	77.23	91.54	75.96	**65.13**	70.18	80.00	76.07	92.66	42.80	97.89	90.39	97.00	80.73	15.56
	CVD	87.15	77.73	90.91	74.33	56.88	68.79	82.33	79.45	92.66	65.80	96.95	89.35	96.00	81.41	12.38
IVDM	CDWL	73.35	69.34	91.12	78.20	58.90	71.53	77.61	77.93	92.00	62.89	97.04	90.37	93.99	79.56	12.38
	VDM	83.30	78.15	86.08	73.03	58.92	71.05	80.33	80.90	91.99	64.12	97.47	88.72	97.00	80.85	11.84
	EBL	83.85	77.82	88.91	75.66	57.89	71.61	82.33	79.83	92.66	64.34	97.36	91.03	97.00	*81.56*	12.14
Euclidean	NW	93.37	72.98	84.25	79.27	50.52	70.62	80.16	73.28	**96.00**	62.25	93.79	96.10	96.00	80.66	14.49
	CDWG	94.76	72.98	85.33	79.03	57.84	70.18	80.16	77.15	**96.00**	60.87	98.00	98.36	96.00	82.05	14.07
	CD	96.72	72.52	85.33	77.75	56.74	70.62	75.00	78.40	**96.00**	65.49	95.89	97.28	97.00	81.90	13.80
	VD	95.04	71.67	83.50	80.72	58.39	70.18	78.33	80.69	**96.00**	61.74	96.42	96.69	**98.99**	82.18	13.88
	MI	**100**	75.29	92.16	77.06	63.12	74.26	82.00	76.88	95.33	42.80	96.42	98.82	97.00	82.40	16.75
	CVD	98.07	73.40	91.16	78.09	55.83	69.66	77.83	77.25	95.33	65.54	95.59	97.73	96.00	82.42	14.09
Euclidean	CDWL	94.18	74.47	86.08	80.57	51.05	76.21	76.86	77.14	95.33	61.35	95.98	96.64	96.00	81.68	14.36
	VDM	94.48	73.15	85.33	79.66	60.54	67.80	81.00	74.93	**96.00**	62.25	95.37	97.73	96.00	81.86	13.45
	EBL	95.89	72.98	87.33	79.06	64.61	73.04	79.33	79.65	**96.00**	64.23	95.26	99.41	96.00	*83.29*	12.49
Manhattan	NW	90.91	74.42	85.08	79.60	51.50	73.95	79.00	73.28	93.99	62.24	93.79	97.28	96.00	80.85	13.90
	CDWG	94.50	74.42	86.33	79.06	54.71	73.95	79.00	77.15	95.33	63.97	97.47	96.60	96.00	82.19	13.64
	CD	95.89	74.48	84.33	77.69	57.17	73.87	78.33	74.09	95.33	65.23	96.00	97.86	95.00	81.94	13.25
	VD	94.78	74.36	84.70	80.69	60.30	75.38	80.33	78.83	95.33	64.26	96.00	97.14	97.00	83.01	12.54
	MI	**100**	**82.15**	92.16	77.09	63.65	78.03	81.50	76.88	**96.00**	42.80	97.36	98.23	97.00	83.30	16.50
	CVD	98.35	74.42	90.16	79.63	53.61	75.69	79.66	77.15	**96.00**	65.57	95.59	96.69	98.00	83.12	14.08
Manhattan	CDWL	95.60	77.18	85.08	80.57	51.05	76.68	77.61	76.00	94.00	64.53	95.46	97.05	96.00	82.06	13.89
	VDM	93.65	75.92	86.33	79.93	58.84	75.38	79.66	74.65	95.33	63.11	95.37	97.64	95.00	82.37	12.78
	EBL	95.87	81.32	87.33	79.69	62.05	75.81	80.66	78.01	**96.00**	65.69	95.78	99.41	96.00	*84.12*	12.16
L'Eixample	NW	90.91	74.42	85.08	79.60	51.50	73.95	79.00	73.28	93.99	62.24	93.79	97.28	96.00	80.85	13.90
	CDWG	98.63	74.42	87.33	79.06	59.94	74.43	79.00	76.87	**96.00**	58.75	96.64	97.19	96.00	82.64	13.91
	CD	98.63	71.51	86.54	77.36	48.14	70.57	78.83	79.49	95.33	64.02	95.89	97.73	97.00	81.62	15.51
	VD	**100**	77.34	86.33	76.00	58.17	66.81	80.00	79.15	95.33	60.82	96.00	97.14	98.00	82.39	14.48
	MI	99.44	79.28	**93.16**	80.03	58.99	**79.54**	76.50	78.32	95.33	62.24	96.00	97.14	97.00	84.07	13.48
	CVD	**100**	74.84	92.16	77.69	56.74	75.73	75.33	76.95	95.33	66.94	95.59	96.05	96.00	83.03	13.58
L'Eixample	CDWL	95.60	77.18	85.08	79.26	51.50	73.95	76.28	74.94	94.00	63.10	94.40	97.05	96.00	81.41	14.07
	VDM	**100**	80.90	89.16	80.03	62.93	78.63	83.50	78.22	95.33	66.31	95.78	**99.50**	95.00	85.02	12.05
	EBL	**100**	79.96	90.33	79.33	63.60	76.29	83.83	78.55	95.33	**68.89**	95.26	99.09	96.00	*85.11*	11.83

Table 3. Generalization accuracy results with no weights (NW), global and local weighting schemas.

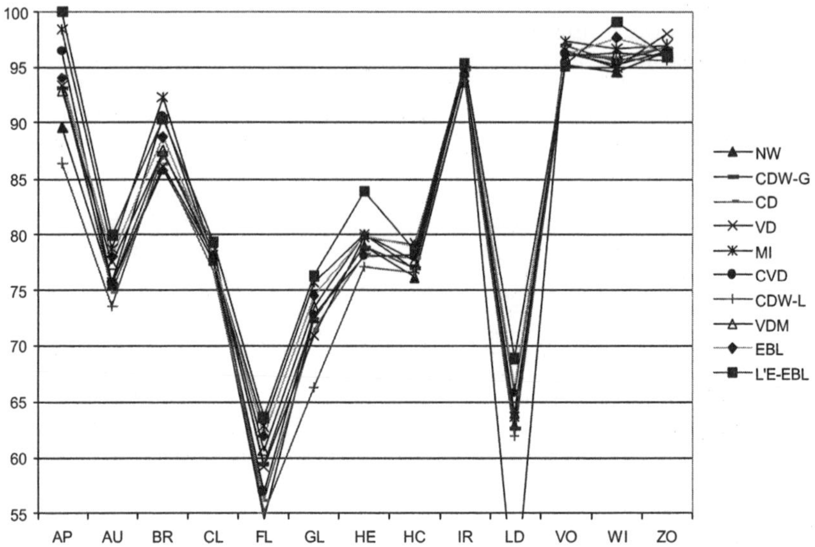

Figure 1a. Average accuracy over all similarity measures for each weighting method and each database

Also, there are four databases where the increase of the accuracy is not very large (Hepatitis, Liver Disorders, Votes and Zoo). We think that the reason is that in those databases, all the features seem to be equally relevant. Thus, good weight assignment cannot improve the predictive accuracy. In fact, it can be argued that perhaps some other relevant features are missed in the database description.

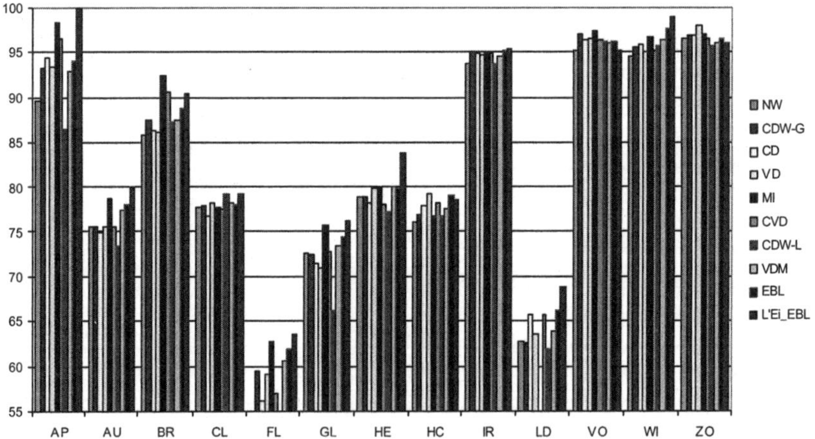

Figure 1b. Average accuracy over all similarity measures for each weighting method and each database

Main conclusion after the comparative study is that local weighting approaches are better than global ones. Obviously this is true within the experimental context undertaken. Thus, all the global measures cannot be tested against all the local measures. But, results obtained seem to be general enough to be extended to other weighting measures.

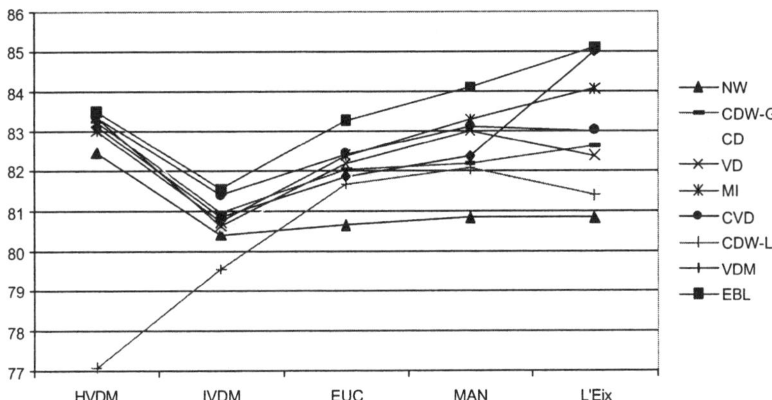

Figure 2. Average accuracy over all databases for each weighting method and each similarity measure.

In this empirical evaluation, it has been confirmed what was found out in a previous study [Núñez *et al.*, 2002]. *L'Eixample* [Sànchez-Marrè *et al.*, 1998] similarity measure, which is very sensitive to weighting schemes and discretization processes, seems to lightly outperform the other measures, in general, although it needs a very accurate weight selection and discretization processes. Although only one table with the CAIM method discretization has been shown, the other tables with the two other methods were equally analysed, and the differences in the accuracy performance are not significant.

A first step has been done in the design of suitable feature weighting techniques, to be used in predictive tasks in instance-based algorithms. Also, the proposed entropy-based local weighting approach (EBL) seems to be a promising feature weighting technique, as its performance is the best within all the weighting schemes. Future work will be focused on the design, study and analysis of other global, and, specially, local weighting algorithms.

Acknowledgments

This work has been partially supported by the Spanish CICyT project TIC2000-1011, and EU project A-TEAM (IST 1999-10176).

References

[1] D. Aha, Feature weighting for lazy learning algorithms, *In H Liu and H. Motoda (Eds.) Feature Extraction, Construction and Selection: A Data Mining Perspective. Norwell MA: Kluwer*, 1998.

[2] C.L. Blake, and C.J. Merz. UCI Repository of machine learning databases [http://www.ics.uci.edu/~mlearn/MLRepository.html]. Irvine, CA: University of California. 1998.

[3] E. Blanzieri and F. Ricci.(1999). Probability Based Metrics for nearest Neighbour classification and Case-Based Reasoning. *Procc. of ICCBR'99*, Munich.

[4] R. H. Creecy, B. M. Masand, S. J. Smith and D. L. Waltz, Trading MIPS and memory for knowledge engineering. *Communications of the ACM* 35:48-64, 1992.

[5] N. Howe, C. Cardie. Examining locally varying weights for nearest neighbor algorithms. *Procc. of the Second International Conference on Case-Based Reasoning*. 1997. pp 455-466.

[7] R. Kerber (1992). Chimerge: Discretization of Numeric Attributes. *In Proceedings of 9th Int'l Conference Artificial Intelligence*.

[8] R. Kohavi, P. Langley, and Y. Yun. The utility of feature weighting in nearest-neighbour algorithms. Procc. of ECML'97.

[9] I. Kononenko, Estimating Attributes: Analysis and extensions of RELIEF, *In Proceedings of European Conference on machine Learning*, Springer, pp-171-182, 1994.

[10] L. Kurgan L. and K.J. Cios (2001). Discretization Algorithm that Uses Class-Attribute Interdependence Maximisation, *Procc. of IC-AI 2001*, pp.980-987, Las Vegas, Nevada.

[11] G.N. Lance and W.T. Williams. Computer Programs for hierarchical polythetic classification ("similarity analyses"), Computer Journal, 9, 60-64, 1966.

[12] T. Mohri and H. Tanaka. An Optimal Weighting Criterion of Case Indexing for Both Numeric and Symbolic Attributes, *Aha, D. W., editor, Case-Based Reasoning papers from the 1994 workshop*, AAAI Press, Menlo Park, CA.

[13] H. Núñez, M. Sànchez-Marrè, U. Cortés, J. Comas, M. Martínez and M. Poch Classifying Environmental System Situations by means of Case-Based Reasoning: a Comparative Study. *Procc of iEMSs'2002*, Lugano, Switzerland, 2002.

[14] M. Sànchez-Marrè, U. Cortés, I. R-Roda, and M. Poch. *L'Eixample* distance: a new similarity measure for case retrieval. *Procc. of 1st Catalan Conference on Artificial Intelligence (CCIA'98)*, ACIA bulletin 14-15 pp. 246-253.Tarragona, Catalonia, EU.

[15] Short R.D. and Fukunaga K. (1981). The optimal distance measure for nearest neighbour classification. *IEEE transactions on Information Theory.* 27:622-627.

[16] C. Stanfill, D. Waltz. Toward Memory-Based Reasoning, *Communications of the ACM,* V. 29, December 1986, pp 1213-1228.

[17] D. Wettschereck, D. W. Aha, and T. Mohri. A review and empirical evaluation of feature weighting methods for a class of lazy learning algorithms. *Artificial Intelligence Review*, Special Issue on lazy learning Algorithms, 1997.

[18] D.R. Wilson and T.R.Martínez. Improved Heterogeneous Distance Functions, *Journal of Artificial Intelligence Research*, 6, 1-34, 1997.

Artificial Intelligence Research and Development
I. Aguiló et al. (Eds.)
IOS Press, 2003

Adding unsupervised learning in the case-base organisation

David Vernet i Bellet, Elisabet Golobardes i Ribé
Grup de Recerca en Sistemes Intel·ligents
Enginyeria i Arquitectura La Salle - Universitat Ramon Llull
{dave,elisabet}@salleurl.edu

Abstract.
This paper describes our ULIC system (Unsupervised Learning in CBR) that organises the Case Base using *clustering* techniques. In previous works we noticed that the organisation of the Case Base in clusters supplied two clear advantages: first, a faster access to the information was provided and second, we can group data in a reliable way, depending on its characteristics. However, one of the problems detected was how to decide the number of clusters in which the information was partitioned. We noticed that the decision taken in a heuristic way implied a loss of information and specially evident problems in order to find the optimum number of clusters. With the aim to solve this drawback, we introduce in this paper a clustering algorithm that predicts in an automatic way the number of partitions must be applied. We specifically have implemented a variant of the WITT Algorithm that we have called *NormWITT* (Normalised WITT); this variant is basically focused on two aspects: firstly, the cohesion factor between the classes is normalised, and, secondly, we adapt the algorithm so as real attributes could be applicable. We show here this variant and how it is included in our system.

1 Introduction

In other works we analised the possibility of restructure the Case Base of our system using the concept of spheres [3, 8]. One sphere is the agrupation of all the cases of the training set depending on the class that classify. So, by means of the calculation of the centroid of each sphere, the operations in the retrieval phase are faster because the cases should be only compared with all the centroids.

In the same way, we noticed that mixing so much cases in the same sphere implied to make several errors in the classification process. Thus, we concluded that in a same sphere we had to distinguish different behaviours and because of this we have introduced clustering techniques into each sphere. We specifically have implemented the K-Means algorithm [6]. It clusters each sphere in K clusters (this technique was called MKM approach). In the figure 1 we show a scheme of the clustering of the Case Base. However, the key to success was based on a good choose of the number of clusters (k) for each sphere. For this reason, this paper presents the introduction of a technique that allows to obtain the optimum number of clusters in an automatic way without any heuristic decision.

The Witt algorithm is an unsupervised algorithm designed by Hanson and Bauer [5] valid for discrete attributes. In this paper we introduce a modification of the algorithm so as to

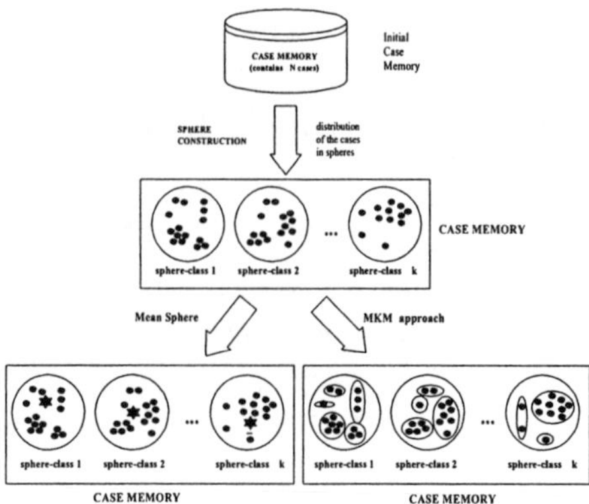

Figure 1: Representation of the system using clustering based on the Mean Sphere and the MKM technique. The ● symbol represents a case and the ⋆ symbol represents the centroid of the sphere.

obtain better results and, in the same way, with the use of discretisation techniques, allow that it was valid for real attributes. The main idea is to achieve an output of the algorithm to indicate in an automatic way the number of clusters in which we have to cluster our spheres.

The paper is distributed as follows: firstly, we study the WITT algorithm and we describe the variations we have applied in it and how we introduce this algorithm in our CBR system. Secondly, we show the testbed and the results obtained. Finally, we present the conclusions and further work.

2   The NormWITT algorithm

In this section we present the algorithm used to cluster the Case Base of our ULIC system. Firstly, we explain the original algorithm and after that, we present the variations applied to perform its introduction in Case-Based Reasoning System.

2.1   The WITT algorithm

In 1989 Hanson and Bauer designed the WITT algorithm [5]. It is located in the inductive learning. It is an unsupervised algorithm, non incremental and it is only valid for discrete attributes.

The algoritm is based on four characteristics:

- The categories tend to have members with no needed characteristics

- The categories have a distribution between their members. So, some members are more representatives than others.

- The categories can be represented using the inter-correlations and the relations between the attributes that describe them.

- The categories appear like a contrast with others.

We have already commented that the representation of the categories is focused on the inter-correlation between the attributes. Is is made using a set of contingence tables for each couple possible attributes. A contingence table is a bidimensional matrix that shows the frequency of co-ocurrence for each possible couple of attributes. The number of contingence tables grows with the quadratic number of attributes.

The WITT algorithm evaluates the categories using the concepts of within-category cohesion (W_c) and the outer-category cohesion (O_c). The cohesion (equation 1) have two aspects into consideration: how much the instances are similar inside a category and how much the instances are different in front of other categories. Its equation is:

$$C_c = \frac{W_c}{O_c} \tag{1}$$

where W_c is the within-category cohesion and O_c is the outer-category cohesion.
The within-category cohesion is computed with the equation 2.

$$W_c = \frac{\sum_{i=1}^{N-1} \sum_{j=i+1}^{N} D_{ij}}{\frac{N(N-1)}{2}} \tag{2}$$

where N is the number of attributes and D_{ij} is the distribution associated to the contingence table of the attributes i and j.

The associated distribution to the contingence tables of two attributes is:

$$D_{ij} = \frac{\sum_{m=1}^{v(i)} \sum_{n=1}^{v(j)} f_{mn} log(f_{mn})}{(\sum_{m=1}^{v(i)} \sum_{n=1}^{v(j)} f_{mn})(log(\sum_{m=1}^{v(i)} \sum_{n=1}^{v(j)} f_{mn}))} \tag{3}$$

where f_{mn} is the frequency of co-ocurrence between the value m of the attribute i and the value n of the attribute j. $v(i)$ is the number of different values that could be token by the attribute i. In the same way for the attribute j. D_{ij} has a range of values that vary between 0.0 (there is no equal characteristic) and 1.0 (when all the attributes are identical).

The outer-category cohesion is computed using the value of B_{ck}:

$$O_c = \frac{\sum_{k=1(k \neq c)}^{L} B_{ck}}{L - 1} \tag{4}$$

where L is the total number of categories and B_{ck} is defined like:

$$B_{ck} = \frac{1}{W_c + W_k - 2W_{c \cup k}} \tag{5}$$

The main algorithm is divided in two parts. The first one, is the preclustering algorithm (figure 2), a greedy algorithm where the evaluation function is the distance between the objects and the condition to finish depends on the parameter F. The categories created are formed with similar instances, depending on the same input parameter. To compute the distance between the objects we have used the Minkowski distance.

After applying the preclustering algorithm the refinement step starts. This step is the most complex one and it includes three operators:

1. Addition of a instance into a category.

2. Creation of new categories.

Figure 2: Algorisme de preclustering

1- Compute the distances between all the
instances and choose the shortest one (D).
Compute the value of $T1 = FxD$

2- Choose the pair of objects
separated by the shortest distance .

    - If the distance is greater than T1 then finish.

    - If the distance is lower combine them in a category.

3- Compute the distance between this new object
and the other and return to the step 2.

3. Fusion of two categories.

In this phase the input parameters are used in order to compute the cohesion of the categories. The first step of the phase consists of computing the cohesion C_c as the result of adding a instance not classified yet, into an existent category. Over all the combinations the one that takes the maximum value of C_c is chosen. If this value is greater to the input parameter T_2, the instance is added into the category and the algorithm is restarted. If the value of cohesion is not much large, it means that the structure of categories created is not adequate. In this case, one category must be created and we start the preclustering algorithm over the remaining instances. But, before considerate the categories returned by the preclustering algorithm as valid, WITT guarantees that these categories were different to the existing ones. In this way, the metric $W_{i\cup j}$ is calculated for all the values of i of the set of existent categories and for all the values of j of the set of categories recently created. If the value is lower than the parameter T_3 for all the cases, the new category is taken as good and it returns to the process of adding instances to the categories. Thus, $W_{i\cup j}$ is computed for all the pairs of existent categories. If this value is greater that T_3 the categories are merged and return to the refinement algorithm. If no new categories are created the algorithm finishes.

2.2 Applied variants - NormWITT

One of the problems detected in the metrics of the original algorithm WITT is that the values of cohesion obtained are really dispersed. Because of this, we proposed the NormWITT algorithm based on two modifications on the computed values of the algorithm. First, we redefine the value of B_{ck} as:

$$B_{ck} = W_{c\cup k} \tag{6}$$

and second the total cohesion value is:

$$C_c = W_c - O_c \tag{7}$$

With this changes we normalise the values obtained and we generate a more stable output.

In the 5 we noticed that if the cohesions of classes c and k were small, the denominator tended to zero and very large values were obtained. Because of the finality of the equation is to compute the sum of the cohesion of the two classes, we have changed the equation by the equation 6, that presents the same behaviour.

In the same way, the original WITT algorithm had problems with the final value of the cohesion. If the cohesion between different classes is very small the results were dispersed. So, we think that a good improvement was to change thr original equation by the equation 7.

3   ULIC framework and integration of the *NormWith* algorithm

The *NormWitt*-based case base organitation presented in this paper is integrated in our previous system, called "Unsupervised Learning in CBR" (*ULIC*), which base based on the *K-Means* algorithm. The main problem of our previous+ approach is that we need to manually specify the number of clusters that *K-Means* will generate for the cases belonging to each domain class. Our new proposal avoids this problem. Figure 3 shows the basic *K-means* algorithm.

Figure 3: Basic K-Means algorithm.

> 1- Initialization. Distribute randomly the cases into K *clusters* and calculate the centroid of each cluster
>
> 2 - Calculation of distance from each case to the centroid of each *cluster*, and asignation of the case to the nearer cluster
>
> 3 - Recalculate the centroids and jump back to step 2
>
> 4 - Repeat steps 2 and 3 until all clusters are stabilized: no case is moved from a cluster to another one.

The *NormWitt* algorithm only works with discrete information. Therefore, we need to use a discretization algorithm is we work with real-valued domains. We have chosen the Fayyad & Irani algorithm [1].

4   Datasets and Results

In this part,we show the data used to test the techniques and the results we have achieved.

4.1   *Test*

To execute all tests we have chosen different datasets/groups. We have used 12 data sets which can be classified in 4 private groups and 8 public groups. Public test groups are *Breast*

Cancer, Sonar, Ionosphere, Multiplexor 11, Iris, Vehicle, Glass i Vowel. All these tests have been acquired from UCI repository [10].

As private data sets, we have used : *Tao-Grid*, a 100Extracted data from an education information system[7]; *Mamografies*, data from FIS project 00/0033 [9, 4] where every sample is a group of microcalcificacions presented in a mammogram in order to make a diagnosis (our data input is a set of matrix); and the last are *Bipsies* [2] Biopsies images digital processed.

In the next table 1, we show a summary of data group testes. For each one we set the name used to present the results, the number of classes and the number of existing instances.

Table 1: Data sets used and their characteristics.

	Problem	Name Used.	Instances	Classes
1	*Biopsies*	*BI*	1027	2
2	*Breast Cancer*	*BR*	699	2
3	*Ensenyament*	*EN*	648	5
4	*Glass*	*GL*	214	6
5	*Ionosphere*	*IO*	351	2
6	*Iris*	*IR*	150	3
7	*Mamografies*	*MA*	216	2
8	*Multiplexor 11*	*MX*	2048	2
9	*Vowel*	*VO*	990	11
10	*Sonar*	*SO*	208	2
11	*Tao-Grid*	*TG*	1888	2
12	*Vehicle*	*VE*	846	4

Table 2: Achieved results applying only Mean sphere. In each problem we show the average percentage obtained , the typical deviation and i CPU time in milliseconds. In the last column, we also show CPU time using traditional CBR 1-NN.

Problema	Encerts	Desv	T CPU	T CPU 1-NN
BI	78.38	4.07	0.78	440.87
BR	96.14	1.83	0.30	108.77
EN	63.12	7.30	0.32	68.65
GL	44.39	9.78	1.15	30.30
IO	72.36	6.31	1.14	208.24
IR	92.67	2.01	0.37	10.41
MA	64.35	9.73	0.69	74.68
MX	50.00	0.16	0.27	409.10
VO	59.80	2.99	0.90	109.61
SO	65.38	11.72	1.87	217.09
TG	83.58	1.87	0.10	92.02
VE	39.24	3.17	1.08	272.16

Table 3: Achieved results using sphere partitioning in cases memory with k-means algorithm. In each problem we show the average percentage obtained , the typical deviation and CPU time (in milliseconds.

Problem	Success	Dev	T CPU
BI	80.04	4.29	0.51
BR	95.72	2.09	0.20
EN	66.39	8.94	0.21
GL	57.66	10.22	1.13
IO	84.48	6.57	0.78
IR	96.71	3.91	0.16
MA	58.02	8.00	0.46
MX	50.00	0.16	0.97
VO	68.59	5.43	0.59
SO	63.59	11.24	1.32
TG	84.24	1.78	0.09
VE	42.64	3.72	0.64

4.2 Results

In this part, we show the results achieved with our ULIC system. For each problem we show the percentage of success, the typical deviation and average time(in milliseconds) to resolve a case. In each data set we have generated 15 random groups of 10-fold stratified cross-validation because we want to ensure the stability of our results (150 executions per problem).

The initial results are shown in table 2. It's the system output when no partition to memory cases is applied. Mean sphere is only used to separate cases according to classifying classes. In the same table, we show the execution time for the case(in milliseconds) using a CBR traditional system.

As shown in table 2, the first result of partitioning cases memory using Mean sphere is an important reduction in time used to resolve the problem. In the last column we have included the time corresponding to traditional 1-NN system to denote the difference obtained.

From these results, we introduce partitioning to original spheres. the first technique used is MKM (Mean K-Means). MKM divides each sphere using *k-means* algorithm. It has the peculiarity that does not generate the number of ideal classes automatically and we had to set it. We have used the value 2 as initial result. The achieved results are shown in table 3 as the previous table.

In the next part, we have included in our ULIC system a partitioning system with automatic divisions. we have now introduced, the technique *NormWitt*, shown previously. This technique configures each sphere in every problem with the ideal number of clusters. In the table 4 achieved results are shown for each data set.

As shown in the table , the results improve in all data sets used, except *Teaching* and *Iris* problems. There are important improves in *Vowel*, *Tao-Grid*, *Vehicle* and *Glass* problems. On other hand, it's important that typical deviation is regular in general or it's reduced and execution time is not affected very much.

Table 4: Achieved results applying spheres partitioning in cases memory using NormWitt algorithm. For each problem, we show the average percentage, typical deviation and CPU time (in milliseconds). A $\sqrt{}$ show the improved results from k-means algorithm.

Problem	Success	Devi	T CPU	
BI	81.02	3.81	0.83	$\sqrt{}$
BR	95.73	2.13	0.54	$\sqrt{}$
EN	66.38	6.01	0.27	
GL	64.70	9.87	7.44	$\sqrt{}$
IO	86.91	4.96	1.36	$\sqrt{}$
IR	96.31	3.74	0.23	
MA	58.58	10.15	0.72	$\sqrt{}$
MX	50.00	0.16	0.48	$\sqrt{}$
VO	91.22	2.61	2.14	$\sqrt{}$
SO	74.62	9.52	2.68	$\sqrt{}$
TG	93.22	1.63	0.08	$\sqrt{}$
VE	58.92	4.37	1.81	$\sqrt{}$

5 Conclusions

We have presented the clustering technique *NormWITT* integrated in our classifier system ULIC. This method is valid with both real and discrete values. We also have not predefine to manually the number of clusters.

We have seen that organising the Case Base in this way implies a great decrement in the CPU time used. The results presented by the NormWITT method improve and it is not bad for CPU time.

As a futher work we want to introduce weighting methods in order to improve the quality of the system. Other clustering techniques must also be tested.

Acknowledgements

This work has been co-financed by the Catalana Occidente and La Salle award. We want to thank the *Ministerio de Ciencia y Tecnología* for his support with the grant TIC2002-04160-C02-02. Finally, we also want to thank *Enginyeria i Arquitectura La Salle* for his support to our Research Group.

References

[1] U. M. Fayyad and K. B. Irani. Multi-interval discretization of continuous-valued attributes for classification learning. In *Proc. of the 13th IJCAI*, pages 1022–1027, Chambery, France, 1993.

[2] J.M. Garrell, E. Golobardes, E. Bernadó, and X. Llorà. Automatic diagnosis with Genetic Algorithms and Case-Based Reasoning. *Elsevier Science Ltd. ISSN 0954-1810*, 13:367–362, 1999.

[3] E. Golobardes. *Aportacions al raonament basat en casos per resoldre problemes de classificació*. PhD thesis, Enginyeria La Salle, Universitat Ramon Llull, Juny 1998.

[4] E. Golobardes, X. Llor, M. Salam, and J. Mart. Computer Aided Diagnosis with Case-Based Reasoning and Genetic Algorithms. In *Journal of Knowledge-Based Systems*, volume 15, pages 45–52, 2002.

[5] S.J. Hanson and M. Bauer. Conceptual clustering, categorization, and polymorphy. *Machine Learning*, 3:343–372, 1989.

[6] J. Hartigan and M. Wong. A k-means clustering algorithm. In *Applied Statistics*, pages 28:100–108. 1979.

[7] D. Vernet i E.Golobardes. Prediction in an Educational Environment using Case-Based Reasoning. In *Proceedings of Learning'00 (in CD)*, Octubre 2000.

[8] D. Vernet i E.Golobardes. An Unsupervised Learning Approach for Case-Based Classifier Systems. In *Proceedings of the 7th UK Workshop on CBR (UKWCBR'2002)*, pages 39–46, Desembre 2002.

[9] J. Martí, J. Español, E. Golobardes, J. Freixenet, R. García, and M. Salamó. Classification of micro-calcifications in digital mammograms using case-based reasonig. In *International Workshop on digital Mammography*, 2000.

[10] C.J. Merz and P.M. Murphy. UCI Repository for Machine Learning Data-Bases [http://www.ics.uci.edu/~mlearn/MLReposi tory.html]. *Irvine, CA: University of California, Department of Information and Computer Science*, 1998.

6. Problem Resolution in AI

Artificial Intelligence Research and Development
I. Aguiló et al. (Eds.)
IOS Press, 2003

Fault Diagnosis based on Detection with Interval Models

G. CALDERON-ESPINOZA[†], J. ARMENGOL[†] and A. ALDEA[‡]
[†]*Departament d' Electrònica, Informàtica i Automàtica.*
Universitat de Girona Campus Montilivi. E-17071 Girona (Spain)
[‡]*Departament d' Informàtica i Matemàtica.*
Universitat Rovira i Virgili Campus Sescelades. Tarragona (Spain)
e-mail: (gcalder,armengol)@eia.udg.es, aaldea@etse.urv.es

Abstract. False alarms in fault detection approaches are often caused by errors in the modelling process. One problem in the modelling task is the uncertainty present in model parameters and the input/output measurements from sensor. Fault detection based on analytical redundancy by using interval models can be considered if knowledge about the system behavior is imprecise. These models make explicit the uncertainty and simulation of them generates numerical envelopes which are formed by all possible behaviors of an uncertain system starting from an initial state.

This paper proposes the use of fault detection based on Modal Interval Analysis (MIA) in fault diagnosis. The use of MIA reduce spurious solutions often present in qualitative methods and which are cause of missed alarms. In addition, the system can avoid false alarms because when a fault is detected it means that a fault really exists. Structural analysis is proposed to determinate which equations will be simulated and after detection task has finished, a tendency analysis is proposed to identify if the deviation of variables is toward smaller or bigger values than those included in the simulated envelopes. A simple example of this proposed architecture is shown and results are presented.

1 Introduction

One purpose of monitoring industrial processes is to avoid and to correct the deviations of normal behavior. In Fault detection and isolation (FDI) a fault is defined as an unpermitted deviation of at least one characteristic property of a variable from an acceptable behavior and according to Isermann the fault is a state that may lead to a malfunction or failure of the system [1]. Faults in a process can stop operation, reduce the production and degrade the equipment, in the worst case can cause accidents.It is for this reason that fault detection and diagnosis systems are necessary to guarantee good operation in processes. Fault detection and diagnosis is an active research area in industries such as automotive, electric and chemistry.

The goal of this paper is to propose a methodology to diagnose faults in dynamic systems like electronic circuits or in the equivalent mechanical and chemical processes. One technique used to diagnose faults is Model-Based Diagnosis (MBD) where the main task is to compare the observed behavior with the predicted one starting from the model in order to detect discrepancies. Under assumption that the model is correct all discrepancies between observed measurements and predicted ones are considered as faults. We start from this basic ideas to propose a fault detection and diagnosis system.

The main problem is that these two behaviors (observed and predicted) are seldom the same because the model is inaccurate due to the uncertainty in the system and modelling errors (hypotheses, assumptions, simplifications, linearizations, etc). One way to take the uncertainty into account is considering it in the modelling procedure. Interval models can represent the uncertainty associated to the systems and intervals can also represent uncertainty in measurements. The reference behavior for fault detection is obtained by simulation of the interval model [2]. In an interval model the parameters are intervals. An example is a n-th order SISO (Single Input, Single Output) system represented by the following difference equation where u are inputs, T the sampling time, and a or b are parameters of the system represented by intervals:

$$y_t = \sum_{i=1}^{m+1} a_i y_{t-iT} + \sum_{j=1}^{p+1} b_j u_{t-jT} \tag{1}$$

The simulation of a real-valued model produces a trajectory for each output variable which is a curve representing the evolution of the variable of the system across time: $y_r(t)$. In the case of an interval model, as it is a set of models indeed, a set of curves (a band) represents the evolution of each variable. The limits of the band are:

$$Y_r(t) = [min(y_r(t)), max(y_r(t))] \tag{2}$$

To compute the band limits is necessary to compute the range of a function in a parameter space at each simulation step, which is a task related to global optimization and usually needs an important computation effort. With the Modal Interval Simulator (MIS) [3] similar results can be obtained at a lower cost by calculating closer external estimations ($Y_{rex}(t)$)of the range of the function at each iteration. After infinite iterations it would calculate the exact range, but it stops when the estimation is sufficiently close to detect the fault, thus saving much computational effort when a fault is detected. However if there is not a fault and the simulator never stops. This drawback can be overcome by using an internal estimation ($Y_{rin}(t)$). The simultaneous use of internal and external estimations obtain the same fault detection results that $Y_r(t)$ but with a much lower computation effort. Both estimations form an error-bounded estimation because although $Y_r(t)$ is not known, it is known that $Y_{rin}(t) \subseteq Y_r(t) \subseteq Y_{rex}(t)$. A useful tool to compute error-bounded estimations of the range of a function in a parameter space is Modal Interval Analysis (MIA) [4] which is an extension of the interval arithmetic.

In this paper we present the use of MIS to generate approximations of envelopes and their use in fault detection and diagnosis by means of structural and tendency analysis. In section 2 we make an introduction to model-based diagnosis system and the problem in simulation due to the modelling process. In section 3 we explain the the detection method based on interval models and modal interval analysis. Section 4 describes the use of structural analysis proposed by Staroswiecki to make fault isolation. Our approach integrating fault detection, structural analysis and tendency analysis is described in section 5. It concludes with an application in a simple electric circuit whose results could be equivalent to a mechanic or hydraulic system.

2 Model-Based Diagnosis

Model-based diagnosis systems reason starting from a model. The model represents in an explicit way the correct behavior of the system to be diagnosed. If behavior of the observed situation is different from the estimation carried out by the model to the same situation, the system concludes that there is a fault. A later analysis about differences tries to identify the component which is cause of the fault [5].

A model about the system to be diagnosed is used to make model-based diagnosis, the model can be well structured according to physical laws or can be made from human experience and data from the process, or combination of both. MBD is based on comparing observations about behavior and the predictions from a model about the process (Figure 1). Model-based diagnosis depends on the model to make diagnosis.

Figure 1: Model-Based diagnosis

Model based diagnosis according to literature can be described in the following way: a) A *system model* which includes a description about the structure of the system and the expected behaviors (normal) from each one of the components. b) A set of *observations* about the current behavior of the system obtained from measurements and c) A set of *symptoms* such as discrepancies between the current behavior (observations) and the expected behavior (prediction by using the model)

2.1 Simulation Problem

As we mentioned above, to make model-based diagnosis a model of the system is required, but some problems arise in modelling task. The parameters that describe the behavior of a large class of man-made systems such as chemical plants are continuous and time-varying, typically modelled by a set of nonlinear differential equations that relate outputs, inputs and system parameters. Solution methods exist if equations are linear. For complex and nonlinear equations numerical techniques may be applied but the solution methods are computationally complex and there is no guarantee that they will converge. Furthermore, quantitative solution methods require complete and precise information to produce reliable results [6]. Quantitative or numeric simulation makes numeric predictions of the system states that which implies the prediction of values of the variables at determined time.

On the other hand the qualitative simulation makes a prediction of the qualitative states in which the system use a non-numeric model. It distinguishes qualitatively (with labels, not with numerical values) the states where the system will be or the values that the variables will have in the future. The qualitative simulators are used when the knowledge about the system has important limitations such as the structure or behavior of the system is not complete or when there are no models of the system, also this simulation is used when it is interesting to have qualitative results.

In qualitative methods the model is often used to simulate the behavior of the process on-line by using some qualitative simulator. Qualitative models present ambiguity, they have no time information and they usually are not correct due to the process of simplification. Due to the form in which they represent uncertainty, some methods such as qualitative fuzzy simulation produce false solutions because of spurious solutions. If quantitative information is added to qualitative methods in order to enhance them, uncertainty of the qualitative state variables is reduced.

The number of qualitative simulators that integrate quantitative knowledge is increasing to deal with these problems, some of them are: QSIM (Qualitative Simulator) [7] where each variable is represented by its value and the value of its derivative. The value of the derivative is expressed in a qualitative way: *inc* for increasing (positive derivative), *dec* for decreasing (negative derivative) or *std* for steady (zero derivative, stationary variable). The value of the variable can be expressed also in a purely qualitative form or, if more information is available, its value space can be split in more than three parts (labels) using landmarks. The model of a system is represented by the relations between its variables (algebraic operations, derivative, monotonicity). Another simulator is FuSim (Fuzzy Qualitative Simulator) [8] which is an extension of QSIM and where values of variables are given by intervals instead of qualitative labels. It is base on the same two phases than QSIM: qualitative generation of all possible transitions and filtering, using numeric information, of the transitions that do not fulfil the constraints. FuSim indicates the time that the system will remain in each state. CA-EN [9] is a model-based supervision system for on-line applications. It includes a semi-qualitative simulator that is based on causal and constraint reasoning. It uses an explicit representation of time given by a logical clock. The value of a variable is an interval of the real axis. The models are represented using two levels: a local constraint level where the influences between the variables are made by the use of an oriented graph and a global constraint level where constraints derived from physical laws are functions relating numeric variables.

Combination of quantitative and qualitative methods are semi-qualitative ones. The semi-qualitative simulation gives quantitative and qualitative information of the predicted states of the system. It combines advantages of the qualitative simulation (ability to work with limited information) and advantages of quantitative simulation (quantitative prediction). Semi-qualitative models are imprecise but more accurate. Methods that use interval arithmetic are defined as semi-qualitative methods because they use more than numeric knowledge. Interval simulation generates numeric envelopes from models. An envelope is formed by all possible behaviors of an uncertain system starting from a specific initial state which can be precise or not, these behaviors form a set of trajectories across time. The generation of envelopes is a difficult goal or even impossible so in many cases approximations to it are obtained. One approximation is an overbounded envelope which is complete but not sound, this means the envelope is wider than the exact one. Another approximation is an underbounded envelope which is sound but not complete, this means the envelope is tighter than the exact one.

3 Fault Detection Module

Model-based fault detection consist on comparing the measurements of variables with the predictions obtained by the simulation of the model. But in real world measurements and predictions are not equal due to uncertainty present in sensors and models. The difference between measurements and predictions is called *residuals*.

The task of residuals evaluation is based on setting thresholds used to decide if there is a fault or not. If the residual is bigger than the tolerance value it is said that a fault exits. Small values of threshold can cause false alarms and big values can cause missed alarms. Generating envelopes is one method to represent these thresholds by adding and subtracting specific values of tolerance to the behavior of the nominal model.

3.1 Envelopes Generation

To calculate an exact envelope that includes all the correct behaviors of a system it is a difficult task and normally it is impossible. A method is to determinate the function range in the parameter space by using global optimization techniques to find maximum and minimum values of a function, but often this task is untractable.

If envelopes are used in fault detection it is said that a fault exists if the measurement is outside of the envelope. This is not always true due to the dynamics of the system since the measurement can be inside the envelope during a time after a fault has taken place and it can not be detected immediately but until after a time. Calculate an exact envelope needs an important computational effort and most of the times results are approximations due to errors of rounding, truncation, etc.

When envelopes are used in fault detection, their characteristics are very important. On one hand an underbounded envelope is tighter than the exact one, so all the points inside belong to the output system, but there are too outputs outside of the envelope that belong to the set of outputs of the system. It is for that reason that if underbounded envelopes are used for fault detection, there can be missed alarms and false alarms.

On the other hand an overbounded envelope is wider than the exact one so all the possible outputs of the system are inside the envelope, but there are points inside that can not belong to any of these outputs. For that reason if overbounded envelopes are used for fault detection, there can be missed alarms too but not false alarms. A deep analysis of the envelopes is presented in [10].

To detect faults we use the Modal Interval Simulator (MIS) [3]. This simulator calculates both envelopes in a simultaneous way, that which defines 3 areas and it guarantees that a fault exits when the measurement is in the outer zone (out of the overbounded envelope), however if the measurement is inside this envelope there can be a fault and not be detected. This is because overbounded envelope includes values that do not belong to the values space of the system represented by interval models. Another reason is the dynamics of the system so more time is needed to be detected. Figure 2 shows the 3 zones generated by the simulator and used for fault detection.

The simulator uses a branch-and-bound algorithm to compute these error-bounded estimations. To calculate the envelopes in a time instant, it uses the values of the interval measurement from the past instant t-window. Using algorithms based on Interval Arithmetic, overbounded results are obtained when there are multi-incidences in the function at a time point because they are not considered. Multi-incidences can be reduced using Modal Interval Analysis (MIA)[4] an extension of Interval Analysis. MIS simulates the behavior of systems with interval models, inputs and initial states.

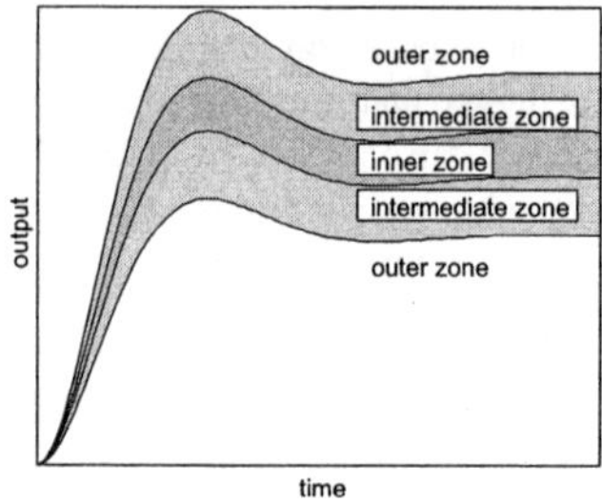

Figure 2: Three zones defined by error-bounded envelopes

4   Fault Isolation Module

The fault isolation module uses the Structural Analysis proposed by Staroswiecki [11] which is the analysis of the structural properties of models. It only represents the links between the variables and the parameters present in the model. It is independent from the values of parameters, for that reason it is independent in the form under this model is expressed (quantitative or qualitative).

In the structural analysis the model of the system is considered as a set of constraints that are applied to a set of variables. Among these variables there is a subset with known values. This subset is formed by sensors present in the process together with the control variables. The set of constraints is given by component models of the system which form the elementary analytical relations (EAR) between the values of variables from physical laws.

The structure of the model is a matrix that represent links between the variables (known and unknown) and the constraints. The matrix contains binary relations between constraints and variables where 1 represents that the constraint applies to the variable and 0 otherwise. Analytical redundancy relations (ARR) defined as relations between known variables can be derived by combining the measurement model with the process model and eliminating unknown variables. These relations will be used in FDI to check the consistency between the observed and the predicted behavior of the process. A constraint that applies only to known variables and parameters constitutes an analytical redundancy relation (ARR) and it can be evaluated from only observed variables, and which can be used in fault detection task [12]. To determinate the redundancy relations is not easy, graph theory and causality conditions are some techniques to deal with this problem to guarantee calculability of the residuals.

The binary vector formed by the set of ARR and the set of faults constitute the fault signature where an "1" represents that some component of the fault is involved in the corresponding ARR and a "0" in the opposite case.

5   Our approach

The system to detect faults introduced above uses interval models to predict the behavior. Unprecise parameters and measurements are considered in the equations of the model. The simulator MIS predicts behavior with the same inputs to the system and two envelopes are computed. Interval analysis make possible fault detection when a measurement is outside of the external envelope indicating in this way that a fault exists.

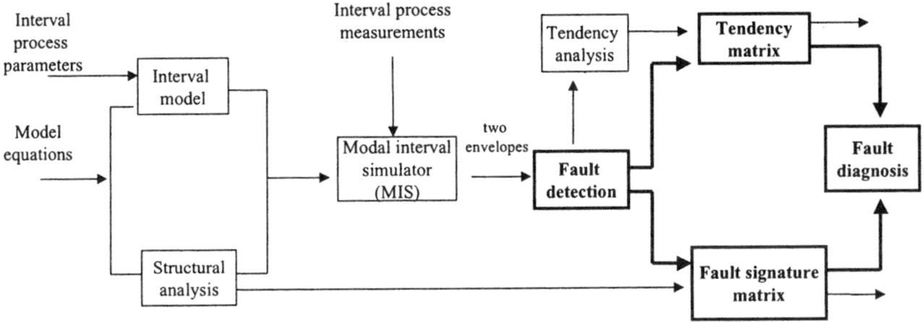

Figure 3: Fault detection and diagnosis

Our approach (Figure 3) consist of two parts: The first one is on-line and second one is off-line. The first part is formed by the following steps: 1) To acquire the knowledge about elementary models of components obtained from elemental physical laws. Knowledge about the system to be diagnose will be presented by a set of equations. 2) To obtain analytical redundancy relations from the structure of the system in order to get the fault signature matrix. 3) To get the characteristic of tendencies for the different classes of faults.

Second part (considered on-line) consists on simulation of the model. Simulation of ARRs is carried on by MIS and the fault detection results are compared firstly with the signature matrix obtained by the structural analysis and secondly the results are compared with tendency matrix. The result is a set of possible diagnostics of the fault detected by the interval simulator. In Figure 3 second part to make diagnosis is indicated in black blocks.

One reason for developing a trend analysis is the subsequent use of the classified trends in fault diagnosis. Typical systems that depend on the use of "event signatures" for fault diagnosis have three main components: (i) A *language* to represent the trends (ii) A technique to *identify* the trends and (iii) A *mapping* from trends to operational conditions [13].

Our tendency analysis consist on analyzing the measurements and the envelopes generated by the interval simulator for each type of fault. In this way we can obtain characteristics from types of faults in order to be able to reduce the fault candidates. With this tendency analysis we can build a fault matrix based on observed deviation of measurements compared with envelopes. We indicate the type of tendency giving information in the form of the following "pair". The pair is formed with a variable and a symbol which indicates the type of deviation:

$$[var, symbol]$$

Where a (-) symbol indicates deviation of the variables toward smaller values, (+) symbol indicates deviation toward bigger values than those included in the envelopes and (o) indicates that the variable is included in the envelopes of normal behavior and no deviation has been detected or that it has been impossible to detect some deviation. In Figure 4 we show these classification of tendencies.

6   Results with a case study

A simple case study has been chosen to test our approach for fault detection and diagnosis. The case study consists on an electric circuit formed by a serial resistor with an inductor in

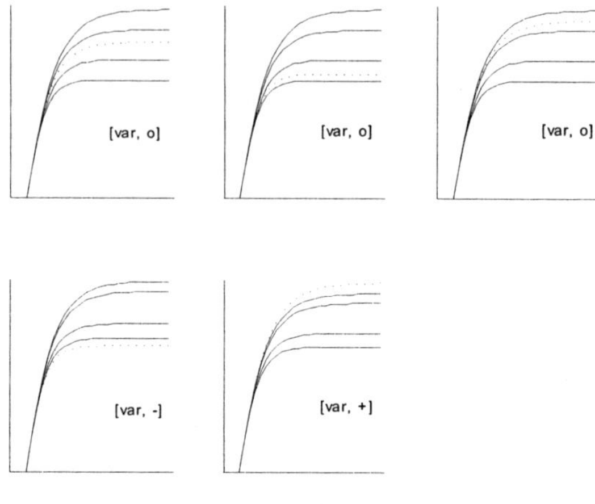

Figure 4: Classification of tendencies

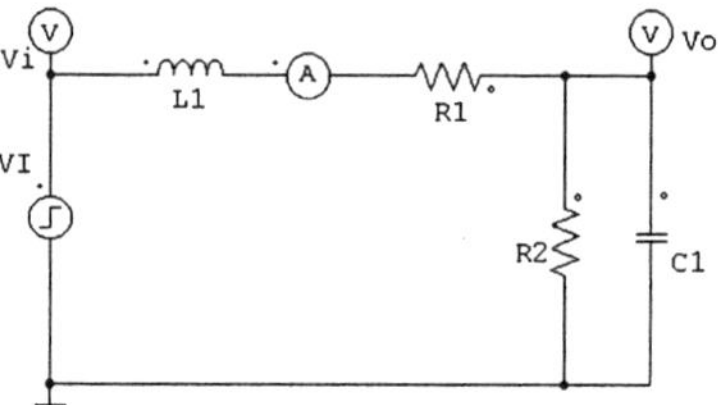

Figure 5: Simple electric circuit

addition with a capacitor in parallel with a second resistor (Figure 5) has been chosen to test our approach. The first step is to have the knowledge about elementary models of components obtained from elemental physical laws, this knowledge is represented in Table 1.

6.1   Structural Analysis

Using structural analysis proposed by Staroswiecki we can obtain analytical redundancy relations and isolate faults. Firstly we obtain the structure of the model in form of matrix using the following representations: in causal relations like an ordinary differential equation, inputs are represented by an "I" and outputs by an "O". In case of no causal relations there is no difference between input and output variables and they are represented by the letter "P" indicating that they are present. The result is shown in the Table 2.

Using elimination rules to deduce ARR we can obtain a set of ARR for diagnosis purpose. The rules are applied to the structural matrix by elimination of unknown variables in the elementary analytical relations (EAR). The rules to obtain the ARR used in [14] have been used. These rules allow to eliminate one variable at each step. The rules vary depending on causality of the used EAR. In this example we use only two of the rules and are the following:

- "Non causal relation". If the same variable appear in two EAR non-causals. It can be

Table 1: Elementary models of the circuit

	Elementary relation	Component
M_1	$L\frac{di}{dt} = Vi - Vo - V_{R1}$	L
M_2	$V_{R1} = R1 * I$	R_1
M_3	$C\frac{dVo}{dt} = I - I_{R2}$	R_2
M_4	$I_{R2} = \frac{Vo}{R2}$	C
M_5	$Vi_m = Vi$	voltage input
M_6	$I_m = I$	current sensor
M_7	$Vo_m = Vo$	voltage sensor

Table 2: Structure of the model

	L	R1	R2	C	Vi	I	Vo	V_{R1}	I_{R2}
M_1	O				I	O	I	I	
M_2		P				P		P	
M_3			O		I	O			I
M_4			P				P		P
M_5					P				
M_6						P			
M_7							P		

eliminated generating a new relation that contain the set of variables of previous relations except the eliminated one.

- "Causal input elimination". Variables of the non-causal relation should be added as inputs of the new causal relation except the eliminated variable. On the other hand, the output of the new causal relation remains the same than the original causal relation.

After using elimination rules the matrix of structure is in the form of Table 3. Taking into account just the components that we want to diagnose, we have the fault signature matrix. Where M_{12567} is ARR1 and the equation obtained from M_{3467} is ARR2 (see Table 4).

6.2 Tendency Analysis

Taking the tendency into account of the different faults we obtain the characteristic behavior of eight type of faults depending on the localization of the measurement respect to the envelope generated by the detection system. The results are shown in Table 5.

Table 3: Analytic redundancy relations

	L	R1	R2	C	Vi	I	Vo	V_{R1}	I_{R2}
M_{12567}	O	I				O			
M_{3467}			I	O			O		

Table 4: Current fault signature

	L	R1	R2	C
ARR1	1	1	0	0
ARR2	0	0	1	1

Table 5: Tendency analysis

Fault number	Type of fault	Measurement property
1	R1 > normal	< Il normal
2	R1 < normal	> Il normal
3	L1 > normal	< Il normal
4	L1 < normal	> Il normal
5	R2 > normal	> Vo normal
6	R2 < normal	< Vo normal
7	C1 > normal	< Vo normal
8	C1 < normal	> Vo normal

In this way we can obtain a matrix formed by pairs with the tendency classification of faults presented in Table 6.

6.3   Simulation and Fault Diagnosis

Simulation results in MIS of two ARRs are shown in form of graphics. In Figure 6 a fault has been detected, while Figure 8 indicates that no fault has been detected. The actual fault signature is resumen in the following way: $ARR_1 = 1$ and $ARR_2 = 0$.

According to the signature fault the first diagnosis is that components L1 and R1 are fault candidates, but there are four possible type of faults that involve these components, these faults are: a) R1 bigger than normal value b) R1 smaller than normal value c) L1 bigger than normal value and d) L1 smaller than normal value. The results of fault detection presented

Table 6: Matrix of tendencies

	[Vo, -]	[Vo, o]	[Vo, +]
$[Il, -]$	Fault 1	Fault 1	Fault 1
	Fault 3	Fault 3	Fault 3
	Fault 6		Fault 5
	Fault 7		Fault 8
$[Il, o]$	Fault 6	No Fault	Fault 5
	Fault 7		Fault 8
$[Il, +]$	Fault 2	Fault 2	Fault 2
	Fault 4	Fault 4	Fault 4
	Fault 6		Fault 5
	Fault 7		Fault 8

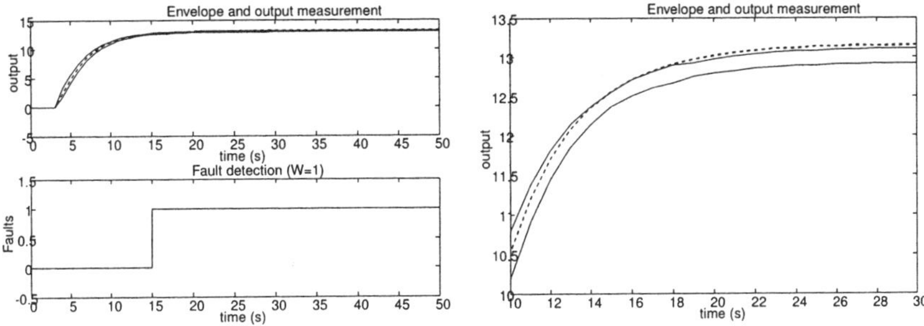

Figure 6: Fault detection in ARR1   Figure 7: Zoom of fault detection in ARR1

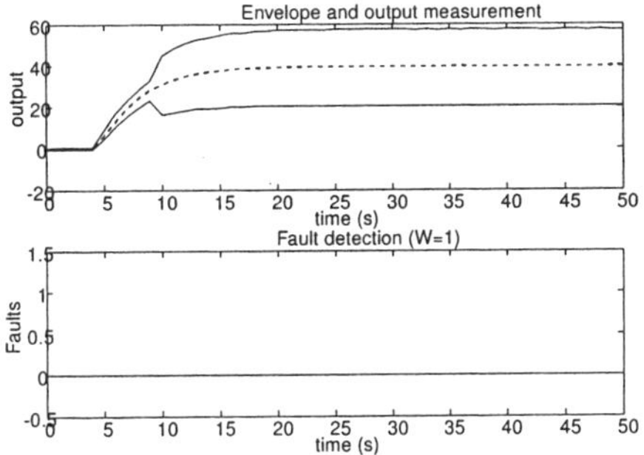

Figure 8: Fault detection in ARR2

in the graphs have the characteristic of tendency $[Il, +]$ in ARR1 (Figures 6, 7) because the measurement is outside the envelope with values bigger than those included in the exact envelope. In ARR2 (Figure 8) the characteristic of tendency is $[Vo, o]$ because no fault has been detected. Results are resumed in the following way:

$$ARR1 \rightarrow [Il, +]$$
$$ARR2 \rightarrow [Vo, o]$$

According to the matrix that shows the tendency analysis, this both tendencies cross in Fault 2 and Fault 4 given as possible diagnosis of the detected fault by the interval simulator.

7 Conclusions

Representing uncertainty in parameters and measurements by means of intervals makes models less precise but more accurate. If we use these models in a fault detection system false alarms are reduced. In this paper we have described the way of using modal interval analysis in fault detection. We have also proposed a methodology to reduce the number of fault candidates in the diagnosis task by means of structural and tendency analysis of faults. The system has the advantages of representing imprecision in models that always is present in physical systems. Another efficient characteristic is related with avoiding false alarms. In the shown example from eight possible faults we have reduced them to two.

Future directions of this work consist of improving the diagnosis system by means of analyzing envelopes to create a possible fault library in order to compare the envelopes generated during detection process, this work includes finding new classes of faults and studying overlapping between faults. Another research topic is the use of different kind of knowledge such as causality to discriminate classes and to reduce the time used in finding the minimal set of possible faults presented in some process.

Acknowledgment

This work has been possible with the support of Agencia Española de Cooperación Internacional.

References

[1] R. Isermann, Supervision, fault detection and fault-diagnosis methods- an introduction, Control Engineering Practice. **5** (1997) 639–652.

[2] J. Armengol, J. Vehi, M.A. Sainz and P. Herrero, Fault detection in a pilot plant using interval models and multiple sliding time windows, 5th IFAC Symposium on Fault Detection, Supervision and Safety of Technical Processes, Washington, D.C., USA. Safeprocess (2003).

[3] J. Armengol, Application of Modal Interval Analysis to the simulation of the behavior of dynamic systems with uncertain parameters, Phd thesis Universitat de Girona (1999).

[4] Group SIGLA /X, Modal intervals, basic tutorial, Applications of Interval Analysis to Systems and Control (MISC'99), Universitat de Girona, Spain. (1999).

[5] J. Gertler, Fault detection and diagnosis in engineering systems, Mancel Dekker Inc. (1998).

[6] G. Biswas, R. Kapadia, and Xudong W.Yu, Combined qualitative-quantitative steady-state diagnosis of continuous-valued systems, IEEE Transactions on systems, man, and cybernetics-Part A:Systems and humans. **27** (1997).

[7] B.J. Kuipers, Qualitative simulation, Artificial Intelligence. **29** (1986) 289–338.

[8] Q. Shen and R. Leitch, Fuzzy qualitative simulation, IEEE Transactions on Systems, Man, and Cybernetics. **23** (1993).

[9] L. Travé-Massuyés and R. Milne, Gas-turbine condition monitoring using qualitative model-based diagnosis, IEEE Expert, Qualitative Reasoning. (1997).

[10] J. Armengol, L. Travé-Massuyés, J. Vehi, and J.L. de la Rosa, A survey on interval model simulators and their properties related to fault detection, Annual Reviews in Control. **24** (2000) 31–39.

[11] M. Staroswiecki and P. Declerck, Analytical redundancy in non-linear interconnected systems by means of structural analysis, IFAC Advanced information processing in automatic control (AIAPAC'89), Nancy, France. (1989) 51–55.

[12] M-O Cordier, P. Dague, M. Dumas, F. Lévy, J. Montmain, M. Staroswiecki, and L.Travé-Massuyé, A comparative analysis of AI and control theory approaches to model-based diagnosis, 14th European control conference on Artificial Intelligence, Germany. (2000) 136–140.

[13] S. Dash, R. Rengaswamy, and V. Venkatasubramanian, Fuzzy-logic based trend classification for fault diagnosis of chemical processes, Computers and Chemical Engineering. **27** (2002) 347–362.

[14] V. Puig, J. Quevedo, T. Escobet, and S. Tornil, Model based fault diagnosis of dynamic processes: comparing FDI and DX methodologies, IV Jornadas de ARCA Sistemas cualitativos y diagnosis. Barcelona, Spain. (2002) 91–99.

Artificial Intelligence Research and Development
I. Aguiló et al. (Eds.)
IOS Press, 2003

331

Human Sequence Evaluation: towards Knowledge-based Scene Interpretations

Jordi Gonzàlez, Javier Varona, F.Xavier Roca and J.J. Villanueva
Computer Vision Center & Dept. d'Informàtica,
Edifici O, Universitat Autònoma de Barcelona (UAB), 08193 Bellaterra, Spain
{poal, xaviv, xavir, villanueva}@cvc.uab.es

Abstract. The term *Video Surveillance* refers to generic systems which describe the actions and interactions of different agents within complex scenes in real-time. In fact, video surveillance is a particular domain of the *Image Sequence Evaluation* framework, which provides a modular scheme to transform image data into high-level descriptions. In this paper, we are centered on human behavior description, denoted to as *Human Sequence Evaluation*. By considering the structure proposed in [9], we adapt the modules involved to cope with humans, and analyze the a-priori knowledge required to design such systems.

1 Introduction

Increasingly, current research in computer vision attempts to deal with video sequences. Improvement of computer resources in terms of capacity and speed, has allowed to develop new algorithms which can cope with the required amount of data. As a result, a new application domain, that benefits from these techniques, has emerged, referred to as *Video Surveillance*. The authors of [4] define it as describing the actions and interactions of different agents (usually humans or vehicles) within complex scenes in real-time. Typical applications are security systems (for example, to monitor buildings or parking lots in order to detect intruders), traffic flow analysis, and military applications.

Due to the complex task to be achieved by Video Surveillance systems, these are subdivided into modules to be robust enough in order to deal with noisy data and to recover from erroneous results generated at any module. Fortunately, it is possible to design applications, which can confront a particular problem, by using a set of specific constraints which reflect different requirements of the application domain. However, the analysis of image sequences involving humans implies additional difficulties. Typically, appearance variability is found in these sequences due to acquisition conditions, clothes, lighting and posture changes.

In this paper, we first review the Image Sequence Evaluation (ISE) framework [9]. ISE systems provide a generic framework which can cope with image sequences, dealing with the required steps from data acquisition to high-level reasoning. Next, we review the problem of handling sequences which involve humans by defining a specific application of ISE called Human Sequence Evaluation (HSE). Subsequently, such an analysis will imply the identification of the a-priori knowledge, in terms of sources of information, required to design a system for HSE. Lastly, conclusions are provided.

2   Image Sequence Evaluation

Video surveillance systems are conceived to describe what is happening in a scene by means of *event* analysis. We consider an event as a noticeable change in the scene, together with the conditions in which these changes are observed. Actually, we will assume that motion analysis is mainly performed based on change detection.

As described in [9], video surveillance systems are a particular domain of generic *Image Sequence Evaluation* (ISE) systems which accomplish two tasks. First, they transform image data into high-level descriptions. As a consequence, the existence of such an abstraction process is reflected in ISE by means of intermediate representations. Second, they are capable to reason about generated descriptions.

In order to achieve such a goal, several issues are involved. First, agents should be properly located within the scene. After that, a motion description for each agent is generated by considering the preceding frames. A sequence of motion descriptions constitutes a *pattern* to be compared with previously learned patterns. The history of recognized patterns is the key to infer the developments in the scene. Lastly, a description of such recorded developments is generated using signal processes or conceptual terms. The former implies to activate different notice or warning signals (such as acoustic alarms, lights, or control signals to mechanisms of access) depending on the observed patterns of motion. A conceptual description requires to associate natural language components, such as verbs, nouns, adjectives, or entire texts, to observations of temporal variations. Conceptual descriptions are preferred to be built in a suitable way (for example, in terms of logic representations), so further reasoning (by means of algorithmic inference engines) about the extracted descriptions is feasible.

It is important to note that *understanding* a scene (considered as dealing with conceptual descriptions) requires of knowledge about the task domain (commonly referred to as *context*). By means of context, the problem domain is constrained, so interpretations are restricted to those which are consistent with such knowledge. Thus, only meaningful semantic descriptions will be generated. Context can be built up from a combination of two sources of knowledge [10]: the physical environment (i.e. representation of its structural properties) and the symbolic world (i.e. representation of rules, prepositions, predicates and algorithms).

3   HSE Architecture

We restrict our domain to human behavior description: we will name *Human Sequence Evaluation* (HSE) the specific application of Image Sequence Evaluation in which the involved agents are humans. As commented before, the complexity of a HSE system suggests to describe these systems by means of a modular scheme. We will consider the structure proposed in [9], which is shown in Fig. 1.

Here we describe the interpretation of human movements as a transformation process of raw video signals into high-level, qualitative descriptions. This abstraction process is subdivided into layers and in each layer, both a suitable representation and the required knowledge are considered. Thus, the combination in each layer of knowledge provided by models and heuristics (by means of assumptions or restrictions) is exploited to reduce the complexity of the problem domain.

The first level is called the *Signal Level*. This layer provides the image data and information about camera parameters (for example, in order to perform calibration). Thus, it is possible to determine the viewing conditions (the recording technique, the viewpoint and the

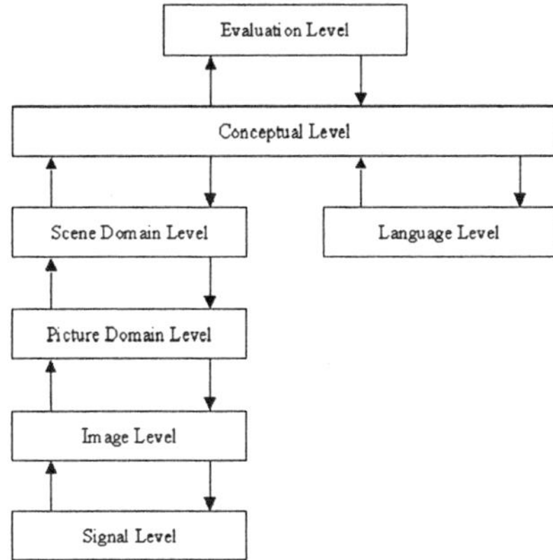

Figure 1: Modular Scheme for Human Sequence Evaluation [9].

image resolution). The camera configuration can also be modified, thus allowing different recording conditions (for example, when the camera zooms in on a human in the scene).

The next level is called the *Image Level*. Here, the sequence of raw image data (called low-level image *measurements*) is processed in order to segment the humans within the scene. This segmentation process is usually performed by means of motion analysis or background modeling. The former implies the extraction of motion information from a sequence of images, which can be achieved by using motion correspondence and optical flow [3]. The latter is scene-dependent: a suitable background model of the scene is computed to robustly determine the foreground pixels (it is usually assumed that detected foreground regions are due to humans). As a result, information about moving or foreground regions in the image (for example, in the form of moving blobs) is provided to the following layer, the *Picture Domain Level*.

In the Picture Domain Level, a 2-D picture-based representation of the human body is calculated from the segmented regions of the Image Level. This representation constitutes the *Picture Domain Cues* (PDC, see [7]), for example, the bounding box or the centroid of the blob, which can be used to perform picture domain-based tracking. This tracking process computes the estimated geometric representation (called the *state* of the agent) of the human body in the image at the next time step. Possible segmentation errors generated at the Image Level should be taken into account here (by means of the context, for example). The tracking process requires a motion model, and the expected state can be sent back to the Image Level in order to assist the segmentation process. The estimated state of the agent is also made available to the *Scene Domain Level*. Furthermore, the picture-based representation of the human body can be enhanced in order to model human attitudes in the time domain. Thus, it is possible to model actions (by means of temporal models, like Hidden Markov Models or non-linear models) and, subsequently, to perform picture-based human action recognition.

In the *Scene Domain Level*, the human is treated as a 3-D body in the scene, so the instantiation of a predefined 3-D human model is mainly used. This 3-D representation is referred to as a *Scene Domain Cue* (SDC, see [7]). This level requires a calibration process which can include two or more cameras. A critical issue relies on how to associate PDCs to SDCs: when dealing with non-rigid bodies like humans, a correspondence process between components of the 2-D representation of the Picture Domain (such as edges) and components of the 3-D human body model (such as cylinders) in the Scene Domain is not straightforward. Commonly, once the 3-D model has been instantiated, it is projected into the image to assist the extraction of PDCs when self-occlusions of limbs or occlusions of part of the body due to static components of the scene (such as trees) occur. When time is involved, we can compute the 3-D human motion characteristics of selected limbs and joints. Thus, it is possible to perform tracking at this level by using a 3-D motion model. Furthermore, we can extend the motion representation to characterize human actions in order to perform scene-based human action recognition, that is, action recognition with respect to the configurations of the 3-D human body model through time. Alternatively, the 3-D human body model can be projected into the Picture Domain Level in order to perform picture-based human action recognition (such an approach is commonly referred to as $2\frac{1}{2}$D). Also at this level, we can use the knowledge about the context (such as the 3-D model of the scene) in order to improve the recognition rate or to simplify the instantiation process of the 3-D human body model.

Note that the human tracking and the human action recognition can be performed in both the Picture Domain Level and the Scene Domain Level. One advantage of dealing with PDC-based approaches is that they are easily adapted to different frameworks, but the recognition process depends strongly on the viewpoint of the camera (2-D single-view representations can turn out to be ambiguous). SDC-based approaches offer a more accurate description of the human motion, but their computational cost can be prohibitive in video surveillance applications. The context plays an important role in both levels: the knowledge of the world (embedded in models) assists the recognition process and helps to alleviate the computational burden of the proposed approaches.

Once the human action is recognized, it is forwarded to the *Conceptual Level* in order to determine the situation [8]. Typically, situation descriptions can be characterized by the following questions:

- What kind of world is shown?
- What are the agents doing?
- What is the next action of each agent?
- Does a situation raise *suspicion(s)* in an observer?

In this level, the set of parameter values which determines the configurations of the 3-D human body model through time are associated to a conceptual representation which should be adequate with respect to a given task. This abstraction process implies the transition from pattern recognition processes to a description process by means of conceptual terms. As a consequence, there exists a data flow in two directions in order to restrict combinatorial explosion of data and reproduction of errors: on the one hand, top-down data flow corresponds to potential situation descriptions (i.e. hypotheses based on expectations) derived from the goal analysis; and, on the other hand, bottom-up data flow amounts to verified hypotheses.

That is, the goal is to instantiate situation descriptions, but also to *verify* them. The Conceptual Layer requires additional information from the Signal, Image, Picture Domain and Scene Domain levels in order to select the most precise concept for the current situation, and to reduce the system *uncertainty* about such a situation. Uncertainty can also be handled by means of *assumptions*. Assumptions to be incorporated into situation descriptions can be *implicit* or *explicit*. The former ones refer to the a-priori knowledge of the context incorporated at the Conceptual Level by means of models. For example, if an agent (a car, in this example) has stopped in front of a traffic light, we can assume that the agent is waiting to cross. However, we can not verify it: maybe the agent has stopped to ask for a particular street. Explicit assumptions refer to the uncertainty due to signal noise, the errors accumulated from the intermediate processes of the systems and the vagueness of the conceptual terms. This uncertainty can be expressed by means of fuzzy logic, for example.

The fourth question presented before implies to determine the system re-actions when the situation is established. Two kinds of system re-actions are commonly considered. First, the re-actions in terms of control signals. In this case, they are fed back to the Signal Level in order, for example, to activate warning signals or to close doors. Second, the re-actions can produce natural language formulations to be reported to human operators. In this case, system re-actions are forwarded to the *Language Level*, which associates the situation representation with natural language components. Thus, the description of the situation can be generated in terms of logic and coherent statements.

Lastly, the current situation is also provided to the *Evaluation Level*. In this level, the expected temporal evolution of situations are modeled a-priori in order to perform spatio-temporal reasoning (see [6] for details in the traffic surveillance domain). So, given a situation, the set of possible successor situations can be determined, thus allowing the system: to reason about the behavior and intention of the agent; to provide data and facilities to the Language Level for natural language text description generation; and to determine the set of possible successor configurations of the agent in order to assist the Image, Picture Domain and Scene Domain levels at the next time step.

To sum up, the system architecture embeds two separated tasks: first, to obtain a geometric description of the scene in terms of quantitative values (task related to the Signal, Image, Picture Domain and Scene Domain levels); and second, to associate the geometric description to qualitative concepts within a proper knowledge representation for further reasoning about the observed behaviors of the agents (task related to the Conceptual, Natural Language and Evaluation levels). Note that there is an explicit cooperation between two different scientific fields: Pattern Recognition and Artificial Intelligence.

4　Sources of Knowledge

Once a modular description of our system has been presented, the required sources of knowledge should be identified. In analogy to [5], this analysis will allow us to determine the requirements of our system in order to detect possible lacks of constraints, and the causes of possible system breakdowns. But even more important, by formulating the sources of knowledge as explicit models, it is possible to design a HSE system which is (to a large degree) independent of the scene in which it is applied: the evaluation in different scenes will imply the substitution of selected models but (hopefully) not a substantial change in our system architecture. Thus, it is feasible to modify, substitute, and evaluate each model independently of the rest of the system. Also, when additional knowledge is required, it is easier to be incorporated by means of an explicit model. Here, we describe generically which would be the required sources of knowledge for HSE systems, and the means by which such knowledge is provided.

The Signal Level

A *camera model* will allow us to change the recording conditions by varying the camera parameters. Such modifications can be required by the Image, Picture Domain and Scene Domain Levels. Therefore, camera resolution can be modified. This can be useful when a human is detected far away in a scene, so a posterior zoom would provide to the system a more detailed image, thus improving segmentation results. Also, the viewpoint of the camera can be changed. Thus, ambiguities can be solved in order to better instantiate a 3-D human body model, for example.

Furthermore, a *digitizer model* is necessary in order to transform the output signals of the camera to image pixel values (the so-called *measurements*). Thus, we determine the *format* of the image data, such as the available rank of pixel values (for example, 8 bits per pixel), and whether the image is gray-level or it contains color information. This model depends on the characteristics of the camera (infra-red, BW, color, or progressive cameras). Lastly, a *decoder model* is required when the image is provided in some encoded format (for example, due to compression or security issues).

Moreover, an *actuator model* can be implemented in order to activate possible signal-based re-actions of the system, such as generating warning alarms or closing/opening admittance doors, depending on the current observations within the scene.

The Image Level

Once image data is available, the system should detect moving or foreground regions. Optical flow analysis or a suitable background model are employed, respectively. In both cases, we can use the knowledge about the continuity of lines (to find lines), the texture primitives (for texture classification), the homogeneity of regions (to build areas), or the gray level changes (for edge detection) in order to aid the segmentation process of agent images in digitized video frames. Also, knowledge about color metrics can be applied to image color transformation (for example, RGB to HSL), depending on the advantages that color information provides to the system.

The Picture Domain Level

At this level, 2-D image features are manipulated in order to obtain a 2-D representation of the agent which constitutes the *2-D human body model*. The representation relies on the output of the segmentation process of the Image Level. Silhouettes and blobs are good examples for constituents of 2-D human body models.

The tracking process is performed by using a *motion model*. Usually the motion model is implemented in discrete form by means of difference equations. Thus, we are able to estimate the next expected position of the human body in the image. But also, the human body parts can be tracked separately, when a suitable 2-D human body model is used (for example, 2-D models based on sticks or joints). Note that tracking is based purely on image features.

Once the human is successfully tracked, the set of parameters, which characterize the model, can be extended over time, thus allowing the analysis of the temporal evolution of the human body parameters in order to perform action recognition. A *2-D movement model* refers to a 2-D human body representation in which time variation is taken into account:

commonly, the movement model represents motion characteristics, or the human pose, or both. For example, in [1] the lower leg limb is analysed for gait recognition. The variation of the parameters of the 2-D human body model (represented as a sequence of 2-D movement model configurations), during an explicitly defined time value, is embedded in the *picture-based action model*, usually in a supervised manner. A similarity measure and a confidence margin should be defined to achieve human action recognition.

Context can provide restrictions which will improve the tracking and action recognition performance. For example, by defining regions of interest, by restricting the plausible human body configurations (by means of *kinematic models* of human motion), or by providing information about the scene.

The Scene Domain Level

When 3-D knowledge is exploited, the 3-D configuration of the human body can be recovered and placed in the scene by means of a predefined *3-D human body model*. Consequently, 3-D human motion can be analysed. 3-D human body models can consist of sticks, but also of polyhedral, ellipsoidal, or cylindrical components.

A *correspondence model* links the scene representation in the Scene Domain with image features in the Picture Domain (usually edges or regions). On the one hand, the correspondence process fits the 3-D person model to the image, by transformation of scene points to image points. This process can be implemented in terms of chained functions which transform body part coordinates to image coordinates, as described in [11]. Differences between the projected model and the image features can be used to calculate corrections of the 3-D human model. On the other hand, the configuration of the 3-D human body model is recovered, or rather estimated, from image features. A calibration process is required to infer 3-D positions within the scene from 2-D positions in the image (also, we can derive the real sizes of objects in the depicted scene). The calibration requires the camera model of the Signal Level, and the anatomical restrictions about allowed body configurations (for example, in terms of kinematic geometry of joint coordinates) can improve this estimation process.

Tracking is applied to a particular instantiation of the 3-D human body model. *3-D human motion models* are required in order to estimate the next expected position and/or configuration of the human model at the next time step. Restrictions due to physically plausible motion of the human body can be incorporated by means of kinematics of human motion, thus allowing to improve the tracking process in terms of time, accuracy and reliability issues. A *3-D scene model* is incorporated to consider occlusions due to the static components of the scene, and to provide context information for activity recognition.

Extension of the human motion analysis to the temporal evolution of 3-D human body configurations will enable action recognition. A *3-D movement model* simplifies the 3-D body representation by considering a reduced set of body characteristics which will be used to learn and recognize actions. For example, if the human body is described in terms of joints and limbs, we can just analyse the angle variations of a reduced set of joints in order to characterize a particular action. The temporal sequence of 3-D movement model parameters constitutes the *scene-based action model*. Similarly to the Picture Domain Level, a similarity measure and a confidence margin should be precisely determined for recognition purposes.

The Conceptual Level

Lastly, the behaviors for each agent should be inferred from the recognized patterns. Specifically, a correspondence process is attained between the identified patterns and the knowledge about the task domain. The aim is to infer the behavior of the human, the relationships of the agent with respect to other components of the scene (static components or additional agents as well) and the selection of possibly occurring situations. All the previously recognized events (provided in quantitative and geometric terms) within the scene are *associated* to conceptual terms at this level. The set of possible situations, that an agent can exhibit, is defined traditionally a-priori. So once an event is recognized, the most suitable situation, which best describes this event, is selected and instantiated. At present, automatic generation of these knowledge structures is becoming an important focus of research [2].

Context helps to reduce the inherent uncertainty about the currently prevailing situation. For example, a *scene model* (2-D or 3-D) provides useful information for spatial reasoning, and the position of the agent within the scene can help to infer the behavior and the goal of such an agent. For example, in order to establish that an agent has come inside a house, we can model the positions in the scene of the visible doors of the buildings (our regions of interest). An agent which disappears at those positions leads to semantic interpretation. Another example is related to human occlusions by static components of the scene: occlusions can be predictable, thus improving the tracking process (in terms of robustness) and interpretation can be achieved.

Next, the relationship between a particular situation and the re-action (that the system generates when such a situation is instantiated) should be established. First, we should define a-priori which re-actions are associated with each possible situation. Thus, given a situation, a subset of system re-actions are selected to be potentially activated. Given the knowledge of the context, and the precise parameter values of the situation, the most suitable re-action(s) are selected. As described before, a suitable scene model can help to determine whether an agent behavior (for example, a human detected too close to a railway line) can be considered as suspicious or not.

We distinguish between language and control signal re-actions. The latter implies to send signals to the actuator (modeled at the Signal Level), which is the interface with, for example, access doors or warning devices. Thus, the communication protocol needs to be known in order to code properly the system re-actions into meaningful control signals. Language re-actions require to associate natural language formulations with the current situation in order to generate conceptual descriptions of what is happening in the scene. This task is achieved in the Language Level.

The Language Level

Language re-actions are fed forward to this level. A natural language text description of the situation is generated, which involves logic and coherent statements by means of natural language formulations. A suitable *grammar* needs to be designed in order to combine the conceptual terms presented in the current situation into meaningful statements.

The situation representation associates quantitative and geometric terms with nouns, motion verbs, adverbs and adjectives. A *generic description* [8] of an agent can consist of the spatial position of the agent, the configuration of the human body model (with respect to pose or motion characteristics), and the goal of the agent. This information can be inferred from the instantiated situation.

Furthermore, the temporal and spatial evolution of situations provides information about the relation of manner or quality, place, time, degree, number, cause, opposition, affirmation, or denial between situations and agents: temporal transitions and spatial relationships between instantiated situations serve to connect properly the statements by means of *adverbs*.

The Evaluation Level

As described in [10], at the beginning of chapter 8: "Knowledge based scene interpretation is a complex task, systems for performing this task tend to be complex, too". We consider here that there is human-computer interaction: users can ask the system about the scene, and the system can generate scene descriptions after reasoning. *Evaluation* (in the sense of explanation) helps to make easy to understand such systems by non-expert users.

At this level, a *knowledge representation language* is designed in order to reason about the behavior and intention of agents. Such a language requires to be independent of the specific context and should obey to several criteria: adequacy for representing the knowledge (to determine which events can not be represented); existence of efficient algorithms (in terms of tolerable complexity) which can handle the knowledge representation; adequacy for handling uncertainty; language logically correct and complete; and language understandable and comprehensible. Although techniques for evaluation depend on the selected knowledge representation language, such as semantic networks, logical, and procedural schemes, there are common requirements to take into account [10].

The first requirement is the evaluation of the performance of the system. Thus, it is possible to *justify* the results of the system reasoning process by controlling the inference process which is applied. The goals are, once a particular evaluation of the scene is required: to trace the computational process which generates the result; to determine the internal information requested by the system; and to reason about the selection of particular re-actions by the system. Therefore, it would become easier to *debug* the system. Also, as a result of this debugging process, the designer can decide to incorporate extra knowledge (restrictions and assumptions) in order to improve the performance of the system in terms of reliability. So there is an increase of *confidence* of the users in the results given by the system.

A second requirement is the evaluation of the knowledge of the system. The user can ask about the content of the knowledge base. Thus, it is possible to obtain a description of *what* is happening in the scene, and even *why*: the system can reason about the availability or no availability of particular knowledge. As context helps to infer the knowledge of the system, the user is actually learning about the context specifications while asking the system: there is a *training* process of the user in the specific task domain in which the system is addressed.

Another requirement is the evaluation of the strategies of the system. This issue is related to the capability of asking about how the system would address the resolution of a particular problem (in terms of the inference steps to be applied). This capability asks for the necessity of control algorithms, which determine the most suitable inference processes to be activated.

Lastly, the relationships between the Evaluation Level and the previously described levels will be pointed out. The user interacts with the system through the Language Level. The inference process of the Evaluation Level reasons about the current instantiated situations at the Conceptual Level, thus allowing the possibility of instantiating the goal of the agent, in the case the goal has not been directly inferred from the scene. Evaluation of numerical results provided in the Image, Picture Domain and Scene Domain levels of the system can also be required. The result of the inference process is fed forward to the Language Level, in order to generate a natural language description embedding the answer of the system, or to the Signal Level, in order to activate signal-based re-actions.

5 Conclusions

In this paper, the Image Sequence Evaluation (ISE) framework [9] is adapted to perform human behavior description, named as *Human Sequence Evaluation* (HSE). First, the modular architecture of HSE systems has been detailed. After that, each module of HSE systems has been described to show the abstraction process that leads to perform high-level reasoning. By means of sources of information, the a-priori knowledge required to transform image data into scene descriptions is presented. By formulating the sources of knowledge as explicit models, it is possible to design a HSE system which is independent of the scene in which it is applied. Furthermore, to modify, substitute, and evaluate each model independently of the rest of the system is guaranteed.

6 Acknowledgements

This work has been supported by project TIC2000-0382 of spanish CICYT.

References

[1] C. Bregler. Learning and recognizing human dynamics in video sequences. In *Proceedings of IEEE Conference on Computer Vision and Pattern Recognition (CVPR'97)*, San Juan, Puerto Rico, 1997.

[2] H. Buxton. Learning and understanding dynamic scene activity: a review. *Image and Vision Computing*, 21(1):125–136, 2002.

[3] C. Cédras and M. Shah. Motion-based recognition: A survey. *Image and Vision Computing*, 13(2):129–155, 1995.

[4] R.T. Collins, A.J. Lipton, and T. Kanade. Introduction to the special section on video surveillance. *IEEE Trans. Pattern Analysis and Machine Intelligence*, 22(8):745–746, 2000.

[5] M. Haag and H.-H. Nagel. Combination of edge element and optical flow estimates for 3d-model-based vehicle tracking in traffic image sequences. *International Journal of Computer Vision*, 35(3):295–319, 1999.

[6] M. Haag and H.-H. Nagel. Incremental recognition of traffic situations from video image sequences. *Image and Vision Computing*, 18(2):137–153, 2000.

[7] T. Kanade. Region segmentation: Signal vs. semantics. *Computer Graphics and Image Processing*, 13:279–297, 1980.

[8] H.-H. Nagel. From image sequences towards conceptual descriptions. *Image and Vision Computing*, 6(2):59–74, 1988.

[9] H.-H. Nagel. Image sequence evaluation: 30 years and still going strong. In *Proceedings of International Conference on Pattern Recognition (ICPR'2000)*, volume 1, pages 149–158, Barcelona, Spain, 2000.

[10] G. Sagerer and H. Niemann. Semantic networks for understanding scenes. In M.D. Levine, editor, *Advances in Computer Vision and Machine Intelligence*. Plenum Press, New York, 1997.

[11] S. Wachter and H.-H. Nagel. Tracking persons in monocular image sequences. *Computer Vision and Image Understanding*, 74(3):174–192, June 1999.

Artificial Intelligence Research and Development
I. Aguiló et al. (Eds.)
IOS Press, 2003

Alba

A Cognitive Assistant for Network Administration

Francisco J. Martin†*and Enric Plaza‡
† *School of Electrical Engineering and Computer Science*
Oregon State University, Corvallis, 97331 OR, USA
‡IIIA - Artificial Intelligence Research Institute
CSIC - Spanish Council for Scientific Research
Campus UAB, 08193 Bellaterra, Catalonia, Spain
fmartin@cs.orst.edu; enric@iiia.csic.es

Abstract
We are developing a fi rst prototype of an agent-aided intrusion detection tool called
Alba (ALert BArrage) that assists a network administrator's decision making, reducing the burdensome output produced by current intrusion detection systems (IDSes).
This work describes the cognitive machinery that allows Alba to reason about computer security incidents and learn the salient features of an incident so that they can be
later employed to recognize similar situations and predict the likely effects of a new
attack.

1 Introduction

Network administrators' responsibilities include, among other perimeter defense tasks, prevention, detection and response to computer security intrusions[1]. Nowadays, Intrusion Detection Systems (IDSes) have become common tools (eTrust, eSafe, IntruShield, RealSecure,
etc) deployed by network administrators to combat unauthorized use of computer systems.
An IDS aims at discovering intrusion attempts and whenever an intrusion (or intrusive behavior) is detected the IDS notifies the network administrator by means of *alerts*. Commonly,
alerts take the form of emails, database or log entries, etc and their format and content vary
according to the particular IDS (Fig. 3 shows an alert signaled by Snort [16]). There are intrusions that require only a single action (hit-and-run intrusions) to cause a malign effect (i.e.
the *Ping of Death* attack[2]). Other intrusions, on the contrary, are sophisticated multi-stage
attacks where each intruder's action is a step intended to result in a change of state of the
target computer system that prepares it to accept the next intruder's action (i.e. the *Mitnick*
attack [15]). Normally, an isolated alert (per se) cannot be correctly classified as malicious
or innocuous. For example, imagine an alert corresponding to a `scan` action coming from
an unknown `IP`. This alert can correspond to a malefactor performing a reconnaissance or
on the contrary it could really correspond to one of our engineers checking at our customer's

---

*On sabbatical leave from iSOCO - Intelligent Software Components, S. A.
[1]The intentional or unintentional access to sensitive information or unauthorized use of a computer system.
[2]http://www.pp.asu.edu/support/ping-o-death.html

office that one of our web services is up. Thus, more evidence is needed before one can go further and initiate a considered response (e.g. creating a new rule in a firewall).

Moreover, the current generation of IDSes generates an unmanageable number of false positive alerts[3] that in turn increases the difficulties for the proper identification of real and malicious attacks. Network administrators are so overwhelmed that they frequently disable the alert device due to the consistent assumption that nothing is wrong reinforced by the fact that the alert device "cried wolf" too often. There are those who even postulate that traditional IDSes not only have failed to provide an additional layer of security but have also added complexity to the security administration task. Therefore, there is a compelling need for developing a new generation of tools that help to automate security administration tasks such as the interpretation and correct diagnosis of IDSes output. The fact of the matter is that as long as the number of networked organizations proliferates and the number of computer security threats increases this need accentuates.

To make the aforementioned tasks more manageable we envisage a new generation of intrusion detection tools under the heading of *agent-aided intrusion detection*. Some recent works can be seen as the prelude of this tendency [4, 8, 12, 18, 19]. This work describes a first prototype of an agent-aided intrusion detection tool called Alba (ALert BArrage) that mediates between an IDS and the corresponding network administrator. Alba rapidly produces an alert triage (i.e. an approximate priorization for subsequent action) on behalf of its network administrator. Alba employs a case-based strategy to analyze the sequence of alerts provided by a conventional IDS, identifying false positives, deeming alerts due to innocuous attacks, and predicting new alerts corresponding to malicious attacks that are still undergoing. We will see how stored cases, in the form of *alert trees* and learnt through frequent episode algorithms, allow Alba to identify subsequences of alerts in the alert stream that are similar to past situations where a computer security incident occurred. Once identified a past situation Alba uses it to predict the likely intentions of an attacker so that the corresponding alerts can be priorized conveniently and the suitable response can be initiated as soon as possible.

This work describes the cognitive machinery that underpins Alba and proceeds as follows. Next Section describes the task that confronts a human network administrator who must detect a human or artificial intruder rapidly and respond appropriately to minimize damage. Section 3 briefly overviews Alba's cognitive architecture. Then, we concentrate on four key components. Firstly, Sec. 4 describes SOID a simple ontology for intrusion detection that allows Alba to reason at a higher level of abstraction than most IDSes. Secondly, Sec. 5 introduces alert trees as the knowledge structure that supports sequence recognition. Thirdly, Sec. 6 explains how an IDS alert stream is analyzed to recognize past episodes. Fourthly, the frequent episode discovery methods deployed by Alba are described in Sec. 7. Finally, Sec. 8 summarizes some approaches addressing the number of alerts that a human network administrator has to handle and Sec. 9 presents some concluding remarks.

2   Network Administration

Responding to intruders (human, artificial or a combination of both) and keeping networks and applications safe encompasses a collection of tasks that are best explained depending on the time at which they are performed by a network administrator: before, during or after the occurrence of an intrusion. See the temporal model depicted by Figure 1.

---

[3]Alerts signaled when there is a manifest absence of intrusive behavior.

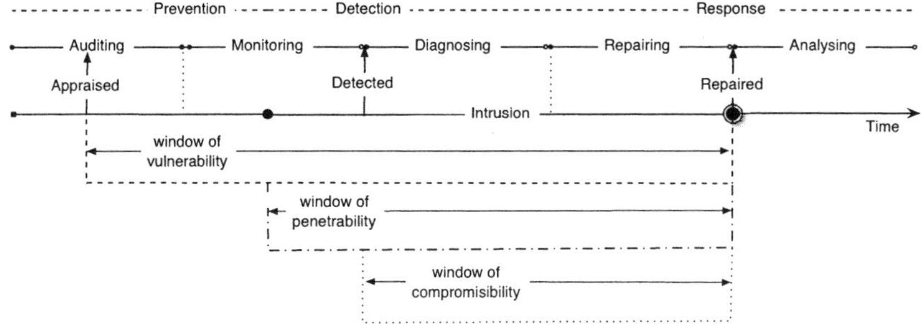

Figure 1: Time axis model of incident prevention, detection, and response tasks.

Prevention Tasks   Network administrators according to the security policy prepare before-hand a collection of procedures to effectively handle future intrusions and to enable rapid reaction. They try to minimize the likeliness of future intrusions by constantly auditing the system and eliminating the greatest number of threats. A network administrator proactively performs security audits testing the computer systems for weaknesses —vulnerabilities or exposures. However scan tools (i.e. Nessus, Satan, Oval, etc) used for penetration or vulner-ability testing only recognize a limited number of vulnerabilities given the ever increasing frequency of newly detected possibilities for breaking into a computer system or disturbing its normal operation. Thus, network administrators continuously update scan tools with new plug-ins that permit to perceive new vulnerabilities. Once the existence of a vulnerability or exposure is appraised, network administrators assess the convenience of discontinuing the service or application affected until the corresponding patch or intrusion detection signature is available. A tradeoff between risk level and service level is made in every assessment. Net-work administrators aim at shrinking the *window of vulnerability*, the time gap between when a new vulnerability or exposure is appraised and a preventing solution (patch, new configu-ration, etc) is provided, as much as possible. A basic strategy to accomplish that objective is based on two conservative tasks: first, minimizing the number of exposures (i.e. disabling unnecessary or optional services configuring firewalls to allow only the use of ports that are necessary for the site to function) and, second, increasing awareness of new vulnerabilities and exposures. Finally, network administrators continuously monitor the system so that pre intrusion behavioral patterns can be understood and used for further reference when an intru-sion occurs. *Monitoring* is a preventive and ongoing task that normally conveys to detect an intrusion.

Detection Tasks   The sooner an intrusion is detected, the more chances there are for imped-ing an unauthorized use or misuse of the computer system. Network administrators monitor computer activities at different level of detail: system calls traces, operating system logs, audit trail records, resources usage, network connections, etc. Normally, they constantly try to fusion and correlate real-time reports and alerts stemming from different security devices (i.e. firewalls, intrusion detection systems, etc) to stop suspicious activities before they have a negative impact (i.e. degrading or disrupting operations). Different sources of evidence are valuable given the evolving capabilities of intruders to elude security devices. The degree of suspicion and malignancy associated to each report or alert still requires continuous human oversight. Thereby, network administrators are continuously overwhelmed with a vast amount of log information and bombarded with countless alerts. Thereabout, network administrators tune security devices to provide an admissible number of false alerts at risk of not detecting real intrusions. The time at which an intrusion is detected directly affects to the damage that an intrusion causes. An objective of network administrators is to reduce the *window of penetrability*, the time span that initiates when a computer system has been broken into and extends until the damage has been completely repaired. The correct diagnosis of an intrusion allows a network administrator to initiate the most convenient response. However, a tradeoff between quality and rapidness is made in every diagnostic. *Diagnosing* is a detection task that conveys to respond an intrusion.

Response and Recovery Tasks   As soon as a diagnostic on an intrusion is available network administrators initiate a considered response. This response tries to minimize the impact on the operations (i.e. do not close all ports in a firewall if blocking a unique IP is enough). Network administrators try to narrow the *window of compromisibility* of each intrusion —the time gap that starts when an intrusion has been detected and ends when the proper response has taken effect— employing a collection of ad-hoc operating procedures that indicate how to respond and recover from a type of intrusion. The responses to an attack range from terminating a user job or suspending a session to blocking an IP or disconnecting from the network to disable the compromised service or host. *Repairing* or damage recovery entails to restore the control, resources, and services of the compromised network entities. Network managers use a disaster recovery process that depending on the severity of the intrusion will even require to regenerate the complete system from scratch. Repairing usually entails keeping the level of service while the system is being repaired what hardens automation. Often, it is impossible to keep the level of service (i.e. when a system reboot is required after a DoS). Once the system in completely recovered from an intrusion, network managers collect all possible data to thoroughly analyze the intrusion, traceback what happened, and evaluate the damages. Thus, system logs are continuously backed up. The goal of *post-mortem analysis* is threefold. First, to gather forensic evidence (contemplating different legal requirements) that will support legal investigations and prosecution. Second, to compile experience and provide or improve documentation and procedures that will facilitate the recognition and rapid repelling of similar intrusions in the future, and, third, to validate the current security policy. *Post-mortem analysis* is a response task that conveys to prevent intrusions.

3 Alba Architecture

Based on Brachman's definition of a cognitive system [3], we have defined a cognitive assistant for network administration as a computer system that is capable of:

- *reasoning* in terms of large amounts of knowledge represented at a useful level of description.

- *learning* from past experiences and continuously improving its workings and results over time.

- *explaining* itself in terms that are meaningful for a network administrator.

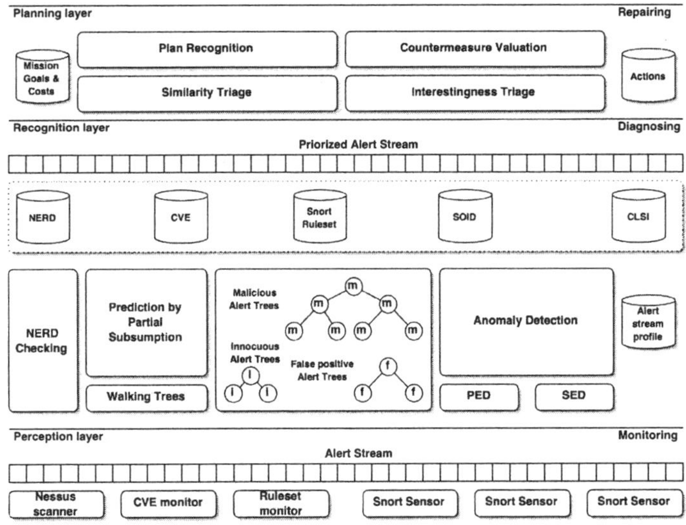

Figure 2: Alba Architecture

- *accepting* direction from a network administrator that tells it what to do.

- *being aware* of its behavior and capabilities (self-aware).

- *responding* in a robust manner and proactively to surprises (survivable).

- *collaborating* with other network administrator's assistants to complete tasks.

In this work, for the sake of brevity, we will only address the first four capabilities. Figure 2 sketches the architecture that provides the primitive resources that allows Alba to reason, learn, accept direction and explain itself meaningfully. Next, we provide a brief description of the complete architecture.

Perception Layer   The first layer provides, on the one hand, a collection of sensors strategically placed to continuously monitor and analyze every packet on the protected network, and, on the other hand, a number of scanners and monitors that allows several sources of knowledge (that we will introduce later on) to be constantly updated. This layer allows Alba to perform preventive tasks such as pinpointing security weaknesses for correction.

Recognition Layer   The second layer provides Alba with deliberative capabilities. First, a collection of models —expressed on top of the concepts defined by SOID, a simple ontology for intrusion detection— allows Alba to reason about security incidents, vulnerabilities, alerts, and the protected network. Second, alert trees permit Alba to represent sequential patterns of malicious and innocuous activity and store past experiences. Third, Alba uses a collection of methods (Checking NERD and Walking Trees) for continuously overseeing the alert stream looking for an explanation for each isolated alert or group of alerts so that they can be conveniently priorized. Forth, the *prediction by partial subsumption* method allows Alba to predict new alerts stemming from attacks that are still underway. Fifth, a collection of methods allows Alba to keep an updated profile of the alert stream and constantly learn new alert trees.

Planning Layer   The third layer provides Alba with reflective capabilities. Firstly, a model of the network mission and costs allows Alba to make savvy judgements on the priorization of certain malicious alerts as well as to keep the number of false positives under control. Secondly, a plan recognition model uses priorized alerts and predicted alerts to properly anticipate the plans of a malefactor and initiate the corresponding plan of countermeasures using a collection of prespecified actions. Thirdly, Alba accepts direction from a network administrator who can provide it with different criteria to estimate the similarity of two sequence of alerts and establishes different measures of interest to properly prune the discovery of new alert trees.

Alba has been coded using Noos, an object-centered knowledge representation language useful for developing knowledge systems that integrate problem solving and learning [1]. Noos also provides agent-programming constructs . The three basic concepts that underpin the Noos knowledge representation language are: *sorts, feature terms*, and *subsumption*. A sort is defined as a symbol that denotes a set of the individuals of a domain. Sorts form a collection of partially ordered symbols. Noos is formalized using *feature terms*. Feature terms are a generalization of first order terms and lambda terms. Feature terms constitute the Noos basic data structure and can be seen as extendable records organized in a *subsumption* hierarchy [1]. Feature terms are represented graphically by means of labeled directed graphs (see Fig. 4 and Fig. 5). In Noos subsumption is defined as an informational ordering among feature terms. A feature term Ψ is subsumed by another feature term Ψ' when all information provided by Ψ' is also provided by Ψ. Subsumption is crucial in our approach since it is at the core of the algorithms that Alba uses to compare sequences of alerts.

In the following, we describe in further detail four different components of the recognition layer aimed at performing an effective alert triage.

4   SOID

SOID aims at providing a domain-specific representation language for alert triage in intrusion detection. At a quick glance, in order to automate the alert triage task we have identified four key sources of knowledge to be conceptualized (networks, incidents, vulnerabilities, and alerts) and built a separate ontology for each of them using the knowledge representation language Noos [1]. Finally, we have merged these partial ontologies in a more global ontology that we have called SOID —a Simple Ontology for Intrusion Detection.

Networks   A network is the computer system to be protected. We have defined a set of concepts and relationships to model a network based on the Network Entity Relationship Database (NERD) proposed in [7]. Properly modelling the network allows the importance of each alert to be correctly assessed. For instance, determining whether a given alert corresponds to an innocuous attack or not. That is the objective of the NERD checking method. Network models based on SOID can easily be coded into Noos and automatically updated translating the reports provided by Nessus (an open source network scanner).

Incidents   An incident is a unauthorized use or abuse of the protected system. We have followed CLCSI [10] that defines an incident taxonomy based on three key concepts: *events*, *attacks* and *incidents*. An event is an *action* directed at a *target* which is intended to result in a change of state of the *target*. An attack is defined as a sequence of actions directed at a target taken by an *attacker* making use of some tool exploiting a computer or network vulnerability. Finally, an incident is defined as a set of attacks carried out by one or more attackers with one or more goals.

Vulnerabilities   A vulnerability is a flaw in a target that could allow an unauthorized result. Knowing the vulnerabilities in our network is the main source of knowledge to automatically decide if a given alert corresponds to an innocuous attack or not. We have incorporated common vulnerabilities and exposures (CVE) dictionary provided by the MITRE corporation into our ontology. A monitor advertises **Alba** of new published vulnerabilities. **Alba** contrasts new vulnerabilities against the network model (NERD) and pintpoints new security weaknesses for correction.

Alerts   We have conceptualized alerts according to the Snort ruleset. Snort is a network IDS where alerts are triggered by a collection of rules [16]. Each Snort rule is composed of a Snort identification number (SID), a message that is included in the alert when the rule is triggered, an attack signature, and references to sources of information about the attack. Each alert is provided with an identifier, time and date, sensor identifier, triggered signature, IP and TCP headers and payload. In Fig. 4 an alert corresponding to an attempt of propagation of the CodeRed worm is shown.

5   Alert Trees

An alert tree is a knowledge structure to describe past security incidents. An alert tree represents the serial structure of a group of alerts that occurred together within a specified window of time at the end of which a particular situation took place (i.e. an concrete attack). The root node represents the goal and target of an attack and the leaf nodes the alerts corresponding to the sequence of actions needed to achieve that goal [17]. An alert tree establishes a partial order among the leaf nodes. An alert tree has two types of intermediate nodes: *a-nodes* (parallel nodes) and *s-nodes* (serial nodes). An a-node indicates that to occur all its subnodes have to occur before (indeptently of the order) and therefore establishes a partial order among them

```
   #(1 - 12064) [2002-11-29 18:47:22]   WEB-IIS CodeRed v2 root.exe access
   IPv4: 80.34.49.201 -> 172.26.0.4
 hlen=5 TOS=0 dlen=112 ID=16914 flags=0 offset=0 TTL=118 chksum=37996
   TCP:  port=3421 -> dport: 80   flags=***AP*** seq=1955827854
 ack=1657159142 off=5 res=0 win=17520 urp=0 chksum=44219
   Payload:  length = 72

   000 : 47 45 54 20 2F 73 63 72 69 70 74 73 2F 72 6F 6F    GET /scripts/roo
   010 : 74 2E 65 78 65 3F 2F 63 2B 64 69 72 20 48 54 54    t.exe?/c+dir HTT
   020 : 50 2F 31 2E 30 0D 0A 48 6F 73 74 3A 20 77 77 77    P/1.0..Host: www
   030 : 0D 0A 43 6F 6E 6E 6E 65 63 74 69 6F 6E 3A 20 63    ..Connnection: c
   040 : 6C 6F 73 65 0D 0A 0D 0A                            lose....
```

Figure 3: CodeRed Worm propagation attempt.

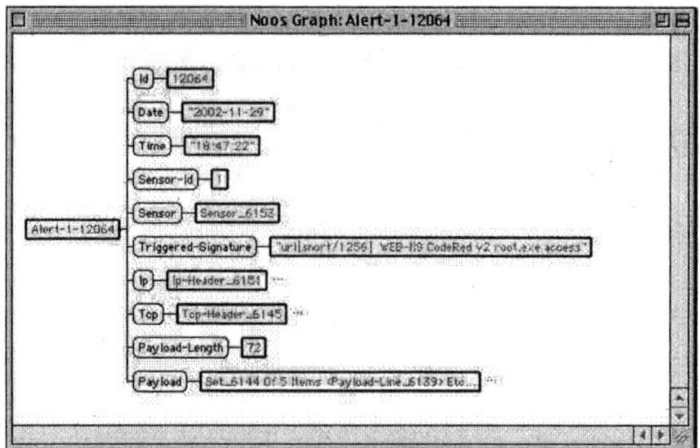

Figure 4: CodeRed alert in Noos

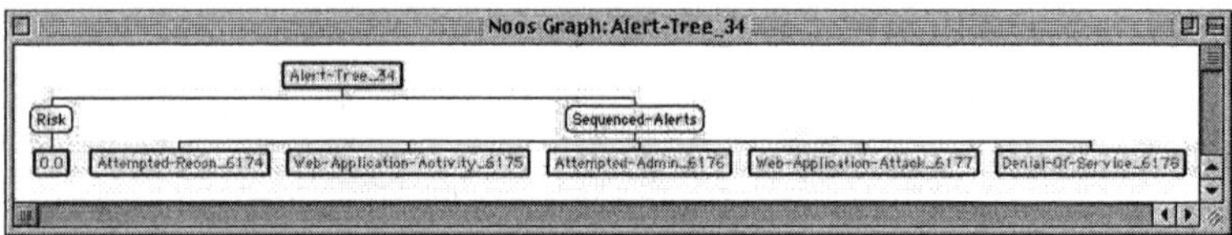

Figure 5: Innocuous Alert Tree.

whereas a s-node indicates that its subnodes are ordered following a total (lexicographic) order. Therefore, an alert tree induces a partial order among all the leaf nodes. We call *episode* to each one of the induced sequences of leaf nodes. The nodes of an alert tree also have other features such as *risk* to indicate the possibilities of suffering the attack at the root node once all its subnodes have occurred and *cost* that indicates the impact of such attack on a give mission. Fig. 5 shows an alert-tree to represent a multi-stage attack as a sequence of Snort alert classes with a null risk factor that indicates that the attack is innocuous.

6 PPS

Alba constantly searches the set of alert trees that best explain the current alert stream. Alba uses a walking tree method —inspired by a family of heuristics to align biologically reasonable strings [5]— to efficiently and incrementally computing the similarity between an alert tree and the alert stream (see Fig. 6). Computing the similarity between two sequences of alerts can be interpreted as the search of evidence that some alerts in the alert stream and a past episode are derived from a common attack pattern perhaps altered using new and undetectable vulnerabilities. The Prediction by Partial Subsumption (PPS) method at any time considers a window ω composed of the last N alerts in the alert stream and looks for partial occurrences of episodes. We define the partial occurrence of an episode and its confidence threshold as follows:

Partial Occurrence A window $\omega = \langle a_{t_{n-N+1}}, \ldots, a_{t_{n-1}} a_{t_n} \rangle$ of length N on an alert stream $\vec{A} = \langle a_{t_1}, .., a_{t_n} \rangle$ is a partial occurrence of episode ε iff the optimal alignment of ε to ω has score at least θ.

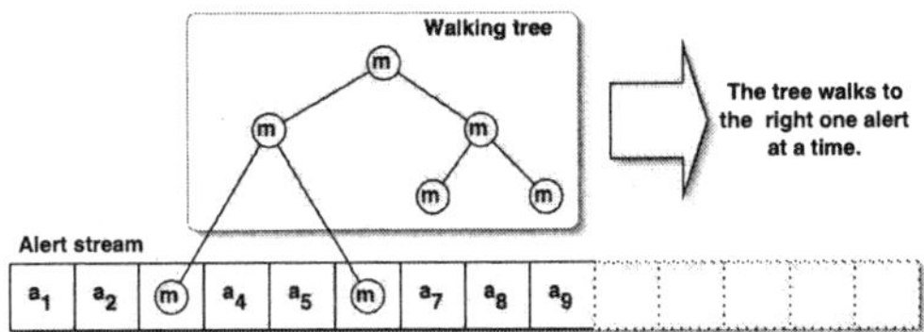

Figure 6: Walking Tree.

Confidence Threshold A window $\omega = \langle a_{t_{n-N+1}}, \ldots, a_{t_{n-1}}, a_{t_n} \rangle$ of length N on an alert stream $\vec{A} = \langle a_{t_1}, .., a_{t_n} \rangle$ such that ω is a partial occurrence of episode ε then we can predict that the whole episode will occur with confidence θ' given by the odds ratio $\prod_i \frac{p_{\omega[i]\varepsilon[i]}}{q_{\omega[i]}q_{\varepsilon[i]}}$. Where $\prod_i q_{\omega[i]} \prod_i q_{\varepsilon[i]}$ represents the probability that both sequences of alerts ω and ε were unrelated or appeared randomly. And $\prod_i p_{\omega[i]\varepsilon[i]}$ can be thought as the probability that the alerts on the window ω of the alert stream have been caused by an incident similar to the episode ε [6].

For each episode ε induced by an alert tree, PPS searches the optimal alignment between a suffix of the window ω and a prefix of the episode ε. When both the decision threshold θ and the confidence threshold θ' are reached or exceeded then Alba is capable of foreseeing that the corresponding suffix of such episode will occur (at least with a level of confidence θ') and therefore preventing the incident $\mathcal{I}'_\varepsilon$. On the other hand, the alerts on which Alba bases this prediction are priorized for further investigation. Notice that once a window ω and a episode ε are deemed to be similar Alba will apply other methods that will look for more evidence before it can conclude that an attack is undergoing (i.e. verifying that the source IP of the different alerts involved are the same). Other issue that deserves attention is that a predictive model is only as good as the trust its user (a network administrator in our case) puts in it. Thus it is fundamental to minimize the number of false positives ("do not cry wolf too many times") while keeping the true positive fraction as high as possible. Alba computes an optimal decision threshold θ with such criteria using ROC analysis. Figure 7 shows the ROC curve generated in a set of preliminary experiments where we employed an alert stream composed of 84168 alerts coming from 8848 different IPs that was generated after four months of real surveillance in a networked organization using 3 Snort sensors, 18 episodes corresponding to well-known attack patterns, an error type weighting of 1:500 (i.e. a cost of 1 for each false positive and a cost of 500 for each false negative), and 12 variants of 3 different multi-stage attacks. The optimal decision threshold corresponded to the iso-performance line with slope equal to 2.2 (see Fig. 7).

7 Frequent Episode Discovery

Alert trees can be provided by a network administrator or learn by means of anomaly detection algorithms[4]. There exists a number of algorithms for frequent episode discovery in sequence of events. Winepi [11], Minepi [11], Seq-Ready&Go [2], etc that are valid for our purpose. These three-phase algorithms exploit the notion that if a given episode is frequent

---

[4]An anomaly detection algorithm is a generalized inductive learning based on past cases that recognizes unusual features of data, i.e. recurrent combinations that occur with greater or lesser frequency than originally might be expected [9].

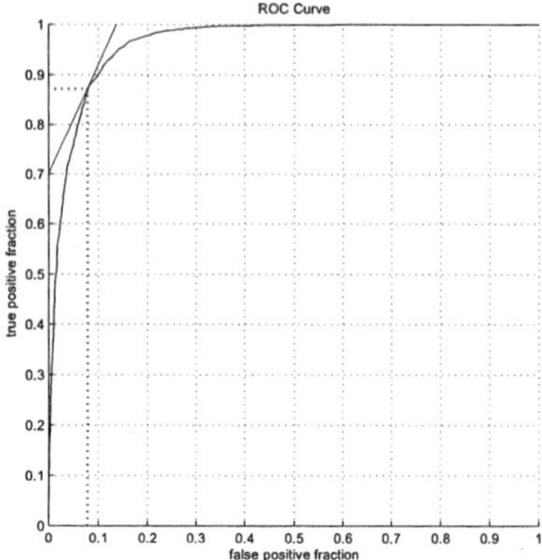

Figure 7: ROC curve and optimal decision threshold.

then all its subepisodes are also frequent. In the first phase, these algorithms generate candidates while in the second phase evaluate the support (the number of times that the candidate occurs) and prune those candidates that are under a preselected *support*. The first two phases are looped until no new candidates can be generated. Then, the third phase generates association rules that are over a given *confidence* threshold. A drawback of these algorithms is the unmanageable number of rules that can generate. For instance, using Winepi to mine an alert stream composed of 31482 alerts corresponding to 3 months of activity of a Snort sensor. After four hours of computation, we found 171566 rules with a minimal confidence of 15% and a minimal frequency of 10% using a window of 30 seconds. Thus, Alba uses a new method based on the Winepi [11] algorithm that is able to support noise data [20] and generalization over a hierarchical taxonomy of sorts [2]. A novelty of this method is that it is also able to use different interestingness measures provided by the network administrator to prune new candidates. We are now experimenting with different interestingness measures such as *general impressions* or *surprisingness* [9]. We have developed two variants one for parallel episode discovery (PED) and other for serial episode discovery (SED) —a-nodes and s-nodes respectively. On the other hand, Alba continually revises models of correct behavior (alert stream profiles i.e. number of alert per minute, frequency of alert sorts, α-rarity, IP sources, etc) and evaluates statical deviation from past history in order to advert meaningful differences.

8   Related Work

The correct interpretation of an IDS alert stream is an active area of research in the intrusion detection community [7, 13]. As our approach M2D2 [13] reuses models proposed by others and integrates multiple interesting concepts into a unified framework. The most significative difference between both approaches is that M2D2 uses the B formal method to model the different sources of information for the alert management task whereas we are using a description logic like language like [7]. Crosbie and Spafford were the first to propose autonomous agents in the context of intrusion detection. Their initial proposal evolved to become AAFID [18]. Other works such as Cooperating Security Managers have proposed a multi-agent system to handle intrusions instead of only detecting them [19]. However, in these works agents lack reasoning capabilities and are used for mere monitoring. More sophisticated agents with richer functionality were provided by [8] where an ontology centered on computer attacks was introduced. That ontology provides a hierarchy of notions specifying a set of harmful actions in different levels of granularity —from high level intentions to low level actions. It has been argued in [4] that a collection of heterogenous software agents can reduce risks during the window of vulnerability introduced between when an intrusion is detected and the security manager can take an active role in the defense of the computer system. Some works have also proposed to deal with intrusion detection at higher level of abstraction. The benefit of dealing with intrusions at higher level of abstraction is twofold: it allows irrelevant details to be removed and the differences between heterogenous systems to be hidden [14].

9   Conclusions

Ideally, the ultimate goal of secure network administration is to make the three windows (vulnerability, penetrability and compromisibility) of each possible intrusion converge into a single point in time. Pursuing that objective is a manpower intensive process. Moreover, the astounding growth of networks and the speed at which Internet software has been developed and released inevitably has led to an exponential growth in the number of current vulnerabilities and exposures and therefore in the complexity of network administration. Only the smart automation of network administration tasks will alleviate the ever increasing manpower needed for secure network administration. This work provides a brief overview of a cognitive assistant, Alba, that reduces the burdensome output produced by current IDSes and contributes to minimize the number of false positives due to innocuous attacks and to increase the predictive power for malicious multi-stage attacks. This work forms part of a more ambitious effort where we are involved in developing CBR techniques for the assessment of dynamic processes in imprecise and adversarial environments.

Acknowledgments

Part of this work has been performed in the context of the MCYT-FEDER project SAMAP (TIC2002-04146-C05-01) and the SWWS EU-funded project under contract number IST-2001-37134.

References

[1] J. L. Arcos and E. Plaza. Inference and reflection in the object-centered representation language Noos. *Journal of Future Generation Computer Systems*, 12:173–188, 1996.

[2] J. Baixeries, G. Casas, and J. L. Balcázar. Frequent sets, sequences, and taxonomies: new, efficient algorithmic proposals. Technical Report LSI-00-78-R, UPC, 2000.

[3] R. Brachman. Developing cognitive systems. a convergence of thinking. Technical report, Defense Advanced Research Projects Agency, 2002.

[4] C. A. Carver, J. M. Hill, J. R. Surdu, and U. W. Pooch. A methodology for using intelligent agents to provide automated intrusion response. In *Proc. of the IEEE WIAS*, pages 110–116, 2000.

[5] P. Cull and T. Hsu. Improved parallel and sequential walking tree methods for biological string alignments. In *Proc. of the ACM/IEEE conference on Supercomputing*, 1999.

[6] R. Durbin, S. Eddy, A. Krogh, and G. Mitchison. *Biological Sequence Analysis*. Cambridge University Press, 1998.

[7] R. P. Goldman, W. Heimerdinger, S. A. Harp, C. W. Geib, V. Thomas, and R. L. Carter. Information modeling for intrusion report aggregation. In *DICEX*. IEEE Computer Society, 2001.

[8] V. I. Gorodetski, L. J. Popyack, I. V. Kotenko, and V. A. Skormin. Ontology-based multi-agent model of information security system. In *7th RSFDGrC*, number 1711 in LNAI, pages 528–532. Springer, 1999.

[9] R. J. Hilderman and H. J. Hamilton. *Knowldege Discovery and Measures of Interest*. Kluwer Academic Publishers, 2001.

[10] J. Howard and T. Longstaff. A common language for computer security incidents. Technical Report SAND98-8667, SNL, 1998.

[11] H. Mannila, H. Toivonen, and A. I. Verkano. Discovery of frequent episodes in event sequences. Technical report, University of Helsinki, 1997.

[12] F. J. Martin and E. Plaza. SOID: an ontology for agent-aided intrusion detection. In *7th International Conference on Knowledge-based Intelligent Information & Engineering Systems*, 2003.

[13] B. Morin, L. Mé, H. Debar, and M. Ducassé. M2d2: A formal data model for ids alert correlation. In *Proc. of the RAID 2002*, 2002.

[14] P. Ning, S. Jajodia, and X. Wang. Abstraction-based intrusion detection in distributed environments. *ACM Transactions on Information and System Security*, 4(4):407–452, 2001.

[15] S. Northcutt. *Network Intrusion Detection. An Analyst's Handbook*. New Riders, 1999.

[16] M. Roesch. Snort - lightweight intrusion detection for networks. In *Proceedings of LISA '99: 13th Systems Administration Conference Seattle, Washington, USA*, November 1999.

[17] B. Schneier. Modeling security threats. *Dr. Dobb's Journal*, 1999.

[18] E. H. Spafford and D. Zamboni. Intrusion detection using autonomous agents. *Computer Networks*, 34:547–570, 2000.

[19] M. White, E. Fisch, and U. Pooch. Cooperating security managers: A peer-based intrusion detection system. *IEEE Network*, 10:20–23, 1996.

[20] Q. Zheng, K. Xu, W. Lv, and S. Ma. Intelligent search of correlated alarms from database containing noise data, 2002.

Artificial Intelligence Research and Development
I. Aguiló et al. (Eds.)
IOS Press, 2003

353

Using a Relevance Model for Performing Feature Weighting

Carlos Mérida-Campos, Emma Rollón
Chemical and Environmental Engineering Laboratory,
University of Girona,
Campus de Montilivi. E17071 Girona, Catalonia, Spain
{dmerida, erollon}@lsi.upc.es

Abstract. Feature Weighting is one of the most difficult tasks when developing Case Based Reasoning applications. This complexity grows when dealing with ill-defined wide domains with a sparse case base. Moreover, most widely-used feature selection and feature weighting methods assume that features are either relevant in the whole instance space or irrelevant through-out. However, it is often the case that specific features are only relevant within the *context* of other features' values (i.e., feature Y is relevant if feature $X = 1$, but irrelevant if $X = 0$). Therefore, features' weight and relevance are Context-Sensitive.

This paper defines a model to capture complex relations of relevance among features using domain knowledge, and suggests a method for mapping the knowledge captured in the model into feature weights, performing in this way *Context-Sensitive Feature Weighting*. The method we suggest is suitable for those domains where no instance based learning algorithm or observation based approach is applicable.

Keywords: Context sensitive Feature Weighting, CBR, Relevance, MBR.

1 Introduction

Feature weighting is a complex task deeply studied in the last years and defined within the *Retrieval* stage of the classical CBR cycle. The complexity of the process is due basically to the fact that expliciting the importance that a feature has among others requires a deep knowledge of the domain (knowledge-based approach) or a good machine learning mechanism to discover it automatically from the stored cases (observation-based approach). In observation-based modelization the role of probability is a central aspect. Thanks to probabilities estimations, these approaches determine whether it exists a relation among the elements of the model and, if sufficient historical or behavioral data is available, provide a quantitative measure of this likelihood. Observation-based approaches, however, need a huge amount of experiences to effectively extract the relationships. Therefore, they can not be successfully applied when dealing with few cases or with ill defined domains. The alternative is to use knowledge-based approaches in which the knowledge to establish the relevance relationships come from an expert. These approaches are useful when few experiences are available in the case base.

Most widely-used feature selection and feature weighting methods assume that features are either relevant in the whole instance space or irrelevant through-out. However, it is often the case that specific features are only relevant within the context of other features (i.e., feature Y is relevant if feature $X = 1$, but irrelevant if $X = 0$). Therefore, features' weight and relevance are context-sensitive.

To exemplify the context-sensitive problem, let us imagine we are computing the global weighting of the feature that defines the color of the smoke in a fire. This attribute must be seriously considered if the fire is in a chemical plant (as it would be the key to know the chemical substance involved). However, if the fire is in a forest, the attribute 'color of the smoke' will not be that *Relevant* in the similarity assessment task and, consequently, a lower weight should be assigned in the weighting process.

Feature weighting methods found in the literature vary in what the weights can depend on, thus varying their degree of context sensitivity. In the representationally simplest schemes, there is one weight per feature, and they are therefore completely context-free [12, 19, 13, 16]. More flexible approaches employ one weight per feature value [18, 22], one weight per feature per class [2], or a combination of the two [6], and thus exhibiting a moderate degree of context sensitivity. The most elaborate algorithms have in effect one weight per feature per instance, assigned either at classification time [5] or at learning time [3, 7], and are consequently fully context-sensitive. Basically, the methods named are based in the observation of the existent cases in the case base (i.e. instance-based approach) for automatically learning the relations among them.

Apart from the instance-based approach we also find other machine learning approaches to learn feature weights from *case order feedback* [21] or methods that use additional structures based on domain knowledge as, for example, ontologies [4] or bayesian networks [1]. Other approaches learn relationships from retrieval failures as the use of *introspective reasoning methods* [9]; or the dynamic system of assignation of bias to each feature used in PRODIGY/ANALOGY [23] and its extension [17] to incorporate explicit weights. Finally, *explanation based learning* (EBL) [14] has also been used for feature weighting purposes in [11] to capture combinations of features that cause failure in the retrieval.

All the mentioned feature weighting techniques appear in systems with well bounded domains and enough cases in the case base for using observation-based approaches to extract hidden relationships, or in environments where a feedback from external sources can be provided to guide the system. However, these techniques are not viable in domains characterized with a huge number of features and few cases available. This paper suggests a method for performing context sensitive feature weighting in wide domains considering relevance relationships established among features and explicited by experts. Starting from the definition of that relevance's feature relation we provide a formalism to capture them in a directed cyclic graph. Afterwards, a method to map the relevance network into feature weights used in the global similarity assessment process allows us to achieve *Context-Sensitive Feature Weighting*.

Our research is done within the scope of the RIMSAT EU Project. RIMSAT aims to design and implement a decision support system that using Case Based Reasoning as well as Model Based Reasoning technology is applied in the management of emergency situations. The context-sensitive feature weighting methodology proposed here is being integrated within the case-based reasoning engine, thus improving the similarity assessment process. This task has major importance in our framework as we are dealing with emergency situations where the usefulness of the action assessed will be determined by the retrieval of the suitable case.

The paper is structured as follows: section 2 specifies the domain model and case representation assumed in the paper, and discusses the option of using a knowledge based approach rather than a observation-based approach. Section 3 characterizes the concept relevance, and provides a methodology for capturing relevances relations in a semantic network. Section 4 describes in detail the proposed methodology for performing case retrieval using the relevances network. Section 5 discusses possible improvements of the proposed methodology and open issues and, finally, in section 6 we conclude by summarizing the proposed method and highlighting its advantages and drawbacks.

2 Dealing with wide Domains

We consider the *Domain Model* as a formal representation of the real world's concepts. In our representation, we have a plain feature-based modelisation:

$$DM = \{Feat_1, Feat_2, \cdots, Feat_n\} \tag{1}$$

where each feature has a set of possible accepted values. A case is represented as a subset of the domain model's features with a value assigned.

The characteristics of the domain will determine the feasible technique to extract possible relations among features. The main influencing aspects are the dimension, that is, the number of features needed for an accurate case representation; and the sampling size, that is, the number of cases stored in the case base.

When dealing with well bounded domains with enough cases in the case base, machine learning techniques fit well. These techniques are based in statistical estimation of a world's sample and, therefore, the reliability of estimation increases with the sample's size and the population's variability.

However, when dealing with high dimensional domains with not enough sampling cases, that are the so called wide domains, machine learning techniques will not guarantee the reliability of the estimations and therefore, they must not be applied. In that case, knowledge based approaches based in the expert knowledge are the ones used to enrich the domain model adding relations as will be explained in the following sections.

3 Enriching the Domain Model with Relevance Relations

In the example of the smoke color and the kind of hazard, we showed how certain values of certain features modify the *relevance* that another feature has for the current case. Our target is capturing all the important relations of relevance in a network. At this point one question arises: Is the Relevance a simple influence relation that can be captured in some of the existent ways of capturing causal relationship?, as for example, bayesian networks or markov models or even trust models? After studying the properties of the relevance relation using examples provided by the domain experts, we saw that certainly the Relevance relation among features has its own behavior, and so none of the existent models could be accurately used for capturing relevance and keeping its properties. The following subsection defines relevance as we understand it, and poses a set of properties that will be kept in our modelisation.

3.1 Relevance definition and quantification

Relevance is a concept relatively easy to interpret from a subjective point of view, but hard to define it formally to provide more than just a couple of examples for characterizing the concept.

Relevance is not a well understood concept in spite of the huge amounts of research on this topic, above all because of an inconsistently used terminology. In the literature, we find many attempts to organize all the research done, from which we highlight the work by Mizzaro in [15]. There, the author states that there are many kinds of valid Relevance definitions, not just one, and that this concept is definable from four different dimensions (Information resources, representation of the user's problem, time and component). We will keep this idea and provide a characterization of the *Relevance* concept following the four dimensional conception of Mizzaro.

We define relevance R of a feature f in a certain instant of time, related to feature weighting task, and given a certain assignation of values to other features (context C) as the importance that feature f has among the other features of the domain in a related time for performing the named task.

Although this generic definition has into account the time, for the sake of simplicity, we will keep it constant and will not appear in the function Relevance as a variable. Thus, we represent formally the relevance as a function of the feature and the context: $R(f, C)$. To this definition we add the effect of the Union operator in the following way:

$$R(f_i, C_j) \cup R(f_i, C_k) = MAX(R(f_i, C_j), R(f_i, C_k)) \tag{2}$$

Relevance quantification is a very prolific topic in the literature (for a deep survey on this topic, we refer the reader to the work by H.Greisdorf [10]). Although the existence of degrees or regions of relevance is accepted, there is no agreement in which are the most useful concrete degrees [20].

Taking into account that the relevance values are going to be specified by an expert, the range should be expressive enough to capture the particularities of the domain knowledge, but clear enough to be easily understood. Note that both an upper and sub specialization will lead to confusion when estimating the relevance hence building an useless relevance model.

The range selected for capturing the relevance in our framework uses the results of the study in [24]. They observed empirically that for capturing relevance, an scale of around seven values is the optimal choice. Our proposed seven values (i.e., Irrelevant=0, Maybe Irrelevant=1, Neutral Relevance=2, Slightly Relevant=3, Medium Relevant=4, Very Relevant=5, Extremely Relevant=6) has been agreed by the RIMSAT's domain experts and, thus, is the scale under study.

3.2   Relevance network model

The relevance relationships that a domain feature is endowed with, will be established by domain experts and, after studying together with them the types of relevances that a feature can be affected by, we define the *incontextual relevance*, that is, the exceptional relevance that a feature can have whatever the context is (i.e. no matter the values of the other features); and *contextual relevance*, that is, the exceptional relevance that a feature has because of the values of other features within an specific context. We will also use in the description the term *neutral relevance* for referring to that relevance value each feature will have by default.

With the conceptualization of *relevance* provided in the previous subsection, we propose a formalisation of a structure that will capture this domain knowledge. Figure 1 shows a relevance model involving three features: f_j, f_k and f_w. Feature f_j is *incontextually relevant*, and the value of this relevance is R_A; feature f_k is relevant when feature $f_j = V_{f_j}$ and $f_w =$

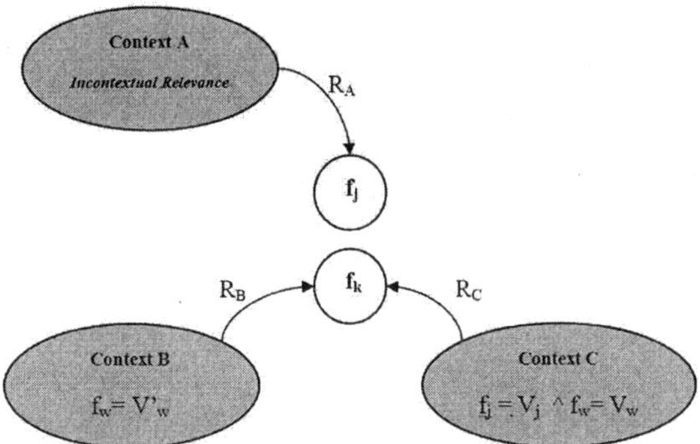

Figure 1: Example of a Relevance Model Conceptualisation

V_{f_w} (both are in the same context $ContextC$) with R_C degree of relevance; and, feature f_k is also relevant when $f_w = V'_{f_w}$, but with R_B value. Other features not considered in the graph or those influencing other features but not being affected by any incontextually or contextually relevance (i.e., f_w) will take the *neutral relevance* as value.

For efficiently implement that conceptualisation without repetition of features among all the possible contexts nodes, our proposal is a cyclic directed graph called *relevance network model* in which nodes represent features, and arrows describe the influence between nodes. Arrows will be tagged with a list of triplets defined as:

$$< Cid_i, V_{f_j}, R_{f_k} > \tag{3}$$

where Cid_i stands for the identifier of a context in which the relevance is applied; and V_{f_j} is the value of the feature f_j that endows the feature f_k with a degree of relevance of R_{f_k}.

If the relevance affecting feature f_k is the same for all the values of feature f_j, an special character $*$, representing all possible values of f_j, is used for clarity and compression purposes.

One additional constrain must be specified for our representation, that is the relation one to one that exist between the context identifier and the relevance value. In other words, all the triplets that have the same Context identifier, must have the same relevance value. Figure 2 shows our proposed representation of the same example showed in Figure 1.

Summarizing, the situations that can be captured by the model are the following:

- A given feature is relevant by itself (influenced by all its values), that is, *incontextual relevant*.

- A given feature is relevant by itself only when it takes certain values.

- A given feature is relevant depending on the values of other features, that is, *context relevant*. Those influences can be constitutive of the same context or be by themselves a different one.

The task of eliciting the relevance relation from domain experts is comparable, to at least some extent, to knowledge engineering for other artificial-intelligence representations and,

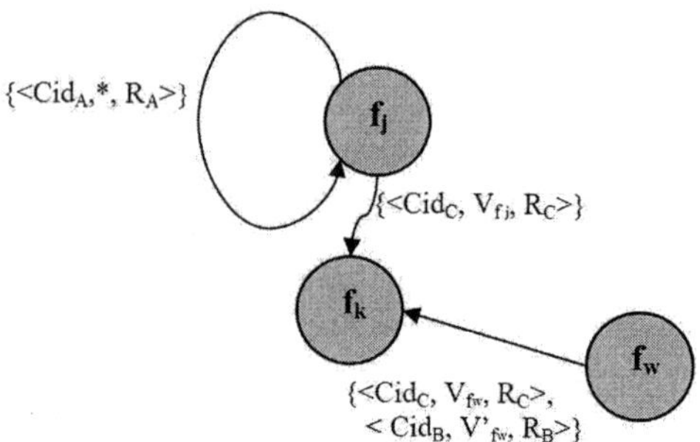

Figure 2: Relevance model example

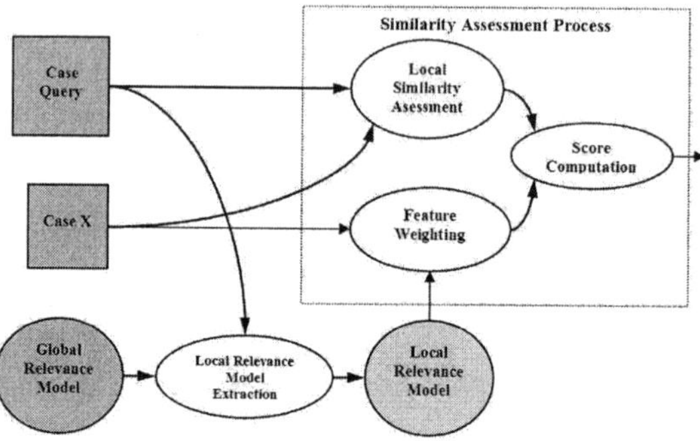

Figure 3: The Similarity Assessment Process

although it may require significant effort, is generally considered doable [8]. The most daunting task in building this kind of networks is the one of obtaining the quantitative part, as is where we decide how much more a feature is considered relevant over those that are not considered specially relevant (contextual or incontextual).

4   Using the relevance network model in case retrieval

The relevance network model is integrated within the case retrieval stage and, more concretely, within the similarity assessment task. Figure 3 depicts where the integration is done and the steps followed from the initial relevance network model to the applicable feature weights. The result of the mapping is a context-sensitive feature weighting technique that takes into account the knowledge specified within relevance relationships.

4.1   Local Relevance Model Extraction

The *relevance network model* describes the whole relevance influences between domain features. However, only the relevance of the features that appear in the Case Query (CQ) are the ones considered to assess the similarity as these are the features that determine the current context of relevance applicability. Thus, the sub-model obtained from the relevance network model by extracting only the nodes that contain feature values that hold in the CQ and the corresponding arrows constitute the so-called *Local Relevance Model (LRM)*. In this way, if the *relevance network model* has captured a contextual relevance of feature f_k, with the triplet $< Cid_i, V_{f_j}, R_{f_k} >$, it just will be part of the LRM if and only if $(f_k \subset CQ) \& (f_j \subset CQ) \& (CQ.f_j = V_{f_j})$.

The LRM is obtained for every new case query presented and depicts the concrete relevance context in which the cases from the case-base are going to be compared.

4.2   *From local relevance model to feature weights*

The translation between the relevance relationships described in the LRM into feature weights is a crucial process called *Feature Weighting*. This translation have to be done for every case from the case-base that is compared with the query case as it considers the specific features of each captured case.

The three subtasks needed to obtain usable feature weights are i) to elicitate relevances, ii) to map relevances into feature weights, and iii) to normalize feature weights.

4.2.1   Elicitating Relevances

The LRM obtained from the case query is merged with the concrete compared case. This merging process consists in searching for those compared case's features that hold in the LRM and in extracting the corresponding relevance.

A special situation can appear when a feature is affected by more than one context and both hold. The consequence is to obtain various relevance values for the same feature. In this case, the *union operator* (described in equation 2) applied to those relevance values is used, thus extracting the definitely relevance value influencing that feature.

4.2.2   Mapping Relevances into Feature Weights

Once we have a Relevance degree for each of the features of the compared case, we will use a mapping method for converting the qualitative degrees of relevance into feature weights. Our proposal has two main assumptions:

1. A feature endowed with the maximum degree of relevance must have more weight that the sum of the rest of weights of the features of the case (considering the rest of features taken neutral relevance).

2. A feature endowed with the minimum degree of relevance (Irrelevant) must have weight 0.

3. There exists a linear relation between degrees of relevance and feature weights.

We will consider z as the value of unnormalized weight of a feature with neutral relevance NR, and k the total number of features with assigned value in Case Query. Following our

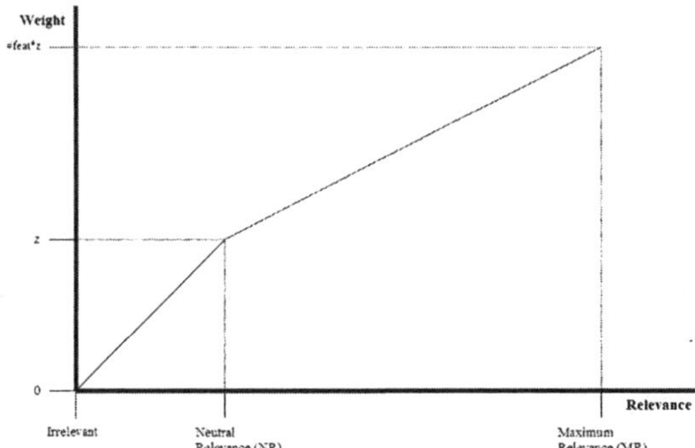

Figure 4: Weighting function representation

conceptualization of maximum relevance, the feature with the highest degree of relevance (MR), will weight k times the value of the neutral relevance weight, i.e.:

$$W(MR) = z * k \qquad (4)$$

Considering assumption 2 and 3, for the weight function $w(Relevance)$ there will exist a linear interpolation between 0 and z for relevance values ranging from irrelevant to NR ones. In the same way, having into account the first assumption, there will exist a linear interpolation between z and $z * k$ for relevance values from NR to MR (see Figure 4).

The existence of a discontinuity point in the function is due to the impossibility for a continuous linear approach to hold our three assumptions.

The election of value z has no effect after the process of normalisation of feature weights. Therefore, and for simplifying the formulae we provide, we have chosen value 1.

The general function for getting the value of the (non-normalized) feature weight from the relevance value ($W(R)$), is computed straightforward, and has the following formalization:

$$W(R) = \frac{R}{NR}; \ \ if \ R \leq NR$$

$$W(R) = \frac{R * (k - 1) - NR * k + MR}{MR - NR}; \ \ if \ R > NR$$

Note that the relevance network model only captures the features whose relevance is modified by the context and those that have an special incontextual relevance. Therefore, the features not affected by the model will take the NR as value.

4.2.3 Normalizing Feature Weights

The normalization of the obtained weights follows the well-known approach that divide each of the feature weights by the sum of all the feature weights of the case.

$$W'_j = \frac{W_j}{\sum_{j=0}^{f} W_j} \qquad (5)$$

Once the whole process has finished we obtain context-sensitive weights ready to be assigned to the compared case's features.

4.3   Similarity Assessment

Similarity assessment is the final step in the whole process and where the context-weighting technique is applied. The task is divided in three processes, that are, Local Similarity Assessment, Feature Weighting, and Score Computation.

The concrete technique for performing *Local Similarity Assessment* must be the most suitable for the kind of features that are going to be compared. The only aspect required at this point is that the value issued by the local similarity functions must be normalized.

The *Feature Weighting* process obtains the specific feature weights. As described in sub-section 4.2, the feature weights take into account domain knowledge and depend on the specific context. The result is a context-sensitive feature weighting technique.

Finally, *Score Computation* process will provide a measure in the range of [0,1] indicating how similar the compared case is with respect the case query. The score will be obtained by using the following formula:

$$Score = \sum_{i=0}^{f-1} (LS_i * FW_i) \tag{6}$$

where LS_i is the local similarity of the value of feature i compared with the value of the same feature in the Case Query; and FW_i is the weight of feature i.

5   Future research

The context-sensitive feature weighting technique described here is under implementation within RIMSAT project. An experimental evaluation will therefore have to wait. Its plausibility, however, is supported by the intuitively approach to the relevance characterization and capture, and the straightforward integration with the case-base reasoning engine.

One of the assumptions made by the model is that exists a linear relation degree between relevance and feature weights. Other relevance-weight transformation functions have to be considered within the tuning parameters task and observe its effect within the whole similarity assessment process.

Currently, the relevance network model does not specify how to capture certain logical constrains as for example a context of relevance that is triggered not only with 'and' operations among features, but also with 'or' operations. At the moment, the way of express the disjunction of feature values is by using different contexts. Therefore, an extension of the model is needed when dealing with domain models in which this requirement of expressiveness exists.

Moreover, we are studying the integration of other ways of making relevance depend on sets of values and thus expressing relations as $>$, $>=$, $<$, $<=$ or $! =$. In the same line, relevance may depend not only on certain feature values but also on the phase in which the incident occurs. Therefore, the "incident time" should be included as part of the context definition.

Finally, we observe the possibility to merge the relevance network model with observation-based approaches as stated in [1] to increase the completeness of the relevance model or to verify its correctness. However, the integration will only be feasible when a greater number of cases is available.

6 Conclusions

Our approach specifies a relevance network model that captures the relevance relationships established among the features that characterize the domain model. The relevance degree specified in the model is translated into feature weights and applied in the similarity assessment task. The result is a *context-sensible feature weighting methodology* whose goal is to take into account the particularities of each context thus increasing the usefulness of the cases retrieved.

The methodology proposed is suitable for dealing with wide domains, with not enough cases for using instance-based approaches to capture in an accurate way existent relations. In such ill conditions, the system proposed will be able to perform an accurate case-retrieval. The payoff for having such flexibility in these adverse conditions is the requirement of having to capture domain knowledge by an expert, with all the risks and inconveniences of this task.

7 Acknowledgements

This work has been funded by the European Commission (Remote Intelligent Management Support and Training (RIMSAT project IST-2000-28655). The authors are thankful to Javier Vázquez and to Dr.Miquel Sánchez-Marré for their valuable advices.

References

[1] A. Aamodt and H. Langseth. Integrating Bayesian networks into knowledge-intensive CBR. Proc. from the AAAI workshop. David Aha, Jody J.Daniels (eds.) Technical Report WS-98-15. AAAI Press, Menlo Park, 1998. pp. 1-6

[2] D.Aha. Incremental, Instance-Based LEarning of Independent and Graded Concept Descriptions. In Proceedings of The Sixth International Workshop on Machine LEarning, 387-391. Ithaca, NY. Ed. Morgan Kaufmann. 1989.

[3] D.W.Aha. Generalizing from Case Studies: A Case Study. In Proceedings of The Ninth International Workshop on Machine LEarning, 1-10. Aberdeen, Scotland. Ed. Morgan Kaufmann. 1992.

[4] E. Armengol and E. Plaza. Similarity of Structured Cases in CBR. Proc. from the CCIA held in Castellon, Spain, 2002.

[5] C.G.Atkeson, A.W.Moore and S.Schaal. Locally Weighted Learning. Artificial Intelligence Review. 1996

[6] R.H. Creecy, B.M. Masand, S.J. Smith and D.L. Waltz. Trading MIPS and memory for knowledge angineering. Communications of the ACM 35:48-64, 1992.

[7] P. Domingos.Contextsensitive feature selection for lazy learners. Artificial Intelligence Review 11:227–253. 1997.

[8] M. Druzdzel, L. van der Gaag, M. Henrion and F. Jensen. Building probabilistic networks: where do the numbers come from. M. Druzdzel, L. C. van der Gaag, M. Henrion, and F. Jensen, editors. Building probabilistic networks: where do the numbers come from?, IJCAI-95 Workshop, Montreal, Canada, 1995.

[9] S.Fox and D.Leake. Using introspective reasoning to refine indexing. In Case-Based Reasoning Research and Development, Procs. of the 1st. International Conference (ICCBR-95) 1010 LNAI, Springer Verlag. 1995.

[10] H.Greisdorf. Relevance: An Interdisciplinary and Information Science Perspective. Special Issue on Information Science Research, Vol. 3 Numb.2. 2000.

[11] L.Ihrig and S.Kambhampati. Automatic storage and indexing of plan derivations based on replay failures. In Proceedings of IJCAI-95. 1995.

[12] J.D.Kelly and L.Davis. A Hybrid Genetic Algorithm for Classification. In Proceedings of the Twefth International Joint Conference on Artificial Intelligence, 645-650. Sydney:Morgan Kaufmann. 1991.

[13] C.Lee. An Instance-Based LEarning Method for Databases: An Information Theoretic Approach. In Proceedings of The Ninth European Conference on Machine Learning, 387-390. Catania, Italy.1994.

[14] S.Minton. Learning Search Control Knowledge: An Explanation-Based Approach. Kluwer Academic Publishers, Boston. 1998.

[15] S. Mizzaro. How many relevances in information retrieval?. In Interacting with Computers journal vol.10 numb.3 pg.303-320. 1998.

[16] T.Mohri and H.Tanaka. An Optimal Weighting Criterion of Case Indexing for Both Numeric and Symbolic Attributes. Aha,D.W., editor, Case-Based Reasoning papers from the 1994 workshop, AAAI Press, Menlo Park, CA.

[17] H.Muoz-Avila and J.Hullen. Feature Weighting by Explaining Case-based Planning Episodes. In I.Smith, B.Faltings (Eds). Proc. European Workshop on case-based Reasoning (EWCBR), LNCS/LNAI, 1996.

[18] R.M.Nosofsky, S.E. Clark, and H.J.Shin. Rules and exemplars in categorization, identification, and recognition. Journal of Experimental Pshichology: Learning, Memory, and Cognition, 15:282-304,1989.

[19] S.Salzberg. A Nearest Hyperrectangle Learning Method. Machine Learning, 6:251-276. 1991.

[20] L.Schamber. Relevance and information behaviour. In M.E. Williams (Ed.), Annual Review of Information Science and Technology, Vol. 29, 3-48. Medford, NJ:American Society for Information Science.1994

[21] A.Stahl. Learning Feature Weights from Case Order Feedback. Eds.D.W.Aha and I.Watson: ICCBR 01, LNAI 2080, pp 504-516. 2001.

[22] C.Stanfill and D.Waltz. Toward memory-based reasoning. Communications of the ACM, 29:1213-1228,1986.

[23] M.Veloso. Learning by Analogical Reasoning in General Problem Solving. PhD thesis, Carnegie Mellon University. 1992.

[24] Towards the Identification of the Optimal Number of Relevance Categories R. Tang, W. M. Shaw, Jr., and J. L. Vevea. Journal of the American Society for Information Science. Volume 50. Number 3.

Artificial Intelligence Research and Development
I. Aguiló et al. (Eds.)
IOS Press, 2003

An iterative constrained quantization algorithm for band discrimination in pulsed field gel electrophoresis

Julià Minguillón[1,2], Pere Coll[3,4], Francesca March[3], Jaume Pujol[2]
[1]*Estudis d'Informàtica i Multimèdia, Universitat Oberta de Catalunya.*
[2]*Combinatòria i Comunicació Digital, Universitat Autònoma de Barcelona.*
[3]*Servei de Microbiologia, Hospital de Sant Pau.*
[4]*Departament de Genètica i Microbiologia, Universitat Autònoma de Barcelona.*

Abstract

In this paper we describe a modified version of the Linde-Buzo-Gray algorithm (LBG) for finding a representative set of bands for a given set of strains using Pulsed Field Gel Electrophoresis (PFGE) as the typing method. Our main goal is to reduce the number of visual comparisons usually needed to determine the correct weight for each band and to generate a set of bands which can be used to obtain a binary string for each strain in the data set for classification and clustering purposes. Results show that the LBG algorithm is very useful for band discrimination purposes, and that the inclusion of several constraints related to the inherent characteristics of the PFGE technique improves the quality of the obtained results: both the number of bands and band locations are closest to the expected values. Despite of its simplicity, our proposal may be an useful tool for band discrimination as the first stage of the current process which involves both automatical and manual tasks.

1   Introduction

Pulsed Field Gel Electrophoresis (PFGE) is a robust technique used in the field of molecular epidemiology for typing. It is an universal technique, as it can be applied to a wide spectrum of typing problems related to different microorganisms. Its robustness under a standardization protocol make it suitable for building the databases used in several centers of reference. In this case, the aim of reproducibility intra and inter-laboratories is the most important goal, in order to correctly identify new strains when compared to those stored in the reference databases, see [8], for example.

Scientists dealing with PFGE need to define a reproducible protocol for creating the gels and obtaining the band weights, in order to obtain comparable results. The need to compare gels by means of visual comparison is an enormous task which is also an important source of errors, even with the aid of specific software packages. We propose a simple algorithm which may help to make decisions regarding band discrimination purposes, thus reducing the number of visual comparisons. This process is usually carried out semi-automatically by means of proprietary software [9, 3], which does not allow the users to fine-tune the process, but only to supervise the process. Other remarkable approaches are [17, 2, 1], for example. Fully documented and validated methods of automated or semi-automated comparison and clustering are needed for expanding the research possibilities in the molecular epidemiology field. Our proposal is a simple way to obtain a reasonably accurate initial clustering which may be used to reduce visual inspection to a small percentage of the total number of strains.

This paper is organized as follows: Section 2 introduces the characteristics of the PFGE technique and the details related to the problem which has to be solved. Section 3 describes the vector quantization algorithm proposed using the Linde-Buzo-Gray algorithm as a starting point. Experiments and simulations are carried out in Section 4. Finally, the conclusions of this paper can be found in Section 5, altogether with some research questions which still remain open.

2 Pulsed Field Gel Electrophoresis

Pulsed-field gel electrophoresis is often considered the "gold standard" of molecular typing methods. This technique has been applied to the subtyping of several bacteria, that is, to identify different clones or clonal groups (strains that have a high degree of genetic relatedness) among isolates of the same species collected from different sources and sites and at different times (discrimination below the species level). PFGE can be used to type a broader array of bacterial species and, for some bacteria, it has greater discriminating capacity than most current molecular typing methods. A good introduction for non-clinicians can be found in [4], for example.

PFGE allows the generation of simplified chromosomal restriction fragment patterns. Because intact DNA is required for PFGE analysis, this technique involves embedding organisms in agarose, lysing the organisms in situ, and digesting the chromosomal DNA with restriction endonucleases that cut infrequently to generate large fragments of chromosomal DNA ranging from 10 to 800kb. These fragments are resolved into a pattern of discrete bands in the gel by cyclically altering the orientation of the electric field during special electrophoretic procedures. Smaller fragments move faster than large fragments. Reference lanes with known molecular weight fragments are included in each gel in order to model the distortion introduced during the electrophoretic procedure.

Gel results can be photographed, and data analysis can be accomplished by using any of a number of commercially available software packages [9]. The DNA restriction patterns of the isolates are compared with one another to determine their relatedness [18]. It is possible to create data banks of PFGE patterns for all organisms, enabling the creation of reference databases to which any new strain could be compared [8].

One of the most difficult problems related to PFGE is the conversion of the weights of the bands detected from each gel to a set of validated bands, where similar band weights are normalized to a single weight, that is, quantized. This process, known as normalization, is carried out by means of a combination of visual comparisons and a software package which helps the user to determine the position of each band. Once this step has been carried out, each strain can be converted to a binary string, where each bit denotes the presence or the absence of a band. Therefore, all strains can be studied as binary vectors of the same length for classification or clustering purposes, and several distance criteria can be computed, see [13] for example. With our proposal, we try to reduce the amount of effort which has to be dedicated to the comparison of similar strains, by obtaining an reduced set of clusters which are known to be different between them.

2.1 Band constraints

There are several restrictions related to the way bands are obtained inherent to the characteristics of the PFGE technique that must be taken into account during the normalization stage:

1. Two or more bands of the same strain cannot be collapsed into a single band weight.

2. Bands that are sufficiently separated (for a given distance criterion) must not be joined.

3. Molecular weights do not follow a linear distribution, but a logarithmic one.

4. Weight precision depends also on band position and it follows a logarithmic distribution.

The problem of band discrimination can be studied as a constrained mixture decomposition problem. Among several possibilities (as the EM algorithm [15], or self organizing maps [11] for example), we consider the LBG algorithm to be more suitable for resolving such problem, mainly due to its interpretability, and that it obtains reasonable results when the number of samples is limited.

3 LBG algorithm

The Generalized Lloyd Algorithm, also known as the Linde-Buzo-Gray algorithm (LBG) [14], is a well known technique for vector quantizer design [10]. It is a probability distribution function (pdf) optimized algorithm, using an iterative approach to refine an initial solution until a minimum (hopefully not local) is achieved. A recent very good compilation of unsupervised learning and clustering techniques can be found in [5].

We propose to use the LBG algorithm for band discrimination but using a modified version which takes into account the constraints described is the previous section. In fact, we are designing pdf optimized scalar quantizers as each band is a single weight, not a vector of weights. Let T be the collection of samples (i.e. band weights) $\{w_i\}$. The LBG algorithm can be summarized as follows:

1. Begin with an initial codebook C_0 of size B from T.

2. Compute the average distortion D for C_0.

3. Given a codebook $C_n = \{y_i\}$, partition the training set into B clusters R_i using the Nearest Neighbor Condition:

$$R_i = \{w \in T \mid d(w, y_i) \leq d(w, y_j) \ \forall \, j \neq i\}.$$

Ties are broken by assigning the weight with smallest index.

4. Using the Centroid Condition, compute the centroids for the clusters found in the previous step to obtain a new codebook $C_{n+1} = \{y_i'\}$:

$$y_i' = \frac{1}{|R_i|} \sum_{w_j \in R_i} w_j \ \forall \, R_i \neq \emptyset. \tag{1}$$

If an empty Voronoi cell is generated, its centroid is not updated and a warning flag is raised.

5. Compute the average distortion D' for C_{n+1}:

$$D' = \frac{1}{B} \sum_{i=1}^{|T|} d(w_i, y'_j) I_{\{w_i \in R_j\}}, \tag{2}$$

where $I_{\{A\}}$ is the indicator function which is one when A is true and zero otherwise.

6. If $(D - D')/D > \epsilon$, set $D = D'$, increase n and go to step 3.

Therefore, the process is determined by the distortion measure d and by ϵ, which is set to 0.01 in our experiments setup.

3.1 Proposed algorithm

Our proposal uses $\text{LBG}(C)$ to generate a new codebook C' from C as the basic step of an iterative process. Basically, the algorithm proposed in this paper can be summarized as follows: start with a number of bands B, trying to find a valid explanation for all strains using the modified LBG algorithm. If B is not enough to represent all different bands for all the strains, increment it and start again. This may happen when the first or the second restrictions cannot be satisfied. If the first constraint is not satisfied, the weight assigned to the band causing the problem is split in two bands by adding a small perturbation, and the process is started again. If the second constraint is not satisfied, a new band is added using the molecular weight which does not satisfy the distance condition.

Once the minimum number of bands B_x for representing all the strains has been found, it is reasonable to ask whether the strains could be represented with a larger number of bands. Nevertheless, it is fair to think that results are more stable when a reduced number of bands is used, because PFGE accuracy is limited and it is impossible to distinguish between bands which are very close to each other. Furthermore, if the number of bands is too large, most bands will be only assigned to a few (or even one) strains, so strains will be far in a number of different bands sense and very different between them, and this might interfere in the posterior epidemiological analysis, as stated in [18]. This process is repeated until an empty Voronoi cell is generated in step 3, meaning that a band weight is no longer needed and, therefore, must be removed. We use this fact as a stopping condition for our algorithm.

3.2 Initial codebook

In order to start the LBG algorithm, an initial codebook is needed. Several options are available:

1. Find the strain with the maximum number of bands and set B to such number, and use such strain as the initial codebook.

2. Find B as above, and distribute the B bands uniformly in the range $[w_m, w_M]$ where w_m and w_M are the minimum and the maximum band weights among all bands of all strains.

3. Set $B = 1$ assigning any valid weight, for example, the first band of the first strain.

Experiments show that the second option usually produces the best results, because the bands in the first case may not be representative, and the third option is the simplest one but usually yields to an initial solution using B bands similar to the second option. In fact, the LBG algorithm ensures convergence if both conditions (defined in steps 3 and 4) are satisfied, so the importance of the initial codebook is relative, although it is well known that the better the initial codebook is, the better the computed final codebook will be. Any information about band positions (direct comparisons with bands within reference lanes, for example) could be used as well. Due to the fact that we are dealing with small data sets, LBG algorithm complexity is not an important issue.

3.3　Including PFGE constraints

One of the most important facts that must be taken into account is the logarithmic relationship between the migration in pixels (that is, the relative position of a band within its lane in the gel) and the weight assigned to such distance. Figure 1 shows this logarithmic relationship for a reference lane in a gel, as described in Section 2.

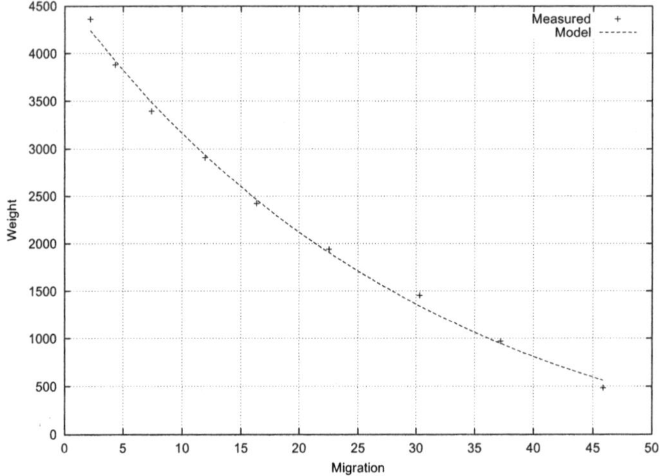

Figure 1: Logarithmic relationship between migration and weight.

It is important to remark that visual inspection compares bands under a migration distance based criterion, not weight, so the proposed algorithm should also use such criterion in some manner. Furthermore, due to the nature of the PFGE technique, accuracy when measuring distances is also variable depending on molecular weight, as small fragments move faster through the gel and distortions are larger than for large fragments. Therefore, the criterion for considering two bands to be different depends also on their molecular weights. Several approaches using linear piecewise interpolation have been proposed, see [12] for example, but they do not reproduce the continuous distortions present in each gel. We use a continuous model which takes into account the logarithmic relationship between migration and molecular weight.

4 Experiments

In order to validate the proposed algorithm we use a database of PFGE patterns representative of the overall *Neisseria meningitidis* population circulating in an open community during an endemic period (30 isolates from patients and 191 from throat cultures of healthy individuals) [6, 7]. This data set contains 134 strains which are known to be different, that is, there are no two strains sharing the same set of bands. The number of bands of each strain ranges from 6 to 15 bands. Therefore, we set $B = 15$ as the initial number of bands, although we know that the expected number of bands will be larger. In fact, using a combination of commercial software and visual inspection, the number of bands seems to be around 60. Figure 2 shows the PFGE of five isolates of *Neisseria meningitidis* and two reference lanes.

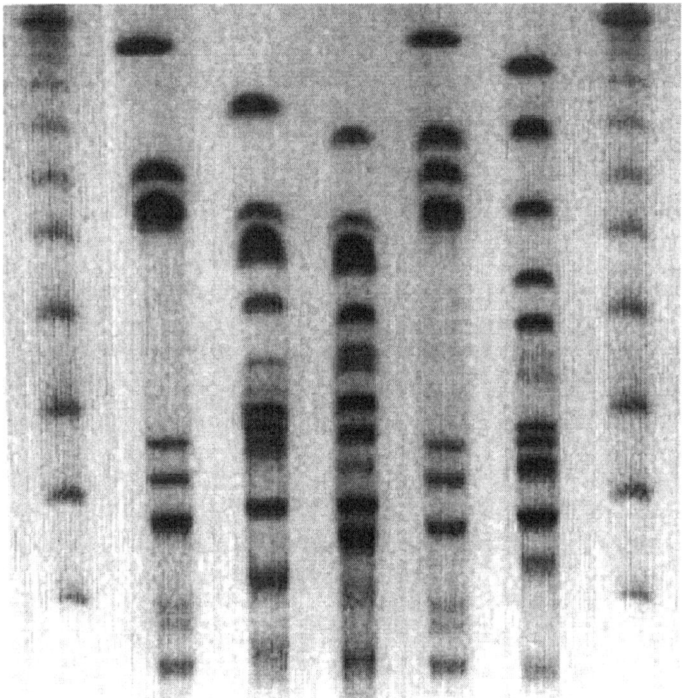

Figure 2: PFGE patterns of chromosomal DNA restriction fragments for *Neisseria meningitidis*. Leftmost and rightmost lanes contain reference molecular weight standards.

We expect our algorithm to minimize the number of clusters found once a binary string is generated for each strain. A cluster would mean that two or more different bands have been erroneously joined. This property, namely discrimination, determines the quality of the output generated by the algorithm, as no clusters should be created for different strains, that is, it is better to consider two similar strains as different than to consider two different but similar strains as identical. On the other hand, if two or more strains are known to form a cluster, the algorithm should also keep the strains within the same cluster.

Figure 3 shows all the weights present in all the strains from the data set, sorted (from left to right) by magnitude. Notice that there are much many bands with small weights than bands with large weights, because small fragments move faster and present a higher distortion than large fragments. Figure 3 also shows the different weight accuracy regions: small weights show a more continuous behavior, varying smoothly, while large weights show a discrete behavior, specially for the largest weights.

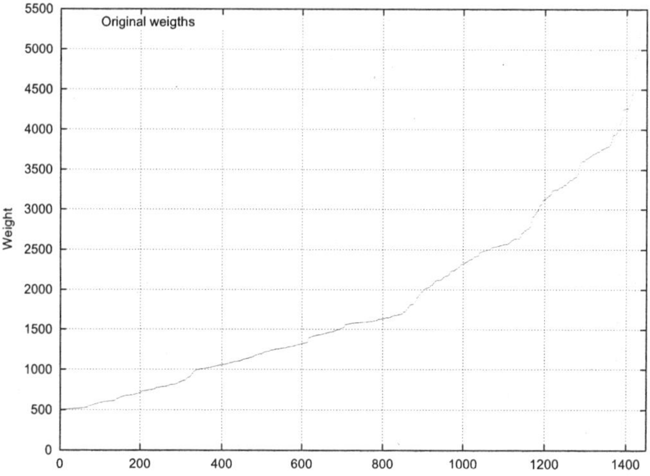

Figure 3: Band weights present in the data set.

4.1 Unconstrained LBG algorithm

For this experiment, we do not use the constraints described in Section 2.1 but the first one, that is, two bands of the same strain cannot be joined.

In this case, the distortion function used in Eq. 2 is the mean square error, as follows:

$$d(x, y) = (x - y)^2,$$

and centroids are computed using Eq. 1 directly without any modification.

With this configuration, the algorithm stops with only 33 bands which is, according to the experts, a small value. Figure 4 shows the weights found by the unconstrained LBG algorithm. The range $[w_i - 3\sigma_i, w_i + 3\sigma_i]$ is also plotted, in order to show possible band overlapping under a Gaussian assumption. Notice that overlapping is approximately similar for all bands, increasing for the largest molecular weight bands.

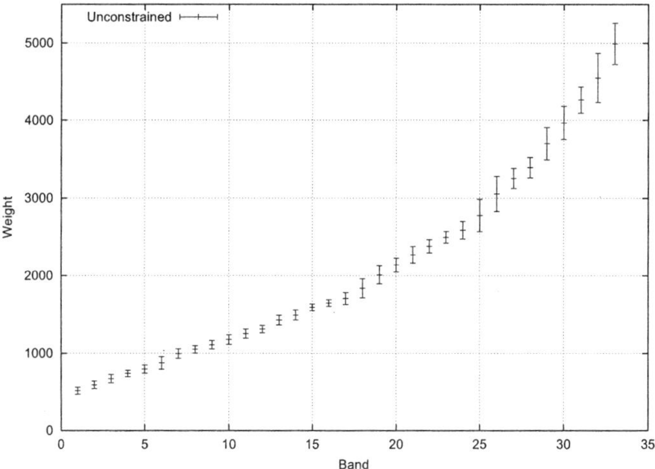

Figure 4: Band weights found by the unconstrained algorithm.

Regarding the discrimination property, this algorithm shows a reasonable behavior but a few mistakes are made: five clusters of two identical strains each one are created by the quantization algorithm. Figure 5 shows the strains which are clustered in pairs. It is easy to see that distortions are higher for large band weights, but most mistakes are made in the small weight region, showing the importance of distance based constraints.

When all the 221 strains are used, the algorithm stops with 34 bands, one more than in the previous experiment. A new band is created between bands 25 and 26 (band weights are 2778.09 and 3055.63, respectively), which are the ones with the largest ratio of weight variance to band weight. This could be used as an indicator of band quality, for example. A complete probabilistic model for fragment lengths (that is, weights) produced by the PFGE technique is needed in order to improve results, such as the one proposed in [16], for example. All the original clusters in the data set were maintained in the quantized version, so the algorithm is useful for creating an initial clustering using all strains, not only those known to be different.

4.2 Constrained LBG algorithm

In this case, we use all the constraints described in Section 2.1. Therefore, the distortion measure and the centroid calculation must be adapted to include the logarithmic behavior of the relationship between migration and molecular weight in order to use a more realistic model. Accuracy is set to a 2% for small band weights and varies exponentially up to a 5% for large band weights.

Regarding the distortion function, we use this distance measure:

$$d(x, y) = |\log(x) - \log(y)|,$$

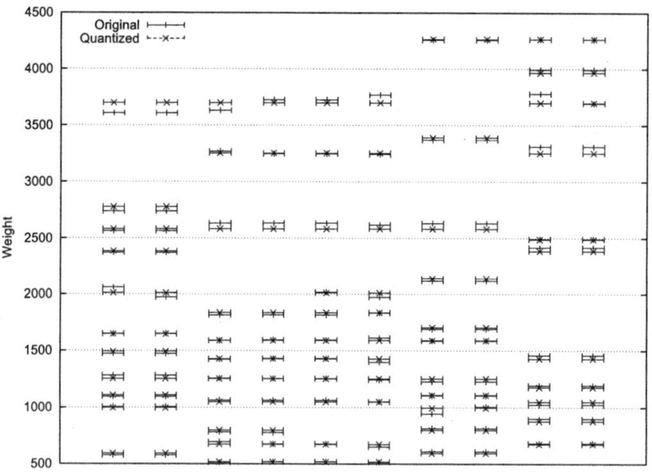

Figure 5: False clusters created by the unconstrained algorithm.

and centroids are computed as follows:

$$y_i' = e^{\frac{1}{|R_i|} \sum_{w_j \in R_i} \log(w_j)}.$$

With this configuration, which is more restrictive than the previous setup due to the inclusion of the second constraint defined in Section 2.1, the algorithm stops with 66 bands, which is a more realistic value for such figure. Figure 6 shows the band weights found by the constrained algorithm.

Notice that in this case band overlapping is reduced, specially for the bands with smaller weights. And except for a few bands with the highest molecular weights, overlapping shows a monotonous increasing behavior, which is more realistic according to the gel model. Regarding the discrimination property, the constrained algorithm shows a much better behavior than the unconstrained algorithm, as only one false cluster with two strains (namely S_{11} and S_{12}) is created instead of five. Both strains share the same band weights but the first one, which is 3725.17 and 3846.36 respectively, while the quantized weight is 3766.06. In this case the mistake is made in the large weight region, which accuracy is set to be stricter. Using a higher value, (3% instead of 2%, for example), causes the algorithm to avoid this problem. This shows the importance of fine-tuning those parameters relative to the logarithmic distortion. When the 221 strains are used, the algorithm stops with 67 bands, one more than in the previous experiment, as happened with the unconstrained case, but in this case more bands are involved, specially those representing large weights. Once again, all the original clusters in the data set were maintained in the quantized version.

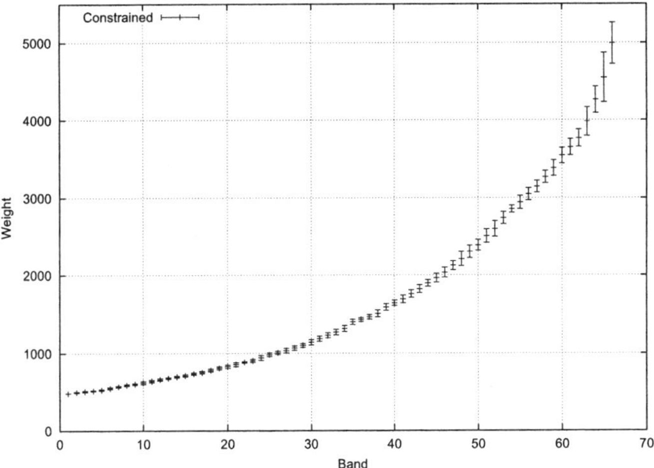

Figure 6: Band weights found by the constrained algorithm.

5　Conclusions

In this paper we have described a simple iterative method based on a modified version of the LBG algorithm for band weight placement, under a set of constraints which try to reproduce the characteristics of the PFGE technique. The main goal is to find a set of bands which is able to represent all the strains in the data set maintaining a high discriminatory power. Our algorithm is able to find a quantized version of the original set of band weights minimizing the number of bands needed to represent the input data set, while maintaining the natural clustering (that is, identical strains in an epidemiological sense) and minimizing the number of false cluster splits. Experiments show that the constrained LBG algorithm using the logarithmic model and a band distance constraint is much better than the unconstrained algorithm. The obtained number of bands is more realistic, and the number of false clusters is also reduced.

Further research in this topic involves several subjects. For example, both the distortion measure and the centroid computation could include a set of parameters to fine-tune the logarithmic distortion for a given experiment. Different accuracies could be used to represent the fact that intra-gel weights variations are smaller than inter-gel variations. Finally, the algorithm should be tested with several data sets obtained from different microorganisms in order to ensure its robustness.

Acknowledgements

This work is partially supported by grant ref. EPAEV - IR 216, funded by IBM / "la Caixa", and by Spanish Government grants TIC2000-0739-C04-01, FIS-94/1442 and FIS-95/0417.

References

[1] A. Akbari, F. Albregtsen, and O.C. Lingjaerde. Adaptive weighted least squares method for the estimation of DNA fragment lengths from agarose gels. *Electrophoresis*, 23(2):176–181, January 2002.

[2] T.H. Alsamarrai, N. Zhang, I.L. Lamont, L. Martin, J. Kolbe, M. Wilsher, A.J. Morris, and J. Schmid. Simple and inexpensive but highly discriminating method for computer-assisted DNA fingerprinting of *Pseudomonas aeruginosa*. *Journal of Clinical Microbiology*, 38(2):4445–4452, December 2000.

[3] G. Cardinali, A. Martini, C. Tascini, and F. Bistoni. Critial observations of computerized analysis of banding patterns with commercial software packages. *Journal of Clinical Microbiology*, 37(3):876–877, March 1999.

[4] Karl Drlica. *Understanding DNA and gene cloning: a guide for the curious*. John Wiley & sons, Inc., 2nd edition, 1992.

[5] Richard O. Duda, Peter E. Hart, and David G. Stork. *Pattern Classification*. John Wiley & Sons, second edition, 2000.

[6] M.E. Verdú et al. Endemic meningococcal disease in Cerdanyola, Spain, 1987-93: molecular epidemiology of the isolates of Neisseria meningitidis. *Clinical Microbiology Infection*, 2(3):168–178, February 1996.

[7] M.E. Verdú et al. Association between asymptomatic carriage and sporadic (endemic) meningococcal disease in an open community. *Epidemiology and Infection*, 127(2):245–259, October 2001.

[8] S. Murchan et al. Harmonization of pulsed-field gel electrophoresis protocols for epidemiological typing of strains of methicillin-resistant *staphylococcus aureus*: a single approach developed by consensus in 10 european laboratories and its application for tracing the spread of related strains. *Journal of Clinical Microbiology*, 41(4):April, 1574–1585 2003.

[9] P. Gerner-Smidt, L.M. Graves, S. Hunter, and B. Swaminathan. Computerized analysis of restriction fragment length polymorphism patterns: Comparative evaluation of two commercial software packages. *Journal of Clinical Microbiology*, 36(5):1318–1323, May 1998.

[10] Allen Gersho and Robert M. Gray. *Vector Quantization and Signal Compression*. Communications and Information Theory. Kluwer Academic Publishers, Norwell, MA, USA, 1992.

[11] Teuvo Kohonen. *Self-Organizing Maps*, volume 30 of *Springer Series in Information Sciences*. Springer, Berlin, Heidelberg, 1995.

[12] T.L. Laber, J.T. Iverson, J.A. Liberty, and S.A. Giese. The evaluation and implementation of match criteria for forensic analysis of dna. *Journal of Forensic Science*, 40(6):1058–1064, November 1995.

[13] Wen-Hsiung Li. *Molecular Evolution*. Sinauer Associates, Inc., 1997.

[14] Yoseph Linde, Andrés Buzo, and Robert M. Gray. An algorithm for vector quantizer design. *IEEE Transactions on Communications*, COM-28(1):84–95, January 1980.

[15] Geoffrey J. McLachlan and Kaye E. Basford. *Mixture Models. Inference and Applications to Clustering*. Marcel Dekker, Inc., 1988.

[16] T. Radivoyevitch and B. Cedervall. Mathematical analysis of DNA fragment distribution models used with pulsed field gel electrophoresis for DNA double-strand break calculations. *Electrophoresis*, 17(6):1087–1093, June 1996.

[17] Hugh Salamon, Mark R. Segal, Alfredo Ponce de Leon, and Peter M. Small. Accommodating error analysis in comparison and clustering of molecular fingerprints. *Emerging Infectious Diseases*, 4(2):159–168, April-June 1998.

[18] F.C. Tenover, R.D. Airbeit, R.V. Goering, P.A. Mickelsen, B.E. Murray, D.H. Persing, and B. Swaminathan. Interpreting chromossomal dna restriction patterns produced by pulsed-field gel electrophoresis: criteria for bacterial strain typing. *Journal of Clinical Microbiology*, 33(9):2233–2239, September 1995.

A Minimal Cover for Declarative Expressions

Margaret Miró-Julià
Universitat de les Illes Balears
Ctra. de Valldemossa, km 7.5, 07122 Palma de Mallorca, SPAIN
margaret.miro@uib.es

Abstract. Descriptive knowledge about a multivalued data table or Information System can be expressed in declarative form by means of a binary Boolean based language.

This paper presents a contribution to the study of an arbitrary multivalued Information System by introducing a non-binary array algebra that allows the treatment of multiple valued data tables with systematic algebraic techniques.

An Information System can be described by means of an algebraic array expression. Furthermore, the same Information System can be described by several distinct, but equivalent, array expressions. Among these, the all-prime-ar expression is singled out. The all-prime-ar expression is a unique expression, although it is not necessarily minimum in the number of prime-ars.

Finally, a completely intensional technique that determines a cover, a minimal prime-ar expression is presented.

1 Introduction

Much of the knowledge one has about its environment is descriptive and can be expressed in declarative form by means of a language. Assuming that the objects to be described are elements of the domain D, different levels of declarations can be established. A first level declaration or itemized description describes one element of the domain. A second level declaration or declarative description refers to subsets of the domain not in terms of the elements of the subset but in terms of the attributes and the values these attributes take. Therefore the idea of attributes and attribute values is equivalent to the idea of a subset of objects having these attribute values. Thus, declarative expressions describe aspects of the reality in terms of subsets of objects described by the attribute values that define them.

The transfer of knowledge from the declarative level to the itemized level is very simple. Given a domain $D = \{x_1, x_2, \ldots, x_n\}$ and an arbitrary subset $A = \{x_i, x_j, \ldots, x_k\}$ the problem consists in finding a definition of the type

$$A = \{x \in D \mid P(x)\}.$$

In general the problem is not trivial because it may have multiple solutions. The need to establish computer programs has brought the problem back to the surface and several groups have designed approaches to it. Directly or indirectly, work by Michalski [3], Quinlan [11],

Pawlak [10], Skowron [1], Miró [4], Wille [12] and Fiol [2] has to do with this problem. However, their efforts are mainly directed to binary descriptions.

The starting point of this research are the itemized descriptions, usually represented by means of a table or Information System. The Information System used to develop the theory considers attributes that take values from a multivalued set.

Definition 1. *Let* $D = \{d_1, d_2, \ldots, d_i, \ldots, d_m\}$ *be an ordered set called domain, of elements* d_i *representing the* m *objects, let* $R = \{r_g, \ldots, r_c, \ldots, r_a\}$ *be a set of the* g *attributes or properties of the objects. The set of values of attribute* c *is represented by* $C = \{[c_{n_c}], \ldots, [c_j], \ldots, [c_1]\}$. *The elements of set* C, $[c_j]$, *are called 1-spec-sets since the elements are defined by means of one specification. An Object Attribute Table (OAT) is a table whose rows represent the objects, and whose columns represent the attributes of these objects. Each element* $[c_i]$ *represents the value of attribute* r_c *that corresponds to object* d_i, *as is shown in Table 1.*

	r_g	$\ldots$	r_c	$\ldots$	r_a
d_1	$[g_1]$	$\ldots$	$[c_1]$	$\ldots$	$[a_1]$
d_2	$[g_2]$	$\ldots$	$[c_2]$	$\ldots$	$[a_2]$
$\vdots$	$\vdots$	$\ddots$	$\vdots$	$\ddots$	$\vdots$
d_i	$[g_i]$	$\ldots$	$[c_i]$	$\ldots$	$[a_i]$
$\vdots$	$\vdots$	$\ddots$	$\vdots$	$\ddots$	$\vdots$
d_m	$[g_m]$	$\ldots$	$[c_m]$	$\ldots$	$[a_m]$

Table 1: Object Attribute Table

In order to handle the multivalued OAT a new multivalued algebra is needed.

2 Theoretical Background

2.1 Symbolic representation of a subset

The initial objective is to offer a general and compact symbolic representation of an arbitrary subset $C_h \subseteq C$ and of the set operations between subsets.

It is well known that the set of all subsets of a given set C (the power set of C), $\rho(C)$, constitutes a Boolean algebra $< \rho(C), \cup, \cap, \hat{}, \emptyset, C >$. If a symbolic representation of the subsets is considered, there is a parallel Boolean algebra $< \mathcal{S}_c, +, \cdot, \hat{}, \vee_c, \wedge_c >$ defined on the set $\mathcal{S}_c$ of all possible symbols representing subsets of C. The zero of this algebra is $\vee_c$ (the symbol representing the empty set). The identity is $\wedge_c$ (the symbol representing set C).

Throughout this paper, the symbol $\rightsquigarrow$ may be read as: "is described by". Therefore, $C_h \rightsquigarrow c_h$ expresses: "subset C_h is described by symbol c_h". The symbolic representations of regular set operations complement ($\hat{}$), union ($\cup$) and intersection ($\cap$) are:

$$\widehat{C_h} \rightsquigarrow \hat{c}_h$$
$$C_h \cup C_k \rightsquigarrow c_h + c_k$$
$$C_h \cap C_k \rightsquigarrow c_h \cdot c_k$$

This symbolic representation has been carefully studied in [6], tables providing operations $+$, $\cdot$ and $\hat{}$ on symbols in hexadecimal representation are also given.

2.2　Fundamental concepts

All the concepts and operations introduced above make reference to only one set, that is, one attribute. A multivalued OAT has more than one attribute.

Let $R = \{r_c, r_b, r_a\}$ be a set of 3 attributes whose attribute values are given by sets $C = \{[c_{n_c}], \ldots, [c_2], [c_1]\}$, $B = \{[b_{n_b}], \ldots, [b_2], [b_1]\}$ and $A = \{[a_{n_a}], \ldots, [a_2], [a_1]\}$. The elements of sets C, B, A are 1-spec-sets (one specification). A 3-spec-set, $[c_k, b_j, a_i]$, is a chain ordered description of 3 specifications, one from set C, one from set B and one from set A. Each spec-set represents itself and all possible permutations. Therefore,

$$[c_k, b_j, a_i] = [c_k, a_i, b_j] = [b_j, c_k, a_i] =$$
$$= [b_j, a_i, c_k] = [a_i, c_k, b_j] = [a_i, b_j, c_k]$$

This idea can be generalized for g attributes. In all definitions that follow, $R = \{r_g, \ldots, r_b, r_a\}$ is the set of g attributes whose attribute values are given by non-empty sets $G, \ldots, B, A$ respectively.

Definition 2. *The cross product $G \otimes \cdots \otimes B \otimes A$ is the set of all possible g-spec-sets formed by one element of G, $\ldots$, one element of B and one element of A.*

$$G \otimes \cdots \otimes B \otimes A = \{[g_x, \ldots, b_j, a_i] \mid [g_x] \in G, \ldots, [b_j] \in B, [a_i] \in A\}$$

It is important to mention that the cross product is not the cartesian product. A g-spec-set represents itself and all possible permutations whereas the elements of the cartesian product are different if the order in which there are written varies.

There is a need to determine an order in a g-spec-set. The basis T is an ordered chain $< G, \ldots, B, A > \equiv T$ which establishes the sequential order in which the spec-sets are always written. The basis considered in this paper is $T = < G, \ldots, B, A >$.

The set of all possible g-spec-sets induced by sets $G, \ldots, B, A$ is called the **universe** U and every subset of the universe, $U_i \subseteq U$, is called a **subuniverse**.

Definition 3. *Let $G_i \subseteq G$, $\ldots$, $B_i \subseteq B$, $A_i \subseteq A$, an array $|t_i| = |g_i, \ldots, b_i, a_i|$ is the symbolic representation of the cross product $G_i \otimes \ldots \otimes B_i \otimes A_i$ where $G_i \rightsquigarrow g_i$, $\ldots$, $B_i \rightsquigarrow b_i$, and $A_i \rightsquigarrow a_i$.*

$$G_i \otimes \cdots \otimes B_i \otimes A_i = \{[g_x, \ldots, b_j, a_i] \mid [g_x] \in G_i, \ldots, [b_j] \in B_i, [a_i] \in A_i\}$$

$$G_i \otimes \cdots \otimes B_i \otimes A_i \rightsquigarrow |t_i| = |g_i, \ldots, b_i, a_i|$$

An array $|t_i|$ is a symbolic representation of a subuniverse. In 2 dimensions (2 attributes) an array can be represented graphically as shown in Fig. 1.

The arrays describe subuniverses (subsets of the universe), therefore regular set operations may be performed with them. The following operations between arrays are introduced. Let $|t_i| = |g_i, \ldots, b_i, a_i|$ and $|t_j| = |g_j, \ldots, b_j, a_j|$ be two arrays.

$$G_i \otimes \cdots \otimes B_i \otimes A_i \rightsquigarrow |t_i|$$

$$G_j \otimes \cdots \otimes B_j \otimes A_j \rightsquigarrow |t_j|$$

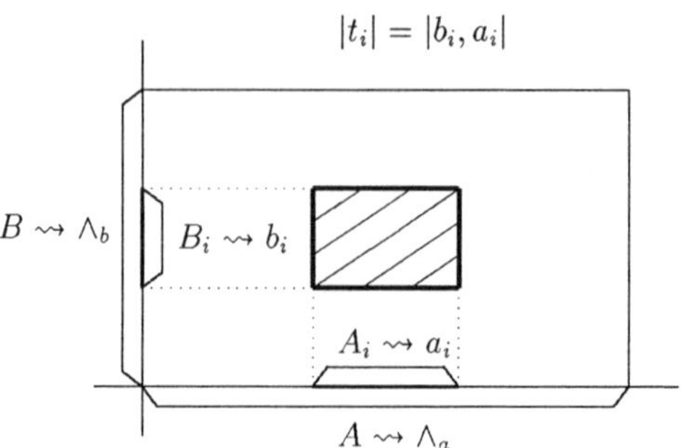

Figure 1: Arrays in 2 dimensions

1. $\sim$ complement of an array respect to the universe

$$\sim (G_i \otimes \cdots \otimes B_i \otimes A_i) \rightsquigarrow \quad \sim |t_i|$$

where $\sim$ is the symbolic representation of the complement respect to the universe (set of all g-spec-sets). In 2 dimensions, the $\sim$ complement of an array can be represented as shown in Fig. 2.

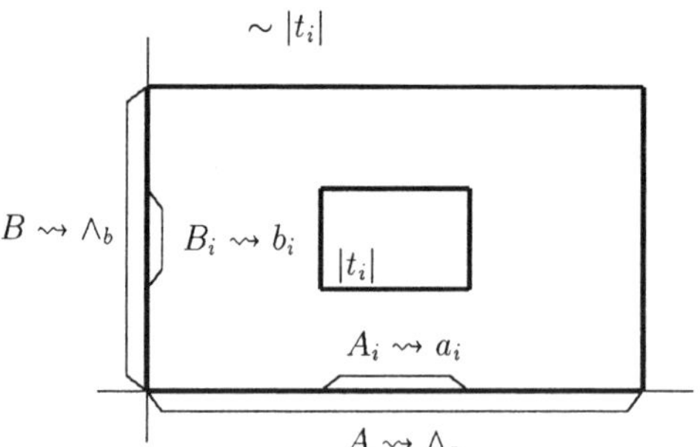

Figure 2: $\sim$ complement of arrays

2. $\ddagger$ sum of arrays

$$(G_i \otimes \cdots \otimes B_i \otimes A_i) \cup (G_j \otimes \cdots \otimes B_j \otimes A_j) \rightsquigarrow |t_i| \ddagger |t_j|$$

$$|t_i| \ddagger |t_j| = |g_i, \ldots, b_i, a_i| \ddagger |g_j, \ldots, b_j, a_j|$$

where the $\ddagger$ sum is the symbolic representation of the union of subuniverses. If only 2 attributes are considered, the $\ddagger$ sum of arrays can be represented graphically as shown in Fig. 3.

3. $\circ$ product of arrays

$$(G_i \otimes \cdots \otimes B_i \otimes A_i) \cap (G_j \otimes \cdots \otimes B_j \otimes A_j) \rightsquigarrow |t_i| \circ |t_j|$$

$$|t_i| \circ |t_j| = |g_i, \ldots, b_i, a_i| \circ |g_j, \ldots, b_j, a_j|$$

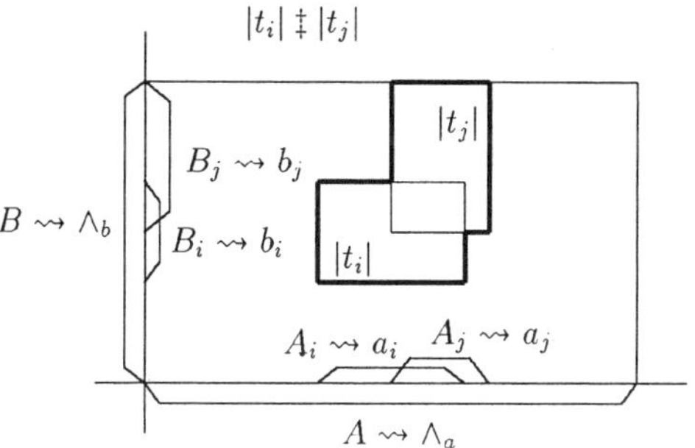

Figure 3: ‡ sum of arrays

where the ∘ product is the symbolic representation of the intersection of subuniverses. Furthermore,

$$|t_i| \circ |t_j| = |g_i \cdot g_j, \ldots, b_i \cdot b_j, a_i \cdot a_j|$$

The ∘ product is a closed operation in the set of all arrays, as can be seen in Fig. 4.

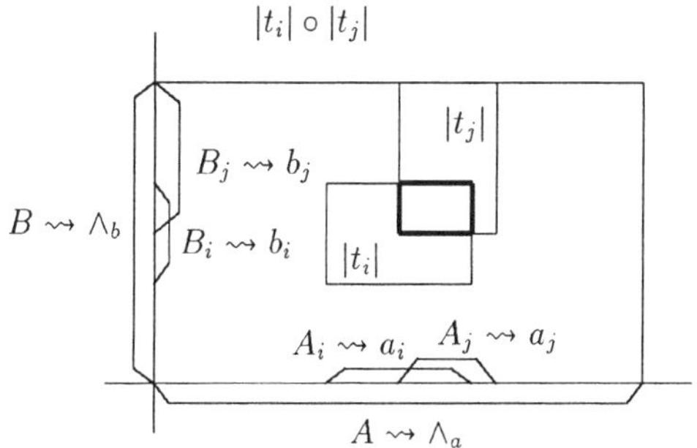

Figure 4: ∘ product of arrays

All the results obtained by use of operations $\sim$, ‡ and ∘ on arrays are symbolic representations of subuniverses. This array algebra has a dual counterpart presented in [9].

There are two subuniverses that deserve special consideration. First, the identity array $\bigwedge$, which is the array representing the universe:

$$U \rightsquigarrow \bigwedge = |\wedge_g, \ldots, \wedge_b, \wedge_a|$$

Second, the zero array $\bigvee$ [8], the array representing the empty universe:

$$\emptyset \rightsquigarrow \bigvee = |\vee_g, \ldots, \vee_b, \vee_a|$$

3 Array Expressions

Subuniverses can be symbolically represented by arrays or by algebraic expressions of arrays. An expression is a symbolic representation of a subuniverse. An expression represents the reality described by an OAT.

Definition 4. *Any combination of arrays using operations $\sim$, $\ddagger$ and $\circ$ (well formed formula) is called an expression E_i.*

$$E_i = \sim |t_i| \ddagger |t_j| \circ |t_k| \ldots$$

Any subuniverse can be described by an expression.

$$U_i \rightsquigarrow E_i$$

Generally, a subuniverse can be represented by more than one expression. Expressions that describe the same subuniverse are said to be equivalent (declaratively). The comparison of two distinct expressions, as far as their declarative describing capability, has been studied in [6] and [5].

Expressions represent subuniverses, therefore an order relation that symbolically represents set inclusion may be introduced:

$$(U_i \subseteq U_j) \rightsquigarrow E_i \preceq E_j .$$

This order relation has been studied in [6] and has been used to find simplified equivalent expressions.

Definition 5. *An expression E_i is called an array expression if it is written as a $\ddagger$ sum of arrays.*

$$E_i = |t_z| \ddagger \cdots \ddagger |t_y| \ddagger \cdots \ddagger |t_x|$$

An array expression in 2 dimensions is shown in Fig. 5.

$$E_i = |t_1| \ddagger |t_2| \ddagger |t_3|$$

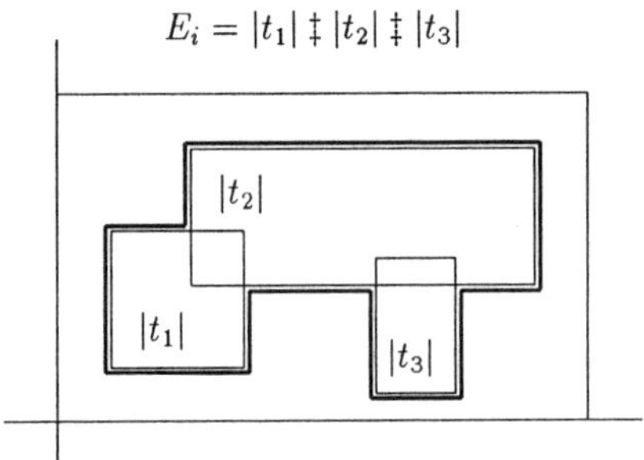

Figure 5: Array expression

Definition 6. *Given an array expression $E_i = |t_z| \ddagger \cdots \ddagger |t_y| \ddagger \cdots \ddagger |t_x|$, $|t_y|$ is a prime array or prime-ar of expression E_i if there is no other array $|t_j|$ such that:*

$$|t_y| \preceq |t_j| \preceq E_i$$

A prime-ar is a "largest" array contained in E_i.

Consider the array expression represented in Fig. 5. Both $|t_1|$ and $|t_2|$ are prime-ars, however $|t_3|$ is not a prime-ar since $|t_3| \preceq |t_j| \preceq E_i$, see Fig. 6. The prime-ars of expression E_i are $|t_1|$, $|t_2|$ and $|t_j|$.

$$E_i = |t_1| \ddagger |t_2| \ddagger |t_j|$$

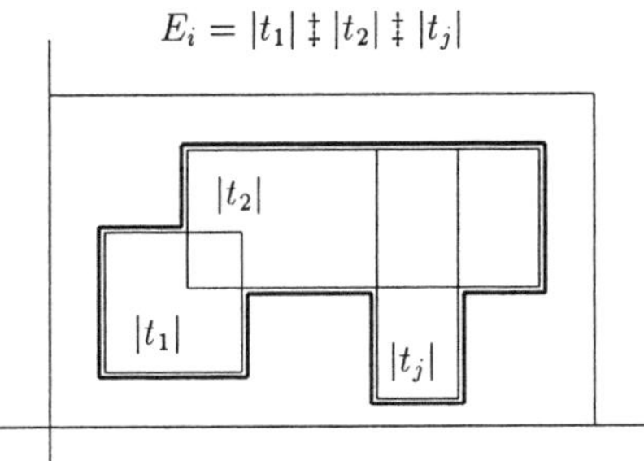

Figure 6: Prime arrays of expression E_i

4 The All-prime-ar Expression

Definition 7. *The $\ddagger$ sum of all the prime-ars of an expression E_i is called the all-prime-ar expression of E_i.*

The same subuniverse can be described by more than one prime-ar expression. The all-prime-ar expression is a unique expression, but the number of prime-ars may not be minimal.

$$E_i = |t_1| \ddagger |t_2| \ddagger |t_3| \ddagger |t_4|$$

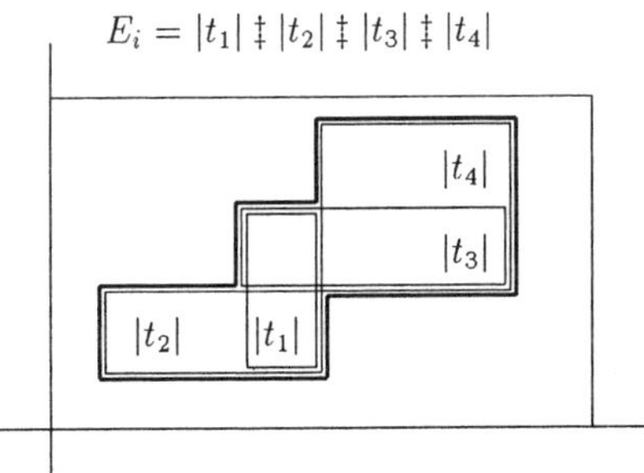

Figure 7: The all prime array expression

Fig. 7 offers a two dimensional insight to these remarks. The unique all-prime-ar expression is $E_i = |t_1| \ddagger |t_2| \ddagger |t_3| \ddagger |t_4|$. Since $|t_1| \preceq |t_2| \ddagger |t_3|$ and $|t_3| \preceq |t_1| \ddagger |t_4|$, two equivalent prime-ar expressions can be found:

$$E_i = |t_2| \ddagger |t_3| \ddagger |t_4|$$

$$E_i = |t_1| \ddagger |t_2| \ddagger |t_4|$$

The same subuniverse can be described by more than one prime-ar expression. How can the equivalency between expressions be studied? A possible way to know if two prime-ar expressions are equivalent is to compare their all-prime-ar expression.

5   Covers of an Expression

The all-prime-ar expression is unique and achievable by means of an algorithm [7]. However, the number of arrays appearing in the expression is not necessarily minimal. In set theory, where sets are extensionally given, a cover is easily obtained. But, can a minimal cover be obtained using a declarative treatment? Algorithmic techniques that provide a minimal declarative expression are presented.

Definition 8. *Given a set of arrays* $A = \{|t_1|, |t_2|, \dots, |t_n|\}$ *an array* $|t_i|$ *is said to be covered by A or is called a covered array respect to A if and only if*

$$|t_i| \preceq |t_1| \ddagger |t_2| \ddagger \cdots \ddagger |t_n|$$

An array that is not a covered array respect to A is called an uncovered array respect to A.

Definition 9. *Given an array expression* $E = |t_1| \ddagger \cdots \ddagger |t_i| \ddagger \cdots \ddagger |t_k| \ddagger \cdots \ddagger |t_z|$ *an array* $|t_i|$ *of the expression is called a redundant array respect to E if and only if*

$$|t_i| \preceq |t_1| \ddagger \cdots \ddagger |t_{i-1}| \ddagger |t_{i+1}| \ddagger \cdots \ddagger |t_z|$$

In other words, $|t_i|$ *is covered by* $A - \{|t_i|\} = \{|t_1|, \dots, |t_{i-1}|, |t_{i+1}|, \dots, |t_z|\}$.

    An array that is not a redundant array respect to E is said to be an essential array respect to E.

$$E = |t_1| \ddagger |t_2| \ddagger |t_3| \ddagger |t_4|$$

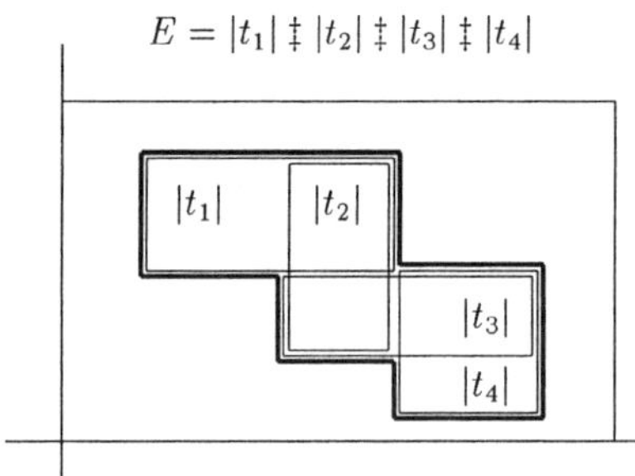

Figure 8: Redundant and essential arrays

If expression E, see Fig. 8, is considered, by close examination of its graphical representation, it can be easily seen that $|t_1|$ and $|t_4|$ are essential arrays respect to expression E, whereas $|t_2|$ and $|t_3|$ are redundant.

$$|t_2| \preceq |t_1| \ddagger |t_3| \ddagger |t_4|$$

$$|t_3| \preceq |t_1| \ddagger |t_2| \ddagger |t_4|$$

Definition 10. *Given an expression E, whose arrays form set A, a subset* $A_c \subseteq A$ *is a cover of E if and only if*

$$E \preceq \Sigma_{|t_i| \in A_c} |t_i|$$

where Σ *represents the* $\ddagger$ *sum of arrays.*

$$C_A = \{|t_1|, |t_2|, |t_4|\}$$

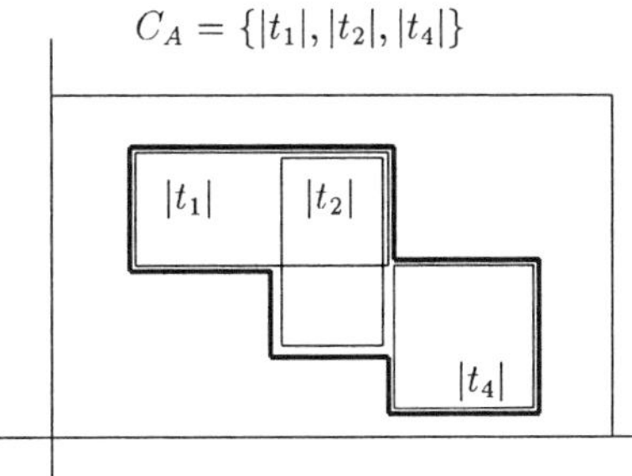

Figure 9: Cover C_A of expression E.

$$C_B = \{|t_1|, |t_3|, |t_4|\}$$

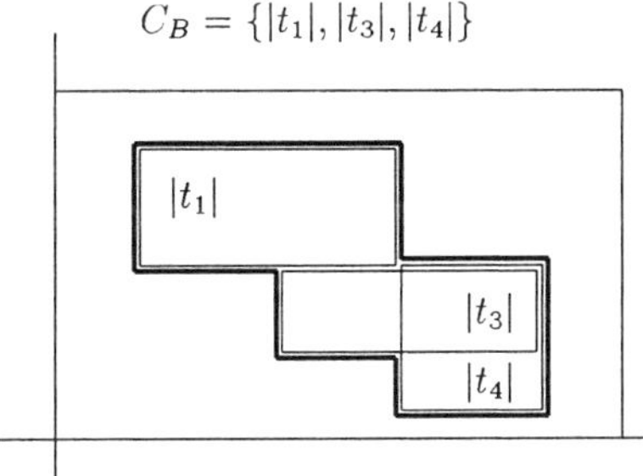

Figure 10: Cover C_B of expression E.

A cover is formed by all the essential arrays of the expression and some of the redundant arrays. The two covers C_A and C_B of expression E represented on Fig. 8 are given in Fig. 9 and Fig. 10.

In order to find a cover of an array expression, the essential arrays must be determined.

5.1 Determination of essential arrays

In order to determine the essential arrays, the redundancy of the array will be checked.

Definition 11. *Given an array expression* $E = |t_1| \ddagger \cdots \ddagger |t_i| \ddagger \cdots \ddagger |t_j| \ddagger \cdots \ddagger |t_z|$ *the remainder of* $|t_i|$ *respect to* $|t_1|$, $R_{i,1}$, *is defined as:*

$$R_{i,1} = |t_i| \circ (\sim |t_1|)$$

the remainder of $R_{i,1}$ *respect to* $|t_2|$ *is defined as*

$$R_{i1,2} = R_{i,1} \circ (\sim |t_2|) = |t_i| \circ (\sim |t_1|) \circ (\sim |t_2|)$$

The remainder of $|t_i|$ *respect to* $|t_1|, |t_2|, \ldots, |t_n|$ *is defined as*

$$R_{i12\ldots,n} = |t_i| \circ (\sim |t_1|) \circ \cdots \circ (\sim |t_{i-1}|) \circ (\sim |t_{i+1}|) \circ \cdots \circ (\sim |t_n|)$$

Given an array expression $E = |t_1| \ddagger \cdots \ddagger |t_i| \ddagger \cdots \ddagger |t_j| \ddagger \cdots \ddagger |t_z|$ an array $|t_i|$ of the expression is redundant if and only if the remainder $R_{i12...,n} = \bigvee$, an array $|t_i|$ of the expression is essential if and only if the remainder $R_{i12...,n} \neq \bigvee$.

The following algorithm finds the essential arrays of given array expression. The procedure consists in determining if an array $|t_i|$ is covered by all other arrays of the expression. The algorithm uses ARRAYLIST formed by all the arrays of the expression and generates REDLIST and ESSLIST. Initially all lists are empty.

1. Create ARRAYLIST with all arrays from the expression (delete repeated arrays, if any).

2. For all $|t_i|$ belonging to ARRAYLIST,

   a) remove $|t_i|$ from ARRAYLIST;

   b) obtain the remainder $R_{i12...,n}$ of $|t_i|$ respect to ARRAYLIST;

   - if $R_{i12...,n} = \bigvee$, include $|t_i|$ in REDLIST;
   - if $R_{i12...,n} \neq \bigvee$, include $|t_i|$ in ESSLIST.

The ESSLIST is formed by all the essential arrays of the expression, the redundant arrays appear in REDLIST.

5.2 Determination of a cover

All the essential arrays are included in a cover but only some of the redundant arrays are necessary. The following algorithm determines whether a redundant array can be dispensed with in a cover. The algorithm uses the REDLIST and ESSLIST generated by the previous algorithm, and generates a NEWREDLIST and a NEWESSLIST. The procedure consists in determining whether an array in REDLIST is covered by the arrays in ESSLIST.

1. Remove those arrays in REDLIST covered by other arrays of REDLIST. For all $|t_i|$ and $|t_j|$ belonging to REDLIST, if $R_{i,j} = |t_i| \circ (\sim |t_j|) = \bigvee$ remove $|t_i|$ from REDLIST.

2. For all $|t_i|$ belonging to REDLIST,

   a) remove $|t_i|$ from REDLIST.

   b) obtain the remainder $R_{i12...,k}$ of $|t_i|$ respect to ESSLIST.

   - if $R_{i12...,k} = \bigvee$, include $|t_i|$ in NEWREDLIST;
   - if $R_{i12...,k} \neq \bigvee$, include $|t_i|$ in NEWESSLIST.

3. Create COVERLIST with all arrays from ESSLIST and NEWESSLIST.

A cover is formed by all essential arrays respect to ARRAYLIST and those redundant arrays respect to ARRAYLIST that are essential respect to ESSLIST.

The results obtained suggest the following comments:

- The cover of an array expression (or set of arrays) has been found without making use of the extensional description of sets.

- The cover is not unique. The ordering of the arrays in the sets and the order in which calculations are performed may change the final outcome.

- A shorter cover may be possible if one (or more) of the remainders $R_{i12...,k}$ is covered by the rest of them.

- If the initial array expression is the all-prime-ar expression then the cover is minimum (no smaller cover can be found).

6 Conclusion

An algebra of arrays that allows the description of an arbitrary OAT by means of an array expression has been presented. The proposed array algebra does not handle raw data, it handles declarative descriptions of the data. Declarative expressions from a multivalued OAT can be obtained using arrays and declarative expressions can be transformed by application of computational techniques.

These array expressions are not unique. In order to find a unique array expression the concept of prime-ar is introduced. The all-prime-ar expression is an unique expression, however the number of prime-ars in the expression is not minimal.

From the many equivalent expressions describing an OAT some may be more economic or elegant. A completely intensional technique has been provided to converge on them. The algorithms presented here find a cover of an expression, by determining the essential arrays and which of the redundant arrays need to be included in the cover.

The procedure presented has a feature that should be mentioned. The computation may be interrupted at any time. The results obtained up to the interruption will always allow to a find a cover. In general the latter the computation has been interrupted, the closer the solution will be to the optimum one.

Acknowledgements

This work has been supported by the Universitat de les Illes Balears through the UIB 2003/11 project.

References

[1] Bazan, J., Skowron, A., and Synak, P. (1994). Discovery of decision rules from experimental data. In *Proceedings of the Third International Workshop on Rough Sets and Soft Computing*, pages 346–355.

[2] Fiol, G., Miró Nicolau, J., and Miró-Julià, J. (1992). A new perspective in the inductive acquisition of knowledge from examples. *Lecture Notes of Computer Science*, 682:219–228.

[3] Michalski, R. (1983). A theory and methodology of inductive learning. *Artificial Intelligence*, 20:111–161.

[4] Miró, J. and Miró-Julià, J. (1993). Uncertainty and inference through approximate sets. In Bouchon-Meunier, B., Valverde, L., and Yager, R., editors, *Uncertainty in Intelligent Systems*, pages 203–214. North Holland.

[5] Miró, J. and Miró-Julià, M. (1995). Equality of functions in CAST. *Lecture Notes in Computer Science*, 1030:129–136.

[6] Miró-Julià, M. (2000). *A Contribution to Multivalued Systems*. PhD thesis, Universitat de les Illes Balears.

[7] Miró-Julià, M. and Miró, J. (2002). Transformation of array expressions. In *Proceedings of the Second IASTED International Conference. Artificial Intelligence and Applications*, pages 273–278.

[8] Miró-Julià, M. The Zero Array: a Twilight Zone (2003). To be published in *Lecture Notes in Computer Science, Computer Aided Systems Theory - EUROCAST'03*.

[9] Miró-Julià, M. and Fiol-Roig, G. (2003). An Algebra for the Treatment of Multivalued Systems. *Lecture Notes in Computer Science*, 2652:556-563.

[10] Pawlak, Z. (1991). *Rough Sets: Theoretical Aspects of Reasoning About Data*. Kluwer Academic Publisher.

[11] Quinlan, J. R. (1986). Induction of decision trees. *Machine Learning*, 1:81–106.

[12] Wille, R. (1982). Restructuring lattice theory: an approach based on hierarchies of concepts. In Rival, J., editor, *Ordered Sets*, pages 445–470. Reidel Publishing Company.

Episode representation and fuzzy classification techniques used to predict unstable conditions in a blast furnace

Juan J. MORA, Joan COLOMER, Joaquim MELÉNDEZ, Francisco GAMERO
Universitat de Girona
Av. Lluís Santaló s/n
17071 Girona, Spain
{jjmora,colomer, quimmel, gamero}@eia.udg.es

Peter WARREN
Corus Group. UK
Peter.Warren@corusgroup.com

Abstract. This paper discusses the analysis of differential pressure signals in a blast furnace stack by a hybrid approach of episode description and fuzzy classification techniques. The objective is to determine whether they can be used to predict when an unstable furnace condition (slip) will occur. Episode analysis is performed on each individual trend. Using the resultant episodes and the raw data, the classification tool is trained both to predict and detect the fault in a blast furnace.

Introduction

Industries have spent large sums of money on sensors and logging devices to measure process signals. These data are usually stored in data bases to be analysed by the process experts. As the amount of data stored increases, the task of extracting useful information becomes more complex and difficult.

In order to provide an adequate supervisory system, which assists the process experts, it is necessary to provide powerful tools to analyse the process variables. Two Artificial Intelligence (AI) techniques working together are proposed, to deal with the signal and to perform data mining tasks respectively.

The first part of the strategy proposes qualitative representations to represent signal trends (tendencies, oscillation degrees, alarms, degree of transient states...) useful in supervision, especially in fault detection and diagnosis. One of these techniques is the representation of signals by episodes [5]. Secondly, having obtained episode based information of each process variable, a fuzzy classification method is proposed to create classes [7]. These classes are related to functional states of the process under analysis. By using the combination of the two Artificial Intelligence techniques proposed (one to extract useful information of a single signal, and the other one aimed at analysing the behaviour of several process variables), it is possible to develop a decision support system applied to industrial process. The application of the proposed approach to the Redcar blast furnace, operated by Corus, is presented in this paper.

In the following section, the process description is given. Next in section 2, the episode based representation of process variables is defined. In 3, the fuzzy classification method is presented. Later on in 4, the episode approach used in this specific case and the model of data arrangement used to obtain the training data are explained. In 5 the test results are analysed and finally the conclusions of this work are presented.

1. Process description

In the blast furnace process, iron oxide is reduced to metallic iron, which is then melted prior to tapping at 1500 deg C. Liquid slag is also removed, the slag being formed from the non-ferrous components of the iron ore (predominantly lime, silica, magnesia and alumina).

The blast furnace itself is a water-cooled vessel, of circular cross-section, about 30m tall. Layers of coke and prepared iron ore (burden) are alternately charged into the top in a controlled manner. Air at approximately 1100 deg C (hot blast) is blown into the bottom of the furnace through copper water-cooled tuyeres. The air reacts with the coke, and supplementary injected oil, to generate both heat to melt the iron and slag, and to form a reducing gas of CO and H2. The burden takes about 7 hours to reduce and melt as it descends the furnace stack; the residence time of the ascending reduction gases is in the order of seconds. The furnace is kept full by charging a fresh batch of burden as soon as the level drops in the top. Burden descent is usually steady at about 5 metres/hour.

The liquid iron and slag collect in the furnace hearth, built from carbon bricks, and are periodically removed by opening a clay-lined taphole.

Redcar blast furnace is the largest in the UK, producing 64000 tonnes of liquid iron per week. Each hour requires the charging of over 5 batches of prepared ore, each at 120 tonnes, and the same number of batches of coke, each of 30 tonnes. Heat is removed at the wall through large water-cooled panels, called staves, installed over 13 rows. These are made from copper in rows 7 to 10, the region of highest heat load, and cast iron above and below these levels.

The Redcar plant has 4 columns of pressure tappings. The pressure is measured at each stave row between row 6 and row 13 in each quadrant. Figure 1 shows the furnace cross section.

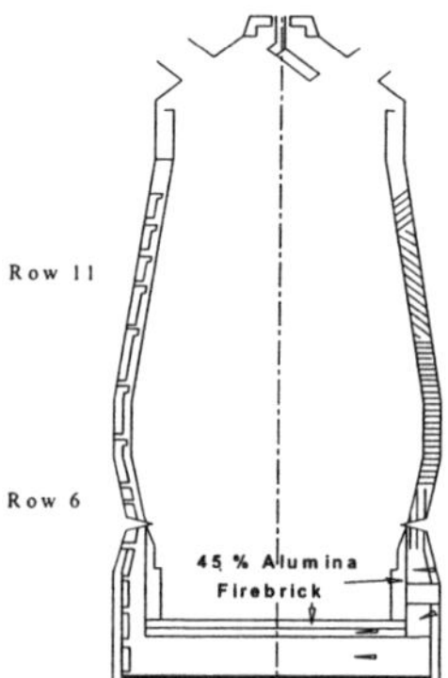

Figure 1: Transverse section of blast furnace

Under normal state, the pressure should reduce gradually between the bottom (row 6) and the top (row 11) of the section of furnace stack under examination.

It has been noticed that trends in differential pressure (pressure drop) between the lower and middle part of the stack can be a good indication that the furnace process will become unstable. The differential pressures found most responsive are the pressure measured at row 6 minus the pressure measured in row 9, for each quadrant individually.

An 'unstable' event is where the material in the furnace stack suddenly 'slips' rather than descend steadily. Such an event can usually be detected by a suddenly change in differential pressure values over the 4 columns of pressure tappings as presented in figure 2.

In figure 2, differential pressure trends are recorded at a frequency of one sample/min. over a 10 hour period. In this figure, it is possible to locate three different unstable conditions (slips) as highlight by the doted lines.

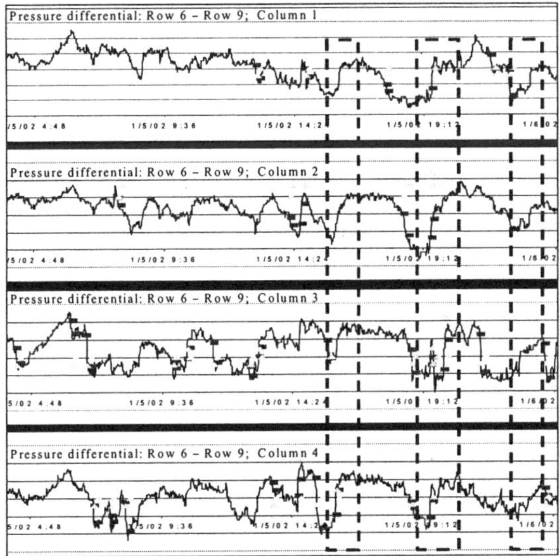

Figure 2: Fault determined by pressure differentials

The objective is to analyse trends of differential pressures, to determine whether they can be used to predict that a slip, as presented in figure 2, will occur.

2. Representation of signals using episodes

Representations by means of episodes provide a good tool for situation assessment. On the one hand, uncertainty, incompleteness and heterogeneity of process data make the qualitative reasoning a good tool. On the other hand, reasoning not only with instantaneous information, but with historic behaviour of processes is necessary. Moreover, since a great deal of process data is available for the supervisory systems, to abstract and use only the most significant information is required. The representation of signals by means of episodes provides an adequate response to these necessities.

The general concept of episode in the field of qualitative reasoning was defined as a set of two elements: a time interval, named temporal extent and a qualitative context, providing the temporal extension with significance [8].

The qualitative representation of process trends is a general formalism for the representations of signals by means of episodes [3]. This formal approach introduces the concept of trend as a sequence of episodes characterised by the signs of the first and the second derivative. It has a practical extension in the triangular and trapezoidal representations.

Later on, in [4] a qualitative description of signals consisting of primitives, episodes, trends and profiles is proposed. Primitives are based on the sign of first and second derivatives (positive, zero or negative). Thus, nine basic types compose the set of primitives. The trend of a signal consists of a series of episodes, and a profile is obtained by adding quantitative information.

In [5] previous formalisms are extended to both qualitative and numerical context in order to be more general. It means that it is possible to build episodes according to any feature extracted from variables. According to this formalism, a new representation allows to describe signal trends depending on the feature or combination of features used. This choice depends on the process and the characteristics that want to be obtained by means of a qualitative representation. Also, this representation can be enriched with quantitative data associated to the temporal extension of the episode.

3. Fuzzy Classification Method

To analyse a set of variables previously represented by episodes, a Learning Algorithm for Multivariate Data Analysis–LAMDA has been used for classification purpose. Taking profit of fuzzy logic and hybrid connectives, the proposed method combines both, numeric and symbolic classification algorithms, [1] [6]. This method is used as a classification technique to obtain the pre-fault and the fault stage prototypes based on the episode description of differential pressures. The following paragraphs resumes the classification principle used in LAMDA.

One object X (set of 4 differential pressures) has a number of characteristics called "descriptors". These descriptors are used to describe the object. Every object is assigned to a "class" in the classification process. Class (ki) is defined as the universe of descriptors, which characterize one set objects as presented in figure 3.

MAD (Marginal Adequacy Degree) concept is a term related to how similar is one object descriptor to the same descriptor of a given class, and GAD (Global Adequacy Degree) is defined as the pertinence degree of one object to a given class as in fuzzy membership functions (mci(x)) [2].

Classification, in LAMDA, is performed according to similarity criteria computed in two stages. First MAD to each existing class is computed for each descriptor of an object. Second, these partial results are aggregated to get a GAD of an individual to a class [1]. The former implementation of LAMDA includes a possibility function to estimate the descriptors distribution based on a "fuzzification" of the binomial probability function computed as (2). This approach was used in this work.

$$MAD(d_i x_j / \rho_{(i/k)}) = \rho_{(i/k)}^{d_i x_j} \left(1 - \rho_{(i/k)}\right)^{\left(1 - d_i x_j\right)}$$ (1)

Where:

$d_i x_j =$ Descriptor i of the object j

$\rho_{(i/k)} =$ Ro of descriptor i and class k

On the other hand, GAD computation was performed as an interpolation between a t-norm and a t-conorm by means of the β parameter such that $\beta = 1$ represents the intersection and $\beta = 0$ means the union.

$$GAD = \beta T(MAD) + (1 - \beta) S(MAD)$$ (2)

The used t-norm is minimun/maximun.

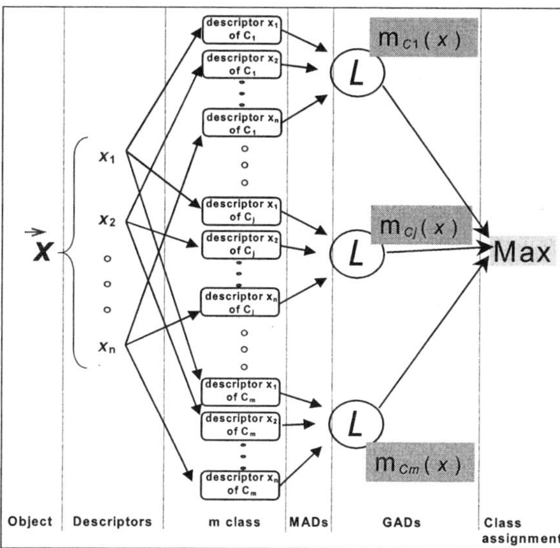

Figure 3: Basic LAMDA recognition methodology

4. Proposed strategy

The strategy approach proposes two Artificial Intelligence (AI) techniques working together, to deal with the signal and to perform data mining tasks respectively.

As first strategy, the episode-based representation of process variables is used to extract quantitative and qualitative information of pressure differentials. Next a procedure to construct the objects used as inputs for the classification method is applied. As a result, the object matrix based on episodes is conformed. Then, a fuzzy classification method is proposed to create classes. These classes are related to functional states of the process under analysis.

The episode based representation and the object conformation for the pressure differentials of the Redcar blast furnace is presented in the next subsections.

4.1   Episode based representation

The necessity of obtaining an effective qualitative representation from the first instants of the episode without waiting until the end of the episode for its identification, leads to the choice of the first derivative as used feature in order to obtain the episodes representation. This simple representation, however, offers enough information to characterize the signals of the analysed process.

Due of the use only the first derivative at the beginning of each episode, only five basic types were possible and used in this approach: A, F, G, H, and L. However, since the previous state to a slip is a fall in pressure followed by a steady trend at low level, a differentiation has been introduced among the episodes of stability according to the value of the signal. So G episode was subdivided in High (Gh), Medium (Gm) and Low (Gl) as presented in figure 4. This representation has been adopted to represent symptoms of blast furnace instability. An example of this representation for two variables is shown in Fig. 5.

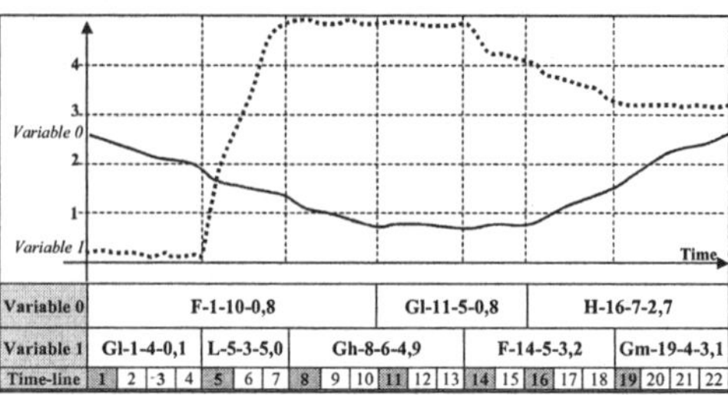

Figure 4: Useful set of episodes

Figure 5: Episode representation of process variables

Process variables presented in table figure 5 are represented by episodes as shown in table 1.

Episode description of variables							
Variable 0				Variable 1			
Type	Starting time	Duration	End value	Type	Starting time	Duration	End value
F	1	10	0,8	Gl	1	4	0,1
Gl	11	5	0,8	L	5	3	5,0
H	16	7	2,7	Gh	8	6	4,9
				F	14	5	3,2
				Gm	19	4	3,1

Table 1: Episode description of variables

4.2   *Object conformation*

Taking into account the fact that the episodes are asynchronous by nature, it is necessary to develop a strategy to conform the set of objects used for the classification stage. The formed objects are synchronized to the change instants of each one of the four differential pressures used to detect the instability state of the blast furnace (slip).

The procedure applied to conform each object is presented as follows:

- Step one: Detect the instant t_{vc} in which one new episode starts in any variable V_c.

- Step two: Identify the type of the new episode (current) and save the type of the previous one in the same variable.

- Step three: Recover the previous and current episodes of all analysed variables.

- Step four: Compute the time between t_c and the time which the current episode starts in all variables. It corresponds to the duration of the current episode.

- Step five: Measure the current value Cv of each process variable.

- Step six: Conform the object using the obtained data.

As example, the object conformation procedure for the variables in figure 5 is presented.

- Step one: t_{v1}=19. V_c=Variable 1.
- Step two: By Variable 1, new episode type = Gm and previous episode type = F.
- Step three: By Variable 0, current episode type = H and previous episode type = Gl.
- Step four: Time between t_{v1} and t_{v0} = 19-16=3.
- Step five: Cv_0=1.5, Cv_1=3.2.
- Step six: The object is presented in figure 6.

Variable 0	F-1-10-0,8				Gl-11-5-0,8		H-16-7-2,7	
Variable 1	Gl-1-4-0,1	L-5-3-5,0	Gh-8-6-4,9		F-14-5-3,2		Gm-19-4-3,1	
Time-line	1 2 3 4	5 6 7	8 9 10	11 12 13	14 15	16 17 18	19 20 21 22	

	Variable 0				Variable 1			
	Current episode	Previous episode	Current duration	Current value	Current episode	Previous episode	Current duration	Current value
	H	Gl	3	1.50	Gm	F	0	3.20

Figure 6: Object conformation of process variables

As a result of the previous procedure application a set of synchronized objects based on the episode representation are obtained as it is presented in table 2. The value is directly taken from the rough data and corresponds to the value of each variable at the time given by the time line column.

The episode variable description presented in table 2 contains the data, which conform the training files used in the learning phase of the fuzzy method. For the first object, the previous type of episodes is supposed equal to the current one.

Time line	Variable 0				Variable 1			
	Current episode	Previous episode	Current duration	Current value	Current episode	Previous episode	Current duration	Current value
1	F	F	0	2.50	Gl	Gl	0	0.20
5	F	F	4	2.00	L	Gl	0	0.18
8	F	F	7	1.30	Gh	L	0	4.90
11	Gl	F	0	0.80	Gh	L	3	4.80
14	Gl	F	3	0.70	F	Gh	0	4.90
16	H	Gl	0	0.80	F	Gh	2	4.00
19	H	Gl	3	1.50	Gm	F	0	3.20

Table 2: Object matrix. Episode based representation of process variables

The obtained results of applying the proposed strategy to four variables are presented in the next section. Each variable consist of a differential between the pressures measured in row 6 and row 9, in the four columns of the blast furnace.

5. Classification tests and results

Several test were performed in order to identify clearly the fault and mainly the pre-fault stage in the Redcar blast furnace. Using data taken directly from the process and presented on table 3, it was possible to select a set of files for training and recognition.

The descriptors used to detect the pre-fault and the fault states are two: The type of the current episode and the value of the pressures differential for each furnace column when a new episode appears in any variable. These descriptors were selected according to the results obtained in the recognition stage.

File Name	Depth of slip
Data set N.1	2.0m
Data set N.2	2.0m
Data set N.3	1.5m
Data set N.4	1.5m
Data set N.5	1.5m
Data set N.6	1m
Data set N.7	1m
Data set N.8	1m
Data set N.9	1m
Data set N.10	1.5m (partial)
Data set N.11	1.5m (partial)
Data set N.12	1.5m (partial)
Data set N.13	0 m (No slip)
Data set N.14	0 m (No slip)

Table 3: Data set used to perform slip prediction

Using these descriptors extracted by the files Data set N. 1, 3, 6, and 10 the classification tool was trained. The files not used by training were used in the recognition stage. The results of the recognition process are presented in table 4

File Name	Depth of slip	Recognition process	
		Pre-fault	Fault
Data set N.1	*2.0m*	*Yes*	*Yes*
Data set N.2	2.0m	Yes	Yes
Data set N.3	*1.5m*	*Yes*	*Yes*
Data set N.4	1.5m	Yes	Yes
Data set N.5	1.5m	Not	Not
Data set N.6	*1m*	*Yes*	*Yes*
Data set N.7	1m	Yes	Yes
Data set N.8	1m	Yes	Yes
Data set N.9	1m	Yes	Not
Data set N.10	*1.5m (partial)*	*Not*	*Yes*
Data set N.11	1.5m (partial)	Not	Not
Data set N.12	1.5m (partial)	Not	Not
Data set N.13	No slips	N/A	N/A
Data set N.14	No slips	N/A	N/A

Table 4: Data set used to perform slip prediction

According to table 4, in most of the files used in training process it is possible to recognise the pre-fault and also the fault state. Not in data set 10 for pre-fault state. In addition, it is also possible to detect the pre-fault ad fault states using different sets of data. This last result is used to test the capability of the proposed approach, to detect faulty situations on the supervised process.

As an example of the presented on table 4, a situation to detect the fault and the pre-fault stage is presented in figure 7. In this figure is possible to see that class 9 is related to the pre-fault state while class 5 is related to the fault state (Slip). The remaining classes are not related to those two states, but they are related to different operative states of the process.

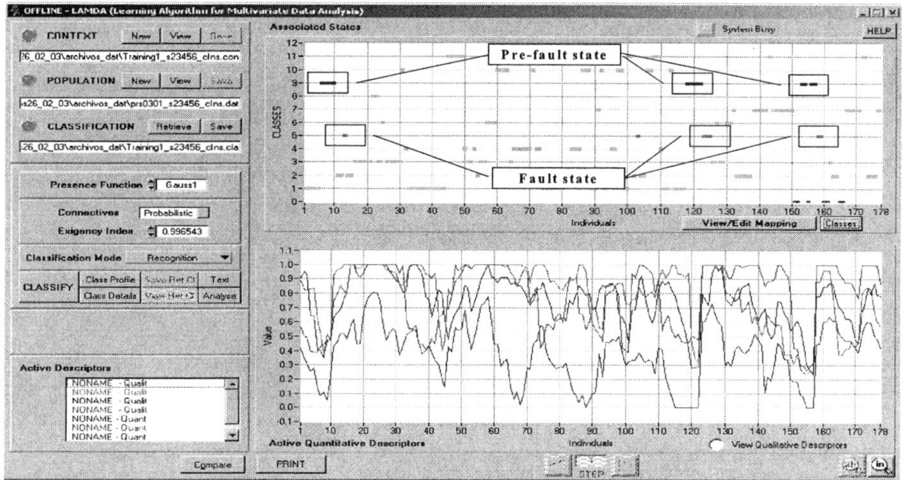

Figure 7: Examples of pre-fault and fault detection. Slip prediction in Redcar blast furnace

Conclusions

In this work, a methodology based in two techniques has been used as complementary strategies to supervise a process. The paper shows the use of the episode representations in the field of diagnosis as it is proposed in the CHEM project. This kind of representation satisfies the necessities of control systems diagnosis regarding to temporal and qualitative reasoning. The object conformation approach, gives a object matrix used as input of the classification method.   This approach reduces the computation time, because the recognition stage is only is performed when the type of episode in any variable changes. The classification method, after the initial training stage, helps to determine classes close related to specific process states at each instant when an object is conformed.

As a result, the previous situations at the fault stage were detected, given an efficient approach to the slip prediction in blast furnaces. In addition, the fault situation is also detected as using both episode type and rough data as input data for the fuzzy classification system.

Acknowledgments

This work is partially supported by the projects "Advanced Decision Support Systems for Chemical/Petrochemical manufacturing processes – CHEM" within the (EC IST program: IST-2000-61200) and CICYT DPI SECSE. DPI2001-2198 (Supervision Experta de la Calidad de Servicio Eléctrico) within the CICYT program from the Spanish government.

References

[1] Aguilar-Martin, J.; López de Mántaras, R. The process of classification and learning the meaning of linguistic descriptors of concepts. *Approximate Reasoning in Decision Analysis*, 1982. p. 165-175.

[2] Aguado, J.C. *"A Mixed Qualitative-Quantitative Self-Learning Classification Technique Applied to Situation Assessment in Industrial Process Control"*. Ph. D. Thesis Universitat Politècnica de Catalunya, 1998.

[3] Cheung, J. T., Stephanopoulos G. *"Representation of Process Trends, parts I and II.* Computers" Chemical Engineering 14, (1990) 495-540.

[4] Janusz, M. and Venkatasubramanian, V. *"Automatic generation of qualitative description of process trends for fault detection and diagnosis".* Engineering Applications of Artificial Intelligence 4 (1991), 329-339.

[5] Meléndez, J.; Colomer, J. *"Episodes representation for supervision. Application to diagnosis of a level control system".* Workshop on Principles of Diagnosis DX'01, (2001) Sansicario (Italy).

[6] Moore, K. *"Using neural nets to analyse qualitative data".* A Marketing Research, 1995, vol. 7, n°1, p.35-39.

[7] Mora, J.; Llanos, D.; Meléndez, J.; Colomer J.; "Classification of sags measured in a distribution substation using a fuzzy tool". International Conference on Renewable Energy and Power Quality – ICREPQ (2003).

[8] Williams, B.C. *"Doing Time: Putting qualitative reasoning on firmer ground".* Proc. of AAAI-86, National Conf. on Artif. Intel., (1986) 105-112.

A Knowledge Representation Approach Suitable to Support Heuristic Search Methods

Mercedes E. NARCISO FARIAS, Miquel Angel PIERA EROLES
Dept. de Telecomunicació i Enginyeria de Sistemes, Universitat Autònoma de Barcelona,
08193 Barcelona, Spain
{mnarciso, miquel}@sunaut.uab.es

Antoni GUASCH PETIT
Dept. d'Enginyeria de Sistemes i Automàtica, IRI, Universitat Politècnica de Catalunya,
08034, Barcelona, Spain
guasch@esaii.upc.es

Abstract. The exact optimal solution of a production, a distribution or a transport system-planning problem is quite complex and difficult, may be impossible to obtain. Simulation models have proved to be useful for examining the performance of alternative system configurations and/or alternative operating procedures for complex systems. However, when applying simulation techniques to improve logistic systems performance, several limitations arises due to its inability to evaluate more than a fraction of the immense range of options available. Different Decision Support Systems (DSS) for particular production schemes has been developed, however, the acceptability of its results are constrained to the particular application field. In this paper we present a generic framework to formalize the behaviour of discrete event systems (manufacturing systems, logistic systems, services systems, etc) that allows the translation of a scheduling or planning problem to a search problem in such a way that different search heuristic algorithms can be tested to deal with an acceptable solution.

The proposed approach is based on the intelligent pruning of a coverability tree that is built dynamically from a system behaviour knowledge representation.

Introduction

For more than 35 years researchers and technologists have built and investigated Decision Support Systems (DSS) [6,10]. Towards 1970 Little in an earlier article identified criteria for designing models and systems to support management decision-making. His four criteria included: robustness, ease of control, simplicity, and completeness of relevant detail. These four criteria remain effective in designing modern DSS.

By the late 1970s, a number of interactive information systems were developed to analyse semi-structured problems. Despite there was not a unified approach neither a formalism to represent system knowledge (mainly based on data and models) all were considered Decision Support Systems.

From those early days, it was recognized that DSS could be designed to support decision-makers at any level in an organization. DSS could support operations, financial management and strategic decision-making. DSS could use spatial data in a system like Geodata Analysis and Display System (GADS), structured multidimensional data and unstructured documents. The type of knowledge representation would depend then on the specific characteristics of the system in study.

Artificial Intelligence (AI) researchers began to work on management and business expert systems in the early 1980s, and the financial planning systems became popular tools of support for decision-making [6].

In the specific field of production planning some DSS have been developed [7,19,21,25], but they have been designed for particular production schemes: Flow Shop [7], Continuous Manufacturing [25], or Flexible Manufacturing Systems (FMS) [19], based on techniques of knowledge representation whose rules or premises must be adapted and some times redefined to the particular characteristics of the application problem.

Due to the economical effort to develop, code and tunne a DSS, some prototypes has been developed that try to increase both: knowledge and decision rules reusability. Thus, at the beginning of 90s, object-oriented technology for building "re-usable" decision support capabilities was widely recommended.

In spite of the ample diversity of knowledge and research areas that include the DSS, since the decision-making process usually goes through stages of problem definition, identification of alternatives, analysis, and evaluation of alternatives, followed by the prescription of the best alternative, in the author's opinion, reusability should be achieved in those fields where the same knowledge representation framework can be used to specify the problem definition stage.

This paper presents a test-bed simulation system to evaluate different heuristic search strategies to deal with the best configuration of the decision variables, of any planning or scheduling logistic problem of a system that can be thought as a discrete event oriented system. Coloured Petri Net formalism is used to represent the knowledge the expert got about the system behaviour, and a discrete event simulator together with a tool to build dynamically the coverability tree has been developed as a reusable technique for the automatic evaluation of alternatives. By considering a DSS as a "... computer technology solutions that can be used to support complex decision making and problem solving" [10], the developed framework can be considered by its self a reusable DSS for the discrete event oriented field.

A summary of different knowledge representation techniques in the field of logistic systems (discrete event oriented) is presented in section 2. Section 3 introduces the main characteristics of Petri Nets (PN) and Coloured Petri Nets (CPN) as knowledge representation formalism for logistic systems. In section 4 the dynamic generation of the coverability tree according to prescription of the best alternative of a DSS is presented. Section 5 illustrates by means of a new heuristic algorithm the benefits of using the test-bed developed to improve the selection of the best alternative task of a DSS.

1. Knowledge Representation

When designing or choosing a Knowledge representation (KR) formalism, both the nature of what will be modelled using the particular method (i.e., the semantic aspect) and the expressive form of the method (i.e., the syntactical aspect) are two aspect that must be taken in care to be sure that the selected formalism will give a proper answer for the application field.

In the particular case of logistic systems, and more broader speaking discrete event oriented system (DEVS), the main characteristic of its behaviour is that the system state remains constant between events, and those usually can appears as a result of a stochastic activity (Figure 1). A typical example is the finalization of a transport or a processing activity.

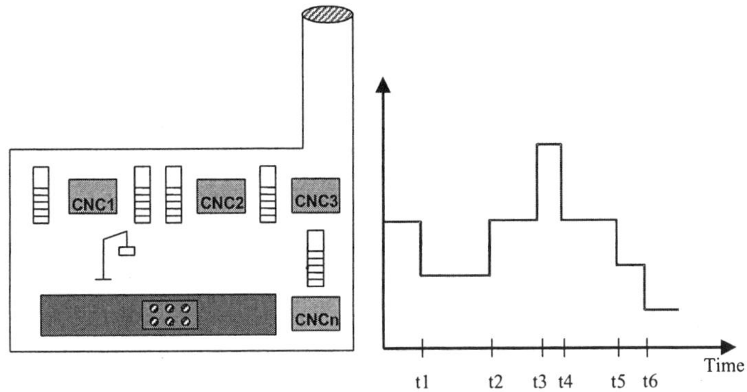

Fig. 1. Amount of pieces in a local CNC stock.

Decision-making complexity in DEVS systems arises because the new state achieved as a result of an event, can block, freeze, delay, enable/disable future enabled/disabled events.

There are many KR formalisms that address data/information only and many that address processes only. In the particular case of DEVS systems the KR formalism should relate these two fundamental kinds of formalisms.

An important aspect related with the KR formalism is that the language used to support the knowledge should be explicit (let alone machine-interpretable). Natural language processing (NLP) has been a driver for much of the work in artificial intelligence. Despite the objective of formally acquiring knowledge by parsing and interpreting text is of interest to a large community of researchers and to industry, knowledge about DEVS system behaviour can not be easily acquired by analysing output data (a DEVS system can show a non bounded amount of different behaviours), but by understanding all the event-relationships, in such a way that the effects of firing an event could be easily predicted, in order to be able to enable or disable the firing of other events.

Another aspect that should be kept on mind when deciding the KR framework to be used to specify the problem definition stage of a DSS is that the expert knowledge about a logistic system, as it is represented in some model, is never complete nor either completely accurate. To be useful, it need only be complete and accurate enough for its intended purpose. Despite the reasoning capabilities of a knowledge representation system is beyond the scope of this paper, it should be point out that when conceptual models are to serve an on-going purpose, the KR formalism should support automatic model improvement and expansion over time, as well as revised to reflect changes in the domain they model.

Thus, when designing or choosing a KR formalism to support knowledge expert got about a DEV System, some aspects inherent to DEVS behaviour should be considered:

- A DEVS can be both: event and/or state driven
- The state space of a DEVS can be discrete or continuous.
- Typical DEVS patterns of behaviour comprise, concurrency, synchronisation and resource sharing

To illustrate the complexity of the KR in such a way that it could be useful to satisfy future DSS demands, lets consider the interacting processes in a manufacturing system: The dynamic nature and the complexity of tooling and synchronization with parts in automated systems require particular attention in order to guarantee streamlined manufacturing. Because all the jobs use the same finite (limited) resources such as machines, stocks, tools, time, etc., the competition for resources makes part flow a vital function for successful manufacturing. The scheduling policy should deal with the timely assignment of manufacturing operations as well as the set of orders that should be ready for processing at each particular station at each particular time, deciding on the sequence in which they will be run and calculating the resulting start and finish times for each operation.

In this sense, the stochastic, dynamic and synchronous nature of production systems demands a technique of knowledge representation that considers all these characteristics and allows representing so much the structure as the different ways in which a system can behave.

The DSS developed until now in the planning and scheduling area, have used different KR formalisms: Markov Decision Processes [20,24], Production Rules [1,19,29], Genetic and Evolutionary Algorithms [13,22], Object-Oriented techniques [1,23, 29], Agents [23,29] and Petri Nets [29,30], among others, which usually deals with complex representations of the system behaviour if a certain low abstraction level is required to deal with a proper plan. Furthermore, most of those techniques separates the knowledge on the structure from the knowledge on the behaviour of the system, which usually is stored in relational databases, constraining in this way the possibility to explore the DEVS performance in those situations not previously modelled, giving poor answers (estimations) during the "evaluation of alternatives" step of a DSS.

The complexity of designing a DSS to deal with the planning and/or scheduling problem of a logistic system is that it requires knowledge about all the event-relationships that affect the system behaviour and its performance. The evaluation of the different states that can reach the system, in order to evaluate all the possible alternatives of the planning problem, is a considered as a NP hard combinatorial problem.

Given the main characteristics of discrete event oriented systems, in the author's opinion, the knowledge representation in an intelligent DSS context should provide both: all the events of the system and the relations among them, in order to represent the whole system behaviour, and to be able to choose the best alternative at each decision step, which will be the one that will allow to reach the industrial targets with the best combination between the use of resources and the time of production.

In the following section PN and CPN formalism are introduced as suitable tools for the knowledge representation of a logistic system.

2. Knowledge Representation by Petri Nets and Coloured Petri Nets

Every modelling or KR paradigm reflects in its fundamental conceptual constructs certain views about the things in the world (the real or imagined world), as well as the concepts we use to represent and describe those things.

2.1 Petri Nets (PN)

Petri net is one of the most popular graphical and mathematical tools available for studying systems of discrete event nature, due to its ability to model the precedence relations and structural interactions of random, concurrent, asynchronous events [2,3,26,27].

Despite there are several formalism that support DEV Systems behaviour description, PN constructs formalism offers several advantages as KR framework in DSS, such as:

- PN can be considered a modelling paradigm with several levels of abstraction and interpretation, which is essential to integrate at the appropriate detail description level the logistic aspects of a system.
- It is possible to carry out both a qualitative analysis (identification of alternatives) and a quantitative analysis (evaluation of alternatives) suitable for DSS.
- There are several mechanisms to determine all the activated events at a particular system state, and all the new events that can be triggered as a consequence of the activation of a certain event.
- They allow the description of a complex system by means of a bottom-up approach.
- PN constitute a model formalism with very few constructors and syntactic rules.

2.2 PN Description

A PN is a particular case of directed, weighed and bipartite graph, with two types of nodes, places and transitions. The marking defines the state of the system that will evolve according to the firings of the transitions when their associated events occur.

Place nodes (represented by circles) are used to describe both logical conditions and stocks, transition nodes represent the system events, weighted arcs are used to describe the logical preconditions to allows the firing of an event, and also the consequences on the system state. Tokens (represented by black points) are used to model the number of elements (pieces, resources, people, etc.) that are stored in stocks (places), or boolean conditions (binary places). Finally, the state of the system can be described by the distribution of tokens in the places, which is known as marking.

One says that a transition is **not enabled** when the number of tokens in anyone of the places at the entrance of a transition is less than the value of the arc weight connecting the place to the transition. Otherwise says that it is **enabled**. When a transition is fired, tokens at the input places are eliminated and added to the output places. The number of tokens eliminated/added is specified by the weight of the corresponding arc of input/output.

2.3 Coloured Petri Nets (CPN)

Despite a PN model might be suffice to describe the logic constraints between a list of resources (processing machines, transport units, local stocks) a list of operations, and their precedence relationships, it lacks of information data representation independent of the system architecture, which is essential to deal in an efficient way with the best logistic policy for a given system state and a given goal state [27].

Simulation Models as evaluation of alternatives mechanism in DSS arises out of an inability to evaluate more than a fraction of the immense range of options available. Most of commercial discrete event oriented simulation packages are designed to perform simulation as an analysis tool. That is, the system to be studied is modelled, perturbed or parameterised in some interesting fashion, and simulated to predict what changes those disturbances or parameter configurations would cause in a real system.

PN models of complex logistic processes consist of large aggregate graph structures due to its inability to describe entity information changes. In general, there a lot of circumstances inherent to logistic systems where it is necessary to distinguish the entities (tokens) that flow through the system. The PN formalism does not facilitate the description of those activities whose behaviour depends on certain information that denominates state of the entities.

Model maintenance and model fitting task inherent to the evaluation mechanism of a DSS becomes a hard and difficult task when models structures are complex.

A suitable KR formalism for a DSS in the logistic field, should offer easy to use modelling constructs to support entity information description to specify aspects such as:

- Entity priorities in a waiting queue.
- Event firing according to entity attribute values.
- Time event functions according to entity attributes.
- Coloured Petri Nets allow a higher level of modelling, by using colours that allows to represent entity attributes of commercial simulation software packages:
- The flow of entities can be specified by describing what it happens to an entity as flows through a sequence of subsystems.
- Transition time can be evaluated as a random function of entity characteristics (attributes).

The CPN offer the necessary modelling tools to represent both the entity attributes (characteristics) that flow through the system, and the object properties that should allow the firing of each system event.

2.4 CPN Description

The main CPN components [12] that empower this methodology as KR formalism in the logistic field are:

- State Vector: The smallest information needed to predict the events that can appear. The state vector represents the number of tokens in each place, and the colours of each token.
- Arc Expressions and Guards: Are used to indicate which type of tokens can be used to fire a transition.
- Colour Sets: Determines the types, operations and functions that can be used by the elements of the CPN model.
- Places: They are very useful to specify both queues and logical conditions.

3. Coverability Tree

Planning and scheduling of logistic systems are considered NP-Hard problems that cannot be solved by means of polynomial time algorithms. Despite important efforts from the OR and AI research communities have been made, these kind of problems are still open research areas due to the economical benefits that a good scheduling algorithm could bring in several fields such as production planning, computer design, logistics, communications, etc.

In this paper a test-bed system for the evaluation of heuristic search algorithms to deal with the planning and scheduling of logistic system is proposed. Our approach consists to open the coverability tree of a system described in the CPN formalism. The main goal of the coverability tree is to find all the markings that can be reached starting at a particular initial state M_0.

The root of the tree consists of the initial marking (M_0). For each node in the tree, all the enabled events are recognized (identification of alternatives), and for each event a new state is calculated (evaluation of alternatives) and its marking is added to the tree together with an arc joining both nodes specifying the transition fired.

This method of analysis, whose formal definition is described widely in [12], is the base for the construction of a generic DSS for DEV Systems, such that given the initial and the goal state, will generate the sequence of transitions that will drive the system to the desired target minimizing a certain cost function [15,16,17].

When applying the proposed methodology to real logistic systems, the amount of nodes (system states) of the coverability tree can grow to computationally prohibited size. On the other hand, the computer time required to explore a tree of these characteristics constrain its use to academic systems.

To tackle this combinatorial explosion problem, an alternative is proposed: To build dynamically the coverability tree according to some heuristics. The underlying basic idea to dynamically build the coverability tree of a logistic system specified in the CPN formalism is to translate a scheduling problem into a search problem, i.e. to obtain a path from a certain system state to a desired goal state in a graph structure that represents the problem space.

This alternative allows the evaluation of different search methods such as Tabu Search, Simulation Annealing, Neighbourhood Search, Agents, and other, [28, 5, 8, 9, 4], to deal with the best sequence of actions that will drive the system to a certain final state.

4. A Generic Test-bed Framework for Search Algorithms.

Computer memory capacity is an important factor to consider at the design phase of a framework for the construction, analysis and maintenance of a coverability tree. It should be noted that the huge amount of decision variables inherent to most logistic systems leads to coverability trees whose dimensions exceed the limits of memory allowed by the computer at a certain moment during the evaluation of alternatives step of a DSS. The design of search algorithms to tackle the combinatorial explosion are needed to "cut" branches of the tree that, according to certain criteria, do not will lead to an acceptable solution. Most of these algorithms are based on the concept of "cost function" to determine which paths are worth to be evaluated.

4.1 Cost Function

The formalization of an objective function to drive the program through the search space, will allow to summarize certain expert knowledge and express it in the mathematical formalism used by the search algorithms. The knowledge expressed through the objective function can be used to select those markings (states) within the solutions space that could lead to the optimal solution.

In industry, production requirements are defined usually as a compromise between time and cost. To assess a production process, the engineer has to be aware of performance indexes such as: total time that a part spends in a queue; total time that parts spend in transport systems; equipment utilization; proportions of time a machine is down (waiting for parts of a previous work station), blocked (waiting for a finished part to be removed), or undergoing setup operations, etc.

Attempting to group the production performance indexes, a corresponding cost function is defined. This cost function is formalized by two components: a place or "work in process" (WIP) component and a time component.

"Work in process" is the current number of pieces (or quantity of material, in the processes industry case) in the production line. In terms of Coloured Petri Nets, the WIP can be obtained by computing the sum of tokens in every place representing a stock. Thus, the cost that a company pays for pieces stored in particular queues (places), can be expressed mathematically by an objective *P-function* (1), where P_i represents the internal values of the place i (number of pieces or tokens stored in queue i), and A_i is a weighting parameter defined by the user.

$$Jp = \sum_{i=1}^{n} A_i \times P_i \tag{1}$$

Note that the performance of the *P-function* depends on the tuning of the weighting parameters. Thus, the final user can penalize those places where tokens should not remain for long (row material places).

4.2 Example

The test-bed framework has been designed under the Object Oriented Programming paradigm to improve its reusability to support both:

- The evaluation of different search algorithms,
- A DSS to generate the best planning policy for a logistic system.

Below, the use of two different heuristics is presented to illustrate the versatility of the proposed tool.

4.2.1 Local Search by Amplitude

Figure 2 illustrates the possibility to open the full tree up to a certain level l, choosing the best n nodes (system states) according to a certain cost function as the root of a new coverability tree. This operation is repeated successively until a goal state is reached. The user specifies parameters l and n.

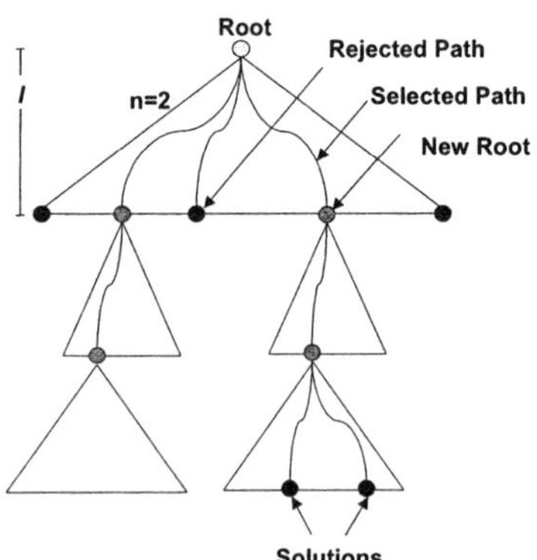

Fig 2. Heuristic Pruning Algorithm.

4.2.2 Linear Regression Estimators

Figure 3 shows a linear regression estimation method used to evaluate the cost function to reach the goal state from the present node:

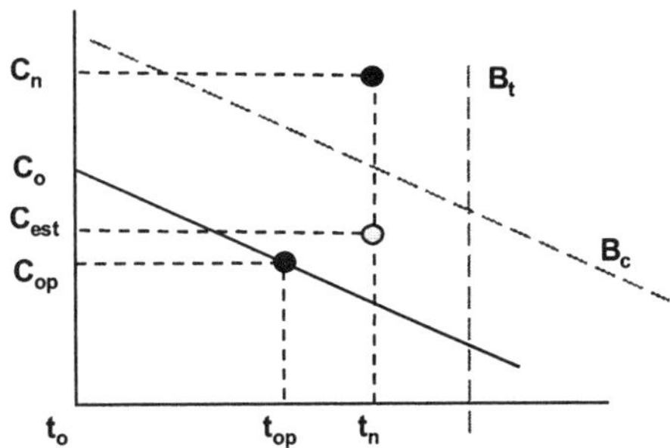

Fig 3. Bounds by Linear Regression.

- *to* and *Co* correspond to the time and cost of the initial marking respectively.
- *Cop* corresponds to the smaller value of cost reached about a marking after the time of arrival top.
- *Cest* corresponds to the estimated cost value of a marking for its corresponding time of arrival *tn*, and represents the value of cost that would have to have to be within the allowed limits of cost. This value is obtained by means of the expression:

$$C_{est} = \left[\frac{t_n - t_o}{t_{op} - t_o} * (C_{op} - C_o) \right] + C_o \tag{2}$$

- *Bc* is an established margin so that the real value of cost of the node, *Cn*, is considered within the bounds of cost allowed
- *Bt* is an established margin so that the value of time of the node, *tn*, is considered within the allowed bounds of time.

On the basis of the previous variables, the method establishes that if the following condition is fulfilled:

$$(C_n > (C_{op} + B_c) \wedge t_n > (t_{op} + B_t)) \vee (C_n > (C_{est} + B_c) \wedge t_n < (t_{op} + B_t))$$

the node is rejected.

4.3 Some Results

The system has been proven, among others, with an example of scheduling for a JobShop system of three machines and three jobs proposed in [9]. The optimum makespan for this problem is know to be 15 time units. The system found the solution in 5 minutes exploring all the possible paths (6.667 nodes of the coverability tree), without heuristic. The solution presented in [9] (a similar system but that uses the ordinary Petri nets to represent the knowledge of the production system), found the same optimal solution, but exploring

36.997 nodes and bounding 40.261 nodes and the execution took 2 h to explore all the accepted paths.

A system well known is benchmarking problem that consist to solve the scheduling problem of 6 jobs into 6 machines in a job shop production system. The machine sequence of each job is known, and each machine can serve only one job at a time. The optimization target consists to minimize the makespan to finish all the jobs. The optimum makespan for this problem is know to be 55 time units. Table A, B y C describe colours, places, and transitions used to model the job-shop production system.

Table A. Colours description of 6x6 JobShop system.

Colour	Definition	Description
J	Int 1..6	Job identifier.
M	Int 0..5	Machine in which the task n° O of job J must be processed.
T	It 1..10	Time units spent processing a certain job in a certain machine.
O	Int 1..7	Sequence position of the job J in the machine M.
Ma	Int 0..5	Machine identifier.
Jo	Product J*M*T*O	Information describing the task characteristics of each Job.

Table B. Places description of 6x6 JobShop CPN model.

Place	Colour	Description
Job	Jo	Tokens stored in place Job represent the information associated to each Job in the production system: Job identifier, machine in which the nest task must be performed, time required for the next operation, and the order of the task in the sequence of operations to finish the Job.
Maq	Ma	Information associated to each machine.

Table C. Transition description of 6x6 JobShop CPN model.

Transition	Description
T_1	Task execution of a Job in a machine.

Figure 4 shows the CPN of the system, and Figure 5 illustrate by means of a Gantt diagram the results obtained when the initial state M_0 corresponds to the vector:

$$[1'(1,2,1,1)+1'(2,1,8,1)+1'(3,2,5,1)+1'(4,1,5,1)+1'(5,2,9,1)+1'(6,1,3,1)]$$

and the goal state is described by the vector M_f:

$$[1'(1,*,*,7)+1'(2,*,*,7)+1'(3,*,*,7)+1'(4,*,*,7)+1'(5,*,*,7)+1'(6,*,*,7)]$$

where the wild card is used to specify that any value can be accepted.

6. Conclusions

A KR formalism to specify the behaviour of discrete event systems has been presented. The main advantages of the proposed formalism have been enumerated, paying special attention to the translation of the scheduling problem to a search problem.

Although there exists other approaches to sort out the scheduling problem by pruning the coverability tree [8], to the best of our knowledge, this is the first approach using CPN as KR formalism.

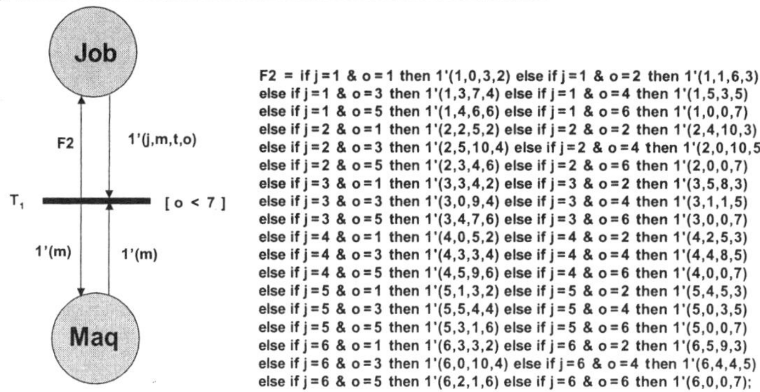

Figure 4. CPN of the 6x6 Job Shop System.

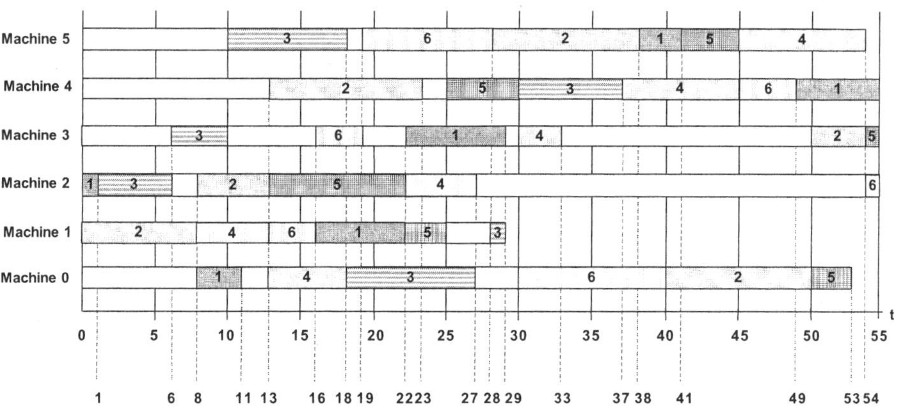

Figure 5. Gantt diagram with the scheduling solution.

Acknowledgements

The authors wish to acknowledge the financial support received from the CICYT Spanish program DPI2001-2051-C01/C02.

References

[1]   A. Mohamed, T. Celik, Knowledge base-system for alternative design, cost estimating and scheduling, *Knowledge-Based Systems*, 15 (2002), 177 - 188.

[2]   A. Zimmerman. Modeling of Manufacturing Systems and Production Routes Using Colored Petri Nets, *Proc. of the 3rd IASTED International. Conference on Robotics and Manufacturing*, (1995), 380-383.

[3]   A. Zimmerman, K. Dalkowski, G. Hommel, G, A Case Study in Modeling and Performance Evaluation of Manufacturing Systems Using Colored Petri Nets, *Proc. of the 8th European Simulation Symposium (ESS '96),* (1996), 282-286.

[4]   B. Yang, J. Geunes, W.J. O'Brien, A heuristic approach for minimizing weighted tardiness and overtime costs in single resource scheduling, *Computers & Operations Research*, Article in Press (2003).

[5]   D-H. Lee, D. Kiritsis, P. Xirouchakis, Operation sequencing in nonlinear planning: Local search heuristics, *Studies in Informatics and Control*, Vol 11, Num. 19 (2002).

[6]   D.J. Power, A Brief History of Decision Support Systems, *DSSResources.COM, World Wide Web*, http://DSSResources.COM/history/dsshistory.html, version 2.7 (2003).

[7]   F. Riane, A. Artiba, An integrated production planning and scheduling system for hybrid flowshop organizations, *International Journal of Production Economics*, 74 (2001), 33 - 48.

[8]   H. Yu, A. Reyes, S. Cang, S. Lloyd, Combined Petri net modelling and AI-based heuristic hybrid search for flexible manufacturing systems-part I. Petri net modelling and heuristic search, *Computer & Industrial Engineering*, 44 (2003), 527 - 543.

[9]   H. Yu, A. Reyes, S. Cang, S. Lloyd, Combined Petri net modelling and AI-based heuristic hybrid search for flexible manufacturing systems-part II. Heuristic hybrid search, *Computer & Industrial Engineering*, 44 (2003), 545 - 566.

[10]   J.P. Shim, M. Warkentin, J.F. Courtney, D.J. Power, R. Sharda, C. Carlsson, Past, present and future of decision support technology, *Decision Support Systems*, 33 (2002), 111 - 126.

[11]   K-C. Ying, C-J. Liao, An ant colony system for permutation flow-shop sequencing, *Computers & Operations Research*, Article in Press (2003).

[12]   K. Jensen, *Coloured Petri Nets: Basics Concepts, Analysis Methods and Practical Use,* vol. 1,2,3, Springer-Verlag, 1997.

[13]   K. Mesghouni, S. Hammadi, P. Borne, On Modelling Genetic Algorithms for Flexible Job-shop Scheduling Problems, *Studies in Informatics and Control*, Vol 7, Num. 1 (1998).

[14]   L. Thiele, Discrete Event Systems: Introduction, *Computer Engineering and Networks Laboratory. Swiss Federal Institute of Technology (ETH)*, www.tik.ee.ethz.ch/tik/education/lectures/ DES/WS02_03/Book/des_book_intro.pdf

[15]   M.A. Piera, M.E. Narciso, A. Guasch, J. Canovas, A Methodology to Improve Simulation Optimization Approach for Process Scheduling through Petri Net Formalism, *2003 Summer Computer Simulation Conference (SCSC'03)*, (2003).

[16]   M.E. Narciso, M. A. Piera, J-C Hennet, Generation de Plan par Exploration Selective d'un Arbre de Couverture, *4e Conférence Francophone de MOodélisation et SIMulation MOSIM'03*, (2003).

[17]   M.E. Narciso, M.A. Piera, A. Guasch, A Modeling and Simulation Approach: Towards True Manufacturing Flexibility, *15th IFAC World Congress on Automatic Control, b'02*, (2002).

[18]   M.E. Narciso, M.A. Piera, Coloured Petri Net Simulator: A Generic Tool for Production Planning, *ETFA'2001 - 8th IEEE International Conference on Emerging Technologies and Factory Automation*, (2001).

[19]   M. Özbayrak, R. Bell, A knowledge-based decision support system for the management of parts and tools in FMS, *Decision Support Systems*, 35 (2003), 487 - 515.

[20]   O. Madani, S. Hanks, A. Condon, On the undecidability of probabilistic planning and related stochastic optimisation problems, *Artificial Intelligence*, Article in Press (2003).

[21]   P. Gazmuri, S. Maturana, Developing and Implementing a Production Planning DSS for CTI Using Structured Modeling, *INTERFACES*, 31 (2001), 22 - 36.

[22]   S. Esquivel, S. Ferrero, R. Gallard, C. Salto, H. Alfonso, M. Schütz, Enhanced evolutionary algorithms for single and multiobjective optimization in the job shop scheduling problem, *Knowledge-Besed Systems*, 15 (2002), 13 - 25.

[23]   S. Feng, L Li, L.X. Cen, An object-oriented intelligent design tool to aid the design of manufacturing systems, *Knowledge-Based Systems*, 14 (2001), 225 - 232.

[24]   S.M. Majercik, M.L. Littman, Contingent planning under uncertainty via stochastic satisfiability, *Artificial Intelligence*, Article in Press (2003).

[25]   S. Mallya, S. Banerjee, W.G. Bistline, A Decision Support System for Production/Distribution Planning in Continuous Manufacturing, *Decision Sciences Journal*, 32 (2001).

[26]   M. Silva, R. Valette, Petri Nets and Flexible Manufacturing, *Lecture Notes in Computer Science, Advances in Petri Nets*, 424 (1989), 374-417.

[27]   M. Zhou, K. Venkatesh, *Modeling, Simulation, and Control of Flexible Manufacturing Systems: A Petri Net Approach*, (1999).

[28]   T. Aldowaisan, A. Allahverdi, New heuristics for no-wait flowshops to minimize makespan, *Computers & Operations Research*, 30 (2003), 1219 - 1231.

[29]   X.F. Zha, A knowledge intensive multi-agent framework for cooperative/collaborative design modelling and decision support of assemblies, *Knowledge-Based Systems*, 15 (2002), 493 - 506.

[30]   X. Li, F. Lara-Rosano, Adaptive fuzzy petri nets for dynamic knowledge representation and inference, *Expert Systems with Applications*, 19 (2000), 235 – 241.

Artificial Intelligence Research and Development
I. Aguiló et al. (Eds.)
IOS Press, 2003

Fuzzy Identification for Fault Isolation.
Application to Analog Circuits Diagnosis

Carles Pous, Joan Colomer, Joaquim Melendez, J. L. de la Rosa
Institut d'Informatica i Aplicacions. Universitat de Girona

Abstract. A fuzzy system that gives estimated parameters value as a result is proposed as a tool for diagnosis proposes. Two fault dictionary methods have been studied in detail. They have been extended for tolerance coverage, fuzzified and then applied to a biquad filter. A comparison between the dictionary and the fuzzyfied one shows the great improvement obtained by the method. The faults considered are parametric, permanent, independent and simple.

Keywords: Fuzzy modelling, parameter identification, fault dictionary, fault diagnosis, analog circuits.

1 Introduction

The main part of supervision of a complex system is focused on to detect and isolate occurring faults and provide information about their size and source, [6]. The most important and difficult task is centered on fault detection and diagnosis where difficulty increases with the real time constrains and complexity of systems (non-linear, coupled dynamics, time dependencies, etc.). The core of the fault diagnosis methodology is the so-called model-based approach, where either analytical or knowledgebased models or combination of both are used together with analytical or heuristic reasoning [6]. The classical procedure of a fault diagnosis system is depicted in Figure 1. This is achieved in three basic steps, residual generation, evaluation and analysis, not always clearly separable.

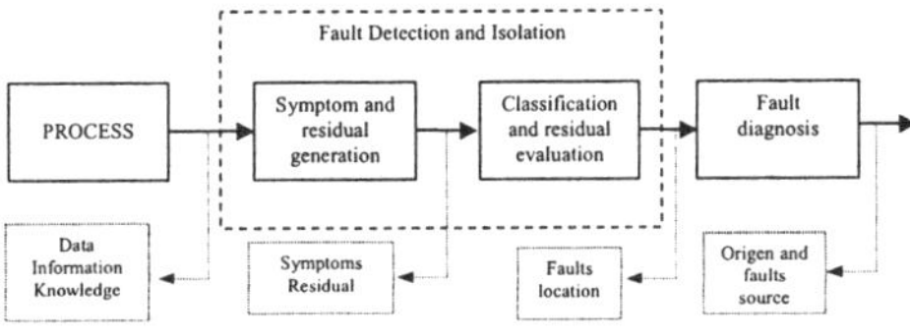

Figure 1: Fault Diagnosis Procedure

Hence, the methodology used in fault detection is clearly dependent on the process and the sort of available information. [12] gives an extensive classification and description of these methods. The evaluation of fault diagnosis and supervision methods is more difficult because of little data, although rule-based reasoning methods are increasingly used and also the number of fuzzy rule-based applications is growing [8]. According to [8], fault detection methods can be classified in the following main groups:

- **Signal-based methods**: They are focused on analyzing signal features. Change detection is measured as a deviation from normal behavior. For this purpose, statistical (mean, variance, entropy, etc. are estimated), frequencial (as filtering or spectral estimations methods for example) and probabilistic (Bayes decision) methods are used. Fault dictionary techniques can be considered into this group.

- **Model-based methods**: Model-based fault detection methods are focused on residual generation, i.e. fault indicators. Residuals are obtained as changes or discrepancies in special features of the process obtained from process variables (for example, output signals, state variables) or coefficients (for example, estimated parameters or other calculated ratios). To achieve this goal, data obtained from the process is compared to the data supplied by models representing normal operating conditions. **Parameter identification** techniques are considered in this category. They are based on the assumption that the faults are provoked by changes in the physical system parameters (mass, friction, resistance, viscosity, etc.). Estimations are compared with the parameters of the reference model, obtained under fault-free conditions. A wider description of those methods and other interesting variants of them are included in [7].

- **Knowledge-based methods**: In the case of noticeable modelling uncertainty, a more suitable strategy is that of using knowledge-based techniques. Instead of output signals any kind of symptoms can be used and the robustness can be attained by restricting to only those symptoms that are not strongly dependent upon the systems uncertainty.

Our proposal is to use fault dictionary techniques as a first approach to the fault diagnosis problem, because they are simpler and the most commonly used in practice. Afterwards, the limitations they have are overcome with the proposed methodology. The methodology is based on building a fuzzy model for parameter identification. It belongs to the three mentioned previously fault detection methods groups because is based on fault dictionaries (signal-based methods), it identifies parameter values (model-based methods), and it models uncertainties (knowledge-based methods).

The selected system to diagnose is an analog electronic circuit. Although almost all circuits are designed using digital technology, a lot of them have analog components. This is due to the analog nature of input and output signals they have to deal with (audio signals, signals from sensors, etc.). So, analog interfaces as filters, AD/DA converters, PLL (Phase Locked Loop), modulators and demodulators are needed [10], [16], [2]. Diagnosis techniques for digital circuits have been successfully developed and automated. But, this is not yet the situation for analog circuits [11], [5]. Analog circuits are more complex to diagnose due to the measures overlapping produced by the components tolerance [3],[4]. These tolerances together with the analog nature of the measured signals, can produce the same symptoms for different failures, giving a set of components as possible diagnosis called *ambiguity groups* [14].

Next paragraphs expose the main limitations of the fault dictionary techniques and the proposed methodology in detail. An example on a analog electronic circuit has been developed to show the improved results obtained by the methodology.

2 Fault Dictionaries and Their Limitations

Fault dictionaries are techniques completely based on quantitative calculations. Once the universe of faults to be detected is defined (Fault 1, Fault 2, ..., Fault m), selected measures are obtained from the system for each considered fault and stored in a table (dictionary).

These values will be then compared with the measures obtained from an unknown faulty system. The comparison is typically performed by the neighborhood criterion, obtaining distances, minimizing certain indexes, and so on. So, the method has two steps: The first one is based on simulation in order to built the dictionary; the second one consists in comparing the measures from the unknown faulty system with the stored ones.

These techniques have a compromise between fault coverage and dictionary length. When the fault dictionary is made larger, the scope of faults detected increases as well. On the other hand, if the faults considered to generate the dictionary are a small set, the dictionary will be shortened, but the world of detected faults will be reduced. So, one of the objectives of the diagnosis designer is to built a dictionary with as few measures as possible that gives a good fault diagnosis coverage.

A lot of systems are seriously affected by tolerances. If the dictionary is obtained simulating the faults only considering the nominal values of the parameters, the measures got from the real system won't match, generally, to the stored ones because of tolerances. In order to find the possible cases produced by the tolerances for a particular measure, several simulation runs have to be carried out. One of the most commonly used methods is Monte-Carlo. It is obvious that increasing the number of Monte-Carlo runs provokes a dictionary spreading, making it unpractical.

The other important fault dictionary limitation is that they can not cope with non previously considered faults. So, more simulations should be done in order to include new situations in the original dictionary.

Two fault dictionary methods are proposed and described in detail in order to be applied to an electronic circuit as a process.

2.1 Frequencial Method

For this method, the stimuli signals are sinusoidal waveforms at different frequencies f1, f2, ..., fn. The measures taken are amplitude, phase or both. The set of frequencies selection at which to perform the measures is based on the one described in [15]. It associates a confidence level index to a set of test frequencies selected. This index has to do with the capability of the selected frequencial measures to separate and diagnose the proposed set of faults. The faults of interest (Fault 1, Fault 2, ..., Fault m) are simulated and the magnitude (Amp) and phase (Ph) responses at these frequencies are stored. Then, the algorithm starts calculating the confidence level beginning with a frequency and a measure (module or phase). If the index is not satisfactory (less than a pre-established minimum), more frequencial measures are introduced. When the confidence level is sufficient, the algorithm stops and provides an optimum set of frequencies and measures to perform. The dictionary for the frequencial method has an appearance like the one shown in Table 1.

Table 1: Frequencial dictionary

Faults	Amp f1	Ph f1	Ph f2	...	Amp fn
Nominal	$A0_{f1}$	$Ph0_{f1}$	$Ph0_{f2}$	...	$A0_{fn}$
Fault 1	$A1_{f1}$	$Ph1_{f1}$	$Ph1_{f2}$	...	$A1_{fn}$
...	...	...	...	...	...
Fault m	Am_{f1}	Phm_{f1}	Am_{f2}	...	Am_{fn}

2.2　*Temporal Method*

In this case, the stored data in the dictionary are certain characteristics of the circuit response
to a saturated ramp input (Figure 2), as proposed in [1].

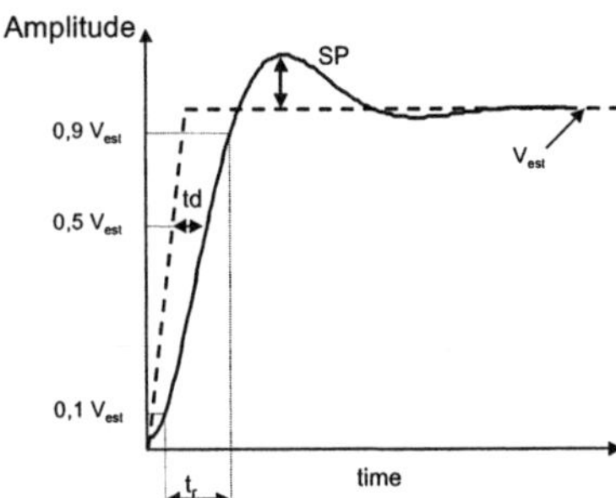

Figure 2: Response parameters to a ramp input

The parameters used to characterize the faults are:

- *Steady state (V_{est})*: Final value at which the output tends to.

- *Overshoot (SP)*: Defined as

$$SP = \frac{V_{\max} - V_{est}}{V_{est}} 100 \qquad (1)$$

where V_{max} is the amplitude maximum value reached at the output.

- *Rising time (tr)*: Time used by the output to rise from the 10% to 90% of the steady state
  value.

- *Delay time (td)*: Interval of time between the moment that the input and the output get to
  the 50% steady state value.

In [1] it is highlighted that choosing a smaller ramp rise time, doesn't imply better diagnostic results. A method to help in the selection of an appropriate ramp rise time is not
provided. The dictionary has an appearance like Table 2.

Table 2: Temporal dictionary

Faults	SP	td	tr	Vest
Nominal	SP0	td0	tr0	Vest0
F1	SP1	td1	tr1	Vest1
...	...	...	...	...
Fm	SPm	tdm	trm	Vestm

3　The Fuzzy Approach

A first solution to the fault dictionary limitations was to refine the diagnosis system by means of fuzzy techniques. Fuzzy sets can be built from Monte-Carlo simulations and the dictionary instances could be compacted in fuzzy rules. The system includes tolerance effects and its output is an estimation of each parameter value. Hence, inputs, outputs, rules and the corresponding operators to combine them, have to be defined.

3.1　Defining the Inputs

Each measure will be considered as a fuzzy system input. For example, for a frequencial method that uses both, magnitude and phase measures at 10 different frequencies, the fuzzy system will have 20 inputs. The number of membership functions belonging to each input will be given by the previously considered universe of faults and the nominal case. That is to say, if the circuit is composed by N parameters, and deviations of $\pm X\%$ for each parameter are considered as desirable identifiable faults, each fuzzy input will have 2N+1 membership functions. Figure 3 shows a possible appearance of the measure i input. Each membership function is related to a possible considered fault. Parameter 1 +X%, Parameter 1 -X%, Nominal (all parameters at their nominal value), and so on. In general, membership functions are not symmetric.

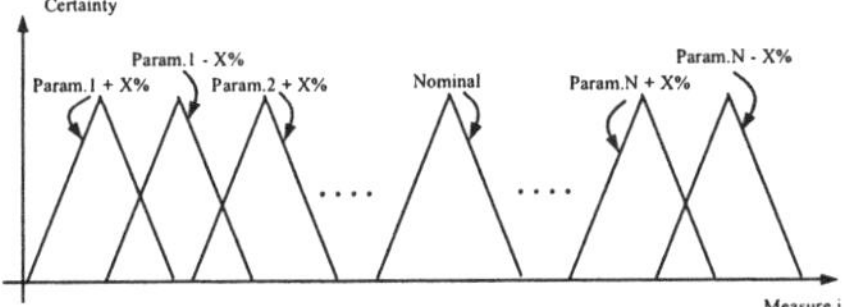

Figure 3: Measure i appearance

The membership function shape has been selected taking advantage of the Monte-Carlo simulation results. An analysis of the *Measure i* faults distribution could be done. For example, *Measure i* for *Fault j* can has the distribution shown in Figure 4 after a Monte-Carlo simulation of L runs.

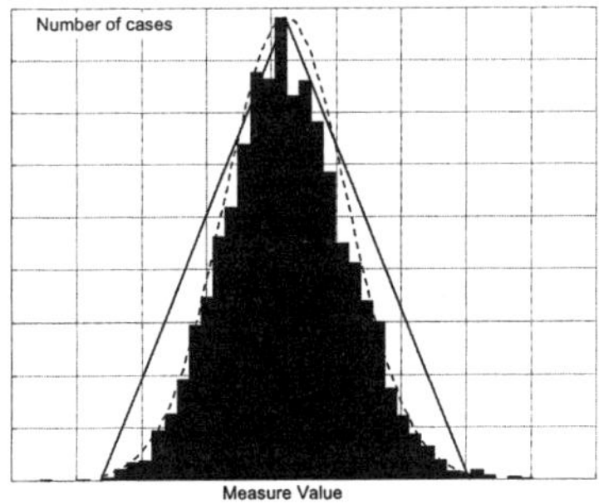

Figure 4: Measure i input distribution for fault j

This distribution could be approximated, for example, by a gaussian or triangular shape as it is depicted in the figure.

3.2 Defining the Outputs

The outputs of the system are the parameter values estimated. Therefore, there will be as many outputs as parameters. Each output will have a membership function for each considered deviation. For example, if deviations of $\pm X\%$ are considered, the parameter *param i* output will look like Figure 5

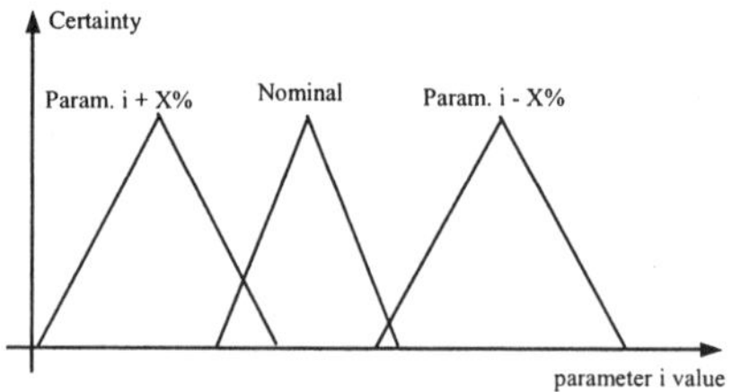

Figure 5: parameter i output appearance

Membership function shape will be taken according to the parameter value distribution. For example, if the parameters correspond to resistors, it is well known that these components have a gaussian distribution probability function.

3.3 Defining the Rules

Once the inputs and outputs are defined, they have to be connected by means of rules. The rule structure for the fault Param. 1+ X% is

if (Meas. 1 is Param. 1+X%)&(Meas. 2 is Param 1+X%)&....(Meas. M is Param. 1+X%) then (Param. 1 is Param. 1+ X%)&(Param. 2 is nominal)&(Param. 3 is nominal)&... (Param. N is nominal).

Hence, there are as many rules as considered faults. The advantage of this method is that it is not necessary to store all cases but the rules and membership functions for the inputs and the outputs. The operator selected to combine antecedents is the product. The main reason is to penalize measures falling outside the memberships scope. If one of the M measures falls outside of at least one of the sets defined by the rule antecedents, the final product will be 0, and the rule won't be fired. On the contrary, the rule will be triggered with a value corresponding to the belonging coefficients product.

The defuzzification method used is the centroid. Then, after computing a set of measures, each output will provide us with an estimated value of the corresponding parameter with a degree of certainty.

4   Example on a Real Circuit

4.1   Circuit Under Test

The selected circuit is a biquadratic filter shown in Figure 6. This circuit is used as a benchmark in the bibliography [1], [9], [13].

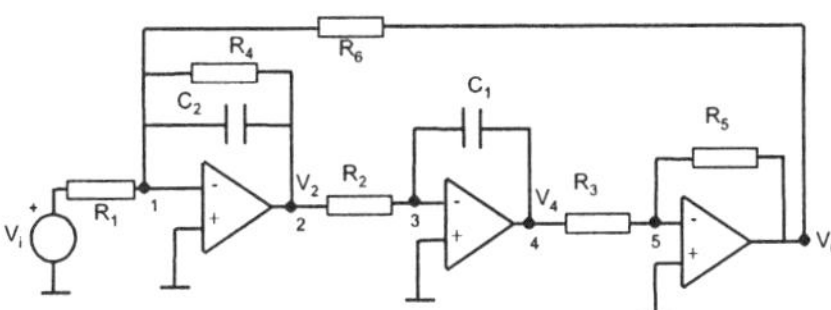

Figure 6: Circuit under test

The nominal values of the components in the example are: R1=2.7K, R2=1K, R3=10K, R4=1.5K, R5=12K, R6=2.7K and C1=C2=10nF. A component is considered faulty when its value differs more than 10% from nominal.

As the circuit under test is frequency dependent, the frequencial method and a temporal one described previously can be used. In order to reduce the set of measures, it has been considered that only voltage measures at the output V_0 are possible.

The initial proposed faults to detect are deviations of $\pm 20\%$ and $\pm 50\%$ from the nominal values of the passive components (a set of 32 faults). So, our dictionary has a row for each fault and the nominal case (33 rows).

4.2   Frequencial Method

Implementing the algorithm proposed in [15] to the biquad filter, a total of 6 measures will be enough to reach a confidence level of 82.28%. Increasing the number of measures doesn't improve the confidence index significantly. The 6 measures selected are: Amplitude at 10000 and 85000 rad/sec. and phase at 9000, 10000, 65000 and 100000 rad/sec. For example, taking the fault $R1 - 20\%$ the following values at V_0 are measured:

Table 3: Measures for R1-20%

Freq.(rad/sec.)	Amplitude (V)	Phase (^{o})
9000		172.17
10000	1.26	171.27
65000		92.89
85000	0.88	
100000		50.19

Hence, a set of 33x6 = 198 measures has to be done in order to built the dictionary.

4.3   Temporal Method

In the case of the temporal response, a ramp input with a saturation value of 1 V and a rise time of $100\mu s$ has been chosen. Thus, taking the case R2+20%, for example, while other components stay at their nominal value, the parameters measured are:

$$SP = 4.51\%,\ td = 19\mu s,\ tr = 76\mu s\ \text{and}\ V_{est} = -0.99V.$$

For all the initially considered faults, the temporal dictionary will has 33 rows and 4 columns, with a total of 33x4 = 132 measures to be done.

5 Implementing the Fuzzy Approach

5.1 Frequencial Method

In the frequencial method, measures at each frequency are taken as fuzzy system inputs (6 inputs are defined). Each fuzzy system input corresponds to the amplitude and phase measures pointed in Table 3, and each one compounded by 33 sets, representing the nominal case and the 32 proposed faults to detect.

Membership functions have been taken triangular shaped. Its maximum value corresponds to the value obtained for this measure and fault, while all the other components are at their nominal value. The triangle extremes are the maximum deviation on this value produced by the component tolerance. For example, for the fault R1-50%, the interval extremes corresponding to the magnitude measurement at 10000 Hz are [1.5278 2.5260], and the value obtained without tolerances is 2.022. After 2000 Monte-Carlo runs with the component values gaussian distributed, each fault distribution is analyzed and it can be seen that a triangular shape approximation is good enough. Taking gaussian distributions doesn't improve the results significantly, as the authors have tested. In some few cases, triangular shape slightly improve the diagnostic. The reason is because in some cases the queues of the gaussian shape introduce overlapping, while triangular membership functions are exactly 0 outside the margin.

There is one fuzzy system output associated to each component (8 for the biquadratic filter). There will be a set of *membership functions* corresponding to the component at its nominal value and one for each possible deviation considered ($\pm 20\%$ and $\pm 50\%$ from the nominal value, giving 5 subsets for each output attribute). So, each output attribute will provide an estimated value for each component. Figure 7 shows the sets considered for the output attribute related to component R1.

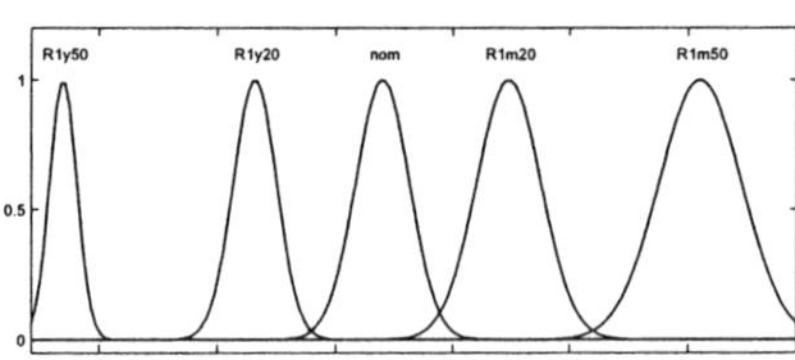

Figure 7: Output attribute sets for R1

Membership functions belonging to the output attributes have a gaussian shape, being this one the typical distribution for electronic components [2].

Rules are simple relations, like the following one

if (phase9000 is R1-20)&(mag10000 is R1-20)&(phase10000 is R1-20)&(phase65000 is R1-20)&(phase100000 is R1-20) then (R1 is R1-20)&(R2 is nominal)&(R3 is nominal)&... (C2 is nominal).

The previous rule corresponds to the case R1-20%. The operator '&' is defined by the product function. When measures of Table 3 are acquired, they belong to a set in a certain degree. Hence, if one of the 6 measures falls outside at least one of the sets defined for this rule, the final product will be 0, and the rule won't be fired. On the other hand, if each of the 6 measures taken falls into the sets defined by the case R1-20%, this rule will be activated with a value corresponding to the belonging coefficients product. If R1-20% was the unique fired rule, the diagnostic would be R1-20% and the other components would have a value belonging to the 10 % tolerance range from nominal. But, due to the overlapping in the sets, sometimes several rules are fired at same time for the same measures set. In this case, the product is the operator selected to combine the fired membership functions. Now, the rules results are added providing the output. A similar procedure is done for each component. The centroid method is used for giving a final estimated value for each component. The final outputs for the case R1-20% are R1=2223, R2=1000, R3=10K, R4=1504, R5=12010, R6=2757, C1=10nF and C2=10nF. Therefore, the conclusion is R1 faulty, since it is the only component that has an estimated value outside the tolerance limits (R1nom=2.7K). For this particular case, fuzzy techniques have allowed to improve the result (diagnostic was R1, R5 and R6 without fuzzy).

There are 4 cases that give a wrong diagnosis: R2-20%, R3-20%, R5-20% and C1-20%. This is because the overlapping fires several rules at the same time, and the centroid averages them giving a wrong value. For example, for the case R2-20%, the output set corresponding to R2 is depicted in Figure 8. The centroid method gives an average of R2=0.911K, therefore, R2 will be considered non faulty. On the other hand, Figure 9 shows the output for R5.

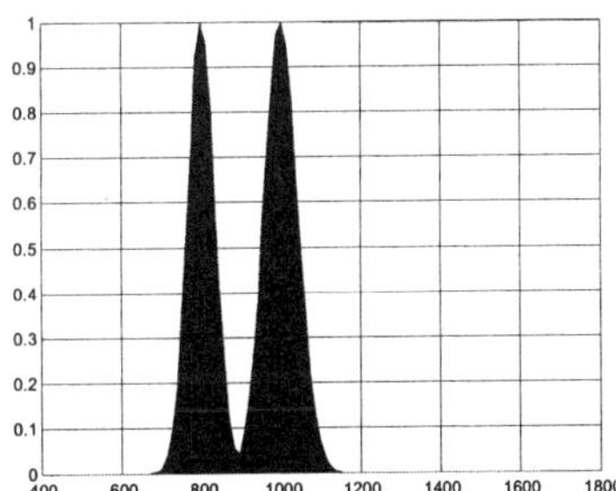

Figure 8: R2 output set for R2-20%

The centroid method applied to this set, produces an output R5= 13.58K. So, R5 is considered as faulty. The produced worsening is not serious, since without fuzzy, it gave much overlapping that makes the situation difficult to diagnose. Something similar happens with the other cases.

As it has been explained in advance, the system has to be able to decide for other unlearned cases. For example, the system was tested with the new cases R1+15%, R6-30%, C2-30% and R3+70%. The diagnosis provided by the system is **R1, R6,C2** and {**R3**,R5,C1}

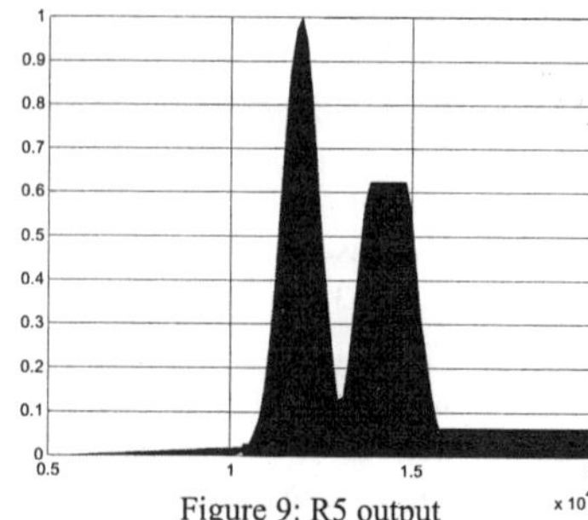

Figure 9: R5 output

respectively. So, the system does what is expected applying fuzzy, it interpolates to conclude about the new situations proposed giving good results. But, circuit responses for the faults C1+30%, R2+20% and R3+20%, are almost identical, so that it will be impossible to distinguish between them with this method.

In a real circuit the components have tolerances, and it should be tested how the diagnosis system cope with this factor. Trying the system with 500 cases for each considered fault, randomly chosen using Monte-Carlo with a gaussian distribution, the percentage of successes shown in Table 4 is obtained for each.

Table 4: Diagnosis success for 500 runs. Freq. method

Fault	Diag. success	Fault	Diag. success
Nom	68%		
R1+20%	87.35%	R5+20%	63.5%
R1-20%	88.15%	R5-20%	38.7%
R1+50%	100%	R5+50%	93.9%
R1-50%	98.25%	R5-50%	97.05%
R2+20%	64.7%	R6+20%	87.45%
R2-20%	0%	R6-20%	89.8%
R2+50%	94.55%	R6+50%	98.1%
R2-50%	96.4%	R6-50%	98.9%
R3+20%	66.6%	C1+20%	68.9%
R3-20%	0%	C1-20%	0%
R3+50%	95.45%	C1+50%	95.45%
R3-50%	96.4%	C1-50%	97.3%
R4+20%	77.55%	C2+20%	84.2%
R4-20%	87.75%	C2-20%	86.9%
R4+50%	99.1%	C2+50%	98.75%
R4-50%	99%	C2-50%	98.9%

The percentage of success means each time the right component is diagnosed, although sometimes it doesn't appear alone. For example, the case R1+50% is detected in 100% of the cases, corresponding to 98.7% R1 and 1.3% to the set R1,R6.

Table 4 shows that in the majority of cases, the successes percentage is good. In the nominal one, it has a lower value because of the overlapping with other sets. For instance, it diagnosis R5 in 11.25% of the cases, and the set R2, R3, C1 in 9% of them. It has to be mentioned as well, that the cases R2-20%, R3-20% and C1-20% are never detected. This is due to that rules 7 (concerning to R2-20%), 11(concerning to R3-20%), 18 (concerning to R5+20%) and 27 (concerning to C1-20%) are fired at the same time due to overlapping. Evaluating the output using the centroid method, the final conclusion is R5 faulty. The same happens with the other non detected cases.

5.2 Temporal Method

Now, the parameters *overshoot, rise time, delay time* and *steady state* will be taken as the fuzzy system inputs. As in the frequencial method, each input attribute is divided into 33 *membership function* triangular shaped. For example, for R2+20% the final diagnosis is R2, R3 and C1. Doing the same for the other faults, it can be concluded that the fact of applying fuzzy does not make worse any of the results obtained with the fault dictionary using the ramp method, and it is able to improve the huge overlapping. Taking into account that real circuits have tolerances, the system is tested making a randomly gaussian distributed sweep in the component values. A total of 500 runs were made for each considered fault, and the percentage of successes is given in Table 5.

Table 5: Diagnosis success for 500 runs. Ramp method

Fault	Diag. success	Fault	Diag. success
Nom	55.15%	R5+20%	81.6%
R1+20%	88.05%	R5-20%	24%
R1-20%	80.70%	R5+50%	99.1%
R1+50%	99%	R5-50%	96.1%
R1-50%	99.05%	R6+20%	85.25%
R2+20%	85.15%	R6-20%	81.7%
R2-20%	0.1%	R6+50%	98.7%
R2+50%	97.1%	R6-50%	99.15%
R2-50%	94.35%	C1+20%	83.7%
R3+20%	84.7%	C1-20%	0.1%
R3-20%	0.05%	C1+50%	96.6%
R3+50%	97.1%	C1-50%	95.4%
R3-50%	94.9%	C2+20%	86.2%
R4+20%	86.25%	C2-20%	82.25%
R4-20%	82.95%	C2+50%	98.65%
R4+50%	98.95%	C2-50%	98.85%
R4-50%	97.35%		

The conclusions are not made worse testing the method with non predicted cases, so the fuzzy system is able to interpolate and predict unlearned cases. But, the cases C1+20%, R2+20% and R3+20%, among others, remain impossible to distinguish, because the responses are almost identical.

6   Conclusions

Two fault dictionary techniques has been shown. One of them based in frequencial measures and the other temporal. Both of them are simple to apply but they show a great overlapping in the final diagnosis due to tolerances.

Then, parameter identification by means of fuzzy modelling is introduced over the previous dictionaries. So, a degree of membership is introduced. Triangular membership function shapes have been tried first, because their simplicity. The authors can state that there are no great differences using the real measures distribution shape observed at the circuit output.

After applying fuzzy modelling to the temporal and frequencial methods, a great improvement in the diagnostic is obtained, because the overlapping is drastically reduced. Furthermore, from the set of faults used to generate the dictionary, the system is able to interpolate an identify faults that were not on the original set.

The system including fuzzy sets has been tested taking into account that real circuits are affected by tolerances. In particular, when testing the fault isolation capability of the system, 2000 cases were generated for each fault considered. The results resumed in tables 4 and 5, depicts that good diagnosis are made despite of tolerances.

References

[1] Balivada, A.; Chen, J.; and Abraham, J., Analog testing with time response parameters. *IEEE Design and Test of computers*,(1996) 18-25.

[2] Boyd, R., *Tolerance Analysis of Electronic Circuits Using Matlab*, Electronics Engineering. CRC Press, ISBN: 0-8493-2276-6, (1999)

[3] Dague, P., Model based diagnosis of analog electronic circuits,*Annals of Mathematics and Artificial Intelligence* (1994). 439-492

[4] Duhamel, P.; and Rault, J., Automatic test generation techniques for analog circuits and systems: A review, *IEEE Transactions on Circuits and Systems*,Cas-26(7), (1979), 411-440

[5] Fanni, A.; Giua, A.; Marchesi, M.; and Montisci, A., A neural network diagnosis approach for analog circuits, *Applied Intelligence 2*,(1999),169-186

[6] Frank, and Koppen-Seliger, New developments using AI in fault diagnosis, *IFAC/IMACS International Workshop. Bled Slovenia*,(1995)

[7] Frank, Analytical and qualitative model-based fault diagnosis. A survey and some new results, *European Journal of Control*, (1996), 6-8

[8] Iserman, and Balle, Trends in the application of model based fault detection and diagnosis of technical processes, *IFAC- 13th Triennial World Congress. Ref 7f-01 1*, (1996)

[9] Kaminska, B.; Arabi, K.; Goteti, P.; Huertas, J.; Kim, B.; Rueda, A.; and Soma, M., Analog and mixed-signal benchmark circuits. First release, *IEEE Proceedings International Test Conference*,(1997)

[10] Milor, L., A tutorial introduction to research on analog and mixed-signal circuits testing, *IEEE Transactions on Circuits and Systems*, (1998), 1389-1407

[11] Mir, S.; Lubaszewski, M.; Kolarik, V.; and Courtois, B., Automatic test generation for maximal diagnosis of linear analog circuits, *Proceedings of IEEE European Design and Test Conference*, USA , (1996)

[12] Pal, K.M., Model based fault detection, *Contribution on TEMPUS project MODIFY. Duisburg*, (1995)

[13] Soma, M., A desing for test methodology for active analog filters, *IEEE Proc. International Test Conference*, (1990), 183-192

[14] Stenbakken, G.; Souders, T.; and Stewart, G., Ambiguity groups and testability, *IEEE Transactions on Instrumentation and Measurement*, 38(5), (1989), 941-947

[15] Varghese, K.; Williams, J.; and Towill, D., Computer aided feature selection for enhanced analogue systems fault location, *IEEE Patern Recognition*, (1978), 265-280

[16] Wey, C., Mixed-signal circuit testing. A review. *IEEE International Conference on Electronics, Circuits, and Systems*. Invited paper. Greece.(1996), 1064-1067

Artificial Intelligence Research and Development
I. Aguiló et al. (Eds.)
IOS Press, 2003

Using Information-Flow Theory
to Enable Semantic Interoperability

Marco Schorlemmer[1]   Yannis Kalfoglou[2]
[1]*Centre for Intelligent Systems and their Applications*
School of Informatics
The University of Edinburgh

[1]*Escola Universitària de Tecnologies d'Informació i Comunicació*
Universitat Internacional de Catalunya

[2]*Department of Electronics and Computer Science*
University of Southampton

Abstract. We observe an ever growing need for integration in today's research agendas across a variety of organisations. The proliferation of ontologies and other similar knowledge-rich and labour-intensive structures as well as their exposure to a distributed environment like the Web, and eventually its successor, the Semantic Web, justifies the need. Although a plethora of solutions have been proposed and used, there are many issues which remain unclear. The most striking one is the antithesis in the availability of solutions for semantic integration as opposed to the abundance of techniques and methods for syntactic integration. In this paper we make the first step towards semantic integration by proposing a mathematically sound application of channel theory to enable semantic interoperability of separate ontologies representing similar domains.

1   Introduction

In the context of a distributed environment like the Web, Uschold and Grüninger point out that, "two agents are semantically integrated if they can successfully communicate with each other" [12], and successful communication means that they understand each other and there is guaranteed accuracy. This is a requirement for complete semantic integration in which the intended models of both agents are the same, that is, all the inferences that hold for one agent, should also hold when translated into the other agent's ontology, the authors continue. This is proposed as the golden standard of semantic integration, but we are skeptical about how or whether it can be achieved in computationally tractable manners. As it has been shown in a recent case study by Corrêa da Silva et al. [3], ontologies, which are naturally believed to be the right vehicle for this task, "fall short in providing adequate solutions in certain knowledge sharing scenarios." These are mostly concerned with problem solving knowledge, where inferential knowledge needs to be made explicit when shared. As the authors state, "there ought to be, beyond the usual ontological correspondence between the communicating systems, a correspondence between the inference engines, in terms of their operators and deduction rules."

Although the debate on adequacy of ontologies is interesting, it is out of the scope of this paper. We tackle the problem of semantic heterogeneity from a theoretical standpoint with attainable practical applications in a variety of knowledge sharing structures, including ontologies. One way to achieve the ambitious goal of semantic integration is to proceed in a step-wise fashion. In our view, to be semantically integrated presupposes to be semantically inter-operable. That's the focus of this paper. Semantic interoperability as a prerequisite for semantic integration. Our aim is to capture semantic interoperability between separate systems and to represent and model it in formal structures in order to reason over those in subsequent integration steps. Having achieved that, we will then be able to establish semantic-preserving exchange of information between the communicating systems, which is the first, and arguably, the most crucial step in achieving the kind of inferential knowledge sharing Uschold and Grüninger [12] and Corrêa da Silva et al. [3] are calling for.

2　The Role of Information Flow

A satisfactory way then, to approach semantic interoperability is via a formal notion of *information flow*. For that reason we will use *channel theory*, a modern theory of semantic information and information flow put forward by Barwise and Seligman in [1]. This theory underlies also Kent's Information Flow Framework [8], which attempts to accomplish this goal of interoperability as well. In Appendix A we list the main definitions we are using in this paper in order to explore how channel theory can help us to put the task of semantic interoperability on a firm theoretical ground. We have been putting the prefix 'IF' in front of channel-theoretic constructions to distinguish them from their standard meaning. For a more in-depth understanding of channel theory we point the interested reader to [1].

The key channel-theoretic construct we are going to exploit is that of a *distributed IF logic*. This is the IF logic that represents the information flow occurring in a distributed IF system. In particular we will be interested in a restriction of this IF logic to the language of those communities we are attempting to integrate. The basic idea is the following.

Suppose two communities **A** and **B** need to inter-operate, but are using different ontologies in different contexts. We use an *IF classification* as a very simple mathematical structure that effectively captures the local syntax and semantics of a community for the purpose of semantic interoperability. The syntactic expressions that a community uses will constitute the *types* of the IF classification. Depending on the kind of semantic interoperation we want to achieve, *types* can be concept or class symbols, relation names, complex queries or logical expressions, or even sets of expressions. The meaning that these expressions take within the context of the community will be represented by the way *tokens* are classified to *types*. Hence, the semantics is characterised by what we choose to be the tokens of the IF classification for a particular community; therefore, these will vary depending on the particularities of a semantic interoperability scenario. *Tokens* may, for example, be particular instances of classes or abstract first-order structures. The crucial point is that the semantics of the interoperability scenario crucially depends on our choice of types, tokens and their IF classification for each community. The example in Section 3 will make this point clearer.

To have communities **A** and **B** semantically inter-operating will mean to *know the semantic relationship in which they stand to each other*. In terms of the channel-theoretic context, this means to know an IF theory that describes how the different types from **A** and **B** are logically related to each other, i.e., an IF theory on the union of types $typ(\mathbf{A}) \cup typ(\mathbf{B})$

that respects the local IF classification systems of each community—the meaning each community attaches to its expressions—but also interrelates types whenever there is a similar semantic pattern, i.e., a similar way communities classify related tokens. In such an IF theory a sequent like $\alpha \vdash \beta$, with $\alpha \in typ(\mathbf{A})$ and $\beta \in typ(\mathbf{B})$, would represent an implication of types among communities that is in accordance to how the tokens of different communities are connected between each other.

This IF theory is the IF theory of the distributed IF logic of an IF channel

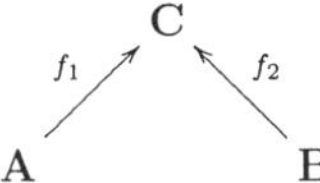

that represent the information flow between $\mathbf{A}$ and $\mathbf{B}$. This channel can either be stated directly, or indirectly by some sort of partial alignment of $\mathbf{A}$ and $\mathbf{B}$. The logic we are after is the one we get from *moving* a logic on the core $\mathbf{C}$ of the channel to the sum of components $\mathbf{A} + \mathbf{B}$.

- Its set of types is the disjoint union of all the types of the component IF classifications: That is the language we speak in a semantic interoperability scenario, because we want to know when type α of one component corresponds to a type β of another component.

- Its IF theory will be over this set of types, hence a constraint $\alpha \vdash \beta$ will represent that every α is a β, together with a constraint $\beta \vdash \alpha$ we obtain type equivalence.

- The IF theory will be induced at the core of the channel; this is crucial. The distributed IF logic is the inverse image of the IF logic at the core; therefore the type and tokens system at the core and the IF classification of tokens to types will determine the IF logic at this core. We usually take the natural IF logic as the IF logic of the core. This seams natural, and is also what happens in the various interoperability scenarios we have been investigating.

- It is interesting though, that since the distributed IF logic is an inverse image, soundness is not guaranteed, which means that the semantic interoperability is not reliable in general. Even if $\alpha \dashv\vdash \beta$ in the IF logic, there might be tokens (instances, situations, models, possible worlds) of the respective components for which this is not the case. Reliable information flow is only achieved for tokens that are connected through the core. The way in which infomorphisms from components to the core are defined in an interoperability scenario is crucial. If these infomorphisms are token-surjective, then the distributed IF logic will preserve the soundness of the IF logic of the core. Proving the token-surjectiveness is hence a necessary task in order to guarantee reliable semantic interoperability.

In the following section we develop the above key ideas using an hypothetical, but realistic example.

3 Interoperability via IF Channels

We elaborate on an imaginative scenario to demonstrate the strengths of channel theory in capturing semantically rich information for alignment purposes. We are dealing with a situation where an agent or a group of agents (human or artificial) are faced with the task of aligning organisational structures and responsibilities of ministries across different governments. This is a realistic scenario set out in the domain of e-governments, and despite its imaginative nature, its complexity and importance differentiates it from mapping ontologies of real world academic departments described in [6], where similar technology was used.

Our agents have to align UK and US governments, by focusing on governmental organisations, like ministries. The focal point of this alignment, is not only the structural and taxonomic differences of these ministries but the way in which responsibilities are allocated in different departments and offices within these ministries.

For the sake of brevity and space reasons, we only describe here four ministries: The UK Foreign and Commonwealth Office, the UK Home Office, the US Department of State, the US Department of Justice (hereafter, FCO, HO, DoS and DoJ, respectively). We gathered information related to these ministries from their web sites[1] where we focused on their organisational structures, assuming that the meaning of these structures is in accordance to the separation of responsibilities. These structures were trivial to extract, either from the hierarchical lists of departments, agencies, bureau, directorates, divisions, offices (which we shall commonly refer to as *units*) within these ministries, or organisational charts and organograms publicly available on the Web. The extraction of responsibilities and their units though, requires an intensive manual knowledge acquisition exercise (typically, a mission statement under a *what we do* hyperlink).

The ministries' taxonomies range from 38 units comprising the US DoJ to 109 units for the UK HO. In this example we focus on the alignment of 3 common responsibilities between these ministries:

- *passport services*, responsibility of HO and DoS;

- *promote productive relations*, responsibility of FCO and DoS;

- *immigration control*, responsibility of HO and DoJ.

Four steps towards semantic interoperability

In order to achieve the semantic interoperability we desire, we will go through the following four steps:

1. We define the various contexts of each community by means of a distributed IF system of IF classifications.

2. We define an IF channel—its core and infomorphisms—connecting the IF classifications of the various communities.

3. We define an IF logic on the core IF classification of the IF channel that represents the information flow between communities.

4. We distribute the IF logic to the sum of community IF classifications to obtain the IF theory that describes the desired semantic interoperability.

These steps illustrate a theoretical framework and need not to correspond to actual engineering steps; but we claim that a sensible implementation of semantic interoperability can be

---

[1] Accessible from www.homeoffice.gov.uk, www.fco.gov.uk, www.state.gov and www.usdoj.gov.

achieved following this framework, as it constitutes the theoretical foundation of a semantic interoperability scenario. In fact, Kalfoglou and Schorlemmer use similar techniques to assist in ontology mapping [6]. In the remainder of this section we apply the above four steps to our hypothetical interoperability scenario.

3.1　Community IF Classifications

UK and US governments use different ontologies to represent their respective ministries; we shall be dealing, therefore, with two separate sets of types:

$$typ(\mathbf{UK}) = \{\mathsf{FCO,HO}\}$$
$$typ(\mathbf{US}) = \{\mathsf{DoS,DoJ}\}$$

We model the interoperability scenario using a separate IF classification for each government, UK and US, whose types are ministries.

To have UK and US ministries semantically inter-operable will mean to know the semantic relationship in which they stand to each other, which we take to be their set of responsibilities. It is sensible to assume that there will be no obvious one-to-one correspondence between ministries of two governments because responsibilities of a ministry in one government may be spread across many ministries of the other, and vice versa. But we can attempt to derive an IF theory that describes how the different ministry types are logically related to each other—an IF theory on the union of ministry types $typ(\mathbf{UK}) \cup typ(\mathbf{US})$ in which a constraint like $\mathsf{FCO} \vdash \mathsf{DoS}$ would represent the fact that a responsibility of the UK Foreign and Commonwealth Office is also a responsibility of the US Department of State.

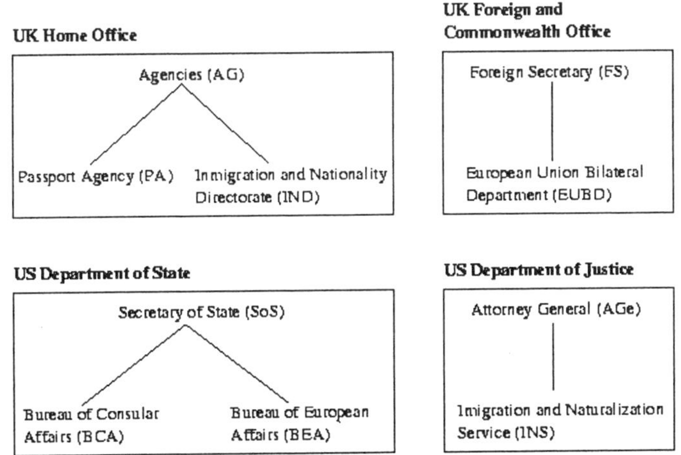

Figure 1: Hierarchical structures of government ministries

We shall construct the IF channel that will allow us to derive the desired IF theory using the hierarchical structure of units shown in Figure 1. Within the context of one government, different ministries represent already the top-level separation of responsibilities.

From the hierarchical structures we extract an IF theory on unit types for each government. Following are the two IF theories of UK and US units, respectively:

<table>
<tr><td>$\vdash$ AG,FS</td><td>$\vdash$ SoS,AGe</td></tr>
<tr><td>AG,FS $\vdash$</td><td>SoS,AGe $\vdash$</td></tr>
<tr><td>PA $\vdash$ AG</td><td>BCA $\vdash$ SoS</td></tr>
<tr><td>IND $\vdash$ AG</td><td>BEA $\vdash$ SoS</td></tr>
<tr><td>PA,IND $\vdash$</td><td>BCA,BEA $\vdash$</td></tr>
<tr><td>EUBD $\vdash$ FS</td><td>INS $\vdash$ AGe</td></tr>
</table>

By extracting responsibilities from the units' web sites we are able to define an IF classification for each government whose tokens are responsibilities and whose types are ministry units, and then classify responsibilities to their respective units. These IF classifications will have to be in accordance to the hierarchy as represented in the IF theories. That is, if a responsibility is classified to a unit, it shall also be classified to all its supra-units. This can be done automatically. In the case of UK units, the IF classification $\mathbf{A}_{UK}$ will be the following:

	AG	PA	IND	FS	EUBD
r_1	1	1	0	0	0
r_2	1	0	1	0	0
r_3	1	0	0	0	0
r_4	0	0	0	1	1
r_5	0	0	0	1	0

Here tokens r_1 to r_5 represent responsibilities extracted from the units' web sites. So, token r_2 stands for the responsibility *immigration control* of the Immigration and Nationality Directorate, and hence also for the Agencies, while token r_3 stands for a responsibility of the Agencies only. For the US units we proceed in the same way:

	SoS	BCA	BEA	AGe	INS
s_1	1	1	0	0	0
s_2	1	0	1	0	0
s_3	1	0	0	0	0
s_4	0	0	0	1	1
s_5	0	0	0	1	0

However, the phrasing of responsibilities in the US web sites might differ form that in the UK web sites, which will result in a separate set of tokens $s_1, \ldots, s_5$ for IF classification $\mathbf{A}_{US}$.

To represent how ministry types (like FCO,HO, etc.) from the IF classification **UK** relates to the IF classification $\mathbf{A}_{UK}$ of ministerial units, we will use the *flip* $\mathbf{A}_{UK}^{\perp}$ of the IF classification table and its *disjunctive power* $\vee \mathbf{A}_{UK}^{\perp}$. The flip classifies ministerial units to responsibilities, and for the UK case it is:

	r_1	r_2	r_3	r_4	r_5
AG	1	1	1	0	0
PA	1	0	0	0	0
IND	0	1	0	0	0
FS	0	0	0	1	1
EUBD	0	0	0	1	0

The disjunctive power of this flip classifies ministerial units to sets of responsibilities, whenever some of its responsibilities is among those in the set. Here is a fragment of this IF classification:

	$\{r_1,r_2,r_3,r_4,r_5\}$	$\cdots$	$\{r_1,r_2,r_3\}$	$\cdots$	$\{r_4,r_5\}$
AG	1		1		0
PA	1		1		0
IND	1		1		0
FS	1		0		1
EUBD	1		0		1

The way ministries relate to these sets of responsibilities can then be represented with an infomorphism $h_{UK} : \mathbf{UK} \rightleftarrows \vee\mathbf{A}_{UK}^{\perp}$:

$$h_{UK}(\mathsf{HO}) = \{r_1,r_2,r_3\}$$
$$h_{UK}(\mathsf{FCO}) = \{r_4,r_5\}$$

Each context for a government, with its ministries, their respective units, and hierarchy captured by an IF theory, is then represented as a distributed IF system of IF classifications. For the UK government this distributed system is the following:

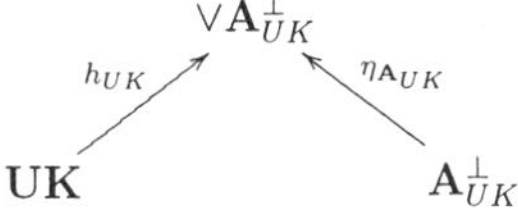

In the next step we use the flips $\mathbf{A}_{UK}^{\perp}$ and $\mathbf{A}_{US}^{\perp}$ to align responsibilities in order to achieve the desired semantic interoperability.

3.2 The IF Channel

We construct an IF channel from a partial alignment of some of the responsibilities extracted from the ministerial units' web sites. This is the crucial aspect of the semantic interoperability, since it is the point where relations in meaning are established. We assume a partial alignment, that is, one where not all responsibilities r_1 to r_5 are related to responsibilities s_1 to s_5. In particular we shall assume the alignment of UK responsibilities r_1, r_2 and r_4 with US responsibilities s_1, s_4 and s_2:

- passport services: $r_1 \longleftrightarrow s_1$

- immigration control: $r_2 \longleftrightarrow s_4$

- promote productive relations: $r_4 \longleftrightarrow s_2$

The focus of this paper is not how this partial alignment is established; various heuristic mechanisms have been proposed in the literature (see e.g., [10]). We assume that we have already applied one of those heuristics. Our purpose here is to provide a framework that shows how a partial alignment of a few responsibilities fits into the larger picture of an alignment scenario as the one described here, and represented as a distributed IF system, and how a global IF theory of semantic interoperability on the level of government ministries is derived from this partial alignment.

The above partial alignment is a binary relation between $typ(\mathbf{A}_{UK}^{\perp})$ and $typ(\mathbf{A}_{US}^{\perp})$. In order to represent this alignment as a distributed IF system in channel theory, we decompose the binary relation into a couple of total functions $\hat{g}_{UK}, \hat{g}_{US}$ from a common domain $typ(\mathbf{A}) = \{\alpha, \beta, \gamma\}$. (For example $\hat{g}_{UK}(\beta) = r_2$ and $\hat{g}_{US}(\beta) = s_4$.) This will constitute the type-level of a couple of infomorphisms. We complete the alignment to a system of IF classifications

$$\mathbf{A}_{UK}^{\perp} \xleftarrow{\;g_{UK}\;} \mathbf{A} \xrightarrow{\;g_{US}\;} \mathbf{A}_{US}^{\perp}$$

by generating the IF classification on $typ(\mathbf{A})$ with all possible tokens, which we generate formally, and their classification:

	α	β	γ
n_0	0	0	0
n_1	0	0	1
n_2	0	1	0
n_3	0	1	1
n_4	1	0	0
n_5	1	0	1
n_6	1	1	0
n_7	1	1	1

To satisfy the fundamental property of infomorphisms, the token-level of g_{UK}, g_{US} must be as follows:

$$\check{g}_{UK}(\mathsf{AG}) = n_6 \qquad\qquad \check{g}_{US}(\mathsf{SoS}) = n_5$$
$$\check{g}_{UK}(\mathsf{PA}) = n_4 \qquad\qquad \check{g}_{US}(\mathsf{BCA}) = n_4$$
$$\check{g}_{UK}(\mathsf{IND}) = n_2 \qquad\qquad \check{g}_{US}(\mathsf{BEA}) = n_1$$
$$\check{g}_{UK}(\mathsf{FS}) = n_1 \qquad\qquad \check{g}_{US}(\mathsf{AGe}) = n_2$$
$$\check{g}_{UK}(\mathsf{EUBD}) = n_1 \qquad\qquad \check{g}_{US}(\mathsf{INS}) = n_2$$

This alignment allows us to generate the desired channel between **UK** and **US** that captures the information flow according to the aligned responsibilities. This is done by constructing a classification **C** and a couple of infomorphisms $f_{UK} : \vee \mathbf{A}_{UK}^{\perp} \rightleftarrows \mathbf{C}$ and $f_{US} : \vee \mathbf{A}_{US}^{\perp} \rightleftarrows \mathbf{C}$ that correspond to a category-theoretic colimit [9] of the following distributed IF system, which includes the alignment and the contexts of each government:

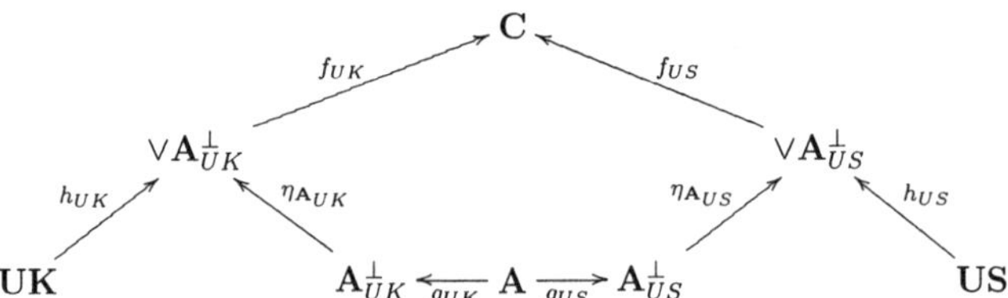

This is a cover of the distributed IF system.

3.3   The IF Logic on the Core

This is how colimit C is constructed: Its set of types $typ(C)$ is the disjoint union of types
of $\vee A_{UK}^{\perp}$ and $\vee A_{US}^{\perp}$; its tokens are connections—pairs of tokens—that connect a token a of
$\vee A_{UK}^{\perp}$ with a token b of $\vee A_{US}^{\perp}$ only when a and b are send by the alignment infomorphisms
g_{UK} and g_{US} to tokens of the alignment IF classification A that are classified as of the same
type. For example, the core C will have a token $\langle \mathsf{AG},\mathsf{SoS} \rangle$ connecting $\vee A_{UK}^{\perp}$-token AG with
$\vee A_{US}^{\perp}$-token SoS, because $\breve{g}_{UK}(\mathsf{AG}) = n_6$ and $\breve{g}_{US}(\mathsf{SoS}) = n_5$, and both n_5 and n_6 are of
type α in A.

The following is a fragment of the IF classification on the core (not all types are listed,
but all tokens are):

	$\{r_1, r_2, r_3\}$	$\{r_4, r_5\}$	$\{s_1, s_2, s_3\}$	$\{s_4, s_5\}$
$\langle \mathsf{FS},\mathsf{BEA} \rangle$	0	1	1	0
$\langle \mathsf{EUBD},\mathsf{BEA} \rangle$	0	1	1	0
$\langle \mathsf{FS},\mathsf{SoS} \rangle$	0	1	1	0
$\langle \mathsf{EUBD},\mathsf{SoS} \rangle$	0	1	1	0
$\langle \mathsf{IND},\mathsf{AGe} \rangle$	1	0	0	1
$\langle \mathsf{IND},\mathsf{INS} \rangle$	1	0	0	1
$\langle \mathsf{PA},\mathsf{BCA} \rangle$	1	0	1	0
$\langle \mathsf{PA},\mathsf{SoS} \rangle$	1	0	1	0
$\langle \mathsf{AG},\mathsf{BCA} \rangle$	1	0	1	0
$\langle \mathsf{AG},\mathsf{SoS} \rangle$	1	0	1	0

It shows the IF classification of all connections to those types of the core that are in the image
of $f_{UK} \circ h_{UK}$ and $f_{US} \circ h_{US}$, which are the infomorphisms we will use in the next step to
distribute the IF logic on the core to the IF classifications UK and US.

As the IF logic on the core we will take the natural IF logic of the IF classification C,
whose constraints are:

$$\{r_4, r_5\} \vdash \{s_1, s_2, s_3\}$$
$$\{s_4, s_5\} \vdash \{r_1, r_2, r_3\}$$
$$\{r_1, r_2, r_3\}, \{r_4, r_5\} \vdash$$
$$\vdash \{r_1, r_2, r_3\}, \{r_4, r_5\}$$
$$\{s_1, s_2, s_3\}, \{s_4, s_5\} \vdash$$
$$\vdash \{s_1, s_2, s_3\}, \{s_4, s_5\}$$

The natural IF logic is the one that captures in its constraints a complete knowledge of the
IF classification. Since we have constructed the IF classification from those in the distributed
system—which captured the contexts of governments together with the alignment of certain
responsibilities—the natural IF logic will have as its IF theory all those sequents that conform
to the government's contexts as well as to the alignment, which is what we desire for semantic
interoperability.

3.4   The Distributed IF Logic

The natural IF logic has an IF theory whose types are sets of responsibilities taken from UK
or US web sites, but we want to know how this theory translates to government ministries, by

virtue of what responsibilities each ministry has. For that reason we take the IF theory of the distributed IF logic of the IF channel:

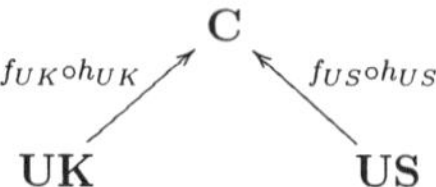

which is the inverse image along $(f_{UK} \circ h_{UK}) + (f_{US} \circ h_{US})$ of the natural IF logic $Log(\mathbf{C})$ generated from the core IF classification. Its theory has the following constraints:

$$FCO \vdash DoS \qquad\qquad DoJ \vdash HO$$
$$FCO, HO \vdash \qquad\qquad \vdash FCO, HO$$
$$DoS, DoJ \vdash \qquad\qquad \vdash DoS, DoJ$$

These constraints capture the semantic interoperability between all ministries, UK and US.

4 Related Work

Previously, Kalfoglou and Schorlemmer have shown that information flow can be used to assist in ontology mapping [6]. Their work demonstrates a practical application of information-flow theory in the area of ontology mapping where the ontologies used were representing academic departments from different universities, which were eventually mapped onto each other.

A complementary agenda is that currently pursued by Kent with his Information Flow Framework [8], which aims at providing a meta-level framework for a standard that will specify an upper ontology, enabling computers to interoperate. Targeted to upper ontologies, his effort is focused on providing the necessary framework for specifying ontologies that define concepts that are meta, generic, abstract and philosophical, and therefore are general enough to address (at a high level) a broad range of domain areas.

Similar work on using the notion of classification of tokens is demonstrated in the FCA-MERGE system [11], where the underpinning theory is that of formal concept analysis [5]. Last, but not least, there is a plethora of less formal approaches for semantic integration, notably the work on using communities of practice and learning algorithms [4], and on constraint-satisfaction-based systems [2]. We refer to [7] for an extensive survey.

5 Conclusions

In this paper we presented a practical application of channel theory to capture and model semantic interoperability in terms of information flow between different systems that needed to be integrated. The strong mathematical foundations of channel theory and their potential transformation to logic programs enabled us to work out a real world integration scenario with semantic-preserving exchange of information. These could provide a better understanding of the foundations for building and deploying semantically integrated systems in distributed environments.

Acknowledgements

This work is supported under the Advanced Knowledge Technologies (AKT) Interdisciplinary Research Collaboration (IRC), which is sponsored by the UK Engineering and Physical Sciences Research Council under grant number GR/N15764/01. The AKT IRC comprises the Universities of Aberdeen, Edinburgh, Sheffield, Southampton and the Open University.

The first author is also supported by a 'Ramón y Cajal' Fellowship from the Spanish Ministry of Science and Technology.

References

[1] J. Barwise and J. Seligman. *Information Flow*. Cambridge University Press, 1997.

[2] S. Bressan and C. Goh. Semantic integration of disparate information sources over the internet using constraint propagation. In *CP'97 Workshop on Constraints and the Internet*, 1996.

[3] F. Corrêa da Sliva, W. Vasconcelos, D. Robertson, V. Brilhante, A. de Melo, M. Finger, and J. Agustí. On the insufficiency of ontologies: problems in knowledge sharing and alternative solutions. *Knowledge-Based Systems*, 15(3):147–167, 2002.

[4] N. Friesen. Semantic interoperability, communities of practice and the CanCore learning object metadata profile. In *11th International World Wide Web Conference*, 2002.

[5] B. Ganter and R. Wille. *Formal Concept Analysis*. Springer, 1999.

[6] Y. Kalfoglou and M. Schorlemmer. Information-flow-based ontology mapping. In *On the Move to Meaningful Internet Systems 2002: CoopIS, DOA, and ODBASE*, LNCS 2519, pages 1132–1151. Springer, 2002.

[7] Y. Kalfoglou and M. Schorlemmer. Ontology mapping: the sate of the art. *Knowledge Engineering Review*, 2003. In press.

[8] R. Kent. The information flow foundation for conceptual knowledge organization. In *Sixth International Conference of the International Society for Knowledge Organization*, 2000.

[9] S. Mac Lane. *Categories for the Working Mathematician*. Springer, second edition, 1998.

[10] P. Mitra and G. Wiederhold. Resolving terminological heterogeneity in ontologies. In *Ontologies and Semantics Interoperability*, CEUR-WS 64, 2002.

[11] G. Stumme and A. Maedche. FCA-Merge: Bottom-up merging of ontologies. In *17th International Joint Conference on Artificial Intelligence*, 2001.

[12] M. Uschold and M. Grüninger. Creating semantically integrated communities on the World Wide Web. In *WWW 2002 Semantic Web Workshop*, 2002.

A Channel Theory

IF classification: $\mathbf{A} = \langle tok(\mathbf{A}), typ(\mathbf{A}), \models_{\mathbf{A}} \rangle$ consists of a set $tok(\mathbf{A})$ of *tokens*, a set $typ(\mathbf{A})$ of *types*, and a binary relation $\models_{\mathbf{A}}$ between $tok(\mathbf{A})$ and $typ(\mathbf{A})$.

Infomorphism: $f : \mathbf{A} \rightleftarrows \mathbf{B}$ from classifications $\mathbf{A}$ to $\mathbf{B}$ is a contra-variant pair of functions $f = \langle f^{\wedge}, f^{\vee} \rangle$ satisfying the Fundamental Property $f^{\vee}(b) \models_{\mathbf{A}} \alpha$ iff $b \models f^{\wedge}(\alpha)$, for each token $b \in tok(\mathbf{B})$ and each type $\alpha \in typ(\mathbf{A})$; f is *token-surjective* if $f^{\vee}$ is surjective.

Flip: $\mathbf{A}^{\perp}$ is the classification whose tokens are $typ(\mathbf{A})$ and types are $tok(\mathbf{A})$, such that $\alpha \models_{\mathbf{A}^{\perp}} a$ iff $a \models_{\mathbf{A}} \alpha$.

IF channel: C is an indexed family $\{f_i : \mathbf{A}_i \rightleftarrows \mathbf{C}\}_{i \in I}$ of infomorphisms with a common codomain $\mathbf{C}$, the *core* of C. The tokens of $\mathbf{C}$ are called *connections*.

Sum: $\mathbf{A} + \mathbf{B}$ of classifications has as set of tokens the Cartesian product of $tok(\mathbf{A})$ and $tok(\mathbf{B})$ and as set of types the disjoint union of $typ(\mathbf{A})$ and $typ(\mathbf{B})$, such that for $\alpha \in typ(\mathbf{A})$ and $\beta \in typ(\mathbf{B})$, $\langle a, b \rangle \models_{\mathbf{A}+\mathbf{B}} \alpha$ iff $a \models_{\mathbf{A}} \alpha$, and $\langle a, b \rangle \models_{\mathbf{A}+\mathbf{B}} \beta$ iff $b \models_{\mathbf{B}} \beta$. Given two infomorphisms $f_{1,2} : \mathbf{A}_{1,2} \rightleftarrows \mathbf{C}$, the sum $f_1 + f_2 : \mathbf{A}_1 + \mathbf{A}_2 \rightleftarrows \mathbf{C}$ is defined by $(f_1 + f_2)\check{\ }(\alpha) = f_i(\alpha)$ if $\alpha \in \mathbf{A}_i$ and $(f_1 + f_2)\check{\ }(c) = \langle f\check{\ }_1(c), f\check{\ }_2(c) \rangle$, for $c \in tok(\mathbf{C})$.

Distributed IF system: $\mathcal{A}$ consists of an indexed family $cla(\mathcal{A}) = \{\mathbf{A}_i\}_{i \in I}$ of classifications together with a set $inf(\mathcal{A})$ of infomorphisms all having both domain and codomain in $cla(\mathcal{A})$.

Cover: An IF channel $C = \{h_i : \mathbf{A}_i \rightleftarrows \mathbf{C}\}_{i \in I}$ covers a distributed IF system $\mathcal{A}$ if $cla(\mathcal{A}) = \{\mathbf{A}_i\}_{i \in I}$ and for each $i, j \in I$ and each infomorphism $f : \mathbf{A}_i \rightleftarrows \mathbf{A}_j$ in $inf(\mathbf{A})$, $h_i = h_j \circ f$.

Disjunctive power: $\vee \mathbf{A}$ of an IF classification $\mathbf{A}$ is the classification whose tokens are the same as $\mathbf{A}$, whose types are subsets of $typ(\mathbf{A})$, and given $a \in tok(\mathbf{A})$ and $\Phi \subseteq typ(\mathbf{A})$, $a \models_{\vee \mathbf{A}} \Phi$ iff $a \models_{\mathbf{A}} \sigma$ for some $\sigma \in \Phi$. There exists a natural embedding $\eta_{\mathbf{A}} : \mathbf{A} \rightleftarrows \vee \mathbf{A}$ defined by $\hat{\eta}_{\mathbf{A}}(\alpha) = \{\alpha\}$ and $\check{\eta}_{\mathbf{A}}(a) = a$, for each $\alpha \in typ(\mathbf{A})$ and $a \in tok(\vee \mathbf{A})$.

IF theory: $T = \langle typ(T), \vdash \rangle$ consists of a set $typ(T)$ of types, and a binary relation $\vdash$ between subsets of $typ(T)$. Pairs $\langle \Gamma, \Delta \rangle$ of subsets of $typ(T)$ are called *sequents*. If $\Gamma \vdash \Delta$, for $\Gamma, \Delta \subseteq typ(T)$, then the sequent $\Gamma \vdash \Delta$ is a *constraint*. T is regular if for all $\alpha \in typ(T)$ and all sets $\Gamma, \Gamma', \Delta, \Delta', \Sigma', \Sigma_0, \Sigma_1$ of types:

1. *Identity:* $\alpha \vdash \alpha$

2. *Weakening:* If $\Gamma \vdash \Delta$, then $\Gamma, \Gamma' \vdash \Delta, \Delta'$

3. *Global Cut:* If $\Gamma, \Sigma_0 \vdash \Gamma, \Sigma_1$ for each partition $\langle \Sigma_0, \Sigma_1 \rangle$ ($\Sigma_0 \cup \Sigma_1 = typ(T)$ and $\Sigma_0 \cap \Sigma_1 = \emptyset$), then $\Gamma \vdash \Delta$.

IF classification generated by an IF theory: Given a regular IF theory T, the classification $Cla(T)$ generated by T is the classification whose tokens are partitions $\langle \Gamma, \Delta \rangle$ of $typ(T)$ that are not constraints of T, and types are the types of T, such that $\langle \Gamma, \Delta \rangle \models_{Cla(T)} \alpha$ iff $\alpha \in \Gamma$.

IF logic: $\mathfrak{L} = \langle tok(\mathfrak{L}), typ(\mathfrak{L}), \models_{\mathfrak{L}}, \vdash_{\mathfrak{L}}, N_{\mathfrak{L}} \rangle$ consists of a classification $cla(\mathfrak{L}) = \langle tok(\mathfrak{L}), typ(\mathfrak{L}), \models_{\mathfrak{L}} \rangle$, a regular theory $th(\mathfrak{L}) = \langle typ(\mathfrak{L}), \vdash_{\mathfrak{L}} \rangle$ and a subset of $N_{\mathfrak{L}} \subseteq tok(\mathfrak{L})$ of *normal tokens*, which satisfy all the constraints of $th(\mathfrak{L})$; a token $a \in tok(\mathfrak{L})$ satisfies a constraint $\Gamma \vdash \Delta$ of $th(\mathfrak{L})$ if, when a is of all types in Γ, a is of some type in Δ. An IF logic $\mathfrak{L}$ is *sound* if $N_{\mathfrak{L}} = tok(\mathfrak{L})$.

Natural IF logic: It is the IF logic $Log(\mathbf{A})$ generated from an IF classification $\mathbf{A}$, and has as classification $\mathbf{A}$, as regular theory the theory whose constraints are the sequents satisfied by all tokens, and whose tokens are all normal.

Inverse image: Given an infomorphism $f : \mathbf{A} \rightleftarrows \mathbf{B}$ and an IF logic $\mathfrak{L}$ on B, the inverse image $f^{-1}[\mathfrak{L}]$ of $\mathfrak{L}$ under f is the local logic on $\mathbf{A}$, whose theory is such that $\Gamma \vdash \Delta$ is a constraint of $th(f^{-1}[\mathfrak{L}])$ iff $f[\Gamma] \vdash f[\Delta]$ is a constraint of $th(\mathfrak{L})$, and whose normal tokens are $N_{f^{-1}[\mathfrak{L}]} = \{a \in tok(\mathbf{A}) \mid a = f(b) \text{ for some } b \in N_{\mathfrak{L}}\}$. If f is token-surjective and $\mathfrak{L}$ is sound, then $f^{-1}[\mathfrak{L}]$ is sound.

Distributed IF logic: Given a binary IF channel $C = \{f_{1,2} : \mathbf{A}_{1,2} \rightleftarrows \mathbf{C}\}$ and an IF logic $\mathfrak{L}$ on its core $\mathbf{C}$, the distributed IF logic $DLog_C(\mathfrak{L})$ is the inverse image of $\mathfrak{L}$ under the sum $f_1 + f_2$.

7. Constraint Reasoning and Planning

Artificial Intelligence Research and Development
I. Aguiló et al. (Eds.)
IOS Press, 2003

435

Improved Branch and Bound Algorithms for Max-2-SAT and Weighted Max-2-SAT

Teresa Alsinet, Felip Manyà, Jordi Planes
Departament d'Informàtica
Universitat de Lleida, Jaume II, 69, 25001-Lleida, Spain
`{tracy,felip,jordi}@eup.udl.es`

Abstract We present novel branch and bound algorithms for solving Max-SAT and weighted Max-SAT, and provide experimental evidence that outperform the algorithm of Borchers & Furman on Max-2-SAT and weighted Max-2-SAT instances. Our algorithms decrease the time needed to solve an instance, as well as the number of backtracks, up to two orders of magnitude.

Keywords: Max-SAT, branch and bound, lower bounds, branching heuristics.

1 Introduction

In recent years we have seen an increasing interest in propositional satisfiability (SAT) that has led to the development of fast and sophisticated complete SAT solvers like Chaff [13], Grasp [15], RelSat [2] and Satz [10], which are based on the well-known Davis-Putnam-Logemann-Loveland (DPLL) procedure [5]. Given a Boolean CNF formula ϕ, such algorithms determine whether there is a truth assignment that satisfies ϕ. Unfortunately, they are not able to solve two well-known satisfiability optimization problems: Max-SAT and weighted Max-SAT. Given a Boolean CNF formula ϕ, Max-SAT consists of finding a truth assignment that maximizes the number of satisfied clauses in ϕ. Given a Boolean CNF formula ϕ, where each clause has a weight, weighted Max-SAT consists of finding a truth assignment that maximizes the sum of the weights of the satisfied clauses in ϕ. When all the clauses have at most two literal per clause (weighted) Max-SAT is called (weighted) Max-2-SAT.

To our best knowledge, there are only two exact algorithms for Max-SAT that are variants of the DPLL procedure. One is due to Wallace & Freuder [16] and the other is due to Borchers & Furman [3]. Both are depth-first branch and bound algorithms, and were developed independently. The former was implemented in Lisp, while the latter was implemented in C and is publicly available. There are other exact algorithms for Max-SAT, but based on mathematical programming techniques [4, 6, 9].

In this paper we first describe novel branch and bound algorithms for solving Max-SAT and weighted Max-SAT that we have designed and implemented. They are variants of the algorithm of Borchers & Furmanm that incorporate more powerful lower bound calculations and variable selection heuristics. We then report on an experimental investigation we have conducted in order to evaluate our algorithms on Max-2-SAT and weighted Max-2-SAT instances. The results obtained provide experimental evidence that our algorithms outperform the algorithm of Borchers & Furman on randomly generated Max-2-SAT and weighted Max-2-SAT instances. Our approach decreases the time needed to solve an instance, as well as the number of backtracks, up to two orders of magnitude.

2   Branch and Bound for Max-SAT

The space of all possible assignments for a CNF formula ϕ can be represented as a search tree, where internal nodes represent partial assignments and leaf nodes represent complete assignments. A branch and bound algorithm for Max-SAT explores the search tree in a depth-first manner. At each node, the algorithm compares the number of clauses unsatisfied by the best complete assignment found so far —called upper bound (UB)— with the number of clauses unsatisfied by the current partial assignment ($unsat$) plus an underestimation of the number of clauses that become unsatisfied if we extend the current partial assignment into a complete assignment ($underestimation$). The sum $unsat + underestimation$ is called lower bound (LB). Obviously, if $UB \leq LB$, a better assignment cannot be found from this point in search. In that case, the algorithm prunes the subtree below the current node and backtracks to a higher level in the search tree. If $UB > LB$, it extends the current partial assignment by instantiating one more variable; which leads to create two branches from the current branch: the left branch corresponds to instantiate the new variable to false, and the right branch corresponds to instantiate the new variable to true. In that case, the formula associated with the left (right) branch is obtained from the formula of the current node by deleting all the clauses containing the literal $\neg p$ (p) and removing all the occurrences of the literal p ($\neg p$); i.e., the algorithm applies the one-literal rule [11]. The solution to Max-SAT is the value that UB takes after exploring the entire search tree.

Borchers & Furman [3] designed and implemented a branch and bound solver for Max-SAT that incorporates two quite significant improvements:

- Before starting to explore the search tree, they obtain an upper bound on the number of unsatisfied clauses in an optimal solution using the local search procedure GSAT [14]. That improvement allows them to solve instances up to seven times faster than when they do not perform that preprocessing [3].

- When branching is done, branch and bound algorithms for Max-SAT apply the one-literal rule (simplifying with the branching literal) instead of applying unit propagation as in the DPLL-style solvers for SAT.[1] If unit propagation is applied at each node, the algorithm can return a non-optimal solution. However, when the difference between the lower bound and the upper bound is one, unit propagation can be safely applied, because otherwise by fixing to false any literal of any unit clause we reach the upper bound. Borchers & Furman perform unit propagation in that case.

Our branch and bound algorithms are variants of the algorithm of Borchers & Furman that incorporate the above improvements. Besides such improvements, there are two factors that have a large impact on the performance of any branch and bound algorithm: the quality of the lower bound, and the heuristic used to select the next variable that has to be instantiated. We consider two lower bounds:

- $LB1 = unsat$. Note that that the number of clauses unsatisfied by the current partial assignment coincides with the number of empty clauses that contains the formula associated with the current partial assignment. That elementary lower bound that does not incorporate underestimation is used by Borchers & Furman.

---

[1] By unit propagation we mean the repeated application of the one-literal rule until a saturation state is reached.

- LB2 $= unsat + \sum_{p \in \phi'} min(ic(p), ic(\neg p))$, where ϕ' is the formula associated with the current partial assignment, and $ic(p)$ $(ic(\neg p))$ —inconsistency count of p $(\neg p)$— is the number of clauses that become unsatisfied if the current partial assignment is extended by fixing p $(\neg p)$ to true (false). Note that $ic(p)$ $(ic(\neg p))$ coincides with the number of unit clauses of ϕ' that contain $\neg p$ (p).

If for each variable we count the number of positive and negative literals in unit clauses, we can know the number of unit clauses that will not be satisfied if the variable is instantiated to true or false. Obviously, the total number of unsatisfied clauses resulting from either instantiation of the variable must be greater than or equal to the minimum count. Moreover, the counts for different variables are independent, since they refer to different unit clauses. Hence, by summing the minimum count for all variables in unit clauses and adding this sum to the number of empty clauses, we calculate a lower bound for the number of unsatisfied clauses given the current assignment. Such a lower bound was considered in [16].

We consider three variable selection heuristics:

- MOMS: selects a variable among those that appear more often in clauses of minimum size. That is the heuristic of Borchers & Furman.

- Jeroslow-Wang (JW) [8, 7]: given a formula ϕ, for each literal L of ϕ the following function is defined:

$$J(L) = \sum_{L \in C \in \phi} 2^{-|C|}$$

where $|C|$ is the length of clause C. JW selects a variable p of ϕ among those that maximize $J(p) + J(\neg p)$.

- Weighted Clause Length (WCL): let ϕ be a formula, let unit-clauses(L) be the number of occurrences of literal L in unit clauses of ϕ, let binary-clauses(L) be the number of occurrences of literal L in binary clauses of ϕ, let w_1, w_2 be natural numbers, and let

$$WCL(L) \quad = \quad w_1 \times \text{unit-clauses}(L) + w_2 \times \text{binary-clauses}(L).$$

WCL selects a variable p of ϕ among those that maximize $WCL(p) + WCL(\neg p)$. We set w_1 and w_2 with values that depend on the ratio *clause/variable*. In most of the cases we set $w_1 = 1$ and $w_2 = 3$. The settings were determined experimentally.

We get several branch and bound algorithms by combining the above lower bounds and heuristics: LB1+MOMS, LB1+JW, LB1+WCL, LB2+MOMS, LB2+JW and LB2+WCL. LB1+MOMS corresponds to the algorithm of Borchers & Furman. LB2+MOMS incorporates the lower bound of [16] into the algorithm of Borchers & Furman. LB2+JW is like LB2+MOMS but uses the Jeroslow-Wang rule as variable selection heuristic. LB2+WCL is like LB2+MOMS but uses the Weighted Clause Length heuristic. LB2+MOMS, LB2+JW and LB2+WCL are our novel branch and bound algorithms for Max-SAT. We have implemented

Input: $\texttt{max-sat}(\phi, ub)$: A Boolean CNF formula ϕ and an upper bound ub
  1: **if** $\phi = \emptyset$ or ϕ only contains empty clauses **then**
  2:    return $\texttt{empty-clauses}(\phi)$
  3: **end if**
  4: **if** $\texttt{lower-bound}(\phi) \geq ub$ **then**
  5:    return ∞
  6: **end if**
  7: **if** $\texttt{lower-bound}(\phi) = ub - 1$ **then**
  8:    $\phi \leftarrow \texttt{unit-propagation}(\phi)$
  9: **end if**
10: $p \leftarrow \texttt{select-variable}(\phi)$
11: $ub \leftarrow \min(ub, \texttt{max-sat}(\phi_{\neg p}, ub))$
12: return $\min(ub, \texttt{max-sat}(\phi_p, ub))$
Output: The minimum number of clauses of ϕ that can be unsatisfied by an assignment

Figure 1: Branch and Bound for Max-SAT

them by modifying the publicly available code of Borchers & Furman. We do not consider $\texttt{LB1+JW}$ ($\texttt{LB1+WCL}$) because its performance is much worse than the performance of $\texttt{LB2+JW}$ ($\texttt{LB2+WCL}$).

Figure 1 shows the pseudo-code of the skeleton of the exact algorithms for Max-SAT we consider here: $\texttt{LB1+MOMS}$, $\texttt{LB2+MOMS}$, $\texttt{LB2+JW}$ and $\texttt{LB2+WCL}$. We use the following notation:

- $\texttt{empty-clauses}(\phi)$ is a function that returns the number of empty clauses in ϕ.

- $\texttt{lower-bound}(\phi)$ is the sum of the number of empty clauses in ϕ plus an underestimation of the number of unsatisfied clauses in the formula obtained from ϕ by removing its empty clauses. In our case, $\texttt{LB1}$ or $\texttt{LB2}$.

- ub is an upper bound of the number of unsatisfied clauses in an optimal solution. We assume that the input value is that obtained with GSAT.

- $\texttt{select-variable}(\phi)$ is a function that returns a variable of ϕ following an heuristic; in our case, MOMS, JW or WCL.

- ϕ_p ($\phi_{\neg p}$) is the formula obtained by applying the one-literal rule to ϕ using the literal p ($\neg p$).

We have also developed improved versions of $\texttt{LB2+MOMS}$, $\texttt{LB2+JW}$ and $\texttt{LB2+WCL}$, which we refer to as $\texttt{LB2-I+MOMS}$, $\texttt{LB2-I+JW}$ and $\texttt{LB2-I+WCL}$. In such versions, we check if we can fix the truth value of any free variable before branching. This amounts to introduce the following code after line 9:

  for all literal l in ϕ **do**
    if $ic(l) > ic(\neg l)$ **and** $\texttt{lower-bound}(\phi) + (ic(l) - ic(\neg l)) \geq ub$ **then**
      $\phi \leftarrow \phi_{\neg l}$
    end if
  end for

instance	unsat	LB1+MOMS	LB2+MOMS	LB2-I+MOMS	LB2+JW	LB2-I+JW	LB2+WCL	LB2-I+WCL
50-100	4	0.03	0.04	0.03	0.05	0.40	0.03	0.03
50-150	8	0.09	0.11	0.09	0.08	0.60	0.07	0.04
50-200	16	6.21	4.06	2.46	1.92	0.79	1.41	0.57
50-250	22	36	7.22	4.64	1.51	0.76	0.87	0.38
50-300	32	526	37	25	23	11	17	7.07
50-350	41	7,593	186	115	66	32	30	14
50-400	45	3,313	79	52	22	12	11	6.58
100-200	5	0.17	0.23	0.24	0.66	0.36	0.22	0.19
100-300	15	720	1,059	795	165	54	141	44
100-400	29	$> 36hrs$	$> 36hrs$	$> 36hrs$	11,602	4,619	4,547	1,525
150-300	4	0.25	0.29	0.34	4.52	1.75	0.34	0.32
150-450	22	$> 36hrs$	$> 36hrs$	$> 36hrs$	$> 36hrs$	$> 36hrs$	$> 36hrs$	128,548

Table 1: Experimental results for Borchers & Furman's Max-2-SAT instances. Time in seconds.

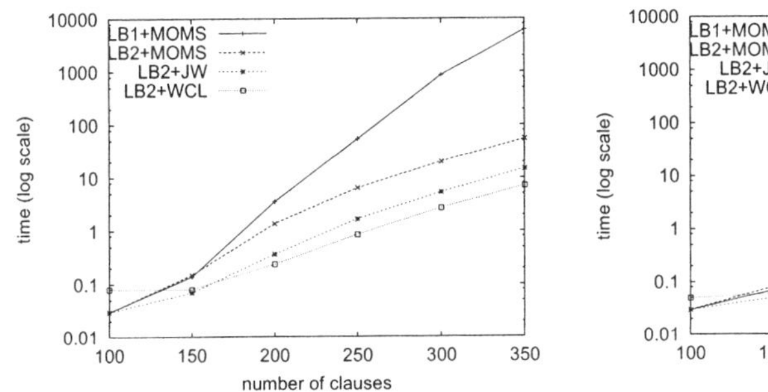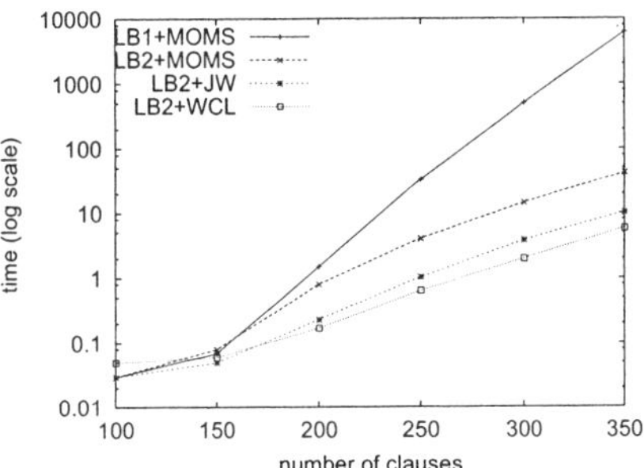

Figure 2: Experimental results for 50-variable Max-2-SAT instances. Left plot: mean time. Right plot: median time. Time in seconds.

We show in the next section that this technique improves considerably the performance of our algorithms.

3 Experimental Results

We conducted an experimental investigation in order to compare the performance of LB1+MOMS, LB2+MOMS, LB2+JW and LB2+WCL, as well as their improved versions. The experiments were performed on a 2GHz Pentium IV with 512 Mb of RAM under Linux.

In our first experiment, we solved the same instances that were used by Borchers & Furman in [3]. They are randomly generated Max-2-SAT and weighted Max-2-SAT instances that differ in the ratio of number of clauses to number of variables.

Table 1 shows the results for those random Max-2-SAT instances that can be solved in less than 36 hours by at least one of the algorithms. For each instance, we give the optimal number of unsatisfied clauses and the seconds needed, by each algorithm, to solve the instance. In the name of the instance, we indicate first the number of variables and then the number of clauses. Observe that our algorithms outperform LB1+MOMS up to two orders of magnitude.

instance	unsat	LB1+MOMS	LB2+MOMS	LB2-I+MOMS	LB2+JW	LB2-I+JW	LB2+WCL	LB2-I+WCL
50-100	16	0.05	0.03	0.04	0.03	0.04	0.04	0.03
50-150	34	0.06	0.04	0.04	0.06	0.04	0.09	0.05
50-200	69	0.70	0.37	0.24	0.26	0.12	0.15	0.09
50-250	96	7.10	2.28	1.38	1.47	0.62	1.25	0.61
50-300	132	27.06	4.14	2.70	1.85	0.87	1.03	0.55
50-350	211	1,278	81	54	42	19	20	8.88
50-400	211	635	23	16	13	6.40	8.42	4.69
50-450	257	2,045	39	27	10	5.71	3.46	2.51
50-500	318	6,113	79	53	57	29	24	14.43
100-200	7	0.13	0.08	0.08	0.08	0.07	0.07	0.08
100-300	67	103	75	16	100	15	105	13.17
100-400	119	36,481	13,381	2,647	9,796	2,568	34,360	4,693
100-500	241	$> 36hrs$	$> 36hrs$	$> 36hrs$	$> 36hrs$	$> 36hrs$	$> 36hrs$	91,742
100-600	266	$> 36hrs$	$> 36hrs$	$> 36hrs$	$> 36hrs$	$> 36hrs$	$> 36hrs$	70,350
150-300	24	0.54	0.37	0.35	5	1.04	0.45	0.41
150-450	9	8,282	5,869	3,012	23,562	4,502	$> 36hrs$	15,188

Table 2: Experimental results for Borchers & Furman's weighted Max-2-SAT instances. Time in seconds.

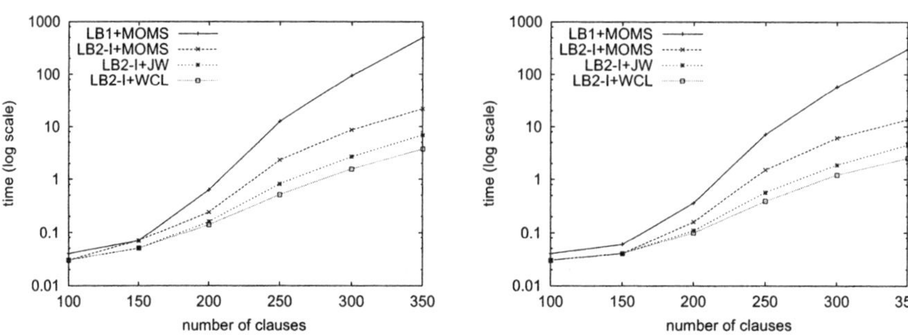

Figure 3: Experimental results for 50-variable weighted Max-2-SAT instances. Left plot: mean time. Right plot: median time. Time in seconds.

As greater is the number of unsatisfied clauses in the optimal solution, the behaviour of our algorithms is better. Also observe that LB2-I+MOMS, LB2-I+JW and LB2-I+WCL outperform considerably LB2+MOMS, LB2+JW and LB2+WCL. Table 2 is like Table 1 but for weighted Max-2-SAT instances. Again, we clearly see that our algorithms provide large performance improvements, which are due to the quality of the lower bounds and variable selection heuristics used.

In our second experiment, we generated sets of random Max-2-SAT and random weighted Max-2-SAT instances with 50 variables and a different number of clauses. Such instances were generated using the method described in [12]. For both Max-2-SAT and weighted Max-2-SAT, we generated sets for 100, 150, 200, 250, 300 and 350 clauses, where each set had 100 instances. The results of solving such instances with LB1+MOMS, LB2-I+MOMS, LB2-I+JW and LB2-I+WCL are shown in Figure 2 (Max-2-SAT instances) and Figure 3 (weighted Max-2-SAT instances). Along the horizontal axis is the number of clauses, and along the vertical axis is the mean and median time (in seconds) needed to solve an instance of a set. Notice that we use a log scale to represent run-time. Clearly, our algorithms outperform LB1+MOMS. It is worth to note that LB2-I+WCL has the best scaling behaviour on both random Max-2-SAT and random weighted Max-2-SAT instances.

As future work, we plan to experiment with other heuristics, define better lower bounds, and incorporate into our algorithms advanced data structures like those defined for SAT solvers in the last years.

Finally, we would like to point out that the algorithms presented here improve the algorithms for solving Max-SAT we described in [1]. After submitting this paper, Zhang, Shen and Manyà [17] have implemented an algorithm for solving Max-2-SAT that outperforms LB1+MOMS and LB2-I+JW. That algorithm incorporates special data structures for binary clauses.

Acknowledgements

Research partially supported by project CICYT TIC2001-1577-C03-03 funded by the *Ministerio de Ciencia y Tecnología*.

References

[1] T. Alsinet, F. Manyà, and J. Planes. Improved branch and bound algorithms for Max-SAT. In *Proceedings of the 6th International Conference on the Theory and Applications of Satisfiability Testing*, 2003.

[2] R. J. Bayardo and R. C. Schrag. Using CSP look-back techniques to solve real-world SAT instances. In *Proceedings of the 14th National Conference on Artificial Intelligence, AAAI'97, Providence/RI, USA*, pages 203–208. AAAI Press, 1997.

[3] B. Borchers and J. Furman. A two-phase exact algorithm for MAX-SAT and weighted MAX-SAT problems. *Journal of Combinatorial Optimization*, 2:299–306, 1999.

[4] J. Cheriyan, W. Cunningham, L. Tunçel, and Y. Wang. A linear programming and rounding approach to MAX-2-SAT. In D. Johnson and M. Trick, editors, *Cliques, Coloring and Satisfiability*, volume 26, pages 395–414. 1996.

[5] M. Davis, G. Logemann, and D. Loveland. A machine program for theorem-proving. *Communications of the ACM*, 5:394–397, 1962.

[6] E. de Klerk and J. P. Warners. Semidefinite programming approaches for MAX-2-SAT and MAX-3-SAT: computational perspectives. Technical report, Delft, The Netherlands, 1998.

[7] J. N. Hooker and V. Vinay. Branching rules for satisfiability. *Journal of Automated Reasoning*, 15:359–383, 1995.

[8] R. G. Jeroslow and J. Wang. Solving propositional satisfiability problems. *Annals of Mathematics and Artificial Intelligence*, 1:167–187, 1990.

[9] S. Joy, J. Mitchell, and B. Borchers. A branch and cut algorithm for max-sat and weighted max-sat. In *DIMACS Workshop on Satisfiability: Theory and Applications*, 1996.

[10] C. M. Li and Anbulagan. Heuristics based on unit propagation for satisfiability problems. In *Proceedings of the International Joint Conference on Artificial Intelligence, IJCAI'97, Nagoya, Japan*, pages 366–371. Morgan Kaufmann, 1997.

[11] D. W. Loveland. *Automated Theorem Proving. A Logical Basis*, volume 6 of *Fundamental Studies in Computer Science*. North-Holland, 1978.

[12] D. Mitchell, B. Selman, and H. Levesque. Hard and easy distributions of SAT problems. In *Proceedings of the 10th National Conference on Artificial Intelligence, AAAI'92, San Jose/CA, USA*, pages 459–465. AAAI Press, 1992.

[13] M. Moskewicz, C. Madigan, Y. Zhao, L. Zhang, and S. Malik. Chaff: Engineering an efficient sat solver. In *Proceedings of the 39th Design Automation Conference*, 2001.

[14] B. Selman, H. Levesque, and D. Mitchell. A new method for solving hard satisfiability problems. In *Proceedings of the 10th National Conference on Artificial Intelligence, AAAI'92, San Jose/CA, USA*, pages 440–446. AAAI Press, 1992.

[15] J. P. M. Silva and K. A. Sakallah. GRASP: A search algorithm for propositional satisfiability. *IEEE Transactions on Computers*, 48(5):506–521, 1999.

[16] R. Wallace and E. Freuder. Comparative studies of constraint satisfaction and Davis-Putnam algorithms for maximum satisfiability problems. In D. Johnson and M. Trick, editors, *Cliques, Coloring and Satisfiability*, volume 26, pages 587–615. 1996.

[17] H. Zhang, H. Shen, and F. Manyà. Exact algorithms for MAX-SAT. In *Proceedings of the 4th International Workshop on First-Order Theorem Proving, FTP-2003, Valencia, Spain*, 2003.

The Interface between P and NP in Many-Valued Clausal Forms

C. Ansótegui, R. Béjar, A. Cabiscol, F. Manyà
Dept. of Computer Science
Universitat de Lleida, Jaume II, 69, E-25001 Lleida, Spain
`{carlos,ramon,alba,felip}@eup.udl.es`

Abstract We study in detail the interface between P and NP in two many-valued satisfiability problems: Mono+pPartiallySigned-2SAT and Regular+pSigned-2SAT. We show that such problems smoothly interpolate between P and NP by mixing together a polynomial and a NP-complete problem, and identify phase transition behavior in each of these problems.

1 Introduction

In recent years we have seen an increasing interest in propositional satisfiability (SAT) encodings. The study of search behavior of random SAT formulas has provided tremendous insights into the hardness nature of such combinatorial problems, beyond the worst-case notion of NP-completeness. In particular, such studies have uncovered an interesting phase transition behavior between an area in which most instances are solvable and one in which most of the instances are unsolvable [3, 14]; the critically constrained area, where the hardest instances occur, coincides with the phase transition.

The identification of very hard instances has in turn led to the development of fast SAT solvers, which in turn is making propositional satisfiability a competitive encoding to solve other NP-complete problems. The approach consists of translating a given problem into propositional satisfiability, solving it with a fast SAT solver and mapping the solution back into the original problem. Examples of domains where propositional encodings have been shown effective include hardware verification [13, 17, 19], planning [7], and other benchmark problems such as graph coloring [18], and the quasigroup completion problem [5].

Our research program is aimed at bridging the gap between propositional satisfiability encodings and constraint satisfaction formalisms. The challenge is to combine the inherent efficiencies of SAT solvers operating on uniform satisfiability encodings with the much more compact and natural representations, and more sophisticated propagation techniques of CSP formalisms. Our path to achieving our research objectives is via gradual enhancement of Boolean satisfiability encodings, while paying careful attention to maintaining the good computational properties of standard satisfiability encodings. As a result, we propose Signed-SAT, which is a new constraint programming language between CSP and SAT that uses the language of the many-valued clausal forms known as signed CNF formulas for encoding problems, and the logical machinery of signed CNF formulas for designing and implementing complete Signed-SAT solvers.

With the aim of generating computationally difficult instances for benchmarking Signed-SAT solvers, as well as with the aim of gaining insights into the hardness nature of Signed-SAT, in this paper we study in detail the interface between P and NP in two new many-valued satisfiability problems: Mono+pPartiallySigned-2SAT and Regular+pSigned-2SAT. We show that such problems smoothly interpolate between P and NP by mixing together a polynomial and a NP-complete problem, and identify phase transition behavior in each of these problems.

This paper is structured as follows. In Section 2 we define the syntax and semantics of signed CNF formulas. In Section 3 we define the Signed-SAT problems we consider here and give some complexity results. In Section 4 we describe the experimental investigation.

2 Signed CNF Formulas

We first formally define the syntax and semantics of signed CNF formulas, which are the most widely used clausal forms in the many-valued logic community, and then present the subclasses of monosigned and regular CNF formulas.

Definition 1. *A* truth value set N *is a finite set* $\{i_1, i_2, \ldots, i_n\}$ *where* $n \in \mathbb{N}$. *The cardinality of* N *is denoted by* $|N|$. *A total order* $\leq$ *is associated with* N, *which may be the empty order.*

Definition 2. *A* sign *is a set* $S \subseteq N$ *of truth values. A* signed literal *is an expression of the form* $S : p$ *where* S *is a sign and* p *is a propositional variable. The* complement *of a signed literal* $S{:}p$, *denoted by* $\overline{S}{:}p$, *is* $(N \setminus S){:}p$. *A* signed clause *is a disjunction of signed literals. A signed clause containing exactly one literal is called a* signed unit clause; *and a signed clause containing exactly two literals is called a* signed binary clause. *The empty signed clause is denoted by* $\square$. *A* signed CNF formula *is a conjunction of signed clauses.*

Definition 3. *An* interpretation *is a mapping that assigns to every propositional variable an element of the truth value set. An interpretation* I satisfies *a signed literal* $S{:}p$ *iff* $I(p) \in S$. *It* satisfies *a signed clause* C *iff it satisfies at least one of the signed literals in* C; *and it* satisfies *a signed CNF formula* Γ *iff it satisfies all clauses in* Γ. *A signed CNF formula is* satisfiable *iff it is satisfied by at least one interpretation; otherwise it is* unsatisfiable.

Once we have defined signed CNF formulas, we present the subclasses of monosigned and regular CNF formulas.

Definition 4. *For all* $i \in N$, *let* $\uparrow i$ *denote the sign* $\{j \in N \mid j \geq i\}$ *and let* $\downarrow i$ *denote the sign* $\{j \in N \mid j \leq i\}$ *where* $\leq$ *is a total order associated with* N. *A sign* S *is* regular *if it is identical to* $\uparrow i$ *(positive) or to* $\downarrow i$ *(negative) for some* $i \in N$. *A signed literal* $S : p$ *is a* regular *literal if its sign* S *is regular. A signed clause (a signed CNF formula) is a* regular clause *(a* regular CNF formula*) if all its literals are regular. A regular CNF formula is* Horn *if each clause contains at most one regular positive literal.*

Definition 5. *A sign* S *is* monosigned *if it is a singleton; i.e. it contains exactly one truth value. A signed literal* $S : p$ *is a* monosigned *literal if its sign* S *is monosigned. A signed* *clause (a signed CNF formula) is a* monosigned clause *(a* monosigned CNF formula*) if all its literals are monosigned.*

Example 1. *Suppose that* $N = \{1, 2, 3, 4\}$. *Then, we have that the signed clause* $\{1, 2, 3\}{:}p_1 \vee \{4\} : p_2$ *can be represented as a regular clause by* $\downarrow 3 : p_1 \vee \uparrow 4 : p_2$, *and as a monosigned clause by* $\{1\} : p_1 \vee \{2\} : p_1 \vee \{3\} : p_1 \vee \{4\} : p_2$.

3 SAT Problems

Signed-SAT is the problem of deciding the satisfiability of a signed CNF formulas defined over a truth value set of size equal to o greater than 3. Signed-SAT, like Boolean SAT, is NP-complete. In the last years, the complexity of a number of subproblems of Signed-SAT has been studied; we refer to [2] for a survey. In this paper we focus on Signed-2SAT (i.e., Signed-SAT with the restriction that each clause has exactly two literals) and two of its sub-problems: Monosigned-2SAT (i.e., Signed-2SAT with the restriction that all the literals are monosigned), and Regular-2SAT (i.e., Signed-2SAT with the restriction that all the literals are regular). It was shown in [12] that Signed-2SAT is NP-complete, but Monosigned-2SAT and Regular-2SAT can be solved in polynomial time like Boolean 2-SAT.

We start by defining PartiallySigned-2SAT, which is a new problem class between Signed-2SAT and Monosigned-2SAT. PartiallySigned-2SAT is defined to be Signed-2SAT with the restriction that each clause has one monosigned literal and one signed literal with a sign of size two.

Proposition 1. *PartiallySigned-2SAT is NP-complete.*

Proof. NP-containment is straightforward to show. The Boolean 3-SAT problem is polynomially reducible to our problem as follows: Let Γ be a 3-SAT instance, let $N = \{0, 1, 2\}$, let $monosigned(p) = \{1\}{:}p$ for each positive literal p occurring in Γ, and let $monosigned(\neg p) = \{0\} : p$ for each negative literal $\neg p$ occurring in Γ. For each clause $C_i = L_{i1} \vee L_{i2} \vee L_{i3}$ of Γ, we introduce a new propositional variable c_i, and define a signed CNF formula Γ' that contains the clauses

$$
\begin{aligned}
(monosigned(L_{i1}) \vee \{0, 1\} : c_i) \wedge \\
(monosigned(L_{i2}) \vee \{0, 2\} : c_i) \wedge \\
(monosigned(L_{i3}) \vee \{1, 2\} : c_i)
\end{aligned}
\tag{1}
$$

for each clause C_i of Γ. Obviously, the reduction is polynomial, and Γ is satisfiable iff Γ' is satisfiable. $\qquad\square$

The above complexity result provides evidence that, by introducing small variations into our signs, we go from P to NP in significant subproblems of Signed-2SAT. To gain insights about the *practical* (in contrast to worst-case) complexity of Signed-2SAT, we introduce two new problems classes which mix together polynomial and NP-complete Signed-2SAT sub-problems:

- Mono+pPartiallySigned-2SAT: it is the problem of deciding the satisfiability of a Signed-2SAT instance in which a fraction of $(1 - p)$ clauses are monosigned, and a fraction of p clauses are partially signed (i.e., each clause has one monosigned literal and one signed literal with a sign of size two). This gives pure Monosigned-2SAT problems for $p = 0$, and gives pure PartiallySigned-2SAT problems for $p = 1$. For any fixed $p > 0$, the Mono+pPartiallySigned-2SAT problem class is NP-complete since the embedded PartiallySigned-2SAT subproblem can be made sufficiently large to encode other NP-complete problems within it.

- Regular+pSigned-2SAT: it is the problem of deciding the satisfiability of a Signed-2SAT instance in which a fraction of $(1 - p)$ clauses are regular, and a fraction of p clauses are signed. This gives pure Regular-2SAT problems for $p = 0$, and pure Signed-2SAT for $p = 1$. For any fixed $p > 0$, the Regular+pSigned-2SAT problem class is NP-complete since the embedded Signed-2SAT subproblem can be made sufficiently large to encode other NP-complete problems within it.

4 Experimental Investigation

We conducted an experimental investigation in order to identify phase transition phenomena in Mono+pPartiallySigned-2SAT and Regular+pSigned-2SAT, and to study the interactions between the polynomial and the NP-complete subproblems of Mono+pPartiallySigned-2SAT and Regular+pSigned-2SAT with the aim of exploring the interface between P and NP.

In all our experiments we used the solver Mv-SAT. It is a complete solver for signed CNF formulas that we designed and implemented. Mv-SAT is based on the Davis-Putnam procedure for signed CNF formulas defined in [6, 10], and incorporates a many-valued extension of the look-ahead branching rule of the Boolean SAT solver Satz [8, 9] in which only variables with minimum domain size are considered in a given state of the search process. We refer the reader to [1] for further details.

Phase transitions occur in SAT, as well as in other NP-hard problems [3]. Mitchell et al. [14] reported results from experiments on testing the satisfiability of classical random 3-SAT instances with the Davis-Putnam (DP) procedure [4]. They observed that (i) there is a sharp phase transition from satisfiable to unsatisfiable instances for a value of the ratio of the number of clauses to the number of variables; such a value is 4.3 for random 3-SAT. At lower ratios, most of the instances are under-constrained and are thus satisfiable. At higher ratios, most of the instances are over-constrained and are thus unsatisfiable. The value of that ratio where 50% of the instances are satisfiable is referred to as the threshold; and (ii) there is an easy-hard-easy pattern in the computational difficulty of solving problem instances as that ratio is varied; the hard instances occur in the area near the threshold.

In our first experiment we executed sets of Mono+pPartiallySigned-2SAT instances for different values of the ratio of the number of clauses to the number of variables ($\frac{C}{V}$), and for fixed values of p, V, and $|N|$. Each set had 100 instances generated uniformly at random, and all the instances of a set had the same value for the ratio $\frac{C}{V}$. We observed a phase transition similar to that identified for SAT, and that the difficulty of the instances of the hard region increases as p increases. While for Random 3-SAT the threshold is for a ratio of 4.3, in our case is for a ratio around 1 like in the polynomial Random 2-SAT problem. A possible explanation is that the polynomial subproblem dominates the problem's satisfiability. Nevertheless, further experiments are needed to see if the threshold remains around 1 for greater values of $|N|$. Figure 1 shows the phase transition we identified for Mono+pPartiallySigned-2SAT

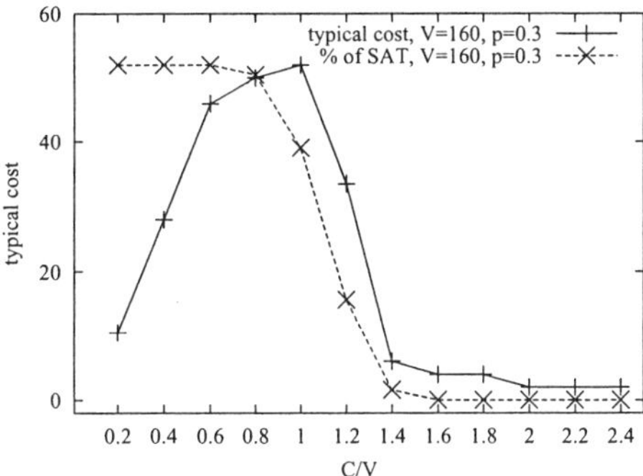

Figure 1: Phase transition for Mono+pPartiallySigned-2SAT ($|N| = 3$)

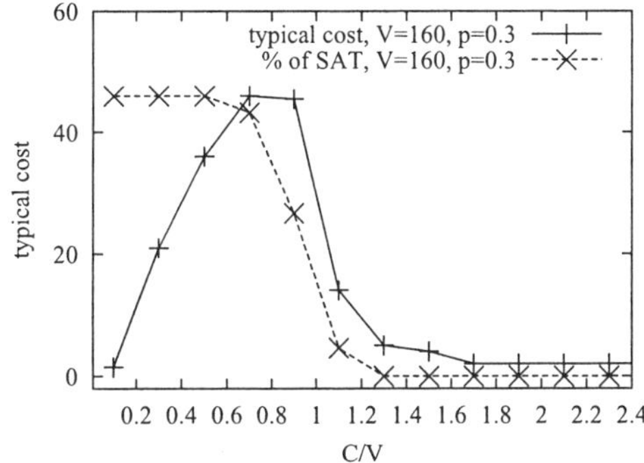

Figure 2: Phase transition for Mono+pPartiallySigned-2SAT ($|N| = 4$)

when $V = 160$, $p = 0.3$, and $|N| = 3$. Figure 2 shows the phase transition we identified for Mono+pPartiallySigned-2SAT when $V = 160$, $p = 0.3$, and $|N| = 4$. Along the vertical axis is the median number of decisions made by Mv-SAT (typical cost). Along the horizontal axis is the ratio $\frac{C}{V}$ in the instances tested. The dashed line indicates the percentage of instances that were found to be satisfiable scaled in such a way that 100% corresponds to the maximum typical cost. One can observe clearly the easy-hard-easy pattern in the computational difficulty of solving instances as the ratio of number of clauses to variables is varied.

Our second experiment was similar to the first, but for Regular+pSigned-2SAT. Figure 3 shows the phase transition we identified for Regular+pSigned-2SAT when $V = 160$, $p = 0.3$, and $|N| = 3$. Figure 4 shows the phase transition we identified for Regular+pSigned-2SAT when $V = 160$, $p = 0.3$, and $|N| = 4$. In this case, the location of the threshold has shifted to the right. A possible explanation is that we need more clauses at the threshold because the clauses for this problem are less constrained than for Mono+pPartiallySigned-2SAT.

In our third experiment we executed sets of 100 instances of the peak of the hard region of

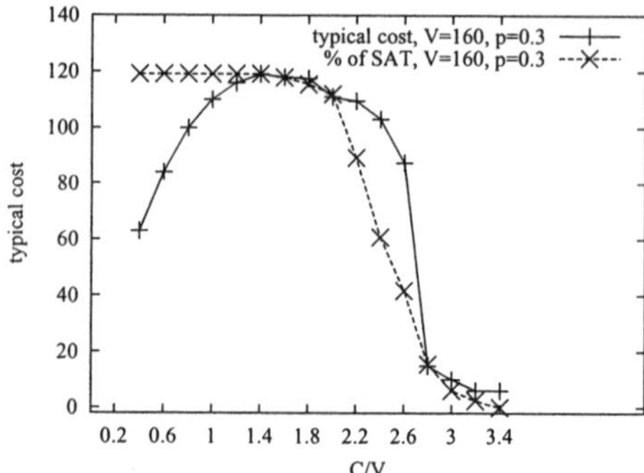

Figure 3: Phase transition for Regular+pSigned-2SAT ($|N| = 3$)

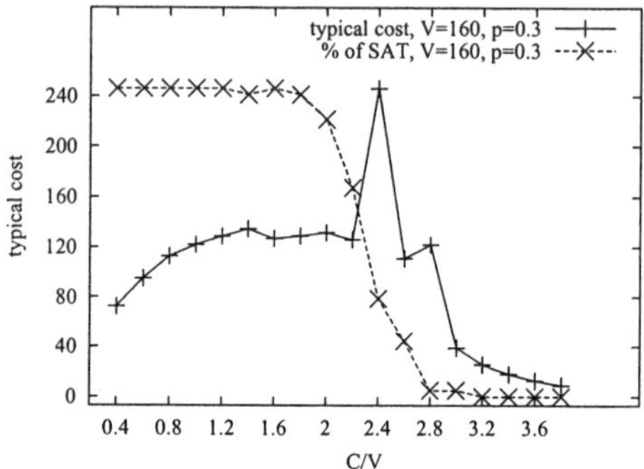

Figure 4: Phase transition for Regular+pSigned-2SAT ($|N| = 4$)

the phase transition of Mono+pPartiallySigned-2SAT and Regular+pSigned-2SAT —where each set had a different number of variables, a fixed value p, and $|N| = 4$— in order to determine if there is a value of p where the search cost appears to move from polynomial to exponential. Figure 5 shows the experimental results obtained for Mono+pPartiallySigned-2SAT for different values of p, and Figure 6 shows the results obtained for Regular+pSigned-2SAT. Along the vertical axis is the typical cost of Mv-SAT (logscale). Along the horizontal axis is the number of variables in the instances tested. For Mono+pPartiallySigned-2SAT, we observe that the typical cost appears to scale in a similar way for all the values of p. In contrast, for Regular+pSigned-2SAT, the cost appears to be polynomial (or at most subexponential) for $p < 0.8$ and exponential for $p \geq 0.8$. Despite Regular+pSigned-2SAT is NP-complete for all fixed and non-zero p, the typical search cost seems to follow a different pattern. Similar results were reported for 2+p-SAT [15, 16] and 2+p-coloring [20]. In these problems the change from polynomial to exponential was observed for $p = 0.4$ and $p = 0.8$, respectively. Further experiments are needed to see if a similar behavior is observed for Mono+pPartiallySigned-2SAT when $|N| > 4$.

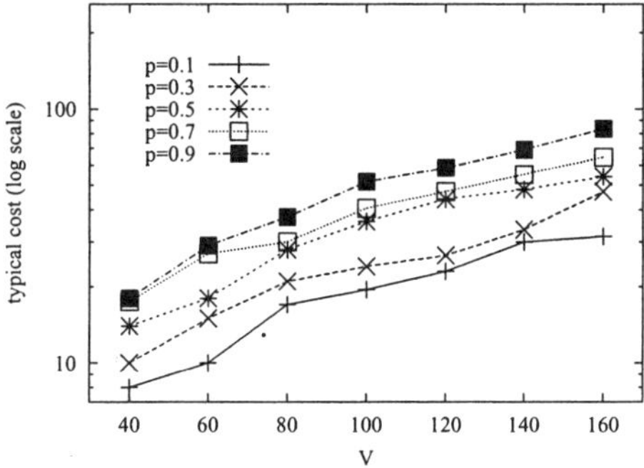

Figure 5: Search cost to solve Mono+pPartiallySigned-2SAT problems at the peak of the hard region of the phase transition for different values of p

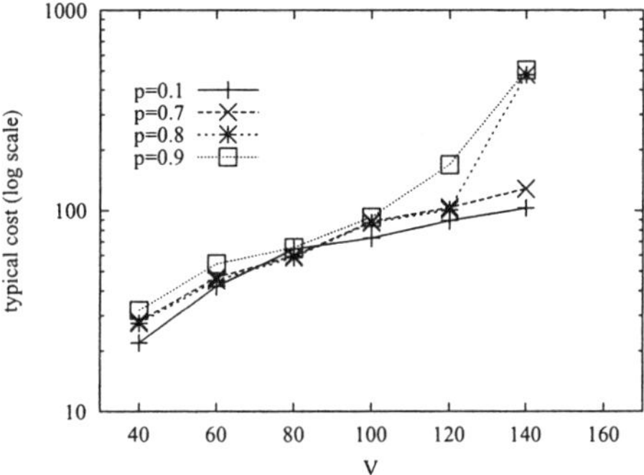

Figure 6: Search cost to solve Regular+pSigned-2SAT problems at the peak of the hard region of the phase transition for different values of p

Acknowledgements

Research partially supported by project CICYT TIC2001-1577-C03-03 funded by the *Ministerio de Ciencia y Tecnología*.

References

[1] C. Ansótegui, R. Béjar, A. Cabiscol, C.-M. Li, and F. Manyà. Resolution methods for many-valued CNF formulas. In *Fifth International Symposium on the Theory and Applications of Satisfiability Testing, SAT-2002, Cincinnati, USA*, pages 156–163, 2002.

[2] B. Beckert, R. Hähnle, and F. Manyà. The SAT problem of signed CNF formulas. In D. Basin, M. D'Agostino, D. Gabbay, S. Matthews, and L. Vigano, editors, *Labelled Deduction*, volume 17 of *Applied Logic Series*, pages 61–82. Kluwer, Dordrecht, 2000.

[3] P. Cheeseman, B. Kanefsky, and W. M. Taylor. Where the really hard problems are. In *Proceedings of the International Joint Conference on Artificial Intelligence, IJCAI'91*, pages 331–337. Morgan Kaufmann, 1991.

[4] M. Davis, G. Logemann, and D. Loveland. A machine program for theorem-proving. *Communications of the ACM*, 5:394–397, 1962.

[5] C. P. Gomes and B. Selman. Problem structure in the presence of perturbations. In *Proceedings of the 14th National Conference on Artificial Intelligence, AAAI'97, Providence/RI, USA*, pages 221–226. AAAI Press, 1997.

[6] R. Hähnle. Exploiting data dependencies in many-valued logics. *Journal of Applied Non-Classical Logics*, 6:49–69, 1996.

[7] H. A. Kautz and B. Selman. Pushing the envelope: Planning, propositional logic, and stochastic search. In *Proceedings of the 14th National Conference on Artificial Intelligence, AAAI'96, Portland/OR, USA*, pages 1194–1201. AAAI Press, 1996.

[8] C. M. Li and Anbulagan. Heuristics based on unit propagation for satisfiability problems. In *Proceedings of the International Joint Conference on Artificial Intelligence, IJCAI'97, Nagoya, Japan*, pages 366–371. Morgan Kaufmann, 1997.

[9] C. M. Li and Anbulagan. Look-ahead versus look-back for satisfiability problems. In *Proceedings of the 3rd International Conference on Principles of Constraint Programming, CP'97, Linz, Austria*, pages 341–355. Springer LNCS 1330, 1997.

[10] F. Manyà. *Proof Procedures for Multiple-Valued Propositional Logics*. PhD thesis, Universitat Autònoma de Barcelona, 1996. Published in [11].

[11] F. Manyà. *Proof Procedures for Multiple-Valued Propositional Logics*. Number 9 in Monografies de l'Institut d'Investigació en Intel.ligència Artificial. IIIA-CSIC, Bellaterra (Barcelona), 1999.

[12] F. Manyà. The 2-SAT problem in signed CNF formulas. *Multiple-Valued Logic. An International Journal*, 5(4):307–325, 2000.

[13] J. P. Marques-Silva and L. Guerra. Algorithms for satisfiability in combinational circuits based on backtrack search and recursive learning. In *Proc. of XII Symposium on Integrated Circuits and Systems Design (SBCCI)*, 1999.

[14] D. Mitchell, B. Selman, and H. Levesque. Hard and easy distributions of SAT problems. In *Proceedings of the 10th National Conference on Artificial Intelligence, AAAI'92, San Jose/CA, USA*, pages 459–465. AAAI Press, 1992.

[15] R. Monasson, R. Zecchina, S. Kirkpatrick, B. Selman, and L. Troyansky. Determining computational complexity for characteristic 'phase transitions'. *Nature*, 400:133–137, 1998.

[16] R. Monasson, R. Zecchina, S. Kirkpatrick, B. Selman, and L. Troyansky. Relation of typical-case complexity to the nature of the phase transition. *Random Structures and Algorithms*, 15(3–4):411–435, 1999.

[17] M. Moskewicz, C. Madigan, Y. Zhao, L. Zhang, and S. Malik. Chaff: Engineering an efficient sat solver. In *39th Design Automation Conference*, 2001.

[18] B. Selman and H. A. Kautz. Domain-independent extensions of GSAT: Solving large structured satisfiability problems. In *Proceedings of the International Joint Conference on Artificial Intelligence, IJCAI'93, Chambery, France*, pages 290–295. Morgan Kaufmann, 1993.

[19] M. Velev and R. Bryant. Effective use of boolean satisfiability procedures in the formal verification of superscalar and vliw microprocessors. In *38th Design Automation Conference (DAC '01)*, 2001.

[20] T. Walsh. The interface between P and NP: COL, XOR, NAE, 1-in-k, and Horn-SAT. In *Proceedings of the National Conference on Artificial Intelligence, AAAI-2002, Edmonton, Canada*, pages 695–700. AAAI Press, 2002.

Pareto-like Distributions in Random Binary CSP *

Christian Bessière[1], Cèsar Fernández[2], Carla P. Gomes[3], Magda Valls[4]

LIRMM-CNRS [1]
161 rue Ada, 34392
Montpellier Cedex 5, France
`bessiere@lirmm.fr`

Dept. of Computer Science [2]
Universitat de Lleida
Jaume II 69, Lleida, Spain
`cesar@eup.udl.es`

Dept. of Computer Science [3]
Cornell University
Ithaca, NY 14853, USA
`gomes@cs.cornell.edu`

Dept. of Mathematics [4]
Universitat de Lleida
Jaume II 69, Lleida, Spain
`magda@eup.udl.es`

Abstract. Much progress has been made in terms of boosting the effectiveness of backtrack style search methods. In addition, during the last decade, a much better understanding of problem hardness, typical case complexity, and backtrack search behavior has been obtained. One example of a recent insight into backtrack search concerns so-called heavy-tailed behavior in randomized versions of backtrack search. Such heavy-tails explain the large variations in run-time often observed in practice. However, heavy-tailed behavior does certainly not occur on all instances. This has led to a need for a more precise characterization of when heavy-tailedness does and when it does not occur in backtrack search. In this paper, we provide such a characterization. In particular, we will identify different statistical regimes in the parameter space of a standard instance generation model. We show that whether backtrack search is heavy-tailed or not depends on the statistical regime of the instance space.

Keywords: constraint satisfaction problems, heavy-tailed distributions, inconsistent search subtrees.

1 Introduction

In recent years we have made great strides in designing more efficient backtrack search methods for solving constraint satisfaction problems (CSP), including Boolean satisfiability problems (SAT). Current state-of-the-art backtrack solvers use a combination of strong search heuristics, fast pruning and propagation techniques, non-chronological backtracking and no-good learning, and more recently randomization and restarts. For example, in areas such as

---

*Research supported by AFOSR, grant F49620-01-1-0076 (Intelligent Information Systems Institute) and F49620-01-1-0361 (MURI grant on Cooperative Control of Distributed Autonomous Vehicles in Adversarial Environments), CICYT, TIC2001-1577-C03-03 and DARPA, F30602-00-2-0530 (Controlling Computational Cost: Structure, Phase Transitions and Randomization) and F30602-00-2-0558 (Configuring Wireless Transmission and Decentralized Data Processing for Generic Sensor Networks). The views and conclusions contained herein are those of the authors and should not be interpreted as necessarily representing the official policies or endorsements, either expressed or implied, of AFOSR, DARPA, or the U.S. Government.

planning and finite model-checking, we are now able to solve large CSP's with up to a million variables and five million constraints. The study of problem structure of combinatorial search problems has also provided tremendous insights in our understanding of the interplay between structure, search algorithms, and more generally, typical case complexity. For example, the work on phase transition phenomena in combinatorial search has led to a better characterization of search cost, beyond the worst-case notion of NP-completeness. While the notion of NP-completeness captures the computational cost of the very hardest possible instances of a given problem, in practice, one may not encounter that many instances that are quite that hard. We now know that, in general, CSP problems exhibit an "easy-hard-easy" pattern of search cost, depending on the constrainedness of the problem [10, 7]. The computational hardest instances appear to lie at the phase transition region, the area in which instances change from being almost all solvable to being almost all unsolvable. "Exceptionally hard instances" seem to defy this pattern: such instances occur in the under-constrained area, they are considerably harder than other similar instances and even harder than instances from the critically constrained area. However, different algorithms encounter different "exceptionally hard instances". Therefore, the "hardness" of exceptionally hard instances does not necessarily reside purely in the instances, but rather in the combination of the instance with the details of the search method [4, 12]. The work on the study of run time distributions of backtrack search algorithms further explains this phenomenon — the performance of backtrack search algorithms can exhibit extremely large variance, even on the *same* instance, *just* by introducing a small element of randomness into its heuristic, for example by breaking ties randomly. Such extreme fluctuations in the run time of backtrack search algorithms are nicely captured by so-called heavy-tailed distributions, distributions that are characterized by extremely long tails with some infinite moments [5, 6]. The decay of the tails of heavy-tailed distributions follows a power law, much slower than the decay of standard distributions, such as the normal, or log-normal, or the exponential distribution, that have tails that decay exponentially. Further insights into the empirical evidence of heavy-tailed phenomena are provided by *abstract* models of backtrack search that show that, under certain conditions, such procedures *provably* exhibit heavy-tailed behavior. In this work *backdoor* variables are a key notion [2, 13]. A set of variables forms a backdoor for a problem instance if there is a value assignment to these variables such that the simplified sub-problem can be solved in polynomial time by the propagation and simplification mechanism of the CSP solver under consideration. Intuitively, the backdoor corresponds to a set of variables, such that when set correctly, the sub-solver can solve the remaining problem easily. A backtrack search algorithm exhibits heavy-tailed behavior when the success probability of the heuristic of the backtrack search method is sufficiently low and the backdoor size is sufficiently small [2, 13].

In this paper we report a different approach. We study the empirical run time distributions of *concrete* backtrack search algorithms across the different constrainedness regions of random binary constraint satisfaction problem models (Model A, B, and E [1, 3]). In order to obtain more accurate empirical run time distributions, all our runs are performed without censorship (*i.e.*, we run our algorithms without a cutoff). Our study reveals dramatically different statistical regimes for randomized backtrack search algorithms across the different constrainedness regions of the CSP models. Figure 1 provides a preview of our results. The figure plots the run time distributions (the survival function, *i.e.,* the complement to one of the cumulative distribution function), of a simple backtrack search algorithm (no look-ahead and no look-back), using variable random ordering heuristic, with random value selection, for different constrainedness regions of model E (instances with 20 variables and domain

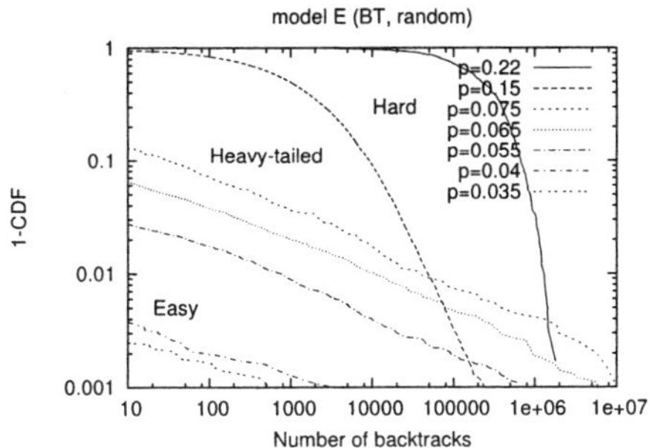

Figure 1: Survival function of the number of backtracks to solve different instances of model E with 20 variables and a domain size of 10. The parameter p captures the constrainedness of the instances. Heavy-tailed regime (curves with linear behavior) and a non-heavy-tailed regime can be identified.

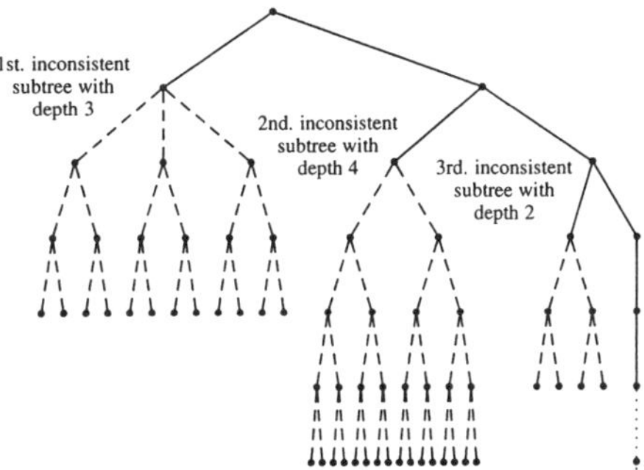

Figure 2: Inconsistent sub-trees in backtrack search.

size 10). Two regions, with dramatically different statistical regimes of the survival function of run time distributions of the backtrack search algorithm can be clearly identified. There is a region in which the tails of the survival distribution decay slowly, exhibiting power law decay. In Figure 1, the curves corresponding to instances with $p \leq 0.075$ exhibit power law decay, which is easily identified by their linear behavior. To some extent the boundary of this region corresponds to a threshold for the backtrack search algorithm. After this region, the instances become too hard for the backtrack search algorithm, all the runs become homogeneously long, and therefore the variance of the backtrack search algorithm decreases and the tails of its survival function decay exponentially (see Figure 1, e.g., the curve corresponding to the instance with $p = 0.22$ exhibits exponential decay, much faster than linear behavior).

In order to get further insights into the statistical behavior of our backtrack search method we study the inconsistent sub-trees discovered by the algorithm during the search, which are associated with the well known phenomenon of *thrashing* in backtrack search (see Figure 2). The distribution of the depth of inconsistent trees is quite revealing: when the run time distribution of the backtrack search method has a power law decay (see Figure 3, left panel, $p = 0.075$), the distribution of the depth of the inconsistent trees decreases exponentially (see Figure 3, right panel, $p = 0.075$). In other words, the backtrack search heuristic has a higher

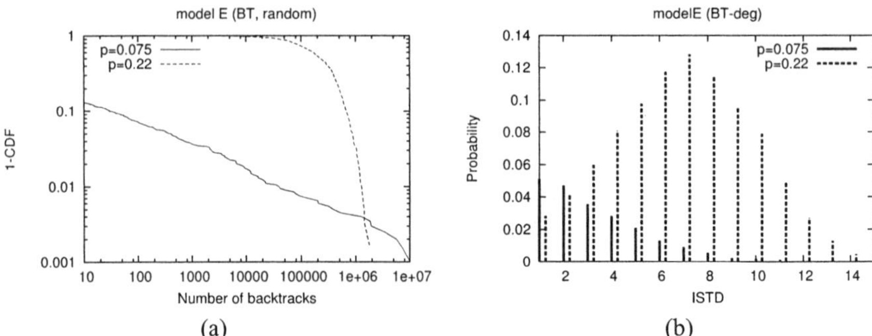

Figure 3: Example of an instance with Pareto-like ($p = 0.075$) and non-Pareto-like run time distribution ($p = 0.22$). The two instances with different regimes in decay of survival function of the run time distributions have also quite different distributions for the corresponding Inconsistency Sub-tree Depth (ISTD). For Pareto-like distributions of the run time, the corresponding ISTD follows an exponential distribution (right panel, $p = 0.075$), which is not the case when the run time distribution has exponential decay ($p = 0.22$).

probability of finding inconsistencies with a few variable assignments, and this probability decreases exponentially as the variable assignments increase. Contrast this behavior with the case in which the survival function of run time distribution of the backtrack search method has an exponential decay (see Figure 3, left panel, $p = 0.22$). In this case, the distribution of the depth of inconsistent trees no longer decreases exponentially (see Figure 3, right panel, $p = 0.22$).

The rest of the paper is organized as follows: in next section we present definitions concerning the random CSP models and concepts used in the paper. We then present empirical results illustrating the different statistical regimes of the run time distributions of our backtrack search methods. We also provide experimental evidence of the different shapes of the distributions of the depth of inconsistent sub-trees, closely related to the tail regime of the underlying run time distributions of the backtrack search method. Finally, conclusions and future work are discussed.

2　Preliminaries

Constraint Networks

A finite binary *constraint network* $\mathcal{P} = (\mathcal{X}, \mathcal{D}, \mathcal{C})$ is defined as a set of n *variables* $\mathcal{X} = \{x_1, \ldots, x_n\}$, a set of *domains* $\mathcal{D} = \{D(x_1), \ldots, D(x_n)\}$, where $D(x_i)$ is the finite set of possible *values* for variable x_i, and a set $\mathcal{C}$ of e binary *constraints* between pairs of variables. A constraint C_{ij} on the ordered set of variables (x_i, x_j) is a subset of the Cartesian product $D(x_i) \times D(x_j)$ that specifies the *allowed* combinations of values for the variables x_i and x_j. A *solution* of a constraint network is an instantiation of the variables such that all the constraints are satisfied. The constraint satisfaction problem (CSP) involves finding a solution of a constraint network or proving that none exists.

Random Problems

The CSP research community has always made a great use of randomly generated constraint satisfaction problems for comparing different search techniques and studying their behavior. Several models for generating these random problems have been proposed over the years. The oldest one, which was the most commonly used until the middle 90's is model A. A network generated by this model is characterized by four parameters $< N, D, p1, p2 >$, where N is the number of variables, D the size of the domains, p_1 the probability of having a constraint between two variables, and p_2, the probability that a pair of values is forbidden in a constraint. Notice that the variance in the type of problems generated with the same four parameters can be large, since the actual number of constraints for two problems with the same parameters can vary from one problem to another, and the actual number of forbidden tuples for two constraints inside the same problem can also be different. Model B does not have this variance. In model B, the four parameters are again $N, D, p1$, and $p2$, where N is the number of variables, and D the size of the domains. But now, p_1 is the proportion of binary constraints that are in the network (*i.e.*, there are exactly $c = \lfloor p_1 \cdot N \cdot (N - 1)/2 \rfloor$ constraints), and p_2 is the proportion of forbidden tuples in a constraint (*i.e.*, there are exactly $t = \lfloor p_2 \cdot D^2 \rfloor$ forbidden tuples in each constraint). Problems classes in this model are denoted by $< N, D, c, t >$. In [1], it was shown that model B (and model A as well) can be "flawed" when we increase N. Indeed, when N goes to infinity, we will almost surely have a *flawed* variable (that is, one variable which has all its values inconsistent with one of the constraints involving it). Model E has been proposed to overcome this weakness. It is a three parameter model, $< N, D, p >$, where N and D are the same as in the other models, and $\lfloor p \cdot D^2 \cdot N \cdot (N - 1)/2 \rfloor$ forbidden pairs of values are selected with repetition out of the $D^2 \cdot N \cdot (N - 1)/2$ possible pairs. Note, however, that there is another way of tackling the problem of flawed variables. In [14] it is shown that some properties on the relative values of N, D, p_1, and p_2, guarantee that the model is sound and scalable, for a certain range of values of the parameters.

Search Trees

A *search tree* is composed of *nodes* and *arcs*. A node u represents an ordered partial instantiation $I(u) = (x_{i_1} = v_{i_1}, \ldots, x_{i_k} = v_{i_k})$. A search tree is rooted at the particular node u_0 with $I(u_0) = \emptyset$. There is an arc from a node u to a node u_c if $I(u_c) = (I(u), x = v)$, x and v being a variable and one of its values. The node u_c is called a child of u and u a parent of u_c. Every node u in a tree T defines a *subtree* T_u that consists of all the nodes and arcs below u in T. The *depth* of a subtree T_u is the length of the longest path from u to any other node in T_u. An inconsistent subtree (IST) is a subtree that does not contain any node u such that $I(u)$ is a solution. The depth of an inconsistent subtree is referred to as ISTD. We denote by $T(A, P)$ the search tree of a backtrack search algorithm A solving a particular problem P, which contains a node for each instantiation visited by A until it reached a solution or proved inconsistency of P. Once assigned a partial instantiation $I(u) = (x_{i_1} = v_{i_1}, \ldots, x_{i_k} = v_{i_k})$ for node u, the algorithm will search for a partial instantiation of some of its children. In the case that there exists no instantiation which does not violate the constraints, algorithm A will take another value for variable x_{i_k}, and start again checking the children of this new node. In this situation, it is said that a *backtrack* happens. The *search cost* of an algorithm A on a particular problem P is the number of total backtracks in $T(A, P)$.

Algorithms

In the following, we will use different search procedures, that differ in the amount of propagation they perform, and in the order in which they generate instantiations. We used three levels of propagation: no propagation (backtracking, BT), removal of values directly inconsistent with the last instantiation performed (forward-checking, FC), and arc consistency propagation (maintaining arc consistency, MAC). We used three different heuristics for ordering variables: random selection of the next variable to instantiate (random), variables pre-ordered by decreasing degree in the constraint graph (deg), and selection of the variable with smallest domain first, ties broken by decreasing degree (dom+deg).

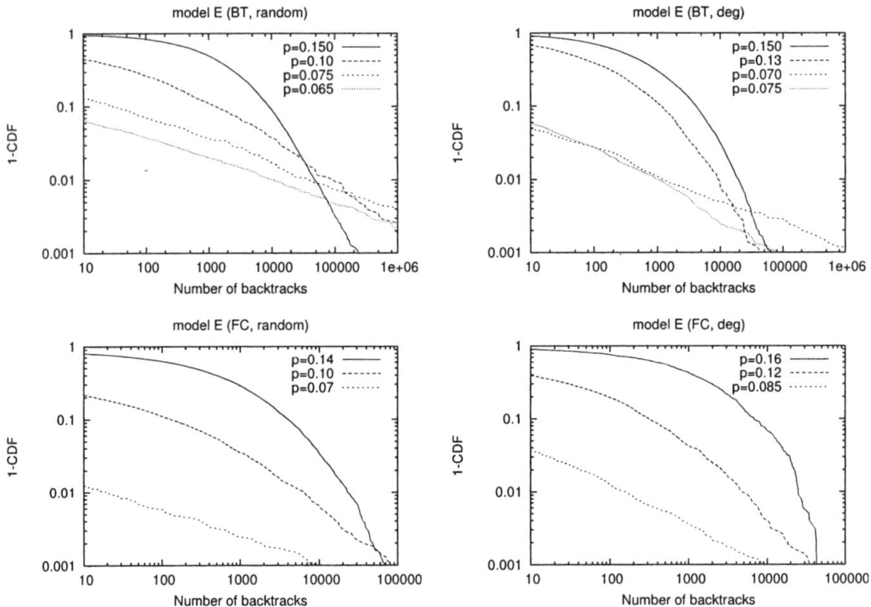

Figure 4: Survival functions of the number of backtracks for some instances generated under model E and solved using different algorithms. All the instances belong to the class $\langle 20, 10, p \rangle$.

Pareto-like Distributions

The runtime distributions of backtrack search methods are often characterized by very long tails or *heavy-tails* (HT). These non-standard probability distributions were first introduced by Vilfredo Pareto in 1897 in the context of income distribution, and have recently received much attention because of their suitability to model stochastic phenomena subject to extreme fluctuations.

Given a general Pareto distribution $F(x)$, the probability that a random variable is larger than a given value x, *i.e.*, its survival function, is:

$$1 - F(x) = P[X > x] \sim Cx^{-\alpha}, \ x > 0,$$

where $\alpha > 0$ and $C > 0$ are constants. These distributions have infinite variance when $1 < \alpha < 2$ and infinite mean and variance when $0 < \alpha <= 1$. If $1 - F(x)$ (the survival function) is plotted in a wide-ranged plot, a perfect L shape is observed. The log-log plot of the survival function of a Pareto-like distribution shows linear behavior with slope equal to $-\alpha$.

3　Empirical Results

In the previous section we formally defined our models and algorithms, as well as the concepts that are key in our study: the runtime distributions of our backtrack search methods and the associated distributions of the depth of the inconsistent subtrees found by the backtrack method. In this section we show how the behavior of these two distributions is highly correlated.

The results presented in this paper concern mainly instances of Model E, using BT and FC algorithms with different heuristics. Nevertheless, we also show some results for harder problems of model B, when using more sophisticated propagation (MAC). We present results for the survival functions of the search cost (number of backtracks) of our backtrack search algorithms. All the plots were computed with over at least 2000 independent executions of a given problem instance. We also present the results for the corresponding inconsistency sub-tree depth distributions (ISTD). The ISTD distributions were computed according to the following procedure:

1. At every node of the search, we translate our CSP problem in conjunction with the already assigned variables, into a SAT problem, in order to use a fast complete SAT-solver. Then we apply `satz` [9, 8] to determine if the remaining problem is consistent.[1]

2. If so, we proceed as in step 1. If not, we have found an inconsistent sub-tree (IST). In order to compute its depth, we mark the current node and proceed with the backtrack search procedure that is the focus of the stufy (e.g., pure backtrack search) until it reaches inconsistency.

3. At this point one inconsistent sub-tree (IST) has been computed. Then, we backtrack up to the marked node in step 2 and proceed as in step 1.

This procedure allows us to compute the ISTD independently of the CSP algorithm employed and skipping all the search inside an IST.

Figure 4 plots the survival functions of the number of backtracks for different instances generated under model E and solved using different algorithms (BT-random, BT-deg, FC-random and FC-deg). All the instances for model E belong to the class $\langle 20, 10, p \rangle$.

The results in Figure 4 show that the threshold for heavy-tailed behavior (*i.e.*, Pareto-like behavior with power law decay) occurs at different levels of constrainedness, depending on how powerful the propagation and the heuristic are. For example, using a simple BT-random algorithm, problems with $p < 0.075$ show Pareto-like distributions, whereas the larger is p beyond this point, the clearer is the exponential drop of the distribution. Considering now FC-deg, the threshold for heavy-tailed (Pareto-like) behavior moves closer to the phase-transition, around $p = 0.085$.

---

[1] Satz outperforms other available CSP solvers on these instances. One could use any fast CSP solver.

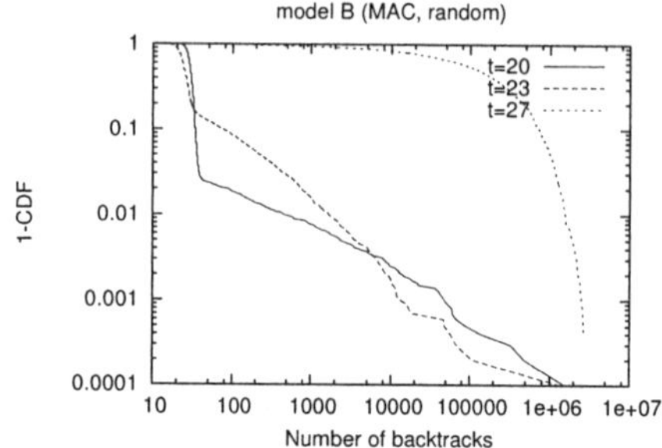

Figure 5: Survival functions of the number of backtracks for some instances generated under model B and solved with MAC random algorithm for problem class $\langle 50, 8, 150, t \rangle$.

Table 1: Model E $\langle 20, 10, p \rangle$. Estimation of α and its corresponding mean square error.

Algorithm	p	α	Error
BT-random	0.065	0.302	0.015
BT-random	0.075	0.318	0.009
BT-deg	0.070	0.418	0.004
BT-deg	0.075	0.448	0.026
FC-random	0.070	0.365	0.003
FC-random	0.100	0.506	0.053
FC-deg	0.085	0.517	0.009
FC-deg	0.120	0.588	0.068
FC-dom+deg	0.120	0.915	0.031
FC-dom+deg	0.140	0.833	0.080

We also observed such a clear separation of two distinct statistical regimes – Pareto-like distribution of the run-time distributions vs. non-Pareto-like distributions – for instances of model B, for different problem sizes and with more sophisticated algorithms. Figure 5 shows the survival functions of run time distributions of instances of model B $\langle 50, 8, 150, t \rangle$, for different levels of constrainedness, solved with MAC-random. Again, the two different statistical regimes of the survival functions are quite clear.

In order to quantify the heavy-tailedness of our Pareto-like distributions we used a QQ-estimator [11]. We estimate the paramter α of our distributions by estimating the slope of the tails using a linear regression of the logarithmic value of the data against the logarithmic values of the probability. Table 1 summarizes the results for model E. The table shows instances of model E in the class $\langle 20, 10, p \rangle$. This table illustrates the following behaviors:

- The heavy-tailedness of the distributions decreases (α increases) as constrainedness increases (p increases);

- The heavy-tailedness of the distributions decreases (α increases) when using more sophisticated search algorithms (e.g., BT-deg exhibits less heavy-tailed behavior (smaller α) than BT-random.)

These results suggest that the existence of heavy-tailed behavior in the cost distributions depends on the efficiency of the heuristic and the pruning mechanisms of the backtrack search

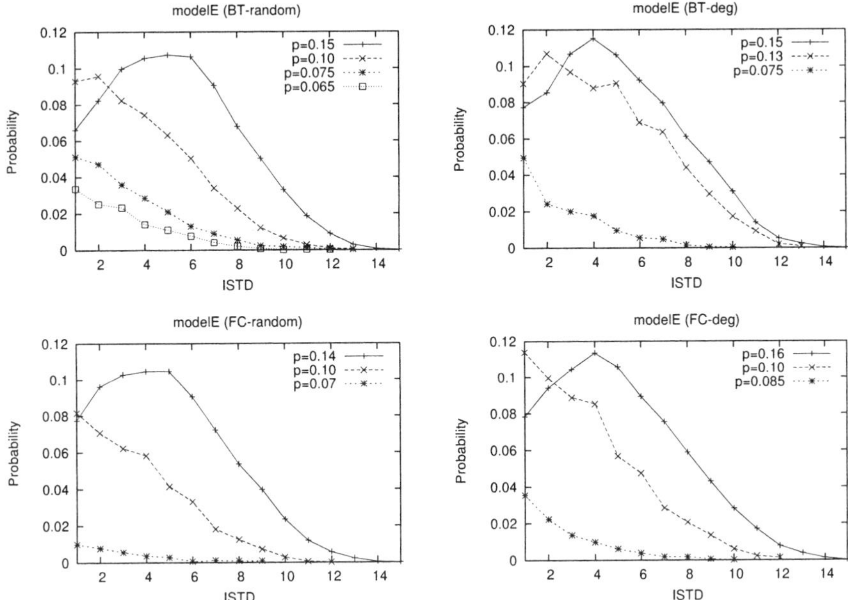

Figure 6: Model E. Distribution of the ISTD for some of the instances plotted in Figure 4.

algorithm as well as on the level of constrainedness of the problem, and of course on the size of the instances. Increasing the algorithm efficiency tends to shift the heavy-tail threshold closer to the phase transition.

A second set of results is related to the distributions of the inconsistency sub-tree detph (ISTD). Figure 6 plots the ISTD distributions for some of the instances plotted in Figure 4. It can be observed that when the cost distribution is Pareto-like, its corresponding ISTD distribution shows an exponential decay. Preliminary studies (out of the scope of this paper) explain this fact from an analytical point of view. On the other hand, as the cost distribution is less Pareto-like, its ISTD distribution moves away from an exponential decay. This effect can be observed clearly in Figure 7.

4   Conclusions and Future Work

We study the run time distributions of complete backtrack search methods on instances of well-known random CSP binary models. Our results clearly reveal different regimes in the runtime distributions of the backtrack search procedures and corresponding distributions of the depth of the inconsistent sub-trees. In the first region (this region starts at the most under-constrained area), randomized backtrack search solvers exhibit heavy-tailed behavior. The boundary of this region corresponds to a threshold for a given backtrack search algorithm. After this region, the instances become harder for the backtrack search algorithm, all the runs become homogeneously long, and therefore the variance of the backtrack search algorithm

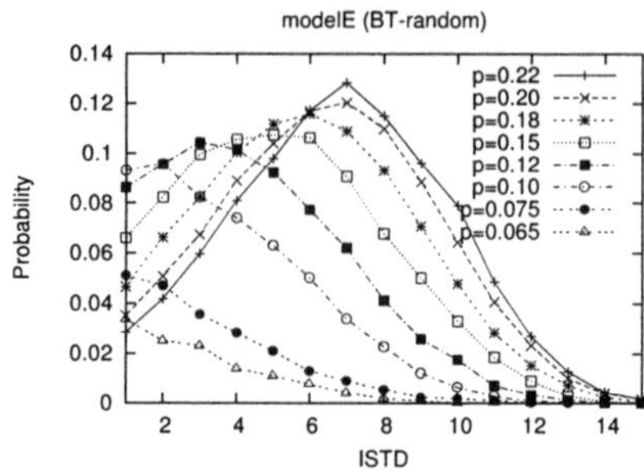

Figure 7: Distribution of the ISTD for some model E instances solved with BT-random.

decreases and the tails of its run time distribution decay exponentially. The location where the transition from the heavy-tailed region to the non-heavy-tailed region occurs depends on the constrainedness of the instances and the efficiency of the propagation and search heuristics of the backtrack search algorithm. The more efficient the backtrack search algorithm, the closer to the phase-transition is the heavy-tail threshold. We also show that there is a clear correlation between the regime of the tail of the run time distributions and the distributions of the depth of the inconsistent sub-trees encountered by the backtrack search method. We believe that we can exploit this correlation to design more efficient restart strategies of randomized backtrack search methods.

References

[1] D. Achlioptas, L. M. Kirousis, E. Kranakis, D. Krizanc, M. S. O. Molloy, and Y. C. Stamatiou. Random constraint satisfaction: A more accurate picture. In *Principles and Practice of Constraint Programming*, pages 107–120, 1997.

[2] H. Chen, C. Gomes, and B. Selman. Formal models of heavy-tailed behavior in combinatorial search. In *Proc. of 7th Int. Conf. of Constraint Programming CP 2001*, pages 408–422, 2001.

[3] I. Gent, E. MacIntyre, P. Prosser, B. Smith, and T. Walsh. Random constraint satisfaction: flaws and structure. In *Constraints, 6(4)*, pages 345–372, 2001.

[4] I. Gent and T. Walsh. Easy Problems are Sometimes Hard. *Artificial Intelligence*, 70:335–345, 1993.

[5] C. P. Gomes, B. Selman, and N. Crato. Heavy-tailed Distributions in Combinatorial Search. In *Proc. of the 3rd Int. Conf. of Constraint Programming (CP-97)*, pages 121–135, Linz, Austria., 1997. Springer-Verlag.

[6] C. P. Gomes, B. Selman, N. Crato, and H. Kautz. Heavy-tailed phenomena in satisfiability and constraint satisfaction problems. *J. of Automated Reasoning*, 24(1–2):67–100, 2000.

[7] T. Hogg, B. Huberman, and C. Williams. Phase transitions and the search problem. *Artificial Intelligence*, 81 (1-2):1–15, 1996.

[8] Chu Min Li. A constraint-based approach to narrow search trees for satisfiability. *Information Processing Letters*, 71(2):75–80, 1999.

[9] Chu Min Li and Anbulagan. Heuristics based on unit propagation for satisfiability problems. In *IJCAI (1)*, pages 366–371, 1997.

[10] D. Mitchell, B. Selman, and H. Levesque. Hard and easy distributions of SAT problems. In *Proceedings of The Tenth National Conference on Artificial Intelligence*, pages 459–465. AAAI Press, 1992.

[11] R. Resnick. Heavy tail modelling and teletraffic data. *Annals of Statistics*, 25:1805–1869, 1997.

[12] B. Smith and S. Grant. Sparse constraint graphs and exceptionally hard problems. In *Proceedings of the International Joint Conference on Artificial Intelligence*, pages 646–651. AAAI Press, 1995.

[13] R. Williams, C. Gomes, and B. Selman. Backdoors to typical case complexity. In *Proceedings of the International Joint Conference on Artificial Intelligence (to appear)*, Acapulco, Mexico, 2003. AAAI Press.

[14] K. Xu and W. Li. Exact phase transition in random constraint satisfaction problems. *Journal of Artificial Intelligence Research*, 12:93–103, 2000.

Artificial Intelligence Research and Development
I. Aguiló et al. (Eds.)
IOS Press, 2003

A Quality-Based Heuristic for Real-Time Scheduling[1]

Luis HERNÁNDEZ, Vicente BOTTI, Ana GARCÍA-FORNES, Mario GONZÁLEZ
*Departament Sistemes Informàtics i Computació, Universitat Politècnica de València,
Camí de Vera s/n, 46022 València, Spain. Fax: +34 96 387 73 59.
{lhernand, vbotti, agarcia, mgonzale}@dsic.upv.es*

Abstract. In this paper, we present a heuristic to be used for scheduling intelligent methods in a real-time agent architecture called ARTIS. This architecture has been designed to build intelligent agents that work in hard real-time environments. To do this, the architecture provides scheduling at two levels. The first level assures the fulfilment of the hard temporal requirements and the second level obtains a result of higher quality. The new heuristic, SSS (slack- slide scheduling), works at the second level, and it manages two types of methods: progressive refinement methods and multiple methods. The SSS also attempts to reuse previous results in order to make better use of the existing CPU time while the first level scheduler fulfils the deadlines.

1. Introduction

The use of Artificial Intelligence (AI) techniques has been widely applied in many areas, one of which is the area of real-time systems. Applications for the control of industrial processes, monitoring of aeronautical systems and similar problems have become more and more common. The reason is the flexibility that these techniques offer for solving problems which are getting more and more complex.

The main disadvantage that usually accompanies the fusion of the real-time and AI areas, is their antagonistic requirements and characteristics. Real-time systems usually require predictable methods, that is, methods that assure that its completion occurs within certain temporary limits. The AI techniques offer better quality answers what are more flexible, but they are unpredictable in the response time.

Artificial intelligence in real time arises as a field which joins both disciplines. Among the many approach available, one of the most widely used are the approximate techniques. These techniques are based on the search for non optimal solutions, but satisfactory solutions that guarantee that the time limits are fulfilled. Our work follows these techniques.

When considering the use of these techniques, the entire system (the real-time system) must be taken into account. One possibility is to use software architectures that can manage these techniques within real-time environments such as CIRCA, PRS, AIS or Phoenix. A description of some of these architectures can be found in [1][2][3]. One of these architectures is ARTIS [4], an architecture for building real-time agents that works in hard real-time environments. The agent guarantees finding solutions within a time limit and it also attempts to improve the quality of the solutions by using AI methods. The agent should have scheduling techniques that assign the available CPU time to the agent's tasks while

---

[1] This work has been funded by grant number DPI2002-04434-C04-02 of the Spanish Government and by grant number CTIDIB/2002/61 of the Generalitat Valenciana.

guaranteeing a minimal quality answer. It should take into account the existing real-time restrictions and it should maximize the quality of the agent's answer in each situation.

In ARTIS the scheduling approach is defined at two levels. The first level is in charge of guaranteeing the strict requirements of real time. The second level must improve the quality of the solutions in the available time. The work presented in this paper is an approximate technique and is centered on the second scheduling level. Our contribution consists in the proposal of a new method for deliberative scheduling based on utility. The objective of this method is to maximize the quality of the agent's answer obtained in the available CPU time, once the execution of the agent's critical tasks have been guaranteed and the real-time restrictions has been satisfied. This new method is called SSS (Slack Slide Scheduling).

First we present the ARTIS architecture. Section 3 describes the two level scheduling. Section 4 presents the new method. Section 5 shows the validation scenario of the method, the tests that were carried out and the results. Section 6 presents our conclusions and future work.

2. ARTIS

ARTIS is an architecture for intelligent real-time agents [5]. The purpose of ARTIS is the development of intelligent agents that are able to operate in hard real-time environments. The agent built under the ARTIS architecture is able to perceive information from the environment through sensors, is able to calculate answers (in a reactive way or with a higher or lower degree of deliberation). It is also able to act on the environment according to the answer by using effectors or by transmitting the answers to other agents.

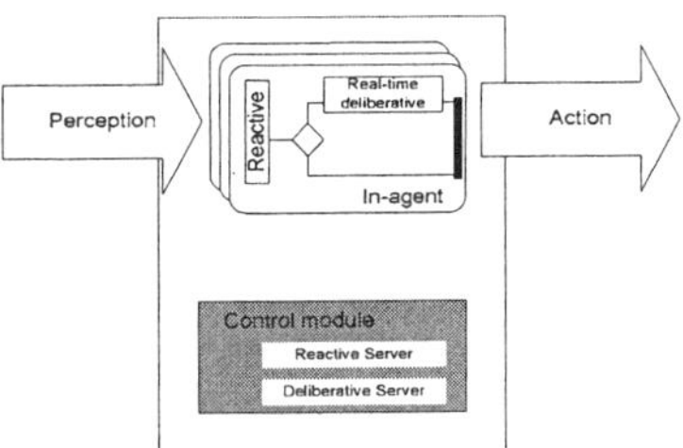

Figure 1. Components of an ARTIS agent.

An ARTIS agent (Figure 1) is composed of a set of in-agents (internal agents) and a control module. Each in-agent (which is in charge of solving a certain subtask) can calculate reactive and/or deliberative answers. The control module decides which in-agents should carry out their function and the order of execution.

An in-agent has associated an activation period, and a deadline or maximum time of execution. Also, it has a series of levels, each of which solves a certain sub-problem. Each level has associated the quality of the answer that it provides. The levels can be of two types:

- Reactive or level 0. These levels are characterized by their worst case execution time. They are used to guarantee the answer in the required time.
- Deliberative or optional. Their function is to obtain a solution in the case of the non-critical sub-problems and to improve the answer of the 0 level in the case of the critical sub-problems. These levels are not time limited; their nature can be very diverse; for example, rule-based systems, neural nets, case-based reasoning, etc. They are characterized by a average execution time.

Since an in-agent has several levels that solve the same sub-problem, the levels are grouped into what we call MKSs -multiple knowledge sources- [4]. An in-agent consist of: a MKS of perception that takes the data that it needs; several cognitive MKSs which are dedicated to calculating the answer in general; and finally an action MKS which is in charge of carrying out the operations indicated by the answer. Each MKS is defined by a group of levels and by its importance. This is a value that reflects the relevance of the MKS in the global agent. The ratio between the execution time and the quality of the levels of a MKS is shown in its execution profile, as in the Figures 2 and 3.

In accordance with the organization of the optional levels, the MKS can be of two types [4]:

- Progressive refinement MKS. In this case each level makes use of the answer from the previous level in order to improve it. A level cannot be executed if all the previous ones have not been executed. This can be considered as an anytime algorithm of thick grain, where the MKS can be interrupted without executing all the levels. The answer chosen is the one which is calculated by the last level that was entirely executed.

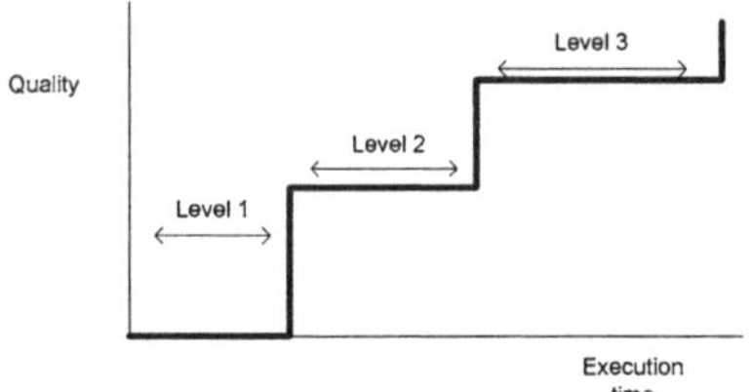

Figure 2. Progressive refinement MKS execution profile

- Multiple-method MKS. In this case, the methods are alternative and represent different possibilities about the same problem. It is not necessary to execute previous levels in order to execute a level.

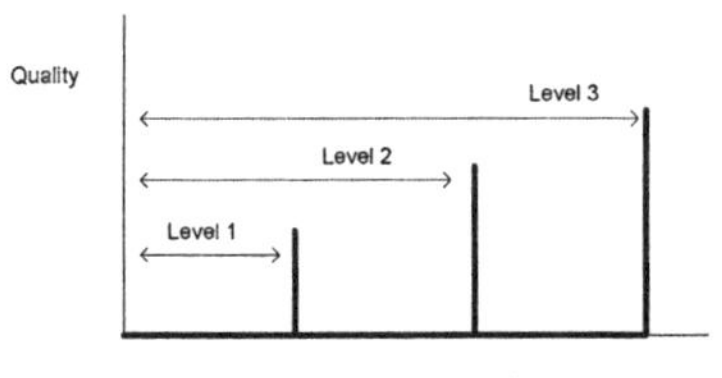

Figure 3. Multiple method MKS execution profile.

2.1 Low-level Model

Each in-agent is translated in a low level task model that consist of one initial mandatory, one optional, and one final mandatory parts [5].

This low-level model is based on a blackboard model [6]. In this model some low level agents or tasks cooperate to find a solution as in the AIS ("Adaptative Intelligent Systems") architecture of Hayes-Roth [2].

In ARTIS, this model is implemented under two operating systems: first, an extension of RT-Linux and, second, Linux. In RT-Linux, which is a operating system designed especially for real-time applications, the critical components of the model will be executed, guaranteeing the execution of their temporal restrictions. To be used in ARTIS,

RT-Linux has been extended so that it can provide more services; this model is called Flexible RT-Linux [7]. During certain temporal periods, RT-Linux allocate CPU time to Linux. The non-critical operations of the system will be carried in Linux. For the example, the deliberative calculation of the answers, the communications with other agents, etc.

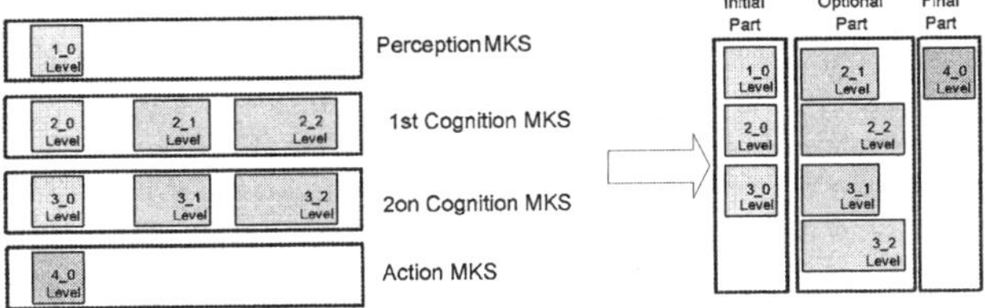

Figure 4. Example of translation to the low-level model

The tasks, which are a low-level translation of the in-agents (Figure 4), are divided into two components:

- A critical component that can be split in two parts: the initial part, which is formed by the 0 levels of the perception and knowledge MKSs, and the final part which is formed by the 0 level of the action MKS (the only level of the action MKSs).
- An optional component which is formed by the optional levels of the perception and knowledge MKSs. This component should be executed after the initial part and before the final part.

Another component of the low-level model is the control component. The control component is split in two parts: the Reactive Server (RS), which is integrated in the RTOS (Real Time Operating System). The RS is run under RT-LINUX and includes the first-level scheduler (FLS). The FLS is in charge of scheduling the critical components. The second part is the Deliberative Server (DS), which run under LINUX and contains the second level scheduler (SLS) for scheduling the optional components.

Another component is the global memory or KDM that allows for the communication among the different in-agents. It is not a passive element because it contains components that take charge of managing the temporary relationships of the information as well as maintaining their logical coherence [6].

3. Scheduling

To reach the objectives of respecting the deadlines and obtaining the best quality, the agent has a control module that negotiates the CPU assignment to the tasks that make up the agent. This scheduling is carried out at two levels. To do this, the control component is divided into two schedulers, each of which is in charge of the critical and optional part components, respectively. The first level scheduler should guarantee that all the critical tasks have an answer before their deadline; the second level scheduler should plan the optional components in order to obtain the best quality results in the available time.

3.1 First-Level Scheduler

From a real-time point of view, a critical in-agent is characterized by a period, a deadline and a worst case execution time of its critical component. If an ARTIS agent is defined by a group of in-agents, the system makes an off-line guarantee test (using the set of low level tasks obtained of the translating process) that indicates whether the system can be scheduled or not. That is, it determines whether the critical components will be able to complete their execution times [5]. To do this, the system is based on a pre-emptive priority scheduling with the assignment of fixed priorities to the tasks [8].

If the test indicates that the system can be scheduled, the FLS decides on-line which initial or final part should be executed. Once the initial part of the task has been executed, the FLS passes the control to the SLS. The SLS can execute the optional component of this task as well as the optional component of other tasks that have also executed their initial part and not their final part.

Every time that the FLS passes the control, it should communicate the existing available time to the following execution of an initial or final part to the SLS, because this temporal hole or slack that the FLS calculates [9] is the time that the SLS has to perform its planning and to execute the optional components. The FLS will also inform the SLS about the deadline of the optional component for each task, named "the execution deadline".
Note that, due to the adopted first-level scheduling policy, the final components of higher priority tasks will be completed before any final component of lower priority tasks, as in the example in Figure 5.

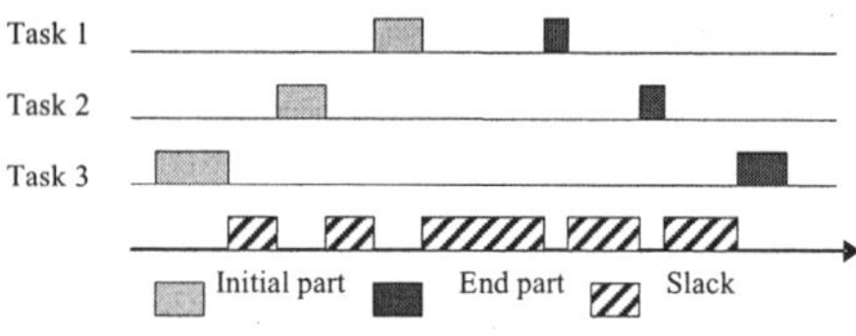

Figure 5. First level scheduling.

The Figure 5 presents an example with the slack generated after the FLS schedules the initial and final parts of three tasks (where the task 1 has the highest priority and the task 3 the lowest priority).

3.2 Second-Level Scheduler

The SLS is in charge of assigning the available slack to the optional components and its objective is to maximize the quality of the global answer. In this case, a temporal requirement does not exist in the sense of obtaining an answer obligatorily, since it is the optional component of a non-critical MKS, or, in the case of the critical MKS, it already has the solution calculated in the 0 level. But, in every case, the solution only is useful if it is obtained before its execution deadline.

Another difference between the FLS and the SLS consists in the information that the SLS uses. The SLS no longer works with the worst-case time, but with the average times. The reason is the nature of the levels. The worst-case execution time is not very representative in these methods (heuristic searches).

Every time that the DS enters, the second level scheduler (SLS) is activated due to the fact that the initial or final part of a task has been executed. This SLS executes a scheduling based on the blackboard system control loop:

- Reception of messages. The SLS receives the initial components that have been executed and the duration of the current slack from the RTOS.
- Triggering. In accordance with the previous information, the SLS inserts the MKS that can be executed, because its initial part has been executed, into a list.
- Condition testing. In this phase, the system filters the previous list, and it eliminates the MKSs that do not complete certain preconditions.

- Rating. The planning is carried out in this phase, using a heuristic to determine the order that the levels should be executed in. The planning is carried out on the list from the previous phase. The MKSs coming from previous activations of the SLS are also included in this list if they continue to be active because the final component has not yet been executed.
- Schedule. The best level from the previous phase is chosen. If it cannot be executed because the foreseen time of execution surpasses the available one, it is not executed but it remains for its possible execution in the following slack hole, and the next best level is chosen.
- Interpret. The level selected in the previous point is executed in this phase. The information managed by the control component is also refreshed, indicating whether the level has been executed correctly, the actual time of execution, etc.

3.3 Scheduling Methods Based on the Utility

When the scheduler decides which level to execute at each moment, it can use two types of methods, either greedy or deliberative ones. The greedy methods are those that use very little information from the levels and they do not make plans. They select the most appropriate level in each moment, according to a method of local decision. Examples of these strategies are the EDF (Earliest deadline first) that selects the level with the next execution deadline (the execution deadline of a level is that of its task) and the HSF (Highest Slope First) that selects the level of highest quality vs execution time ratio among the executable ones. These strategies are simple to implement, but they don't take good advantage of the system characteristics, as they do not look at the whole extension of the slack nor future slacks.

The deliberative methods [1][10] are those that generate level plans and always use the approach of maximizing utility. This measure indicates the kindness or quality of the results. There are different techniques such as the deliberative planning of Boddy and Dean [11], the marginal heuristic of Etzioni [12] or the design-to-time techniques of Garvey and Lesser [13]. These techniques have difficulties to be applied to our model:

- Most of these techniques are centered on only one algorithm type, anytime algorithms in the case of deliberative planning and multiple method algorithms in marginal heuristic and design-to-time techniques. Our in-agents can have progressive refinement MKSs and multiple method MKSs simultaneously.
- The anytime algorithm techniques [14], are not applicable to the model of successive refinement. Although based on the anytime algorithms, these algorithms are not interruptible in intervals of any duration, something that anytime algorithms use to obtain optimal plans.
- The existence of several slack holes (which is the result of the planning of critical components), that break the available time into fragments. Most of these techniques uses only one interval with different deadlines.

A new technique has been developed to offset these disadvantages.

4. Slack-Slide Method

Section 3 addresses the need for a new method for second-level scheduling. The method must create plans that use several slack holes and can use two types of MKSs.

An additional characteristic is also necessary to comment. Not all the slack holes are equal, but rather depend on the critical component type that constitutes the right side of the slack. There are two types:

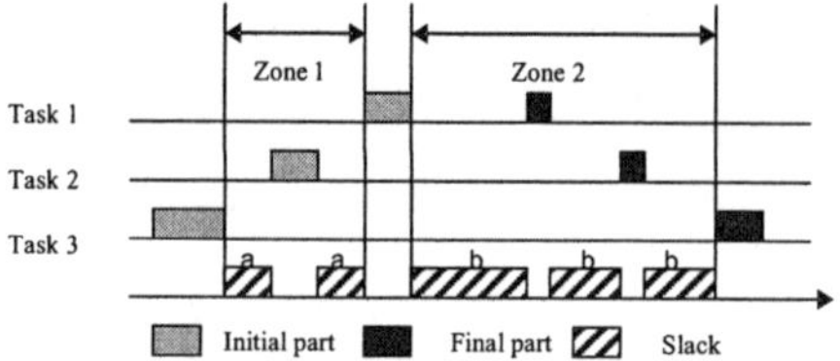

Figure 6. Slack types

- Slacks that end with an initial part (type a in Figure 6). In this case, the duration of the slack is the one specified by FLS, because it is not appropriate to delay the execution of an initial part nor to advance its activation (because its period should be respected).
- Slacks that conclude with a final part (type b in Figure 6). In this case, the SLS can indicate its advance to the FLS (never its delay for the same reasons as in the previous case). The scheduler will make use of this characteristic, since it is advisable to apply the results as soon as they are obtained and cannot longer be improved.

4.1 Heuristic SSS

The proposed SSS (Slack Slide Scheduling) algorithm divides a typical situation such as the one in Figure 6 into two zones. The first zone (zone 1 in Figure 6) is the zone that corresponds to all the slacks from the first to the slack that concludes with the last initial part (the part of the highest priority agent). It is composed of slacks that end in an initial part (type a), such as it has been commented previously. Each slack is planned independently and is assigned for different levels progressively according to their quality vs execution-time ratio, since any optimal scheduling is NP-complete.

The second zone (zone 2 in Figure 6) is the zone composed of all those slacks which have concluded in a final part. The algorithm studies this zone as a whole set. At the beginning of the first slack of this zone, when there are no plan, the SLS plans the whole zone. This can be done at this point since the scheduler knows the longitude of the holes of this zone in advance, and it knows the deadline of all the active tasks.

The scheduler begins with the last slack. This is similar to what is done by Boddy and Dean [11]. This is due to the fact, that in the first hole, all the tasks are active. In the last hole, only one task is active. This takes advantage of the fact that those tasks with a lower level of priority have a bigger slack to be executed. An example of this scheduling is shown in Figure 7.

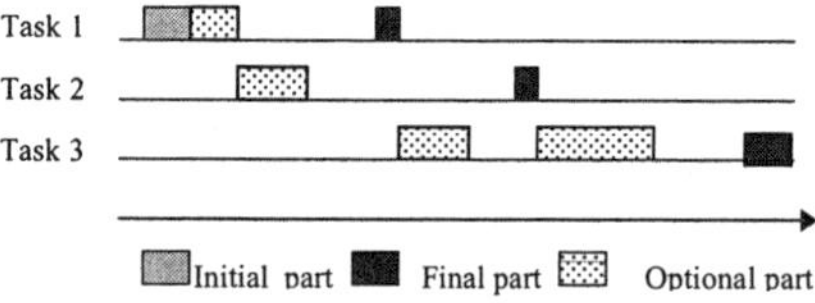

Figure 7. Second level scheduling

Once the level assignment is completed, a relocation of holes is carried out. To be able to take advantage of the holes, the SSS method carries out a second step, from the first interval to the last one, where the system plans an advancement of the final parts. This advancement is communicated to the FLS when it is needed. When advancing a final part, the unused interval of a slack is merged to the following one, enlarging the interval and even facilitating the entrance of unassigned levels. To merge the intervals has some advantages:

In certain conditions a level cannot be interrupted and next resumed its execution. In these cases we cannot execute part of the level in a interval and another in the next interval, but the level can be executed in the new larger interval. Also, if the system executes a level only in an interval, context switching is not needed and the system is more efficient.

Figure 8 shows the result of enlarging an interval since the final part of task 1 is moved, and a new level can be assigned.

Finally, the final parts are moved forward so the levels are only executed in the slack that is defined by its own final part. This way the final part is executed as soon as the last level, which belongs to that task, can be executed, and the use of the results is not delayed.

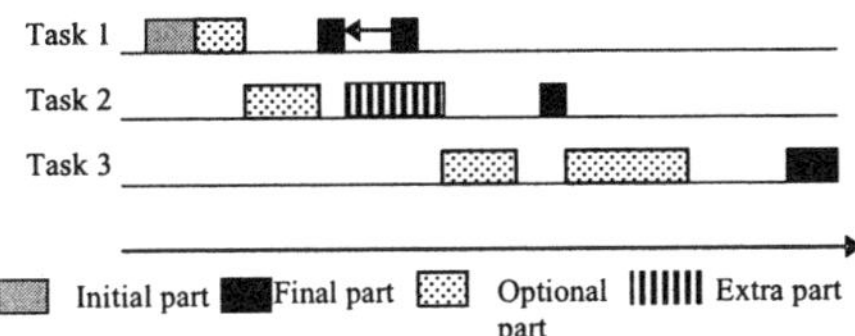

Figure 8. Slack displacement

4.2 Handling of MKS Types

The handling of the two types of MKS (successive refinement and multiple methods) is carried out simultaneously. The levels are put in descending order since the election decision is carried out keeping in mind the quality vs execution time ratio. Not all the levels of successive refinement MKSs are considered in this arrangement. Only the unscheduled lower-order levels that are not planned are considered (one for each MKS).

The multiple-method MKSs do not have this limitation as they do not need to be executed in a chained way. However, as they are alternative methods, it is not necessary to execute a method that provides lower quality, if another method of higher quality can be executed with a somewhat longer time of consumption. When the SLS decides if it can include a level of this type instead of another level of lower quality that is in the plan, it does not use all its time of execution, but only the extra time that it needs. If it decides to plan the new level, the lower-quality level is eliminated from the plan.

4.3 Algorithm

This point presents the SSS heuristic algorithm and explains the functions that it uses. The algorithm is:

```
Data
        Let L be the list of active MKS
        N, new active MKS
        LH, the list of slack holes
        Slack, the current slack hole
        LPF, the list of final parts
Begin
    If slack.type == zone_1
            assign_levels (slack.duration, L)
            save_holes (LH, N)
```

```
If slack.type == first slack of zone_2
        save_holes(LH, N)
        for all s ∈ LH from final(LH) until first(LH)
                assign_levels_in_section(s, L, LH)
        for all s∈ LH from first(LH) until final(LH)
                assign_levels_in_section (s, L, LH)
                mark_to_move_forward (s, LPF)
End
```

- Assign_levels. This selects levels among the active MKSs for the current slack. The approach used is the quality vs execution time ratio, keeping in mind that the available time in this hole diminishes with each assignment and with the limitations according to the type of MKS.
- Save_holes. To create the plan for the second zone, the control continues to keep the information corresponding to the execution deadline of each MKS that is activated (the deadline of the task that it belongs). By doing this, it knows the limits and the duration of the next slack holes. It produces the list of slack holes.
- Assign_levels_in_section. This is similar to Assign_levels, but it is not applied to current slack. It is applied to the following ones that have been saved in the previous function in the list of slack holes. It also refreshes the information of the slack holes as they decrease their free space.
- Mark_to_move_forward. This groups the levels of the MKS belonging to the following final part, so they are the only ones that are executed in this hole. Once the total duration of these levels is determined, it plans the execution of the final part by advancing it as much as is possible so that its execution is done as soon as possible.

An important aspect is the cost of the heuristic. The cost of SSS depends on the creation of the ordered lists, and it is similar to the cost of the HSF. This cost is $(N+M)Log_2M$ (With N the number of levels and M the number of MKSs).

4.4 SSS with Memory

This algorithm can be completed using another characteristic of the system: the active character of the global memory. This memory knows the data that is relevant to each in-agent and when some modification is made, it warns the corresponding in-agent. This mechanism implements a maintenance reasoning system that is used by the architecture to be able to carry out meta-reasoning operations. It can be also used to complete the SSS algorithm, creating the SSS with memory (SSSM).

The technique consists of taking advantage of the fact that there are different algorithms for solving the same problem, and that, many times, two serial inputs of an in-agent have the same entrance data. If the same methods are applied, the answer would be the same one. To reuse it, each in-agent maintains the highest-quality executed level and the results that it provided.

This algorithm is increased by a new function that is the first one to be executed each time that the control is activated. This function determines whether the active in-agent remains unchanged from its last execution (if the in-agent has not received any message indicating the contrary). If it has not changed, the scheduler does not plan the levels that were already used to obtain the result. This result is already there. The scheduler only plans the levels that provide it with higher quality. This way, the system will try to schedule levels that improve the answer even more, knowing that it already has answers of the same quality from the last time that it was executed.

Each in-agent can store the methods that it has executed and as well as the duration of each one of them. This allows each in-agent to be able to refine the mean execution time that has been assigned to it in its definition. The planner can be more precise in its plans when using times more adjusted to reality.

5. Validation scenario

When validating the behaviour of the developed heuristic, it is necessary to compare it with other heuristics. It becomes necessary to generate a great number of tests, with variations in the characteristics (number of in-agents, deadlines, etc). To make this, a simulator of the architecture has been generated. The reason for using the simulator and not the architecture is due to the fact that the ARTIS agent requires the specification of a great number of elements, the implementation of the code that constitutes the levels, etc. This is not viable for the great number of tests that are required to be able to reach valid conclusions. In any case, we have tested the ARTIS architecture using the new heuristics in two real environments: a sewage purifier plant and a miniature train model. The results are satisfactory but no statistical data can be compared.

The simulator is constituted of two modules. First, a generator of random tests and, second, a simulator of the agent's behaviour. The generator is able to generate batteries of tests that are used by the simulator.The result that each test provides is the absolute final quality. This is defined as the sum of the quality of each executed level multiplied by the importance of the MKS to which it belong. Although this measure would be the one that would be used in a real application, we cannot use it when making statistical tests, since the quality that we obtain in two tests with different parameters can be very different and, therefore, not directly comparable.

To have a measure that allow us to compare different tests independently of their specifications, the relative quality is defined. This is the quotient between the absolute final quality and a higher bench mark of the optimal quality. The optimal quality would be the maximum quality that one could obtain in a given specification. However, this measure is not available, since obtaining it would mean carrying out the optimal scheduling, which is an NP-complete problem. This measure is substituted by a higher bench mark that is easily calculable: for each activation of an in-agent the mark suppose that all the levels of all the MKS are executed (or the level of highest quality in the case of multiple methods).

5.1 Results

First, the tests are used to compare the SSS heuristic with the HSF heuristic (the greedy heuristic that provides the best results). We do not use the deliberative ones because they are not applicable to our model.

Next, the tests have been repeated using several repeat ratios to prove the SSSM. The repeat ratio indicates when a significant change in the inputs occurs. It is expressed as the number of activations of the highest priority in-agent until a change occurs. Figure 9 presents the results (the HSF only presents a line because it is independent of the repeat ratio, SSSM_RRn indicates the SSSM heuristic with a repeat ratio n in the test).

The results of the tests shown in the Figure 9 present that (independently of the in-agent number) the new heuristic increase the quality, specially when the input data is stable and the SSSM can work.

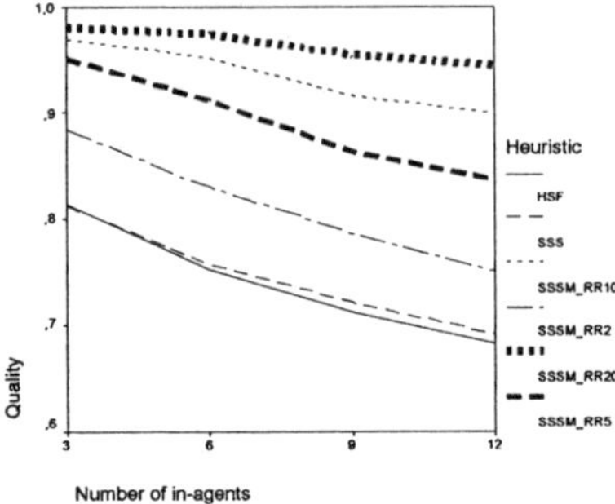

Figure 9. Results of the tests

6. Conclusions

In this work, a heuristic has been presented to work with two types of algorithms, the algorithms of progressive refinement and multiple methods. This heuristic is designed to be applied in an architecture (ARTIS) that allows for the guarantee of the execution of critical tasks but it could be applied to other ones. It also uses AI techniques (that will be planned by the heuristic SSS) to improve the quality of the results.

The tests show that the SSS heuristic has a better behaviour than the best greedy heuristic, the HSF, which simply uses the quality vs execution time ratio as the election method. Although this improvement is slight in very dynamic situations of the environment, it is necessary to point out that in most of the cases there is improvement when using the new heuristic.

The use of the SSSM heuristic is even more appropriate when the problem begins to show stable behaviour, since it allows the use of previous results to improve the system. Whenever it is possible it uses the execution time to improve the solution existent, instead of repeating the same calculations. This is especially important because it is a characteristic which the other of heuristic lacks. In stable behaviour this can mean a great saving in calculations, leaving the system free for make new calculations.

The next step is to improve the learning mechanisms that allow the system to adjust the computation times. The calculations carried out by the planner will be more exact, and will provide more utility. Each in-agent will have a learning module that can refine the execution profiles in accordance with each execution. This refinement principally affects the execution times, as well as the quality.

References

[1] Garvey, A., Lesser, V., A Survey of Reseach in Deliberative Real-Time Artificial Intelligence. Real-Time Systems, 6 (1994), 317-347.

[2] Hayes-Roth, B., An Architecture for Adaptative Intelligent Systems. Artificial Intelligence, 72 (1995), 329-365.

[3] Musliner, D. J., Hendler, J. A., Agrakala, A. K., Durfee, E. H., Strosnider, J. K., Paul, C. J., The Challenges of Real-Time AI. Computer IEEE January (1995), 58-66.

[4] Botti, V., Carrascosa, C., Julian, V., Soler, J., Modelling Agents in Hard Real-Time Environments. Lectures Notes in Artificial Intelligence, 1647, (1999), 63-76.

[5] García-Fornes, A., Terrasa, A., Botti, V., Crespo, A., Analyzing the Schedulability of Hard Real-time Artificial Intelligent Systems. Engineering Applications of Artificial Intelligence, 10 (1997), 369-377.

[6] Botti, V., Barber, F., Crespo, A., Towards a Temporal Coherence Management in Real-time Knowledge-based Systems. Data & Knowledge Engineering, 25 (1998), 247-266.

[7] Terrasa, A., García-Fornes, A., Botti, V., Flexible Real-Time Linux. Real-Time Systems Journal, 2 (2002), 149-170.

[8] Burns, A., Preemptive Priority Based Scheduling: an Appropiate Engineering Approach. Real-Time Systems Research Groep. Department of Computer Science. University of York, UK. Report number YCS214 (1993).

[9] Davis, R.I., Approximate Slack Stealing Algorithms for Fixed Priority Pre-emptive Systems. Department of Computer Science, University of York, Technical report YCS217 (1993).

[10] Horwitz, E., Zilberstein, S. (Eds.) Special Issue: Computational tradeoffs under bounded resources. Artificial Intelligence, 126, vol 1-2, (2001).

[11] Boddy, M., Dean, T., Deliberation Scheduling for Problem Solving in Time-Constrained Environments. Artificial Intelligence, 67 (1994), 245-285.

[12] Etzioni, O., Embedding Decision-Analityc Control in a Learning Architecture. Artificial Intelligence. 49 (1991), 129-159.

[13] Garvey, A., Lesser, V., Design-to-Time Real-Time Scheduling. IEEE Transactions on Systems, Man and Cybernetics, 23(6) (1993), 1491-1503.

[14] Horvitz, E., Rutledge, G., Time-Dependent Utility and Action under Uncertainty. Proceedings of the 6th Conference on Uncertainty in Artificial Intelligence (1991).

Artificial Intelligence Research and Development
I. Aguiló et al. (Eds.)
IOS Press, 2003

PN to CSP methodology: Tighter constraints

Daniel Riera[†] , **Miquel A. Piera**[†] , **Antoni Guasch**[‡]
[†]*Departament de Telecomunicació i d'Enginyeria de Sistemes,*
Universitat Autònoma de Barcelona, Bellaterra, Catalonia
[‡]Instituto de Robótica e Informática Industrial, UPC/CSIC,
Universitat Politècnica de Catalunya, Barcelona, Spain
{Daniel.Riera,MiquelAngel.Piera}@uab.es; Guasch@esaii.upc.es

Abstract Traditional production planning techniques are constrained by large numbers of decision variables, uncertainty in demand and time production, and non-deterministic system behaviour (intrinsic characteristics in manufacturing). This paper presents an improvement to a methodology which generates automatically Constraint Satisfaction Problems (CSP), using Petri-nets (PN) to model the problem and Constraint Programming (CP) in the solution.

The methodology combines the modeling power of PN to represent both manufacturing architecture and production logistics, together with the optimisation performance given by CP. While PN can represent a whole production system, CP is effective in solving large problems, especially in the area of planning. The presented improvement raises from the addition of new constraints related to both the number of firings of the transitions and complex structures of the PN.

Introduction

In the last few years, many methods and tools have been developed to improve production performance in the manufacturing industry. Most approaches try to tackle changes in production objectives such as *high production diversity* (instead of *high production volume*), *make to order* (instead of *make to stock*), and *zero stock* policies. Although Operations Research (OR) methodologies have proved to perform well for certain problems, they fall short in tackling present flexible manufacturing scheduling production demands [17].

Petri-nets have been shown to be successful tools for modeling Flexible Manufacturing Systems (FMS) due to several advantages such as the conciseness of embodying both the static structure and the dynamics, the availability of the mathematical analysis techniques, and its graphical nature [7, 8, 12, 13]. Furthermore, PN are very suitable for modeling and visualising patterns of behaviour comprising concurrency, synchronisation and resources sharing, which are the main characteristics of a FMS. Thus, PN formalism allows to formalise both the production and logistic constraints inherent to the system.

Constraint Programming has been mainly chosen because of its good optimisation performance. Since CP is usually embedded in declarative programming, the user does not need to write an algorithm to solve the problem but only to model the problem to be solved. Therefore, once the model is generated, CP can optimise it without requiring an expert to rule it.

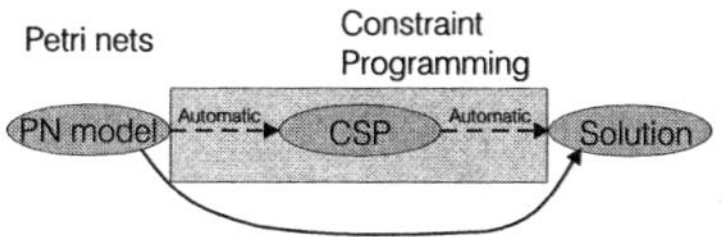

Figure 1: Presented methodology

In [9] the main aspects of a PN analysis methodology to deal automatically with all the constraints of a production system were presented. The aim of this methodology is to automatise the constraints modeling phase of a production system — described previously in PN formalism — in order to generate an optimal scheduling for a particular system state and production goal, making the optimisation phase hidden from the user (See Fig. 1).

It should be noted that several PN analysis tools for improving system performance may only be used when the PN model shows certain characteristics, which is not always the case of PN models of production systems. On the other hand, while CP offers a powerful technology to deal with the best planning policy for a production system, it requires a deep knowledge in both the production system and the CP technology, and time to develop the CP model. Thus, the PN to CSP methodology attempts to combine the main advantages of both PN and CP in order to offer good scheduling policies, to minimise the time spent in the modeling and optimisation tasks, and to allow the use of PN simulators to validate the results. Despite there are other works studying the relationship between PN and constraint graphs [6], the presented methodology is an original approach.

The foundations for the analysis on a PN and the generation of the CP model and later improvements are introduced in [9, 10, 11]. The analysis is made by the detection of certain structures in the PN, which are translated directly into the CSP constraints. Since the kind of problems to be solved using this methodology are more and more complex, the reduction of the solutions search tree becomes a necessity. The current work presents sets of constraints related to both the number of times a transitions is fired and global structures of the PN. The former replaces the preprocessing algorithms presented in [10], and the latter improves the lower bound of the cost function.

In Sections 1, 2 and 3, Petri-nets, Constraint Programming and 'PN to CSP' are introduced. Section 4 describes the new constraints presented. Section 5 illustrates the whole methodology by means of an example. Finally, Sections 6 and 7 discuss the benefits of the proposed improvements, and present the conclusions and future work.

1 Petri-Nets Background

A *Petri-net* is a particular kind of directed graph, together with an initial state called the *initial marking*. An ordinary PN is a 5-tuple $N = (P, T, I, O, M_0)$:

- $P = \{p_1, \ldots, p_n\}$ is the set of places, represented graphically by circles.

- $T = \{t_1, \ldots, t_m\}$ is the set of transitions, represented graphically by bold lines or rectangles.

- $I : (P \times T) \rightarrow \mathbb{N}$ is a function that defines the weight of directed arcs from places to transitions.

- $O : (T \times P) \to \mathbb{N}$ is a function that defines the weight of directed arcs from transitions to places.

- M_0 is the initial marking.

A *marking* is an array that assigns to each place a non-negative integer. If a marking assigns to place p a value k ($k \in \mathbb{Z}^+$), p is marked with k tokens, represented graphically by black dots. In this paper two special markings are used: M_0 is the initial marking or state, and M_f is the final marking or state (the aim is to reach it in the minimum time).

Given a PN, a transition $t_i \in T$ and a place $p_j \in P$, the following sets are defined:

- Set of input places of t: ${}^{\cdot}t = \{p \in P | I(p,t) > 0\}$

- Set of output places of t: $t^{\cdot} = \{p \in P | O(t,p) > 0\}$

- Set of input transitions of p: ${}^{\cdot}p = \{t \in T | O(t,p) > 0\}$

- Set of output transitions of p: $p^{\cdot} = \{t \in T | I(p,t) > 0\}$

A transition t is said to be enabled by a marking M, if $\forall p \in {}^{\cdot}t : M(p) \geq I(p,t)$. An enabled transition can be fired, generating a new marking M' computed by withdrawing $I(p,t)$ tokens from each input place of t, and adding $O(t,p)$ tokens to each output place of t.

In manufacturing terms, *transitions* are used to model events (firing a transition can represent a task or process initiation or an ending of a task), *places* are used to model buffers and resources status, connecting *arcs* specify logical relationships and resource constraints among operations, and *tokens* represent material and resources conditions.

Although a number of PN classes have been defined in the literature, the proposed methodology has been designed to work with deterministic timed PN [16]. In these PN, a time $time_i$ is defined for each transition t_i representing the duration of the associated event.

2   Constraint Programming Background

Constraints arise in most areas of human endeavour. A constraint is simply a logical relation among several unknowns (or variables), each taking a value in a given domain. The constraint thus restricts the possible values that variables can take. CP is the study of computational systems based on constraints. The main idea is to solve problems by stating constraints (requirements) about the problem area and, consequently, finding a solution satisfying all the constraints.

The earliest ideas leading to CP may be found in the Artificial Intelligence (AI) with the *scene labeling* problem [15] and the *interactive graphics* [14].

Gallaire [2] and Jaffar and Lassez [4] noted that logic programming was just a particular kind of CP. The basic idea behind Logic Programming (LP), and declarative programming in general, is that the user states *what* has to be solved instead of *how* to solve it, which is very close to the idea of constraints.

Recent advances promise that CP and Operations Research (OR), can exploit each other, in particular, the CP can serve as a roof platform for integrating various constraint solving algorithms including those developed and checked to be successful in OR.

CP combines ideas from a number of fields including Artificial Intelligence, Combinatorial Algorithms, Computational Logic, Discrete Mathematics, Neural Networks, Operations Research, Programming Languages and Symbolic Computation.

The problems solved using CP are called Constraint Satisfaction Problems. A CSP is defined as:

- a set of variables, $X = \{x_1, \ldots, x_s\}$

- for each variable x_i, a finite set D_i of possible values (its *domain*), and

- a set of *constraints* restricting the values that the variables can simultaneously take.

3 Petri-Net to CP Models

In order to analyse the PN model and generate the CSP problem, the first step is to identify the elements composing the CSP. These elements are:

- **Variables** There is a time variable for each firing of a transition. Hence, every transition has a time variables list associated: $t_i \rightarrow T_i = [t_{i_1}, \ldots, t_{i_f}]$

  The length of this list is given by the number of times the transition is fired. These are called *transition variables*.

  The second kind of variables are those representing the number of times a transition is fired (F_i is the number of firings of t_i). These variables are called *firing variables*.

  Finally, there are *Boolean variables*, which set the paths followed by tokens in bifurcations.

- **Domains** The domains of the *transition variables* are defined using knowledge of the problem. Usually the fact of reducing the domains on the variables quickens the search.

- **Constraints** They are generated in the PN structures detection phase (See Section 3.2) and restrict the paths which can be followed by tokens and the times when transitions can be fired.

3.1 Calculation of the Bounds of the Transitions Firings

In the presentation of the methodology [9], an algorithm based in the initial marking (M_0) of the PN was proposed. Later, [10] presented a two-phases algorithm — by the addition of a new part based on the final marking (M_f) — which improves the bounds calculations. These algorithms have been replaced by a set of constraints on the *firing variables* (See 4).

3.2 Petri-Net Structures Detection

PN structures are extracted in order to generate the constraints and reduce the search space. Each structure corresponds to a set of automatically generated constraints. There is one structure on the transitions (T), and five regarding the places (IS, S, M, B and MB).

3.2.1   Structure T (*Transition*)

T constraints (See (1)) are generated for every single transition (t_i) in the PN. This is not a real structure but a way of removing symmetries from the problem. Since there is a variable for each firing of a transition, by using T constraints, the values of these variables (and hence the firings) are given a unique order.

$$t_{i_j} \geq t_{i_{j-1}} \forall j = 2, \ldots, F_i \tag{1}$$

3.2.2   Structure S (*Sequence*)

This structure is formed by a place p with one input and one output transitions (i.e. $\sharp^1(\overset{\bullet}{p}) = \sharp(\overset{\bullet}{p}) = 1$). Each firing time of the exit transition is related with one of the source transition (See (2)).

$$
\begin{aligned}
&\forall i, j = 1 \ldots F_{\text{in}}(= F_{\text{out}}), \; t_{out_i} \geq (t_{\text{in}_j} + \texttt{time}_{\text{in}}) \cdot B \\
&B = ((M_0(p) + j \cdot O(t_{\text{in}}, p) \geq i \cdot I(p, t_{\text{out}})) \wedge \\
&(M_0(p) + (j-1) \cdot O(t_{\text{in}}, p) < i \cdot I(p, t_{\text{out}})))
\end{aligned}
\tag{2}
$$

3.2.3   Structure B (*Branch*)

This structure (See Fig.2(a)) is formed by a place p with a single input transition ($\sharp(\overset{\bullet}{p}) = 1$) and multiple output transitions ($\sharp(\overset{\bullet}{p}) > 1$). A list of *Boolean variables* are used to select the path followed by tokens crossing through the structure. These variables enable or disable constraints depending on their correspondence to the selected path (See (3)).

$$
\begin{aligned}
&t_{\text{out}_i} \geq (t_{\text{in}_j} + \texttt{time}_{\text{in}}) \cdot B \\
&\forall t_{\text{out}} \in \overset{\bullet}{p}, \forall i = 1, \ldots, F_{\text{out}}, \forall j = 1, \ldots, F_{\text{in}} \\
&B = ((\sum_{s=1}^{r} B_{\text{out},s} = i) \wedge (M_0(p) + j \cdot O(t_{\text{in}}, p) \geq \sum_{x \in \overset{\bullet}{p}} \sum_{v=1}^{r} B_{x,v} \cdot I(p, t_x)) \wedge \\
&(M_0(p) + (j-1) \cdot O(t_{\text{in}}, p) < \sum_{x \in \overset{\bullet}{p}} \sum_{v=1}^{r} B_{x,v} \cdot I(p, t_x)))
\end{aligned}
\tag{3}
$$

3.2.4   Structure M (*Meet*)

This is complementary to structure B: a place p with multiple input transitions ($\sharp(\overset{\bullet}{p}) > 1$) and a single output transition ($\sharp(\overset{\bullet}{p}) = 1$) (See Fig.2(b)). *Boolean variables* are also necessary in this case (See (4)).

---

[1] $\sharp$ stands for the cardinality of a set or list.

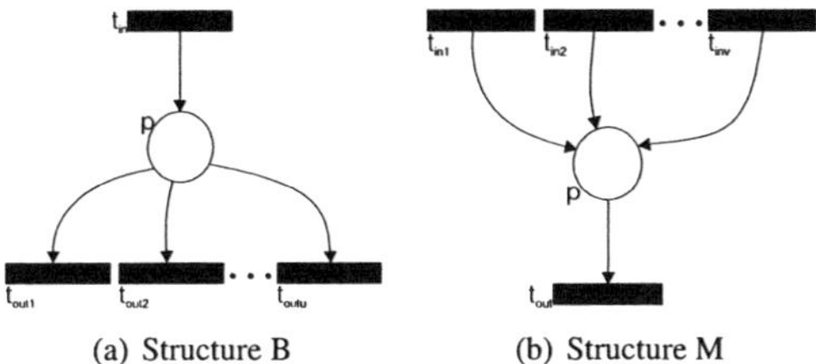

(a) Structure B　　　　　　(b) Structure M

Figure 2: Structures Branch and Meet

$$t_{\text{out}_i} \geq (t_{\text{in}_j} + \texttt{time}_{\text{in}}) \cdot B$$
$$\forall t_{\text{in}} \in \dot{p}, \forall i = 1, \ldots, F_{\text{out}}, \forall j = 1, \ldots, F_{\text{in}}$$
$$B = ((\sum_{s=1}^{r} B_{\text{in},s} = j) \wedge (M_0(p) + \sum_{x \in \dot{p}} \sum_{v=1}^{r} B_{x,v} \cdot O(t_x, p) \geq j \cdot I(p, t_{\text{out}})) \wedge \tag{4}$$
$$(M_0(p) + \sum_{x \in \dot{p}} \sum_{v=1}^{r-1} B_{x,v} \cdot O(t_x, p) < j \cdot I(p, t_{\text{out}})))$$

3.2.5　Structure MB (*Meet-Branch*)

This is the most complex structure, where a place p has multiple input and output transitions ($\sharp(p) > 1, \sharp(\dot{p}) > 1$). This structure also requires the use of *Boolean variables* (See (5)).

$$t_{\text{out}_i} \geq (t_{\text{in}_j} + \texttt{time}_{\text{in}}) \cdot B$$
$$\forall t_{\text{in}} \in \dot{p}, \forall t_{\text{out}} \in \dot{p}, \forall i = 1, \ldots, F_{\text{out}}, \forall j = 1, \ldots, F_{\text{in}}$$
$$B = ((\sum_{s=1}^{r} B_{\text{in},s} = j) \wedge (M_0(p) + \sum_{x \in \dot{p}} \sum_{v=1}^{r} B_{x,v} \cdot O(t_x, p) \geq \sum_{w \in \dot{p}} \sum_{f=1}^{y} B_{w,f} \cdot I(p, t_w)) \wedge \tag{5}$$
$$(\sum_{z=1}^{y} B_{\text{out},z} = i) \wedge (M_0(p) + \sum_{x \in \dot{p}} \sum_{v=1}^{r-1} B_{x,v} \cdot O(t_x, p) < \sum_{w \in \dot{p}} \sum_{f=1}^{y} B_{w,f} \cdot I(p, t_w)))$$

3.3　*CSP Labeling Definition: Dichotomic Search*

Since the objective of this methodology is to find the optimum, seeking the first solution is not sufficient. Optimality must be proved. The aim is to avoid the generation of the complete solutions tree. The strategy is based on the construction of a cost function containing only one variable. In this case, optimality can be proved by labeling that variable first and selecting its values from better to worse solutions. Thus, in the moment a solution is found, all the possible better solutions have been already rejected. Optimality is proved and further search is not necessary.

　　The use of dichotomic search (on the cost variable) was considered in [11]. This technique reduces to $\log \sharp D_{Cost}$ the number of subtrees generated before finding the optimal solution,

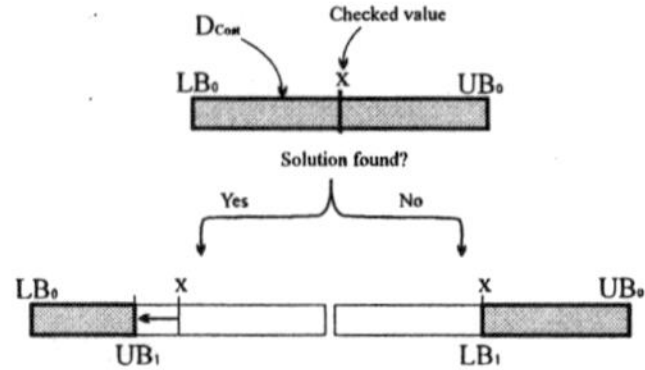

Figure 3: Dichotomic choice point

where D_{Cost} is the domain of variable $Cost$. A single step of this labeling mechanism is pictured in Fig. 3.

4 New Constraints

4.1 Constraints on the Transition Variables

The structures and nomenclature used to define these constraints are the same as in Section 3.2. Furthermore, two new structures are considered: initial stocks (IS) and collectors (C). These constraints depend on the number of firings of transitions, the weights of the arcs and the initial and final markings. Note that the final marking of a place may be undefined. Then, the constraint becomes softer.

4.1.1 Structure IS (*Initial Stock*)

This represents an initial stock (i.e. a place p with $\cdot p = \emptyset$ and $p^{\cdot} \neq \emptyset$).

$$\sum_{t_i \in p^{\cdot}} F_i \cdot I(p, t_i) = M_0(p) - M_f(p) \tag{6}$$

4.1.2 Structure C (*Collector*)

This represents a collector or final stock (i.e. a place p with $p^{\cdot} = \emptyset$ and $\cdot p \neq \emptyset$).

$$\sum_{t_i \in \cdot p} F_i \cdot O(t_i, p) = M_f(p) - M_0(p) \tag{7}$$

4.1.3 Structure S (*Sequence*)

$$F_{in} \cdot O(t_{in}, p) + M_0(p) = F_{out} \cdot I(p, t_{out}) + M_f(p) \tag{8}$$

4.1.4 Structure B (*Branch*)

$$F_{in} \cdot O(t_{in}, p) + M_0(p) = \sum_{t_j \in p^{\cdot}} F_j \cdot I(p, t_j) + M_f(p) \tag{9}$$

4.1.5 Structure M (*Meet*)

$$\sum_{t_i \in p} F_i \cdot O(t_i, p) + M_0(p) = F_{out} \cdot I(p, t_{out}) + M_f(p) \tag{10}$$

4.1.6 Structure MB (*Meet-Branch*)

$$\sum_{t_i \in p} F_i \cdot O(t_i, p) + M_0(p) = \sum_{t_j \in \dot{p}} F_j \cdot I(p, t_j) + M_f(p) \tag{11}$$

4.2 Global Constraints

These constraints raise from the seek of a lower bound (LB) for the cost variable. A good LB allows the search to avoid the generation of part of the subtrees which, apart from being useless, make the search slower. Are specially undesirable those which fail, because the whole search tree is generated. These subtrees are built on values of the cost variable lower than the optimal solution.

4.2.1 Binary Shared Resources (*BSR*)

A BSR consists of a place p with non-zero input and output transitions sets ($\dot{p} \neq \emptyset, p\dot{} \neq \emptyset$) and always marked with either one or zero tokens ($M(p) \in \{0, 1\}$).

By definition of shared resource, the firings of the transition variables in $BSR(p) = \dot{p} \bigcup p\dot{}$ are disjoint. Hence, the total time the system spends to reach the final marking is at least the addition of the times corresponding to the transitions in $BSR(p)$. Then, for each BSR there is a constraint (See 12).

$$Opt \geq \sum_{x \in \dot{p}} F_x \cdot O(t_x, p) + \sum_{y \in p\dot{}} F_y \cdot I(p, t_y)) \tag{12}$$

5 Example

Flexible Factory

The system is composed by two machines which can perform two different operations on each kind of piece (A and B). The former is to process totally the piece, and the latter, to perform a faster and simpler operation after/before the other machine starts/completes the process (i.e. both machines collaborate to process a piece). Note that the transport systems used are not considered in the model. Hence, the possible ways to manufacture a piece are:

A → M1(20 min)∨	B → M2(20 min)∨
M1(5 min), M2(9 min)∨	M2(5 min), M1(9 min)∨
M2(8 min), M1(5 min)∨	M1(8 min), M2(5 min)∨
M2(22 min)	M1(22 min)

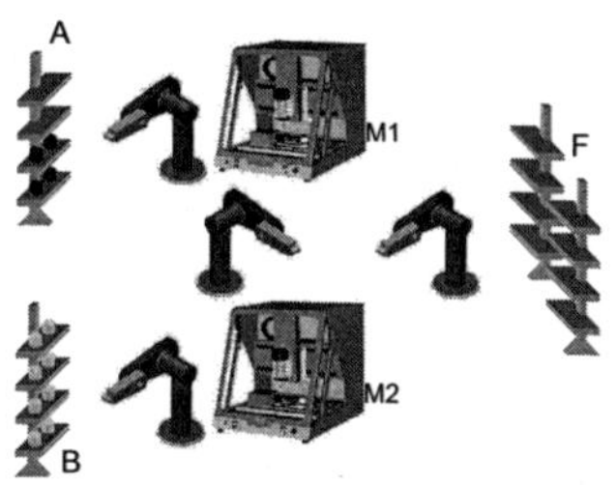

Figure 4: The studied system

Furthermore, a setup time (1 min) has to be considered when a machine changes the tools to process one kind of piece to the necessaries for the other kind. The system can be seen in Fig. 4.

The aim is to process 2 of each type. In the initial state there are 10 and 5 pieces respectively.

5.1   Petri-Net of the System

The PN of the studied system (See Fig.5) has the following components:

Places:

$p_1[p_9]$: Stock of pieces A[B].

$p_2[p_{10}]$: M1 processing piece A[B].

$p_3[p_{11}]$: M1 free and ready for piece A[B].

$p_4[p_{12}]$: M2 processing piece A[B].

$p_5[p_{13}]$: M2 processing piece A[B].

$p_6[p_{14}]$: M1 processing piece A[B].

$p_7[p_{15}]$: Stock of pieces A[B] processed.

$p_8[p_{16}]$: M2 free and ready for piece A[B].

$p_{17}[p_{18}]$: M1[M2] setup.

Transitions:

$t_1[t_9]$: Move piece A[B] to M1.

$t_2[t_{10}]$: Move piece A[B] to M2.

$t_3[t_{11}]$: Retire final piece A[B] from M1.

$t_4[t_{12}]$: Move piece A[B] from M1 to M2.

$t_5[t_{13}]$: Move piece A[B] from M2 to M1.

$t_6[t_{14}]$: Retire final piece A[B] from M2.

$t_7[t_{15}]$: Retire final piece A[B] from M2.

$t_8[t_{16}]$: Retire final piece A[B] from M1.

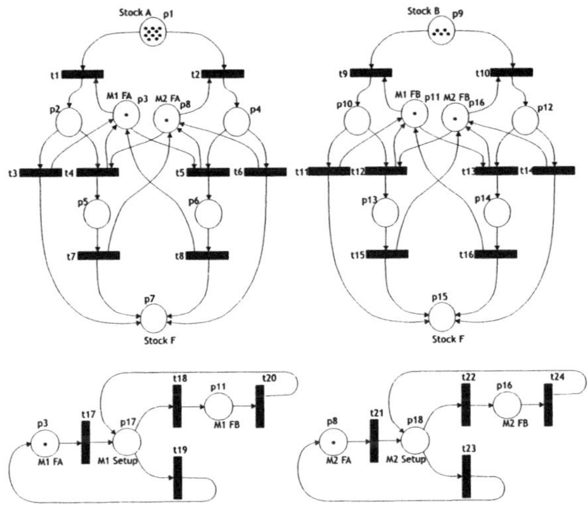

Figure 5: The Petri-net of the system

$t_{17}[t_{21}]$: Start M1[M2] setup from A.

$t_{18}[t_{22}]$: Assign M1[M2] to piece B.

$t_{19}[t_{23}]$: Assign M1[M2] to piece A.

$t_{20}[t_{24}]$: Start M1[M2] setup from B.

Note that some of these places and transitions can seem redundant but they are different depending on the number of processes they have previously received.

Initial and final markings:

$$M_0 = [10, 0, 1, 0, 0, 0, 0, 1, 5, 0, 1, 0, 0, 0, 0, 1, 0, 0],$$
$$M_f = [\_, \_, \_, \_, \_, \_, 2, \_, \_, \_, \_, \_, \_, \_, 2, \_, \_, \_],$$

where M_0 represents the initial state, with 10 pieces in stock A and 5 in stock B; and both machines $M1$ and $M2$ are free and ready to work with pieces of type A. M_f sets the final state, which states the objective: the construction of 2 processed pieces of each type.

5.2 Structures Found

The structures found and automatically translated into constraints are as follows:

T: $t_1, \ldots, t_{23}$

IS: p_1, p_9

C: p_7 and p_{15}

S: p_5, p_6, p_{13} and p_{14}

B: p_2, p_4, p_{10} and p_{12}

M: $\emptyset$

MB: $p_3, p_8, p_{11}, p_{16}, p_{17}$ and p_{18}

5.3 Search

Given an initial domain, 13..60 for the cost variable, the values checked by the algorithm presented in [11] are 37, 49, 43, 40, 42 and 41. The optimal solution to the problem is 41.

5.4 Results

The number of firings for the transitions in the optimal solution are:

$$F = [2, 0, 2, 0, 0, 0, 0, 0, 0, 1, 0, 0, 0, 1, 0, 0, 0, 0, 0, 0, 1, 1]$$

The firing times found are:

$$F = [[0, 20], -, [0, 20], -, -, -, -, -, -, [1, 21], -, -, -, [1, 21], -, -, -, -, -, -, [0], [1]]$$

Thus, the optimal time for the process of 2 pieces of type A and two pieces of type B is 41 minutes ($t_{14_1} + \texttt{time}_{14}$).

6 Benefits of the Proposed Methodology

The proposed approach improves several aspects of actual scheduling tools, some of which are:

- The specification of the logistics of complex production systems using the PN formalism together with the presented analysis tool is a useful procedure to improve the overall system performance.

- The use of the CP technology to avoid local optimisation in front of global optimisation gives better solutions.

- The possible validation of the scheduling policy by means of a PN simulator. Note that the CP model does not consider the stochastic aspects of manufacturing systems.

7 Conclusions and Future Work

This methodology has proved to work for academic examples and small manufacturing systems, reducing the new constraints the size of the search tree. Currently, more global constraints and heuristics are being studied to quicken the search. Having studied more complex manufacturing systems, the inclusion of incomplete search seems to be necessary. On the other hand, Coloured Petri-nets (CPN) [5] are currently being considered. A next step is the application to non-deterministic PN.

Acknowledgements

The authors wish to acknowledge the financial support received from the CICYT Spanish program DPI2001-2051-C01/C02.

References

[1] S. French, Sequencing and Scheduling: An Introduction to the Mathematics of the Job-Shop, Willey, New York (1982)

[2] H. Gallaire, Logic Programming: Further developments, IEEE Symposium on Logic Programming, Boston (1985)

[3] A. Guasch and M.A. Piera and J. Casanovas and J. Figueras, Modelado y simulación, Edicions UPC, Barcelona (2002)

[4] J. Jaffar and J.L. Lassez, Constraint Logic Programming, The ACM Symposium on Principles of Programming Languages, ACM (1987)

[5] K. Jensen, Coloured Petri-Nets: Basics Concepts, Analysis Methods and Practical Use, Springer-Verlag, (1), Berlin (1997)

[6] C. Mancel and P. Lopez and N. Rivière and R. Valette,Relationships between Petri nets and constraint graphs: Application to manufacturing, IFAC b'02. 15th World Congress, Barcelona (2002)

[7] T. Murata, Petri Nets: Properties, Analysis and Applications, Proceedings of the IEEE, 77 (4), 541–580 (2002)

[8] J.L. Peterson, Petri Net Theory and the Modeling of Systems, Prentice-Hall, N.J. (1981)

[9] D. Riera and M.A. Piera and A. Guasch, CSP Generation from Petri-nets Models, IFAC b'02. 15th World Congress, Barcelona (2002)

[10] D. Riera and M.A. Piera and A. Guasch, PN to CSP Methodology: Improved Bounds, LNAI/LNCS (CCIA'02) (2002), Springer-Verlag

[11] D. Riera and M.A. Piera and A. Guasch, PN to CSP Methodology: Dichotomic Search, CESA'03. IEEE, Lille (2003)

[12] M. Silva, Las Redes de Petri: en la Automática y la Informática, AC, Madrid (1985)

[13] M. Silva and R. Valette, Petri Nets and Flexible Manufacturing, Lecture Notes in Computer Science, vol. 424, Advances in Petri-Nets (1989), 374–417

[14] I. Sutherland, Sketchpad: a man-machine graphical communication system, Proc. IFIP Spring Joint Computer Conference (1963)

[15] D.L. Waltz, Understanding line drawings of scenes with shadows, in: Psycology, of Computer Vision, McGraw-Hill, New York (1975)

[16] L. Wang and S. Wu, Modeling with Colored Timed Object-Oriented Petri Nets for Automated Manufacturing Systems, Computers and Industrial Engineering 34 (2) (1998) 463–480

[17] M. Zhou and K. Venkatesh, Modeling, Simulation and Control of Flexible Manufacturing Systems. A Petri Net Approach. Intelligent, Control and Intelligent Automation, World Scientific Publishing 6 (1999)

Artificial Intelligence Research and Development
I. Aguiló et al. (Eds.)
IOS Press, 2003

Integration of agent interactions in real-time environments

J. Soler, V. Julian, V. Botti
Departamento de Sistemas Informaticos y Computacion
Universidad Politecnica de Valencia
Camino de Vera s/n Valencia, 46071
{jsoler, vinglada,vbotti}@dsic.upv.es

Abstract. The application of multi-agent systems to real-time environments constitutes, nowadays, an area of increasing interest. One of the problems that appears is the
efficient integration of high-level communication processes of multi-agent systems
in environments of this kind. In this article, we present an approach that allows the
interaction between real-time agents based on ARTIS agent architecture. The article
raises a simple example on mobile robotic in order to illustrate the above mentioned
approach.

1 Introduction

Multi-agent systems constitute an appropriate approximation to solve inherently distributed
problems, where clearly different and independent processes are distinguished. In addition,
these problems need to exchange information. Examples of problems with these characteristics are robot teams, in which several mobile robots develop a common task, or the problems
of control and management of intelligent buildings. In these systems a set of sensors and
effectors are distributed throughout the building, and they must be coordinated to reach acceptable safety and efficient use of resources. These problems can also be typical examples
of real-time systems, which might make multi-agent systems applicable in environments of
this kind.

A real-time system (RTS) is defined as a computer system in which the correctness of the
system depends not only on the logical results of computation, but also on the time at which
the results are produced [14]. Nowadays, the majority of real-time systems are implemented
as concurrent applications formed by a set of tasks with temporal restrictions, where each of
these tasks solves a certain part of the problem. Current real-time systems are characterized
by their increasing need to be flexible and adaptive. The above mentioned characteristics are
intrinsic to the multi-agent systems.

Following this line of research, it is possible to define a real-time agent as an agent with
temporal restrictions in the accomplishment of some of its responsibilities or tasks [10].
Therefore, a real-time multi-agent system (RTMAS) is a multi-agent system where at least
one of its agents is a real-time agent.

The main advantage of the RTMAS as opposed to classical RTS is the possibility of high-
level communication by means of Agent Communication Languages (ACL), which allow for
the exchange of knowledge. It is important to differentiate RTMAS from real-time distributed

systems. In the former, the communication process is a high-level weighted process, while in the latter, there are usually dedicated buses that allow real-time communication and where the communication is limited to the mere exchange of parameters.

There are few works related to real-time agent development and real-time multiagent systems. The ARTIS real-time agent architecture is one of these [1] [12]. The main goal in ARTIS is to provide an agent architecture where it is possible to merge hard real-time characteristics with intelligent components.

There can be no doubt about the importance of ACL for developing autonomous and intelligent agents. When we try to use these languages in RTMAS, the efficiency of the implementation of these languages becomes relevant. The standard FIPA [3] describes the need for an efficient codification of the messages at some point in the specification. Howewer there are other aspects that are also important and that can improve the efficiency of the communication process.

This problem becomes clear in the implementations of different platforms that support the FIPA specification. In any of them, the knowledge of the agent is divided into simpler, normally independent, structures (tasks in FIPA-OS [7] or behaviors in JADE [8]). The problem arises when the developer has to distribute the messages that are sent to the agent among these elements.

If we take a look at the case of JADE, the agent has a list of received messages. The behaviors can obtain messages from this list according to a few specified templates. Recovering a message does not imply that this message can be treated by the behavior that recovers the message. It will always be necessary to check the content. In the worst case, the message will be returned to the list to be recovered by other behaviors. The questions of how many behaviors must investigate in the message content until the message can be treated and wether it is possible for the messages to remain for an indefinite time in the message lists must be answered. This additional agent work must be minimized in RTMAS. Increasing the efficiency of the entire communication process also improves the probability of success of the system development.

In this article we present a communication model for agents based on the ARTIS agent architecture. A specific agent platform appears for real-time agents (SIMBA), which allows for the interoperability with other FIPA-compliant platforms . The remainder of this article is structured as follows: the agent platform is presented in point 2, an example of application is described in point 3, and finally, some conclusions are presented in point 4.

2 SIMBA agent platform

SIMBA (Multi-agent system based on ARTIS) [11] is an agent platform that allows us to develop RTMAS in accordance with the definition presented above. The architecture of this platform is shown in Figure 1.

The SIMBA platform is constituted by a set of ARTIS agents and a special agent (Manager Platform Agent - MPA-) which is in charge of the services that are specified in the standard FIPA [5]: agent management services and white pages service (AMS), directory management services or yellow pages (DF). This agent also is in charge of the interoperability with other FIPA platforms across an agent communication channel (ACC).

With this platform, the ARTIS agents are transformed into social real-time agents that can communicate with other agents by means of an agent communication language (ACL). It is

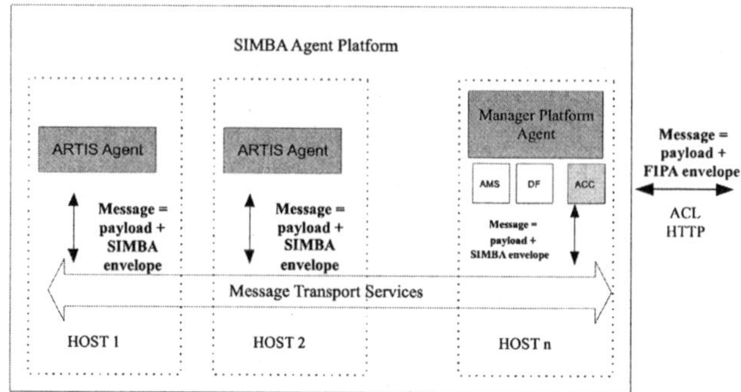

Figure 1: SIMBA platform architecture

important to emphasize that hard real-time communication has not been introduced, and it is not guaranteed to receive the packets in time or without errors.

The main characteristics of the SIMBA platform are [13]:

- Distributed platform. Each agent in the platform is executed in a different host.

- FIPA ACL [4] is used as a communication language.

- The size of messages is bounded in order to fit into a network packet.

- UDP/IP network protocol is used in the communication between agents in the platform.

2.1   The service model in SIMBA

The ARTIS agent architecture splits the problem resolution knowledge into minor entities called *in-agents* and *control knowledge sources*. This division of knowledge is similar to other approaches. The communication has been organized on the concept of service in order to facilitate the whole process of message distribution among these entities and in order to control mistakes. The agents are autonomous entities that are capable of executing services. These services are registered in the DF of the platform so that other agents can find them and perform requests on them. Therefore, an ARTIS agent gives a set of services and performs requests on other services. These services are formed by interactions, which are sequences of messages that follow one of the FIPA interaction protocols and/or the interaction protocols defined by the user. The relation between these elements is shown in figure 2.

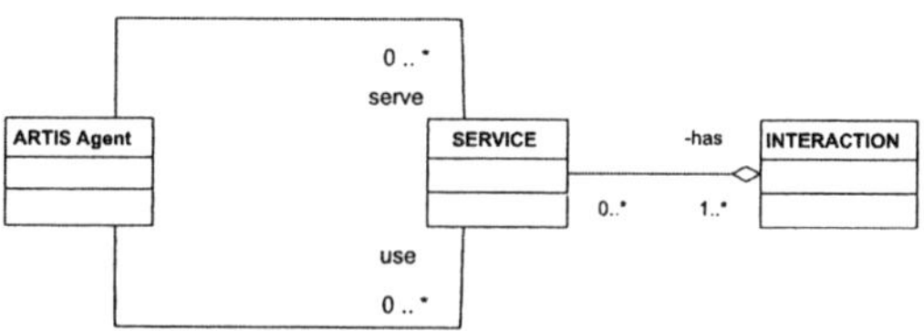

Figure 2: Service model

Conversations are instances of these services. Any conversation in which an agent takes part must be associated with a service given by him or with the request of a service from one or more other agents.

The accomplishment of this model is based on two features:

- Classification of the conversations according to services. Any received (or sent) message will be related to one of the services. In the opposite case, this message is an untreatable message for the agent, and is considered an erroneous message.

- Incorporation of the service attribute in the messages, with the value of the service referred by the message. This field will facilitate the previous classification. The function of this attribute is similar to the content field in a mail message. It permits the organization of the received messages and their elimination in case of erroneous or unrecognized messages.

This model does not prevent the interoperability between different agent platforms. It also does not suppose that the agent should use intra-platform messages and inter-platform messages in a different way. This is explained in the following sections.

2.2 ARTIS agent communication

As has been mentioned above, in an ARTIS agent, the problem resolution knowledge is divided into *in-agents* which are in charge of performing the different subtasks of the agent. Moreover, these in-agents are divided into knowledge sources (KS) which are the subentities that make use of the communication functions. For a detailed description of these elements, refer to [12]. The high-level architecture that supports the communication model described in this paper is shown in Figure 3.

The elements that make up the architecture are:

- A Message Transport Service, which is responsible for preparing the messages to be sent across the net. The messages between the platform agents are sent by means of a proprietary transport protocol.

- A Conversation Manager (CM), which is in charge of the control and classification of the conversations and the messages that make up these conversations.

- A Conversation Service, which is made up of a set of functions used by the KS to be able to send and to receive the messages.

2.3 The conversation manager

The CM is a component that is in charge of controlling conversations inside every ARTIS agent. This component has a set of structures and a few access functions to these structures. These structures constitute the conversation services. The three main structures that make up the CM are the following (see Figure 4):

- ACTIVE Conversations. These are the set of conversations that are currently being used by the agent. Each one of these conversations has an identifier which will always appear in messages sent or received inside these conversation.

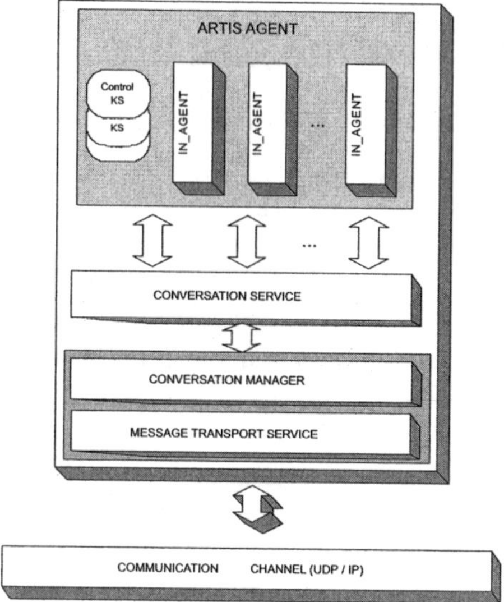

Figure 3: Communication model in an ARTIS agent

- PENDING Conversations. These are conversations that other agents try to establish with the agent. These conversations will always be associated with some of the services that the agent has registered in the DF (active services).

- ERRONEOUS Messages. If a received message cannot be classified inside one of the active services of the agent, then the message cannot be treated. These messages are stored to be answered with a mistake message. The treatment of these messages is automatic and does not require extra code from the developer.

The messages received from other platforms do not contain the additional information that facilitates their classification in any service. In this case, an initial message of a conversation can be associated to several services. This is possible if the protocol of the message is included in these services. These messages will be accepted or rejected by the suppliers of the service, depending on the analysis of the content. In the case of rejection by all the services, the messages will pass to the list of erroneous messages.

2.4   The transport service

The transport level is in charge of coding/decoding and sending/receiving the messages. At this level, the message is coded. This codification converts the message into a useful load for the transport message. Additional and necessary information is added in this transport message in order to support the platform communication model. This information is basically the service identification. This process is similar to the process described in the transport services of FIPA. A graphical view of this transformation process is shown in Figure 5.

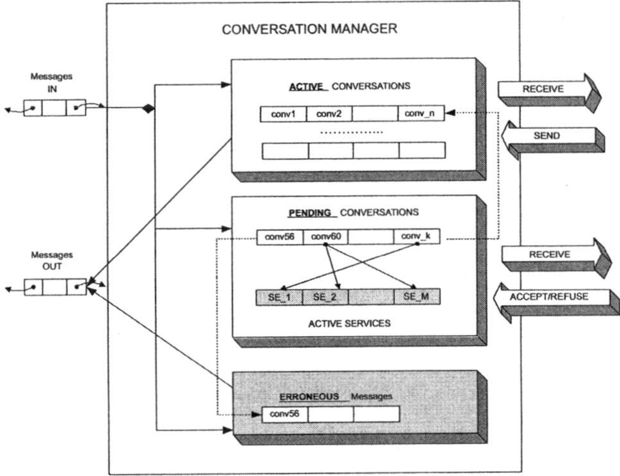

Figure 4: The conversation manager

2.5   The inter-platform communication

The communication among different FIPA platforms is guaranteed by the manager platform agent (MPA). Basically, the MPA implements an ACC communication channel that uses the FIPA transport protocols HTTP and IIOP. Moreover, the MPA canalizes the whole message flow among agents of different platforms. When a message is sent out from the platform, the ACC is in charge of changing the message envelope. That is, it transforms the transport message, from the internal transport of the platform to an understandable transport for the external agents. When the platform receives an external message the process is the inverse one.

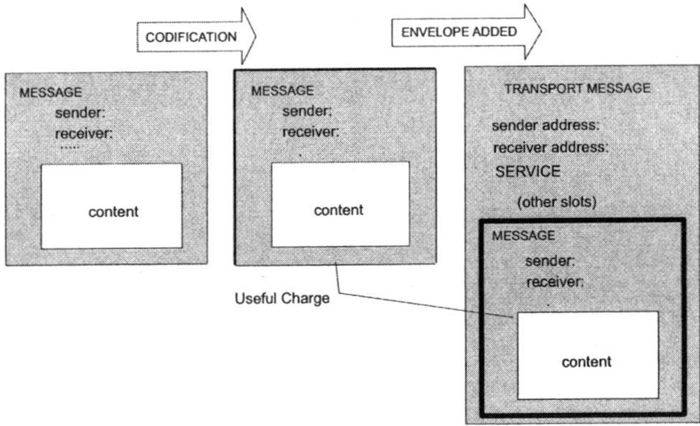

Figure 5: Transport message

Throw the use of parametrized attributes, the MPA also limits the number of messages received from other platforms. This is done in order to avoid the collapse of the real-time agent tasks inside the platform.

3　Example of application

An application example will be used in order to illustrate the integration of the communication process in SIMBA, as well as in an ARTIS agent. The example consists of developing a system that manages different robots which are placed in a closed environment. These robots try to jointly move an object from an initial position to a final position.

The required functionality of the system can be summarized in the following sequence of phases:

1. The object movement action is introduced into the system through an interface agent.

2. The robot team is created to move the object.

3. The planning for positioning the robots is done.

4. The robots move to the initial positions.

5. The object is moved by the robots.

6. The movement is monitored to be able to take corrective action if necessary.

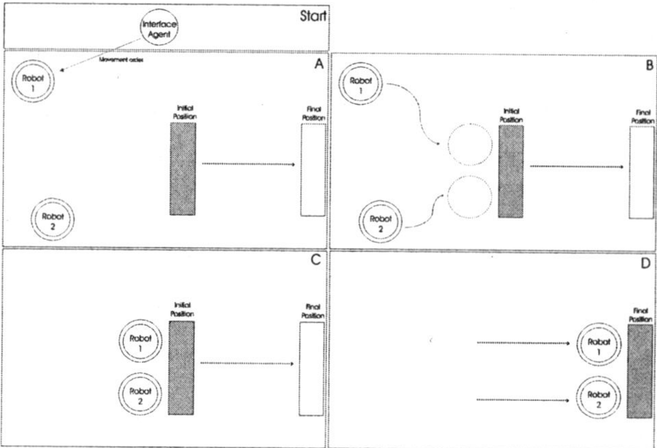

Figure 6: Application example scenario

A sequence of these steps starting from a possible initial scenario is shown in Figure 6. In this case, an interface agent indicates to a robot agent that it must move an object to a specific position. This agent creates a team with other possible robot and they begin to move the object from the initial position together. During this process, every robot agent must monitor its integrity, doing critical tasks in order to avoid hitting other objects. Each robot agent must also calculate its position or control the charge of its battery. For a complete specification of the example see [9].

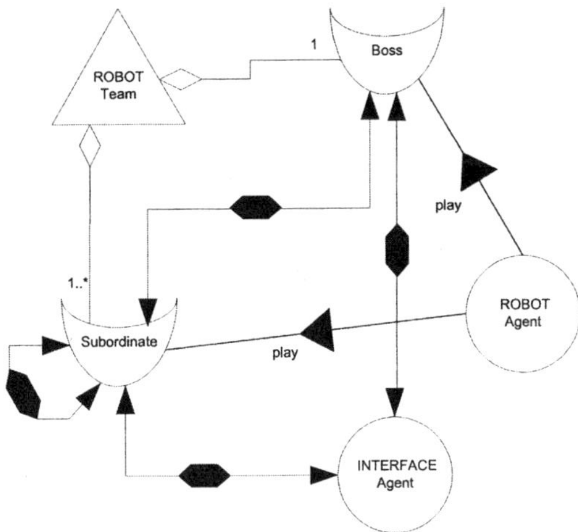

Figure 7: Organization diagram

3.1 Analysis of services and interactions

A simple diagram of the proposed system organization is shown in Figure 7. The figure follows the iconography proposed in the RT-MESSAGE method for real-time multi-agent system development [9], which is based on the MESSAGE methodology [2]. The above mentioned diagram shows the different roles and agents that make up the system, as well as their interrelationships.

Once the system analysis has been dones, the possible interactions are the following:

1. Make a request (I1). The interface agent makes a movement request to a robot agent of the system.

2. To create a team (I2). Once there is a movement goal, the robot team must be created. This process must be started by the robot that receives the request from the interface. This agent assumes the *boss* role of the team.

3. Request position (I3). On some occasions, a robot agent can request positions to other robot agents.

4. Request state (I4). The robot agent that has the boss role requests what another robot is currently doing.

5. Send orders (I5). The boss robot will interact with the rest of robot agents by sending action orders to accomplish the system goal.

This specification allows for the later definition of a set of services that will integrate the different interactions of the system. The services are the following:

- The boss role will incorporate a service called *move_object*, which integrates the interaction I1. It will also incorporate another service named *get_position*, which integrates the interaction I3.

Table 1: Specification of interactions I3 and I4

Interaction I3	
Motivation	To ask for current position information
Initiator	Boss, Subordinate, Interface
Collaborator	Boss, Subordinate
Inputs	Robot agent identification
Outputs	Current robot position
Process	To update the position in order to determine the next action
Restrictions	This interaction has an estimated period of 1000 ms
Interaction I4	
Motivation	To ask for the current state
Initiator	Boss, Interface
Collaborator	Boss, Subordinate
Inputs	Robot agent identification
Outputs	Current robot agent state information
Process	To check the process evolution in order to calculate the following actions
Restrictions	This interaction has no temporal restrictions

- The subordinated role will also incorporate the service *get_position* as well as a service named *be_subordinate*, which integrates the interactions I2, I4 and I5.

If only interactions I3 and I4 are considered, both consist of information requests that will be modelled by means of a FIPA-QUERY protocol. Therefore, the system relates the subordinated role to the possibility of receiving two query messages (request of position or state). These two messages are associated with different services (*get_position* and *be_subordinate*).

Table 1 shows a more specific description of interactions I3 and I4, in accordance with the notation proposed in RT-MESSAGE.

With respect to the messages and, specifically, to their content, Figure 8 shows examples of how interactions I3 and I4 exchange messages. The use of FIPA-SL [6] can be observed in the message content. There are expressions (predicates and actions) in the content language that must be understandable to each pair of robots.

The predicates and actions employed in this set of interactions are the following:

- The *position* predicate allows us to exchange information about the current robot situation. It is defined as follows:

```
position( position_x position_y  angle )
```

- The *state* predicate allows us to exchange the information about the current state of the robot. It is defined as follows:

```
state( value_state )
```

- The set of actions to be employed is:

  - To propose the movement of an object:
    ```
    move-object( position_x  position_y )
    ```

  - To order the movement to a specific position:
    ```
    go-to( position_x position_y  angle  time )
    ```

```
( query-ref                                                          I3
      :sender boss_robot_id
      :receiver subordinate_robot_id
      :content ( iota  ( sequence ?x ?y ?th )
                       ( position ( ?x ?y ?th ) ) )
      :language FIPA-SL
      :reply-with query_position  )


( inform
      :sender subordinate_robot_id
      :receiver boss_robot_id
      :content (  ( = ( iota  ( sequence ?x ?y ?th )
                              ( position ( ?x ?y ?th ) ) )
                       (sequence <value>  <value>  <value> ) ) )
      :language FIPA-SL
      :in-reply-to query_position  )
```

```
( query-ref                                                          I4
      :sender boss_robot_id
      :receiver subordinate_robot_id
      :content ( iota   ( ?status )
                        ( state ( ?status ) ) )
      :language FIPA-SL
      :reply-with query_state  )


( inform
      :sender subordinate_robot_id
      :receiver boss_robot_id
      :content (  ( = ( iota  ( ?status )
                              ( state ( ?status ) ) )
                              ( <value> ) ) )
      :language FIPA-SL
      :in-reply-to query_state  )
```

Figure 8: Example of messages for I3 and I4 interactions

- To order stop:
  ```
  stop( time )
  ```
- To order push:
  ```
  push( )
  ```


3.2 Implementation

A SIMBA platform with two ARTIS agents has been used for the implementation of the system. There is one for every physical robot. For simplicity, the interface agent has been implemented as a dummy agent on a JADE platform. The initial messages are written by and sent from this agent to the robot that assumes the boss role.

The service *get_position*, which corresponds to interaction I3, is integrated in the boss and subordinate role. It is implemented as an aperiodic KS (Knowledge Source). This KS will be activated when a message associated with this service is registered in the CM. Figure 9 shows the code of this KS.

On the other hand, the service *be_subordinate*, which incorporates interactions I2, I4 and I5, has been implemented as an in-agent. This is due to the complexity of this service.

The protocol of interaction I4 is the same as the previous service, though the treatment is obviously different. These two similar protocols are associated with two different services. There is no possibility of confusion with regard to the internal entity of the agent that must be activated in each case. When a query message arrives, the CM will know the correct service associated with the message. Therefore, the CM will also know which entity is in charge of dealing with this message.

It is very important to activate the correct entity (in-agent or KS). This is because, the optional scheduler will execute it as soon as possible depending on its priority.

Besides the above mentioned interactions, the robot agent also performs other tasks that

```c
/*****************************************************************
 function that implements get_position service
 protocol: query  rol: participant
 ****************************************************************/

#include "Mensaje.h"
#include "CoMo.h"
#include <string.h>

void get_position(){

/* declaration of necessary variables */
int x, y, th, error=0;
conversación my_conv;
message r_message, s_message;
content my_cont;

/* Init of conversation and receive message */
if (my_conv = receive_conversation("get-position")) {

        r_message = receive_message(my_conv,NULL);


        /* message treatment , content reading     */
        if Is_iota(r_message.content, 0)
           if is_sequence(r_message.content, 1)
                if equals("posicion", r_message.cont, 2)) {
                   /* resto de los terminos del mensaje */


                } else error=1;
            else error=1;
        else (  /* is another service */
            reject_conversation(my_conv, "get-position");
            return;
        }
        /* We construct the response message */
        s_message = menssage_to_reply(r_message);
        if (error) {  /* respondemos not-understood  */
             set_performative(s_message, NOT-UNDERSTOOD);
             strcpy(s_message.content, r_message.content);
        } else (      /* respondemos con un inform  */
             set_performative(s_message, INFORM);
             add_str(s_message.content, " = ");
             add_str(s_message.content, r_message.content);
             /* lectura de los valores en el KDM  */
             KDM_Get_Slot_Value(Robot.position.x, &x);
             KDM_Get_Slot_Value(Robot.position.y, &y);
             /* resto del contenido  */


        }
        /* response message */
        send_message(res_mas);

    } /* end if receive_conversation */
}
```

Figure 9: Code of *give_position* service

are critical. For example, making sure that the robot does not collide with objects or that the battery does not run down. These tasks must not be affected by the interactions of other agents. This is because the proposed communication model does not affect the execution model of an ARTIS agent.

4　Conclusions

The interaction processes related to an agent society are a powerful tool that allows for the transfer of knowledge between autonomous entities. The possibility of using these mechanisms in real-time environments permits the development of more flexible and adaptable systems. In this article, a communication model is presented together with an agent platform, called SIMBA, which allows the interaction between real-time agents based on the ARTIS agent architecture. These interactions are done in an efficient way and without affecting the execution of the critical tasks associated with each agent in the system.

As future work, we are planning the validation and testing of the platform with diverse application examples. This will allow us not only to evaluate the interaction between different real-time agents, but also to exhaustively analyze the interoperability with other agents of different platforms.

5 Acknowledgements

This work has been funded by grant number DPI2002-04434-C04-02 of the Spanish government and by grant number CTIDIB/2002/61 of the Generalitat Valenciana.

References

[1] Botti, V., Carrascosa, C., Julian, V., and Soler, J. (1999). Modelling agents in hard real-time environments. In MAAMAW'99, volume 1647 of LNAI, pages 63-76. Springer-Verlag.

[2] EURESCOM (2001b). MESSAGE: Methodology for engineering systems of software agents (Final). Technical Report P907-TI1, EURESCOM.

[3] FIPA, http://fipa.org/

[4] FIPA. Agent ACL Message Structure Specification. Technical Report S00061F, http://www.fipa.org/

[5] FIPA. Agent Management Specification. Technical Report S000231, http://www.fipa.org/

[6] FIPA. FIPA SL Content Language Specification. Technical Report S00008H, http://www.fipa.org/

[7] FIPA-OS, http://sourceforge.net/projects/fipa-os/

[8] JADE, http://sharon.cselt.it/projects/jade/

[9] Julian, V. RT-MESSAGE: Desarrollo de Sistemas Multiagente de Tiempo Real. PhD thesis, Universidad Politecnica de Valencia, 2002.

[10] Julian, V., Botti. V. Developing Real-Time Multi-Agent Systems. En Actas de 4th Iberoamerican Workshop on Multi-Agent Systems, Malaga. 2002.

[11] Julian, V., Carrascosa, C., Rebollo, M., Soler, J. and Botti. V. SIMBA: an Approach for Real-Time Multi-Agent Systems. In Proceedings of V Conferencia Catalana d'Intel.ligencia Artificial, Castellon. Springer-Verlag, 2002.

[12] Soler J., Julian V., Carrascosa C., and Botti V.. Applying the ARTIS agent architecture to mobile robot control. In Proceedings of IBERAMIA'2000. Atibaia, Sao Paulo, Brasil, volume I, pages 359- 368. Springer Verlag, 2000.

[13] Soler J., Julian V., Rebollo M., Carrascosa C., and Botti V.. Towards a real-time MAS architecture. In Proceedings of Challenges in Open Agent Systems. AAMAS'02, Bolonia, Italia, 2002.

[14] Stankovic, J. (1988). Misconceptions about real-time computing. IEEE Computer, 12(10):10-19.

Author Index